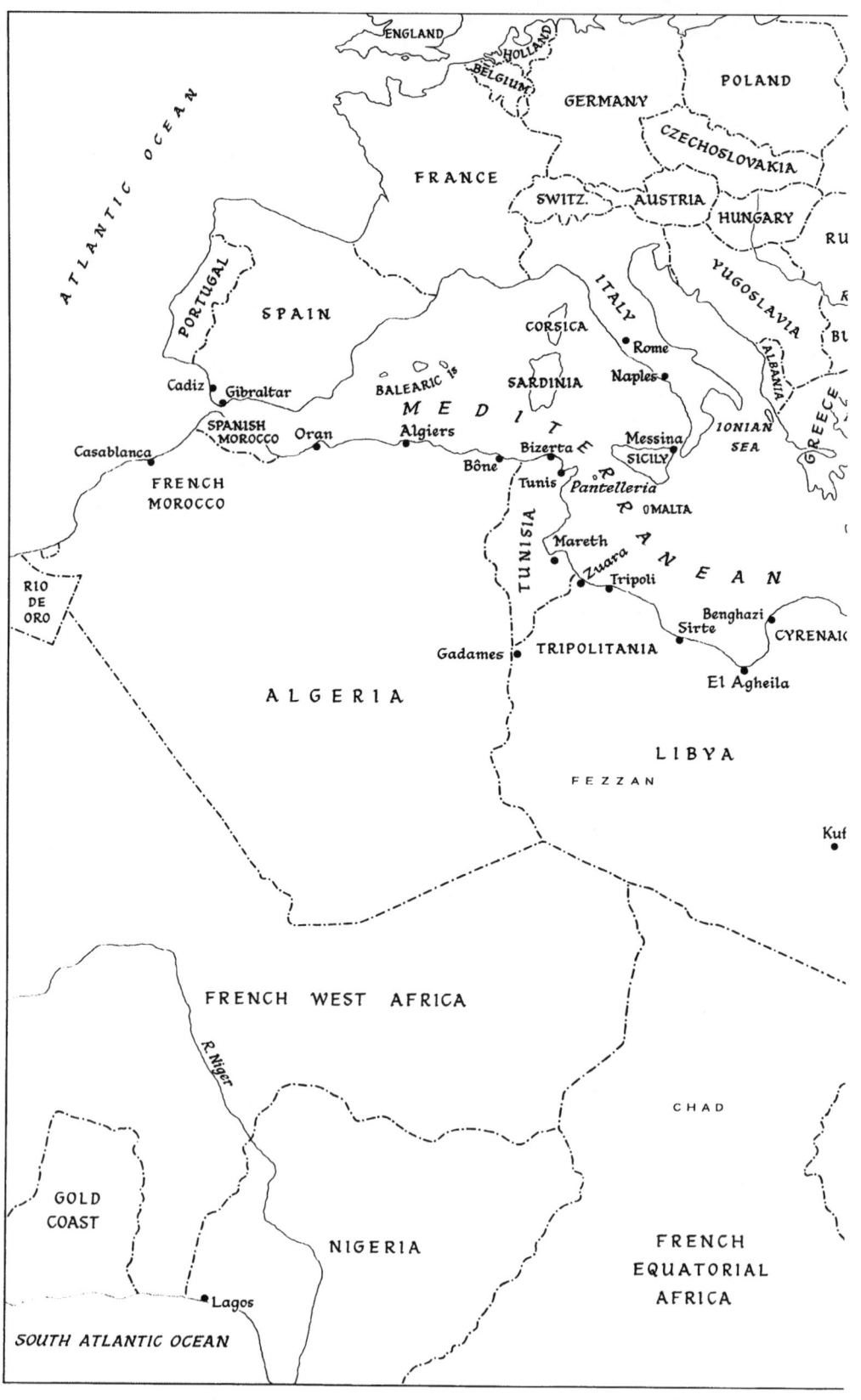

Map 1

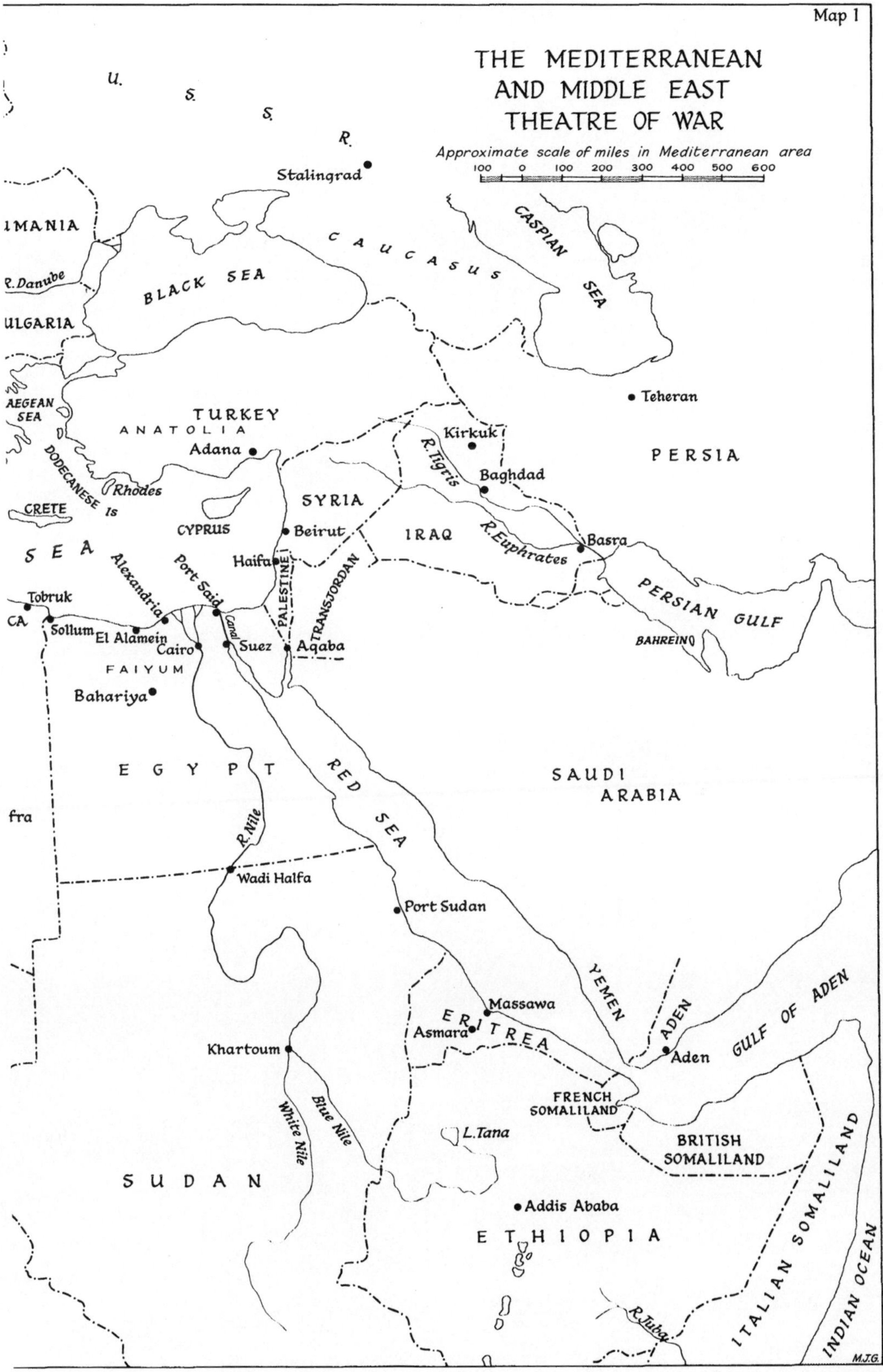
THE MEDITERRANEAN AND MIDDLE EAST THEATRE OF WAR
Approximate scale of miles in Mediterranean area
100 0 100 200 300 400 500 600
U. S. S. R.
Stalingrad
MANIA
R. Danube
BLACK SEA
ULGARIA
CAUCASUS
CASPIAN SEA
Teheran
AEGEAN SEA
TURKEY
ANATOLIA
Adana
Kirkuk
R. Tigris
PERSIA
Baghdad
DODECANESE Is
Rhodes
CRETE
CYPRUS
SYRIA
Beirut
IRAQ
R. Euphrates
Basra
SEA
Alexandria
Port Said
Haifa
PALESTINE
TRANSJORDAN
PERSIAN GULF
Tobruk
CA
Sollum
El Alamein
Canal
Cairo
Suez
Aqaba
BAHREIN
FAIYUM
Bahariya
EGYPT
RED SEA
SAUDI ARABIA
fra
R. Nile
Wadi Halfa
Port Sudan
YEMEN
ADEN
GULF OF ADEN
Massawa
ERITREA
Asmara
Khartoum
Aden
FRENCH SOMALILAND
BRITISH SOMALILAND
White Nile
Blue Nile
L. Tana
SUDAN
Addis Ababa
ETHIOPIA
ITALIAN SOMALILAND
INDIAN OCEAN
R. Juba
M.J.G.

HISTORY OF
THE SECOND WORLD WAR
UNITED KINGDOM MILITARY SERIES

Edited by Sir James Butler

The authors of the Military Histories have been given full access to official documents. They and the editor are alone responsible for the statements made and the views expressed.

THE MEDITERRANEAN
AND
MIDDLE EAST

VOLUME IV
The Destruction of the Axis Forces in Africa

BY

MAJOR-GENERAL I. S. O. PLAYFAIR
C.B., D.S.O., M.C.

AND

BRIGADIER C. J. C. MOLONY

WITH

CAPTAIN F. C. FLYNN, R.N.
GROUP CAPTAIN T. P. GLEAVE, C.B.E.

This edition of The Mediterranean and Middle East: Volume IV
first published in 2004
by The Naval & Military Press Ltd

Published by
The Naval & Military Press Ltd
Unit 10 Ridgewood Industrial Park,
Uckfield, East Sussex,
TN22 5QE England
Tel: +44 (0) 1825 749494
Fax: +44 (0) 1825 765701
www.naval-military-press.com

The Mediterranean and Middle East: Volume IV first published in 1966.
© Crown copyright. Reprinted with the permission of
the Controller of HMSO and Queen's Printer for Scotland.

In reprinting in facsimile from the original, any imperfections are inevitably reproduced and the quality may fall short of modern type and cartographic standards.

Printed and bound by Antony Rowe Ltd, Eastbourne

CONTENTS

	Page
INTRODUCTION	xv

CHAPTER I. PRELUDE TO EL ALAMEIN (SEPTEMBER–OCTOBER 1942)
The basic plan	1
Reorganization and re-equipment	7
Training	13
Administration	15
The deception plan	17
Some operations in September	19
The enemy picture	24

CHAPTER II. EL ALAMEIN: THE BREAK-IN ('LIGHTFOOT') AND DOG-FIGHT (23RD–26TH OCTOBER)
Air action (19th to 23rd October)	31
Tasks of the three British Corps	34
Initial attacks (night 23rd/24th)	37
Successes and failures on 24th and 25th . . .	43
From the enemy's point of view	49
The decision to regroup (26th October) . . .	51

CHAPTER III. EL ALAMEIN: THE DOG-FIGHT CONTINUED AND THE BREAK-OUT ('SUPERCHARGE') (26TH/27TH OCTOBER–DAWN 4TH NOVEMBER)
The fighting in the Kidney Ridge area (26th–27th October)	53
The Australian attack of 28th/29th October . .	58
Intentions of the two Army Commanders . .	59
The Australian attack renewed (30th/31st) . .	60
The Air Force in the 'dog-fight' phase . . .	62
Operation 'Supercharge' (2nd–4th November) .	64
Reflections on the twelve-day battle . . .	76

CONTENTS

                                                                                     Page

Chapter IV. THE PURSUIT TO EL AGHEILA (4TH–23RD NOVEMBER)

4th November: the retreat begins	81
5th–7th November: the attempts to cut off the enemy	84
The 13th Corps' front	92
Rommel breaks clear	93
The advance of the Air Forces	98
Logistic problems and the L. of C.	101

Chapter V. 'TORCH': THE BIRTH OF THE FIRST GREAT ALLIED ENTERPRISE

The decision for 'Torch'	109
Creation of the Allied Command	112
The progress of planning	115
The outline plan	125
First moves	130
The enemy's intelligence	134

Chapter VI. 'TORCH': THE LANDINGS (8TH–13TH NOVEMBER)

The approach and the ships taking part	137
Algiers	140
Oran	146
Morocco	150
Bougie, Djidjelli, Bône	153
Axis reactions at sea	155
The attitude of the French	158

Chapter VII. 'TORCH': THE EXPLOITATION EASTWARDS (November and December)

The build-up of British land and air forces	165
The Axis reacts rapidly	170
The Allies' attempts to capture Tunis	173
The Axis counter-attack	180
Rain puts an end to Allied hopes	186
The assassination of Darlan	190

Chapter VIII. MALTA AND THE WAR AT SEA (October–December 1942)

Malta's last 'Blitz' and final relief	193
The war against Axis reinforcements and supplies	200

CONTENTS

CHAPTER IX. FROM EL AGHEILA TO TRIPOLI
(12TH NOVEMBER 1942–23RD JANUARY 1943)
The attack on the Agheila position 215
To the Buerat position and Tripoli 228

CHAPTER X. THE WAR AT SEA
(JANUARY AND FEBRUARY 1943)
The Mediterranean theatre at the beginning of 1943 . 239
Axis maritime communications with Tunisia in January . 240
Axis maritime communications with Tunisia in February 246
Allied maritime communications with Tunisia . . 252
Allied maritime communications in the Eastern and Central Mediterranean 254
The situation at the end of February 259

CHAPTER XI. THE CASABLANCA CONFERENCE AND THE FIGHTING IN TUNISIA IN JANUARY 1943
The Casablanca Conference 261
Axis and Allied policies for Tunisia; and operations . 267

CHAPTER XII. THE FIGHTING IN TUNISIA IN FEBRUARY 1943: SIDI BOU ZID AND KASSERINE
Further Axis policies 287
Fighting at Sidi Bou Zid and Kasserine . . . 289
Some details of the creation of 18th Army Group . . 303
Some details of the creation of the Mediterranean Air Command, and its effects 306

CHAPTER XIII. THE AXIS AT BAY
(26TH FEBRUARY–30TH MARCH 1943)
British plans 315
Axis plans 322
Medenine 324
Operations '*Ochsenkopf*' and '*Ausladung*' . . . 326
The battle of Mareth 329

CONTENTS

Chapter XIV. THE AXIS AT BAY: THE BATTLE OF WADI AKARIT AND THE ACTION AT FONDOUK (April 1943)

	Page
British plans	357
Axis plans	359
The terrain at Wadi Akarit and the enemy's dispositions	362
8th Army's plans	363
The Air Forces	368
The battle of Wadi Akarit, 6th April	369
9th Corps at Fondouk	376

Chapter XV. THE ALLIED FORCES FACE THE BRIDGEHEAD (March–April 1943)

Plans of 18th Army Group and 1st Army	383
Some administrative matters	384
1st Army: further plans; reinforcements; terrain	388
The Air Forces	390
The mood of the enemy	393
1st Army attacks	395
8th Army at Enfidaville	401

Chapter XVI. THE WAR AT SEA (March, April, and May 1943)

Axis maritime communications with Tunisia (March and April)	407
Allied maritime communications (March and April)	419
The last days of the African campaign, and the month of May in the Mediterranean	422

Chapter XVII. '. . . . WE ARE MASTERS OF THE NORTH AFRICAN SHORES'. (22nd April–15th May 1943)

Plans for the final offensive against Tunis and Bizerta	429
A glance at the enemy	431
1st Army's offensive begins	432
The Air Forces' part	439
A change of plan	441
8th Army checked	441
More of the air	443
The enemy's views	444
Fresh plans for the finish	446
The last offensive	449
The end	453
The surrenders	457
Compliments; what some soldiers thought	461

Index	531

APPENDICES

	Page
APPENDIX 1. Principal Commanders and Staff Officers in the Mediterranean and Middle East	463
APPENDIX 2. Principal German and Italian Commanders and Staff Officers	471
APPENDIX 3. Messages between Hitler, Rommel, and Comando Supremo, 2nd–4th November 1942	475
APPENDIX 4. Some types of landing ships and craft in use in 1942	478
APPENDIX 5. Strength of the opposing fleets	480
APPENDIX 6. Distribution of the Army	483
APPENDIX 7. Order of Battle of 5th Corps, 6th December 1942	486
APPENDIX 8. Outline Orders of Battle, R.A.F. and U.S.A.A.F.	488
APPENDIX 9. A note on Army equipment	498
APPENDIX 10. Some particulars of British and enemy aircraft	511
APPENDIX 11. Telegram from General Eisenhower to his Chief of Staff in London 5th December 1942	525
APPENDIX 12. Operational Code Names	529

MAPS AND DIAGRAMS

1.	The Mediterranean and Middle East Theatre of War *Frontispiece*	
	Facing page	
2.	The Eve of El Alamein—enemy positions on 23rd October 1942	3
3.	Plan for raid on Tobruk 13th/14th September 1942	21
4.	Operation 'Lightfoot'. Plan of 10th and 30th Corps 23rd/24th October	35
5.	Operation 'Lightfoot'. Situation early on 24th October	35
6.	Operation 'Lightfoot'. Plan of 13th Corps 23rd/24th October	43
7.	1st Armoured Division's attack on 'Snipe' and 'Woodcock' 26th/27th October	53
8.	9th Australian Division's attack night 28th/29th October	53
9.	9th Australian Division's attack night 30/31st October	53
10.	Plan of operation 'Supercharge' night 1st/2nd November	65
11.	The final attacks at El Alamein	65
12.	The pursuit to Matruh 4th–7th November 1942	81
13.	The Western Desert, Winter 1942/43	91
14.	Benghazi–El Agheila area 18th November 1942	99
15.	Sea communications with the Middle East and French North Africa	109
16.	'Torch': area of operations	113
17.	Tunisia	117
18.	Operation 'Torch'. The assault on Algiers	141
19.	Operation 'Torch'. The assault on Oran	147
20.	First Allied attempt to reach Tunis	165
21.	Allied and Axis airfields on the north Tunisian front	178
22.	Enemy attack on Tebourba Gap, 1st–3rd December 1942	181
23.	Axis sea and air transport routes to North Africa, October 1942–May 1943	193
24.	Minefields in the Sicilian Channel and Axis convoy routes	195
25.	Benghazi to Tripoli, Winter 1942/43	215
26.	The New Zealand left-hook at El Agheila	218
27.	1st Army positions, dawn 14th February 1943	275
28.	Operation *'Eilbote'*, January 1943	279
29.	The German offensive, 14th–22nd February 1943: Kasserine Pass and Thala	287
30.	The Mareth Line outflanked, 19th–28th March 1943	315
31.	Battle of Mareth	321

MAPS AND DIAGRAMS

Facing page

32. Battle of Medenine 325
33. Highwater mark of Operation '*Ochsenkopf*' . . . 327
34. Battle of Tebaga Gap, 26th March 1943 . . . 347
35. Battle of Wadi Akarit, 6th April 1943 363
36. Plan of 9th Corps' attack on Fondouk 377
37. Capture of the Tunis bridgehead 383
38. Plan for attack on Enfidaville position, 19th April 1943 . 395
39. The fighting in the El Kourzia area, 22nd–26th April . 435
40. Progress of 5th Corps' attack, 23rd–28th April . . 435

PHOTOGRAPHS

Most of the photographs are Crown Copyright and are reproduced by courtesy of the Imperial War Museum and the Ministries concerned; No. 42 by courtesy of the United States Air Force.

1. A ploughed-up Axis airfield. Tripolitania
2. Western Desert. Royal Artillery O.P. Shell-fire
3. American medium tanks, General Sherman
4. A 'Scorpion'
5. Sweeping an airfield for mines
6. A Desert landing ground before rain.
7. The same, after rain

following page 108

8. Air Chief Marshal Sholto Douglas, the Prime Minister, General Brooke. Cairo 1943
9. General Alexander, General Eisenhower
10. Air Chief Marshal Tedder, Brigadier-General Strickland, Air Marshal Coningham
11. Air Vice-Marshal Broadhurst
12. General Montgomery, Air Marshal Coningham
13. General Clark, Admiral Cunningham, General Anderson
14. Marshal Messe, General Montgomery, General Freyberg
15. Colonel-General von Arnim

following page 134

16. Landing water for 8th Army
17. Discharging stores from L.C.T. Benghazi
18. A Landing Craft Infantry (Large)
19. Landing weapons and equipment from Landing Craft Mechanized
20. Landing craft manoeuvring in surf
21. Destroyer lays a smoke-screen around a transport off Oran
22. 'Stoneage' convoy to Malta
23. R.A.F. attack on Benghazi

following page 190

24. Before Mareth. A patrol of the Gordon Highlanders
25. Wadi Akarit. Part of the battlefield
26. British Infantry tanks, Churchill
27. German 'Tiger' tank, Pzkw. VI
28. British 17-pdr anti-tank gun
29. Tunisia. Djebel Bargou area
30. Tunisia. Heidous area. Shell-fire
31. Medjez el Bab. Bridge over the River Medjerda

following page 280

32. R.A.F. Bostons over Tunisian mountains
33. Tunisia. Longstop Hill
34. Tunisia. Pack-mules
35. Tunisia. Crags above Kelbine
36. Tunisia. Heidous Hill
37. British 7·2-inch howitzer
38. The *Cathay* on fire off Bougie after air attack
39. Anti-aircraft fire at night. Algiers

following page 406

40. R.A.F. Mosquito over Malta
41. United States 'Flying Fortresses'
42. United States Mitchells. South African Air Force Baltimores
43. Enemy aircraft wrecked by Allied air attack
44. Enemy seaplane hangars wrecked by Allied air attack

following page 450

INTRODUCTION

THE first of this series of six volumes covered the opening stages of the War in the Mediterranean and Middle East, where by early in 1941 the British had won great successes against the Italians. The Germans then came to the help of their ally, and our second volume described the outcome. The British suffered reverses in Greece and Crete, and in the 'Desert War', yet held their vital bases, Gibraltar, Malta, and Egypt, and in the winter of 1941 tried once more to drive the Axis forces from the Western Desert. Our third volume continued the story. The British offensive ('Crusader' or the Winter Battle) succeeded but Rommel quickly recovered from his defeat. There followed terrible misfortunes for the British. The Mediterranean Fleet had heavy losses; Malta was battered almost into helplessness by the enemy's aircraft; the 8th Army was defeated at Gazala; Tobruk fell; the fighting on the 'Alamein line' in July 1942 greatly exhausted the British although it put a stop to the enemy's advance. The nature of the events suggested the third volume's title, 'British Fortunes Reach Their Lowest Ebb'.

Nevertheless the last scene in that volume, the defeat of Rommel at Alam Halfa, prefigured the contrast presented in this fourth volume, 'The Destruction of the Axis Forces in Africa'. British fortunes turned to the flood. Malta, sustained with difficulty, had resumed its attacks upon the enemy's lines of supply to Africa. The air forces were growing—towards a strength ten times that of 1940. Reinforcements, and equipment of all kinds poured into Egypt, and a new Commander-in-Chief of land forces, and a new Commander for the 8th Army were appointed. The tremendous power of America stood ready to intervene, now in the tangible forms of her armed men.

And so in this volume the Allies take the strategic initiative, and assail the enemy from both ends of the North African seaboard—at the eastern end the battle of El Alamein marks the beginning as do, at the western end, the Allied landings at Algiers, Oran and Casablanca. The two campaigns, though complementary, were very different in appearance. The 8th Army and its supporting Air Forces won the pitched battle of El Alamein and then set out on an anabasis of eighteen hundred miles pointed by battles and actions: El Agheila, Tripoli, Mareth, Wadi Akarit, to name some. This campaign was supported by an administrative achievement that is among the greatest in military history. At the western limit of the theatre the Anglo-American 'Torch' expedition, at that time the largest that had ever sailed for a possibly hostile shore, descended from the sea. This was a tremendous exercise of naval power. French opposition to the landings was shortlived and slight, and a force, mainly British, then tried to seize Tunis and Bizerta by coup de main from the Axis forces which were rushing in. This attempt failed but was no more than a check to the first great joint enterprise of Britain and America, and their fruitful experiment in unified command. In time the Allied arrays from east and west united, and the Axis arms in Africa were beaten down and destroyed. It can scarcely too often be said that this renowned victory was the work of fighting Services, sea, land, and air, which had learned much and were learning more, of how to wage one war, not separate wars, in three elements.

The Mediterranean now lay open once more to the Allies, and the way was clear for landings wherever on the Italian islands or mainland strategy might decide. Truly the Mediterranean and Middle East was the workshop in which the weapon of invasion was forged and the trial-ground on which it was proved. Here the highest commanders learned how to handle it.

We feel, as keenly as ever before, how little is the amount which we have recorded when compared with the multitude of events which we have come to know. The battleground, surveyed in this volume, was more than two thousand miles across, and beyond it stretched the oceans and the skies above them, and by sea, land, and air the fighting men and their panoply came to the battles, almost from 'the round earth's imagined corners'. Thronging events preserved in thousands of documents have continually reminded us that our purpose has been '. . . to provide a broad survey of events from an inter-Service point of view . . .' And this purpose, though far-reaching enough to exceed our powers of fulfilling it, has imposed very great compression. Our volume, too, is part of the United Kingdom Military Series and therefore we have thought it right to give almost all its space to the works and deeds of the forces of the British Commonwealth. The few words, in comparison, which we have given to Allies do not mean that we are ignorant of their achievements or that we rate these cheaply. We hold their deeds and names in high account. There is scarcely a scene of action which does not recall to us the men of other nations who fought beside us. This is true also of the many units and formations of our own forces which are unmentioned, especially of the administrative services, the merchant navy, and the merchant air services. If these had not done their whole duty their comrades would have carried their arms not to victory but to death or captivity in the vast and inhospitable wastes.

INTRODUCTION

We have relied, for the facts of our story, upon the evidence given by the documents of the time. Our treatment of particular problems will, we hope, appear from the telling. But, as an illustration, there is the case of air operations. In general, when dealing with Allied air activity, we have expressed the power exerted in one mission or in a series in terms of sorties flown. When there is evidence for the results of an operation we give it, and we often try to estimate the effects of multiple operations over a period because cumulative effects can sometimes be observed though the details remain obscure. We have seldom been able to apply our methods to the operations of the Axis air forces because the records are not complete. As regards the enemy's losses in aircraft, Italian records have virtually dried up, while German records describe a proportion of losses on operations in terms of which we have not found an accurate explanation.[1] Broadly speaking these casualties amount to a quarter of the aircraft lost, and have been omitted from our reckoning.

In all matters we have tried to use hind-sight sparingly, to avoid the cloudy land of Might-have-Been, and not to mistake our desks for the battlefield. History at times may assume an air of certainty, but sure it is that nothing is certain in war.

The photographs in our previous volume were chosen to illustrate conditions in the Desert and other fronts, and equipment. In this volume therefore we have chosen photographs of French North Africa, of personalities, and of some new equipment.

We have to thank many persons who have helped our work whether by comment, or criticism, or by the works from which we have gained knowledge. We alone are responsible for our mistakes and shortcomings.

We are indebted to the Official Historians and their assistants: of Australia, Mr. Gavin Long; of New Zealand, the late Sir Howard Kippenberger and Brigadier M. C. Fairbrother, also Major-General W. G. Stevens; of the Union of South Africa, Mr. J. A. I. Agar-Hamilton. In likewise to the Chief of Military History, Brigadier-General Hal C. Pattison, and to Doctor Stetson Conn, Doctor George F. Howe, Mr. Charles V. P. von Luttichau, Office of the Chief of Military History, Washington, D.C., as also to Rear-Admiral S. E. Morison, U.S.N.R. (Retired) the official historian to the U.S. Navy Department. We have had much help from the Heads of the Historical Branches in the Service Departments of the Ministry of Defence, Commander P. K. Kemp, Lieutenant-Colonel W. B. R. Neave-Hill, Mr. L. A. Jacketts and sometime Mr. J. C. Nerney; also from the Archivists, Librarians,

---

[1] e.g. 'Not by enemy action', 'Unknown'. The puzzle is because these headings, when compared with other information available to us, appear to express more than their obvious meanings.

and keepers of the various records in the Cabinet Office, the Ministries, the Imperial War Museum and their Staffs. We have had the use of narratives compiled by Major G. S. Keane, Lieutenant-Colonel M. E. S. Laws, Captain G. C. Wynne, Squadron Leader W. M. Mills, Mr. T. Milne and Wing Commander P. G. Scott. We owe much to the administrative narratives of Brigadier W. P. Pessell. On German and Italian documents we have had the expert help of Mr. B. M. Melland and Commander M. G. Saunders, of Mrs. N. B. Taylor, and sometime of Mrs. J. M. Hamilton, and of Doctor G. W. S. Friedrichsen who handled for us the German material in the United States. The maps have been drawn by Mr. M. J. Godliman of the Cabinet Office Mapping Section under the direction of Colonel T. M. Penney. General research has been done throughout by Miss Jean Burt and Miss D. F. Butler, and sometime by Mrs. R. Matthews. In particular, Miss Butler has done most valuable work in connection with the preparation of maps, as has Miss Burt in preparing the index, and Miss D. G. Plant in secretarial matters and in her accomplished typing of drafts. To all these, and to the Editor for his unfailing support and advice, we wish to express our gratitude.

Ill health compelled Major-General I. S. O. Playfair to give up before work on this volume was finished. His place was taken by Brigadier C. J. C. Molony.

C.J.C.M.
F.C.F.
T.P.G.

CHAPTER I
PRELUDE TO EL ALAMEIN
September—October 1942

IN the autumn of 1942 the War, viewed as a whole, showed bright spots as well as dark. By September, for instance, the monthly figures for Allied world-wide shipping losses had fallen well below the desperately high figure for June, though mastery of the U-boats was still not in sight. Attacks by the Royal Air Force on Germany were steadily becoming heavier. In southern Russia there was violent fighting near Stalingrad, and in the Caucasus the Germans were still advancing, though more slowly than before. In the Far East the British had been driven out of Burma and were awaiting the end of the monsoon to start winning the country back again. In the Solomon Islands the great battle for Guadalcanal had begun, and in New Guinea the Japanese attempt to seize Port Moresby by an advance over the Owen Stanley range had been held. The battle of Midway Island, in which the Japanese lost heavily, had removed the danger to shipping in the Indian Ocean from aircraft carriers, while the Allied landing in Madagascar had reduced the danger from submarines—German as well as Japanese—by depriving them of a possible refuelling base. These results were of great importance to the Middle East, which depended so largely upon shipping from India and Australia and up the east coast of Africa. Indeed, a steady flow of men and equipment was now pouring into Egypt by the Cape route. Meanwhile the British and Americans had together decided to send a large expedition to land in North-West Africa, and this was already being prepared.[1]

In the Middle East some changes had been made in the high command of the land forces, and a new 'Persia and Iraq Command' had been created with the object of leaving the Commander-in-Chief, Middle East, freer to attend to the Western Desert.[2] 'I should be most reluctant,' wrote the Prime Minister, 'to embarrass Alexander with remote cares at a moment when all our fortunes turn upon the speedy and decisive defeat of Rommel.'

General Alexander's instructions to General Montgomery (confirmed in writing on 19th August) were to prepare to attack the

---
[1] Operation 'Torch'—described in Chapter V. The first ships sailed from the United Kingdom on 2nd October.
[2] Volume III, Chapter XV.

Axis forces with a view to destroying them at the earliest possible moment. Montgomery was also ordered to hold the 8th Army's present positions. This secondary task receded into the background after Rommel had been soundly beaten, in the early days of September, when he attempted to crown his successes of May and June by smashing the 8th Army where it stood. This was the battle of Alam el Halfa.[1]

The two armies were now in close contact on a front of nearly forty miles between the sea and the Qattara depression. Both sides were improving their positions, and adding to the profusion of mines in and about them. It was thought unlikely that the enemy would withdraw, because nowhere east of Tobruk was there another position with both flanks naturally secure. Rommel's army was much depleted and its supply position was known to be bad and getting worse. The British, on the other hand, were daily growing stronger on land and in the air, and the initiative was theirs for the taking.

The timing of the British offensive led to the familiar argument in which, broadly, the commanders on the spot wanted time and the Prime Minister wanted action. It was clearly desirable to win a resounding victory over Rommel before the Anglo-American forces landed in Algeria and Morocco early in November, on account of the influence it might have on French and Spanish opinion. It was also very important to replenish Malta by convoy from Egypt, for which purpose it was essential to have the use of the airfields of Cyrenaica by mid-November to enable fighter cover to be extended sufficiently far westwards. On the other hand, there were many British reinforcements to absorb and train, new equipments to master, and preparations of all sorts to make. Moonlight would be essential for the start of the land battle because only in moonlight might defended minefields be tackled. General Montgomery insisted that he could not be ready by the September full moon period but that by the fourth week of October he would be in a position to guarantee success. General Alexander supported this view and 23rd October was chosen.

The 8th Army could count on having the following formations— a more detailed order of battle is given later.

> Three armoured divisions
> Two armoured brigade groups
> One brigade of 'I' tanks
> Seven infantry divisions
> Two Fighting French and one Greek infantry brigade groups[2]

---

[1] Described in Volume III.
[2] Early in April 1942 General de Gaulle gave the name 'Fighting France' to what had been 'Free France', and formally notified the Allies of the change.

BATTLE OF EL ALAMEIN
23rd October – 4th November 1942

LEGEND FOR MAPS 2 & 4-11

British troops are shown in red, German in blue and Italian in green

Headquarters of Armies
- 8th (Montgomery)
- Panzerarmee Afrika (Stumme/Rommel)

Headquarters of Corps
- 10th (Lumsden)
- 13th (Horrocks)
- 30th (Leese)
- DAK (von Thoma)
- 10th (Pafundi)
- 20th (Stefanis)
- 21st (Navarrini)

- Headquarters of Divisions
- Headquarters of Brigades (or equivalent)
- Divisions (51, 90, Pavia)
- Armoured Divisions (10, 21, Ariete)
- Brigades; Panzergrenadier or Italian Infantry Regiments (6NZ, 125, 62)
- Armoured Brigades or mixed enemy battle groups (2)
- Battalions and smaller Units (2RB, I/382, II/61)
- Armoured Regiments or Battalions (3H, II/8, IV/133)
- Recce Units or patrols
- Inter Corps boundary
- Inter Divisional boundary
- Inter Brigade boundary
- Field Maintenance Centre (96)
- Enemy minefields, main alignment
- Dummy enemy minefields
- Scattered anti-tank mines
- Airfields and landing grounds

Arabic Terms
- Naqb or Bab..........a pass or cutting
- Qaret....................a low hill
- Deir......................a depression
- Ras......................a cape
- Tell......................a mound

Map 2

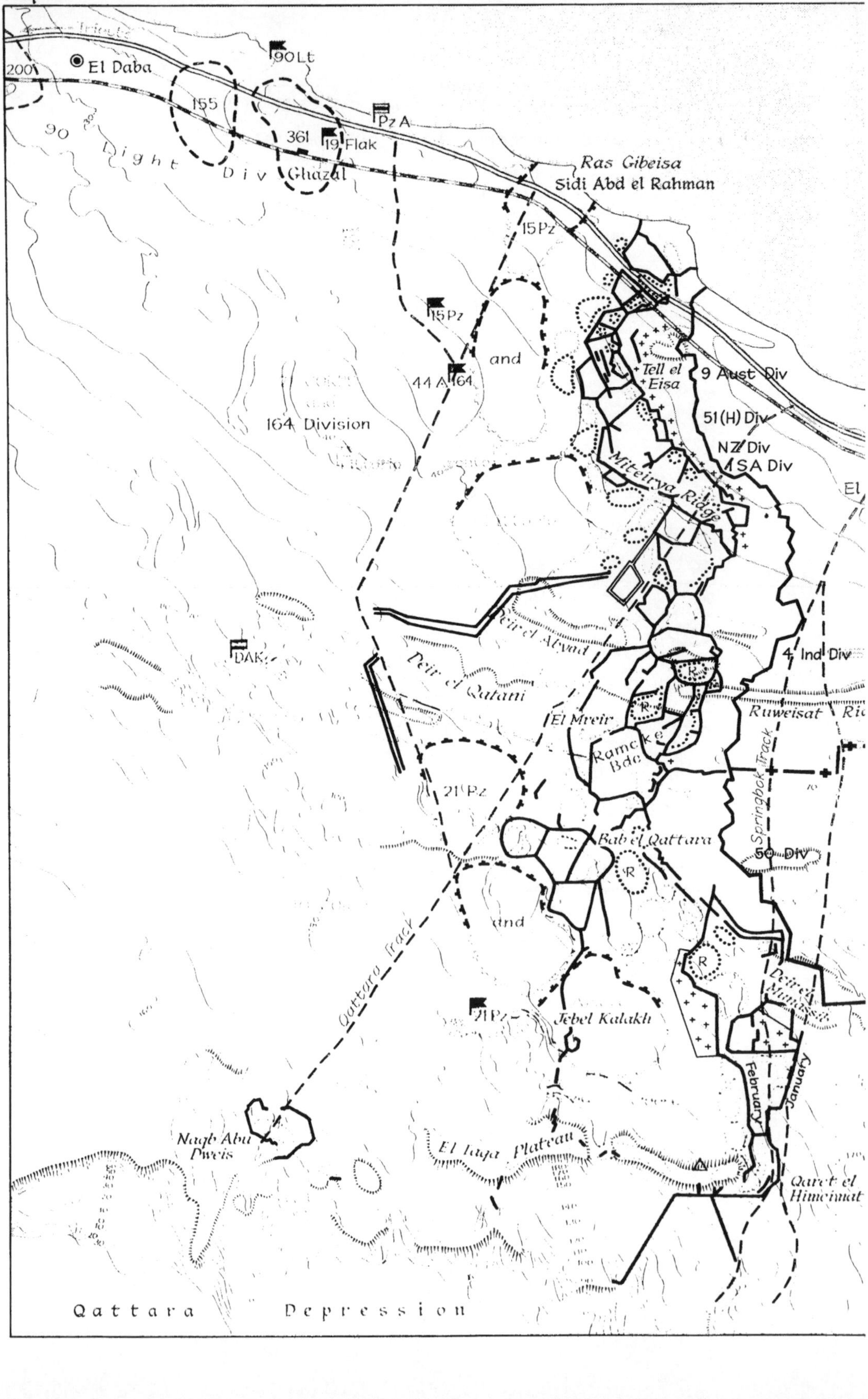

El Daba
200
90 Lt
155
361
19 Flak
Pz A
90 Light Div
Ghazal
Ras Gibeisa
Sidi Abd el Rahman
15 Pz
15 Pz
and
44 A 164
164 Division
Tell el Eisa
9 Aust Div
51(H) Div
NZ Div
SA Div
Miteirya Ridge
El
Deir el Abyad
Deir el Qatani
DAK
4 Ind Div
Ruweisat Ri
El Mreir
Ramcke Bde
R
R
21 Pz
Springbok Track
Bab el Qattara
50 Div
R
and
R
Deir el Munassib
Qattara Track
21 Pz
Jebel Kalakh
February
January
Naqb Abu Dweis
El Taqa Plateau
Qaret el Himeimat
Qattara Depression

THE EVE OF EL ALAMEIN
Enemy Positions on 23rd October 1942

Forward line of British minefields............

5 4 3 2 1 0   5   10
MILES

Form lines at 10 metres

Tac 8
30
201
Alamein
10

102
El Hammam

202
1 Armoured Div
El Imayid   Assembly Area

30 CORPS

10 Armoured Div
Assembly Area
Alam el Halfa

96

13 CORPS

97

13

44 Div

7 Armd Div

Qaret el Humur

MJG

compared with
- *German*
  - Two armoured divisions
  - One motorized division
  - One (partly) motorized division
  - One parachute brigade
- *Italian*
  - Two armoured divisions
  - One motorized division
  - Four infantry divisions
  - One parachute division.

The Axis array was much weaker than it appears, since nearly every formation was very short of men and equipment. Replacements had not kept pace with losses, owing mainly to the successful British attacks by sea and air against shipping. The British were to be greatly superior in artillery and tanks, and were at last to have numerous 6-pdr anti-tank guns, as well as stores and equipment of all kinds in plenty, and ample petrol, transport, and ammunition.

Air preparations for the coming battle were greatly furthered by the fact that Air Chief Marshal Tedder and Air Vice-Marshal Coningham knew each other's minds and worked in a mutual confidence and respect born from their long association in war. Tedder's policy had been to disrupt the enemy's supply to North Africa by attacking his sea convoys and unloading ports, and—as D day came nearer—to subdue his air forces. This policy was to continue after D day and Tedder intended then to strengthen the Desert Air Force, in its support of 8th Army, by allotting to Coningham, on call, some of the strategic bomber, maritime, and other aircraft. He had at his disposal in the Middle East the equivalent of 104 squadrons.[1] In the squadrons available to support the army were about 750 aircraft (530 serviceable) apart from 54 transport aircraft. The Axis air forces in North Africa consisted of 275 German aircraft (150 serviceable) including 80 dive-bombers but no bombers, and 400 Italian aircraft (200 serviceable)—or about 350 serviceable aircraft in all. In addition the Germans had about 225 (130 serviceable) long-range bombers based in Greece, Crete, Sicily, and Sardinia. There was also a fleet of German and Italian transports numbering about 300 aircraft.

See Map 2

Many of the difficulties in which the British found themselves during the past year's campaigning in the Western Desert, and the chances they had missed, were caused in part by the awkward

---

[1] Including incomplete squadrons these were: Royal Air Force 64; Fleet Air Arm 7; South African Air Force 16; Royal Australian Air Force 6; Royal Canadian Air Force 2; Rhodesian 1; United States Army Air Force 13; Greek 2.

system of command at the top.[1] It is appropriate therefore to remark upon the relations between the new Commander-in-Chief, Alexander, and the new Army Commander, Montgomery.

It will be recalled that at the time of the changes in the high command in August 1942, General Auchinleck had been acting both as Commander-in-Chief and Army Commander. The burden on the Commander-in-Chief was very great; what was wanted was a separate, able, and energetic commander for the 8th Army. General Montgomery certainly met these requirements, and, what is more, Alexander and he were old friends and military colleagues who knew each other well. In the early months of the present War they had commanded adjacent divisions on the Western Front, which led to close contacts. Back in England after Dunkirk, Alexander at Southern Command had Montgomery as a Corps Commander and found his views on military tactics very similar to his own. When General Alexander was appointed to be C.-in-C., Middle East, he was satisfied that the new 8th Army Commander was better qualified for the post than any other British officer of his acquaintance.

General Montgomery, for his part, was fortunate in having a Commander-in-Chief who understood him so well, had confidence in him, and was determined to help him in every possible way. For instance, General Alexander could ensure that the Army Commander would have no problems to deal with except those connected directly with the 8th Army's operations. His method was to establish a small advanced camp close to 8th Army Headquarters and staffed from G.H.Q. He kept himself thoroughly conversant with the Army Commander's ideas and intentions, visited him frequently, discussed all major issues, and gave his approval when necessary. In the operations which began with El Alamein he never had cause to override his Army Commander. On one occasion, as we shall see, he may have been very near to doing so, but the need did not arise.

In starting a battle in the Desert it had become customary to demonstrate (sometimes rather perfunctorily) somewhere near the coast while a mobile striking force containing all or most of the armour swung round the inland flank. In September 1942 conditions at El Alamein ruled out this manoeuvre, because there was no open flank round which to pass. It would therefore be necessary to force a passage right through the defended zone, with its strong points and minefields, and this the armour alone could not be expected to do without prohibitive losses. The gap would have to be made and secured by the infantry, and, in General Alexander's

---

[1] Volume III, pp. 285, 376.

words, the defences were so strong that this would involve a battle on the grandest scale.

Soon after taking command of the 8th Army General Montgomery had made up his mind to attack in two sectors simultaneously, with the main effort in the north, where success would unhinge the whole front. On 14th September he issued his 'General Plan' for operation 'Lightfoot', which began with this definition of the object: 'To destroy the enemy forces now opposing Eighth Army. The operations will be designed to "trap" the enemy in his present area and destroy him there. Should small elements escape to the West, they will be pursued and dealt with later'.

In outline the plan was for the infantry of 30th Corps, with massive artillery support, to breach the enemy's defences in the north. The bulk of the armour (10th Corps) would pass through the breach and position itself 'on ground of its own choosing astride the enemy supply routes'. This would force the enemy's armour to attack, and the more powerful British armour would destroy it. The Axis infantry would then be rounded up.

The secondary attack in the south by 13th Corps would be more than a mere demonstration; it would be real enough to prevent the enemy from moving troops to reinforce the northern sector. It had the further object of enabling a light mobile force to pass into the enemy's back area and swing north towards El Daba.

This, then, was the broad conception which formed the basis for tactical planning and detailed preparations, for reorganizing, regrouping, and training the army formations, for the move forward of large quantities of ammunition and stores of all kinds, and for the deception plan.

General Montgomery did not follow the British custom of having one principal staff officer for general staff matters ('G') only, and another one for administration ('A and Q'). Instead he nominated a 'Chief of Staff' who was responsible for co-ordinating the whole work of army headquarters, though the Army Commander himself was available for consultation by senior officers. The appointment of Brigadier F. W. de Guingand as Chief of Staff marked the beginning of a notable partnership. Three others in positions of great responsibility at H.Q. 8th Army were: the Brigadier, Royal Artillery, Brigadier S. C. Kirkman; the Chief Engineer, Brigadier F. H. Kisch; and the head of administration, Brigadier Sir Brian Robertson.

The Army Commander now felt free to devote most of his energy directly to his troops. He was out and about, seeing and being seen, sizing up his subordinate leaders, talking to officers and men and arousing their interest and enthusiasm, and generally inspiring confidence and raising the spirits of the whole army to fighting pitch.

Long before the details of the land offensive were settled Air Vice-Marshal Coningham had so planned the activities of the Desert Air Force that as the time drew near he had to intensify, rather than change, the pattern of air operations. From 19th October he would aim at reducing the risks of heavy air attacks on the assembling British troops, and winning for his own forces conditions which would favour future air operations in support of the battle. To do this he would attack the enemy's forward airfields by day and night, provide fighter defence of the army's forward area, and constantly reconnoitre the enemy's defences and dispositions, while preventing him spying out the British preparations. Once the battle on land was joined, Coningham intended to be ready to attack the enemy's forces in the battle area as continuously and intensely as possible.

The naval plans for supporting the army excluded bombardment by warships because this would probably have little effect and because many fighters would have to be diverted from protecting the army to protecting the ships. Deceptive demonstrations at points on the coast were arranged, however, and destroyers and motor torpedo-boats were to stand by at Alexandria to attack coastal shipping. But the principal naval task was to organise and work the line of supply by sea as the army advanced. For this purpose naval port parties were assembled for use at all the Desert ports up to and including Benghazi. Tugs, schooners, mobile lighters, and other small craft were held ready, and ships suitable for the Western Desert run were docked and prepared.

As September wore on General Montgomery began to have doubts about his plan. He feared that he might be asking too much of his 'somewhat untrained troops'. He decided—the record is dated 6th October—to alter the design of the battle on the front of the main attack, after the infantry had broken into the enemy's defended zone. Under the new plan the infantry, still enjoying very strong artillery support, would widen the breach to north and south and methodically destroy the enemy's holding troops. This process he called 'crumbling'. The enemy's armour could not stand idle while the defences crumbled away, and it would be obliged to move to the help of its infantry. The British armour, having passed through the original breach, should be well placed to intervene—its object being still to destroy the opposing armour. The revised plan had the merit of giving the enemy no respite, for if the crumbling attacks started soon enough the initiative would remain with the British. General Montgomery hoped in this way to destroy all the enemy's holding troops. 'Having thus "eaten the guts" out of the enemy he will have no troops with which to hold a front. His Panzer Army may attempt to interfere with our tactics, and may launch counter-attacks; this would be what we want, and would give us the opportunity of inflicting casualties on the enemy's armour. When we have succeeded in destroying the enemy holding troops, the eventual fate of the Panzer Army is certain—it will not be able to avoid destruction.'

Except for the short interruption caused by the battle of Alam el Halfa, reorganization of the 8th Army went on apace. In its simplest terms the problem was how to group the available formations and units in the most effective way in view of the coming battle and how best to allot the material resources, old and new.

One of General Montgomery's first decisions on taking command of the 8th Army had been to form what he called a reserve corps, strong in armour, characteristically referred to by Mr. Churchill as 'the mass of manoeuvre'. This Corps—the 10th—was originally to consist of the 1st, 8th and 10th Armoured Divisions and the New Zealand Division, but as the 8th could not be provided with a lorried infantry brigade this Division was broken up. The New Zealand Division was to be lent to the 30th Corps for the 'break in' phase, but was to revert to the 10th Corps later. This Division had an armoured brigade under its command, an arrangement of special interest in view of the disappointing results of the attempts made by the armour and the New Zealanders to co-operate during the July fighting—particularly on the morrow of a night attack.[1]

The intention was to have three types of division: *Armoured*, of one armoured and one lorried infantry or motor brigade; *Mixed*, of one armoured and two infantry brigades; and *Infantry*, of three infantry brigades. Each type would have the appropriate divisional troops. The Brigade Group organization was to be abolished except in the French and Greek contingents; divisions were to be handled as divisions. In principle a brigade was not to be detached from its parent division, though it will be seen that in practice, for a temporary and particular purpose, it often was.

In outline the finished structure was as follows:

30*th Corps* (Lieut.-General Sir Oliver Leese)
    23rd Armoured Brigade Group.
    51st (Highland) Division (Major-General D. N. Wimberley):
        152nd, 153rd, 154th Infantry Brigades.
    4th Indian Division (Major-General F. I. S. Tuker):
        5th, 7th, 161st Indian Infantry Brigades.
    9th Australian Division (Lieut.-General Sir Leslie Morshead):
        20th, 24th, 26th Australian Infantry Brigades.
    New Zealand Division (Lieut.-General Sir Bernard Freyberg, V.C.):
        5th, 6th New Zealand Infantry Brigades.*
        9th (U.K.) Armoured Brigade.
            *The 4th New Zealand Infantry Brigade was away, changing into an armoured brigade.

---
[1] Volume III, Chapter XIV.

1st South African Division (Major-General D. H. Pienaar):
  1st, 2nd, 3rd South African Infantry Brigades.

13th Corps (Lieut.-General B. G. Horrocks)
  7th Armoured Division (Major-General A. F. Harding):
    4th Light Armoured Brigade, 22nd Armoured Brigade, 1st Fighting French Brigade Group.
  50th Division (Major-General J. S. Nichols):
    69th, 151st Infantry Brigades, 1st Greek Infantry Brigade Group, 2nd Fighting French Brigade Group.
  44th Division (Major-General I. T. P. Hughes):
    131st, 132nd Infantry Brigades.

10th Corps (Lieut.-General H. Lumsden)
  1st Armoured Division (Major-General R. Briggs):
    2nd Armoured Brigade, 7th Motor Brigade.
  10th Armoured Division (Major-General A. H. Gatehouse):
    8th, 24th Armoured Brigades, 133rd (Lorried) Infantry Brigade.
  8th Armoured Division (Major-General C. H. Gairdner):
    Divisional H.Q. and certain divisional troops only.

Among the weapons now arriving in good quantities were some newcomers to the Middle East. The most important was the American Sherman tank, of which 300 had been given by President Roosevelt to the Prime Minister on that black day in June when news reached them that Rommel had taken Tobruk.[1] The Sherman was a well-armoured and mechanically reliable vehicle whose main weapon was a high-velocity 75-mm gun firing either H.E. or capped armour-piercing shell. Unlike the Grant—which in its turn had been so welcome—the Sherman carried its gun in the turret, with all-round traverse. Another newcomer was the British Crusader Mark III, which mounted a 6-pdr gun. About one quarter of all the Crusaders in the 8th Army were of this Mark. It had been keenly awaited for a long time in the Middle East and was expected to be a big improvement on tanks armed with the 2-pdr, which had been the standard British tank and anti-tank gun. But before long the Mark III was being criticized for displaying most of the weaknesses of the earlier Crusaders, and, like them, for having no capped ammunition.[2]

---

[1] On 15th July seven ships sailed from the U.S.A. with these tanks. The next day one ship was torpedoed and sunk, but the loss was made good by sending 52 more tanks. By 11th September 318 Shermans had arrived in the Middle East.

[2] In Palestine there was a brigade of three RTR regiments equipped with a searchlight in a special turret on a Matilda chassis and called (for secrecy) CDL. This purported to stand for Canal Defence Lights but in reality the light was to be used to dazzle the enemy and make it impossible for him to see, let alone aim, up to some 1,000 yards. Anything in its flickering beam was illuminated. It was thought that it might be able to help maintain the momentum of the advance at night. Many who saw it in operation were impressed by its possibilities. General Alexander was one of those who believed in it, but the 1st Tank Brigade only started training in October 1942, too late for El Alamein.

TANKS

The distribution of tanks among the various formations is shown in the following table. They totalled 1,029 fit and ready for action, with 200 of various types available as replacements. This gives a grand total of roughly twice as many as the German and Italian tanks put together, while about another 1,000 were in workshops, being repaired or modified.

Fit Tanks in Formations on the evening of 23rd October

(The figure below the name is the main armament)

	Grant 75-mm	Sherman 75-mm long	Crusader 2-pdr or 3-in. How	Crusader III 6-pdr	Stuart 37-mm	Valentine 2-pdr
10 *Corps*						
1 Armd Div	2	—	—	—	—	—
2 Armd Bde	—	—	8	—	—	—
	1	92	39	29	—	—
10 Armd Div	—	—	7	—	—	—
8 Armd Bde	57	31	33	12	—	—
24 Armd Bde	2	93	28	17	—	—
13 *Corps*						
7 Armd Div	—	—	7	—	—	—
4 Lt Armd Bde	14	—	—	—	67	—
22 Armd Bde	57	—	42	8	19	—
30 *Corps*						
9 Armd Bde†	37	36	37	12	—	—
23 Armd Bde*	—	—	—	—	—	194
N.Z. Div Cav	—	—	—	—	29	—
9 Aust Div Cav	—	—	15	—	4	—
Total	170	252	216	78	119	194

† Under command of New Zealand Division.
* One regiment of this Brigade was attached to each of these divisions: Australian, 51st, and South African; the fourth was in Corps reserve.

GERMAN TANKS IN THE D.A.K.*

Pzkw	(II)	III 5-cm short	III Sp 5-cm long	IV 7.5-cm short	IV Sp 7.5-cm long	Comd
Fit	(31)	85	88	8	30	7
Under repair	(2)	17	1	2	—	1

* Divided almost equally between 15th and 21st Panzer Divisions. Since June all reinforcements were either III Specials or IV Specials. Pzkw II was too light to count in combat, and hereafter is not included in tank strengths unless so stated.

ITALIAN TANKS

	Medium 47-mm	(Light)
Ariete Division	129	—
Littorio Division	115	(20)
Trieste Division[1]	34	—
Total	278	(20)

A new artillery weapon was the American 105-mm self-propelled (SP) Howitzer—the 'Priest'. Two British experimental SP equipments were present in small numbers: the 25-pdr mounted on the chassis of a Valentine tank ('Bishop'), and the 6-pdr anti-tank gun mounted on a four-wheel chassis ('Deacon'). The 'Bishop' proved unsatisfactory and was soon dropped.

The total of the 8th Army's artillery weapons was formidable indeed. Over 900 medium and field pieces were ready for action on the eve of the battle. Of 2-pdr and 6-pdr anti-tank guns there were 554 and 849 respectively, distributed broadly as follows: to each infantry battalion, eight 2-pdrs; to each motor battalion, sixteen 6-pdrs; to each anti-tank regiment R.A. (in armoured formations) sixty-four 6-pdrs, or (in infantry formations) forty-eight 6-pdrs and sixteen 2-pdrs.

The enemy's anti-tank guns at this time were of various types, among the most effective being the 7·65-cm of which there were 68, and the 5-cm Pak 38 of which there were about 290. Rommel had repeatedly asked for more 8·8-cm Flak guns, which had done so well as anti-tank weapons ever since they first landed early in 1941. These had belonged to Flak Regiment 135, a *Luftwaffe* unit. In August 1942 Headquarters 19th Flak Division came over to Africa, together with Flak Regiment 102. On 1st October there were 86 8·8-cm Flak guns in the *Panzerarmee's* area, but not all had the primary role in battle of defence against tanks. A further 52 were deployed in the back area for the anti-aircraft defence of airfields and ports; these were not under the 19th Flak Division.

The growth of the U.S. Army Middle East Air Force made it necessary to arrange between the Allies for its control.[2] At the Commanders-in-Chief's level the Commanding General, U.S.A.M.E.A.F. (Major-General Lewis H. Brereton) and the

---

[1] Not an armoured division.
[2] Its creation in June 1942 is referred to in Volume III.

Air Officer Commanding-in-Chief, in consultation with the other Commanders-in-Chief as necessary, laid down the policy.[1] Operational control of the American heavy bomber squadrons was vested in IX Bomber Command, U.S.A.A.F. (which came into being on 12th October 1942) and that of the American medium day-bomber and fighter squadrons in the A.O.C., Western Desert Air Force. The day before the battle began a small American Task Force Headquarters was set up to work alongside the Desert Air Force's Advanced Headquarters and look after the interests of the American squadrons.

The need to form the best available hard-hitting fighter aircraft into the spearhead of an advance, and the influx of American tactical air squadrons, called for some reorganization within the Desert Air Force. A new fighter group headquarters (No. 212) and a new fighter wing headquarters (No. 244) were therefore set up, and an additional day-bomber wing headquarters (No. 232) was brought forward from Palestine. The twenty-five British and American fighter squadrons were divided between the two fighter groups, the best types of fighter aircraft being concentrated in No. 211 Group to form the spearhead—known as Force A. The remainder—Force B—came under No. 212 Group. The distribution of the Desert Air Force squadrons on 27th October was as follows:

Fighter
  No. 211 Group (Force A)
    No. 233 Wing (Three squadrons of Kittyhawks and one of Tomahawks).
    No. 239 Wing (Five squadrons of Kittyhawks including one from the U.S. 57th Fighter Group).
    No. 244 Wing (Three squadrons of Spitfires and one of night-flying Hurricanes).
    U.S. 57th Fighter Group (Two squadrons of Kittyhawks).*
    Two tank-destroying Hurricane squadrons.
    * The American 'Group' was similar to the British 'Wing'.
  No. 212 Group (Force B)
    No. 7 (S.A.A.F.) Wing (Four squadrons of Hurricanes).
    No. 243 Wing (Four squadrons of Hurricanes).

Day-bomber
  No. 3 (S.A.A.F.) Wing (Two squadrons of Bostons and one of Baltimores).
  No. 232 Wing (Two squadrons of Baltimores).
  U.S. 12th Medium Bombardment Group (Three squadrons of Mitchells).

---

[1] On 5th December 1942 the Commanding General U.S.A.M.E.A.F. (by then re-designated Ninth Air Force) was made a formal member of the Cs.-in-C's Committee.

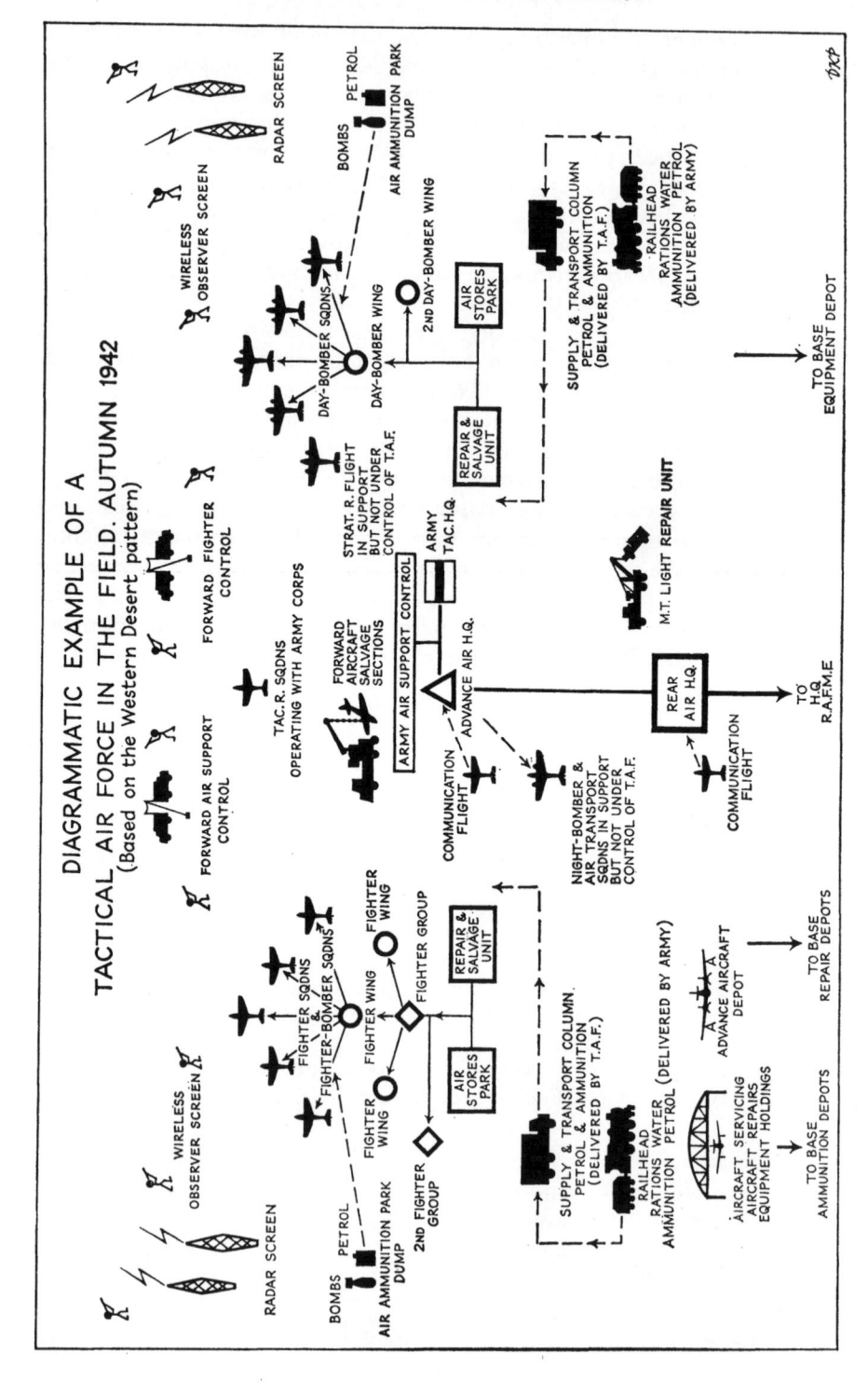

DIAGRAMMATIC EXAMPLE OF A TACTICAL AIR FORCE IN THE FIELD. AUTUMN 1942
(Based on the Western Desert pattern)

Reconnaissance
  No. 285 Wing:
     Two tactical reconnaissance (Hurricane) squadrons.
     One strategical reconnaissance (Baltimore) flight.
     One survey reconnaissance (Baltimore) squadron.
     One photographic reconnaissance (Spitfire) flight.

Certain other units were available to reinforce the Desert Air Force in direct support of the 8th Army. These were two squadrons of long-range twin-engine fighters (Beaufighters) from No. 201 Group; six squadrons of medium night-bombers (Wellingtons) from No. 205 Group; two pathfinder squadrons (Albacores) from the Fleet Air Arm; and four squadrons of various types of transport aircraft from No. 216 Group. The operations of many other units were also designed to support the battle, though less directly; in effect, almost all the Allied air forces in the Mediterranean area were involved in one way or another.

As for the aircraft themselves, there were some drawbacks to be overcome. After the battle of Alam el Halfa there had been a shortage of Spitfires and Kittyhawks, and though this became steadily less, thanks largely to the efforts of the repair organization, there was no reserve with which to meet wastage or replace the obsolescent Hurricanes. Moreover, little more than half the available fighter aircraft could compare in performance with the Me. 109F or G. Air Vice-Marshal Coningham relied on the medium night-bomber force to complete his programme of round-the-clock bombing, but there was a shortage of Wellingtons in No. 205 Group, and even by the third week of October there were only fifty serviceable, mainly on account of transfers to India and the needs of Bomber Command. But as regards the day-bomber force Air Vice-Marshal Coningham had good reason to feel satisfied. Strengthened by another Baltimore squadron and three American squadrons equipped with the Mitchell—an aircraft with a much greater bombload and longer range than the Boston or the Baltimore—it was the most powerful force yet seen in the desert.[1]

General Montgomery had quickly seen that his Army was badly in need of training, and, as time was short, he insisted on training for the particular type of battle he had devised. It was not easy to hold the front and train hard at the same time. It proved possible, however, for the armoured divisions of the 10th Corps and the New Zealand Division to train as divisions well behind the line,

---

[1] The Orders of Battle of the Royal Air Force and U.S. Army Air Force in the Middle East as at 27th October 1942, together with details of aircraft employed, are at Appendices 8 and 10.

though the 10th Armoured Division was hampered by the late arrival of equipment, which delayed the reorganization of the 133rd Infantry Brigade as a lorried infantry brigade. The Division's additional armoured brigade, the 24th, only came under General Gatehouse's command on 10th October. For the other divisions a complicated system of reliefs made short periods of training possible, mostly by a brigade at a time. Exercises were so arranged that units (unwittingly—for reasons of security) rehearsed their parts in the coming battle.

Very particular attention was given to the problem of passing large bodies of troops through minefields by night. This problem had been steadily growing in difficulty and importance, and it was now clear that all else would be in vain if it were not satisfactorily solved. One of the traditional tasks of the engineers—that of breaching the walls of the fortress—had appeared in a new guise, and the 8th Army's Minefield Clearance School was charged with devising a drill for clearing lanes through minefields and teaching this unenviable duty to the engineer troops. Nearly 500 detectors of various patterns, mostly of that known as 'Polish', were issued, but failures and damage meant that more often the desperately slow and risky method of prodding the ground with bayonets had to be used.

Among the items of equipment specially designed for clearing a way through mines was the 'Scorpion'. This was a Matilda tank fitted in front with a revolving drum to which lengths of chain were fastened. An auxiliary engine, mounted in a sponson and driven by a Sapper, turned the drum whereupon the chains thrashed the ground like flails and detonated any mines in the path. Twenty-four Scorpions, manned by men of 42nd and 44th R.T.R. and a party of Royal Engineers, were ready by 23rd October. Unfortunately these early machines were unreliable and very slow in action, so that almost all gaps in minefields had to be made by hand.[1]

The training of the Royal Air Force and its attached American squadrons had to be worked in with essential air operations and rest. An item of training not previously referred to was smoke-laying, to which considerable importance was attached by the army. It was practised by Bostons of Nos. 12 and 24 Squadrons, S.A.A.F. and needed much skill. Other items of training to which

---

[1] Dust in the Desert was bad enough in any event, but the cloud raised by a Scorpion had to be seen to be believed. The machine had thus to be driven practically "blind". If the flail driver looked out he would be deluged with sand, and bombarded by stones, scrub, and an occasional mine! An Italian prisoner was reported to have said that more frightening than the barrage was this slowly advancing pillar of dust out of which came dreadful noises of clanking, grinding, and rattling of chains.

After the War the Royal Commission of Awards to Inventors recommended awards totalling £20,000 to be made to eleven individuals for their share in developing the Scorpion. Five of these were officers of the Union Defence Force.

particular attention was given were the standards of discipline in the use of radio-telephony in the air and the dispersal of aircraft on the ground. Squadrons were to prepare for and practise rapid movement in an advance.

To extend the range of the Hurricanes two airfields were constructed near El Hammam, forty miles ahead of the main group of fighter airfields around Amiriya. On Ruweisat Ridge a forward fighter control post was set up, and all fighter aircraft were fitted to carry long-range fuel tanks.

In the preparation of the Desert Air Force for the coming battle, Air Commodore G. R. Beamish, the Senior Air Staff Officer, played an important part.

In the administrative field the British had made the most of the opportunity given them by the run of the summer campaign, when they had been pressed back nearly to their base. The size and regularity of the ocean convoys, supplemented by fast and independently-routed personnel ships, had ensured a steady delivery of men, munitions, supplies and stores of all kinds on a vast scale. By now the base was far better equipped and able to receive and deal expeditiously with the flow than ever before. To give one example: because vehicle assembly plants were now working in the Middle East, vehicles could be shipped dismantled, which meant that more could be carried in each ship.

Thus the British had in plenty commodities, including ammunition, with which to build up, in the 8th Army's area, stocks to provide for the move of the troops to their assembly position, and for the subsequent battle.[1] Equally important, the lines of communication from the base in the Canal zone were short and well served by rail and road, and there were satisfactory numbers of transport vehicles—not that anybody would ever admit to having enough. To give some idea of the quantities, over and above vehicles on the establishment of units and formations, it was planned to provide the 8th Army with the equivalent of thirty-six 3-ton General Transport (GT) Companies, six Tank Transporter Companies, nine Water Tank Companies, and one Bulk Petrol Transport Company.[2] This intention was very nearly fulfilled, and G.H.Q. still had seven General Transport Companies in reserve.

---

[1] Some 268,000 rounds of 25-pdr and 20,000 rounds of medium ammunition were dumped for immediate use. As a reserve in the forward area seven days' at double the 8th Army's normal scale was provided: approximately 18,000 tons.

[2] 'Equivalent' because some GT Companies were equipped with 10-ton lorries. The standard lift of a GT Company was 300 tons. Between 1st August–23rd October 1942 8,700 General Service vehicles were issued to, or earmarked for, 8th Army out of a total intake of 10,300.

The ration strength of the 8th Army was now around 231,000, and from 1st to 23rd October (the peak period of the build-up) an average of 2,500 tons of stores a day was delivered at the various railheads situated about Amiriya and Burg el Arab. By 22nd October all the Field Maintenance Centres held at least the planned requirement of five days' stocks, and a further two days' was on wheels. Many miles of water pipe-line from 4-inch to 10-inch were laid, and three new water-points were built near El Alamein.

A major decision on policy by the War Office led on 1st October to a change in some duties of the technical branches of the army. A new Corps of Royal Electrical and Mechanical Engineers was created, to be responsible for the inspection and repair of guns, vehicles and other equipment.[1] The Royal Army Ordnance Corps remained responsible for provision, storage, and distribution. The chain of workshops serving the 8th Army became R.E.M.E. units —mainly a change of title at first—and the shortage of skilled British artificers was overcome by skinning technical units in other parts of the Middle East.[2]

The organization for replacing damaged tanks was overhauled. A Tank Reorganization Group had been formed from the 1st Armoured Brigade to receive from the Base all replacement armoured vehicles, inspect them and carry out minor repairs, and provide tool kits, fuel, and crews. The vehicles were then to be passed to units through the Tank Delivery Regiment and it was hoped that they would arrive in a thoroughly battleworthy condition.

Two further administrative matters deserve mention. A special organization was set up to deliver quickly from the base any stores which were so scarce or so varied and complex that it was not feasible for every advanced ordnance unit to hold a complete range. Secondly, the 8th Army had the satisfactory number of 25 pioneer and labour companies, and there were 24 more in G.H.Q. reserve.

It is evident that the powerful 8th Army rested on a broad and solid administrative foundation—at all events, for any fighting that might occur as far east as the El Alamein positions. Measures for supporting a subsequent advance were prepared also, but it will be convenient to describe them in a later chapter.

The main interest in the administrative preparations made by the R.A.F., and in which, as regards the Desert Air Force, Air Commodore T. W. Elmhirst had a principal hand, lies in the steps taken to ensure that Force A (the spearhead fighter force) should lack nothing. It was to be kept up to strength from Force B, and

---

[1] The new Corps was formed by the amalgamation of the engineering side of the R.A.O.C. with the bulk of that of the R.A.S.C., plus certain Royal Engineers.

[2] Among the 8th Army's workshops was one American unit.

was to have its own air stores park (ASP), a section of an advanced salvage unit (ASU) and a repair detachment. An ASP and the remainder of the ASU were allotted to Force B; and an ASP was retained by the day-bomber squadrons. A fourth ASP and the normal wing repair and salvage units (RSU) were to follow in the wake of the advance. Each ASP was to carry four weeks' stock of equipment. The repair and salvage units were to take spare aero engines with them and those in the rear would also hold reserves of aircraft which would be replenished by ferrying direct from the maintenance units. Before the offensive opened each fighter squadron was to have thirty pilots and each wing a reserve of ten, who would travel with the wing's RSU. An important feature of the maintenance policy was that Force A should not be burdened with any aircraft or vehicles it could not repair within forty-eight hours. Other new administrative measures of a general nature were: the issue to every unit of seven days' supply of spare parts, rations, water and M.T. fuel, with a further three days' supply of rations and water to each vehicle (for its crew) and enough petrol for 300 miles; the holding at all times, for rapid despatch forward, of one complete re-arm of ammunition and bombs for every squadron, and 24 long-range tanks for all Hurricane, Kittyhawk and Spitfire squadrons. The Chief Engineer, 8th Army, undertook to clear captured landing-grounds of obstacles and mines as a matter of high priority. There was to be a regular daily air freight and passenger service between the Base area and Force A, and 40 Hudson aircraft were to be available for ferrying forward bombs, ammunition, fuel, or any other items urgently needed by the 8th Army or the Desert Air Force.

In February 1942 the R.A.F. Regiment had come into being in the United Kingdom. Not until September, however, were steps taken to form the 7,800 'ground gunners' in the Middle East into flights of the new Regiment, armed with rifles, machine-guns, and a few 20-mm cannon. Their tasks were to clear from airfields any enemy who had been missed by the army, and mines which the Royal Engineers had not had time to remove; to protect airfields; and to guard R.A.F. convoys. Though in October 1942 the new organization was still in its infancy, it was able to provide a number of units to meet the requirements of Force A.

After his failure at Alam el Halfa in the early days of September, Field-Marshal Rommel was bound to expect the 8th Army to take the offensive itself as soon as it could. General Montgomery therefore decided to go for tactical surprise—that is, to deceive the enemy about when, where, and how the attack would be delivered. As he had made the basic plan for the battle in good time, it was possible to take some elaborate steps to encourage the enemy to draw false deductions.

The concealment of the numerous dumps of ammunition, supplies, and stores of all kinds required care and ingenuity. Old slit trenches and borrow-pits were used, existing dumps were unobtrusively added to, and boxes were built up into the shape of vehicles. But owing to the lack of natural cover in the desert many preparations could not be concealed. The bold policy was therefore adopted of letting the enemy become accustomed to them in the hope that he would be misled as to what they really were. For example, the 10th Corps' training ground was near Wadi Natrun, far to the east, and it would be impossible to conceal the mass of vehicles when the Corps moved up through staging areas to an assembly position close to El Alamein. But if these areas had already been occupied by an equal number of soft vehicles, and if the vehicle density could be made to appear unchanged in spite of fresh arrivals, it seemed possible that the enemy would cease to be suspicious about them. Accordingly by 6th October—seventeen days before D day—the correct number of vehicles (drawn from 13th and 30th Corps) and dummies were stationed in the staging and assembly areas. Some of the dummies, known as 'sunshields' and 'cannibals', were designed to cover and disguise tanks and guns. As each tank, gun, or vehicle arrived in its new area it disappeared beneath a sunshield or cannibal awaiting it, or took the place of a vehicle already there. The replaced vehicles moved off, and some —and dummies—occupied the areas from which the fresh arrivals had come. By morning the density of the various concentrations seemed unchanged.

Something of the sort was also done for the 51st and New Zealand Divisions, and an interesting detail was that some of the slit trenches from which the infantry would advance to the assault were dug about a month before they would be used. They thus became part of the landscape.

An essential part of the Army Commander's plan was to deceive the enemy into thinking that the main blow would fall in the south. Several dummy dumps and administrative camps were built to support this impression; and to suggest that a new water-supply system was being provided for the southern sector a bogus pipe-line was laid, but at a pace which suggested that it would not be ready until early November. Finally, to draw further attention to the south the 10th Armoured Division moved openly to a position behind the 13th Corps. From here it departed by night for its real destination to the north of Alam el Halfa and was replaced by a life-like dummy replica.

These stratagems were supplemented by strict orders on security discipline, and every precaution was taken to maintain a uniform volume and pattern of wireless traffic, which would give nothing away to the enemy's intercept service. Some realistic bogus traffic helped to suggest that the 10th Armoured Division remained in the south after it had in reality moved away.

How far did the deception plan succeed? The situation as viewed by the enemy will be described presently, and it will be seen that, briefly, he expected to be strongly attacked sooner or later, but did not know where. On the whole, he considered the most likely front of attack to be in the vicinity of Deir el Munassib.

During the weeks of preparation the 8th Army's operations consisted almost entirely of patrolling, to find out everything possible about the enemy's dispositions and minefields. In the Desert Air Force the policy was to restrict the activities of the fighters and day-bombers to a minimum until 19th October. The aircraft on all-important reconnaissance duties were hampered by cloud and gales but did great service. The night-bombers had no respite; they and the squadrons of No. 201 Group and those in Malta continued to attack the enemy's unloading ports and sea convoys as heavily as possible.[1]

An exception to the general air policy occurred on 9th October, after photographic reconnaissance had shown some of the enemy's forward airfields to be flooded. The day-bombers and fighter-bombers took advantage of the conditions to drop over 100 tons of bombs on airfields at El Daba. They had a strong escort of British and American fighters and there were several combats in the air. During a total of 196 day-bomber and fighter-bomber sorties, and 464 flown by the fighters, 14 aircraft were lost—all British. German records show that two of their aircraft were destroyed and nine damaged on the ground, and two more were lost in combat. Italian records show two lost in combat and one on the ground. The same night the Wellington force bombed the Fuka landing grounds, destroying four aircraft and damaging four more. On 9th October, also, Bisleys and Beaufighters destroyed a train carrying guns and ammunition. All this activity on one day was exceptional. In fact the day-bombers averaged only about ten sorties a day, and the fighter-bombers even less, throughout the six weeks. Because enemy air activity was slight the fighters, too, were not hard pressed. Their average of 160 sorties a day gave them ample opportunity to rest and train.

---

[1] The attacks on convoys in October are described in Chapter VIII.

Meanwhile, the medium and heavy bombers took Tobruk and Benghazi as their main targets. The Wellingtons flew 700 sorties, and the Halifaxes and Liberators 100 to drop 850 tons of bombs on Tobruk. Only the Liberators could reach Benghazi, and the British and American squadrons dropped 150 tons of bombs on the port in 50 sorties. Bombs from American aircraft sank one ship, the *Apuania* of 7,949 tons, and damaged several others. Attacks were also made on airfields and minor ports, and American aircraft laid some mines and made a few attacks on shipping at sea.

Between 8th September and 18th October, excluding air operations from Malta and the anti-shipping operations of No. 201 Group, the Royal Air Force flew 8,606 sorties (or just under 210 each day) and the Americans 444. The British lost 54 aircraft, the Americans 7, and the Axis air forces 77, of which 50 were German.

See Map 3

Plans to harry the enemy's lines of communication by raiding the shipping, harbour facilities, and fuel storage at Tobruk and Benghazi had been under consideration ever since the withdrawal from Cyrenaica. It was felt at Headquarters in Cairo that something of the sort ought to be done to play on the enemy's nerves and cause losses he could ill afford. Plans for a series of raids were sponsored by the three Commanders-in-Chief and worked out by their staffs. Air Chief Marshal Tedder did not like the operation because of the impossibility of providing fighter cover, but felt that he could not carry his dislike to the point of refusal. The 8th Army Commander had no part in making the plans or in carrying them out and, indeed, disliked the whole operation.

The concept was a bold one. It relied greatly on surprise and the belief, mistaken as regards Tobruk, that the garrisons consisted of low-grade Italian troops. A party of Special Service troops, guided by the Long Range Desert Group by way of Kufra to within striking distance, was to penetrate the Tobruk perimeter at dusk and seize an inlet (Mersa Sciausc) to the east of Tobruk harbour, just outside the boom defence. Here, if successful, this party—Force B—would be reinforced by troops carried from Alexandria in MTBs (Force C). The combined forces would then work west, capturing coast defence and Flak batteries on the way. At 3.40 a.m. Royal Marines were to land from the destroyers *Sikh* and *Zulu* (Force A) on the coast north of Tobruk town, cross the intervening tongue of land, capture the guns on the north side of the harbour and enter the town. To occupy the enemy's attention heavy bombing attacks were to be made on Tobruk during the night. As soon as

Map 3

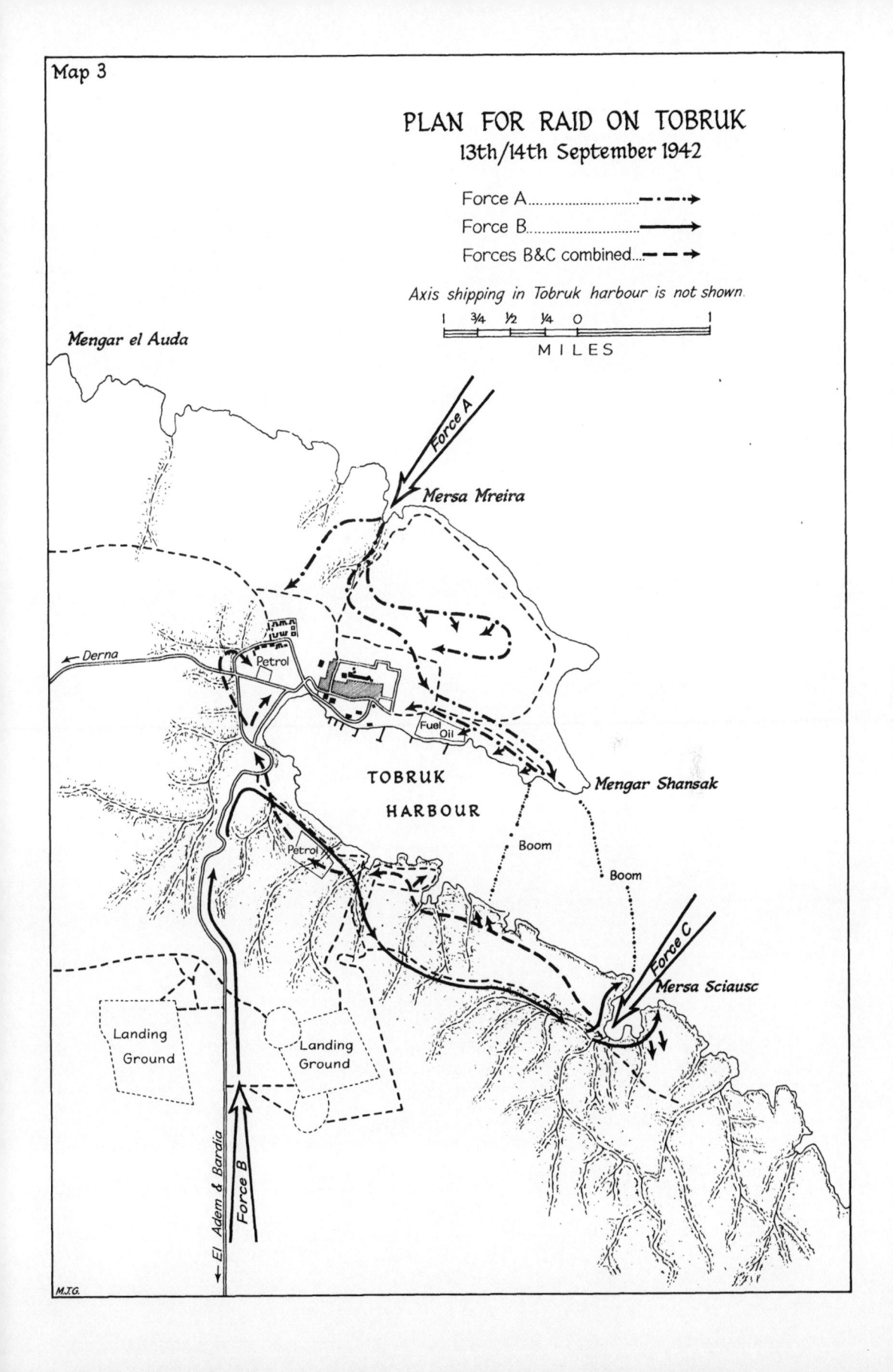

PLAN FOR RAID ON TOBRUK
13th/14th September 1942

Force A .... — · — →
Force B .... ———→
Forces B & C combined .... — — →

Axis shipping in Tobruk harbour is not shown.

MILES

Mengar el Auda

← Derna

Petrol

Fuel Oil

Force A

Mersa Mreira

TOBRUK HARBOUR

Mengar Shansak

Boom

Boom

Petrol

Landing Ground

Landing Ground

Force C

Mersa Sciausc

← El Adem & Bardia

Force B

M.J.G.

the bombing ceased the MTBs were to attack shipping at the east end of the harbour. After the guns protecting the harbour had been captured the *Sikh* and *Zulu* were to enter and land demolition parties. In the afternoon some of the forces ashore were to be embarked for return passage to Alexandria; the remainder in captured transport were to be ready to move westward for further tasks of destruction.[1]

The raid on Benghazi was to be made by Force X, from Kufra, with the objects of blocking the inner harbour, sinking all ships in harbour, and destroying the oil storage and pumping plants. Force X was then to retire to Jalo and continue raiding for three weeks.[2]

To provide a base for the continued operations of Force X, Jalo was to be captured on the night 15th/16th September by Force Z —a detachment of the Sudan Defence Force from Kufra, guided by a patrol of the Long Range Desert Group.

The Royal Air Force was to co-operate by bombing Benghazi and by dropping dummy parachutists on Siwa. Feints on land were also to be made on suitable dates: a raid on Barce by two patrols of the Long Range Desert Group, and a demonstration against Siwa by a motor battalion of the Sudan Defence Force, from Bahariya Oasis.

On 22nd August Force B, guided by a patrol of the Long Range Desert Group, left Cairo on its 1,700 mile journey to Tobruk. The force halted for a few days at Kufra and set out again on 5th September. It struck northwards, skirting Jalo, and on 13th September was ready to begin its task. The plan was daring indeed. The assaulting party, 83 strong, travelled in three lorries displaying German markings. The party posed as prisoners of war and its weapons were concealed. The 'escort' was provided by a number of German speakers dressed in German uniforms.[3] The plan was to drive openly through the perimeter posts and then to the jumping-off place for the assault. This daring gamble came off. At last light on the 13th the party drove past an Italian check post and on to the chosen point, where the 'escort' changed into British uniforms.

---

[1] The main units of the several forces were:
   Force A *Naval* (Captain St. J. A. Micklethwait, R.N.): H.M.S. *Sikh*; *Zulu*.
   Military (Lieut.-Colonel E. H. M. Unwin, R.M.): 11th Battalion Royal Marines; detachments R.A., R.E., R.Sigs., R.A.M.C.
   Force B (Lieut.-Colonel J. E. Haselden): D Squadron 1st Special Service Regiment; detachments R.A., R.E., R.Sigs.
   Force C *Naval* (Commander J. F. Blackburn, R.N.): 16 MTBs. and 3 MLs.
   Military (Captain A. N. Macfie): D Company 1st Argyll and Sutherland Highlanders; detachments 1st Royal Northumberland Fusiliers; R.A., R.E., R.Sigs., R.A.M.C.

[2] Force X (Lieut.-Colonel A. D. Stirling): L Detachment 1st Special Air Service Brigade, S.1 and S.2 Patrols Long Range Desert Group, detachment R.M.

[3] These men, led by Captain H. C. Buck and Lieutenant T. C. D. A. Russell, would have been liable to execution if they had been captured while thus disguised.

Meanwhile the air-raid alarm had sounded. Between 10.25 p.m. and 3.30 a.m. 91 Wellingtons, Halifaxes, Liberators and Fortresses dropped 70 tons of bombs on Tobruk and started several fires. Under cover of the bombing Force B attacked and captured the inlet at Mersa Sciausc.

The stage was now set for the appearance of Forces C and A. Unfortunately Force C had straggled during the last stage of its passage from Alexandria, a number of MTBs had not intercepted the success signal from Force B, guiding lights (which it was Force B's responsibility to establish) were difficult to distinguish, and MTBs attempting to make the entrance to the inlet were met with gunfire from several directions. Only two boats succeeded in entering, and landed a section of machine-gunners.

Force A arrived about two miles off the north coast shortly after 3 a.m. on the 11th. The swell had prevented folbotists landing from the submarine *Taku* to mark the landing place, a great deal of trouble was experienced with the improvised landing-craft, and by 5 a.m. only about 70 Marines had landed—near Mengar el Auda, about two miles west of the correct beach.[1] They fought their way towards Tobruk but were overwhelmed. No more Marines reached the shore because of the situation at sea. There the two destroyers, in search of returning landing-craft in which to land the second flight of Royal Marines, closed to within a mile of the coast and came under accurate shell fire. The *Sikh*'s steering gear was put out of action. The *Zulu* took her in tow but a shell parted the towing wire and both ships were repeatedly hit. Captain Micklethwait ordered the *Zulu* to retire and later the *Sikh* to be scuttled. Survivors from the ship's company and the Marines were taken prisoner. Force B had meanwhile blown up the coastal guns at Mersa Sciausc and fought on against increasing numbers as long as it could. Its commander, Lieut.-Colonel Haselden, was killed while leading an attempt to break out.

The enemy was using fighter-bombers and dive-bombers based in North Africa and some long-range bombers from Crete. At about 11.15 a.m. the anti-aircraft cruiser *Coventry*, coming up with six Hunts to support the retiring *Zulu*, was hit by four bombs and had to be sunk. After surviving several further air attacks the *Zulu* herself was hit and sank after an attempt to tow her had failed. In the course of the day three MTBs and two MLs were also sunk by air attack, and one of the two MTBs which had entered Mersa Sciausc was stranded and abandoned.

Besides the loss of these warships, and eight British and American aircraft, this gallant endeavour cost in killed, wounded, and

---

[1] 'Folbot' was the trade name for some of the canoes used in clandestine landings.

captured, about 280 naval officers and men, 300 Royal Marines, and 160 soldiers. The main causes of failure were the great hazards of the plan, the distance to the objective—beyond the reach of all but a few of the British fighters—lack of experience of landing operations and of suitable craft, and underestimates of the enemy. No evidence has been found to show that the enemy had become aware of any part of the plan, but there is irony in the fact that the unusually heavy air attacks aroused the suspicions of Major-General Deindl (commanding the Rear Army Area) who alerted all the German troops, of which there were over 2,000 in Tobruk. The Italian troops also acted with speed and resolution.

The other operations, with one exception, fared little better. Force X appears to have been detected on its way towards Benghazi. The Liberators made their attack as planned, but Force X had dropped behind its time-table and was hotly opposed when it made contact with a road block. Dawn was near, surprise had been lost, and Colonel Stirling decided to withdraw. His Force was attacked from the air throughout the next day.

Force Z reached Jalo on the night 15th/16th as planned, but found the enemy watchful and strong enough to repel the attack. On the 19th GHQ ordered the Force to withdraw. The demonstration against Siwa caused no apparent reaction. At Barce the L.R.D.G. scored the only success when Major J. R. Easonsmith's two patrols, in five Jeeps and twelve 30-cwt trucks, having covered 700 miles from the Faiyum, reached their objective up to time and roamed over the airfield shooting up aircraft and hurling grenades into military buildings. The Italians reported sixteen of their aircraft destroyed and seven damaged on 14th September 'by British armoured cars'—a tribute to the dash and efficiency of the L.R.D.G. The party—47 strong—had 21 casualties (many from air attacks the next day) and had 15 vehicles destroyed out of 17.

Thus the results of the raids were on the whole disappointing. They led to a general overhaul of the defensive arrangements on the enemy's lines of communication and to a decision to reinforce Siwa, Jarabub, and Jalo. Three German replacement or draft-holding battalions were posted at Sollum, and for a short time the Pavia Division was kept at Matruh instead of moving forward. Finally, there was much talk of capturing Kufra, but nothing came of it.

An operation of a different kind took place on 8th Army's front at the end of the month. This was an attack by 131st Infantry Brigade (of 44th Division) on the Deir el Munassib.[1] The main object was to capture an additional deployment area for the artillery

---

[1] Deir = a depression.

in preparation for the coming offensive; another was to continue to draw the enemy's attention to the southern sector of the front. The attack was straightforward, covered by strong fighter forces, and supported by a few day- and fighter-bombers and by one medium and nine field artillery regiments. It began at first light on 30th September. The 1/6th and 1/7th Queen's met little opposition, but 1/5th Queen's was not so fortunate, for its objectives were held by the 9th Battalion of the good (Italian) Folgore Parachute Division and part of the Ramcke Parachute Brigade. The Queen's took heavy casualties and were pinned down. Brigadier E. H. C. Frith decided to resume the attack in the evening, but there were delays and confusion in the preparations which led to postponements, and on 1st October the Corps Commander, General Horrocks, called the operation off. The ground gained in the north of the depression was consolidated and taken over by 132nd Infantry Brigade (Brigadier L. G. Whistler). The main causes of the partial failure were thought to be that much of the artillery support was wasted owing to faulty information about the enemy's dispositions, the brigade was inexperienced, and the ground very difficult.

September and October were, for the enemy, months of anxiety and frustration. Alam el Halfa had given a taste of what to expect now that the British—especially their air forces—were becoming so much stronger in Egypt. But the troubles of the Axis were not confined to North Africa. The German offensive in Russia was not prospering, and on 24th September General Halder (Chief of the General Staff since 1938) was dismissed by Hitler for voicing misgivings about its prospects. Hitler still cherished his Russian plans and gave a bad second place to the African theatre and its needs. Mussolini took a gloomy view and thought that Italy no longer had the ships to win the struggle, especially as the Americans would probably land in North Africa during the coming year. Hitler, however, was more concerned with the Eastern Mediterranean and the Aegean, and directed that Crete was to be reinforced and Field-Marshal Kesselring made responsible for those parts of the Mediterranean and Aegean coasts which were occupied by German forces outside the *Panzerarmee's* area.[1] Kesselring asked the Italians whether they were strengthening the defences of such

---

[1] Towards the end of 1941 Hitler had appointed Field-Marshal Albert Kesselring to be Commander-in-Chief South (*Oberbefehlshaber Süd*) with the task of establishing naval and air superiority in the zone between Italy and North Africa. Kesselring was subordinate to the Duce and had a mixed German and Italian staff. Under him were *Fliegerkorps II* and *X*, and he could issue directives to certain German and Italian naval forces. He was to co-operate with the Axis forces in North Africa, but Rommel was not under his orders. From August 1942 he (Rommel) was made directly responsible to *Comando Supremo* for operations; previously he had been under Bastico.

places as the islands of Rhodes and Scarpanto, and was told that they were.

This defensive outlook was very different from the bright mirage seen only a short time before when Rommel was chasing the retreating British eastwards deep into Egyptian territory. If only Malta had been captured, as was originally intended! The alternative plan had failed, and recriminations were in the air. Amid a welter of appreciations, directives, orders, plans, and opinions relating to the affairs of the African and Mediterranean theatre, the German Naval Staff seems to have hit the mark in recording on 8th September:

> 'In order to safeguard our position in the Mediterranean, to protect Italy, to prevent a planned British offensive, to frustrate the enemy's plans for a defensive front and to create the prerequisites for a direct connexion between Germany and Japan, the Naval Staff believes that the following requirements must be met:
>
> 1. North Africa must be held, if at all possible, from the Alamein position.
> 2. The *Luftwaffe* must be greatly reinforced.
> 3. Malta must be seized.
> 4. The plan of an offensive against Suez at a later date must be adhered to.'

But the writer cautiously added 'Until further notice this opinion must not be passed on.'

As the summer passed the condition of the *Panzerarmee* grew worse. The Royal Navy and Royal Air Force took steady toll of the Axis merchant ships, of which, by the end of September, the shortage had become serious.[1] To make matters worse there was not enough oil fuel to keep the escorting warships at sea. Moreover, the whole administrative machine was clumsy and neither partner was in full control. For example, there was much friction over the proportion of cargo space allotted to the Germans. (Rommel never ceased complaining of this.) Promises to provide this or that—whether it was railway material, labourers, anti-aircraft guns, heavy tanks, or engineer troops—were almost always qualified by 'if' or 'when', and usually ended in nothing happening. Most of the German and Italian high officers saw the ills and suggested the remedies, but most of the prescriptions remained on paper because there was no longer time to make them up even if all the ingredients had been available.

---

[1] Details of the twelve merchant vessels of over 500 tons sunk in September are given in Volume III, pages 327 and 382n. 20% of military cargo was lost. In October the figures rose to seventeen ships and 44% of cargo.

Early in September, as soon as the battle of Alam el Halfa died down, it was arranged that Field-Marshal Rommel should go for medical treatment to Germany, his place being taken by 'armoured' General Georg Stumme from the Russian front. On 11th September Rommel sent a long appreciation to *OKH* and *OKW* in which he pointed out the many shortcomings of the Italian troops (largely, he said, the result of poor equipment), and enumerated his own essential requirements. Broadly, these were the reinforcement of the *Luftwaffe*, the transfer to Egypt of the 22nd Air Landing Division before the end of the month,[1] a substantial increase in the flow of ammunition, rations and petrol—35,000 tons of supplies in all were needed every month—and the transfer of the 11,000 German drafts and reinforcements waiting in Italy and Germany. He saw clearly enough that there was now no chance of renewing the offensive or even of fighting the sort of mobile defensive battle he would prefer. Also that it was too late to neutralize the British preparations by withdrawing his whole army from the Alamein positions—to Sollum, for example—even supposing that Hitler and Mussolini would have sanctioned such a course. The *Panzerarmee* had not enough motor transport to enable the whole to withdraw quickly, and the British would certainly not allow it to extricate its non-mobile formations. Rommel nevertheless gave an encouraging address to his Corps and Divisional commanders before handing over to General Stumme, and told them of the intention to provide the defences with greater depth and free the mobile troops from static tasks. On 19th September Stumme arrived; on the 22nd he took command, and the next day a sick and despondent Rommel set off to lay the *Panzerarmee's* troubles before Hitler and Mussolini.

Entries in the *Panzerarmee's* diaries and reports to *OKH* furnish a key to General Stumme's deductions and expectations at the time. For instance, on 3rd October he informed Marshal Cavallero that the recent British activities at Munassib, their landing at Tobruk, and their long-distance raiding into Cyrenaica all presaged a major offensive. However, the re-deployment of the German and Italian forces to provide defence in considerable depth would be complete by 20th October. Further items of intelligence followed from day to day. On the 7th there were references to the observed move forward of supply depots, the increased activity of the R.A.F., and extremely active patrolling in the southern sector of the front. This prompted Stumme to tell his Corps and Divisional commanders that the offensive would soon begin, with its main axis probably somewhere between Ruweisat and Himeimat. An advance on either side of the coastal road was also to be expected, and

---

[1] But the Division was sent to Crete. The *Panzerarmee* was offered instead the 47th Infantry Regiment 'when the supply situation had been stabilized'.

possibly a landing near Sollum. By 15th October expectations had hardened to 'either side of Munassib', 'near Ruweisat', and 'at and south of the coast road'. On the 20th Stumme issued an order telling his subordinate commanders that the British attack might now come at any time and at any point. The indications were that the main effort would be concentrated against the 'northern part of our southern sector'.

General Stumme had frequently protested to *OKH*—as had Rommel before him—about the failure to keep the army adequately supplied. The last report of its condition before the storm of the British offensive broke on its head is dated 19th October. There was then enough fuel in the country for about eleven days at current rates of consumption, and enough ammunition for roughly nine days' fighting. Bread was sufficient for 21 days at about 1 lb per man daily, but many items—in particular, lemons and vegetables —were short. Tyres and spare parts for vehicles were badly wanted, and nearly one-third of all the vehicles were under repair. The railway was affording some slight relief to the motor transport, which, however, was now further burdened by having to make long journeys to fetch water, as the system in the forward area had partially failed. As regards men, reinforcements had fallen far below the numbers needed to fill establishments and make good wastage. Under-nourishment was common and the sick rate was high and increasing.

Then came news that the tanker *Panuco*, due at Tobruk on 20th October with 1,650 tons of bulk and cased petrol, had been hit by a torpedo-bomber (in fact it was a Wellington of No. 69 Squadron) off Cape Stilo. She was forced to put in to Taranto, where her cargo lay useless for over a fortnight.

See Map 2

Field-Marshal Rommel's decision to add to the depth of his defences deserves a word of explanation. Broadly speaking there were at least two belts of mines all along the Axis positions. These belts were connected at intervals by other minefields to form 'boxes' which would localize and restrict any penetration by the British, and, in particular, deprive their armour of room for manoeuvre. The front face of each box was to be lightly held by 'battle outposts' (*Gefechtsvorposten*) guarding the foremost mine-belt and disposed in depth. The rest of the box was to be unoccupied, but sown with mines and explosive traps of all kinds. The front line of the main defensive zone (*Hauptkampffeld*) was drawn back behind the second mine-belt, and from here the zone extended to a depth of at least two kilometres. In a directive of 20th September

Rommel laid down the frontage of a battalion as about $1\frac{1}{2}$ kms and the depth about 5 kms. One company was to man the battalion's battle outposts, while the remainder occupied its main defensive zone. The larger anti-tank guns would be held well back. In reality the whole system—forward and main zones and the 'Devil's Garden' in between—covered anything from $2\frac{1}{2}$ to $4\frac{1}{2}$ miles from front to rear. Some of the guns of 15th Panzer and Littorio Divisions were dug in on a line running due south from Sidi Abd el Rahman, so that they could join in with defensive fire if the British were to attack somewhere between the railway and the Miteirya Ridge. Southwards of El Mreir the Axis defences were less elaborate, but the principle was the same, and it will be noticed that they included the two British mine-belts (January and February) which the enemy had kept after his withdrawal from Alam el Halfa early in September. Farther west a second, but incomplete, system of defences, dating from August, ran from Bab el Qattara to the El Taqa plateau.

An interesting point arises over the role of the two German and two Italian armoured divisions, which were placed in pairs in two separate areas, and split up into battle-groups capable of acting independently. It was thought by many that General Stumme must have been responsible for such an apparently mistaken idea, for Rommel would surely not have spread his armour in this way, and had he not often criticized the British for using their armour piecemeal?

The reason was that in September Rommel had decided that he could not afford to let the British armour break out into the open country. For one thing it was so strong, and for another his own shortage of petrol would prevent him from manoeuvring to fight a major armoured battle in his own way. Therefore he must try to confine the battle to the defended zone, where the movement of British tanks would be greatly restricted. It was of course important to oppose the attack strongly, and this required, in his opinion, that German troops should stiffen the front by alternating with Italians. Hence the dispositions, for example, of the four battalions of the staunch Ramcke Parachute Brigade. By this means Rommel hoped to prevent a sudden breakthrough occurring on a fairly wide front. A narrow penetration would have to be dealt with before it could be enlarged. A policy of plugging the gaps, in fact, which required a portion of the mobile reserves to be stationed within a short distance of every part of the front. Accordingly, the 15th Panzer and Littorio Divisions were placed behind the northern half of the front, and the 21st Panzer and Ariete behind the southern. Each mixed pair was organized in three battle-groups capable of independent action. The battle headquarters of the appropriate

German and Italian formations were placed alongside each other, so that their actions might be concerted. To comply with Mussolini's wish that Italian troops should be led by their own commanders, the *Panzerarmee* addressed its orders jointly to German and Italian commanders—a system which worked fairly well, for it seems that in practice the Germans took the decisions on which they and the Italians then acted. To complete the picture, farther back and near the coast were the *Panzerarmee's* reserves, 90th Light and Trieste Divisions[1].

Anti-tank mines had been used in the Desert from the start of hostilities, though at first in small numbers.[2] Both sides gradually used them more and more, not only on the perimeter of defended places like Bardia and Tobruk, but also in the open as at Gazala in May 1942. In the fighting near El Alamein in July the British tanks suffered heavily from mines, but the tables were turned a month later when the enemy, intending to strike at the Alam el Halfa ridge, made a bad start by underestimating the time needed to cross two British mine-belts. Both sides then realized that the use of mines in large numbers might have a great influence upon the coming battle. In a report dated 21st October the German Engineer Commander estimated a total of over 445,000 mines in the Axis positions, about 14,000—or three per cent—of which were anti-personnel mines.[3] In an earlier document the aim was laid down that one-third of all mines should be of anti-personnel type. It was fortunate for the British that this figure had not nearly been reached at El Alamein. In the months ahead these and many other devices were to be used to make finding and lifting anti-tank mines much more difficult. For the present, things were difficult enough because of the gaps in our knowledge. Aerial photographs yielded much useful information, but only personal reconnaissance could establish the facts the mine-clearing parties wanted to know. As it was very difficult for patrols to explore any but the foremost belts it was hard to say whether the mines as a whole would turn out to be merely a nuisance—though no doubt a big one—or whether they would paralyse the battle. The fact that the enemy, though short of many important items of equipment, was strong in anti-tank guns (both in quantity and quality), added to the British

---

[1] Although General Stumme expected the main blow to fall somewhere in the centre, he did not alter the dispositions but adhered to Rommel's plan for smothering any break-in before it could spread, no matter where it came.

[2] In Wavell's offensive of December 1940 six precious Matildas were caught by mines just outside Nibeiwa Camp. Volume I, page 268.

[3] The German 'S' anti-personnel mine could be set off by being trodden on, or by a slack or taut trip-wire. It jumped in the air like a jack-in-the-box and then burst, scattering steel pellets in all directions. The Italian A.P. mine did not jump. The German 'Teller' anti-tank mine usually did no more than break the victim's track, thus stopping it completely. If driven over by a wheel, a Tellermine would usually wreck the vehicle.

uncertainty of what the minefields held in store. This uncertainty was a real cause for anxiety.

The following broad comparisons show the advantages enjoyed by the British. The 8th Army had a vigorous and inspiring commander, whose enthusiasm was infectious: the *Panzerarmee*, on the other hand, was without its trusted and almost fabulous leader. Reinforcements and material of all kinds for the British were steadily flowing in along the ocean routes, while the short sea passages from Italy to Africa, the lifeline of the Axis forces, were uncertain and dangerous. British units were more or less up to strength, but nearly every German and Italian unit was well below its establishment. The figures available do not permit of an accurate comparison of the total fighting strengths, but if the fighting strength of the 8th Army is taken as 195,000 it is probably fair to assess that of the Germans in the *Panzerarmee* as about 50,000 and of the Italians 54,000.[1] Of infantry battalions the numbers were British 85 of all kinds (including eight machine-gun and two reconnaissance battalions), German 31 and Italian 40.[2]

In material the British had ample supplies of almost everything—fuel, food, transport, and ammunition. Of the most important items of army equipment they had, ready for action in units and formations, and not counting reserves:

> Armoured cars: 435, compared with 192.
> Tanks (other than light): 1,029, compared with 496.
> Field and medium guns: 908, compared with 200 German and between 260 and 300 Italian, plus 18 German heavy howitzers.
> Anti-tank guns: 1,451 (849 being 6-pdrs) compared with 550 German (even including 86 8·8-cm Flak) and some 300 Italian.

In the air, the R.A.F. looked likely to establish a definite superiority, which would enable them to give the Army the best possible support. On the night 18th/19th October the Army began its series of moves into battle positions, and on the morning of the 19th the Desert Air Force started its operations to subdue the enemy's air forces.

---

[1] The figure 50,000 includes the 19th Flak Division and the Ramcke Parachute Brigade, both of the *Luftwaffe*. There were a further 77,000 Italian troops on African soil but not under the *Panzerarmee*.

[2] The figure 85 excludes four Greek and five Fighting French battalions.

CHAPTER II

EL ALAMEIN: THE BREAK-IN ('LIGHTFOOT') AND DOG-FIGHT

(23rd-26th October)

THE plan for the move forward of the two armoured divisions of the 10th Corps was described on page 18 as part of the general scheme of deception. There were some anxious moments on 16th and 17th October, when gales and sandstorms wrecked many of the dummy vehicles, but the damage was repaired in time and the whole programme carried through successfully. Thus there was reason to hope that the 1st Armoured Division would appear to the enemy to be still back in its training area, while the 10th, if detected at all, would be thought to have moved forward to the southern half of the front.

The concentration of the 30th Corps was less complicated. The 9th Australian, 1st South African, and 4th Indian Divisions were already holding the line and had only to make small adjustments. The 51st and New Zealand Divisions, however, had to move up, and the 9th Armoured Brigade—which made its earlier moves as part of the 10th Corps' series—had to join the New Zealand Division. The nights covered many other activities, such as the occupation of gun positions, the dumping of ammunition, the coming and going of hundreds of lorries as part of the deception scheme or for many other purposes, and, towards the end, the clearing of gaps through the British minefields, the marking of start-lines and of routes to them. The infantry completed their moves by the night of 22nd/23rd October, and at daylight on the 23rd all was ready—a triumph of careful planning, well executed. Concealment in daytime, and throughout, demanded good discipline from all whose business it was to stay concealed, but now several thousand men had to endure the ordeal of lying up all day in cramped trenches just behind the foremost defended localities.

At 6.30 p.m. on the 23rd General Montgomery's Intelligence Staff was able to report to him that the enemy showed no sign of expecting to be attacked that night. And this was true. Dusk, for the *Panzerarmee*, ended just one more day of a period of foreboding. 'Enemy situation unchanged', ran the evening report to *OKH*.

During the five days and nights taken by the 8th Army to deploy, the Desert Air Force and its attached American squadrons broke the comparative lull in the air. Air Vice-Marshal Coningham had two main aims: first, to lessen the risk of the Army being heavily attacked from the air during this rather precarious time; second, to win conditions which would favour his own operations in support of the land battle. The first step was to subdue the enemy's fighters in the forward area. The main German fighter force was based on and around El Daba, with a few Italian fighter units at Fuka. The German dive-bombers were based at Sidi Haneish, and a substantial Italian bomber force was at Matruh. Practically the whole of the *Luftwaffe* in North Africa was within reach of El Alamein, whereas nearly two-thirds of the Italian *5th Squadra* was spread between Derna (over 400 miles away) and Tripoli. Just before the land battle began some of the Italian squadrons at Fuka moved back out of range. Shortly after, the Germans sent more of their long-range bombers from Sicily to Crete. They moved some fighters from Crete to the Desert, and brought forward the few which had been stiffening the Italian air defences in rear. These also were replaced from Sicily. The broad picture, then, is of the *Luftwaffe* gathering its forces and replacing some of the Italian squadrons in the process. In Chapter VIII we describe the defeat, by 19th October, of the enemy's last attempt to neutralize Malta by air attack. The attempt, and the losses incurred in it put the *Luftwaffe* on the wrong foot, and made the process just mentioned more complicated.

On 19th October the attack on the enemy's fighter force in the forward area was begun by Baltimores of Nos. 55 and 223 Squadrons and fighter-bombers of Nos. 2 and 4 Squadrons, S.A.A.F., and No. 450 Squadron, R.A.A.F. The main targets were the airfields at El Daba, on which attacks were continued into the night by Bostons and Albacores. On the 20th it was the turn of the Fuka airfields, though that night the Bostons of Nos. 12 and 24 Squadrons, S.A.A.F., were back again over El Daba. The next night the Wellingtons joined in, and until the morning of the 23rd—when the day-bombers were withdrawn to prepare for a strenuous day on the 24th—the attacks on the El Daba airfields went on at the scale of one hundred aircraft every twenty-four hours. On the 23rd fighter patrols were kept continuously over all the enemy's forward fighter airfields, and the fact that they were never challenged showed that the Allies had won the first round. Their operations were so successful in protecting the British staging and assembly areas and preventing reconnaissance by hostile aircraft that the 8th Army was unmolested during its concentration and no information reached the enemy from aerial observation.

There were many other activities in the air. Wellingtons of No.

205 Group flew 65 sorties over Tobruk and the lesser ports. The daybombers and fighter-bombers attacked ground targets by day, and by night Hurricanes of No. 73 Squadron, in addition to their defensive tasks, harassed transport and made intruder flights over the forward airfields. All in all—apart from the operations against enemy shipping and those by other aircraft based on Malta—the British squadrons flew between dawn on the 19th and dusk on the 23rd October 2,209 sorties (or about 490 every twenty-four hours) and the American squadrons a further 260. Some 300 tons of bombs were dropped. The British lost 17 aircraft, the Americans 1, and the Germans 13; the Italian losses are not known. The Allied air operations were modest in proportion to the aircraft available, but the necessary strength was well judged and the effort well applied, so that by the end of the preparatory period the air forces were ready and able to give support on a scale that the army may have imagined but had never known.

The measure of air superiority thus gained had an immediate and valuable result in making possible many reconnaissance flights over the battle area (which were ordinarily very hazardous) for a variety of purposes. Targets here and on the enemy's airfields were examined and many of them photographed by the Reconnaissance Wing, supplemented by certain Baltimores and American Mitchells which took photographs in addition to dropping bombs. Much last minute information was obtained about the enemy's dispositions and defences—including minefields—and especially about the location of his guns.

On the eve of the offensive the Desert Air Force was deployed as follows. Two wings of fighters had moved forward to the advanced landing-grounds at El Hammam; the reconnaissance units were at Burg el Arab; and the main fighter force and day-bombers were around Amiriya. No. 205 Group had two squadrons of Wellingtons based near Cairo and the remainder in the Canal Zone.

Air Vice-Marshal Coningham's plans for 23rd/24th, the first night of the offensive, were to illuminate and bomb gun positions and concentrations, attack with low-flying night fighters, jam the R/T communications of the enemy's armoured formations by specially equipped Wellingtons, and create confusion by dropping dummy parachutists and laying smoke. At daybreak on the 24th day-bombers and fighter-bombers would attack prearranged targets, and thereafter, with the smoke-laying aircraft, were to be on call to meet the army's requests for air support. The fighters were to provide general cover, protect the advancing armour, escort bombers and reconnaissance aircraft, attack distant targets, and make armed reconnaissance of the battlefield. All these plans were subject to the proviso that part or the whole of the air effort might have to be used at any time to meet an enemy challenge in the air.

See Map 4

The main tasks of the three British Corps at the beginning of the battle were briefly as follows.

At 10 p.m. on 23rd October three simultaneous attacks were to be made—
  (i) by 30th Corps, to secure before dawn on 24th October a bridgehead (objective 'Oxalic') beyond the enemy's main defended zone, and help 10th Corps to pass through it:
  (ii) by 13th Corps, to penetrate the enemy's positions near Munassib and pass the 7th Armoured Division through towards Jebel Kalakh. This Division was, however, to be kept 'in being'; it was not to be exposed to serious losses in tanks:
  (iii) also by 13th Corps, using the French Forces, to secure Qaret el Himeimat and the el Taqa plateau.

Both 13th and 30th Corps were then to proceed with the methodical destruction of the enemy's static troops by the crumbling operations referred to on page 6 of Chapter I.

The task of the 10th Corps was to follow 30th Corps and pass through its bridgehead ('Oxalic') with the aim of bringing on an armoured battle where full use could be made of the superior weight of British armour and armament to destroy the enemy. If no immediate opportunity should occur of doing this, the 10th Corps would prevent the enemy's armour from interfering with 30th Corps' crumbling operations. Hence 10th Corps' first bound would be to the line 'Pierson', just west of the infantry's objective 'Oxalic'. The subsequent advance to the area 'Skinflint' was intended to challenge attack by blocking an important lateral track.

The 30th Corps was responsible for clearing all the necessary lanes through the British minefields. Forward of this each Corps was responsible for clearing its own. The 10th Corps' lanes were to be made within the limits of two corridors, each about one mile wide— one for each armoured division. The armour was to move off from the Springbok track at 2 a.m. on 24th October, by which time it would not be known how far the lanes through the corridors had been cleared.[1] The leading armoured brigades were therefore to be prepared to deploy and if necessary fight through to open country. But General Lumsden warned them that they must on no account 'rush blindly on to the enemy's anti-tank guns or try to pass through

---

[1] Springbok track is shown on Map 2.

Map 4

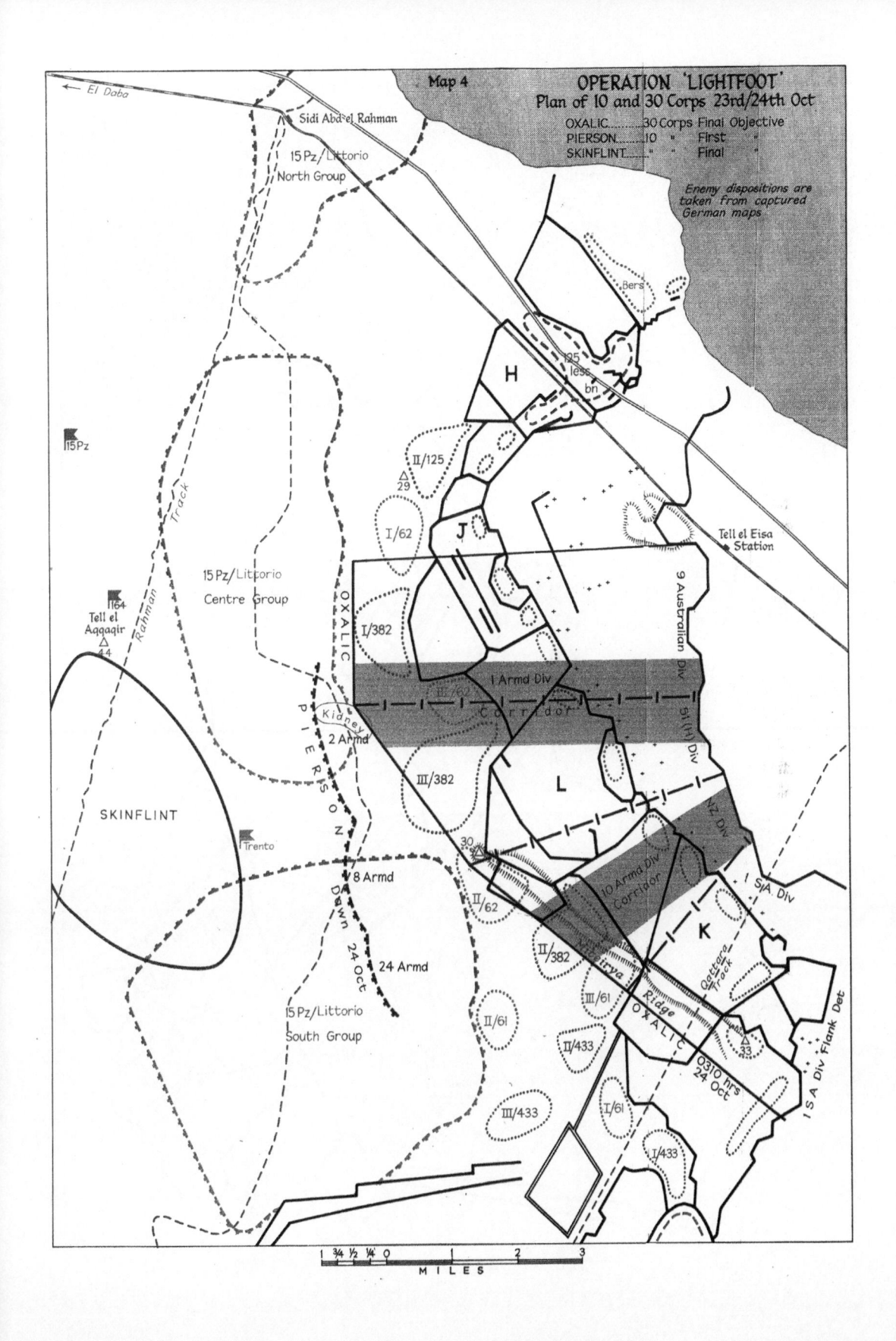

OPERATION 'LIGHTFOOT'
Plan of 10 and 30 Corps 23rd/24th Oct

OXALIC .... 30 Corps Final Objective
PIERSON ...... 10 "   First   "
SKINFLINT ..... "   "   Final   "

Enemy dispositions are taken from captured German maps

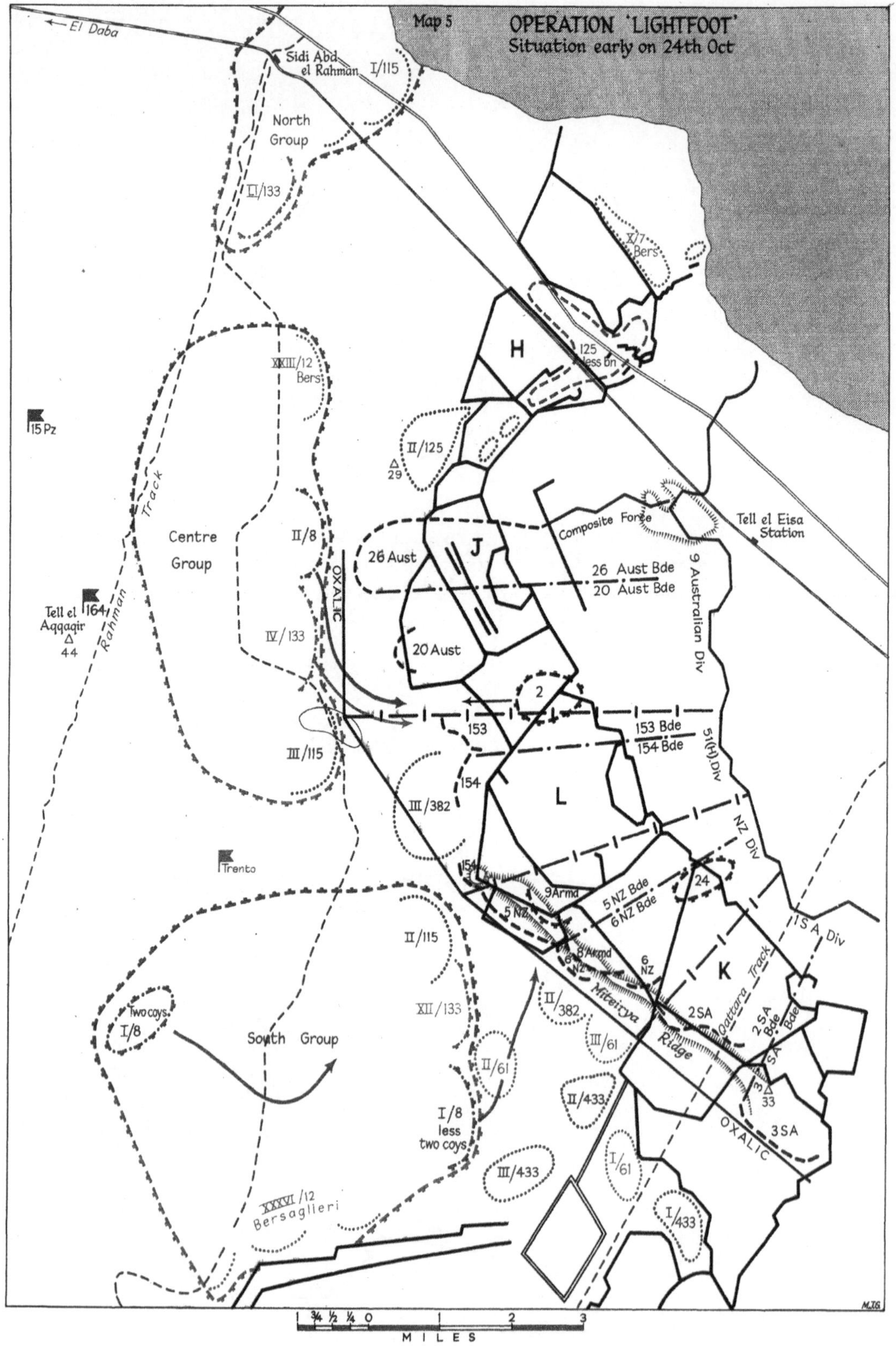
Map 5
OPERATION 'LIGHTFOOT'
Situation early on 24th Oct
El Daba
Sidi Abd el Rahman
I/115
North Group
II/133
X/7 Bers
H
125 less bn
XXIII/12 Bers
15 Pz
II/125
29
Rahman Track
Centre Group
II/8
OXALIC
J
26 Aust
Composite Force
Tell el Eisa Station
9 Australian Div
26 Aust Bde
20 Aust Bde
Tell el Aqqaqir
164
44
IV/133
20 Aust
2
153
153 Bde
154 Bde
51(H) Div
III/115
154
L
III/382
NZ Div
Trento
154
9 Armd
5 NZ Bde
6 NZ Bde
24
5 NZ
II/115
1 SA Div
6 NZ
9 Armd
6 NZ
K
Qattara Track
Miteirya Ridge
Two coys
I/8
XII/133
II/382
2 SA
2 SA Bde
1 SA Bde
South Group
III/61
II/61
II/433
3 SA
33
I/8 less two coys
OXALIC
3 SA
III/433
I/61
XXXVI/12 Bersaglieri
I/433
M.J.G.
MILES

a narrow bottleneck which is covered by a concentration of enemy tanks.' In such cases 'a proper co-ordinated plan must be made'.

There is no doubt that General Lumsden was very uneasy about the role given to his Corps, and in the warning quoted above he was trying to lessen the dangers inherent in the plan, particularly if the armour became stuck owing to the narrowness of the lanes and exits. Three experienced divisional commanders in the 30th Corps—Generals Freyberg, Morshead, and Pienaar—told General Leese that they doubted the armour's ability to break out as intended. Their doubts probably arose partly from what they had seen of the power of anti-tank weapons and of the cramping effect of minefields in the desert, and partly from their low opinion of the armoured formations. General Leese reported the matter to the Army Commander. Brigadier de Guingand did so too after attending a conference at 10th Corps which had left him doubtful of General Lumsden's intention. General Montgomery then gave orders that the operations would be carried out exactly as he had directed.[1] Not that he had visions of a rapid victory; on the contrary he foresaw a long dog-fight. At his final address to all senior officers on 19th and 20th October the note for his talk reads: 'Organise ahead for a "dog-fight" of a week. Whole affair about 12 days'.[2]

In the Desert the enemy had learned to respect the British artillery from the first. As we have seen, however, the 25-pdrs had often to be used on anti-tank and other tasks involving dispersion, at the expense of their true field artillery role. With the arrival of 6-pdr anti-tank guns in good numbers, and the powerful 75-mm mounted in the new Sherman tanks, this need had ceased. Not only were the 25-pdrs themselves now present in large numbers, but the command of them could be centralized and their effect greatly enhanced. Strong forces of artillery could be used to support first one and then another of the set-piece attacks which were to play a very important part in this battle. Fortunately no restriction needed to be imposed on the expenditure of ammunition in any of the major attacks.[3]

The bombardment with which the battle opened provides a good example of centralized control. Because there were not enough guns to neutralize effectively and simultaneously the enemy's batteries

---

[1] General Montgomery had made it known throughout the 8th Army that there was to be no 'belly-aching' about orders received. 'Orders,' he said, 'would no longer form the basis for discussion, but for action.'
[2] The figure 12 was written in as a correction to 10.
[3] In twelve days' fighting 834 25-pdrs fired altogether over 1 million rounds, an average of 102 rounds per gun per day. The rates for the mediums were even higher—133 for the 4·5-in. and 157 for the 5·5-in.

and his defended localities, almost every available gun was used on a co-ordinated programme designed to neutralize as many batteries as possible just before zero hour. Great pains had been taken to fix the positions of the Axis guns by all the means available—ground observation, flash spotting, sound ranging, aerial reconnaissance, and the R.A.F.'s excellent vertical photographs. A special counter-battery organization had been set up to co-ordinate and distribute information and allot the various tasks. On the main front—that of the 30th Corps—were deployed the 25-pdrs of the five attacking divisions, 336 in all, plus 72 attached from 10th Corps, together with 48 medium guns; a total of 456 guns all under the Commander of the 30th Corps Artillery, Brigadier M. E. Dennis.[1] On this front the enemy was estimated to have in action 200 field, 40 medium, and 14 heavy guns. The concentrations fired against them worked out at 22 to 1 at the most, and 10 to 1 at the least. The 13th Corps also fired a neutralization programme, but on a much smaller scale. It used 136 field guns and lasted from 9.25 to 9.55 p.m. The concentrations against hostile batteries on this front averaged $3\frac{1}{2}$ to 1.

On 30th Corps' front fire was opened at 9.40 p.m. and lasted fifteen minutes. The Royal Air Force added weight to this programme: forty-eight Wellingtons, some flying two sorties during the night, with naval Albacores as pathfinders dropped nearly 125 tons of bombs on known gun positions or on any hostile guns which opened fire. The results of these counter-battery operations appeared most satisfactory, in that there was no shelling of the troops assembled for the assault. It is, however, a fact that General Stumme had twice emphasized the importance of controlled fire: guns would engage only known targets and were not to open fire too soon. The tremendous shelling between 9.40 and 9.55 p.m., aided no doubt by the jamming of radio-telephony by the specially equipped Wellingtons, thoroughly disrupted the enemy's signals system, so that some time elapsed before the Axis gunners and higher headquarters knew what was happening. For these reasons the response by the enemy's guns was for several hours only spasmodic.

Zero-hour for the attacks by 30th and 13th Corps was 10 p.m. If, as the 8th Army's Chief of Staff has recorded, there remained nothing to be done at the higher headquarters, darkness released great activity in the fighting formations.[2] Men emerged thankfully from their slit trenches; final checks and adjustments were made, hot meals were eaten, commanders went the rounds, and units moved to their start lines to await zero. On the main front the

---

[1] Strictly speaking the 4th Indian Division was not initially one of the attacking divisions, but had a raiding task.
[2] F. de Guingand: *Operation Victory* (London 1947).

thunderous roll of the guns and their sheet-lightning flashes came as a general surprise, for none but survivors of the First World War had seen or heard anything like this before. For five minutes before zero the guns were silent. Then they opened up again, this time on the enemy's forward defended localities. It was the signal for the leading infantry to move up close to the bursting shells in readiness to assault directly the artillery fire lifted. The battle, which Mr. Churchill had said might well be be the key to the future, was on. The evening was clear and the moon bright, but a haze arose from the dust kicked up by explosives, vehicles, and men, and hung over the battlefield, making it hard to see more than a very short distance.

See Map 5

For seven minutes the enemy's forward defences received a tremendous pounding by the full weight of 30th Corps' artillery. Then, at zero plus 7, the fire support began to vary with each division's needs; it consisted mainly of concentrations lifting at given times from locality to locality, except in two places where it took the form of a barrage. The whole elaborate programme lasted about $5\frac{1}{2}$ hours. The physical strain on the gunners was very great, and so was the mechanical strain on the guns. This was artillery support indeed.

The four divisions of the 30th Corps attacked in line, each on a two-brigade front. Each division had one regiment of Valentine tanks of the 23rd Armoured Brigade (Brigadier G. W. Richards), except the New Zealand Division which had a whole armoured brigade—the 9th (Brigadier J. C. Currie)—under its command. The total frontage was about six miles, fanning out to nearly eight miles when measured along the final objective 'Oxalic'. The distance from the British forward line of defended localities to 'Oxalic' varied from five miles on the right to about three on the left. Various intermediate objectives and report-lines were given, but for clarity they are omitted from the map. There was a pause of an hour on a line some 2,000 yards short of 'Oxalic', to give the troops a chance to get sorted out and be off to a good start to the final objective.

In general the experience of each of the eight attacking brigades was similar in that they had no great difficulty in overcoming the first line of defended localities—Rommel's weakly held 'battle outposts'. After that, resistance became stronger, which will cause no surprise in view of the intended conduct of the defence explained on page 28.

On the 9th Australian Division's front the right brigade reached 'Oxalic' after some stiff fighting, but the brigade on the left was checked about a thousand yards short. Meanwhile a composite force including light tanks of the Divisional Cavalry, anti-tank guns, machine guns and pioneers established a chain of six posts and a minefield to protect the Division's newly extended right flank. A feint attack was staged on the enemy's positions astride the main road, and succeeded in attracting his attention.

The attack by the 51st Division ran up against several centres of resistance and only on the extreme left was the final objective reached. There had been a good deal of artillery, mortar, and light automatic fire, and the right brigade—the 153rd—had considerable losses. The squadrons of Valentine tanks, one with each brigade, were checked by mines some distance short of 'Oxalic'.

Except on its extreme left the New Zealand Division gained its objectives, but the time taken to clear mines delayed the forward move of the supporting weapons. Owing to an unsuspected minefield on the Miteirya Ridge the 9th Armoured Brigade had not succeeded in getting forward of 'Oxalic' by dawn.

On the left of 30th Corps' front of attack the South African Division also had mixed fortunes. At dawn its right brigade was still some way short of 'Oxalic' and was somewhat disorganized, but the left brigade reached its objective on Miteirya Ridge with little loss. The arrangements made for securing the left flank worked satisfactorily.

A word is required about the crucial matter of passing through the enemy's minefields. It will be remembered that each division in 30th Corps was to make its own gaps. Trials with the novel 'Scorpions' had not been very convincing, and no great reliance was placed on them. Rather were they looked upon as an extra which might be worth trying but was unlikely to replace the human hand. Actually, on this occasion the Scorpions were of some use, but not much; the Matilda chassis were old and several of them broke down. In the New Zealand Division's sector the Scorpions did fairly well, but the two with the Australian Division seized up very quickly.[1]

Briefly, the results were as follows. The Australian Division's engineers and pioneers succeeded in their task, though some delay was caused by patches of scattered mines—obstacles which often gave more trouble than regular minefields. In the 51st Division the engineers helped by infantry made the gaps as intended, but with more difficulty and more delay than had been expected. Here, too, trouble came from scattered mines. The New Zealand Division's engineers cleared a way on the right of their divisional front up to the Miteirya Ridge, but the field on and beyond the ridge was still not breached by dawn. In the South African Division all the

---

[1] Nevertheless the 'flail' type of mine-clearing tank had come to stay. In 1943 it developed into the Sherman Crab, a great improvement on the original Scorpion in every way.

necessary gaps were made, but here too the task took longer than expected.

Close on the heels of 30th Corps' leading infantry came the advanced parties of the minefield task forces of the 10th Corps.[1] By making the armoured divisions responsible for clearing their own lanes through the enemy's minefields it was hoped to avoid the mistakes and misunderstandings which had occurred in July. The main task of each Force was to clear and mark four lanes within its divisional corridor up to the 'Oxalic' line. The difference in composition of the two task forces was that the 1st Armoured Division's included troops to fight for the gaps if necessary and protect the Engineers at work. Each lane was to be 16 yards wide to begin with, and later to be widened to 32 yards. In the event some gaps began with 8 yards.

In the 1st Armoured Division's corridor there was trouble with scattered mines, but by dawn one lane was cleared as far as the Australians had reached. The other lanes had not been cleared further than half-way through the defended area owing to difficulties of various sorts and some opposition from hostile posts. In 10th Armoured Division's corridor, in spite of delays and the need to mop up parties of enemy here and there, four lanes had been cleared up to, but not over, the Miteirya Ridge by dawn.

The Minefield Task Forces had therefore proved their worth, but it must be remembered that the cleared lanes were narrow and to move off them was dangerous. Gaps do not create elbow-room, and this was a very important restricting factor in the subsequent operations. Moreover the work of clearing mines had been slower than was expected, and the armoured divisions fell behind time in their advance.[2]

In these conditions mine-lifting caused great nervous and physical strain on the sappers. There was the deliberate sweeping with sensitive detectors—each man going forward slowly and intently, eyes on the ground, earphones in position, the distracting sounds of battle all around; or else kneeling or lying and prodding with a bayonet. Then followed the cold-blooded investigation and lifting of each mine, with always the chance that some new trap or anti-

---

[1] *1st Armoured Division's Minefield Task Force.* Comd: O.C. 2nd Rifle Brigade; one troop from each Bays, 9th Lancers, 10th Hussars; 7th and 9th Field Squadrons and 572nd Army Field Company, R.E.; 2nd Rifle Brigade (less one company); Signals and Provost detachments.

10th Armoured Division's Minefield Task Force. Comd: Division's C.R.E.; 3rd Field Squadron, 571st and 573rd Army Field Companies, and 141st Field Park Squadron, R.E.; Signals and Provost detachments.

[2] In the 8th Army's pamphlet 'Lessons from Operations October and November 1942' it was stated that 'under average operational conditions' one section or troop R.E. could clear a 16-yard wide gap to a depth of 400 yards in two hours. This is obviously only a very rough guide, but it shows that the times allowed in 'Lightfoot' were not enough.

lifting device had been added to *this* one .... In October 1942 these devices were few, but before long not only they but every imaginable sort of lethal booby-trap were to be met in a profusion which posed further problems for the sappers to solve.

At last light on 23rd October the two armoured divisions of 10th Corps were in their assembly areas some 16 to 19 miles east of Springbok track. Secrecy required them not to leave these areas before dark; they then advanced by six carefully prepared parallel tracks to the regulating station at Springbok track. Here they topped up with fuel and waited for 2 a.m., the hour for the further advance to begin. From Springbok track to the enemy's forward localities, now in 30th Corps' hands, was a distance of six to nine miles. The purpose of the whole long and intricate approach-march, admirably planned and executed, was to project the two armoured divisions with their vast numbers of fighting and attendant vehicles into an area some four miles by six, which, for the past few hours, had been a battlefield, and where now, it was hoped, the divisions of the 30th Corps had left only the debris of the enemy's defences in their wake. It was not known for certain how these divisions had fared, but General Montgomery decided not to wait for this information; the most important consideration was that the armour should cross the line 'Oxalic' as soon as possible.

Punctually at 2 a.m. on the 24th the leading troops of the 1st and 10th Armoured Divisions left the Springbok track and resumed their advance. The intention was that both Divisions, after passing through the 30th Corps' objective 'Oxalic', should deploy on 'Pierson' while their two armoured car regiments drove ahead and reconnoitred to locate the 15th Panzer and Littorio Divisions (which were known to be on this part of the front) and to look for any signs of the 21st Panzer and Ariete Divisions moving up from the south. The 2nd Armoured Brigade (Brigadier A. F. Fisher), after leading the way along the 1st Armoured Division's corridor, would deploy when it reached 'Pierson'. The 7th Motor Brigade (Brigadier T. J. B. Bosville) would come up on its right and push out an anti-tank screen. From the southern corridor the 10th Armoured Division would emerge and deploy with the 8th Armoured Brigade (Brigadier E. C. N. Custance) on the right and the 24th (Brigadier A. G. Kenchington) on the left. When these Brigades were in position, and when the anti-tank screen of 7th Motor Brigade was ready to give some protection, the 2nd Armoured Brigade would advance, moving from fire position to fire position, to 'Skinflint'. As soon as possible the 133rd Lorried Infantry Brigade (Brigadier A. W. Lee) was to come up into position on the left of the 24th Armoured

Brigade and form a defensive flank facing south-west. At a suitable time both the 8th and 24th Armoured Brigades were to prepare to advance to 'Skinflint'. These dispositions and manoeuvres were designed to enable the 10th Armoured Division to take on any armoured forces approaching from the west or south, and also help the 1st Armoured Division and cover any exploitation by the New Zealand Division.

The achievements of 10th Corps fell a long way short of these intentions. The 2nd Armoured Brigade led the 1st Armoured Division from Springbok track, driving with difficulty in thick clouds of dust at three miles in the hour, crossed the old British front line ahead of time and reached the former German front line a little after 4 a.m. Then the advance gradually slowed to a standstill mainly because of scattered mines and unsubdued enemy posts. By first light the Bays reported that two squadrons were through the last enemy minefield. It was, however, as throughout this battle, remarkably difficult to fix the position of troops on ground and map where the country was featureless, and harder still in dust and smoke. The actual position of the Bays was uncertain to their brigade and divisional headquarters, but 2nd Armoured Brigade as a whole was still about three miles short of 'Pierson'.[1] The slowing down had of course affected every one behind; the 12th Lancers' armoured cars had not yet crossed the old no-man's land, while the 7th Motor Brigade had not left Springbok track. Farther south, in 10th Armoured Division's corridor, the 8th Armoured Brigade had made good progress to the Miteirya Ridge, but when it tried to cross the ridge in the first light it met mines and anti-tank fire. The Staffordshire Yeomanry lost two tanks and the Nottinghamshire Yeomanry sixteen. The Brigade went into hull-down positions behind the ridge in an area already occupied by New Zealanders and their supporting tanks. The armoured cars of the Royals were unable to pass through to start their reconnaissance. The 24th Armoured Brigade had moved off from Springbok track at 4.30 a.m. and by dawn had reached the former enemy front line. The 133rd Lorried Infantry Brigade, waiting its turn to advance, had not left Springbok track. In short the 10th Corps had successfully accomplished its night march, but had nowhere broken out from 30th Corps' partly formed bridgehead.

It is now time to see what was occurring elsewhere. First, on the northern flank. Shortly before midnight on 23rd October the Royal Navy made a demonstration on the coast to the west of Ras el Kenayis, a promontory near Fuka. In daylight on that day twelve

---

[1] As an example of the difficulty, the best estimates and calculations of two neighbouring divisions differed persistently by more than a thousand yards in describing one particular point.

tank landing-craft escorted by three destroyers and eight motor torpedo-boats had sailed westwards from Alexandria, followed by four merchant ships. The hope was that hostile observers would spot and report a 'raiding force'. After dark all vessels but the MTBs turned back; the MTBs then closed the beaches, opened fire, and put up Verey lights, while a Boston aircraft laid a smoke screen along the coast. Night-flying Hurricanes roamed over the coastal strip firing at whatever they could see, and self-destroying dummy parachutists were dropped near Fuka. All this may have added to the enemy's anxieties; anyway, the 90th Light Division, responsible for this part of the coast, recorded next day that Italian aircraft had 'attacked and dispersed the British naval units reported north of El Daba.' In fact one MTB was slightly damaged by cannon fire from an aircraft.

The 4th Indian Division, on the left of 30th Corps, made two small raids and a mock attack near the Ruweisat Ridge to draw attention to this part of the front.

See Map 6

It remains to give a brief account of the operations of the 13th Corps, the first phase of whose task was to penetrate the January and February minefields and establish an armoured force just beyond. This was to be done by the 7th Armoured Division, which, it will be recalled, the Army Commander had ordered was not to be seriously weakened. The plan entailed an approach-march by its two armoured brigades of some thirteen miles, through gaps made previously in three British minefields. The 22nd Armoured Brigade (Brigadier G. P. B. Roberts) was then to breach the enemy's minefields at four places, using a specially organized force corresponding to the minefield task forces in the 10th Corps. The plan required the 22nd Armoured Brigade to penetrate to a depth of some 6,000 yards, followed by the 4th Light Armoured Brigade (Brigadier M. G. Roddick). The attack was to begin at 10 p.m., simultaneously with that of 30th Corps, behind a barrage fired by four field regiments. The northern flank would be protected by the 131st Infantry Brigade (of 44th Division), while on the southern a smoke screen would be laid by aircraft and artillery. Farther still to the south the 1st Fighting French Brigade Group (Brigadier-General M-P. Koenig) under command of 7th Armoured Division, had the task of advancing about ten miles and capturing, in the first place, the high ground at Naqb Rala.

For this occasion the 44th Reconnaissance Regiment (equipped with carriers) had under its command the 4th and part of the 21st Field Squadron, R.E., one Stuart troop of the Scots Greys and six

Map 6

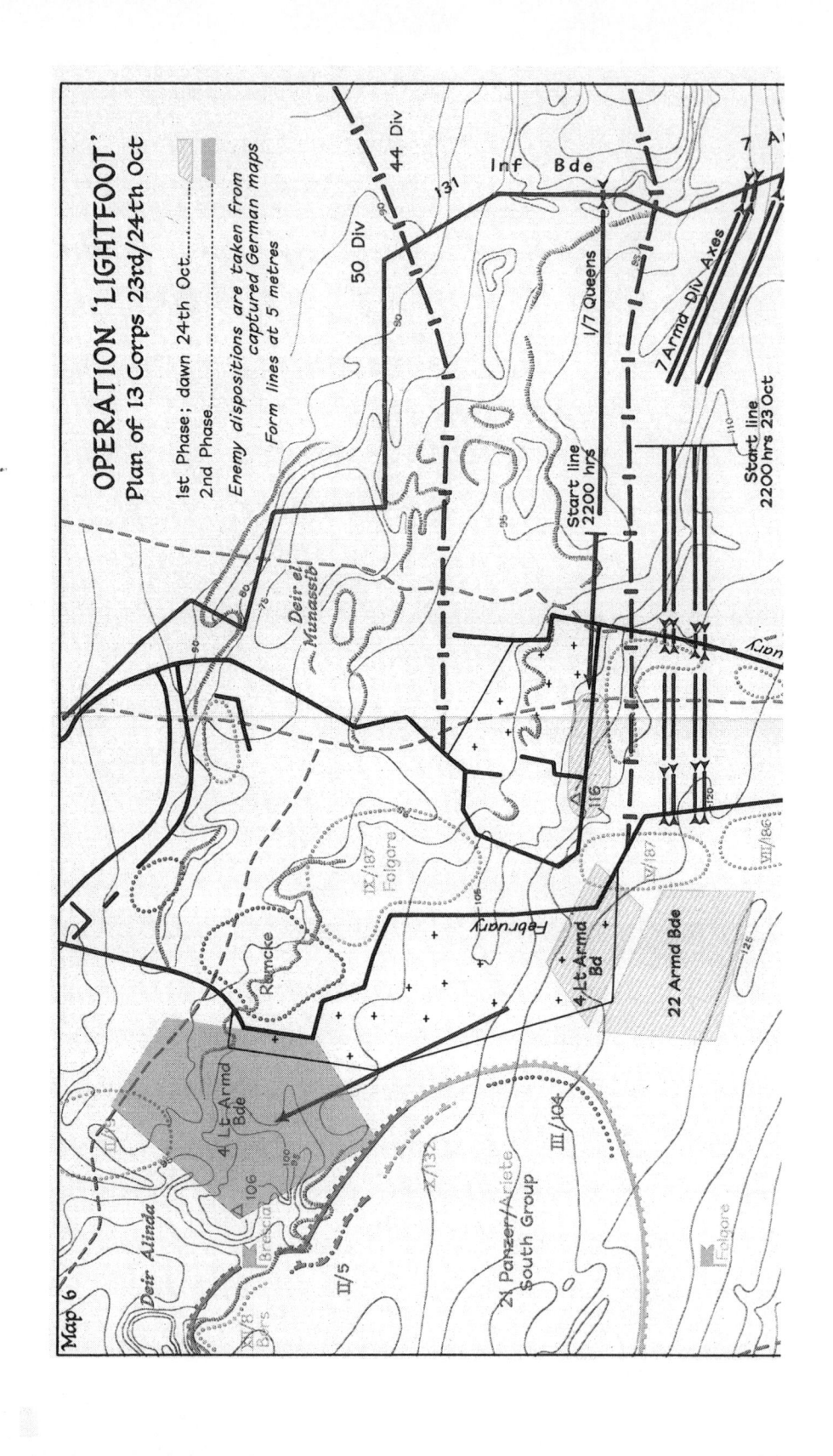

OPERATION 'LIGHTFOOT'
Plan of 13 Corps 23rd/24th Oct

1st Phase; dawn 24th Oct.
2nd Phase.

Enemy dispositions are taken from captured German maps
Form lines at 5 metres

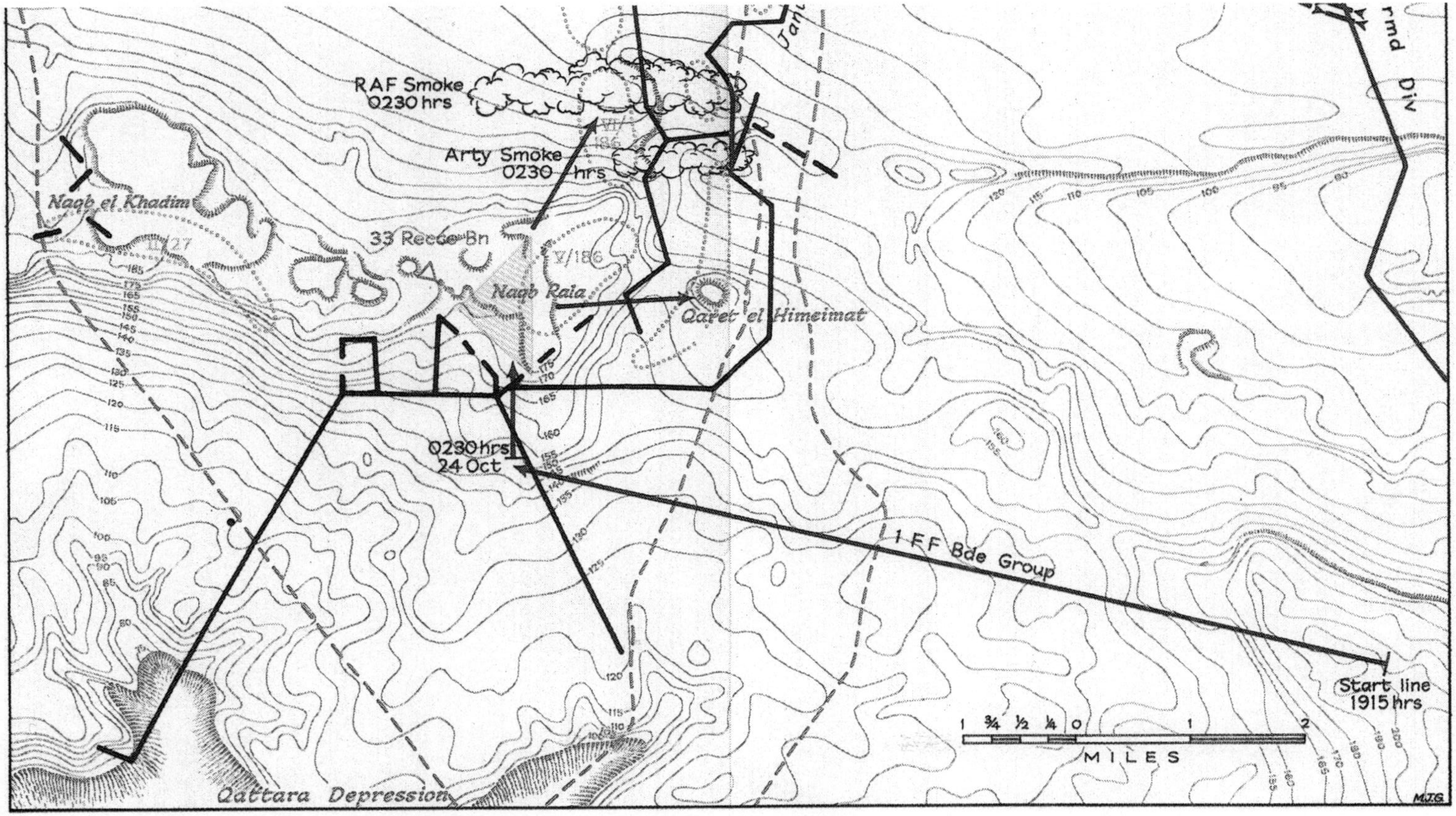
RAF Smoke
0230 hrs
Arty Smoke
0230 hrs
Naqb el Khadim
33 Recce Bn
V/186
Naqb Raia
Qaret el Himeimat
0230 hrs
24 Oct
1 FF Bde Group
Start line
1915 hrs
1 ¾ ½ ¼ 0 1 2
MILES
Qattara Depression
rmd Div
M.J.G.

Scorpions. It had to make four lanes through the January and February minefields, which were believed to be respectively 350 yards and 1,000 yards deep. A method of co-operation between carriers, Scorpions, sappers, and tanks had been practised. Bad going, a few scattered mines which caused the Scorpions to start flailing more than half a mile short of January, and enemy fire impeded the approach to this minefield, but by shortly after 11 p.m. parties were at grips with it. Breakdowns and casualties gradually eliminated the Scorpions, which were most doggedly handled, and lifting went on by hand. The two southern gaps were clear by about 2.30 a.m., but several unsubdued enemy posts had to be tackled by the 1st Rifle Brigade's two companies in the advance-guard, and part of the Greys. By about 4 a.m.—by one gap or another—5th R.T.R., the Greys, and the two Rifle Brigade companies were through and organizing a bridgehead. Shortly after 5 a.m. the mine-clearing force, much reduced by casualties, set out to clear two gaps—it was too weak to tackle all four—in February minefield. Heavy fire and daylight frustrated the attempt. Thus the 22nd Armoured Brigade had made and held gaps through one minefield only, at a cost of about 200 casualties. Meanwhile the 131st Infantry Brigade's attempt to protect the northern flank by capturing with one battalion a chosen point in the enemy's defences, ended in confusion and failure after a fair start.[1] The smoke-screens to protect the southern flank and to help 1st Fighting French Brigade Group were successfully laid between 2.30 and 3 a.m. on 24th October by Boston aircraft and a field battery. The French attacked at 2.30, met strong opposition, had trouble with their supporting weapons on the bad going, and secured no more than a lodgment south of Naqb Rala.

On 13th Corps' front, therefore, daylight on 24th October saw a somewhat unsatisfactory situation. General Horrocks was about to investigate it before deciding whether to push 7th Armoured Division on, or begin 'crumbling' operations between the January and February minefields.

At dawn on 24th October reconnaissance by No. 208 Squadron showed no great change in the enemy's dispositions.

General Montgomery's intentions (confirmed by a message timed 9.45 a.m.) were briefly as follows. On 30th Corps' front to clear the northern corridor; the New Zealand Division to exploit southwards from the Miteirya Ridge; and the Australian Division to plan a

---

[1] In this action 1/7th The Queen's Royal Regiment had about 180 casualties. The rest of the brigade was later to have taken over 22nd Armoured Brigade's bridgehead but the operation did not get so far.

crumbling operation for the night 24th/25th. In 13th Corps, if the 7th Armoured Division could not punch a hole through February minefield, a brigade of the 44th Division would have to lead the way with a night attack.

Later in the morning, after he had learnt the views of Generals Leese, Lumsden, and Freyberg, the Army Commander decided to adhere to the original idea of first deploying the armour on 'Pierson'. Accordingly, the 10th Armoured Division would advance as soon as possible, with strong artillery support. He told Lumsden that he was prepared to accept casualties provided the armoured divisions broke through, so that they could protect the New Zealand Division when it exploited southwards.

Except for the operations of the 1st Armoured Division and the 51st Division in the northern corridor during the afternoon, the main activity on 24th October was in the air. The Army Commander asked for maximum air support to be given on 30th Corps' front, and most of the available day-bombers and fighter-bombers spent the daylight hours shuttling to and fro and attacking principally 15th Panzer and Littorio Divisions' battle-groups. Casualties to British and American aircraft were high—eight day-bombers were shot down and twenty-seven damaged by gunfire. In the extreme south, near Naqb Rala, cannon Hurricanes put out of action a German unit of captured British tanks, destroying seven Stuarts and damaging five more. The remaining day-bombers and fighter-bombers attacked the landing-grounds at Qotafiya and El Daba. All these tasks made large demands on fighter escorts, and when dust put two of the fighter airfields out of action just after midday, fighter patrols over the enemy's forward landing-grounds and the battle area were called off so that there should be sufficient fighters to cover the bombers. In the course of this busy day the Desert Air Force flew nearly 1,000 sorties, almost all in support of the Army; the U.S.A.A.F. flew a further 147.

On the ground the enemy's artillery everywhere became active. Signs of counter attacks were reported but no serious threat developed. The 51st Division, helped by a diversionary attack by Valentines of 50th R.T.R., cleared up two enemy posts which were holding up the further progress of 1st Armoured Division's Minefield Task Force. This Force went on improving the lanes it had made, and helping the 2nd Armoured Brigade to continue its advance westward. Mines and the fire of field, tank, and anti-tank guns combined to make this a slow business, and the Shermans had considerable losses. But they gave as good as they got, and by evening most of the Brigade had reached the line 'Oxalic' between the Australian and 51st Divisions.

Meanwhile preparations were being made for two operations to

10TH ARMOURED DIVISION'S ATTACK

take place that night—24th. The 10th Armoured Division was to advance to gain positions from which to cover a further thrust south-westwards by the New Zealanders, while on the 13th Corps' front the 131st Infantry Brigade, backed by the 22nd Armoured Brigade, was to breach the February minefield.

The 10th Armoured Division's intention was to advance over the crest of the Miteirya Ridge, 24th Armoured Brigade on the right and 8th on the left, and occupy the part of 'Pierson' that had been the objective for the previous night. To clear the mines on and beyond the ridge each brigade would use its attached field squadron of Royal Engineers. A battalion of 133rd Lorried Infantry Brigade was to form a 'pivot of manoeuvre' on the Miteirya Ridge. The 9th Armoured Brigade (still under the New Zealand Division) was to help by advancing on the left of the 8th Armoured Brigade to about the same distance, returning later to the ridge.[1] The operation was to be supported by the artillery of 10th Armoured, New Zealand, and 51st Divisions, and the 30th Corps' medium artillery, firing a counter-battery programme, concentrations, and a barrage. In the air No. 205 Group would continue to bomb the enemy's armoured battle-groups with every Wellington it could muster, assisted by pathfinder Albacores. Night-flying Hurricanes would again patrol the area.

The night's operations were ill-fated from the start. There were far more mines on and beyond the Miteirya Ridge than had been expected, and the lifting of them, amid many distractions, took a long time. There was a good deal of shell-fire round about the gaps that were being made, and just after zero hour—10 p.m.—an attack from the air caught the 8th Armoured Brigade at an unlucky moment, when formed up ready to advance. Many vehicles were set on fire, and the blaze attracted more bombing and more shelling, which affected, to a lesser extent, the 9th and 24th Armoured Brigades also. To minimize casualties the regiments dispersed as best they could, but much delay and some disorganization resulted. It was much too late now for the tanks to catch up the barrage, and at about midnight Brigadier Custance reported to the Divisional Commander, General Gatehouse, that in his opinion it was inadvisable to go on with the advance. General Gatehouse feared that daylight would find his Division disorganized, with its tanks either out on an exposed forward slope or still partly caught up in the minefields. He spoke in this sense to General Lumsden, who reported the matter to Army Headquarters. Here the Chief of Staff decided that the situation called for the intervention of the Army Commander, and summoned the

---

[1] The 9th Armoured Brigade had then only two regiments, as the Royal Wiltshire Yeomanry had lost many tanks and handed over the remainder to the other regiments

two Corps Commanders to meet at 8th Army's Tactical Headquarters at 3.30 a.m.[1]

Having heard what his two Corps Commanders had to say General Montgomery affirmed his earlier orders and left Lumsden in no doubt that the 10th Armoured Division was to do its utmost to break out during the night. He spoke also to General Gatehouse on the telephone, and Lumsden told Gatehouse that the 24th Armoured Brigade must be on its objectives by dawn and that the 8th was to maintain one regiment forward in contact with the right (western) flank of the 9th. These orders seem to have been issued at about 4.20 a.m.

What apparently happened, however, was that the 24th Armoured Brigade had started to pass through its one available gap shortly after 3.45 a.m., and by dawn reported two of its regiments on 'Pierson', though there was some doubt whether they were really as far forward as this. (It now seems that they were not.) By dawn, too, all three regiments of the 8th Armoured Brigade had also emerged from the minefields through only one gap. Meanwhile the 9th Armoured Brigade and the New Zealand Divisional Cavalry, impeded less by mines than by gunfire, got about half-way to their objective. At daybreak the Brigade found itself without cover and under fire from well-sited tanks and anti-tank guns about a thousand yards away. Before pushing on in order to deal with this opposition Brigadier Currie considered that he would need more fuel, and proposed to withdraw behind the Miteirya Ridge to get it, but was ordered by General Freyberg to stay where he was. The 8th Armoured Brigade came under ever-increasing fire, and, because no hull-down positions could be found, Brigadier Custance withdrew it just east of the Miteirya Ridge at about 7 a.m. The 133rd Lorried Infantry Brigade had pushed two battalions up to the Miteirya Ridge in the 5th New Zealand Infantry Brigade's area, which was now decidedly congested.

On the 13th Corps' front the fresh attempt to breach the February minefield failed of its purpose. The two battalions of the 131st Infantry Brigade (of 44th Division), which were under command of the 7th Armoured Division for the operation, got through the minefield but were pinned down just beyond it. Two lanes were cleared of mines by the sappers—mostly by hand—under a good deal of fire. When, in bright moonlight, the 22nd Armoured Brigade tried to follow along the lanes it came under heavy and effective anti-tank

---

[1] This was one of the few occasions on which Brigadier de Guingand found it necessary to wake General Montgomery, who was to write (in 21st Army Group's pamphlet *High Command in War*, June 1945): 'The wise commander will see very few papers or letters; he will refuse to sit up late at night conducting the business of his army; he will be well advised to withdraw to his tent or caravan after dinner at night and have time for quiet thought and reflection. It is vital that he should keep mentally fresh.'

fire; 31 tanks were disabled and the attempt was called off. The infantry remained where they were, pinned to the ground in their narrow and shallow bridgehead.

British night-bomber activity had been directed mainly against concentrations of vehicles of 15th Panzer Division on or near the Rahman track. Over 135 tons of bombs were dropped; several large fires were started and three road convoys on the move were straddled with bombs. To prevent a repetition of the air attacks on the 8th Armoured Brigade, none of which was intercepted by the night-flying Hurricanes, night-fighter patrols, intruder flights, and attacks on the enemy's landing-grounds were stepped up.

General Montgomery's first intentions on 25th October were for the New Zealand Division to strike south; for one armoured brigade of 10th Armoured Division to remain on the Miteirya Ridge to form what he termed a 'hinge'; and for the 1st Armoured Division (plus 24th Armoured Brigade) to act offensively against the enemy's armoured group. Shortly after noon he changed his mind. He now thought that the operations proposed for the New Zealand Division would be too costly, and cancelled them. Instead of exploiting to the south as intended, the 30th Corps, while firmly holding the Miteirya Ridge, was to strike north towards the coast with 9th Australian Division. The 10th Corps was to press west and north-west from the positions gained in the northern corridor. All three Corps were to patrol constantly to detect any signs of a withdrawal by the enemy.

During 25th October the 1st Armoured Division made no headway against the enemy's anti-tank defences and lost about 24 tanks. On the other hand it held off an attack in the early afternoon by German and Italian tanks. The dispositions of the 10th Armoured Division were unchanged during the day, and the Army Commander decided to withdraw it during the night to reorganize, except for the 24th Armoured Brigade which was to join the 1st Armoured Division. The 9th Armoured Brigade was withdrawn also at dusk behind the Miteirya Ridge.

Those, briefly, were the facts. That evening General Alexander sent the C.I.G.S. his impressions of the battle: '. . . It is clear that the enemy intends to fight in his forward positions and that the struggle for mastery will be fierce and probably prolonged over a considerable period, so that for about a week it will not be possible to give reliable appreciation of how events will develop. The first phase of the battle—the break in—opened and proceeded much according to plan . . . The second phase—the debouchment of armour west of minefields—did not progress as rapidly as was hoped, but by this morning it had been completed and operations following on from that are now in progress but are not yet clearly defined . . .' It is evident that, as regards the armour at any rate, the information from which these impressions were gained was on the optimistic side.

Most of the day-bomber and fighter-bomber effort had been used to help in dispersing small concentrations opposite the Australian and 1st Armoured Divisions. Tactical reconnaissance aircraft reported when they saw parties of enemy collecting, and in 210 sorties British and American aircraft dropped 112 tons of bombs, the best targets being those found in the Deir el Abyad area. A few fighter-bomber attacks were made on 13th Corps' front and for the rest the day-bombers attacked enemy landing-grounds, over which Allied fighters patrolled without interference. Indeed, so subdued were the enemy's fighters that tactical air reconnaissances, carried out in obsolescent Hurricane aircraft, were flown without any escort at all. During the afternoon Beaufighters intercepted some of the enemy's air transports carrying fuel to North Africa and destroyed one of them.

The focus must now shift to the 9th Australian Division on the right of the 30th Corps, and events elsewhere can be summarized as follows. During the night 25th/26th October the 51st Division made some ground towards part of its original objective 'Oxalic' that it had not yet reached. Patrols on the rest of 30th Corps' front found no signs that the enemy intended to withdraw. On the southern front the two battalions uneasily deployed just west of February minefield were withdrawn at dusk. An attempt to pierce the minefield, this time farther north, by a brigade of the 50th Division, failed. A brigade of the 44th Division took over the ground gained by the 7th Armoured Division. Thus the operations of 13th Corps were disappointing in themselves, though in so far as the 21st Panzer and Ariete Divisions had been kept behind the southern front, and serious losses in the 7th Armoured Division had been avoided, they had achieved their purpose.

The 9th Australian Division's attack on the night 25th/26th October was the first of three elaborate set pieces which were to give worthwhile results. The objectives—Pt 29 and the 'high' ground to the right of it—lay north and north-east at about one mile's distance. Pt 29 was in itself an inconsiderable feature, but one which in the almost featureless surroundings had value as an observation post.[1] The task was given to the 26th Australian Infantry Brigade (Brigadier D. A. Whitehead) supported by the 40th R.T.R. (with about thirty fit Valentines), and two medium and five field regiments of artillery. One thousand rounds of medium shell and fourteen thousand of 25-pdr were allotted for the artillery's programme.

---

[1] Pt 29 was marked on many German maps as '28'. The British version only will be used here, to avoid confusion.

General Morshead was of course prepared for this crumbling operation to be ordered by the Army Commander. The 26th Brigade's patrols had found that although the objectives seemed strongly held there were very few mines about. This was confirmed on the evening of the 25th when a patrol captured two senior officers of the 125th Regiment, both of whom carried marked maps and were talkative.[1] The Australian plan was simple: at midnight 2/48th Battalion was to advance north and capture Pt 29, and forty minutes later 2/24th Battalion was to advance north-east to its own objective. The artillery, besides firing a counter-battery programme, was to put down timed concentrations for each battalion in turn, and the tanks were to stand by to meet a counter-attack at first light. This neat plan came off exactly, and both battalions took their objectives after short fights, and with them about 240 prisoners. Casualties were not high and the ground won was quickly consolidated. Private P. E. Gratwick was the first Australian to win a Victoria Cross in this battle; single-handed he had destroyed a German mortar's crew and was killed when attacking, again single-handed, a machine-gun position.

During the night Wellingtons and Albacores flew 79 sorties and dropped 115 tons of bombs on targets in the battle area. The D.A.K. whose Battle Headquarters was repeatedly raided, remarked upon the incessant bombing attacks. To prevent retaliation seven Wellingtons and six Bostons dropped fourteen tons of bombs on the Stuka base at Sidi Hancish, while night-flying Hurricanes, flying a maximum effort of thirty sorties that night, intruded over the enemy's forward landing-grounds and also patrolled the battle area, from which several hostile aircraft were driven away without doing any damage.

It is time to take a look from the enemy's point of view. The process of thinning out the front-line troops and redisposing them in greater depth had been completed by 20th October, just as the moon was approaching the full. If the British should attack and penetrate the main defensive zone they were to be counter-attacked at once, in order to seal off any crack while still small. It will be recalled that the mobile reserves had been placed well forward—indeed several German and Italian units of the 15th Panzer/Littorio Group were deployed, with guns dug in and tanks hull-down, roughly along the line 'Pierson' (which had been chosen as the first bound of the British armour). These units formed the backbone of an anti-tank screen which gave the British much trouble.

---

[1] The 2nd Battalion, 125th Panzer Grenadier Regiment, held the objectives, and the other two battalions lay between it and the coast. These were of 164th Light Division.

Reports received by the *Panzerarmee* during the morning of 24th October showed that the British had attacked on a broad front, but that such penetration of the main defences as had occurred should be within the power of local counter-attacks to seal off. Early in the morning Stumme had gone forward to learn at closer quarters the state of affairs at Minefield 'J' (in the 9th Australian Division's sector of attack). He ran into trouble; the officer with him was shot dead, and Stumme himself died of a heart attack. His body was found the next day; until then there had been no news of him except that he was missing. Lieut.-General Ritter von Thoma, who assumed command of the *Panzerarmee* in Stumme's absence, decided about noon that no large-scale counter-measures were called for.

The *Panzerarmee's* evening report on the 24th was not alarmist, though it foretold a resumption of the British attack next day with fresh forces and perhaps a landing from the sea somewhere in the back area. The fuel situation would be critical if promised supplies failed to arrive.[1]

Already on the 24th Hitler had decided to ask Rommel to leave his sanatorium and return to Africa. Rommel flew next morning to Rome, where he tried once more to impress *Comando Supremo* with the seriousness of the shortages of fuel and ammunition. He then flew on to Africa and took over his old command late in the evening of 25th October.[2] He was feeling far from confident, and his evening report for 25th October struck a serious note. Losses in the northern sector had been particularly heavy owing to the great superiority of the British air forces and artillery. The Trento Division had lost more than half its infantry and most of its artillery. The 164th Light Division had lost most of two battalions and several guns. Local counter-attacks by 15th Panzer and Littorio Divisions, though successful (sic), had been costly. He had already directed that the armour was to be husbanded and that British tanks must be taken on by guns—particularly the 8·8-cms.

Rommel's main concern on 26th October was to restore the position at Pt 29, where he expected the British to follow up their success by thrusting north-west to the coast road. A counter-attack was ordered by troops from 15th Panzer Division, the Italian 20th Corps, and the 164th Light Division, but after much manoeuvring under bombing by Baltimores and Mitchells, and heavy shelling by

---

[1] A rule-of-thumb calculation of Rommel's was that a day's fighting used up about 60 miles' worth of fuel per vehicle. German stocks for the *Panzerarmee* were enough for about 180 miles' running per vehicle; of this quantity about one-third was at Benghazi. The Italian situation was equally precarious.

Rommel's worst fears were realized, for on 26th October the *Proserpina* was sunk at sea with over 3,000 tons of fuel, and the same day the *Tergestea*, with 1,000 tons of fuel and 1,000 tons of ammunition, was sunk entering Tobruk harbour.

[2] On this day the *Panzerarmee Afrika* was renamed *Deutsch–Italienische Panzerarmee* by agreement between *OKW* and *Comando Supremo*.

the artillery covering the Australian Division, this came to nothing. The enemy's fighters strove hard to protect their troops and several fighter-bomber and dive-bomber attacks were launched in support of the intended counter-attack, but in the face of exceptionally strong opposition by Allied fighters these achieved little. During the day Rommel decided to move most of 90th Light Division from El Daba to just south of Sidi el Rahman, and replace it with the Trieste Division from Fuka.

Another big question was whether to call up some or all of the 21st Panzer/Ariete battle-groups from the southern sector of the front. Rommel realized that he might not have enough fuel to move them back again, if he should want to, but on the 26th decided that it was imperative to reinforce the 15th Panzer/Littorio sector.[1] At 9 p.m. the 21st Panzer Division received the order to move north. Three hours later it was on its way, accompanied by about one-third of the Ariete. Progress was slow because the battle area and the routes leading into it were heavily bombed during the night. It may be of interest to note that while Rommel was feeling the need to have 21st Panzer Division nearer to the *Schwerpunkt* in the north, Montgomery could afford to leave its 'opposite number'—7th Armoured Division—in the south.

October 26th was a day of important decisions for General Montgomery also. Operation 'Lightfoot' had not achieved all that had been hoped of it; in particular, the deployment of the armour beyond the 30th Corps' bridgehead had not gone well, and the crumbling operations had not begun as early as the Army Commander had said it was vital that they should. On the other hand, the enemy had been heavily engaged on a wide front and his policy of making piecemeal counter-attacks with small forces was causing him considerable losses. The relative strength of the two sides was so heavily in favour of the British that, as a matter of cold statistics, the battle might be said to be going well for them so long as German and Italian soldiers and equipment were being put out of action; the *Panzerarmee* simply could not afford to be weakened much further. At the time it was impossible to make more than a rough estimate of the total Axis losses, but the haul of prisoners—628 German and 1,534 Italian—was not very big.[2] Losses in aircraft had been light on both sides—16 British and 12 German. The 8th Army's estimate

---

[1] Axis losses in tanks had amounted to about 127, leaving fit for action 221 Italian and 148 German, of which 15th Panzer Division had only 40—a figure not reached again until 31st October.

[2] The Axis losses in killed, wounded and missing had been 1,700 Germans and 1,955 Italians.

of casualties from the evening of 23rd October until dawn on the 26th was about 6,140 killed, wounded, and missing—4,640 in the 30th Corps, 1,040 in the 13th, and 460 in the 10th. The 30th Corps' figure was made up of nearly 2,000 in the 51st Division, 1,000 Australians, 1,000 New Zealanders, and 600 South Africans. Not many replacements, however, were available for the New Zealand and South African Divisions, and General Montgomery saw that he would have to go carefully with his infantry.

The gist of his first orders, issued about noon, was: 10th Corps not to be responsible in any way for the bridgehead so far gained by 30th Corps, but to make ground west and north-west; 30th Corps to hold its sector against any form of attack, to prepare for major operations later and meanwhile to undertake minor operations to help 10th Corps—in particular, 51st Division was to mop up the parties of enemy still holding out in its sector. The 9th Australian Division was to renew its attack northward on the night 28th/29th October. General Horrocks was to ensure that the 7th Armoured Division was not exposed to casualties in offensive operations.

The Army Commander spent 26th October considering the position. About 300 British tanks had been put out of action, but many of these were recoverable and could fight again.[1] The 10th Corps had 93 actually under repair, and there were altogether about 900 fit tanks ready for action in the 8th Army. General Montgomery realized that the impetus of his offensive was on the wane and he decided to regroup his army to create a reserve with which to restore it. (This simple-sounding action was a feature of his methods.) In effect, the 30th and 13th Corps were to redistribute their formations in a manner directed by the Army Commander in order that he could draw into reserve the New Zealand Division (including 9th Armoured Brigade), the 10th Armoured Division, and possibly the 7th Armoured Division also. The regrouping was to be complete, except for small changes, by dawn on 28th October.

---

[1] Made up of Shermans and Grants together 127, Crusaders III 28, other Crusaders 77, Valentines 39, and Stuarts 31.

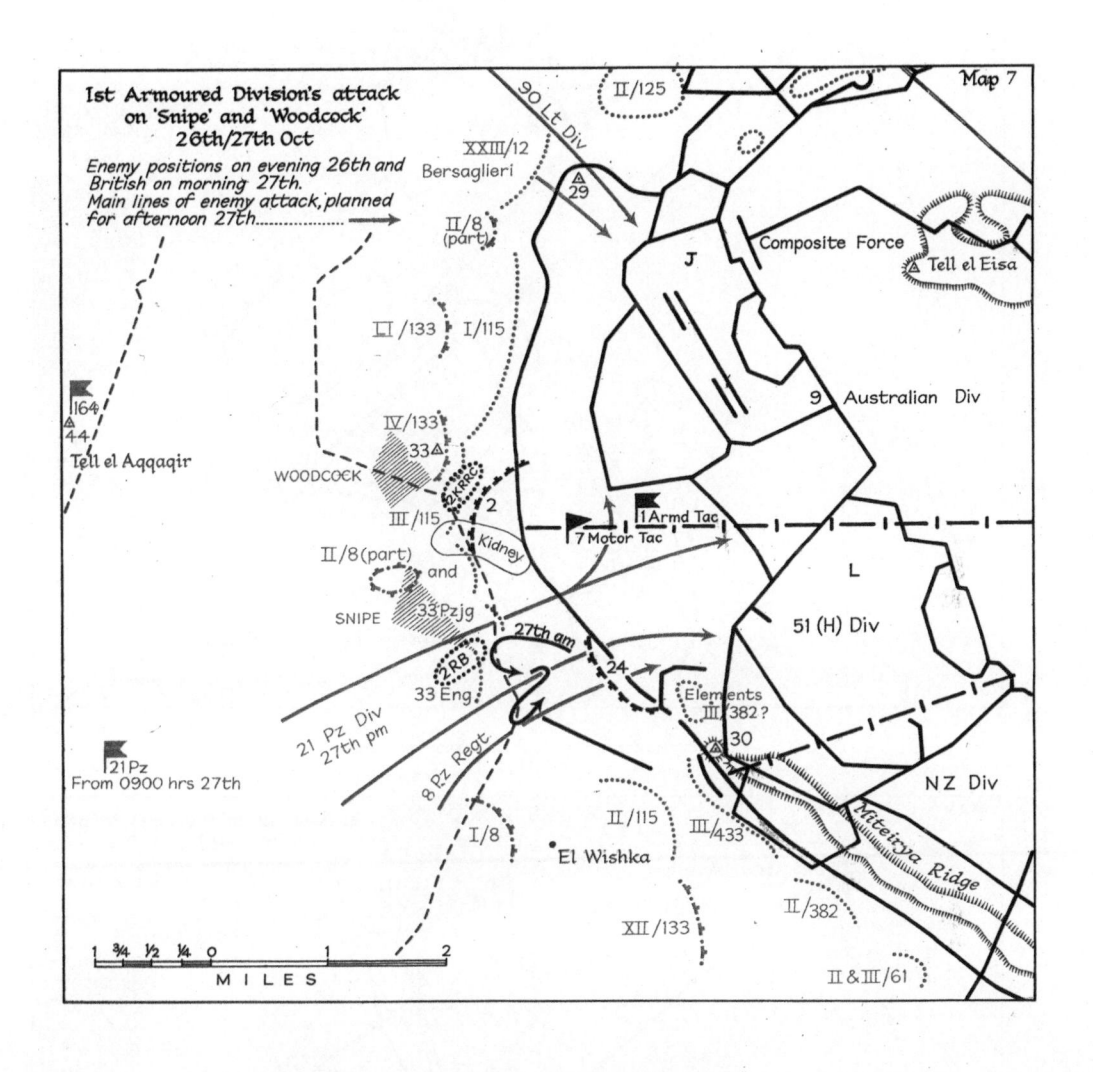

1st Armoured Division's attack on 'Snipe' and 'Woodcock' 26th/27th Oct

Enemy positions on evening 26th and British on morning 27th.
Main lines of enemy attack, planned for afternoon 27th..................→

Map 7

LEGEND MAP 8

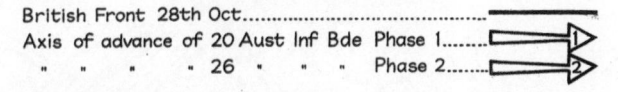

British Front 28th Oct.................................. ▬▬▬
Axis of advance of 20 Aust Inf Bde Phase 1........ ⇨
 "   "   "   " 26 "   "   " Phase 2........ ⇨

LEGEND MAP 9

British Front 30th Oct.................................. ▬▬▬
Axis of advance of 26 Aust Inf Bde Phases 1-4..... ⇨

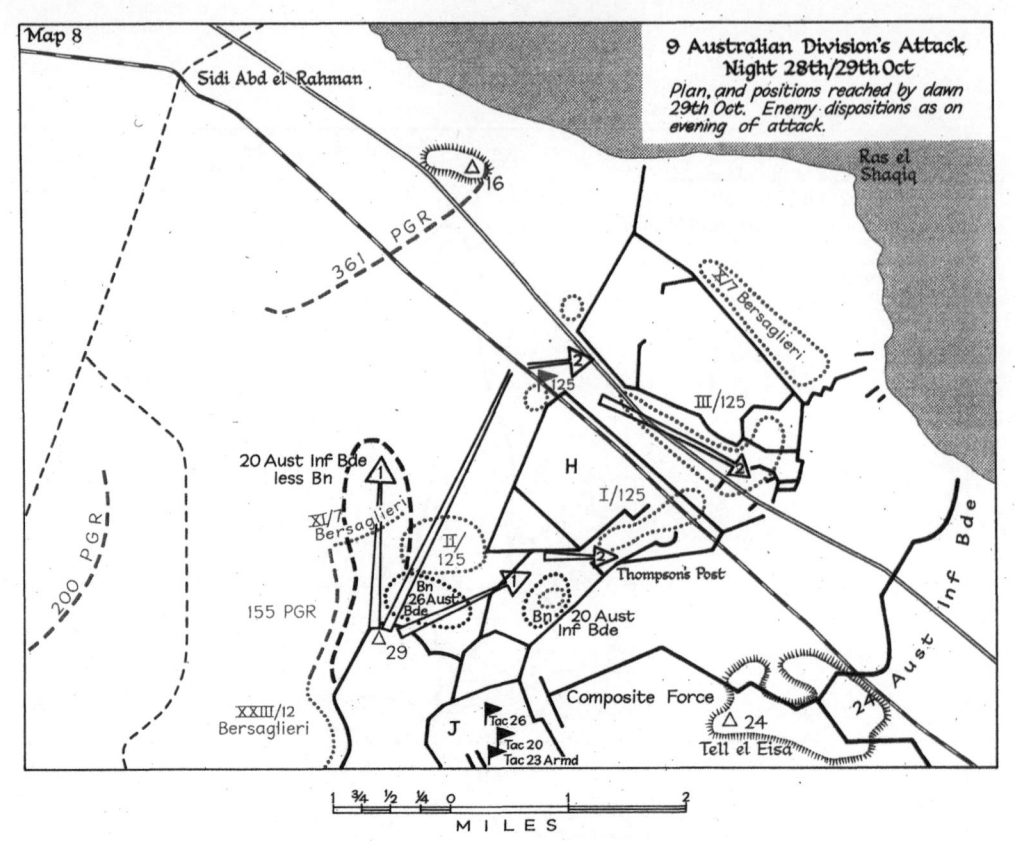

Map 8

9 Australian Division's Attack Night 28th/29th Oct
Plan, and positions reached by dawn 29th Oct. Enemy dispositions as on evening of attack.

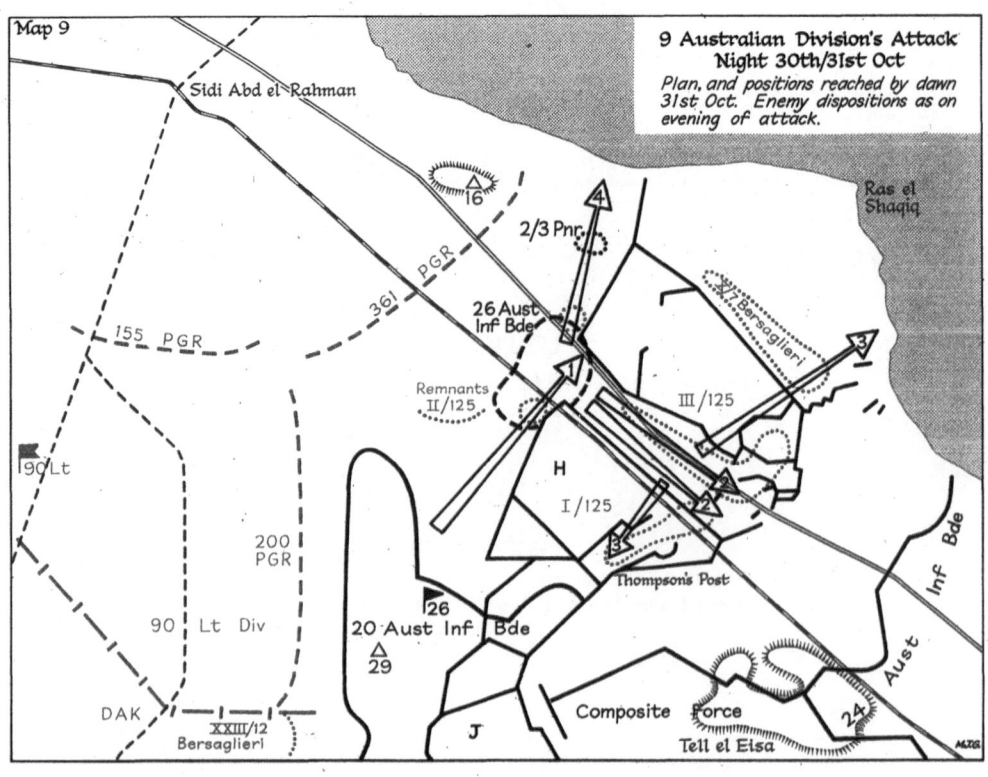

Map 9

9 Australian Division's Attack Night 30th/31st Oct
Plan, and positions reached by dawn 31st Oct. Enemy dispositions as on evening of attack.

CHAPTER III

EL ALAMEIN: THE DOG-FIGHT CONTINUED AND THE BREAK OUT ('SUPERCHARGE')

(26th-27th October—Dawn 4th November 1942)

See Map 7

IN the week from 26th October to 1st November much of importance happened. First, the attempts by the 1st Armoured Division to gain ground westward from the mouth of the northern corridor. Little ground was in fact gained, but the attempts led to the repulse of several counter-attacks with heavy losses to the enemy, especially on 27th October. The next day the British attacks in this area were called off. That night, 28th/29th, and again two nights later the Australians attacked the enemy in the coastal bulge with considerable success. Even though they did not gain all their objectives, they did enough to add greatly to Rommel's anxieties and increased his expectation that a new major attack would be coming from near Pt 29 in the direction of Sidi Abd el Rahman. Meanwhile, by milking the southern front General Montgomery was creating a new striking force with which to deliver what he hoped would be the knock-out blow. This was to be called 'Supercharge'.

Before describing the attempts of the 1st Armoured Division to advance from the northern corridor, a word is necessary about the ground which here is almost featureless. Opposite the extreme right of the 51st Division's sector was a conformation shaped—on maps—like a kidney bean, and known as Kidney Ridge. Opinions differed widely over where it was in fact, and even whether it was a ridge at all. Nearly a mile to the north-west of it, and about the same distance to the south-west, lay two localities known as 'Woodcock' and 'Snipe', centres of resistance which it was decided to capture. The difficulty was to determine exactly where they were. The best estimates of the two Divisions differed by as much as a mile—enough to spell chaos in a set-piece attack.[1]

---

[1] Subsequent evidence showed the 51st Division's map-reading to have been the more accurate. The Germans, too, had their difficulties, especially over the position of Pt 29.

The plan was to use two battalions of the 7th Motor Brigade—the 2nd K.R.R.C. against 'Woodcock' and the 2nd Rifle Brigade against 'Snipe'—supported by all available guns in the 10th and 30th Corps. Zero for both attacks would be 11 p.m. on the 26th, and at dawn on the 27th the 2nd Armoured Brigade would pass round the north of 'Woodcock' and the 24th Armoured Brigade round the south of 'Snipe'.

The 2nd K.R.R.C. began its attack in a murk compounded of darkness and dust kicked up by vehicles and shells. Some opposition was met, and direction was hard to keep; at first light the battalion found itself south of 'Woodcock' in a position which the battalion commander saw would be untenable by day. He moved quickly and the battalion began to dig in just to the south-east of Pt 33, not having reached 'Woodcock'. Farther south the 2nd Rifle Brigade found the going very bad and the dust stifling, and had difficulty in fixing the position of the start line and the direction of the objective. The British bombardment, presumed to be falling accurately on the target, appeared unexpectedly far to the north. Lieut.-Colonel V. B. Turner decided to march towards the shell bursts and the battalion changed direction and advanced about two miles against little opposition. There, concluding they were at 'Snipe', they started to dig in.

Elsewhere on the front of 30th Corps, the 51st, New Zealand, and South African Divisions worked forward during the night without much difficulty to the original objective ('Oxalic') wherever they had been short of it.

At about 6 a.m. on the 27th the 2nd Armoured Brigade began to advance, but reported stiff opposition and by noon was still slightly to the east of the K.R.R.C. The 24th Armoured Brigade started a little later and made contact with the Rifle Brigade (after shelling them for a while). For some hours confused fighting occurred in which Italian tanks of the Littorio and troops of both Panzer Divisions took part[1]. The enemy was particularly anxious about III/115th Panzer Grenadier Regiment and the 33rd Panzerjäger Battalion, but these resisted strongly and the 24th Armoured Brigade could not get on. The nineteen 6-pdr anti-tank guns (thirteen of the Rifle Brigade and six of the 239th Battery R.A.) greatly distinguished themselves. But General Briggs concluded there was little chance of the armour gaining any more ground during the day and General Lumsden decided to bring up the 133rd Lorried Infantry Brigade (of 10th Armoured Division) to reinforce the 7th Motor Brigade during the night 27th/28th with a view to making a further advance.

---

[1] The Italian tanks belonged to XII/133 Regiment and had moved up from south-east of El Wishka.

Since his return, Rommel had made a number of requests which he must have known could not be met—certainly not in time to be of use. He reported to *OKH* that his troops were showing signs of exhaustion, not only because of the weight of metal that they had to endure from the British artillery and aircraft, but also because many of the German and Italian soldiers who had been in Africa more than eighteen months were no longer equal to the strain. He wanted more infantry, more air support, and more supplies. He appealed to Barbasetti and Kesselring for more fuel; the former promised to have road tankers sent from Tripoli to Benghazi, and the latter guaranteed to fly 300 to 400 tons of fuel daily. He asked *OKW* for the 47th Infantry Regiment to be sent to him from Crete; to this Hitler replied that Rommel could have supplies or men by air, but not both. In any case this regiment was not fully equipped.

For the present battle it was quite clear to Rommel that he would have to do his best with the resources he had. His policy of making immediate local counter-attacks had served its purpose fairly well, but he felt that the situation now demanded something bigger. The 21st Panzer and 90th Light Divisions had been ordered up to the main battlefront overnight and Rommel decided to use them both, together with certain units of 15th Panzer and 164th Divisions, in an attempt to drive the British back from the six miles of front between Pt 29 in the north and El Wishka in the south.[1] The main thrusts would be made by the 90th Light Division against the Pt 29 area and by the 21st Panzer Division to the south of 'Snipe'. The operation was to take place in the afternoon of 27th October and would be preceded by a five-minute bombardment and an attack by Stukas.

In the afternoon the Stukas, about twenty in number, accompanied by C.R. 42s and strongly escorted by Me. 109s, were met and engaged by sixteen American Kittyhawks and twenty-four British Hurricanes. The hostile formation was broken up—five of its aircraft being destroyed for the loss of three Hurricanes. German records show that all the air operations that day were cramped by the great fighter superiority of their opponents.

Rommels' counter-attack began at about 4 p.m. and fell most heavily on the 'Snipe' area. This day—27th October—has been called by the Rifle Brigade's historian the most famous of the Regiment's war.[2] The 2nd Battalion, with its 6-pdr anti-tank guns and those of the 239th Anti-Tank Battery, R.A., stood its ground and did great execution, particularly among enemy tanks advancing against the 24th Armoured Brigade. More than once it seemed that

---

[1] A battle-group of the Ariete Division, including a battalion of tanks, moved up with the 21st Panzer Division but returned south on 28th October.
[2] R. H. W. S. Hastings: *The Rifle Brigade in the Second World War* 1939–1945 (Aldershot, 1950).

the Battalion must be overrun. Coolness and courage averted this fate and led, instead, to the decisive defeat of the enemy at this important point. Later in the evening the Battalion was mistakenly withdrawn, but it had set an example of what resolute troops could do to defend themselves against tanks. The Victoria Cross awarded to Lieut.-Colonel V. B. Turner of the Rifle Brigade honoured his own gallantry in the action and that of all under his command.[1]

Elsewhere on the front the enemy had little or no success. At Pt 29 the other main thrust of his attack was broken up by heavy defensive artillery fire, backed by some devastating bombing by 90 British and American day-bombers, and the 90th Light Division never closed with the Australians. They reported having captured Pt 29, but later admitted that this was a mistake. As their diary put it 'It was very difficult to determine the exact position of Point 29, and under enemy fire quite impossible.'

In short the enemy's counter-stroke had failed utterly, which at this stage of the battle was most significant. At 8 p.m. General von Thoma reported the situation to Rommel, who ordered that all positions were to be held, that full use must be made of defensive artillery fire, and that no major penetration by the enemy could be allowed.

Meanwhile the 133rd Lorried Infantry Brigade (Brigadier A. W. Lee) had been unable to learn the exact situation of 7th Motor Brigade's foremost troops, as ground reconnaissance of the 'Woodcock-Snipe' area was impossible by daylight. During the evening it was learned that neither 'Woodcock' nor 'Snipe' was in British hands, whereupon the 133rd Lorried Infantry Brigade set out to capture them. The artillery plan had to be very simple in view of the confused situation. Zero, after a postponement to give battalions more time to move up, was fixed for 10.30 p.m. The advance of the 4th Royal Sussex on the right took them through ground already held by the 1st Gordons (of 51st Division), and there was an unfortunate clash which caused some casualties. Then considerable fire broke out from the left; the reserve company was sent to deal with it and was almost destroyed. By 1.30 a.m. the Commanding Officer judged that he had reached 'Woodcock' and ordered consolidation —not easy in the rocky ground. Communications with Brigade Headquarters and the artillery had broken down. The Battalion seems to have touched the eastern end of 'Woodcock' and to have got among some German and Italian units which soon began to react. At dawn the 2nd Armoured Brigade was moving up on the northern flank, much as it had done twenty-four hours previously,

---

[1] An official committee of investigation subsequently put the 'bag' of hostile tanks as 22 German and 10 Italian.

but before its two regiments were in place the enemy suddenly attacked and overran the 4th Royal Sussex.[1]

The other two battalions had better fortune, and reached and dug in on positions believed to be the objectives but in fact well short of them. Both Panzer Divisions made a sustained attempt to advance against the 10th Corps, but they were checked and finally halted by powerful artillery, tank, and anti-tank gun fire. Early in the afternoon, when the enemy attempted to re-form for a further attack, the British day-bombers were switched from airfield targets to the concentrations of vehicles near the Rahman track on 10th Corps' front. For two and a half hours the Bostons and Baltimores carried out crippling bombing attacks and the enemy's attempt was defeated even before he could complete forming up.

The foregoing brief account of the two days' fighting from 26th to 28th October shows how reverses can occur locally during a battle which is nevertheless being steadily won. For the enemy had suffered losses he could not afford: the fit tanks in the *D.A.K.* fell from 148 to 77, and the Littorio lost 27. The change from attack to defence had favoured the British, and General Montgomery directed that the 'Woodcock-Snipe' area was now to become a defensive front. His next attack was to be made that night, farther to the north.

By this time the regrouping of the 8th Army was under way and proceeding smoothly, although it entailed some complicated reliefs and movements owing to the need to hold the front and not give the enemy too much breathing space. By 31st October the following principal moves had taken place. Side-stepping by the 4th Indian and South African Divisions enabled the New Zealand Division, together with the 9th Armoured Brigade, to be withdrawn into reserve. The 1st Armoured Division was also taken out for a quick refit. The 10th Armoured Division came temporarily under the 30th Corps, thus simplifying the command in the Kidney Ridge area. The 7th Armoured Division (less 4th Light Armoured Brigade) was ordered north from 13th Corps and the 131st Infantry Brigade (from 44th Division) joined it as an improvised lorried infantry brigade. The Army Commander's idea was to use the skill and experience of General Freyberg and his New Zealand Division for a decisive attack westward along the coast. In view, however, of the shortage of New Zealand infantry the Division was to be reinforced by two infantry brigades—the 151st (from 50th Division), and the 152nd (from 51st Division). Among other adjustments the 4th Indian Division passed to the command of 13th Corps and 152nd Brigade

---

[1] The 4th Royal Sussex's casualties were 47 killed and wounded and 342 missing. The incident revived some of the old recriminations between infantry and armour, but it is hard to see how the armour could have intervened.

of the 51st Division reached out to its right and took over part of the front from the 20th Australian Brigade.

See Map 8

On the night of 28th/29th October the Australian Division made the second of its set-piece attacks—an essential preliminary to the Army Commander's plan for launching the reinforced New Zealand Division westward along the coast. The plan was elaborate. Broadly, it aimed at enlarging the ground already gained at Pt 29 as a firm base from which to thrust north-eastwards over the railway as far as the main road; from here to advance south-east along the line of the road and railway and get behind the enemy holding the nose of the coastal salient. Finally, to attack the salient itself from the south-east. All three Australian Infantry Brigades were required for this plan. The artillery support was again very powerful, but the directions of the various attacks were so different that the artillery programme was somewhat complicated.[1]

The attack began at 10 p.m. The 20th Australian Infantry Brigade (Brigadier W. J. V. Windeyer), with 40th R.T.R. in support, took its objectives after some trouble with anti-personnel mines and shell-fire. The advance of 26th Australian Infantry Brigade and 46th R.T.R. towards the road fared less well. Because of the distance to the objective, and in the hope of winning surprise, some of the infantry rode on the Valentine tanks and others on carriers. The advance began in difficulties owing to darkness, dust, and—vexingly —mines which had been laid to protect the Australian positions, as well as those which had been scattered by the enemy. Very soon the tanks ran into anti-tank fire, and machine-gun fire forced the infantry to dismount. Communications failed, and the armour and infantry, preoccupied with their own actions, lost touch. A general mêlée followed and some infantry may have reached the railway, but the 2/23rd Battalion's commanding officer decided that it was not possible to continue the attack and dug in about half a mile north-east of Pt 29, with the remaining seven runner tanks of 46th R.T.R. in support.[2] Meanwhile the 26th Australian Infantry Brigade was preparing to continue the attack with its two other battalions and 40th R.T.R., but it soon became clear that not enough of the night was left to give this plan any chance of success. The Australian Division's operation had fallen short of its ambitious

---

[1] *Panzerarmee* Battle Report refers to 'the heaviest artillery fire which had so far been experienced'.
[2] Australian casualties were 27 killed and 290 wounded. The 46th R.T.R. had fifteen tanks knocked out besides those damaged. All were recovered later.

aims but had nevertheless achieved a solid success. It had punched a hole between II/125th Panzer Grenadier Regiment and 90th Light Division's Battle Group 155, and had to all intents destroyed the former unit. A battalion of Bersaglieri had also been overrun. At dawn part of the 15th Panzer and Littorio Divisions moved as if to counter-attack towards Pt 29, but this came to nothing.

Rommel was by now seriously worried and was considering a general withdrawal. He could not bring himself to make the decision because fuel was so short and the opposing armies were at such grips that there seemed to be no chance of extricating the non-motorized infantry. Moreover, even if a fairly large part of his army did manage to get away, shortage of fuel was likely to prevent it from ever using the mobile tactics which alone seemed likely to be fruitful. It was on the morning of the 29th that he received news that the important tanker *Luisiano* had been sunk. He expected the British to press on without pause towards Sidi Abd el Rahman. He therefore decided to have a defensive position reconnoitred at Fuka and gave some temporizing orders. The 21st Panzer Division (with 60 tanks) was to be taken out of the line to become a mobile reserve north of Tell el Aqqaqir, being relieved by the Trieste Division; Battle Group 155 of 90th Light Division and the remains of II/125th Panzer Grenadier Regiment were to withdraw the same evening (29th) to the south-east of Sidi Abd el Rahman; the rest of 125th Panzer Grenadier Regiment was to hold on to the present positions until the night 30th/31st October. Command in the coastal sector would be taken over by 90th Light Division.

Thus Rommel had judged correctly what the British Army Commander had been intending to do. It happened however that General Montgomery had changed his mind! Early on the 29th, as a result of the Australian operation which had just taken place, information was obtained which showed that the 90th Light Division was committed to the sector between Pt 29 and the coast. This meant that the enemy probably expected an attack in the direction of Sidi Abd el Rahman, and that no fresh German formations were now available in reserve. General Montgomery then decided to launch his assault farther to the south, a course which had been strongly advocated by his Chief of Staff (among others). To keep Rommel's eye on the coastal sector he ordered the Australian Division to renew its attack northwards on the night 30th/31st. The reinforced New Zealand Division would launch its attack westward on a front of about 4,000 yards, with its right near Pt 29. This blow, he hoped, would land mainly upon Italian troops. It would take place during the night 31st October/1st November, and its object was defined by the Army Commander as to 'bring about the disintegration of the whole enemy army.'

At this moment a flutter occurred in London. Mr. Churchill had not forgotten General Montgomery's exposition, made in August, of the outline of the British offensive and his forecast of about a week's hard fighting. A situation report of 28th October—the fifth day of 'Lightfoot'—gave details of the 8th Army's regrouping which the Prime Minister found disquieting. He feared that Montgomery's offensive operations were now on too small a scale, moreover, a standstill would be proclaimed as a defeat. The C.I.G.S., General Brooke, explained that the reorganization going on was almost certainly a prelude to a further offensive. He later wrote 'It was fortunate that on that day I had not yet received a letter from Monty which arrived a few days later telling me what his feelings were at this juncture of the battle.'[1] Whatever General Montgomery's inner feelings may have been, a reassuring telegram from General Alexander, to which he had agreed, and another from Mr. Casey, the Minister of State, left no doubt that the offensive would be vigorously pressed. The incident serves as a reminder of the importance of the timing of 'Lightfoot'. A resounding victory in the Desert a few days before 8th November might make the difference between success and failure of the 'Torch' landings.

See Map 9

The last of the Australian Division's three set-piece attacks, which contributed so markedly to the successful outcome of the battle, took place on the night of 30th/31st October. Broadly, General Morshead's intention, with a few additions, was for 26th Australian Infantry Brigade to complete the operation that had been broken off early on the 29th. The first phase would be an advance north-east to seize positions astride the main road and railway from which to make further thrusts. These were, as before, to be made south-eastwards down the railway—this being phase two—capturing whatever positions lay in their paths, and getting close behind the enemy in the nose of the salient. In the third phase two further thrusts were to be made, one north-eastwards to the sea and one in the opposite direction to capture the work known as Thompson's Post. As a fourth phase one battalion was to advance from the area seized in the first

---

[1] Arthur Bryant: *The Turn of the Tide* (London, 1957) p. 513. This letter has not been found. It may have been destroyed at the moment of receipt.

phase and strike northwards to the sea. Shortly before dusk on the 30th a concentrated attack by bombers and fighter-bombers was to be carried out in the area immediately north of the Australian positions 'to soften up' the enemy defences. The artillery plan included a counter-battery programme, barrages, and timed concentrations, and was remarkable for the enormous volume of fire to be controlled by the C.R.A., for the need to support the infantry in so many different directions, and for the adoption of three zero hours in one night. The 'I' tanks were not to join in the first attack, but 40th R.T.R. was to move to a central position from which it could go where it was needed. Thus the plan was bold, complex, and ambitious, and asked much of the skill and endurance of the troops. The fighting won the award of a V.C. to a second Australian soldier in this battle—Sergeant W. H. Kibby, for heroic conduct on no less than three occasions, beginning on 23rd October. On the last, during the night 30th/31st, he was killed when attacking a machine gun alone.

In preparation for the first phase, and throughout daylight on the 30th, the fighter-bombers roamed the coastal area attacking targets wherever they could be found. Shortly before dusk they joined the Bostons and Baltimores of Nos. 21 and 24 (both S.A.A.F.) and 55 Squadrons in forty minutes of concentrated bombing, 150 aircraft taking part all told and dropping 85 tons of bombs on enemy strongpoints and A.F.V.s in front of the Australians sometimes at distances of only 1,000 yards from their positions. Results appear to have been excellent. Zero hour for the first phase was 10 p.m. The 2/32nd Australian Battalion, after some opposition from the 1/125th Panzer Grenadier Regiment, captured and consolidated its objectives, though it could not mop up every hostile post in the area. Zero hour for the second phase was 1 a.m. on the 31st. The 2/24th and 2/48th Australian Battalions made considerable progress down the railway, but they lost touch with each other and both suffered heavy casualties. Realizing that they were too weak to reach their objectives both battalions drew back to near the positions of the 2/32nd Battalion, and it became clear that there was no chance of carrying out the third phase of the operation. The fourth phase however was not dependent on the progress of the third, and at 4.25 a.m. the 2/3rd Australian Pioneer Battalion, in its first action as infantry in the attack, set off north towards the sea. When about half way it met stubborn resistance and the battalion was later withdrawn behind the railway.

Although the operation did not achieve all that was hoped for, the 26th Australian Infantry Brigade had inflicted substantial casualties and taken over 500 prisoners. It now held positions astride the main road and railway which would make it hard for the enemy to withdraw from the salient. If, on the contrary, Rommel decided to rescue the remainder of 125th Panzer Grenadier Regiment he would have to counter-attack over ground dominated by the British artillery. Whichever course he chose, the coastal sector would remain a cause of anxiety to him.

A probe by 361st Panzer Grenadier Regiment early on the 31st was stopped by artillery fire. Rommel then ordered up in support a battle-group from 21st Panzer Division (containing about half the Division's tanks, self-propelled anti-tank guns and artillery) to take part in an attack down the railway at about 1 p.m. The attack was pushed home and for the next half hour there was a sharp fight involving 2/32nd Australian Battalion and 40th R.T.R. but the main British positions remained firm. Much the same thing happened at about 4 p.m., although 40th R.T.R., after losing twenty-one Valentines, was forced to withdraw. Rommel ordered the attack to be renewed the following morning. This led to some hard fighting: ground was lost, retaken, and lost again, but in general the Australians managed to hold their own. Rommel also was satisfied on the whole, since he had established contact with 125th Panzer Grenadier Regiment.

The newly won Australian positions were congested with men and vehicles and invited air attack. The Australians asked for special cover and on the 31st the Desert Air Force responded with fighter sweeps amounting to about 200 sorties.

Day-bombers and fighter-bombers operated in support, and one attack against 90th Light Division soon after midday was described by the Australians as 'right in the middle of the target'.

This is a suitable moment to remark on the part played by the air forces during the period between 'Lightfoot' and 'Supercharge'. There is plenty of evidence of the cumulative effect on both Germans and Italians of the persistent round-the-clock bombing to which they had been subjected for some time. But bombing, whether by day or night, caused few casualties among men crouching in narrow trenches or among vehicles or guns sunk in pits, and at the start of 'Lightfoot' even the mobile battle-groups of 15th Panzer and Littorio Divisions had some protection of this kind. But during the dog-fight phase of the battle (25th to 31st October) there was much movement of troops behind the enemy's front for one reason or another, and the air forces found good targets among men and vehicles on the move, and even to some extent concentrated—for instance when forming up preparatory to making a counter-attack. Sometimes the weather prevented the air forces from intervening, but on several occasions they were able to break up and disorganize an intended counter-attack in its early stages—before it had begun, one might say. Then it was a shaken and wavering enemy who, after running the gauntlet of air attack, was faced with having to cross the inferno of the powerful British artillery's defensive fire.

Tanks, even in the open, suffered little damage by bombs, except from a direct hit which was rarely obtained. The tank-destroying fighters—Hurricane IIDs armed with two 40-mm cannons firing armour-piercing shot—were most effective, but these aircraft had to come down very low to aim and they became the targets for all the small arms and anti-aircraft guns within reach. This was the main reason for confining these Hurricane IIDs to the southern sector, where targets and ground defences were more dispersed.

The night bombing attacks made by the skilful and experienced team of Wellingtons and flare-dropping Albacores never wanted for targets among the leaguers and transport concentrations and the various activities that went on by night in what may be called the front of the back area. Certain other standing activities were at this stage as important as ever: for example, reconnaissance of all kinds, strategical, tactical and photographic—the last being of particular value to the artillery. Finally, all these tasks were additional to that of keeping the enemy's air forces subdued, which entailed making fighter sweeps and frequently attacking his airfields, especially Sidi Haneish, Fuka and El Daba.

The Army Commander was well aware of the value of the Air's contribution, and later wrote:

'The moral effect of air action is very great and out of all proportion to the material damage inflicted. In the reverse direction, the sight and sound of our own air forces operating against the enemy have an equally satisfactory effect on our own troops. A combination of the two has a profound influence on the most important single factor in war–morale.'

The Desert Air Force could well be proud of the great part it played at this critical time in lowering the enemy's will to resist.

Meanwhile, his capacity to do so was being further sapped by the British successes in the struggle for seaborne supplies, and it happens that three more sinkings occurred during the phase now under review. On the evening of 28th October the tanker *Luisiano*, carrying 1,459 tons of petrol, was sunk by a torpedo from a Wellington off the west coast of Greece, and on 1st November the *Tripolino* of 1,464 tons, laden with petrol and ammunition, was sunk, also by a Wellington, to the north-west of Tobruk. Another ship of the same convoy, the *Ostia*, was torpedoed and sunk by a Beaufort.

The critical state of Rommel's fuel supply having caused the Germans to fly fuel from Crete, a force of heavy bombers of No. 205 Group attacked Maleme on 27th October. This marked the renewal of strong attacks on the main airfield used by the Ju. 52s. On this occasion four of these transport aircraft were destroyed and other damage was done.

It has been explained why, on 29th October, General Montgomery decided to change the front and direction of 'Supercharge'. His final choice is shown on Map 10. This front happens to have corresponded roughly with the sector for which the *D.A.K.* (General von Thoma) was now responsible. In order to bring the 21st Panzer Division into reserve it was relieved by the Trieste Division on 30th October, but the latter's infantry was so weak that a battalion of the German 104th Panzer Grenadier Regiment was left in position when the 21st Panzer Division withdrew to the vicinity of the Rahman track. British estimates of the current strength, morale, and general condition of German and Italian formations and units were not far wrong. Nevertheless they credited the enemy with more tanks than he had, believing about 280 German and Italian mediums to be available within reach of the main front, including 40 of Ariete's. German records show that here, on 1st November, *D.A.K.* had a total of 102: 7 with H.Q., 51 in 15th Panzer Division, and 44 in the 21st; a detachment of some 15 to 25 more was under 90th Light Division near the coast. Littorio and Trieste held 65 between them. In addition 52 German tanks were under repair. All the Ariete's tanks were now back again in the southern sector.

'Supercharge' was in many respects a repetition of 'Lightfoot'. For instance, the basic idea was for the infantry to attack by night, with the armour following as closely as possible and passing through the infantry's objective. There would again be a tremendous volume of supporting fire, but on this occasion there were enough guns to allow the counter-battery neutralization programme and the barrage to be fired simultaneously, beginning at zero. As for mines, it was realized that there would not be any elaborate belt to deal with like those met in 'Lightfoot', but that there might be numerous patches of scattered mines, and it had been learned during 'Lightfoot' how troublesome these odd mines could be. The same methods and means of gapping would be used, including Scorpions. The fact that the moon would be in its last quarter, rising on 1st November just before 1 a.m., meant that zero hour would have to be later than it had been on 23rd October if there was to be moonlight to help the engineers locate and clear the mines.

The problem of passing the armour through without allowing the attack to lose its momentum had not been satisfactorily solved in 'Lightfoot'. This time it was tackled slightly differently. The break-in attack by 30th Corps, on a front of about 4,000 yards, was to be made by two (British) infantry brigades attached for the purpose to

Map 10

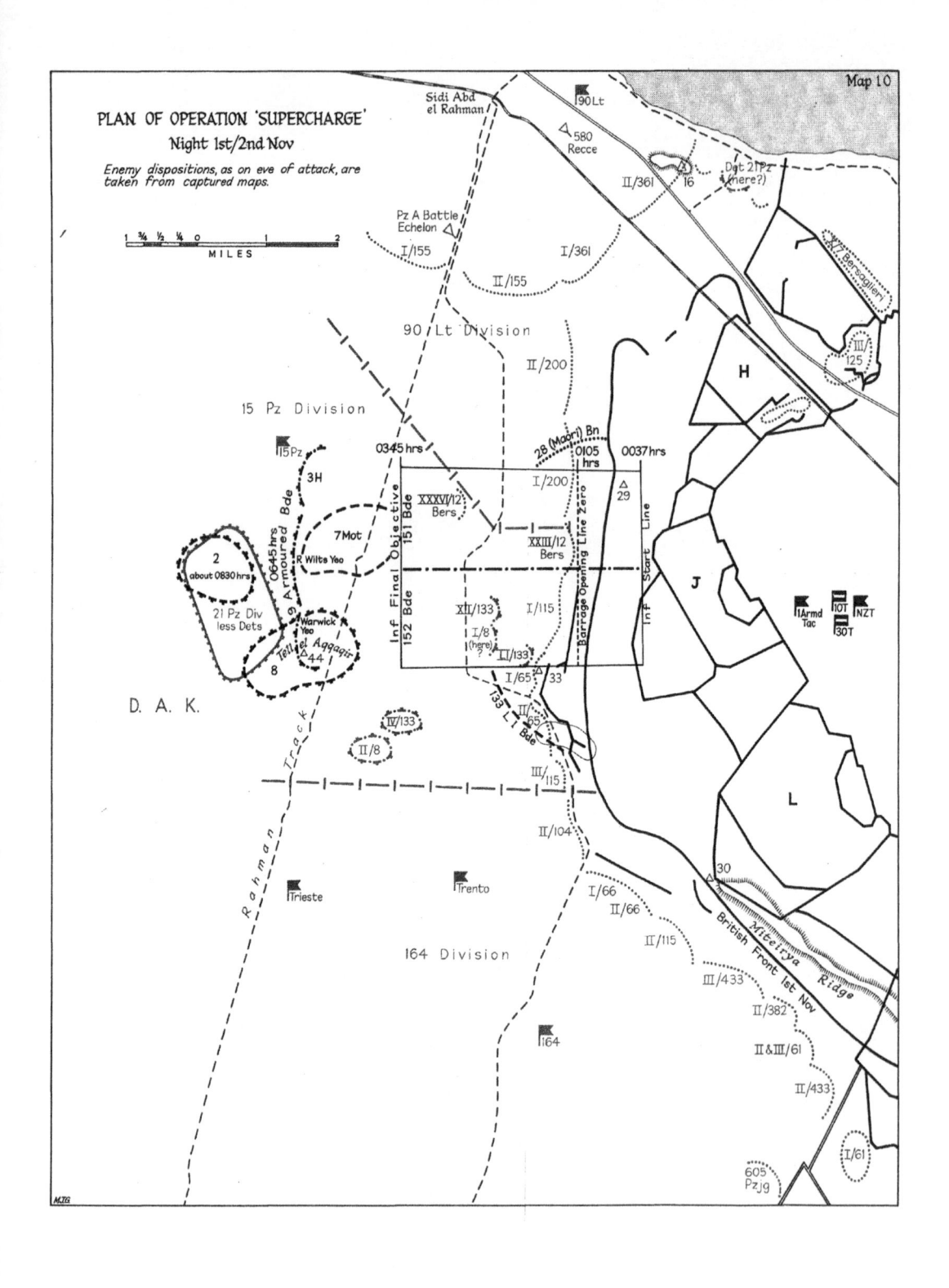

PLAN OF OPERATION 'SUPERCHARGE'
Night 1st/2nd Nov

Enemy dispositions, as on eve of attack, are taken from captured maps.

Map 11

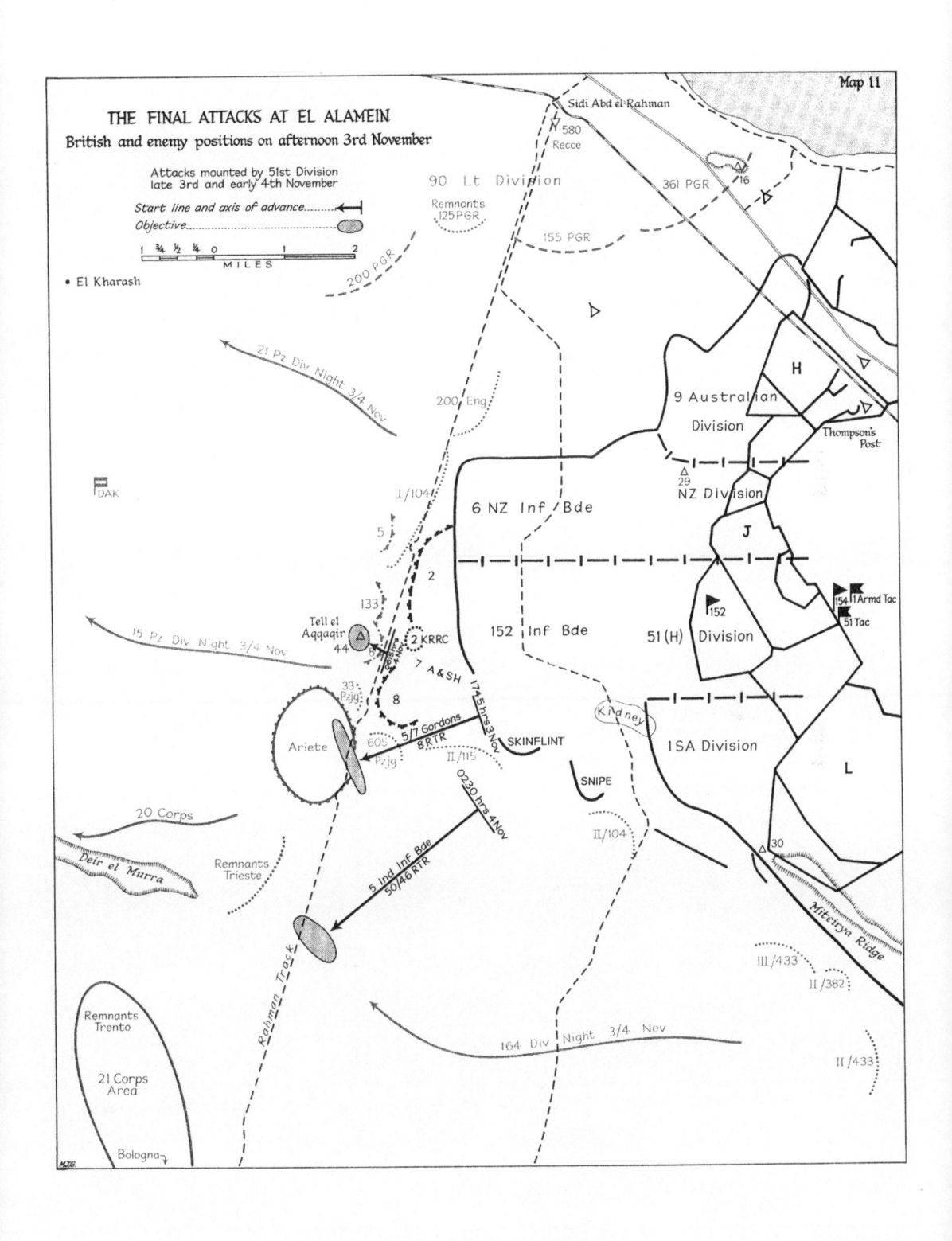

THE FINAL ATTACKS AT EL ALAMEIN
British and enemy positions on afternoon 3rd November

Attacks mounted by 51st Division late 3rd and early 4th November

Start line and axis of advance..........→
Objective..........⬬

the New Zealand Division. Each was to have a regiment of Valentine tanks in support. Behind them would be the 9th Armoured Brigade (of three tank regiments) also under command of the New Zealand Division. This Brigade was to take up the advance from the infantry's objective for about another 2,000 yards under a barrage, and would, it was hoped, smash or capture the defences situated on and around the Rahman track. Moving forward all this time would be the 1st Armoured Division of 10th Corps, which in its turn would cross the Rahman track and prepare to do battle with the enemy's armour in the open.[1]

This, in bare outline, was the plan for operation 'Supercharge'. General Montgomery had intended to launch it on the night 31st October/1st November, but early on the 31st, at General Freyberg's suggestion, he reluctantly postponed it for twenty-four hours on account of the tiredness of many of the troops, and the shortness of time for collecting all the units (a business entailing an intricate chain of movements in congested areas) and for reconnaissance. Zero hour was fixed for 1.05 a.m. on 2nd November.

The 13th Corps, after being milked to reinforce the other two corps, now had three weak infantry divisions and a light armoured brigade with which to hold a front of some thirty miles. Its task in 'Supercharge' was to lead the enemy to think that something important was in train in the southern sector.

At 9.15 p.m. on 1st November a force of 68 Wellingtons and 19 Albacores opened a seven-hours' attack on targets in the area Tell el Aqqaqir, Sidi Abd el Rahman, and Ghazal station. Six tremendous explosions and more than twenty large fires were counted, and it was later learned that at *D.A.K.* Advanced Headquarters the signals

---

[1] The 8th Armoured Brigade (of 10th Armoured Division) had been lent to the 1st Armoured Division for 'Supercharge'. The 24th Armoured Brigade had not been made up after its severe losses in 'Lightfoot'. The 10th Armoured Division was therefore off the board. The 7th Armoured Division (less 4th Light Armoured Brigade) was under 10th Corps for administration, but was still under the control of 8th Army as a reserve.

Table showing fit tanks on 1st November (other than Valentines and Stuarts)

Formation	Grants	Shermans	Crusaders III	Crusaders II
1 Armoured Division	—	—	—	6
2 Armoured Brigade	—	90	26	40
8 Armoured Brigade	39	23	20	27
7 Armoured Division	—	—	—	4
22 Armoured Brigade	54	—	10	16
9 Armoured Brigade	40	39	24	29
Totals	133	152	80	122

system was wrecked. Night flying Hurricanes patrolled the battlefield and intruded over the Stuka base at Sidi Haneish.

A small naval demonstration was staged in the bays off Ras el Daba and Ras Gibeish where torpedo boats simulated landings by dropping rafts and flares.

The New Zealand Division's attack started under a powerful barrage at 1.05 a.m., after what was for the infantry a trying wait in the cold. The attack was led on the right by the 151st Infantry Brigade (of 50th Division) and on the left by the 152nd (of 51st Division), each advancing on a frontage of about 2,000 yards with two battalions up.[1] Close behind came the 8th and 50th R.T.R. (each with about 38 Valentines) with the task of protecting the foremost infantry from hostile armour at dawn on 2nd November. On the northern flank the 28th (Maori) Battalion attacked and captured a position which would strengthen the right shoulder of the new salient, while the 133rd Lorried Infantry Brigade performed a similar task on the left flank. Overcoming some opposition and taking a number of German and Italian prisoners, the main attack reached its objective 4,000 yards distant up to time and without excessive losses. Battalion vehicles were soon forward, two field companies of New Zealand Engineers having cleared five lanes through the mines. As expected, only one substantial minefield was met, but there was a little delay in destroying odd patches of enemy whom the moppers-up had missed.

In order to take immediate advantage of this early success two armoured car regiments tried at once to slip out into open country. One of them, the Royal Dragoons, after having no luck near Tell el Aqqaqir, tried again farther south and succeeded. Darting out to the westward two squadrons spent the day doing mischief before halting for the night south of El Daba.

On 29th October General Montgomery had taken the important decision to bring the 9th Armoured Brigade up to strength as a first priority, and it had now 79 Shermans and Grants and 53 Crusaders. It had left its rest area near El Alamein station by 8 p.m. on 1st November and its approach march had not been made without trouble. The dark and the dust were very trying, and the 3rd Hussars Group's motor-infantry and anti-tank guns were unlucky in having some casualties from shell-fire. The number of tanks in the three regiments which failed to arrive for one reason or another—a disappointingly large number—left 94 fit to go into action. At Brigadier Currie's request the next phase of the attack, in which his

---

[1] 151st (Brigadier J. E. S. Percy)—8th and 9th Durham Light Infantry; 152nd (Brigadier G. Murray)—5th Seaforth Highlanders and 5th Queen's Own Cameron Highlanders.

Brigade was to take up the advance at 5.45 a.m. behind a barrage, was postponed half an hour.

Accordingly at 6.15 a.m. on 2nd November (that is about half an hour before first light) the 9th Armoured Brigade in three regimental groups passed through the infantry's objective and advanced behind the barrage. The 3rd Hussars and Royal Wiltshire Yeomanry met only slight opposition at first, but nearer the Rahman track they came under heavy anti-tank fire and only a few tanks got across the track. The Warwickshire Yeomanry, on the left, ran into trouble even sooner. All three regiments had heavy losses but gallantly strove to maintain their ground so that the 1st Armoured Division could pass through. On arrival of the 2nd Armoured Brigade the nineteen remaining tanks of the 9th Brigade rallied on the right and continued the fight.[1] When the Brigade was withdrawn in the evening it had had 230 casualties to officers and men, and 70 (out of 94) tanks put out of action, many of them of course recoverable.

The 10th Corps' plan was based on the belief that the enemy would react to the New Zealand Division's thrust by counter-attacking strongly from north or west. If therefore the 1st Armoured Division, in addition to the 9th Armoured Brigade, could be deployed in a favourable position there was every chance that the superior British armour would be able to crush those enemy tanks that still remained. The 2nd Armoured Brigade was directed to a deployment area two miles north-west of Tell el Aqqaqir, the 8th Armoured Brigade to Tell el Aqqaqir itself, and the 7th Motor Brigade to a position between the two.

Soon after 7 a.m. the 2nd Armoured Brigade began to deploy in rear of the 9th. Preceded by the 1st Armoured Division's Minefield Task Force (composed as for 'Lightfoot') it had led the way from Springbok Track and had been on the move since 3 a.m. Visibility was bad and made worse by the dust of battle and smoke from burning tanks. Very soon all three regiments ran into fire from tanks and anti-tank guns and came to a standstill. At about 10.15 a.m. the 8th Armoured Brigade came up on the left of the 2nd and was ordered to make ground to the south-west. But it, too, was brought to a halt by heavy fire. The losses in these two Brigades were 14 tanks lost and 40 others damaged or broken down. If little ground had been gained the Division had clearly attained its object of 'finding and destroying enemy tanks'. In fact *D.A.K's* strength in fit tanks fell by over 70 during the day.

During the morning targets for the British air force were not plentiful, but in the afternoon, when a concentration of tanks and

---

[1] Just after 9 a.m. the 9th Armoured Brigade came under command of 1st Armoured Division.

vehicles was found by air reconnaissance west of the Rahman track, a shuttle service of fighter-bombers and British and American day-bombers was laid on, and by evening 310 sorties had been flown and 163 tons of bombs dropped. 'Air raid after air raid' wrote Rommel to his wife. Reports from the forward troops confirm that the bombing had been very accurate and after the last raid of the day (by South African Bostons) on targets near Tell el Aqqaqir 200 enemy troops surrendered. All the available Hurricanes were employed in protecting the British armour, but the enemy made only two attempts to intervene, once with twelve Stukas and once with forty, each time with fighter escort. The first attack was met by the Hurricanes of Nos. 33 and 238 Squadrons and the second by those of No. 1 Squadron S.A.A.F. and No. 213 Squadron. Both attacks were repelled, and in one of them the dive-bombers jettisoned their bombs among their own troops. Two German fighters were shot down for the loss of two Hurricanes. The remaining Allied fighters made constant sweeps over the battlefield, the Spitfires in particular giving special protection to the Royal Dragoons in their raid.[1]

The information which General Freyberg received early on the 2nd led him to think that for all practical purposes the reinforced New Zealand Division had performed its task. By 7.30 a.m. he was worried by the slow progress of 1st Armoured Division and asked General Leese to get it hurried up. By 10 a.m. he felt—and told General Leese—that the situation was becoming static and that chances might be missed. At H.Q. 30th Corps the situation seemed satisfactory; the night's operations had not resulted in heavy casualties, a good bag of prisoners had been made, and mine-free routes were open for the armour to advance west. General Montgomery also had reason for satisfaction in that Rommel had not reacted with his usual speed and it seemed that 30th Corps and 10th Corps would be well placed to deal with the expected counter-attack when it came. General Montgomery gave orders allotting responsibilities for holding the newly captured ground as a firm base for further operations. The 2nd Armoured Brigade was to advance west across the Rahman track. The localities 'Skinflint' and 'Snipe' were to be captured the same evening. Two South African regiments of armoured cars were to attempt to break out westwards. The 7th Armoured Division was to move up to Tell el Eisa and pass from Army reserve to 10th Corps. The 4th Light Armoured Brigade was to be sent up at once from 13th Corps to 10th Corps. A shuffle amongst the infantry was to be made

---

[1] The same day the *Zara* of 1,976 tons, carrying amongst its cargo 235 tons of fuel, was sunk near Tobruk by a Beaufort torpedo-bomber of No. 39 Squadron. The *Brioni* of 1,987 tons, carrying 295 tons of ammunition, reached Tobruk safely only to be destroyed at its moorings by American Liberators at dusk. Of 4,244 tons of fuel promised to the *Panzerarmee* between 27th October and 1st November only 893 tons had arrived.

with the purpose of collecting four brigades in reserve under 30th Corps.[1] General Montgomery meant to keep up the pressure and to strengthen 10th Corps, and was again showing his skill in creating reserves.

At 8.15 p.m. on 2nd November General von Thoma gave Rommel his report of the situation. He considered that he had checked the British advance and that the front was holding, but only just. The enemy's air superiority was very great. Forty or fifty American-type bombers kept up perpetual attacks over the battle area, even at night. The British outnumbered, out-tanked, and out-gunned him. Next day he would have at most thirty-five tanks in action. The German infantry, artillery, and 8·8-cm dual-purpose guns had been reduced to about one-third of their strength at the beginning of the battle. The 5-cm anti-tank guns could penetrate Shermans and Grants only at short range and were being overwhelmed. As for the Italians, only their artillery was any good. There were no more German reserves and if the British continued to attack they would inevitably break through. Yet their methods were so deliberate that he felt there was a chance of getting at least the German troops away.

Rommel thereupon decided that the time had come to start withdrawing to the positions which had been reconnoitred at Fuka. The Ariete Division would move to Tell el Aqqaqir at once, to swell the remnants of 20th Corps. The 21st Corps was to pull back to the right of the 20th. In the southern sector the 10th Corps was to withdraw that night behind the western minefield which stretched from El Taqa to west of Bab el Qattara. The Ramcke Parachute Brigade was to continue the line to the Qatani minefield. The distance of these withdrawals was only about eight to ten miles, and Rommel hoped to provide all these formations with some extra transport by the evening of 3rd November. The mobile formations—20th Italian Corps, *D.A.K.*, 90th Light Division and 19th Flak Division—were to make a 'fighting withdrawal' in such a way that by the evening of the 3rd they could still deny to the British a line north and south through Ghazal station. The *D.A.K.* and the 20th Corps would withdraw south of the railway. The 90th Light Division was to take 125th Panzer Grenadier Regiment along with it somehow; the remainder of 164th Light Division would probably be carried in 15th Panzer Division's vehicles. The *Panzerarmee's* reserve would consist of 33rd and 580th Reconnaissance Units and its own 'Battle Echelon'.[2]

---

[1] 5th Indian, 151st, 5th New Zealand, and 154th.
[2] *Panzerarmee's* Battle Echelon was a small mixed force with an establishment of about 700 all ranks. It was intended for protecting Army headquarters, but was used by Rommel for a variety of tactical tasks.

Rommel was thus doing what he could in a bad situation, banking upon the hope that the British would follow up hesitantly. But he knew that lack of transport would prevent a planned withdrawal by the marching formations and that even the mobile formations might be unable to disengage completely. This pessimistic view was included in a situation report to *OKW*, which ended thus: 'In these circumstances we must therefore expect the gradual destruction of the Army, in spite of the heroic resistance and exceptionally high morale of the troops.'

Meanwhile the 51st Division had made ready to capture 'Skinflint' and 'Snipe' (shown on Map 11), as ordered by General Montgomery earlier in the day. The attack on 'Skinflint' was to be made at 6.15 p.m. on 2nd November by the 2nd Seaforth Highlanders (of 152nd Infantry Brigade) and 50th R.T.R., supported by eight field and two medium regiments; that on 'Snipe' a little later by 5th Royal Sussex (133rd Lorried Infantry Brigade) also with strong artillery support. This plan was completely successful: 'Skinflint', saturated by artillery fire, offered little opposition and yielded about 100 prisoners from the Trieste Division for very few British casualties; at 'Snipe' 60 of the Trieste, terrified by the plastering of 'Skinflint', surrendered out of hand.

General Lumsden had received from General Montgomery a certain latitude in making his plans, and until the evening of 2nd November had in mind a rather deep westward thrust by the whole of the 1st Armoured Division. The enemy's screen of guns along the Rahman track seemed to be the only real obstacle left to a breakthrough to the west, and at 8.30 p.m. General Lumsden finally decided to call upon his infantry once more and gave orders for the 7th Motor Brigade to seize the Rahman track along a front of about two miles stretching north-east from Tell el Aqqaqir. The 2nd and 8th Armoured Brigades would advance in succession through the captured area to a distance of about three and a half miles. On the morning of 3rd November the 7th Armoured Division was to pass through the 1st and head for Ghazal station.

Unfortunately, the attack by the 7th Motor Brigade was a failure. The Brigade received its orders late, it had no detailed information about the positions it was to capture, and the failing light precluded any useful reconnaissance. At 1.15 a.m. on 3rd November the three battalions advanced to the attack. The artillery support was certainly strong but information about it is incomplete—in fact the whole story is very difficult to piece together. It is clear however that a misunderstanding about the time of zero lost one battalion the benefit of the artillery support, and the enemy was very wide awake.

Another battalion ran into heavy fire and became scattered, while the third, after some trouble with posts which had been by-passed, was withdrawn because it had reached a position which would be untenable by day. When it was realized that the attack had failed, the orders to the armoured brigades were modified, although 10th Corps' headquarters, because of inaccurate reports and, it seems, some faulty map reading, believed until a late hour on the 3rd that the 2nd K.R.R.C. was holding Pt 44 at Tell el Aqqaqir. The 4/6th South African Armoured Car Regiment, seeking a way through, and believing that the infantry had taken Tell el Aqqaqir, came to grief on various obstacles such as scattered mines and disused gun pits.

See Map 11.

The modified task of the 1st Armoured Division was for the 2nd Armoured Brigade to support the 2nd K.R.R.C. while the 8th Armoured Brigade worked forward to the south-west. In the event the 2nd Armoured Brigade was held up by elements of both Panzer Divisions and tanks of the Littorio disposed along the Rahman track. Farther to the south-west the few remaining guns of the 33rd and 605th Panzerjäger Battalions and three troops of 8·8-cm guns, backed later by the Ariete, engaged in sporadic duels with the 8th Armoured Brigade.[1] In the afternoon the Nottinghamshire Yeomanry tried a 'rush' attack, and some Crusaders reached the Rahman track before being driven off—events which probably occasioned exaggerated reports of the brigade's progress. The strength of the two brigades fell that day by some 16 Grants and Shermans and at least 10 Crusaders. Behind the enemy's lines the Royal Dragoons continued to make a nuisance of themselves and were credited by the enemy with doing a good deal of damage: their own claims were one tank, nineteen lorries, and, surprisingly, one aircraft.

During the night 2nd/3rd Wellingtons and Albacores, at maximum strength, battered the enemy for eight hours while night-flying Hurricanes patrolled overhead. The principal targets were presented by vehicles near Ghazal station, and when the last aircraft turned for home thirty good fires were blazing. Meanwhile Liberators of No. 160 Squadron and Halifaxes of No. 462 Squadron, R.A.A.F., dropped forty tons of bombs among dispersed transport aircraft at Maleme in Crete. Here, too, a huge fire was caused, but no aircraft were thought to have been hit.

The same night the Australians noticed that the enemy in the

---

[1] If these three troops of 19th Flak Division were up to strength there would be twelve guns in all.

coastal bulge showed signs of withdrawing, as it was expected he might do since the local tactical situation had become so unfavourable for him. But before 10 a.m. on the 3rd General Montgomery received word from 13th Corps that there were signs of withdrawal in the southern sector too. Reports during the morning that the 1st Armoured Division was slowly making ground suggested that the enemy was everywhere loosening his grip. At about noon General Montgomery directed that the 51st Division was to capture (i) the Rahman track west of 'Skinflint' at 4.45 p.m., and (ii) Tell el Aqqaqir and the Rahman track about eight miles south of that place, during the small hours of the 4th. South African armoured cars were to make another attempt to break out to the west.

During the evening it seemed to General Montgomery that the enemy was on the brink of a general withdrawal. If Rommel decided to make a stand it would probably be on the escarpment above Fuka and perhaps also at Matruh, where field defences of a sort existed. General Montgomery accordingly gave instructions for exploiting the success which he expected his night attacks would achieve. Briefly, the task of the 10th Corps would be to strike north at the coast road while the New Zealand Division, suitably reinforced, would move westwards across the desert preparatory to making for the Fuka escarpment from the south. Depending on the situation at Fuka the Division was to be prepared to send a detachment to Matruh, in which event the 10th Corps might have to send an armoured division to Fuka. Warning orders were given to the 30th and 13th Corps for mopping up the enemy on their fronts.

At this point it will be interesting to use later knowledge and learn what was happening to Rommel. By 3 p.m. on the 3rd the withdrawals in the southern sector had gone as planned, as also in the sector of 90th Light Division. The 20th and 21st Italian Corps were moving into their new positions south of the *D.A.K.*, but 164th Light Africa Division remained grounded for want of transport. Rommel deduced from the small scale of British activity, worrying though it was, that the 8th Army was busy regrouping and that a brief opportunity offered to get some of his infantry away to Fuka. He ordered 10th Italian Corps to filter north-west to Deir el Harra as a first step; the Ramcke Parachute Brigade to an area about twenty-five miles south of Daba; 21st Italian Corps to positions near Fuka. At 3.30 p.m. his confidence was shattered by the arrival of an order from Hitler that the *Panzerarmee* was to hold its ground to the last and 'not to yield a step'. A similar order was issued by Mussolini through Cavallero.[1] Rommel was angry and dismayed because he felt that the High Command did not grasp, or were shutting their eyes to,

---

[1] The text of these and certain other relevant telegrams is given in Appendix 3.

the danger in which his army stood, and he knew that if the present opportunity to withdraw was missed he might never have another. He read the orders on the telephone to von Thoma, who at once declared that *D.A.K.* could not possibly continue to hold its present positions and escape destruction. He suggested that it must withdraw at least as far west as Ghazal. Rommel was in a quandary and after much hesitation tried to escape from it by compromise. He ordered 10th and 21st Italian Corps and 90th Light Division to stand fast; *D.A.K.* was to withdraw to a line about six miles west of Tell el Aqqaqir; 20th Italian Corps was to conform and the Ariete Division, on arrival from the south, was to take post on *D.A.K.'s* right. These withdrawals would begin after dark. He replied to Hitler, detailing his heavy losses but confirming his determination to hold the battlefield. It was not until the next morning (4th November) that he asked permission to withdraw to Fuka. Incidentally, the interference by the two Dictators had spoiled any slight chance Rommel may have had of lifting some of the Italian marching formations at least part of the way back. As he noted later in his memoirs he often found it necessary, after this experience, to get round the orders of his superiors. The whole episode illustrates the inefficiency of the Axis arrangements for the higher direction of the war.

On 3rd November the Allied air effort reached its peak. Soon after dawn fighter-bombers attacked motor transport on the Rahman track and beyond. An hour later the first day-bombers took off to attack targets north-east of Tell el Aqqaqir and Bostons dropped eight tons of bombs on them. From then onwards all the available day-bombers and fighter-bombers concentrated on the Aqqaqir area on which 93 tons of bombs were dropped by noon. Signs that the enemy was withdrawing were seen. Reconnaissance was intensified and as a result the bombing was switched to the coast road in the El Daba area; later, after a noticeable thinning out of traffic, it was switched to the desert tracks. By dusk a further 100 or more tons of bombs had been dropped, fighters had flown nearly 200 'strafing' sorties and the Ghazal-Fuka road was studded with burning vehicles. In the south the cannon Hurricanes were given a free hand, and they attacked tanks, armoured cars, half-tracked vehicles and motor transport over a wide area. No fighter escorts were provided and none were required.

The enemy's total air effort had declined still further, but his few fighters scored some successes in the afternoon while attempting to break up the Allied fighter patrols covering attacks on the coast road traffic. He also launched two Stuka raids. The first, of twenty

Ju. 87s escorted by twelve Me. 109s, came in soon after dawn and was intercepted by twenty-four Hurricanes of Nos. 33 and 238 Squadrons which were quickly joined by nine Spitfires of No. 145 Squadron. The Stukas were forced to jettison their bombs among their own troops. The second raid, made up of thirty Ju. 87s and twenty Me. 109s, came in soon after midday, and the Stukas were again forced to jettison their bombs when attacked by Hurricanes of Nos. 80 and 127 Squadrons. In all one Stuka and one Me. 109 were destroyed in these raids against a heavy British loss of two Spitfires and seven Hurricanes. This brought the total British fighter losses for the day to sixteen, and eleven damaged.

It had been the busiest and, despite the heavy fighter losses, probably the most successful day of the battle for the Desert Air Force. With its reconnaissance flights it had flown 1,094 sorties and dropped 199 tons of bombs. Together with the previous night's effort, this means that the Royal Air Force had flown 1,208 sorties in the twenty-four hours and dropped 396 tons of bombs on the enemy—and this after two and a half weeks of large scale operations. American day-bombers flew a further 53 sorties and the fighters 72.[1]

During 3rd November there were further signs on 30th Corps' front that the enemy was beginning to withdraw. Patrols detected some thinning out—for example, in the Australian Division's sector the notorious 'Thompson's Post' was found empty. The focus, however, must now be on 51st Division, which was ordered to stage three set-piece attacks. First, 5/7th Gordon Highlanders (under command 152nd Infantry Brigade) and 8th R.T.R. (23rd Armoured Brigade) were to capture a portion of the Rahman track about two miles south of Pt 44 (Tell el Aqqaqir) starting at about 5.45 p.m. on the 3rd. Second, the 5th Indian Infantry Brigade was to capture a stretch of the same track some four miles south of Pt 44, starting in the early hours of 4th November. Third, the 7th Argyll and Sutherland Highlanders (of Brigadier Houldsworth's 154th Infantry Brigade) were to capture Pt 44 itself at 6.15 a.m. on the 4th. These attacks were to be the prelude to what General Montgomery intended to be the final reckoning with the *Panzerarmee* described in the next chapter. Meanwhile the 9th Australian Division was to mop up the coastal sector and clear all mines and other obstacles from any parts of the coast road that it might capture.

The first of the three attacks was to be a straight-forward joint affair preceded by an air bombardment and with weighty artillery

---

[1] The squadrons operating were: *Night of 2nd/3rd November*—Nos. 37, 40, 70, 73, 104, 108, 148 and 162 R.A.F.; Nos. 821 and 826 F.A.A. *Day of 3rd November*—Nos. 6, 33, 55, 80, 92, 112, 127, 145, 208, 213, 223, 238, 250, 260, 274, 601 and 1437 Flt., No. 2 P.R.U., R.A.F.; Nos. 1, 2, 4, 5, 7, 12, 15, 21, 24, 40 and 60 S.A.A.F.; Nos. 3 and 450 R.A.A.F.; No. 335 Hellenic; 64th, 65th, 66th, 82nd, 83rd and 434th U.S.A.A.F.

support. Most unfortunately it was believed (wrongly) at H.Q. 1st Armoured Division that the 8th Armoured Brigade had already passed beyond the objective now set for the infantry and that the enemy had withdrawn from it. The outcome of this muddle was that the 152nd Infantry Brigade informed its units that the air and artillery programmes were cancelled except for a guiding smoke-screen, and suggested that some infantry should ride forward on tanks to take over the objective. The Officer Commanding 8th R.T.R. protested but was overruled, and 'A' Squadron advanced carrying three platoons of Highlanders on the tanks. The enemy had not in fact withdrawn and gave the tanks a hot reception. A good deal of confusion followed. 8th R.T.R. were ordered not to press on if the opposition was too stiff; attempts to reorganize the artillery support were made; important wireless links failed, as at awkward times they were apt to do. Finally the Gordons dug in well short of the objective, supported by the tanks; between them these two units had 94 casualties including 16 officers; 9 Valentines were destroyed and 11 damaged out of about 32.

As regards the second attack, there were moments during the evening when it must have seemed impossible for the 5th Indian Infantry Brigade to be ready in time. The Commander, Brigadier D. Russell, got zero hour postponed one hour to 2.30 a.m., which required some quick work by the C.R.A. New Zealand Division who was controlling all the artillery. Even so, one field regiment at at least did not receive the order in time. Brigadier Russell also made a last-minute change of roles between two of his battalions, and managed to stage the attack more or less as planned. It met practically no opposition—for the enemy was already withdrawing—and about a hundred German prisoners were taken.

The attack by the 7th Argyll and Sutherland Highlanders on Tell el Aqqaqir met some shelling, but the enemy had almost melted away and the Battalion was on its objective by 6.45 a.m. Two squadrons of 4/6th South African Armoured Car Regiment and Headquarters and one squadron of the Royal Dragoons slipped out south of the 5th Indian Infantry Brigade and by 6.30 a.m. were in the open desert. In the coastal sector the Australians pushed up to west of Ras el Shaqiq, found nothing, and began to patrol westwards and clear the main road of mines.

Signs of the enemy's intention to retreat had already been seen from the air and every serviceable Wellington was out during the night 3rd/4th, attacking in particular a mass of vehicles between El Daba and the sea and later in the night concentrating on the point where the main road climbed the escarpment at Fuka. Crews reported a vast number of fires reaching all the way to Fuka, so many that it seemed the enemy must be firing his own dumps.

Before passing on to describe the enemy's retreat from the field of El Alamein it will be convenient to review briefly the circumstances in which this great twelve-day battle was fought. For although it provided the climax to two years of to-and-fro struggle in the Western Desert, it differed from previous encounters in many important respects. It was nothing new for the British to have a numerical advantage in men or material, but never before had this been so complete, applying as it did to fighter aircraft, tanks, field and anti-tank guns, and armoured cars, as well as to stocks of ammunition, fuel, and supplies of all kinds, backed by ample transport and workshops and by the many benefits that go with a short and well-established L. of C. Nor was the advantage now only quantitative—as witness the new and powerful Sherman tank. On top of all this, and largely because of it, the morale of the 8th Army was very high. Perhaps the most important single factor which kept it so high, and did much to lessen the enemy's, was the superiority of the Western Desert Air Force, which made it possible for the enemy to be attacked incessantly from the air, while the inevitably crowded areas behind the British lines were raided neither heavily nor often.

On the ground the battle-front was restricted, with both flanks secure; there was no way round for the familiar sweep of a mobile force. The alternative—punching a way through—was made harder by the fact that the two sides had been in contact for many weeks during which the enemy had greatly strengthened his field defences and had laid anti-tank mines in vast numbers. Mr. Churchill has referred to this as 'the tremendous shield of minefields of a quality and density never known before'.[1] Although the position of most of the Axis fields—or, at least, of their front edges—was known to the British, the full extent of the clearing to be done could only be guessed at. Fortunately the enemy had sown comparatively few anti-personnel mines, and, in the northern sector, had not put up enough barbed wire obstacles to be really troublesome.

The minefields made their presence felt long before the battle began by compelling General Montgomery to make his break-in attack ('Lightfoot') in moonlight. The enemy rightly judged that this would be so, and Rommel clearly had it in mind when he ordered the re-deployment of the Axis troops in greater depth to be completed by 20th October—four days before the full moon. On the British side vigorous training was going on, also conditioned by the minefields. For the tanks, which in 1917 had led the infantry across the barbed wire, had now themselves to be helped through the mines; in fact the roles of infantry and tanks had become reversed. So infantry formations practiced attacking over flat featureless ground

---

[1] *The Hinge of Fate* (London, 1951), p. 541.

by night, while the engineers cleared the mines. The armoured forces rehearsed the crossing of minefields, also by night, and the break-out at first light into open country.

This break-out was a cause of worry to the armoured formation commanders. They feared that their tanks, on emerging from a minefield, would come under effective fire from anti-tank guns sited for the purpose and dug in. In fact this happened again and again, for the British armour frequently failed to make full use of the supporting arms.[1] It would have suited the tanks if the infantry's objective could have included this gun area, but in 'Lightfoot' the infantry had to advance a long way as it was, and could not be expected to do more. Which suggests that in laying out his anti-tank defences the enemy had seen the problem very clearly.

When 'Lightfoot' only partially succeeded, and its momentum was on the wane, General Montgomery, resilient but resolute, did not hesitate to change his plan. He realized that in order to get his armour into the open another big infantry attack on the same pattern would be needed and the preparations would take time. His task was still 'to take or destroy at the earliest opportunity the German-Italian army together with all its supplies and establishments in Egypt and Libya', and he could afford little delay. The landings in French North Africa were to take place on 8th November and it was hoped to precede them by a resounding victory over Rommel a few days before. Secondly, it was essential for the success of the 'Stoneage' convoy bound for Malta that the Martuba airfields should be available for the R.A.F. by 16th November—and from El Alamein to Martuba is 450 miles. Clearly, the *Panzerarmee* ought to be destroyed without delay. Radiating confidence and determination amid all the stress and urgency, General Montgomery proceeded with his new plan ('Supercharge'). If he felt anxious—and there is reason for believing that he did—he never showed it. Firmly convinced that morale is what matters most he strove to keep it high, in spite of considerable infantry casualties and the misgivings of the armoured commanders.

His opponent, Field-Marshal Rommel, was pitch-forked back into Egypt to resume command of the *Panzerarmee* after being away sick for a month. He was not at his best, and the odds against him lengthened as the process of attrition took toll of both sides; unless General Montgomery made a cardinal mistake Rommel was almost certain to be beaten. Yet the Rommel legend died hard, and he was still widely regarded by the British as an unusually dangerous enemy, especially if he had just suffered a reverse, for he had gained a reputation for suddenly rebounding and snatching success.

---

[1] In spite of General Lumsden's warning quoted on page 34.

Air Vice-Marshal Coningham succeeded admirably in applying the strength of the Desert Air Force to the two main tasks of subduing the enemy's air forces and of giving the Army the best possible direct support. The result was that the Army enjoyed complete protection from serious air attack and, at the same time, had the benefit of such close co-operation and continuous air support as never before. Coningham's handling of the Desert Air Force and its attached American squadrons drew a generous tribute from General Montgomery, which covered also the indispensable contribution by the R.A.F. medium night-bombers and the skilled pathfinders of the Fleet Air Arm. General Alexander telegraphed to Mr. Churchill '... Work of R.A.F., Dominion Air Forces, and U.S.A. Air Corps was beyond praise and our air superiority had a great moral effect on the soldiers of both sides'. The practical result was that the Allied Air Force dominated the air throughout the battle.

In achieving this success the British lost 77 aircraft and the Americans 20; the Germans lost 64 and the Italians an estimated 20. These figures should be related to the numbers of sorties, of which the Royal Air Force flew 10,405 (not counting those from Malta and against ships), the Americans 1,181, the Germans 1,550 and the Italians an estimated 1,570.

The 8th Army lost approximately 2,350 officers and men killed, 8,950 wounded, and 2,260 missing—a total of 13,560.[1] They had nearly 500 tanks put out of action, mostly repairable; in fact over 300 had already been repaired. They had also lost 111 guns of various kinds. Figures can mislead, but these show clearly that although General Montgomery never let go of the initiative, and chose when and where to strike next, the battle was anything but a walk-over. The 8th Army thoroughly deserved its success, for the German troops put up a magnificent defence and retained their soldierly qualities in the face of stronger forces backed by much greater resources both on the ground and in the air. Those Italian formations that were closely engaged fought with spirit, but they were inadequately equipped for a struggle of this sort, and were out-classed.

The enemy's losses were tremendous, the German formations being reduced to skeletons and the Italian broken to bits. What the losses had totalled by the morning of 4th November can only be guessed; the Trento, Trieste and Littorio divisions had been almost wiped out and several others both German and Italian severely mauled. For the next few days Rommel had little idea of what men and equipment he had left, but he knew on the 4th that some 36 German tanks (including a few IIs) remained out of a total of 249

---

[1] Percentages of the total losses were borne by U.K. troops 58; Australians 22; New Zealanders 10; South Africans 6; Indians 1; Allies 3.

of all types. The Italians had still about half the 278 with which they began, but they were to lose them nearly all before the day was out in a long encounter with 7th Armoured Division. Figures for prisoners can be given with more certainty; by the 5th those taken during the battle, as distinct from the subsequent round-up, were 2,922 Germans and 4,148 Italians; by the 11th the figures had risen to 7,802 and 22,071, or about 30,000 in all.

The Battle of El Alamein may be said to have ended at dawn on 4th November, with the enemy breaking away and the British setting out to catch him (as described in the following chapter). Whether they could have captured or destroyed more of the *Panzerarmee* than they did will be argued as long as military history is read. But the twelve-day battle was a clear and indisputable victory in which forces beyond the battlefield had played important parts. Thus the sustained offensive against Axis shipping carried on by the Royal Navy and the maritime air forces had deeply cut into (as by the end of the next seven months it would almost cut off) the enemy's means of living and fighting in Africa. The whole battle was an impressive instance of co-operation by Commonwealth and Allied forces, by the three Services—sea, land and air—and by the several arms and branches of the 8th Army and G.H.Q.

Seldom can a communique have been more welcome to the Allies, nor, indeed, to the free world at large, than the announcement from Cairo on 4th November that the Axis forces were in full retreat. The British had had many disappointments in 1942; and the public badly wanted some good news: now they had got it. Confidence in General Montgomery had risen sharply after Alam el Halfa, where he had shown his skill in conducting a big defensive action. Now he had followed this up by bringing off a major offensive against an enemy entrenched in fortified positions far more formidable than any hitherto met in the Desert war, and his stock soared to new heights.

Mr. Churchill has praised the whole achievement as one which will always make a glorious page in British military annals, and observes that 'It marked in fact the turning of the "Hinge of Fate" '.[1]

---

[1] Op cit., page 541.

Map 12

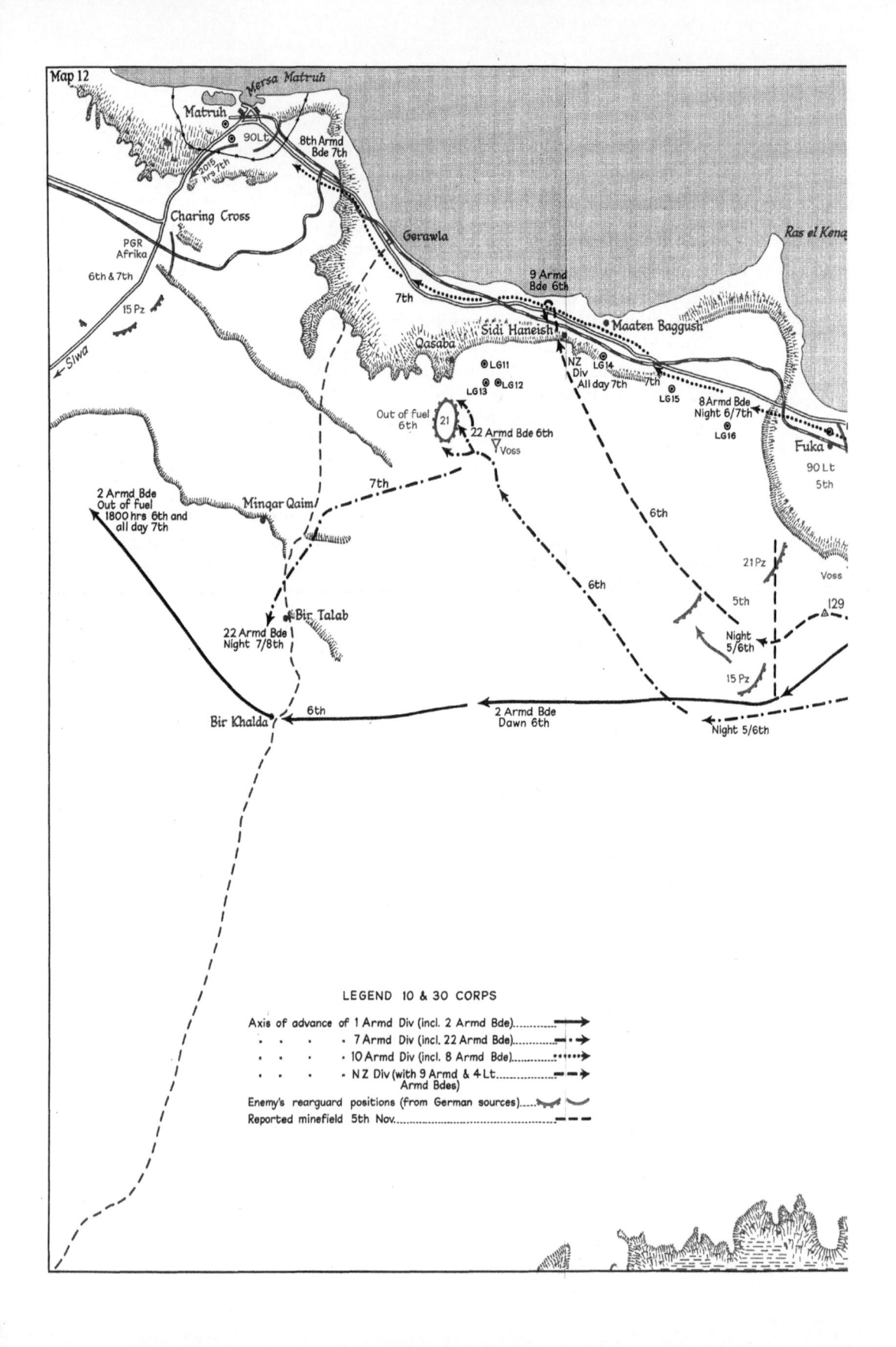

Mersa Matruh
Matruh
90 Lt
2015 hrs 7th
8th Armd Bde 7th
Charing Cross
PGR Afrika
6th & 7th
15 Pz
Siwa
Gerawla
Ras el Kenayis
9 Armd Bde 6th
7th
Qasaba
Sidi Haneish
Maaten Baggush
LG11
LG13 LG12
NZ Div All day 7th
LG14
7th
LG15
8 Armd Bde Night 6/7th
LG16
Fuka
90 Lt 5th
Out of fuel 6th
21
22 Armd Bde 6th
Voss
2 Armd Bde Out of fuel 1800 hrs 6th and all day 7th
Minqar Qaim
7th
6th
6th
21 Pz
Voss
129
Bir Talab
22 Armd Bde Night 7/8th
Night 5/6th
5th
15 Pz
Bir Khalda
6th
2 Armd Bde Dawn 6th
Night 5/6th

LEGEND 10 & 30 CORPS

Axis of advance of 1 Armd Div (incl. 2 Armd Bde).............. ⟶
" " " " 7 Armd Div (incl. 22 Armd Bde)............... ‣⟶
" " " " 10 Armd Div (incl. 8 Armd Bde)................ ••••▶
" " " " NZ Div (with 9 Armd & 4 Lt. Armd Bdes).............. ⤏
Enemy's rearguard positions (from German sources)....⌒⌒
Reported minefield 5th Nov....................................... ▬ ▬

The Pursuit to Matruh
4th – 7th November 1942

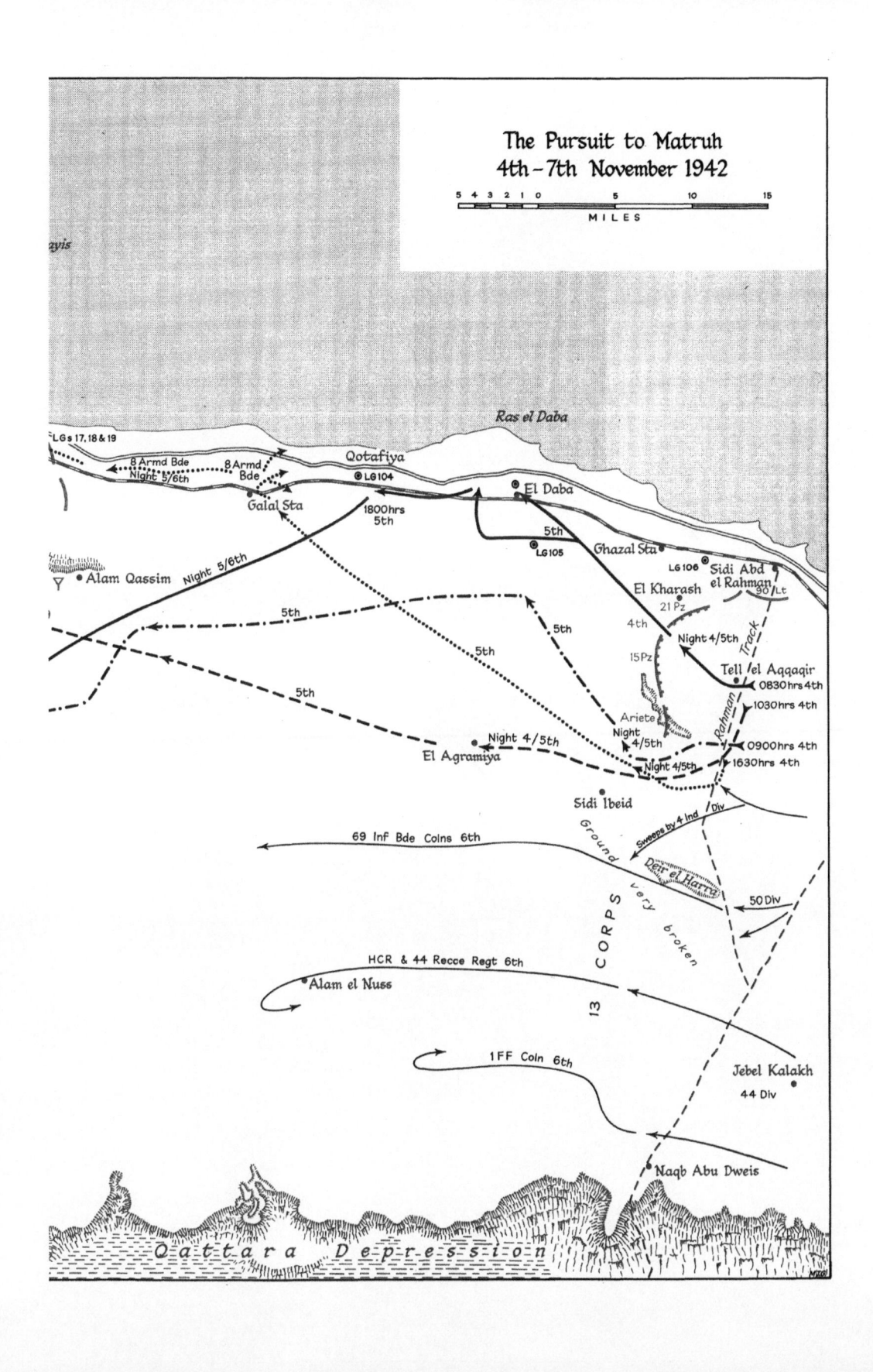

CHAPTER IV

THE PURSUIT TO EL AGHEILA
(4th to 23rd November)

See Map 12

THE two final British attacks, described on page 75, were made early in the morning of 4th November while it was still dark. Opposition to the first was slight and to the second negligible, because Rommel had ordered the *D.A.K.* and 20th Italian Corps to withdraw a few miles during the night in an attempt to reconcile what he knew to be the correct tactical move —namely, to break away—with what he had been told by the Führer, which was 'not to yield a step'.

General Montgomery's instructions for exploiting the expected success of these two attacks were briefly referred to in the previous chapter, as indicating his outlook on the evening of 3rd November. These instructions became amplified as follows. The New Zealand Division, with its two infantry brigades lorry-borne and with the 9th Armoured and 4th Light Armoured Brigades under command, was to move west by desert tracks through Sidi Ibeid to the escarpment above Fuka—a distance of about sixty miles from the Rahman Track. The 13th and 30th Corps were given various tasks on their own fronts, mainly to keep contact with the enemy's troops and round them up. General Lumsden's intention was for the 10th Corps to get west of Sidi Abd el Rahman, cutting off and destroying enemy forces in that area. To this end the 1st Armoured Division was directed on El Kharash and the 7th on Ghazal. The 1st was later to be prepared to go to Fuka, followed by the 10th.[1] The general advance would begin at first light on 4th November.

Because of the course taken by the battle since 23rd October there was no strong mobile formation fresh, concentrated, and poised for distant pursuit, as, for example, had been Allenby's Desert Mounted Corps at Megiddo in September 1918.[2] Nevertheless a plan had been made for a force under Major-General C. H. Gairdner (commander of the skeleton 8th Armoured Division),

---
[1] The 8th Armoured Brigade reverted to the 10th Armoured Division's command at 7 a.m. on 4th November.
[2] On that occasion the Desert Mounted Corps was ordered on no account to become involved in the operations of the infantry who were to make the gap.

with an air component, to be formed ready to dart forward to some point in the enemy's back area, possibly even as far as Tobruk. This force was to be self-contained for several days, but as it could only be made up of units taken from here and there General Montgomery cancelled the project and decided instead to use formations already in the forward area. His message to the troops issued at 9.15 a.m. on 4th November shows that he was confident that the operations he had ordered by the 10th Corps and the New Zealand Division would succeed in destroying the *D.A.K.*, 90th Light Division, and any other German forces in the north.[1] This would mean the end of Rommel's Army, for the marching divisions in the south would wither away or be captured. The message ran:

> 'The present battle has now lasted for twelve days, during which all troops have fought so magnificently that the enemy is being worn down. The enemy has just reached the breaking point and he is trying to get his Army away. The Royal Air Force is taking heavy toll of his columns moving west on the main coast road. The enemy is in our power and he is just about to crack. I call on all troops to keep up the pressure and not to relax for one moment. We have the chance of putting the whole Panzer Army in the bag and we will do so. I congratulate all troops on what has been achieved. Complete victory is almost in sight. On your behalf I have sent a separate message to the Royal Air Force thanking them for their quite magnificent support.'

During the twelve-day pitched battle the air support had indeed been magnificent, and now, with its operational efficiency scarcely impaired, the Desert Air Force was looking forward with relish to the excitements of the chase. Air Vice-Marshal Coningham hoped to harry relentlessly the retreating columns and weaken and delay them for the army to catch and destroy. The organization of the British and American fighters into two Forces was described on page 11. Force 'A', the spearhead, comprised the Spitfires, Tomahawks, and Kittyhawks. Advanced ground-parties stood ready to move to newly won landing-grounds to which their parent squadrons would fly when the word was given. Force 'B', of Hurricanes, with the principal task of protecting the L. of C., was to move in the wake of Force 'A'. As all these squadrons were relatively economical to maintain, Coningham decided to use them to the full and keep the day-bombers on call as usual. As regards the forces outside his control, advanced wings of No. 205 Group and of the American heavy bombers were to move up to airfields as

---

[1] General Montgomery had all along intended the motorized New Zealand Division to form part of the 10th Corps, but placed it under 30th Corps for 'Lightfoot'. It was to come under 10th Corps, probably on reaching Fuka.

they were vacated, starting with those in the Amiriya area. Their subsequent movements and those of No. 201 Group would depend largely upon the development of road, rail, and sea communications.[1]

Aircraft on reconnaissance early on 4th November saw little movement except near Fuka. They encountered heavy anti-aircraft fire from 'flak' posts along the main road, over which enemy fighters were patrolling. In flying 206 sorties during the day the British fighter-bombers lost seven of their number—four of them to 'flak'. In the afternoon enemy traffic on the road dwindled, and air attacks were therefore switched farther south. The sole Stuka raid of the day was successfully intercepted over Tell el Aqqaqir.

On land desultory fighting was still going on at dawn on 4th November, and there was a great deal of shelling. The moves of the 10th Corps and the New Zealand Division, which were to give effect to the Army Commander's intentions, were seriously hampered by congestion behind the front. Ceaseless work had been done on widening and improving the mine-free lanes, but with constant heavy use the surface had been pulverized and passage along the lanes was very slow and tiring. It was fortunate that the enemy's air forces were in no position to attack in strength the many large traffic blocks.

General Freyberg's force was particularly badly affected because its components were so widely scattered. The 4th Light Armoured Brigade, which was to lead the advance, was right back on the Springbok Track and at dawn on 4th November it began to move forward.[2] The state of the lanes and the simultaneous moves of many units of 10th Corps caused so much confusion that the Brigade did not leave the Tell el Aqqaqir area until nearly 10.30 a.m. The 9th Armoured Brigade which was to follow did not begin to move until 2 p.m., just as the 6th New Zealand Infantry Brigade, whose relief by a brigade of the 51st Division had fallen behind schedule, also got under way. Briefly, the position at last light was that the leading formations of General Freyberg's force had leaguered at El Agramiya, fourteen miles due south of El Daba, but the 9th Armoured Brigade was just west of the Rahman Track and the 6th

---

[1] In November changes occurred in the United States Army Air Forces in the Middle East. On the 8th another airman, Lieutenant-General Frank M. Andrews, succeeded Major-General Russell L. Maxwell as Commanding General. On 12th November the 'U.S. Army Middle East Air Force' became the U.S. Ninth Air Force (Major-General Lewis H. Brereton, Commanding General) and included the U.S. IX Bomber Command which had been in existence since 12th October but was not officially so designated until 27th November.

[2] The 4th Light Armoured Brigade had 23 Grants and 56 Stuarts. The 9th consisted of only one regiment, the Warwickshire Yeomanry, which, after taking over the fit tanks of 3rd Hussars and Royal Wiltshire Yeomanry, had 14 Grants and Stuarts and 10 Crusader IIs.

New Zealand Infantry Brigade had moved hardly at all.[1] General Freyberg decided that he must concentrate his sprawling forces and hoped to push on again at 11 p.m. It will be seen that this hope was not realized.

The 10th Corps had been wheeling north in accordance with General Lumsden's intention to get west of Sidi Abd el Rahman and cut off and destroy the enemy's forces in that area. Its strength in fit tanks was about 270.[2] It has been mentioned that the Corps was hampered by the congestion behind the front, but there were other causes of delay. The 1st Armoured Division's advance was postponed until 6.15 a.m. while its artillery continued to support the 5th Indian Infantry Brigade. Ground mist then delayed the start until 8.30 a.m. An hour later the 2nd Armoured Brigade made touch with 21st Panzer Division and gradually pushed it back and by last light had advanced about eight miles. The 7th Armoured Division, resuming its advance at 9 a.m., spent most of the day engaged with the Ariete (armoured) Division, which resisted stoutly but was almost annihilated in spite of an attempt by the 3rd (German) Reconnaissance Unit to come to its help.

The reconstitution of the 10th Armoured Division was almost complete by 7.30 a.m., with the 8th Armoured Brigade just west of Tell el Aqqaqir. At noon General Lumsden gave orders to General Gatehouse for this Brigade to pull out and make a detour to the south-west to get behind the enemy who were holding off the other two armoured divisions. The Brigade was warned to get ready to make a seventeen-mile night march with the object of reaching El Daba at first light on the 5th.

The advance of the British armour on 4th November had not been spectacular but late in the morning Rommel knew that D.A.K. and 90th Light Division were hard pressed, and that farther to the south the front was in danger of collapse. Elements of 21st

---

[1] Distances covered by the N.Z. Division during daylight on 4th November were: 4th Light Armoured Brigade 35 miles; 9th Armoured Brigade 12 miles; 5th N.Z. Infantry Brigade 28 miles; 6th N.Z. Infantry Brigade 2½ miles.

[2]

Formation	Grants and Shermans	Crusaders III	Stuarts and early Crusaders
2 Armd Bde of 1 Armd Div	49	19	23
22 ,, ,, ,, 7 ,, ,,	52	10	42
8 ,, ,, ,, 10 ,, ,,	50	12	13
Total	151	41	78

Corps were reported to be streaming westward and the Ariete Division of 20th Corps was under heavy attack. Convinced of the need to fall back to Fuka Rommel telegraphed to ask Hitler's permission. (His request and Hitler's belated consent are given in Appendix 3). The blows he feared soon followed. The *D.A.K's* front was broken in several places and General von Thoma, forward with his 'Battle Echelon', was taken prisoner;[1] Ariete reported that it was encircled; Trento also sent its last message. Rommel could wait no longer, and at 5.30 p.m. gave orders for the retreat. The 10th and 21st Italian Corps and the Ramcke Brigade were to break contact and move at once. The 90th Light Division, *D.A.K.*, and 20th Italian Corps were to withdraw after dark with the 90th astride the coast road and railway, *D.A.K.* south of the railway and 20th Corps farther south still, through the desert. The *ad hoc* Voss Group of Reconnaissance Units was also to move south of the railway.

These orders committed fairly few troops to the use of the main road, and even these had elbow-room on either side of it. By far the greater part of the German/Italian *Panzerarmee* in the northern sector withdrew across the desert towards the plateau above the Fuka escarpment. Fuka, with its wayside railway station and group of landing-grounds, lies a few miles east of (i.e. below) the main stretch of the escarpment which here runs north and south. About seven miles south of the point where it is climbed by the road and railway, the escarpment turns east and becomes less steep, until at about Alam el Qassim it merges with the general run of the desert. Thus from the east there are two ways of approaching the point where the road climbs the escarpment; one straight along the road itself, and the other across country, passing south of Alam el Qassim and keeping above the escarpment all the way.

The latter was the route General Freyberg was following. He found it so difficult, however, to close up his scattered force in the dark at El Agramiya that he decided to postpone his further advance from 11 p.m. to 5.30 a.m. It is interesting that the *D.A.K.* was having much the same difficulties, assembling as best it could about eight miles north of El Agramiya. From here its line of retreat ran due west about six miles south of the railway, while the axis of advance of the New Zealand Division also ran roughly parallel to the railway but about fourteen miles from it. As both forces were bent on reaching the plateau as soon as possible, it was inevitable that there should be occasional encounters between them.[2]

---

[1] Colonel Bayerlein, Chief of Staff *D.A.K.*, took over the command—not for the first time.
[2] The enemy had the great advantage of having been able to reconnoitre the route by daylight.

The other British attempt to save time by making a long night march—that of the 8th Armoured Brigade to El Daba, already referred to—was a failure. The Brigade set out at 7.30 p.m. on the 4th, but halted after covering only one and a half miles in two and a half hours in dense darkness. It then leaguered with the intention of starting again when there might be a little light from the moon, which was only two days from new.

At 2.45 a.m. on the 5th the R.A.F. reported a solid mass of vehicles head to tail between El Daba and Fuka. Army Headquarters passed this news to 10th Corps, urging it to push on boldly. General Freyberg, on being told by 30th Corps, replied that he hoped to reach his objective by 10 a.m. In order to deepen the thrusts by the armour the 1st Armoured Division was now directed on El Daba, the 7th on the road between El Daba and Galal, and the 10th on Galal and later Fuka. During the night Wellingtons and F.A.A. Albacores flew 90 sorties against targets on the road as far west as Fuka, and the enemy's 90th Light Division recorded heavy casualties among the Army's transport and supply troops. Another night activity was a sweep by motor torpedo boats and launches as far as Matruh to intercept any enemy who might be trying to escape by sea.

The 8th Armoured Brigade, whose objective had been changed from El Daba to Galal before it started off at 6 a.m., covered the thirty miles to Galal in just over four hours. On the way, and also after arriving, it had several encounters with parties of retreating enemy, notably with a column of tanks and lorries, mainly Italian, which it intercepted and destroyed. Soon after 1 p.m. the Brigade received orders to sweep the road and railway towards Fuka.[1] It moved at about 3.30 p.m. and covered nine miles before halting for the night.

General Freyberg's expectation of reaching his objective by 10 a.m. was not fulfilled. His force had moved off from El Agramiya shortly before 6 a.m. and by noon the leading troops had covered some thirty miles and were in touch with elements of the 21st Panzer Division. They then struck what seemed to be a minefield, and three hours passed in finding and proving a gap.[2] There was a good deal of shell-fire and by dusk only the 4th Light Armoured Brigade and the 5th New Zealand Infantry Brigade had passed through the suspected field. This episode was a stroke of luck for the enemy, for the reports of *D.A.K.* and its divisions show that although most of their troops had arrived on the plateau before General Freyberg's force, they were nevertheless very thin on the

---

[1] It was important to bring the road and railway into use for supply purposes as rapidly as possible.
[2] The 21st Field Squadron, R.E. noted that the field was a dummy.

ground.[1] The 15th Panzer Division complained that it had had no time to organize serious resistance. The position and strength of the remaining Italians were uncertain.

From 3.45 p.m. onwards reports from *D.A.K.* stated that the British had penetrated between the two Panzer Divisions but did not seem to be acting very vigorously. If, however, the *D.A.K.* was to avoid encirclement it must be permitted to withdraw at nightfall. To this Rommel agreed.

General Montgomery, realizing that, if good numbers of the enemy were to be cut off, the thrusts by the armour would have to be made deeper, had given orders for the 7th Armoured Division, then heading for the road west of El Daba, to move instead to the area of the airfields near Sidi Haneish and Qasaba, which it would approach from the south. The 1st Armoured Division, whose 2nd Armoured Brigade was about nine miles west of El Daba, was to make an even wider detour by night to Bir Khalda, thirty-five miles south of Matruh, preparatory to advancing on Matruh next day. Neither of these moves was entirely successful. The 7th Armoured Division tried to follow the axis of advance of the New Zealand Division and only avoided becoming involved in General Freyberg's operations by turning south-west. An encounter with a supposed minefield—very like the experience of the 4th Light Armoured Brigade described above—ended in the Division halting for the night with 22nd Armoured Brigade leading, twenty miles short of its destination, having covered more than fifty miles in the day. The night march of the 1st Armoured Division will be related presently.

On the evening of the 5th General Montgomery sent a personal message to General Lumsden saying how important was the early capture of Matruh and giving as a future object to seize the area Derna—Tmimi—El Mechili. This was the first day of what General Montgomery has called 'the pursuit proper.'[2] As such it was disappointing, for the New Zealand Division did not reach its objective and the three armoured divisions only rounded up one large and several small parties of straggling enemy on or near the main road in the wake of the 90th Light Division. For the R.A.F. the day was even more disappointing, in spite of the order having been given for Force 'A' to make ready to hop on to captured airfields. Two were in fact occupied during the day—landing-grounds 105 and 106—and nine brand new Me. 109s were found, apart from

---

[1] The *D.A.K.* reported as a rough (and pessimistic) estimate at about noon: 15*th Panzer Division* 8 tanks, 200 infantry, 4 anti-tank guns, 12 field guns. No 8·8-cm guns. 21*st Panzer Division* 30 tanks, 400 infantry, 16 anti-tank guns, 25 field guns. No 8·8-cm guns. 164*th Light Africa Division* about 600 officers and men of three Panzer Grenadier battalions. No 8·8-cm guns.

[2] *The Memoirs of Field-Marshal Montgomery* (London, 1958), p. 140.

fifty other aircraft in various states of repair and thirty-nine wrecks. But on this day to which all our pilots had been eagerly looking forward, many, to their astonishment, were given nothing to do. The daylight effort of the Desert Air Force and the squadrons of the U.S. Army Air Force during the 3rd, 4th, and 5th November in terms of sorties was as follows:

Date: November	Sorties by the Desert Air Force			Sorties by the U.S. Army Air Force		
	3rd	4th	5th	3rd	4th	5th
Day-bombers	219	141	67	53	42	18
Fighter-bombers	129	206	53	72	58	31
Fighters	734	279	238*			
Reconnaissance	12	15	9	—	—	—

* Includes 111 bomber escort sorties, mostly in the afternoon. About 100 sorties were flown on sweeps mainly to protect the New Zealand Division.

The pattern of the 8th Army's operations on 5th November clearly made it very difficult to choose workable bomb-lines, beyond which anything might be attacked from the air. Armoured cars were still roaming the desert, the New Zealand Division was making a long outflanking move, and the three armoured divisions started by each heading for a different part of the road between Sidi Abd el Rahman and Fuka. But the enemy's transport columns were still reported thick between Fuka and Matruh, and the machinery of Army/Air co-operation, which had been working so well, was apparently unable to adapt itself quickly enough to the new conditions. There was no trouble from the weather, yet on this day of all days less than one-third of the possible day-bomber and fighter-bomber sorties were flown. (The Army only called for air support five times during the day). It was fortunate for Rommel that the British air attacks referred to in his daily report for the 5th November as 'uninterrupted and very heavy' were not as heavy or continuous as they might have been.

The *Luftwaffe* in Egypt and Libya was by now in a bad way. Some of its advanced units had moved back, destroying many damaged aircraft where they stood. On 5th November German fighters made a few spirited but unsuccessful attempts to challenge the R.A.F's fighter cover, but by this time all the German units were quitting Egypt, salvaging what aircraft and equipment they could. The disorganization, want of fuel, losses in the air and on the ground, and poor state of the remaining aircraft had greatly reduced the *Luftwaffe's* power. It was still possible, however, that reinforcements of aircraft would be flown over to Africa. Indeed on 4th November *Comando Supremo* told Rommel that German air reinforcements were on their way. Before anything came of this the 'Torch' landings on 8th November created new problems for Kesselring and the *Luftwaffe*.

On the evening of 5th November Rommel sent to *OKW* an exaggerated account of the day's fighting and added that he intended to withdraw again during the night. This was done—the 90th Light Division by the main road towards Matruh, 21st Panzer Division to Qasaba, and the rest of *D.A.K.* and various odds and ends to the area of Charing Cross. These moves were harassed during the night by Wellingtons, reinforced by eleven Halifaxes. Night-flying Hurricanes were out also, and at dawn on the 6th Kittyhawks and other Hurricanes joined in. By that time beyond Fuka it was impossible, except at Sidi Haneish and Qasaba, for the pilots to tell friend from foe, for the weather, which had become cloudy with rainstorms during the night, was growing worse.

Most of 10th Corps halted for the night, but at 6 p.m. on the 5th the 1st Armoured Division, led by 12th Royal Lancers and 2nd Armoured Brigade, set out on its night march to Bir Khalda. 'B' Echelon had come west of El Daba to top up the Division with fuel, and was to travel with it during the night.[1]

The march did not go well; the darkness was intense and the going bad. The 12th Lancers encountered an enemy leaguer and made a detour; the 'B' Echelon vehicles became scattered and lost touch. By dawn on the 6th the 2nd Armoured Brigade had all but completed the first leg—to sixteen miles east of Bir Khalda—but shortly afterwards it ran out of fuel. One reason was that some of the Shermans, long overdue for engine overhaul, were using fantastic quantities of fuel in the heavy going—up to three gallons a mile. 'B' Echelon did not begin to arrive until about 11 a.m., and then could only partly refuel two of the three regiments. Accompanied by the Divisional Commander the Brigade, less one regiment, set off at a smart pace, still hoping to be in time to cut off the enemy. About twenty miles south-west of Charing Cross however the tanks ran dry and there they stuck—'everyone fuming'.

The Division's second line transport (the R.A.S.C. Companies) had replenished the 'B' Echelon vehicles near Tell el Eisa during the morning and had then returned to Nos. 201 and 202 Field Maintenance Centres at El Alamein and El Imayid to refill. A special replenishment convoy was formed which set out westward on the evening of the 5th. The going on the tracks, not only those

---

[1] The term 'B' Echelon meant the vehicles of a unit's own first-line transport which carried petrol, ammunition, food, water, etc. They were replenished from the vehicles of the R.A.S.C. Companies, normally once every twenty-four hours. The latter in their turn refilled at a Field Maintenance Centre.

through the minefields, was now very bad indeed with ruts up to two feet deep, and the convoy covered little more than twenty miles by midnight. It persevered in the pitch dark, but many vehicles stuck in soft sand or in old slit trenches and others strayed. At 3 a.m. on the 6th the convoy leaguered to await daylight. It then went on again but at midday rain began to fall heavily and three hours later the convoy was bogged, still about forty miles from where it was to have met 'B' Echelon.[1]

This episode has been related in some detail to show how serious was the petrol situation of the 1st Armoured Division even before rain prevented all cross-country movement by wheeled vehicles. The 9th and 22nd Armoured Brigades were also to have trouble from shortage of petrol on the morning of the 6th.

That morning, the 6th, the New Zealand Division, led by the 9th Armoured Brigade, advanced towards Sidi Haneish. Meanwhile the 8th Armoured Brigade (of 10th Armoured Division) had occupied landing-grounds 17, 18 and 19 at Fuka and then went on to take the escarpment position without much trouble; after rounding up a number of prisoners it halted for the night above the escarpment in drenching rain. The 133rd Lorried Infantry Brigade of this Division was still back at Galal, where it collected nearly one thousand prisoners.

The most noteworthy engagement of the day fell to the 22nd Armoured Brigade of 7th Armoured Division. Moving at first light towards Qasaba it soon became engaged with the Voss Reconnaissance Group and then with the 21st Panzer Division, whose tanks were reported too short of fuel to manoeuvre. In a series of actions lasting most of the day in heavy rain the 22nd Armoured Brigade inflicted considerable losses on the enemy and almost encircled him. Sixteen German tanks and numerous guns were destroyed or wrecked and abandoned. In the evening a much weakened 21st Panzer Division and the Voss Group escaped on wheels to Matruh.

See also Map 13

Quite early in the morning the weather had become bad for flying, and apart from early reconnaissance there were no air operations until the afternoon. Then, on four occasions, British and American Kittyhawks attacked transport west of Matruh, but no more than 107 fighter sorties of all kinds were flown. The daybombers once again were hardly called upon. On the credit side,

---

[1] The whole trip Tell el Eisa—El Alamein—Bir Khalda was about 120 miles, whereas a 24-hour march over 'fair' desert going was held to be about 80 miles for transport vehicles.

Map 13

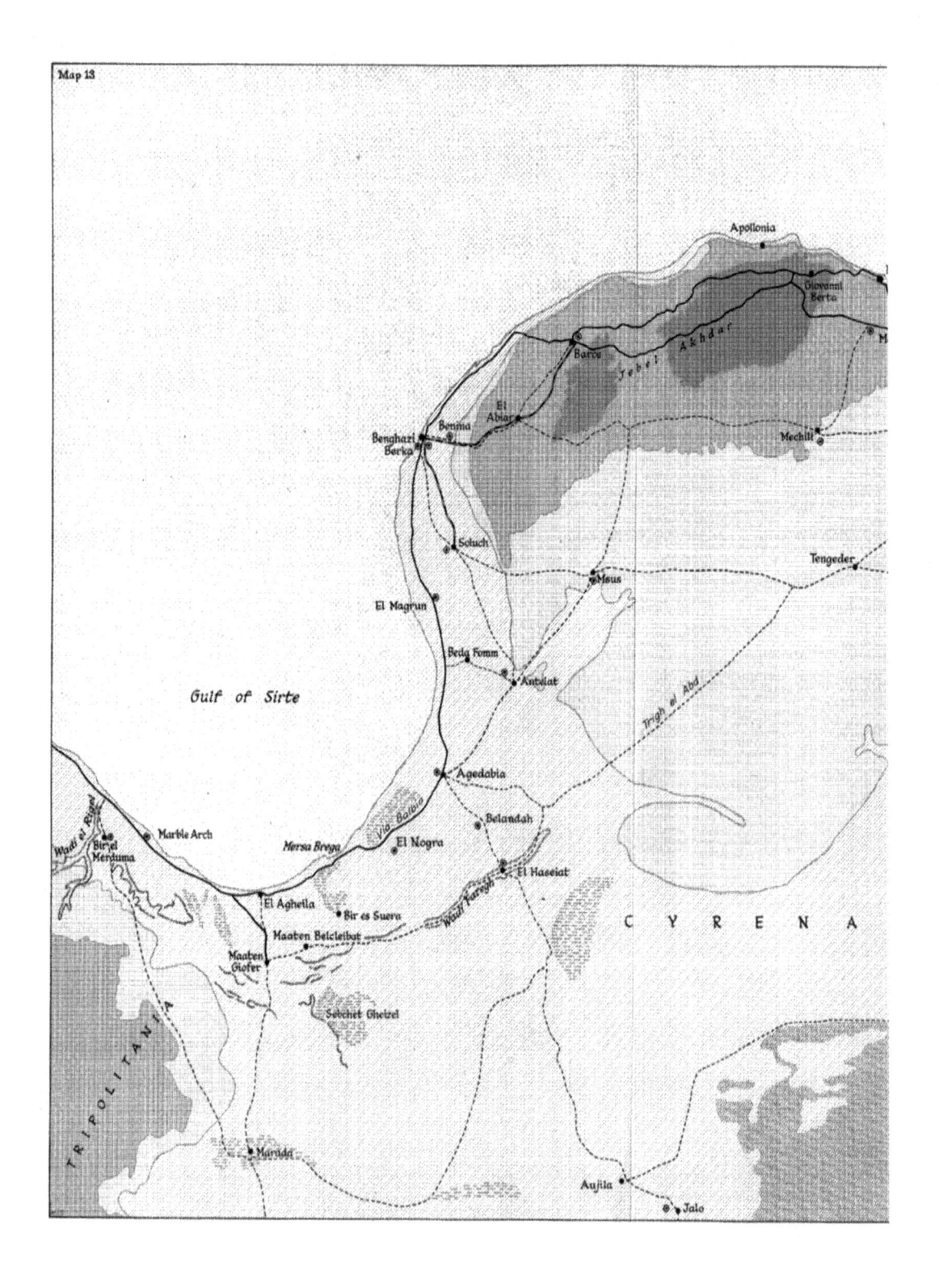

THE WESTERN DESERT
Winter 1942/43

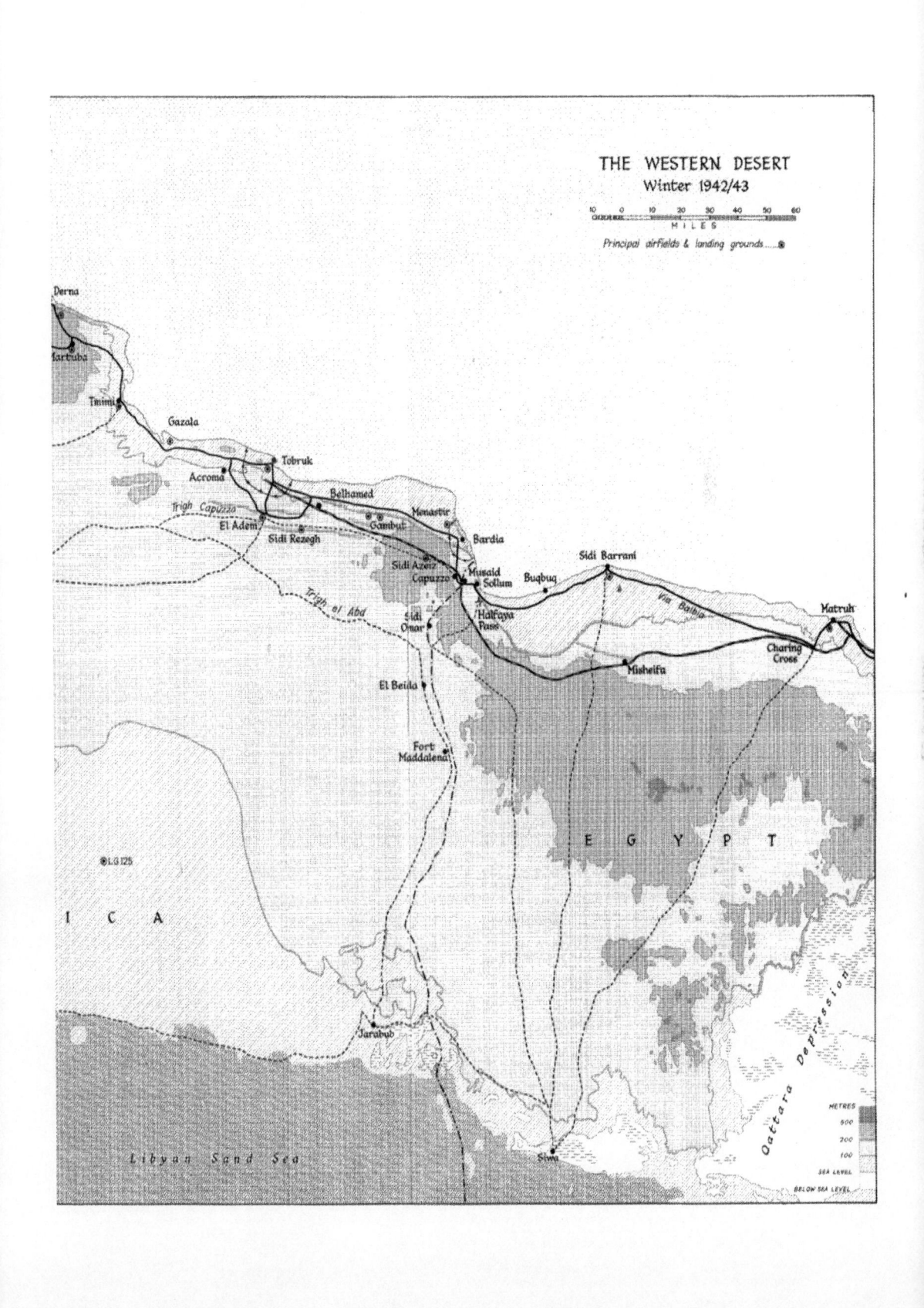

Principal airfields & landing grounds ⊕

however, five American Fortresses attacked Tobruk harbour in daylight and sank the *Etiopia* (2,153 tons) and damaged other ships. Towards evening 21 American Liberators attacked Benghazi harbour, sank the *Mars* (369 tons) and set on fire the tanker *Portofino* (6,424 tons) with her precious cargo. During the night 6th/7th 43 Wellingtons and 8 Halifaxes were available for operations, but targets beyond Matruh were out of reach of the path-finding Albacores, and bad weather was a further handicap to the bombers. Nevertheless 84 tons of bombs were dropped on vehicles at Buq Buq, the Halfaya Pass and Sollum, and thirty fires were started.

On the morning of the 7th most of 90th Light and 21st Panzer Divisions were at Matruh, the rest of *D.A.K.* was in the area of Charing Cross, and 20th and 21st Italian Corps were withdrawing west of it. Heavy rain had fallen all night, and it was not until the afternoon of the 7th that a strong wind began to dry the ground. Before this even tracked vehicles could barely move off the road; in any event most of 10th Corps was out of petrol and its wheels were stuck or floundering in the quagmire that the desert had become. Matruh remained the Corps' immediate objective; beyond it the New Zealand Division was given Sidi Barrani, and the 7th Armoured Division Sollum.

The 7th was a comparatively uneventful day in the air, for the weather was bad for flying. Fighter protection for 10th Corps still held first place. Air reconnaissance covered the country as far as Tobruk. The day-bombers did not fly, and thirteen fighter-bombers reported little success in two raids. British and American Kittyhawks shot up vehicles between Sidi Barrani and Sollum, and Spitfires attacked grounded aircraft and vehicles at Sidi Barrani. The enemy's air force was now on the airfields at Menastir, Gambut, and Tobruk and showed some activity, including a dive-bomber raid on the 1st Armoured Division. German transport aircraft were also active, apparently ferrying petrol to the forward area. There were several air combats, in which three Ju. 52s, two Ju. 87s and one Me. 109 were shot down as against three Kittyhawks.

On the ground the main activity fell to the 10th Armoured Division, which had petrol and a road on which to move. Its 8th Armoured Brigade was told to clear the road from Fuka to Matruh, while its lorried infantry and engineers went on clearing up around Galal and along the main road. Soon after midday the Brigade struck a road block and anti-tank weapons just outside the Matruh perimeter. After attempts to dislodge the enemy had failed, the 133rd Lorried Infantry Brigade was sent for.[1] Before it could

---

[1] This Brigade was widely dispersed on its clearing-up duties. It received the order calling it forward at 1 a.m. on the 8th. Largely owing to traffic congestion the move took all day.

arrive Lieut.-Colonel G. H. G. Smith-Dorrien, commanding the 1st Buffs (Motor Battalion), thoroughly reconnoitred and probed the enemy's positions. At 6.45 a.m. on the 8th he went forward with two companies of his Battalion and two tanks, and found the birds flown. The Germans who fought this copy-book rearguard action were of 90th Light Division.

During the night 47 Wellingtons and 8 Halifaxes were sent to carry out 'the maximum destruction on traffic in the Halfaya Pass area'. The 86 tons of bombs they dropped, including some of 4,000 lb, took their toll of vehicles and added to the strain on the enemy's transport, already handicapped by losses, the effects of the rain, and the numerous traffic blocks—especially at the passes.

Meanwhile in the south the 13th Corps had been active, although the main battle had swirled away out of its reach. By nightfall on 3rd November patrols had penetrated to about three miles on most of the front. No ambitious pursuit could be made for lack of transport, so much having been taken away to serve the rest of the Army. A broad 'sweeping up' operation was laid on for dawn on the 4th, but by then the enemy had disengaged almost everywhere. However, the 44th Division met some opposition south of Jebel Kalakh, and General Horrocks, who was present, ruled out a full scale attack, presumably for humane reasons; he decided to try instead the effect of artillery fire accompanied by propaganda utterances by the 'Sonic Unit'.[1] Neither produced any noticeable effect and by the early morning of the 5th the enemy had gone. The 13th Corps resumed its 'search and sweep' operations and was rewarded after one encounter by the surrender of 2,000 Italians. Many other small actions yielded prisoners, of whom the Corps took about 6,000 in the day. Next day only handfuls of stragglers were encountered moving west, the sole exception being when the 44th Reconnaissance Regiment and the Household Cavalry Regiment (armoured cars) came up with the Ramcke Parachute Brigade and bits of the Folgore Division. A sharp little fight ensued, but though the British took 450 prisoners they were unable to capture the rest, who appeared to have enough transport. The sequel was that on 7th November Major-General Ramcke and about 600 of his men, it is said very angry with the German Army, rejoined Rommel after an adventurous and determined retreat.[2]

---

[1] A broadcasting device mounted in an armoured car, from which it could transmit speech or recorded noises.

[2] The Parachute Brigade was a *Luftwaffe* formation and felt that it had been left in the lurch.

The 13th Corps continued to collect prisoners, but the task of finding them became so difficult, and their condition when found was so pitiable, that No. 208 (Tactical Reconnaissance) Squadron, R.A.F., was allotted to the 13th Corps to help in what amounted to an errand of mercy. Between 5th and 14th November some 17,000 Italian prisoners reached the base, most of them having been collected by 13th Corps, which, with the best of intentions, was hard put to water, feed, and transport them from its own modest resources.

The hindmost of Rommel's troops slipped away from Matruh during the night 7th/8th November. His immediate intention was to fight a delaying action at Sidi Barrani to see the army through the bottle-neck made by the passes up the escarpment at Halfaya and Sollum. There now began an exchange of views upon high policy with *Comando Supremo*, Mussolini, and finally Hitler, which, if summarized at this point, will form a background to the events of the next fortnight.

On 8th November—the day of the Anglo-American landings in Algeria and Morocco—Rommel reported his short-term intentions as above. In his reply Cavallero quoted Mussolini as insisting that the Halfaya—Sollum—Sidi Omar position should be held as long as possible. On the 10th the Duce again urged that failure to do so would prejudice the plan to establish a defensive position at El Agheila, but that if the retreat was to continue it must be systematic, and the Italian non-motorized formations and resources in general must be got away. Rommel replied that to organize resistance at El Agheila was impossible with the forces available. He intended to make an orderly retreat to Sirte and the stages would depend upon how much pressure the British applied. On the 13th Cavallero came to Africa to confer with Bastico, but did not see Rommel. Between them they decided that the area Mersa Brega—El Agheila—Marada must be held and that the Spezia and Young Fascist Divisions and the Centauro Armoured Division would be available as fresh reinforcements.[1] Tanks (mainly German), artillery, ammunition and so on would have to be sent across from Italy as soon as possible. The *Panzerarmee* must delay the British east of this area for at least a week, and must thereafter hold it long enough for the Axis forces to be re-built. Rommel protested furiously at Cavallero's neglect to see him, but received no more than a confirmation of these views. On the 16th Mussolini

---

[1] The Spezia Division was already in the area. The Centauro was moving up from Tripoli. The Young Fascist was moving back from Siwa.

telegraphed to assure Bastico that no situation was serious unless the commander felt it to be so. Notwithstanding this, *Comando Supremo* admitted that if the El Agheila position collapsed the *Panzerarmee* was unlikely to last very long. On the 17th Rommel sent details of the state of his shattered army to *Comando Supremo*, hoping to convince the Italians that the *Panzerarmee* was not strong enough to hold the El Agheila position. The report had no effect, however, except to cause Mussolini to ask Hitler for more artillery and aircraft. Rommel then sent General De Stefanis, commander of the Italian 20th Corps, to explain matters in Rome and to say that Buerat and Homs—Tarhuna were the best positions on which to offer resistance.[1] Cavallero's opinion however was that reorganization was the first need and that the line El Agheila—Marada was the best position behind which to attempt it. He felt that the *Panzerarmee* would be strong enough to hold out against anything except a full scale attack, which would take the British about a month to prepare. Hitler now took a hand and on 22nd November gave orders for the El Agheila position to be held to the last. This dismayed Rommel, who told Bastico that it meant certain destruction. He thought the only hope lay in avoiding battle. He supported this opinion in another report on the state of the *Panzerarmee*, sent to *OKW* and others, and privately decided to do what he thought best. Later he wrote in his memoirs 'The German-Italian authorities had still not reached a strategic decision on the future of the African theatre of war ... They did not see things as they were, indeed they did not want to ...'[2]

By the evening of 9th November the enemy's rearguards were forced out of Sidi Barrani—one day sooner than Rommel intended they should leave. The New Zealand Division was advancing on Sollum and the 7th Armoured Division was making a wide detour to the south—it was then to turn north and head for Capuzzo and Sidi Azeiz. By the evening of 10th November the 4th Light Armoured Brigade had reached the foot of Halfaya Pass. In the early hours of the 11th Brigadier Kippenberger (5th New Zealand Infantry Brigade) sent two companies of the 21st New Zealand Battalion to storm the Pass, which they did with complete success, taking 600 Italian prisoners. This admirable feat was most valuable, for, as it turned out, the road up the escarpment at Sollum had been demolished. The 4th Light Armoured Brigade then drove up Halfaya Pass and made for Musaid.

---

[1] Rommel informed Bastico (who now commanded all the Axis forces in Libya), *OKW* and *OKH* of De Stefanis's mission.
[2] *Krieg Ohne Hass*, draft version.

Meanwhile on 10th November the 22nd Armoured Brigade (of 7th Armoured Division), which had been awaiting petrol, reached the frontier near El Beida. It forbore to chase a hostile column moving west about fourteen miles away, reported by the 11th Hussars as containing about 18 tanks, for the reason that the Brigade's objective was Capuzzo. The next morning the loss of Halfaya Pass sent the Axis forces scurrying off at full speed. At about 9.30 a.m. some of them could be seen heading towards Bardia; the British armoured regiments pursued but failed to come to grips. The day ended with the Egyptian frontier clear of the enemy.[1] The Army Commander had already directed on the 10th that the main bodies of formations were not to move at first west of the area Bardia—Capuzzo—Sidi Azeiz because of the difficulty of maintaining them. Instead, armoured cars and artillery were to continue to pursue.

The fact that Rommel had managed to break away with even a small force probably seems more of an anticlimax in retrospect than it did at the time to the Army at large. The British had accomplished so much during the past week; they had driven the *Panzerarmee* from the field and pursued it for 250 miles; prisoners were still streaming in; weapons, vehicles and equipment of all kinds were lying about everywhere; all the signs of victory were plain to see, and overhead the Desert Air Force's control of the air was virtually complete.

Many German and Italian troops in the back area had already got away by 4th November, since Rommel had seen for some days that to withdraw would be inevitable. But the escape of German formations that had been in contact with the British until dark on 4th November is remarkable, especially in view of Hitler's intervention which caused Rommel to countermand the orders for a withdrawal already being acted on. This added greatly to Rommel's anxieties, and there were three places where he feared the retreating *D.A.K.* might be headed off—Fuka, Matruh, and Sollum.

It has been related how, on 3rd November, with a break-out clearly in sight, General Montgomery had decided to exploit with

---

[1] The strengths of the principal German formations on or about 10th November were recorded as follows:
    90th Light Division: 1,000 all ranks; 10 anti-tank guns; 2 troops field artillery.
    15th Panzer Division: 1,177 all ranks; 5 anti-tank guns; 11 field guns; no tanks.
    21st Panzer Division: 1,009 all ranks; 5 anti-tank guns; 6 field guns; 11 tanks.
    Ramcke Parachute Brigade: 700 all ranks; 5 anti-tank guns; 2 field guns.
    19th Flak Division: 24 heavy (8·8-cm) and 40 light (2-cm) anti-aircraft guns, having lost 50 heavy and 60 light.
    164th Light Division: (on 17th November) about 2 battalions and 2 troops field artillery.

the mobile formations that were already well forward—the 10th Corps and the New Zealand Division. This was the quickest thing he could have done, but the execution fell short of the conception. For on 4th November General Lumsden's 10th Corps, turning sharply north, spent most of the day pushing against the enemy where he was strongest, and nowhere reached the main road. At the time it might have seemed rash to by-pass the *D.A.K.* and cut the road much farther west; the magic of Rommel's name undoubtedly conjured up extra wariness. Rommel himself frequently commented on what he regarded as lack of enterprise on the part of the enemy, and of this particular occasion he wrote 'The British command continued to observe its usual caution and showed little evidence of ability to make resolute decisions'.[1] At all events, Rommel disengaged and slipped away during the night.

The motorized New Zealand Division was an obvious choice for the move to the plateau above Fuka, but it will be recalled that the Division was widely dispersed, as were the other troops who were to join it; farthest away of all was the 4th Light Armoured Brigade which was to lead the way. The appalling congestion behind the front, especially in the 'Supercharge' area and in the tracks through the minefields, caused great delay. The conditions called for vigorous traffic control, but from all accounts both traffic control and driving discipline generally were thoroughly bad. Could the difficulties have been foreseen and overcome by the 8th Army, General Freyberg's force might have been above Fuka before the *D.A.K.* had even begun to move back. And if one of the British armoured divisions could have gone there too, either to fight and destroy the *D.A.K.* or to penetrate deeper still into the enemy's back area—to Charing Cross, for example—the express aim of General Montgomery to 'put the whole Panzer Army in the bag' might have been achieved. The Armoured Divisional Commanders themselves felt that a deep thrust should be made into the enemy's back area, and suggested fitting-out at least one armoured division to make it self-sufficient for several days, but this was not done.

The rain of 6th and 7th November hampered the British more than it did the enemy. The Desert Air Force was grounded by low cloud and flooded airfields, and on land the rain prevented the shortage of petrol being made good. Rain was not to blame for everything, but it did wash away an opportunity which had not been firmly grasped.

At the third of Rommel's danger points, Sollum, delays in delivering petrol to the 7th Armoured Division enabled the last of his

---

[1] *Krieg Ohne Hass*, draft version.

troops to get away. He had narrowly escaped disaster at all three places.

After the capture of Halfaya Pass on 11th November it seemed to General Montgomery that Rommel would almost certainly draw right back to El Agheila (as he had done from Gazala at the end of 1941) without offering much resistance on the way. But Montgomery had made up his mind that his advance to the El Agheila area was not going to be followed by one of Rommel's rebounds; it was to be an irreversible step towards driving the Axis forces from North Africa. In no circumstances would he expose himself to a counter-stroke such as had twice turned the tables on the British and deprived them of most of their gains. This time he was going to capture the El Agheila position, and in the meanwhile would station a strong force of armour in the area Tmimi—Mechili.

On 12th November the 4th Light Armoured Brigade with two armoured car regiments—the Royals and the 4/6th South African Regiment—was given a harassing role as far as Acroma, just west of Tobruk. Tobruk itself was entered on the 13th without opposition.

On 14th November General Lumsden set in motion four columns, all under command of 7th Armoured Division and provided with extra transport. These columns were built round (*a*) the 12th Lancers, (*b*) H.Q. 4th Light Armoured Brigade, (*c*) the 11th Hussars, and (*d*) the Royal Dragoons. Each had detachments of field, anti-tank, and anti-aircraft artillery, and of engineers. Column (*b*) had in addition one troop of Grant tanks. The three cavalry regiments were equipped with armoured cars.

Columns were given tasks as follows. Column (*a*) was to secure the airfields at Martuba—which it did on the 15th—and then the one at Derna. (It will be remembered that 'Martuba by mid-November' was one of General Montgomery's objectives, to be taken in time for air cover to be given by the R.A.F. for the 'Stoneage' convoy to Malta). Column (*b*) was also directed on Martuba en route for Benghazi by the road through the Jebel Akhdar. The other two columns were to leave El Adem on the 15th, seize Msus landing-ground, and then harass the enemy on the road between Benghazi and Antelat.

The enemy was having renewed trouble over petrol, which on the 15th caused the *D.A.K.* and the Italian 20th Corps to halt near Barce. The 90th Light Division had just enough for its rearguard to pull back from Giovanni Berta a few hours before the first troops of Column (*b*) arrived there. On the 16th, a day of particularly heavy rain, neither side could move at all. On the 17th the 4th Light Armoured Brigade made contact with the German rearguards, but on the 18th it was much delayed by demolitions and mines. Meanwhile the *Panzerarmee* had received some fuel and got on the move again. The 18th was the critical day according to Rommel, and Map 14 shows the dispositions of his forces against the expected British attempt to cut the main road.

On the morning of the 18th General Montgomery, realizing that the enemy's retreat was being delayed for want of fuel, urged General Lumsden to hasten on his southern columns to cut the enemy off. But owing to the bad going, made much worse by the rain, these columns and the transport serving them were all in difficulties.[1] Actually the 11th Hussars were engaged all day near Sceleidima, while the Royals, heading south-west from Msus, had patrols in Antelat. Next day the 11th Hussars entered Soluch and Ghemines and the Royals leaguered just east of Antelat, where tanks had been reported. On the Axis side *D.A.K.* and 90th Light Division slipped away to Agedabia, and the Young Fascists to El Agheila.

On the 20th, for the third and last time, the British entered Benghazi. The next step was for the 7th Armoured Division to gain touch with the Mersa Brega—El Agheila positions, into which the enemy finally withdrew on the night 23rd/24th November.

The advance of the Desert Air Force's spearhead had closely matched the progress of the Army. The clearing and repair of newly-won airfields had been satisfactory, though in many cases the landing areas were unserviceable owing to the rain or from being cut up, while wet, by heedless vehicles. The method adopted was as follows. At each airfield an R.A.F. reconnaissance party and mine-clearing and construction parties R.E. would move in first with a detachment of the R.A.F. Regiment for local protection.[2] Next came an advanced ground party from the appropriate fighter squadron, and finally the squadron itself flew to its new landing-ground. Many transport vehicles were employed in moving stores, and suffered from, and added to, the congestion on the road. Gradually more use was made of transport aircraft for ferrying forward men and equipment.

---

[1] It may be wondered to what extent the situation could have been eased by air supply. On 17th November the 10th Corps asked for an airlift to Msus of petrol, Bofors ammunition, rations and water, for the southern columns. The weather was so bad that not until the 20th could any worth-while deliveries be made. By the 28th when airlift to Msus ceased, at least 58 tons of these items had been delivered.

[2] All newly-occupied airfields had to be searched for mines and booby-traps—a long and tedious process. The first airfield found to be systematically prepared was Derna; Benina, Barce and Berka were even worse, having been furnished with a great variety of infernal devices.

Map 14

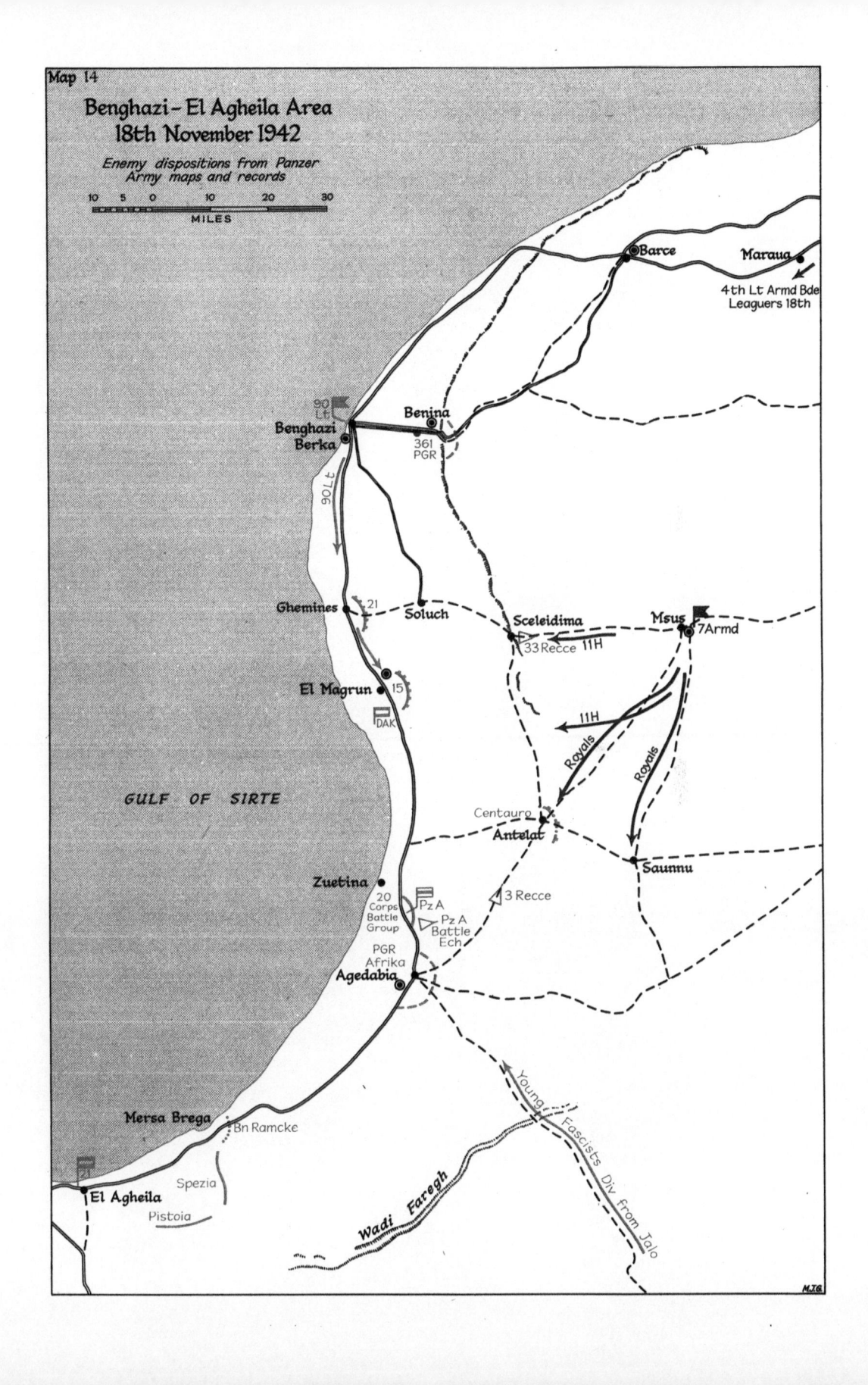

Benghazi – El Agheila Area
18th November 1942

Enemy dispositions from Panzer Army maps and records

A few examples will show the kind of progress made. On 12th November advanced ground parties of Force 'A' reached Sidi Azeiz, Gambut and Sidi Rezegh, and next day fighter squadrons flew to the two first named. (Farther back this enabled three Wellington squadrons to move forward on the 13th to El Daba and a Halifax squadron to Jebel Hamzi, west of Cairo.) By the 15th Gazala was in use by fighters, and next day advanced ground parties reached Martuba. This airfield was flooded, but Gazala was serviceable and was used by fighters covering the 'Stoneage' convoy to Malta. To complete the picture, on the 17th Advanced Air H.Q. opened at Gambut and H.Q. No. 211 Group at Martuba. A week later a fighter control party (called Sector A) and a wing of Spitfires arrived at Msus.

It will be seen therefore that fighter squadrons of Force 'A' were well forward, ready to act in both their protective and ground-strafing roles. But the story of the fighter-bombers and day-bombers is unhappily very different. After 9th November the enemy, in this phase of the campaign, no longer presented the day-bombers with targets which were worth-while in view of the distances involved. Consequently the strong and experienced day-bomber force dropped right out of the battle for the time being. After 14th November the same fate befell the fighter-bombers, because it was becoming impracticable to send large quantities of bombs from their bases to landing-grounds so far ahead.

The enemy's air force seldom appeared except on 11th November, when the British caught up with it at Gambut. On this day 43 Kittyhawks and Tomahawks of No. 260, and Nos. 2, 4 and 5 (all S.A.A.F.) Squadrons attacked Gambut airfields which were vigorously defended. The German fighters were driven off these fields and the enemy's main terminal for air transports, Tobruk, became exposed to air attack. On the same day No. 2 (S.A.A.F.) and the 64th and 65th U.S. Squadrons successfully intercepted a formation of Stukas with fighter escort. In all, on the 11th, three Ju. 52s, one Ju. 88, and seven Ju. 87s were shot down. Not until the 18th November did the Germans again try to attack in any numbers. The British fighters were so well forward and the Axis so short of fuel that at this time the 8th Army seldom felt air attack other than occasional nuisance raids.

In order to surprise the enemy and harass his retreat by suddenly attacking the road and airfields as far west as Agedabia, Air Vice-Marshal Coningham decided upon a bold venture to be run entirely by the R.A.F. It depended upon the use of 'Landing ground 125' in the deep desert about a hundred miles north-west of Jarabub. On 12th November, transport aircraft of No. 216 Group flew stores to this landing ground, screened by No. 2 Armoured Car Company,

R.A.F. Next day thirty-six Hurricanes of Nos. 213 and 238 Squadrons followed, together with more transport aircraft carrying maintenance crews. The whole was commanded by Wing Commander J. Darwen.

That afternoon twenty-seven Hurricanes, carrying long-range tanks, flew off L.G. 125 and successfully attacked traffic on the Benghazi—El Agheila road. Next day both Squadrons were out morning and afternoon, attacking the road and Agedabia airfield. On the 15th further attacks were made on the road, where a small Italian column was shot up, and on Jalo airfield. By the 16th it was clear to Wing Commander Darwen that the enemy would soon discover his hideout, which had neither radar nor anti-aircraft guns.[1] Before he withdrew to Maaten Baggush, however, he sent twenty-one Hurricanes to attack a column of the Young Fascist Division heading for Agedabia from Jalo. Altogether, in addition to destroying and damaging many transport vehicles, the squadrons were confident that they had destroyed twelve aircraft on the ground. The fighters had flown 119 sorties, in which three Hurricanes were lost and another four damaged. So ended an operation out of the ordinary run, an eagle's stoop.

After an invaluable spell of three weeks of operating in direct support of the Army, the British night-bombers now rejoined the American heavies in their attacks on more distant targets, for example: on the 10th/11th Tobruk; on the 13th/14th, and again on the following night, Benghazi; on the 18th in daylight, Benghazi; on the 21st in daylight Tripoli harbour and again during the night. Airfields in Crete were attacked on the 23rd/24th. The results of all these operations—to which the British night-bombers contributed over 150 sorties in the fortnight—cannot be precisely assessed, but there is no doubt that they considerably worsened the bad logistic situation of the Axis forces.

Attacks upon ships were most important, and here some confirmed successes can be given, and not only those of aircraft based in Africa. On the night 17th/18th two Fleet Air Arm Albacores and a Wellington from Malta sank the *Giulio Giordani* (10,534 tons) with 4,000 tons of fuel. On 21st November the *D'Annunzio* (4,537 tons) had to be beached following British-American air attacks on Tripoli, and several other ships were damaged. On the 25th the *Algerino* (1,371 tons), with a cargo of ammunition and fuel, was sunk off the Tripolitanian coast by a Beaufighter from Malta.

From 5th to 25th November the Allied air effort in the Desert and Eastern Mediterranean, excluding that of Malta and the anti-shipping operations, amounted to 4,278 sorties or about 200 every

---

[1] In November 1941, as part of operation 'Crusader', the Oasis Force, accompanied by two R.A.F. fighter squadrons, had used this landing-ground as a base for the capture of Jalo and Aujila. The enemy undoubtedly knew of its existence.

24 hours. The British lost 45 aircraft, the Americans 6, the Germans 123 (of which they themselves destroyed 78), and the Italians an estimated 25 or so.

The British well knew that in pursuing Rommel's Army to El Agheila they would feel the drag of a long and rapidly lengthening line of supply across Cyrenaica more heavily than ever before. Immediate requirements were not the sole consideration; the necessary stocks and reserves would have to be built up for an attack by the 8th Army at El Agheila at the earliest possible date and General Montgomery, immediately after the capture of Halfaya Pass, gave instructions for this to be done. It is appropriate, therefore, to consider the logistic measures that had been taken to support the advance.

The growth of the Middle East Base has been described in previous volumes of the History. Lieut.-General Sir Wilfrid Lindsell had succeeded Sir Thomas Riddell-Webster in July 1942 as the head of the whole vast project. During the last two and a half years the ports and railways had been extended and improved; inland water transport developed; airfields constructed; workshops, depots and camps built and equipped; signal communications greatly extended; an almost inexhaustible supply of fuel received and stored; and depots stocked with great quantities of ammunition, bombs, vehicles, supplies and commodities of every sort.[1] All this, and a great expansion of local manufactures, had enabled the Base to provide the 8th Army and Desert Air Force with practically everything they wanted for the pitched battle of El Alamein.[2]

The problem of nourishing the ensuing pursuit was far harder because the distances from the Delta would be very great and much would depend on the state of the desert railway, the ports, the coastal road, and the water supplies, after the enemy had gone. Enough was known in advance to make it certain that the task and the difficulties were going to be vast. The success achieved was the outcome of close collaboration at all stages, including early planning between the staffs and services of G.H.Q. on the one hand and of

---

[1] A few examples will give some idea of the scale of working at about this time:
   (i) Ammunition in Base installations October: 272,000 tons.
   (ii) Total tonnage of military stores received from overseas in October: 253,000.
   (iii) Vehicles received in September and October: 18,480.
   (iv) Anti-tank mines manufactured in August: 530,000.
   (v) Parachutes and harness made for supply-dropping: 25,000 sets.

[2] It may be recalled that the Army habitually performed certain administrative services for the R.A.F. (Volume I, page 59). Among them were the carriage of fuel, rations, and explosives as far as railhead, roadhead, or seahead. The R.A.F. used its own transport columns onward from these points, but the Army helped with more transport when possible.

the 8th Army on the other. This collaboration was strikingly stream-lined in that the 8th Army dealt with one co-ordinating staff section of G.H.Q. instead of with many sections. The DQMG, Brigadier G. Surtees, was the officer responsible at G.H.Q. In principle the 8th Army was responsible for framing demands and for the use made of what was provided; G.H.Q. for deciding what could be provided and how. In practice this system worked very well.

Rail, road, and sea were to be used to the full in providing the administrative backing which made the advance possible. The desert railway, capable of carrying some 2,500 tons a day, was of prime importance. In the spring of 1942 the line had been built by the British as far as Belhamed, just outside the Tobruk perimeter, and the enemy had extended it to within seven miles of the harbour. But he made little use of the railway as a supply line for want of locomotives and rolling stock. The British now intended to develop it to its full capacity, by opening successive railheads at El Alamein, El Daba, Matruh, Capuzzo and Tobruk, to which as much as possible would be carried by rail and lifted onward by motor transport. Obviously the sooner the railway could be opened the better, and engineer troops stood ready to search the track and begin restoring it. The track proved to be free from serious damage anywhere west of El Daba, though the search of the whole 335 mile stretch from El Alamein to Tobruk discovered 141 mines and 39 live charges, apart from 280 demolitions and obstructions of various kinds. The table on page 104 shows the rate of progress.

The running of the railway through the desert depended largely upon providing enough good water for the steam locomotives. In 1941 the British placed an order in the U.S.A. for Diesels, of which twenty-one arrived in October 1942—just in time. Locomotives of this type used very little water and would therefore be invaluable for the run between Capuzzo and Tobruk. The preparations for 'Crusader' in 1941 had included the laying of a water pipe-line to Misheifa, 70 miles short of Capuzzo, making it possible to pump Nile water to this point 270 miles from Alexandria. Four hundred breaks had now to be mended, five miles of piping replaced, many miles relaid and many damaged reservoirs repaired. Preparations were also made for developing the sources of water between El Daba and Sidi Barrani which were nearly all found to be demolished or polluted. Men and plant were ready to sink new wells and repair the aqueducts at Matruh, Buq Buq and Bardia. As an extra insurance large numbers of containers were held at Alexandria for carriage by sea or overland as required, and three water barges were equipped to take in water from water-ships and pump it ashore. The net result was that the daily ration in the 8th Army was half a gallon per man, and only on one day did lack of water curtail traffic on the railway.

Road construction units were ready to start work at once on the coastal road. Except through the battlefield area and up the escarpment at Sollum the damage was not enough to impede traffic seriously anywhere east of Tobruk. The road was nevertheless in bad condition at many points, though there was fortunately no need to undertake repair over long stretches.

Preparations had also been made to use the 'small ports' of Matruh, Sollum, and Bardia. Six small ships and three landing-craft were ready, loaded, and a variety of other small craft had been assembled.[1] Port and dock operating companies were ready also. By 9th November two small ships and two landing-craft had discharged petrol at Smugglers' Cove, a beach to the east of Matruh. Matruh was in use for six days and Bardia for eight, at 300 tons a day each.

The first port of any real consequence was Tobruk, where it was intended to discharge as much as possible up to the estimated maximum of 1,500 tons a day. Some jetties were found still intact, and the lighter wharves were able to receive landing-craft (carrying cargo) almost at once. All the bulk petrol installations except one had been destroyed, as had both the water distilleries and all the sources of water to the west of the town.

The first sea convoy arrived at Tobruk on 19th November and during the first week an average of 865 tons was discharged daily against an estimated 500. The next week a fire in a merchant ship prevented the new target of 750 tons being reached; thereafter the figure soon rose to 880 tons a day.

Benghazi, captured on the 20th, was a larger port than Tobruk, but having no natural harbour it depended entirely on artificial works, easy to demolish. (The outer breakwater, for instance, had been damaged on five separate occasions by one or other retreating army.)[2] The Naval Base party and Army dock parties began work on 21st November. On the 23rd H.Q. No. 83 Area moved in from Capuzzo, and by the 26th two ships and three tank landing-craft were able to start discharging. The same day the Senior Naval Officer, Inshore Squadron, established his headquarters at Benghazi.

The growth of this new Advanced Base (for that is what Benghazi was) belongs to the story of the advance to Tripoli, told in a later chapter. With the opening of the port of Benghazi a change came over the pattern of the L. of C., in that the aim became to deliver

---

[1] In all 28 landing-craft, 12 powered lighters, 40 other lighters, 8 tugs and 3 launches. Ten store-ships had been earmarked for G.H.Q. and ten more were on call.

[2] A hydrographical survey showed 101 wrecks in Tobruk and 86 in Benghazi ranging from lighters to merchant vessels and warships.

as much as possible by sea to Benghazi. Tobruk would cease to be an importing port for other than local purposes, its main function being now to despatch cargoes by road, and to some extent by sea also, to Benghazi. As stocks at Benghazi increased, the lift by road from Tobruk would be reduced until practically all load-carrying vehicles were employed in supplying the Army and Air Forces on their way to Tripoli—a road haul of nearly 700 miles from Benghazi.

The following table shows the dates of opening railheads and ports:

Place	Miles from Alexandria	Date entered	Railhead opened†	Port opened†
El Alamein	60	—	5th Nov.	—
El Daba	95	5th Nov.	9th Nov.	—
Matruh	190	8th Nov.	14th Nov.	15th Nov. Closed 20th except for water.
Bardia	360	12th Nov.	—	19th Nov. Closed 26th.
Capuzzo	350	12th Nov.	20th Nov.	—
Tobruk	435	13th Nov.	1st Dec.*	20th Nov.
Benghazi	741	20th Nov.	—	26th Nov.

† A railhead 'opened' when the first supply trains arrived there, but a couple of days or so elapsed before it became a fully going concern. The same sort of qualification applied to a port.

* The construction train reached Belhamed on 22nd November.

Good as this progress was, it was not—and could not be—quick enough to have a direct or immediate effect on the logistic support of the troops and air forces following the retreating enemy through Cyrenaica. For example, on 14th November, the day after the British entered Tobruk, no ports were yet open and railhead was 245 miles away at Matruh. At that moment this stretch could only be spanned by motor transport, and it is appropriate at this point to consider the vital part played by the transport companies.

The introduction of the Field Maintenance Centre (FMC) as an essential feature of the supply system in the Desert has been described in earlier volumes of this History. The second-line transport of formations (for example, the Divisional R.A.S.C. Companies) normally refilled at a FMC which in its turn was fed by third-line transport that had been loaded at a railhead, seahead or roadhead. One or more FMCs usually served a Corps, and during an advance a new FMC would leap-frog forward to replace one which was dropping out of reach of the second-line transport, whose task it was to deliver to the 'B' Echelons of units every day. When possible the FMC was not more than fifty miles from the units it served.

Examples of the opening of FMCs are: at El Adem on 15th November; at Tmimi (a further 60 miles) on the 16th; and at Msus (200 miles from Tobruk) on the 21st.

Third-line transport was organized in General Transport Companies, each capable of carrying 300 tons. These companies did not belong permanently to formations or units but were usually allotted to Corps, each Corps being given a number of them to carry the requisite tonnage over a stage of 80–100 miles from railhead or seahead, or from both, to FMCs. In the rapid advance through Cyrenaica there were times when the forces outstripped the extension of the rail and sea links behind them. But since a road existed which could carry heavy traffic forward, and which could be put to use more quickly than the rail and sea links could be extended to successive railheads and seaheads, the opportunity was seized to push forward roadheads. Roadheads were fed by extra links of third-line transport provided and controlled by Army Headquarters, and from them the Corps third-line transport carried supplies to FMCs in the usual way.[1] For example, a roadhead was opened at Matruh on 10th November while railhead was still at El Daba, and, later, another at Capuzzo while railhead was at Matruh. As soon, however, as a further extension of the rail or sea links was made, the appropriate roadhead gradually closed, and the Army third-line transport serving it became available to set up another or for other tasks. The system was not rigid, and road, rail, and sea transport were always simultaneously working, though at differing gaits, to extend the L. of C. But road transport was more flexible, readier, and more quickly extensible than rail or sea and was therefore the maid-of-all-work.

Thus during the 10th Corps' advance through Cyrenaica the bulk of its requirements and of those of the Desert Air Force was carried by motor transport from Matruh and Capuzzo.[2] The effects of working day after day over such great distances were many and should be understood. Examples are: the severe strain on drivers of whom there were not enough to provide proper reliefs; ceaseless wear and tear of vehicles which made heavier the task of maintaining them; and the fact that the greater the distance the greater is the amount of transport needed to keep up a given bulk of deliveries.

To illustrate how deliveries fall off with distance, the lift from Matruh to Tobruk between 14th and 20th November, whether for

---

[1] G.H.Q. had ultimately of course to provide all the companies. From the 31st October 1942 to April 1943 it added about sixteen to 8th Army.
[2] The forces to be maintained west of the Egyptian frontier in the first stage were as follows:
 10th Corps (New Zealand Division and 1st and 7th Armoured Divisions and Corps troops)—63,500 mouths.
 R.A.F. component, and A.A. Artillery for airfield defence—11,500 mouths.

carrying onward to the advanced troops or for building up stocks, meant covering a distance of 245 miles. If a company with a total lift of 300 tons ran 100 miles a day (a figure which may seem on the low side to a peace-time eye but which takes account of such matters as stops for minimum rest and maintenance, economic speed, road space, and so on) this distance meant a six-day turn-round, giving an average daily delivery (or 'pay load') of one-sixth of the total load carried, or 50 tons. In this distance, therefore, to deliver the 400 tons needed daily by an armoured division would have required eight transport companies, and even more if in the meantime the 'customer' had moved farther forward.

Further, delivering supplies for troops and for building up stocks was only part of the work of the transport companies. Developing the L. of C. created many other demands upon them such as clearing ports and railheads, shifting commodities in depots, moving large medical units such as Casualty Clearing Stations, and carrying Pioneer companies wherever needed. Moreover there were operational tasks such as troop lifting which were likely to arise when least desired from the point of view of administration. Small wonder that it was vital to open railheads and seaheads as far forward, and as quickly, as possible. There is much truth in the Army's saying 'When G walks a mile, Q must run three.'

To sum up the supply situation. For a long time the British had been accumulating resources in their Middle East Base, which now contained practically everything they could want. The problem was to deliver maintenance requirements and reserve stocks to the 8th Army and Desert Air Force along a rapidly lengthening line of supply. Such hitches as occurred during the first few days of the pursuit, mainly in the delivery of petrol to the armour, were caused partly by sudden changes of plan in a desperate attempt to make up for the poor and unambitious start of the pursuit, and partly by the very bad going across the 'Lightfoot' and 'Supercharge' battlefields, and then over the desert routes in the rain.

Fortunately the damage done by the enemy to the ports and desert railway was not as bad as it might have been, and was soon largely repaired. This enabled sea and rail to take their share of the total burden fairly quickly; on the long view, therefore, the situation was satisfactory. Meanwhile the much more flexible motor transport companies were bearing the brunt. For them it was the start of a gruelling spell of convoy work in preparation for, and in support of, the long haul to Tripoli.

The enemy, harried by the 7th Armoured Division, finally withdrew into the Mersa Brega—El Agheila positions on the night of

23rd November and the British pressed on with their preparations for attacking them. General Leese, with his 30th Corps Headquarters, moved up to take over command in the forward area from General Lumsden. As soon as possible the 30th Corps (7th Armoured, 51st Highland, and the New Zealand Divisions) was to be concentrated south of Benghazi.

The story of the advance from El Agheila to Tripoli, with its many special problems, must wait until a later chapter. We leave the 8th Army and Desert Air Force gathering strength to attack at El Agheila, and turn now to the Western Mediterranean to follow the fortunes of the first great Allied landing from the sea.

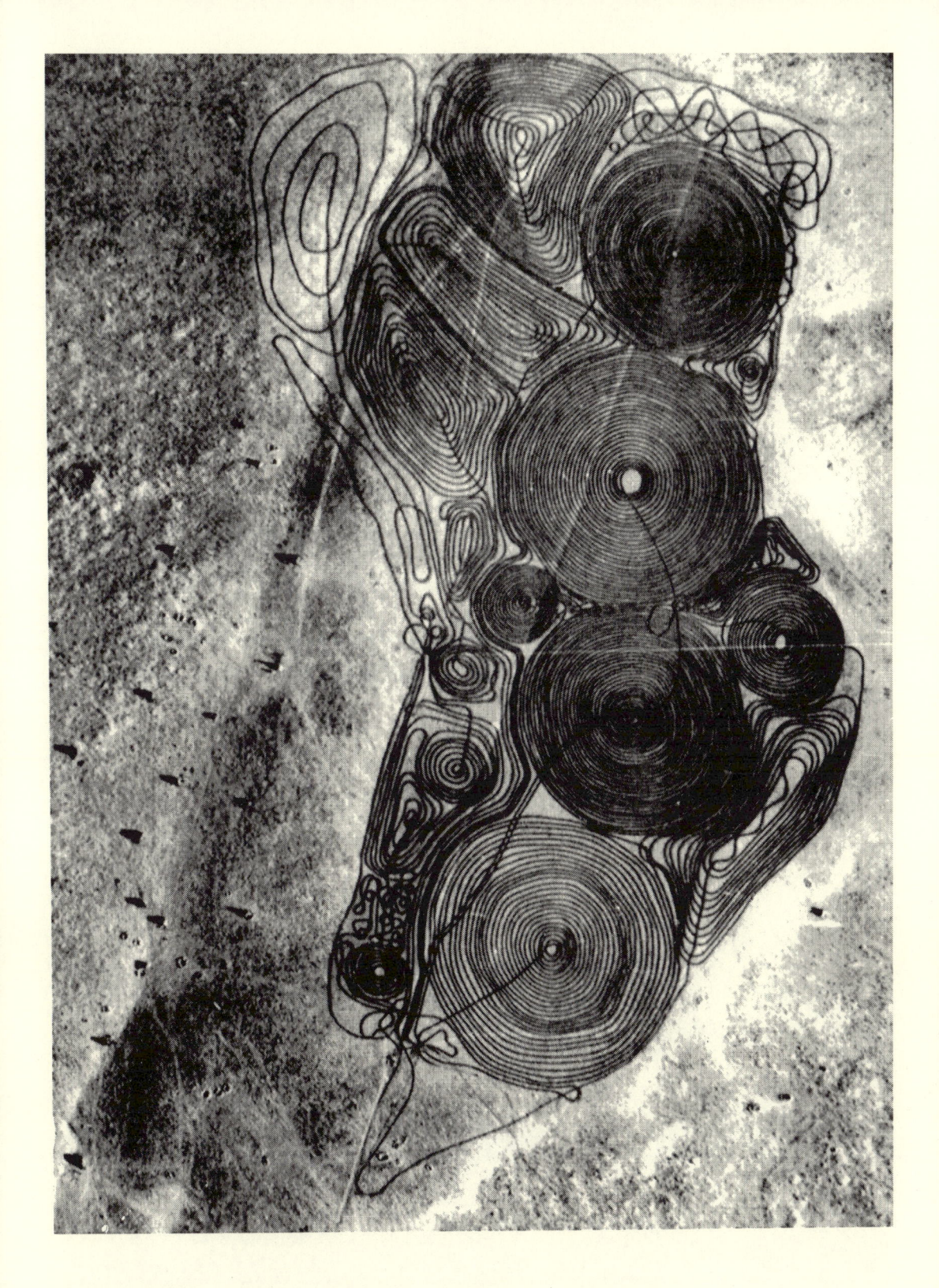

1. Axis airfield in Tripolitania, obstructed by ploughing (probably with three tractors) before capture by British.

2. Western Desert. Royal Artillery O.P. party. Shell-fire.

3. American medium tanks, General Sherman.

4. A Scorpion; Matilda tank with flails to destroy mines.

5. Sappers sweeping an airfield with mine-detectors.

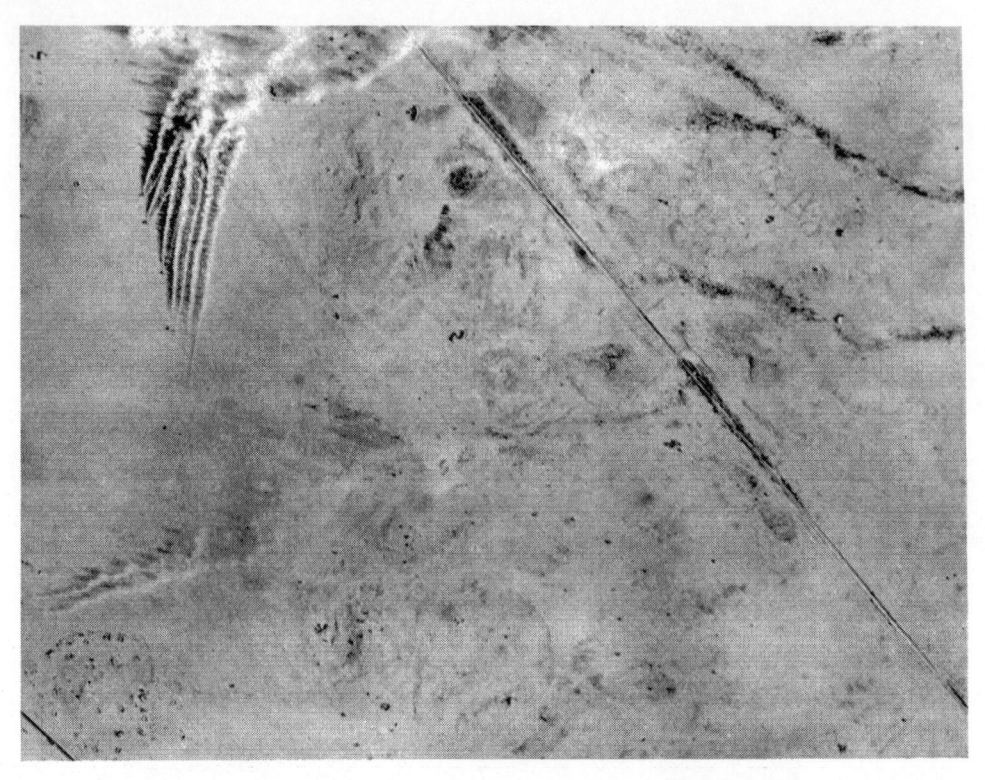

6. A Desert landing ground before rain. Aircraft top left, taking off. November 1942.

7. The same landing ground after two days' rain. Dark patches are water and mud.

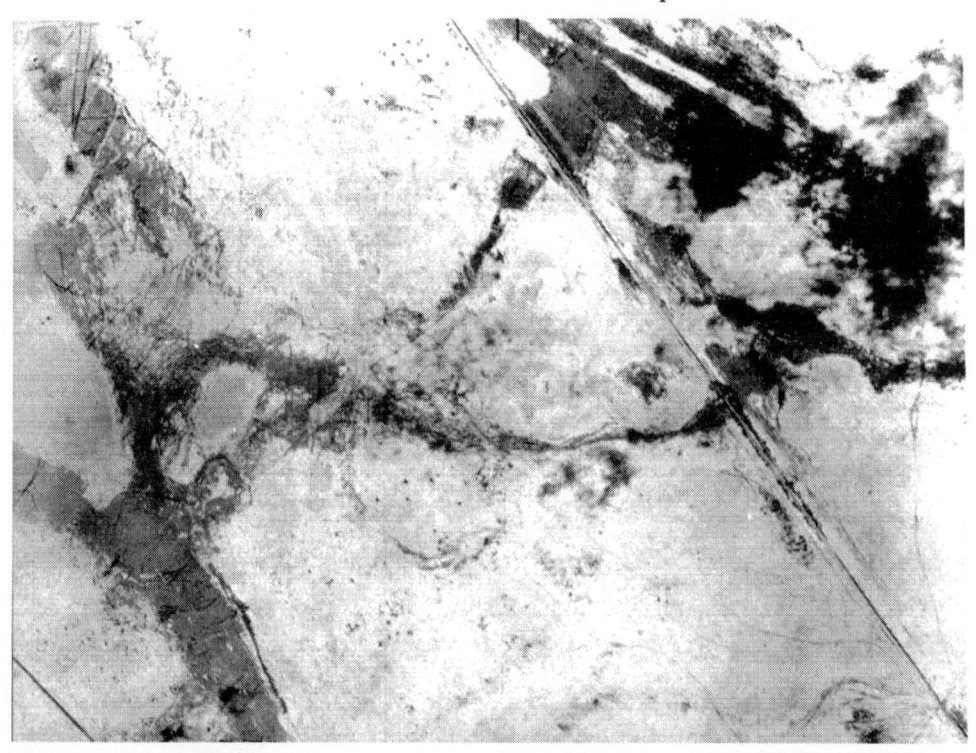

Map 15

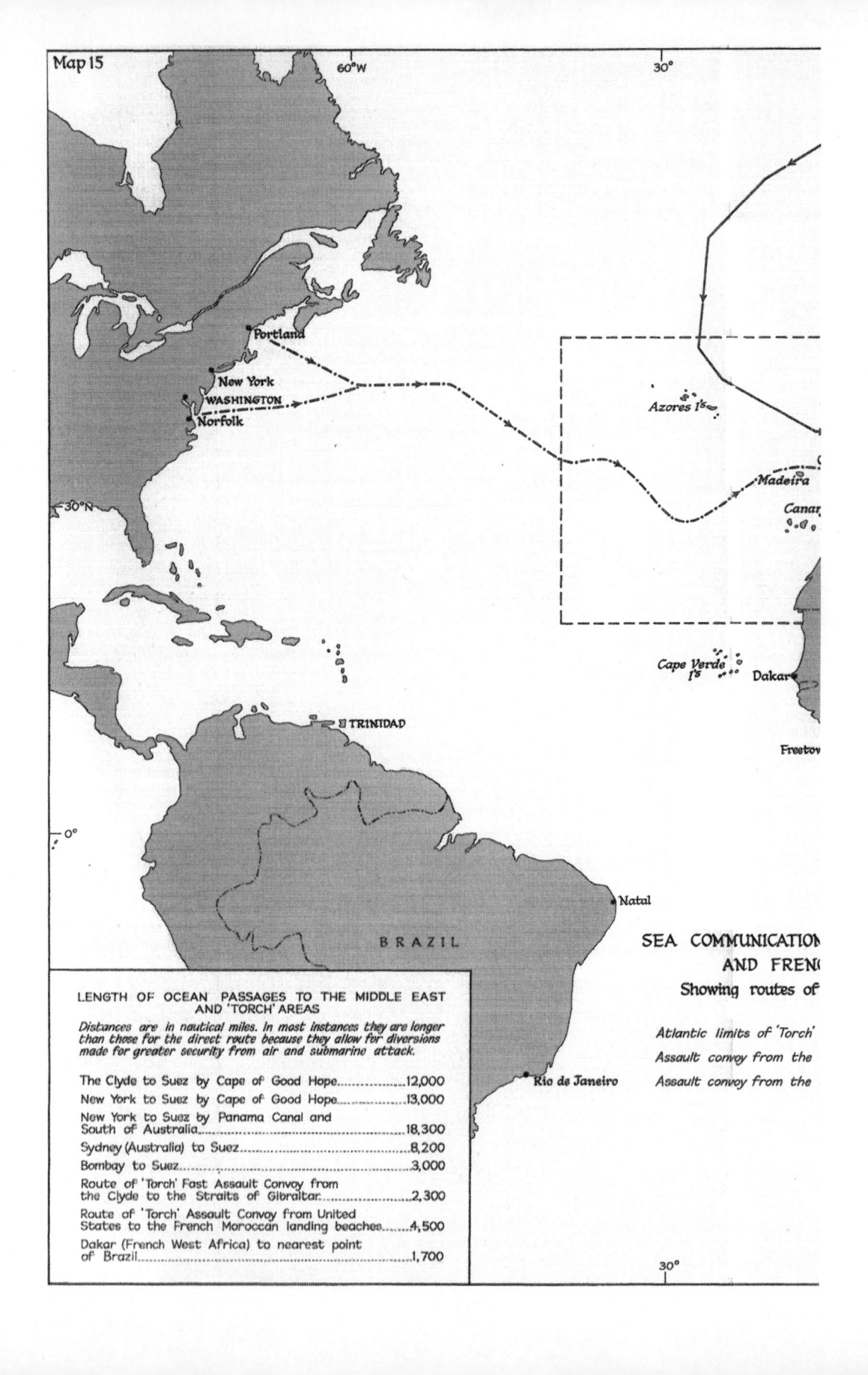

LENGTH OF OCEAN PASSAGES TO THE MIDDLE EAST
AND 'TORCH' AREAS

Distances are in nautical miles. In most instances they are longer than those for the direct route because they allow for diversions made for greater security from air and submarine attack.

The Clyde to Suez by Cape of Good Hope	12,000
New York to Suez by Cape of Good Hope	13,000
New York to Suez by Panama Canal and South of Australia	18,300
Sydney (Australia) to Suez	8,200
Bombay to Suez	3,000
Route of 'Torch' Fast Assault Convoy from the Clyde to the Straits of Gibraltar	2,300
Route of 'Torch' Assault Convoy from United States to the French Moroccan landing beaches	4,500
Dakar (French West Africa) to nearest point of Brazil	1,700

SEA COMMUNICATION
AND FREN
Showing routes of

Atlantic limits of 'Torch'
Assault convoy from the
Assault convoy from the

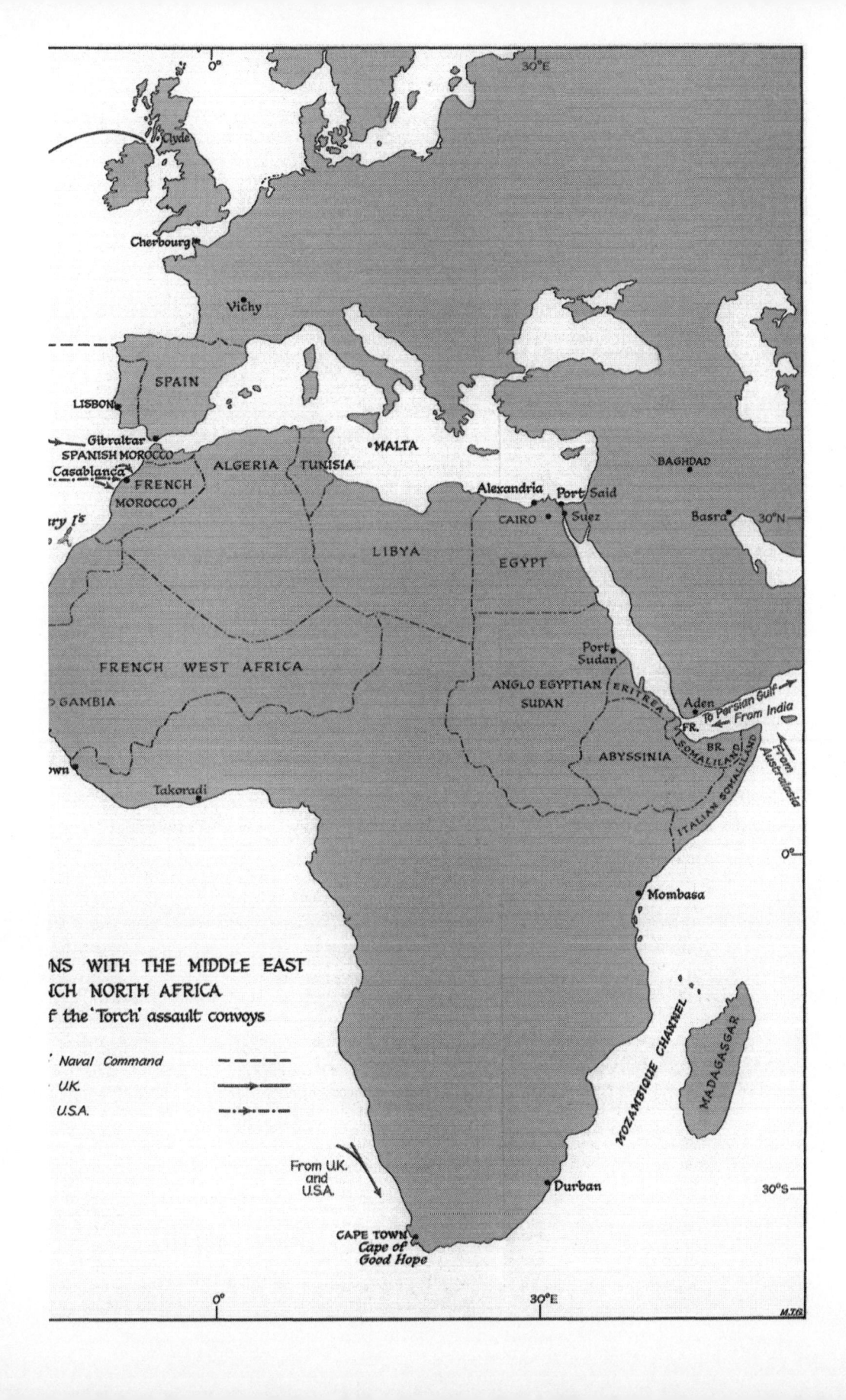

NS WITH THE MIDDLE EAST
CH NORTH AFRICA
f the 'Torch' assault convoys

Naval Command
U.K.
U.S.A.

From U.K. and U.S.A.

CHAPTER V

'TORCH': THE BIRTH OF THE FIRST GREAT ALLIED ENTERPRISE

See Map 15

THE fall of France in 1940 aroused British and American interest in French territory in North and West Africa, for neither Government wanted to see these areas occupied by the enemy. To the U.S.A. a German occupation of French West Africa or French Morocco would appear to threaten the western hemisphere, since between Dakar and Brazil the Atlantic is at its narrowest, and German warships and aircraft could obtain some measure of control over this 1,700 mile stretch of ocean. German influence in South and Central America, already considerable, would grow and might present a threat not only to the Monroe Doctrine but to the Panama Canal. The British, for their part, saw an added danger to shipping, especially on the Cape route, and a threat to the air routes to Egypt. With their strong views on the importance of the Mediterranean and Middle East the British regarded a German occupation of Algeria or Tunisia as also highly undesirable, for it would turn the Western Mediterranean into an Axis lake and make another gap in the blockade of Germany.

Thus the attitude of both countries was mainly defensive. The Americans, while still neutral, did consider from time to time the possibility of occupying the Atlantic Islands and Dakar themselves, while the British examined also the question of occupying Algeria and Tunisia, to give them control of the Western Mediterranean and a back door to Libya.[1] When the time came these territories should be useful as a springboard by which to enter southern Europe. The difference in the point of view of the two countries was only to be expected, and will be seen to continue after they had become allies in arms as well as in ideas.

For more than two years no military action against French territory in North and West Africa resulted from the fall of France,

---

[1] The British also made plans for occupying the Canary Islands and the Azores, Madeira and Cape Verde Islands. See J. R. M. Butler: *Grand Strategy*, Volume II.

with the exception of the abortive attack on Dakar in September 1940. Neither the British nor the Americans had forces to spare, and the Americans, with, as they believed, good reason, pursued a policy of appeasement towards the Vichy Government and of giving economic aid to French Africa. On one occasion, however, the British seriously contemplated military action: this was during the autumn of 1941, when it was hoped to exploit success in operation 'Crusader' by advancing across Tripolitania to the Tunisian frontier. These hopes led the British to prepare to enter French North Africa if French invitation and help were forthcoming. At the first Washington Conference in December 1941 (when the policy of first defeating Germany and then Japan was confirmed) this British project, known as 'Gymnast', was enlarged into an Anglo-American 'Super Gymnast'.

The results of 'Crusader', however, were disappointing, and the 8th Army was presently forced back to Gazala. Action against French North Africa consequently lost its urgency. Moreover, the shortage of shipping so limited the force which could be landed that the project came to depend too much on the wholehearted co-operation of the French. And now that the U.S.A. was herself at war, her point of view had changed; she wanted not a preventive occupation but a direct and early attack on the dominant Axis partner. By April 1942 work on 'Super Gymnast' was stopped and the Combined Chiefs of Staff agreed to concentrate on making a plan ('Round-up') for landing in north-western France in 1943.[1] But 'Super Gymnast' was never far from the Prime Minister's thoughts—nor from the President's either—and in July 1942 it came to life again as 'Torch'. In the meantime Anglo-American policy was being forged to the accompaniment of mounting shipping losses and Allied reverses in Russia and Egypt, and, until the

---

[1] The Combined Chiefs of Staff consisted of the British and American C.O.S. sitting together, but as the former were seldom in Washington they were represented there by the principals on the British Joint Staff Mission. The agreed terminology was that 'Joint' should denote the Inter-Service collaboration of one nation, while 'Combined' would apply to collaboration between two or more of the United Nations. In practice the U.S.C.O.S. came to be known as the Joint C.O.S., and the British remained the British C.O.S.

In August 1942 the holders of these appointments were:
British Chiefs of Staff
  General Sir Alan Brooke (Chairman)
  Admiral of the Fleet Sir Dudley Pound
  Air Chief Marshal Sir Charles Portal
United States Chiefs of Staff
  Admiral William D. Leahy (Chairman; also C.O.S. to the President)
  General George C. Marshall
  Admiral Ernest J. King
  Lieut.-General Henry H. Arnold (U.S. Army Air Force)
British Joint Staff Mission in Washington
  Field-Marshal Sir John Dill
  Admiral Sir Andrew Cunningham
  Air Marshal D. C. S. Evill

situation was relieved in June by the American victory at the battle of Midway Island, in the Far East as well. The story is fully told in another volume of this series.[1] Here it is sufficient to mention the differences which had to be reconciled before it was finally agreed that the main Anglo-American effort in 1942, and America's first large-scale operation, was to be the occupation of French North Africa.

The basic question which had been exercising British and Americans between April and July was how best to employ the available Allied forces, in 1942 if possible, so as to relieve German pressure on the Russians. The U.S. Chiefs of Staff wished the main 1943 operation ('Round-up') to be preceded by smaller landings in France during 1942. The first proposal was for a series of raids, which soon hardened into a single operation ('Sledgehammer') as large as the available landing-craft would permit. The locality favoured was the Cherbourg peninsula and the idea of a large-scale raid gave place to that of establishing a bridgehead from which 'Round-up' would break loose in 1943.

The British Chiefs of Staff, for their part, were quite ready to mount Commando raids against various points along the enemy-held coasts, and, indeed, were already doing so. They were naturally alive to the advantages of any operation, large or small, for which the United Kingdom could be used as a launching platform and base, but the more they studied the implications of a large operation across the Channel in 1942, the more convinced they were that it would fail. It could not be large enough to draw Germans from the Russian front, for the German land and air forces already in France were adequate to contain, and perhaps expel, any Anglo-American force sent to occupy the Cherbourg peninsula. A failure would not help the Russians and would be disastrous for the French resistance movement. In the opinion of the British Chiefs of Staff 'Sledgehammer' would be a waste of men and resources and would delay 'Round-up'. It would not even 'blood' many American troops, since most of the troops would have to be British. Only in the unlikely event of a sudden German collapse did the British look upon 'Sledgehammer' as justifiable.

The Americans, who had not the same experience in weighing what was desirable against what was practicable with available resources such as shipping, landing-craft, and aircraft, began to suspect the British of being lukewarm about any Channel crossing, even in 1943. The Prime Minister in particular seemed to them to prefer, perhaps with some post-war imperialistic aim in view, indirect attack to head-on collision, while the British Chiefs of Staff

---

[1] J. M. A. Gwyer and J. R. M. Butler: *Grand Strategy*, Volume III.

appeared to be more immediately concerned for the security of sea communications and of the Middle East and its oil—as indeed they were.

At the second Washington Conference in June it was agreed to continue with preparations for 'Round-up', but the fate of 'Sledgehammer' was left undecided. By then the President had become more impressed by the practical difficulties of landing in France in 1942, but not wishing to oppose his own advisers, he sent Mr. Harry Hopkins, General Marshall, and Admiral King to London in July to try to persuade the British to agree to 'Sledgehammer'. If they failed they were to choose another place where American troops should fight in 1942. Fail they did, and acknowledging with a good grace that it was no use pressing an unwilling partner, they turned once more to the best alternative acceptable to both countries—a landing in French Africa. This was the decision which the Prime Minister ardently desired, and the President welcomed it as the happiest solution. It would probably mean postponing 'Round-up' until 1944, though training and preparations were to continue. Whatever the critics of 'Torch' thought of the decision on the plane of Grand Strategy, they had to admit that, besides the tremendous gain to Allied shipping which would follow the re-opening of the Mediterranean, it offered a number of other advantages: 'Torch' required fewer landing-craft than 'Sledgehammer'; it would provide more suitable initial experience for raw American troops; it would close a minor gap in the blockade of Germany; and it might encourage Frenchmen to align themselves once more on the side of the Allies.

On 6th August 1942 Lieut.-General Dwight D. Eisenhower, commander since June of the U.S. Army in the European Theatre of Operations, was appointed 'Commander-in-Chief, Allied Expeditionary Force', responsible to the Combined Chiefs of Staff. It was particularly appropriate to appoint an American to command 'Torch', for not only would the troops be mostly American, but it was believed that even if the French in Africa did not actually welcome an ostensibly American invasion they would not seriously oppose it.

At Allied Force Headquarters (A.F.H.Q.) in London was gathered a staff of officers drawn from the three Services of both nations. General Eisenhower's deputy was Major-General Mark W. Clark, an American, so that if the Commander-in-Chief were incapacitated, the fiction of an almost exclusively American expedition would be preserved. The Chief of Staff was Brigadier-General Walter Bedell Smith, U.S. Army.

Map 16

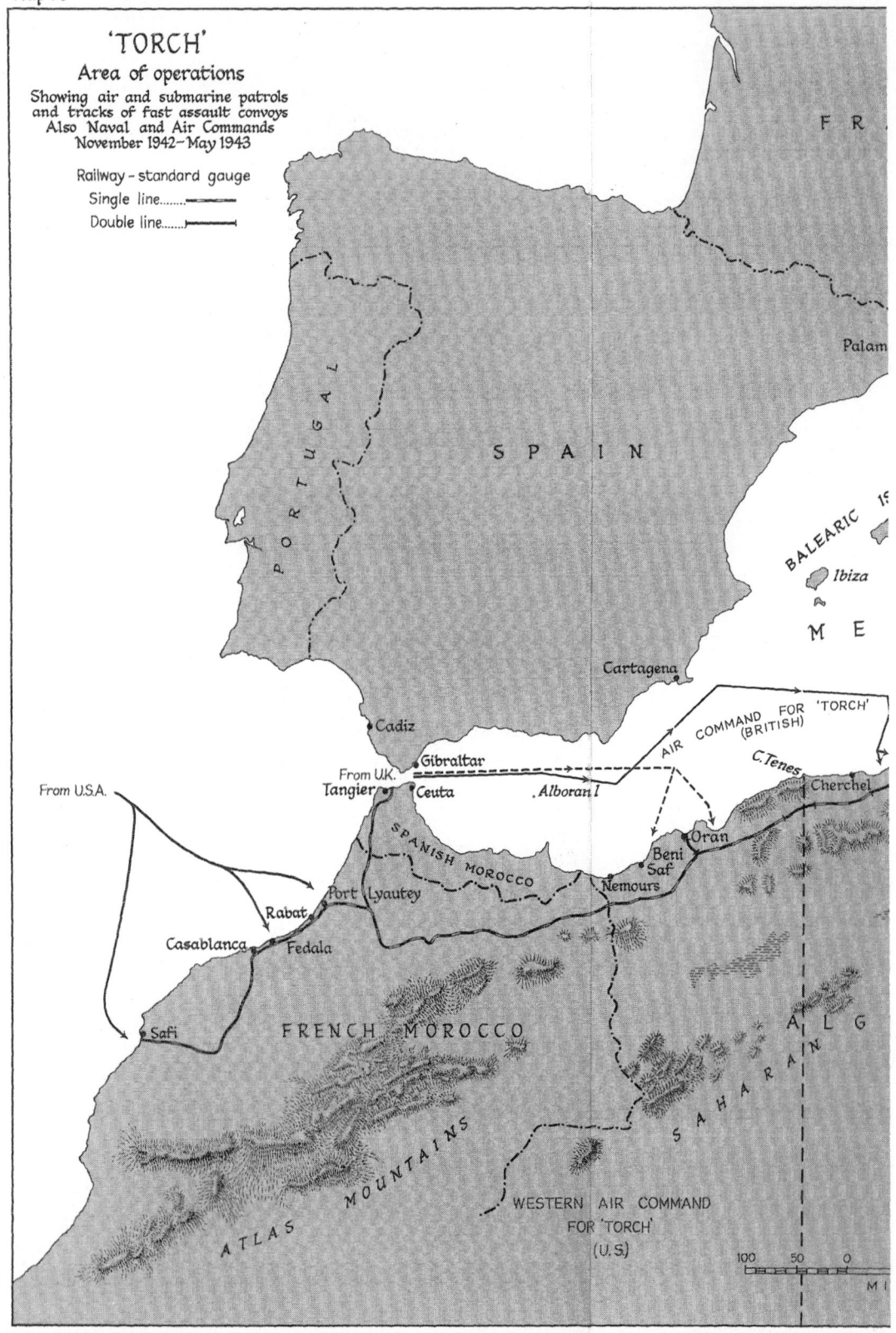

'TORCH'
Area of operations
Showing air and submarine patrols
and tracks of fast assault convoys
Also Naval and Air Commands
November 1942 – May 1943

Railway - standard gauge
Single line........
Double line........

EASTERN AIR COMMAND FOR 'TORCH' (BRITISH)

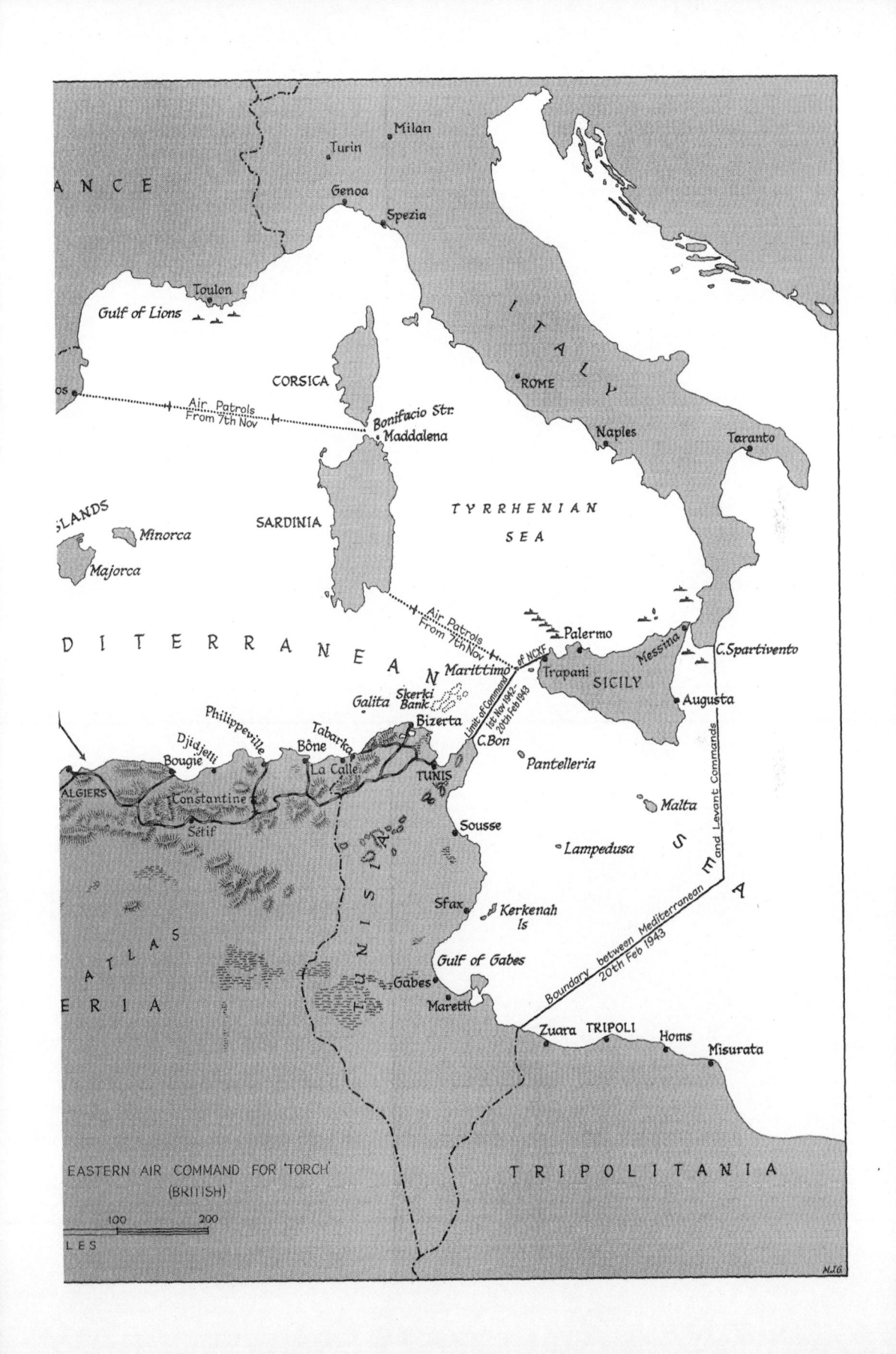

Command of the British land forces underwent some vicissitudes. First Lieut.-General Alexander was appointed, but early in August he was suddenly required to succeed General Auchinleck in the Middle East, and Lieut.-General Montgomery took his place in 'Torch'. Next day Lieut.-General Gott, who was about to take command of the 8th Army, was killed, and Montgomery was appointed to replace him.[1] Finally Lieut.-General K. A. N. Anderson succeeded to the command under Eisenhower, to whom Mark Clark remarked that he hoped the turn over of American generals in Africa would be less rapid.

The 'Allied Naval Commander, Expeditionary Force' (N.C.X.F.) under General Eisenhower was to be Admiral Sir Andrew Cunningham, who was thus to return to the Mediterranean after an absence of seven months, for four of which he had been at Washington as British Naval member of the Combined Chiefs of Staff's Committee. His deputy, Vice-Admiral Sir Bertram Ramsay, was already famous in combined operations for his command of the evacuation from Dunkirk. The Mediterranean was divided into two: Admiral Harwood, still holding the title of Commander-in-Chief, Mediterranean, was to command the eastern half and Admiral Cunningham the western and a large area of the Atlantic to the west of Gibraltar as well.[2] Admiral Cunningham was responsible to the Allied Commander-in-Chief for the security of the sea communications of the expedition once it entered this area, for supporting the army in further amphibious operations in the Western Mediterranean, and for the seaward defence of the North African coast and ports. For the British naval forces in the Western Mediterranean and around Gibraltar that were being used for purposes other than the African operations, he was responsible directly to the Admiralty.

For the Allied Air Command General Eisenhower would have liked some similar arrangement, but deferred to the wish of others for separate commands. Accordingly Brigadier-General (later Major-General) James H. Doolittle, the bomber of Tokyo, was appointed to command the American air forces assigned to the expedition and Air Marshal Sir William Welsh the British.[3] Both officers were directly responsible to General Eisenhower, who had, in addition, two Air advisers on his staff—Air Vice-Marshal A. P. M. Sanders, R.A.F., and Brigadier-General Howard Craig. This was an awkward arrangement and it was a pity that the experience gained in the Middle East in the handling of large air

---

[1] For a fuller account of the changes in the Middle East see Volume III.
[2] See Maps 15 and 16. Admiral Cunningham's area in the Atlantic extended to 40° west between latitudes 43° and 20° north.
[3] Brigadier-General Doolittle had led a bombing attack on Tokyo on 18th April 1942 from the U.S.S. *Hornet*, then 668 miles from the target.

forces by a unified command, which included the integrated British and American tactical air forces, was not drawn upon when the Allied Air Command for 'Torch' was being set up.

General Eisenhower was determined to make of this first great Anglo-American command a truly Allied Force. This he achieved, largely by the strength of his own example, though this is not in any way to belittle the loyal co-operation of his Commanders nor the support he received from the Combined Chiefs of Staff. He has mentioned as an example of this support the immediate concurrence of the British Chiefs of Staff with his request that their directive appointing General Anderson should be amended to limit the British General's right of appeal to the War Office to occasions of the gravest emergency, and then only after giving General Eisenhower his reasons for wishing to do so.

In organizing his Allied Force Headquarters General Eisenhower, in his own words, 'proceeded as though all its members belonged to a single nation'. Throughout the General Staff sections (there were no Naval or Air Staff sections) he aimed at integrating and balancing Americans and British. On the administrative side, however, the two systems differed so much, and in many matters were rooted in their country's law, that separate and parallel American and British sections were appointed to work their own systems. A (British) Chief Administrative Officer, Major-General H. M. Gale, was appointed to co-ordinate the operational logistics of the Allies and the work of the administrative staffs.

General Eisenhower's directive from the Combined Chiefs of Staff was dated 13th August and read: 'The President and the Prime Minister have agreed that combined military operations be directed against Africa as early as practicable with a view to gaining, in conjunction with Allied forces in the Middle East, complete control of North Africa from the Atlantic to the Red Sea ...' It went on to explain that this should be achieved in three stages. First, by establishing firm and mutually supporting lodgements in the Oran—Algiers—Tunis area on the north coast, and in the Casablanca area on the north-west coast. Second, by exploiting these lodgements to acquire complete control of all French North Africa and if necessary Spanish Morocco. Third, by thrusting eastward so as to take the Axis forces in the Western Desert in the rear and annihilate them. At the same time air and sea operations against Axis installations in the Mediterranean area were to be intensified in order to ensure through sea communications and to facilitate operations against the Axis on the European continent.

Within this framework it was General Eisenhower's task to make a plan.

The problem of occupying French Africa was beset with unknowns, any one of which might interfere seriously with the Allies' plans. Spain was certainly pro-Axis, and although General Franco would probably not wish to be drawn into the war, the Spanish could soon render Gibraltar unusable as a naval and air base, and make the passage of the Straits—which are only eight miles wide—hazardous for Allied ships. With or without Spanish consent the Germans might conceivably decide to move in to attack Gibraltar and command the Straits themselves. General Franco might be unable to resist Axis pressure to join in, or at least to place airfields at Germany's disposal. Whatever happened in Spain, it seemed certain that as soon as the Allies landed in French Africa—if not before—the Germans would send forces by air and sea to Tunisia. They might also move into Unoccupied France in order to establish air and submarine bases on the Mediterranean coast and defend it against assault. They might well try to seize the French Fleet at Toulon. For all this, however, there might be no need if French reactions—which were habitually unpredictable—were strongly unfavourable to the Allies.

As will be related presently the Americans had reason to believe that if they were not at once welcomed by the French they would at least not be seriously opposed. However, many Frenchmen in Africa had less reason for hating Germans than had their countrymen in Metropolitan France, and in common with the native population might look upon the Americans, if not as enemies, at any rate as disturbers of the peace. It was to be expected that the attitude of Spain, of Vichy, and of the French in Africa would be greatly influenced by first impressions. Consequently it was most important that the initial landings should be immediately successful and give an impression of overwhelming strength.

Much of what the Americans knew, or thought they knew, about feelings in French Africa, was based on reports from Mr. Robert D. Murphy. As Counsellor of the U.S. Embassy at Vichy Mr. Murphy had been sent to visit Algiers and Dakar in December 1940 to learn what he could of conditions and of the leading personalities in French Africa. From this visit had sprung an American undertaking to send food and supplies, which General Weygand, Vichy's Delegate-General in North Africa, and M. Boisson, Governor of French West Africa, had contended would help them to organize resistance to German penetration. The British had agreed to grant a limited number of navicerts on the understanding that the Americans would ensure that no benefit should accrue to the Axis. Early in 1941 Mr. Murphy was sent to Algiers as Consul-General, with a team of young Americans to supervise distribution. From this network the United States collected intelligence on a wide range of subjects and learned something of those leading French personalities who genuinely favoured the Allies.

The French land forces in North Africa were limited by the terms of the 1940 armistice to 120,000 men, of whom about 55,000 were in Morocco, 50,000 in Algeria, and 15,000 in Tunisia. They consisted mainly of native infantry units with French officers, but there were also units of the Foreign Legion, of Chasseurs d'Afrique (Frenchmen on foreign service), and Zouaves—African born Frenchmen. The human material was good and the military tradition high, but weapons, ammunition, and equipment were scarce and obsolete, and training had fallen out of date. The French were believed (correctly) to have about 500 aircraft of obsolete types in North Africa.

The French naval forces were far from negligible. In the Mediterranean at Bizerta and Oran there were only destroyers, submarines, and smaller craft, but at Casablanca were one 6-inch cruiser, seven destroyers, eight submarines, and the battleship *Jean Bart* (uncompleted, but able to fire her turret guns); at Dakar there was the modern battleship *Richelieu* with three more cruisers. The Fleet at Toulon consisted of 3 capital ships, 7 cruisers, 28 destroyers and 15 submarines. The Italian Fleet serviceable in August 1942 comprised 6 capital ships, 9 cruisers, 28 destroyers and 35 submarines. Both these navies were seriously short of fuel. Finally, there were 15 German submarines in the Mediterranean.

The threat presented by the Axis air forces in the Central Mediterranean had just been vividly illustrated by the experience of 'Pedestal', the August convoy to Malta from the west, in which nine out of fourteen merchant ships were lost from all causes. The Air Ministry's forecast of the aircraft the Axis would have in Sicily and Sardinia at the end of October was 395 German and 530 Italian. Actual strengths were 298 German, 574 Italian. Most of these aircraft in Sicily and Sardinia were less than 200 miles from Tunis or Bizerta, and their numbers could be quickly increased. Account had also to be taken of the large German air transport fleet which could give the *Luftwaffe* considerable mobility and might be used also to carry army units and light equipment to Tunisia.

See Maps 16 *and* 17

In carrying the war into French North Africa at the start of the rainy season the Allies were committing themselves to a campaign in conditions very different from those in the Western Desert of Egypt. Morocco, Algeria, and northern and western Tunisia are all

Map 17

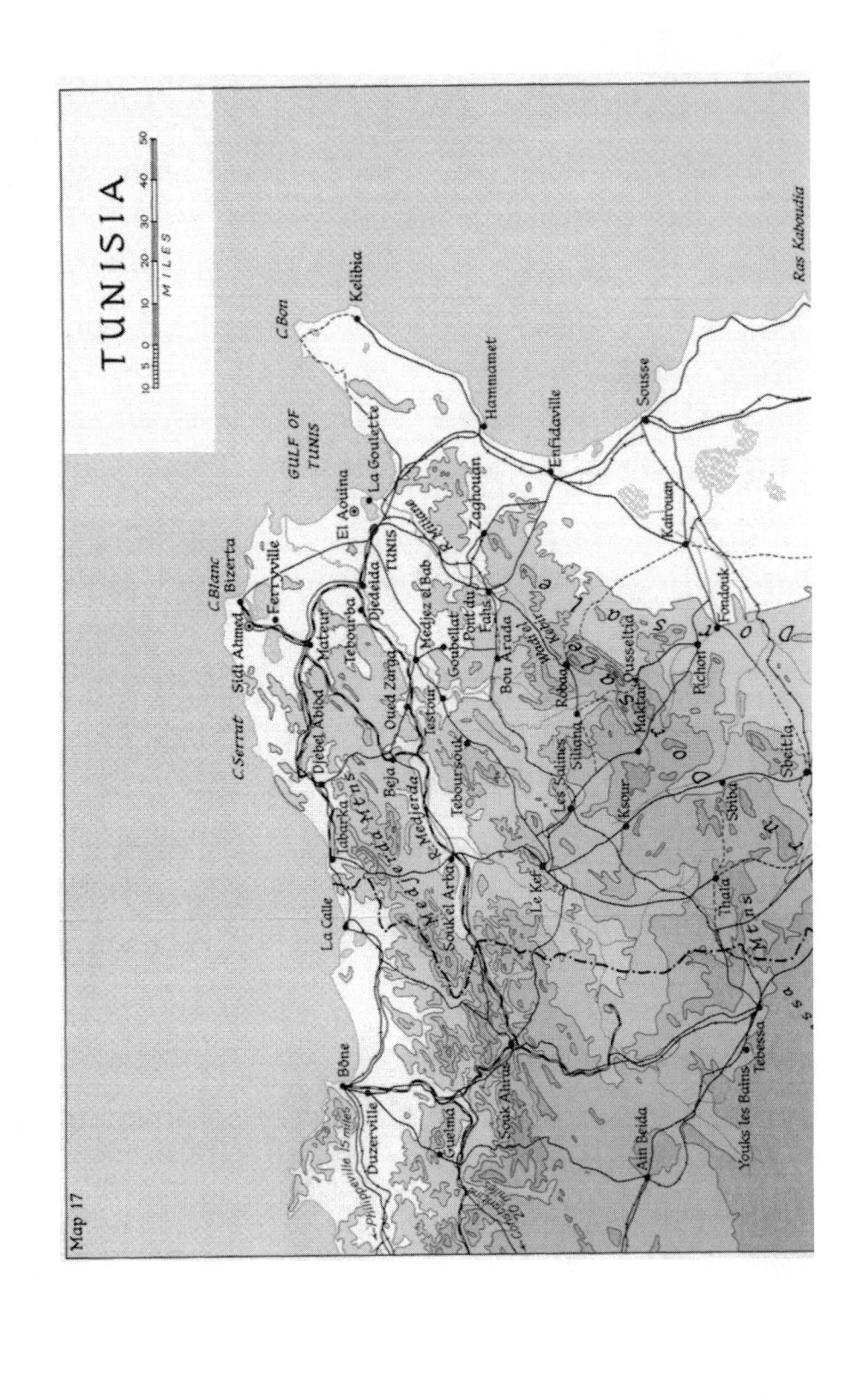

TUNISIA

MILES
10 5 0 10 20 30 40 50

C. Blanc
Bizerta
C. Serrat Sidi Ahmed
Ferryville
Mateur
Djebel Abiod Tebourba
Oued Zarga Djedeida
Beja   Medjez el Bab
Tabarka   Testour
            Goubellat   Pont du Fahs
Medjerda   Teboursouk Bou Arada
Souk el Arba   Robaa
            Les Slainés Siliana   Ousseltia
La Calle   Maktar
            Le Kef   Ksour
                                 Pichon
                        Sbiba
Bône   Thala
Duzerville   Sbeitla
Philippeville 15 miles
Guelma
Souk Ahras
            Ain Beida
Youks les Bains
Tebessa

El Aouina
La Goulette
TUNIS
GULF OF TUNIS
C. Bon
Kelibia
Hammamet
Zaghouan
Enfidaville
Sousse
Kairouan
Fondouk
Ras Kaboudia

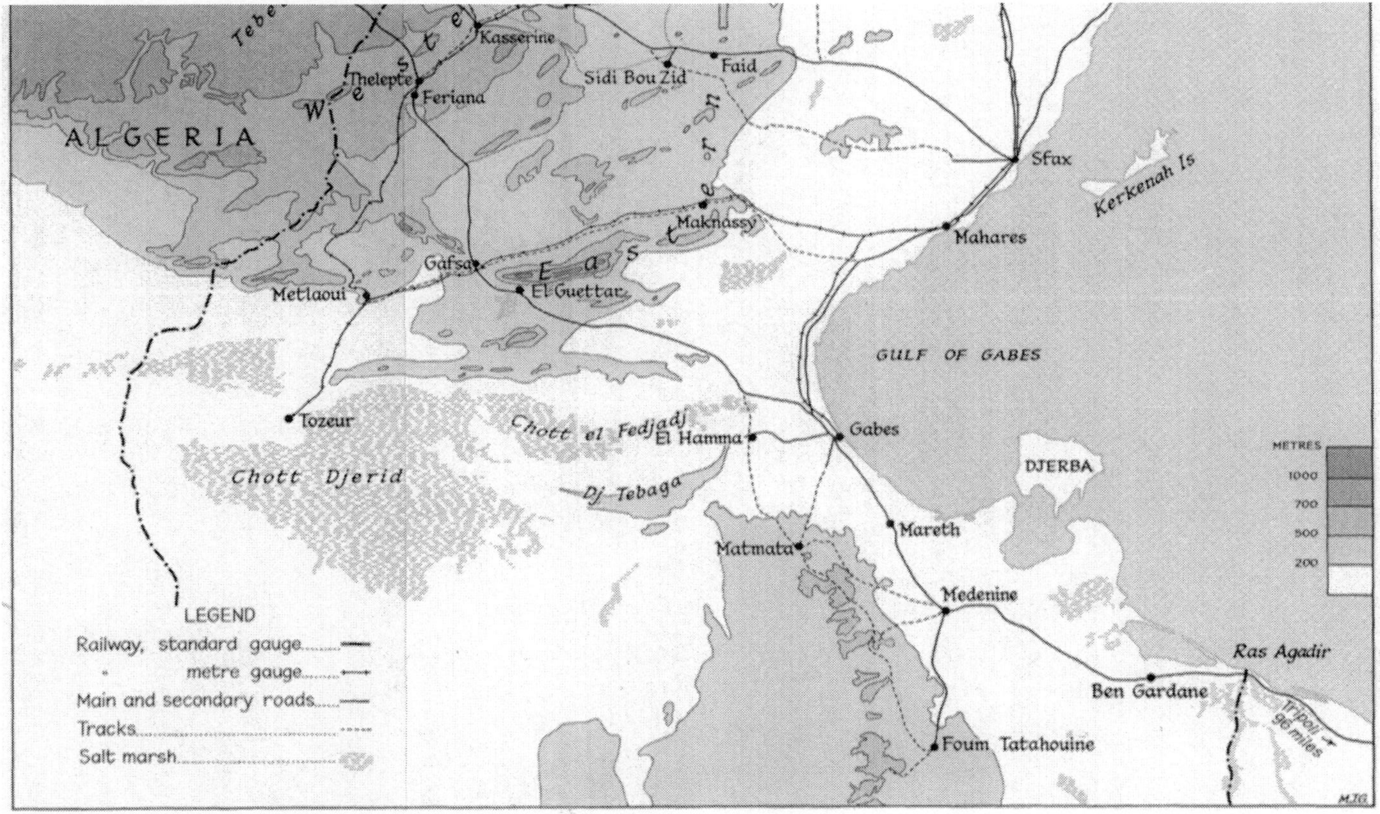
ALGERIA
Western
Eastern
Kasserine
Thelepte
Feriana
Sidi Bou Zid
Faid
Sfax
Kerkenah Is
Maknassy
Mahares
Gafsa
El Guettar
Metlaoui
GULF OF GABES
Tozeur
Chott el Fedjadj
El Hamma
Gabes
DJERBA
Chott Djerid
Dj Tebaga
Mareth
Matmata
Medenine
Ras Agadir
Ben Gardane
Tripoli 96 miles
Foum Tatahouine
METRES
1000
700
500
200
LEGEND
Railway, standard gauge
" metre gauge
Main and secondary roads
Tracks
Salt marsh
MJG

mountainous, being traversed by the Atlas range, which, with its subsidiary chains, runs from the Atlantic coast of Morocco nearly to Tunis—a distance of 1,200 miles.[1] This long stretch was threaded by a single standard-gauge railway, which ran for 600 miles from the Atlantic coast to Oran, another 250 miles to Algiers and a further 500, roughly speaking, to Tunis. This shows how large was this new theatre of war, and how far apart were some of the proposed landing-places. The main scenes of the campaign to which the 'Torch' landings were the prelude were laid in eastern Algeria and Tunisia; a brief description will give some idea of the setting.

Eastward of Algiers the mountains close in on the coast and dominate it—except for a small plain at Bône—as far as Bizerta in the extreme north of Tunisia. Two subsidiary and lower ranges run from a knot of hills just south of Tunis; these are the Eastern and Western Dorsales. The Eastern stretches south to Maknassy, the Western towards Tebessa and Gafsa. Both ridges are pierced at only a few points. To the east of the Eastern Dorsale lies the Tunisian coastal plain, whose features, and their influences on the 8th Army's advance from Tripolitania, will be described later.

In a theatre where the distances are so great the railways are obviously very important. The single standard-gauge line runs eastward from Algiers to northern Tunisia through Ouled Rahmoun (a few miles south of Constantine), and Souk Ahras. Branch lines lead in from the ports of Bougie, Philippeville and Bône. A connected metre-gauge system serves the Tunisian plain and the ports of Gabes, Sfax and Sousse. This system is joined to the standard-gauge system by two branches to Tebessa—one from Ouled Rahmoun, the other from Souk Ahras. The direct line from Tebessa to Tunis is metre-gauge.

Thus the railways were not well suited to the Allies' purposes: a break of gauge is the enemy of the smooth carriage of freight, and apart from the possibility of damage by sabotage, the railway system as a whole was in poor shape. Locomotives and rolling-stock were old and worn, and spare parts and lubricants were very scarce. Worse still, French Africa produced no suitable coal and imported stocks had run down. So if the Allies wanted to use the railways, as of course they did, they would have to bring with them a great deal of stores and equipment.

Two main roads ran from Algiers to northern Tunisia. First, the coast road through Bougie, Philippeville and Bône to Bizerta. This had a tarred surface but was so narrow and winding as to be in

---

[1] The name 'Morocco' will be used to mean French Morocco unless stated otherwise.

places unsafe for heavy military traffic, even one way. Farther inland the second main road followed the general line of the railway to Tunis; it had a tarmac surface wide enough for two way traffic for most of its length, and was joined by feeder roads from the ports, notably Philippeville, Bône, La Calle and Tabarka.

There were also many secondary roads, some fairly good, others mere rocky or earthy tracks. Thus the road system in general was not suitable for modern armies, seeing that there were only two main west-east routes, neither fit to take the flow of a great volume of traffic. The north-south routes and those of the secondary system were rambling and often steep—laid out for the needs of peace and farming. Moreover, traffic was often road-bound, except on the Tunisian coastal plain in dry weather.

The theatre in short was one which would present difficult logistic problems, aggravated by the fact that the French territories were so hard-up economically as a result of the war that an invading force would have to be self-sufficient in every way.

Besides the general features that have been mentioned there were many others which set tactical problems, large and small. North of the Medjerda valley the hills were high and rugged, and thick scrub and cork forests were common. Elsewhere the hills often had barer slopes. Valleys were heavily cultivated and as a rule seamed with gullies; cover round villages and farms was often thick. The broken and hilly country caused numerous bottle-necks on the various routes. To take a few examples: in the Medjerda valley at Medjez el Bab; in the Western Dorsale at Pont du Fahs, Maktar, Sbiba and Kasserine; and in the Eastern Dorsale at Pichon, Fondouk, Faid, and Maknassy. These bottle-necks especially lent themselves to defence. The country did not favour armour (except on the Tunisian plain) and, generally speaking, hindered mechanized movement. It could help troops who knew something of the arts of fighting and living in hills, but held many pitfalls for those who knew little (as did most of the British and Americans). In many places it could tax the skill of experts. The rain which was known to fall heavily in normal years between November and March would turn valleys and level ground into quagmires, impassable to vehicles and difficult for infantry and pack animals. It would also put airfields out of action unless they were weatherproofed at a cost in transport whose prohibitive amount was not at first realized. Cold, rain, and mud would make life very hard for the troops.

Broadly speaking, then, country and climate favoured the defence, which can usually profit from conditions with which the attack can do nothing but struggle.

An additional and most serious physical factor affecting the planning of a landing was the surf which breaks on the beaches of the Atlantic coast of Morocco. After the end of October it could be expected to make landing on open beaches impracticable on four days out of five.

From 'Torch' onwards almost every British and American campaign began with a landing from the sea. It is therefore appropriate to examine the state of preparedness for what were known as 'Combined Operations' and to indicate the trend of British ideas about them. Between the Wars the British had given much thought to the problem. Experience at Gallipoli in 1915 had shown that the fire-power of modern weapons would make opposed landings on open beaches practically impossible unless some protection could be given to the assaulting force during the last few hundred yards of its approach from the sea, and while it was obtaining a footing ashore. The British theoretical solution lay partly in devising special equipment, such as armoured landing-craft and means for giving covering fire, but between the Wars money was only available for such purposes on a niggardly scale. When, however, in the summer of 1940 the British were thrown out of the continent, they had to recognize that any plan for wresting the initiative from the Axis Powers would almost certainly necessitate a landing from the sea as a first step. But so urgent were the demands on British and American shipbuilding capacity for other classes of vessels, that ships and craft specially designed for landing operations were not given a high priority until mid-1942.

Most of the craft and some of the ships specially built or altered were designed to discharge men or material direct on to the beaches. If the sea passage was short, an assault force and its immediate needs could be given a through carriage, as it were, from shore to shore. Longer sea passages, on the other hand, might compel the use of larger ships unsuitable for beaching; in this case men and material would have to be transferred before landing to small craft carried as part of the larger ships' equipment.

In spite of the benefits which accrued from the introduction of special equipment, it was still thought essential to obtain surprise if the assault was to succeed. Even tactical surprise could scarcely be expected unless the final approach to the beaches was made under cover of darkness. But individual beaches were often very difficult to find in the dark, and deployment from them was difficult too. These and many other factors had to be weighed when deciding on the time to land.

The tasks of the air forces in a landing from the sea, while of great importance, would be unlikely to differ from those for which they were normally trained. It would be essential to possess command of the air over the areas in which landings were taking place—a time when ships and troops would be at their most vulnerable. To gain this the invading air forces would of course require suitable bases from which to operate. Should the landing beaches be out of range of shore-based fighters, cover would have to be provided by carrier-borne aircraft until suitable airfields could be captured and brought into use.

The approach to battle in ships and landing-craft required the army to be disposed in a special way. Broadly, it was divided into assault formations, which normally included a floating reserve; follow-up formations; and build-up formations. The first of these were 'assault stowed', which means men and equipment so loaded that they can emerge in a predetermined order very quickly. The build-up formations were stowed normally, an arrangement which results in the most economical use of shipping space. Between these two extremes came 'tactical stowing', with some of the features of both the other systems.

A few other terms should be explained. A 'flight' was a naval formation of landing-craft and the troops in them. It usually carried a complete military unit, and to ensure that the troops landed in the right tactical order the flight might be sub-divided into 'waves'. All the landing-craft in a 'wave' were meant to touch down as nearly as possible at the same moment. While the first waves of troops fought their way to their objectives it was important that more men, weapons, vehicles, and stores should be passed quickly and smoothly across the beaches to selected places. Indeed, the success of a landing operation depended to a great extent on a good beach organization and good communications. The principle was accepted in 1940 that specially trained permanent Beach Groups would be required, but no training did in fact begin until April 1942.

It is important to realize that a force of any size could not be maintained indefinitely over beaches. The early use of a deep-water port was essential to the build-up of almost every Combined Operation. Beaches selected for the initial landings would therefore have to be so near to such a port as to make possible its early capture.

Responsibility for developing this form of warfare, including raids which entailed a landing from the sea, had been entrusted to the 'Combined Operations Organization', a descendant of a small 'Inter-Service Training and Development Centre' established at Portsmouth in 1938. The organization grew with the times and may be said to have come of age in March 1942 when its then head (Commodore Lord Louis Mountbatten) was appointed 'Chief of

Combined Operations', with three-fold rank as Vice-Admiral, Lieutenant-General, and Air Marshal, and became a member of the Chiefs of Staff's Committee.[1] Put very briefly it is broadly correct to say that in 1942 the Combined Operations Organization under the C.C.O.:
- (a) Provided expert advice on every aspect of combined operations from a joint-Service point of view.
- (b) Formulated the doctrine of combined operations, and controlled training in the United Kingdom.
- (c) Experimented with and examined craft and equipment, and concerned itself with their development.

Between the fall of France in 1940 and the 'Torch' landings nearly two and a half years later, the British had launched a number of landing operations, mostly raids, against German-occupied France and Norway. Farther afield there was the long-range operation against Madagascar in May 1942, and three months later the costly raid on Dieppe. The former achieved surprise and was successful; the latter met strong opposition and was costly in lives and equipment, but some extremely valuable lessons were learned.

Many types of craft were built and many ships specially built or converted to meet the needs of landing operations. The main categories can be reduced to five:
- (i) Ships for carrying the assault forces to the point where the assault landing-craft were lowered—Landing Ship Infantry (LSI); and the American Combat Loader.
- (ii) Craft to carry the assault flights—Landing Craft Assault (LCA); Landing Craft Vehicle or Personnel (LCV or P); and Landing Vehicle Tracked (LVT).
- (iii) Ships and craft for discharging tanks and vehicles direct on to the beaches—Landing Ship Tank (LST) and Landing Craft Tank (LCT).
- (iv) Craft to unload the ships—Landing Craft Mechanized (LCM) and DUKWs.[2]

---

[1] Earlier styles of the chief figure in combined operations were:
1938–   Commandant, I.S.T.D.C.: Captain L. E. H. Maund, R.N.
1940–June   Commander of Raiding Operations: Lieut.-General A. G. B. Bourne, Royal Marines.
    –July   Director of Combined Operations: Admiral of the Fleet Sir Roger Keyes.
1941–October Adviser on Combined Operations: Commodore Lord Louis Mountbatten.
The changes of title indicate generally the march of ideas.

[2] In manufacturer's code:
D —year of origin (1942, fourth year of war)
U —utility
K —front-wheel drive
W—six-wheeled.

(v) Craft to give support with gun or rocket fire, or to provide anti-aircraft defence, e.g. Landing Craft Support (LCS).

By the outbreak of war in 1939 no special ships had been designed in the United Kingdom, and landing-craft were still experimental. In the U.S.A. technical development was in much the same condition. Even so, both countries were ahead of any others except Japan, who had sprung a surprise in China in 1937 by producing a 'mother ship' of some 7,500 tons fitted with stern doors through which vehicles and small ramped landing-craft were discharged. British landing-craft available in September 1939 consisted of twelve L.C.A., ten obsolete L.C.M., one new L.C.M. and one L.C.S. All these were lost in the spring of 1940 at Narvik.

By May 1940 nine new L.C.A. and two new L.C.M. had been built of which six were lost at Dunkirk. A fresh batch of craft and three L.S.I. were ordered in June 1940 but could be given no priority because of the urgent need for warships of other classes.

In the autumn of 1941 plans for the invasion of France began to receive serious attention, and before long shipbuilding capacity in the U.S.A. was directed to the production of L.S.T. and various types of landing-craft.

The first British-built L.S.T., known as Winettes, were not completed until early 1943. They drew too much water and their ramping system was unsatisfactory. Three converted shallow-draught Maracaibo oilers did good work in 'Torch' at Oran, but were unseaworthy in bad weather owing to a fault in their bow doors, and they left a wide water-gap on any but the steepest beaches.

Meanwhile the L.S.T.2, embodying British experience, were being built in the United States and were to prove very successful, though they also drew too much water for beaching on flat shores. The first was completed in November 1942—just too late for 'Torch'.

The problem of the water-gap to be crossed after the craft had touched down and lowered its ramp was solved by various means —by the use of pontoons or special pierheads, by constructing suitable hards in captured ports, or, if the rise and fall of the tide was enough (which in the Mediterranean it was not), by drying out. Another solution was to waterproof the vehicles by sealing the joints, as was done in the Madagascar landing in May 1942. At Dieppe in August and again in 'Torch' this method was used for many of the tanks. It could be used only where the water was shallow, for waterproofing of this sort did not turn a tank into an amphibian.

The L.C.T. was of course much smaller than the L.S.T. and could discharge its relatively small load on the flattest of beaches. Some of the earliest British models were shipped in sections to the Middle

East in 1941 and were of great value in the supply of Tobruk and in the evacuation of Greece. In fact both the L.C.T. and L.S.T. proved to be extremely useful maids-of-all-work. Two L.C.T.s were used at Oran during 'Torch'.

The first ships converted to L.S.I. (large) were the three Glen line ships of between 9,000 and 10,000 tons which had been sent to the Mediterranean early in 1941 carrying Special Service troops. Of these only the *Glengyle* took part in 'Torch'. During 1940 several cross-channel steamers were taken over for conversion to L.S.I. (medium) or L.S.I. (small). In 1941 and 1942 nine other ships were converted to White Ensign L.S.I., while others, used temporarily, remained under the Red Ensign. It was important that an L.S.I. should be able to lower its L.C.A. fully loaded and stow these craft inboard when at sea, but these requirements were seldom met except in the larger ships permanently taken over by the Royal Navy.

Some 400 landing-craft were used in the initial landings at Algiers and Oran; their characteristics and those of the specially converted ships are shown in Appendix 4.

In fixing the date for D day a compromise had to be made. Planning, preparations, and training all needed time, but the risk of leakage to the enemy, the approach of winter, the situation in Russia and Egypt, and the importance of not interfering with 'Round-up' all called for the earliest possible date. As it turned out there was little change from General Eisenhower's first proposal (presented on 9th August) in which he mentioned 5th November. D day was finally settled for 8th November—a date which proved to be well chosen in relation to the outcome of the fighting at El Alamein.

Among the factors affecting the decision where to land, the question of air cover loomed large. Convoys would need protection from the time when, while still in the Atlantic, they came within reach of German long-range maritime aircraft. Aircraft carriers were few, and as many of their fighters as possible would have to be conserved for the period between first light on D day and the time when Allied fighters could operate from newly captured airfields.[1] But a number of carrier-borne fighters would have to be kept ready to protect the Fleet against attack by shore-based aircraft. How far to the east troop convoys could safely go would

---

[1] Although fighter aircraft using long-range tanks could have reached Oran from Gibraltar and returned without refuelling, the short time available on patrol would not have been worth-while. From Algiers a return flight without refuelling, even with long-range tanks, was out of the question.

depend therefore on the scale of air attack that the carrier-borne fighters could be reasonably expected to tackle. This fixed the eastward limit at about Bône, and so, although it was highly desirable to forestall the enemy in Tunisia, it was accepted at this stage that Bizerta and Tunis would have to be captured by an advance overland rather than by an assault from the sea. The possibility of using airborne troops to seize these places had not yet been raised.

At first sight, then, it seemed simple enough to fix where the landings should take place—the limits would be Bône in the east and Casablanca in the west. But in between lay Algiers and Oran, important ports and centres of influence with good airfields near by, and there were not enough American troops or British and American ships and landing-craft for landings in more than three areas in all. This was what made it so difficult to agree on a plan, and for four weeks proposals and counter-proposals shuttled to and fro between Washington and London to the embarrassment of General Eisenhower and his staff.[1]

At this time the U.S.C.O.S. were particularly anxious about the security of the expedition's communications. They did not like the idea of routeing many of their ships through the Straits of Gibraltar, which, they felt, would be like putting one's head in a bag. The necessity of ensuring that America's first large-scale operation of war should be a success precluded the taking of too many risks. The U.S.C.O.S. wanted no rash adventures. There were plenty of voices in Washington ready to foster these feelings—those, for example, who disliked 'Torch' because it was a peripheral operation and not an attack on Germany, and those whose war was first and foremost against Japan. At first, therefore, the U.S.C.O.S. favoured landings at Casablanca, Oran, and Algiers, but cut out Algiers when it appeared that the resources available were too few for even three areas. The B.C.O.S. had the vital importance of reaching Tunisia rather more constantly in mind. If the Germans got there first in strength they might rob the Allies of the potential gains of the whole operation. The effect on Spain and on the French and native population in North and West Africa would be disastrous. The B.C.O.S. recognized some risk to the sea communications, but the naval view was that the enemy could probably not close the Straits of Gibraltar any more than he had closed the Straits of Dover. Moreover, there was the unwelcome fact (mentioned on page 119) that the surf on the Atlantic coast would, after October, permit a landing to be made on only one day in five.

The First Sea Lord and the Chief of the Air Staff favoured

---

[1] A full account of these discussions is given in Michael Howard: *Grand Strategy*, Volume IV.

simultaneous landings at Bône, Algiers, and Oran, but the C.I.G.S., anxious to have more port capacity and impressed by the air threat from Sardinia and Sicily, preferred to see the forces earmarked for Bône augmented as necessary and used at Casablanca. General Eisenhower and his planning staff agreed with the First Sea Lord and the Chief of the Air Staff but like them wanted more forces to be found in order to widen the front and land at Bône, Algiers, Oran and Casablanca. The difference in the American and British point of view towards French Africa as a theatre of operations had made it difficult to reach agreement on the objectives. And now here was General Eisenhower favouring Bône, and the C.I.G.S. Casablanca.

The B.C.O.S. and General Eisenhower were unanimous, however, in regarding a landing at Algiers as essential if the enemy was to be prevented from establishing himself in Tunisia; the U.S.C.O.S., on the other hand, placed first emphasis on having secure sea communications with North-West Africa. But the will to agree existed, and gradually, with help from the customary personal exchanges between Prime Minister and President, ideas grew closer. By 6th September a compromise had been found—simultaneous landings at Casablanca, Oran and Algiers but not at Bône (nor at Philippeville, which had joined the list of possibles). Enough Combat Loaded Transports to lift in all 10,000 men were to be withdrawn from the Oran and Casablanca forces to form the nucleus of an Algiers force; the balance to be made up with British troops. Escorts and landing-craft were just sufficient for these adjustments. The all-American aspect of the assault at Algiers was surrendered, but as all the warships inside the Mediterranean were to be British this deception would, in any case, disappear with daylight.

The plan issued on 20th September provided for landings on the Atlantic coast of Morocco and, inside the Mediterranean, at a number of beaches on either side of Oran and Algiers. All the troops landed in Morocco and at Oran were to be American; those at Algiers half American and half British. After seizing the initial objectives, which included in each case the port and neighbouring airfields, the Morocco and Oran forces were to join hands to form the American Fifth Army, ready to meet a German threat through Spain or trouble from Spanish Morocco.[1] The forces at Algiers, on the other hand, were to be turned by the wave of a wand into the (British) First Army, ready to move eastward towards Tunisia. Obviously, everything depended on the attitude of the French,

---

[1] In Spanish Morocco there were 130,000 troops of uneven quality.

particularly at Algiers. Plans had to be as flexible as possible to meet anything from full-scale opposition to mere token defence or even positive co-operation. These conditions however called for two different ways of stowing stores and equipment, neither of which could be altered once the convoy had sailed. Ships were therefore loaded as if full-scale opposition would be met, and the disadvantages that would arise if a rapid eastward advance proved possible had to be accepted.

All the troops for Algiers and Oran were to sail from the United Kingdom; the Royal Navy would be responsible for their transport and for all naval operations within the Mediterranean. The troops for Morocco were to come direct from America; the U.S. Navy would be responsible for their transport and for all naval operations off the west coast of Morocco. Planning for the Moroccan landings had necessarily to be done in Washington.

The total Assault Forces (Eastern, Central and Western) numbered about 65,000. The Eastern (Algiers) Assault Force was composed of the 39th and 168th U.S. Regimental Combat Teams (9,000), the 11th and 36th British Brigade Groups (9,000), and the 1st and 6th Commandos (2,000) of both American and British troops.[1] Troops, equipment, and stores were to be transported from the United Kingdom in 15 L.S.I., including 4 American Combat Loaders, and 16 merchant ships. The force was charged first with seizing the port of Algiers and the airfields at Blida and Maison Blanche. To give the impression that the enterprise was wholly American it was to be commanded initially by Major-General Charles W. Ryder, U.S. Army, who was to hand over at a suitable moment to Lieut.-General K. A. N. Anderson, commander designate of the (British) 1st Army. General Anderson was to thrust eastward to capture the port of Bougie and the airfield at Djidjelli, and then advance into Tunisia.

The Central (Oran) Assault Force was composed of the 16th, 18th and 26th U.S. Regimental Combat Teams (13,500), a Combat Command from the 1st U.S. Armoured Division (4,500) with 180 tanks, and the 1st Ranger Battalion (500).[2] It was to be transported from the United Kingdom in fifteen L.S.I. Major-General Lloyd R. Fredendall was to be in command and his first task was to capture Oran and the airfields of Tafaraoui and La Senia. Here the follow-up troops were American.

The Western (Moroccan) Assault Force, commanded by Major-General George S. Patton, comprised five Regimental Combat

---

[1] A Regimental Combat Team was roughly equivalent to a British infantry brigade group.
[2] This Combat Command was roughly equivalent to a British armoured brigade group. Rangers were the equivalent of British commando troops.

Teams (22,500), one Armoured Combat Team of two battalions (2,000) with 250 tanks. Its passage from the United States would be made in American ships escorted by the U.S. Navy, the whole commanded by Rear-Admiral H. Kent Hewitt. If the surf on the coast of Morocco was too heavy to make landings on D day possible, and the French attitude precluded using the ports, the Western Assault Force, after waiting several days in the offing for conditions to improve, would enter the Mediterranean and land at a point between Oran and the eastern border of Spanish Morocco. To counter possible German or Spanish action from Spanish Morocco before the American forces from Oran and French Morocco were securely installed, a force was held in England ready to be landed in the Tangier-Ceuta area. This force continued to be held in readiness until February 1943.

The movements of such numbers of men and their equipment, vehicles, and supplies across thousands of miles of sea made unprecedented demands on the Allied Fleets and Merchant Navies.[1] The necessary warships could only be provided by drawing heavily on the Home Fleet, by reducing the Atlantic escort forces, and by suspending convoys to North Russia and those between the United Kingdom and the South Atlantic. So far as merchant ships were concerned, the transports, store-ships, and auxiliaries of all sorts which had to be taken out of normal circulation seriously upset the Allied shipping programme throughout the world. The United States could give little direct help beyond providing the merchant ships and escorts for the Moroccan landings. However, it was hoped that by January 1943 the whole of North Africa from the Atlantic to Port Said—with the probable exception of Spanish Morocco—would be in Allied hands and this would give great relief to shipping.

The Royal Navy and United States Navy between them would provide surface escort and cover for convoys on passage, and cover and support for the assaults. Within the Mediterranean, Force 'H', commanded by Vice-Admiral Sir Neville Syfret and made up to three capital ships, three carriers, three cruisers and seventeen destroyers, was to prevent the Italian and French Fleets from interfering. The warships attached to each Assault Convoy would be powerful enough to deal with French ships based on Oran and Algiers. An oiling force of two tankers with their own escort would enable ships to fuel without returning to Gibraltar. Two British cruisers and three destroyers (Force 'G') were to cruise to the south of the Azores to give additional cover to the Moroccan landings.

The Royal Navy's task would not be finished when the army

---

[1] It was 2,760 sea miles from the Clyde to Algiers as the assault convoys were routed. Assault convoys from the U.S.A. to Morocco steamed about 4,500 miles.

and air forces were established ashore. It was to continue to supply and support them, in particular during the hoped-for rapid advance of the 1st Army into Tunisia. In co-operation with the R.A.F. and U.S.A.A.F. the Navy would aim at cutting the enemy's communications across the narrow Sicilian Straits. In addition there would be a long succession of build-up and homeward-bound convoys which would need escorts, both in the Mediterranean and outside.

The circumstances in which the Allied air forces came to be grouped in two separate commands, each directly under General Eisenhower, were described on page 113. The Eastern Air Command, formed on 1st November from No. 333 Group, R.A.F., was to support the Algiers Assault Force, while the Western Air Command—i.e. the United States Twelfth Air Force—would support the Oran and Morocco Assault Forces. The boundary between Air Commands was a line north and south through Cape Tenes. At first the headquarters of both Commands would be at Gibraltar.

As the landings could only be supported by carrier-borne aircraft, it was essential to seize French airfields and fly in shore-based fighters as quickly as possible. From Gibraltar 160 fighters were to fly in to Oran, 160 to Casablanca, and 90 to Algiers, within three days of the landings. The initial total of Allied aircraft of all kinds depended not only on the number of suitable squadrons available in the United States and United Kingdom, but on the speed with which cased fighters could be erected at Gibraltar and passed through that bottle-neck. In the case of aircraft flown in from the United Kingdom, a ruling factor would be the ground crews, fuel, stores, equipment and motor transport for which shipping and unloading berths could be found. The planned build-up in all types of aircraft to be reached after seven weeks was 1,244 (including 282 reserve aircraft) in the Western Air Command and 454 in the Eastern.[1] Between them these aircraft were to provide cover for ships, troops, and shore bases, and anti-submarine patrols for convoys. They would also provide air support for the land operations which were to follow the assault phase. Once suitable bases had been secured, the strategic air forces—principally American—were to be built up to attack Axis installations that might have sprung up in Spain, and other targets in the Mediterranean area.

From the time the Assault Convoys sailed until $D+4$ the co-

---

[1] The Orders of Battle showing the British and American air formations and squadrons available to support 'Torch', together with the types and roles of the aircraft used, are at Appendix 8.

ordination of all operations by general and photographic reconnaissance aircraft to meet Naval needs was to be the responsibility of the A.O.C.-in-C. Coastal Command. Photographic reconnaissance of Dakar was to be undertaken from Gambia; of Casablanca, Oran and Algiers from Gibraltar; of Toulon from the U.K.; and of the Italian ports and Tunis, Bizerta, Bône and Philippeville from Malta. Within the Mediterranean and in the Atlantic as far south as the Cape Verde Islands an elaborate system of patrols would keep watch for Axis and French warships. Anti-submarine patrols and fighter cover for the Assault Convoys from the U.K. were to be provided by Home-based aircraft of Coastal Command to the limit of their range, while long-range aircraft lent by Bomber Command, R.A.F., and by the Eighth Air Force, U.S.A.A.F., were to strengthen the anti-submarine patrols in the Bay of Biscay. The Assault Convoys were routed too far west to remain under the protection of U.K.-based aircraft; carrier-borne aircraft would therefore have to be used for this task until the convoys came within range of aircraft from Gibraltar. Helped by American flying-boats based at Freetown, aircraft from Gibraltar would also cover the convoys from the U.S.A. as they approached the Moroccan coast. Initially no squadrons other than those at Gibraltar would be available as a striking force to attack enemy surface vessels; this would be a further task for the squadrons already there, until others could be established in North Africa for the purpose. Aircraft from Gibraltar were also to drop propaganda leaflets over Casablanca, Oran and Algiers on D day.

Early in October two additions were made to the plan, both for action on D day. The first was for seizing the Oran airfields—Tafaraoui and La Senia—by American parachute troops flown all the way from England. Air Marshal Welsh strongly opposed this project, and would have preferred to see the limited number of transport aircraft and all the available British and American parachute and airborne troops given the task of seizing the airfields at Bône, Tunis, and Bizerta to forestall a build-up of enemy forces in Tunisia. He suggested that paratroops should arrive at Algiers in the first sea convoy, the transport aircraft being flown direct from the U.K. to the Algiers airfields as soon as these were secured. General Anderson and Admiral Burrough (the Eastern Naval Task Force Commander) supported this suggestion because it seemed the only way of getting to Tunis and Bizerta before the Germans, whose best reply to the Allied landings would be to move air units to Tunisia and then ferry troops across in transport aircraft. General Eisenhower, however, decided to stick to his plan for first using his airborne resources to help capture the airfields at Oran, but intimated that thereafter he would give first consideration to operations to further a rapid advance eastward.

The other addition was for the use of warships to make frontal attacks on the ports of Oran and Algiers. However swift and successful the landings on the neighbouring beaches might be, troops could not hope to reach the ports in time to prevent sabotage and scuttling if the French were so minded. At Algiers the direct attack was to be made by two British destroyers, and at Oran by two American cutters manned by the Royal Navy. At each place the intention was to force the boom and put ashore parties, predominantly American, to capture the port intact.

For assaults within the Mediterranean on the scale intended there were not enough British and American forces in the U.K. trained in combined operations. As many as possible were therefore rushed through a programme of training in the west of Scotland, handicapped by the need to overhaul and conserve the landing-craft already in use, and to assemble and work up the many craft which continued to arrive from the U.S.A. up to the last moment.

The immense and complex movement by sea, which was to involve some 370 merchant ships and over 300 warships, began on 2nd October (six days before the final version of the plan was issued) with the sailing of the first of six advance convoys from the U.K. to Gibraltar. These comprised colliers, tankers, ammunition ships, cased petrol carriers, and all the various auxiliaries needed to service the warships and assault forces. Aircraft for erection at Gibraltar were among the important items carried. One advance convoy consisted of only one ship—a liner carrying signal and radar ratings and additional anti-aircraft gun crews for Gibraltar.

Between 22nd and 26th October the Assault Convoys left the Clyde and Loch Ewe. A slow convoy carrying vehicles, tanks, equipment and stores sailed first, followed four days later by a fast convoy carrying troops. Many of the escorting warships stayed with these convoys to take part with them in the landings; other warships were to join before D day. The Assault Convoys carrying the American Forces for the Morocco landings sailed in their several groups from Portland (Maine) and Norfolk (Virginia) around 23rd October. They totalled 38 transports and store-ships and 56 escorts, including battleships, aircraft-carriers, and cruisers.

It was an anxious time for the Admiralty, who well knew how quickly a large number of U-boats could concentrate in the path of the expedition if the enemy had guessed our intentions. Good fortune, however, attended the ocean passages. Between 26th

October and 3rd November the enemy received five reports (four from U-boats and one from a Focke-Wulf aircraft) of warships and convoys on southerly courses, but failed to deduce that anything unusual was afoot. Two U-boats were sunk by patrolling aircraft, and a number of other U-boats to the west of Gibraltar drew away to attack, with considerable success, a mercantile convoy homeward bound from Freetown as it was passing across the front of the approaching Assault Convoys, which slipped through in safety. On 4th November, some 300 and 400 miles west of Gibraltar, the Slow and Fast Assault Convoys from the U.K. split into their Algiers and Oran sections.

We have referred to the tasks of R.A.F. Coastal Command in photographic and sea reconnaissance and anti-submarine patrols. There was another preliminary to the landings, carried out this time by R.A.F. Bomber Command. Targets in Northern Italy had been attacked in June and August 1940, in September 1941, and in April 1942, principally to bring home to the Italian people what the Prime Minister called the severity of war, and to hamper the war effort. On the night of 22nd/23rd October, with the object of pinning down Italian fighters and A.A. guns to the protection of the 'industrial triangle'—Genoa, Turin, Milan—Bomber Command began a new series of attacks lasting on and off for seven weeks. By 8th November Milan had been bombed once by day and once by night, causing damage to industrial property and dislocation to the railway. At Genoa, which by then had had four visits by night, damage was done to the port, industrial buildings, the railway, and to the *Augustus*—one of the two liners being reconstructed as an aircraft-carrier. A raid on Turin during the night 28th/29th November was the occasion of a splendid feat of valour and endurance. Flight-Sergeant R. H. Middleton, R.A.A.F., of No. 149 Squadron, R.A.F., though desperately wounded, contrived to fly his shattered aircraft back to England, enabling most of his aircrew to land safely by parachute. Then the aircraft, petrol exhausted, crashed, killing Middleton and two comrades who had chosen to stay by him. Flight-Sergeant Middleton was awarded a posthumous V.C.

An attempt by Malta's Wellingtons on the night of 7th/8th November to attack two airfields in Sardinia with delayed action bombs was frustrated by the weather, but on each of the next three nights they succeeded in finding and bombing them.

In deciding to occupy French Africa the Allied governments had set the future course of the war—a course which could not have been followed in 1942 had there been no British base at Gibraltar.

The air plan for 'Torch' depended very largely on Gibraltar's one airstrip—exposed though it was to Spanish guns and hostile bombers. Large numbers of fighters, including Spitfires for American squadrons, had been shipped to Gibraltar for assembly there. Additional R.A.F. technicians who had been sent to assist in the work of erection arrived by mistake in the Middle East! However, Air Vice-Marshal J. M. Robb, who had been specially appointed by the Chief of the Air Staff to control air preparations in, and air operations from, Gibraltar, drove everything ahead. With the assistance of troops of the garrison, the Royal Air Force at Gibraltar succeeded in assembling, and making serviceable, just in time, all the aircraft required for the opening stage of 'Torch'. By the early hours of 8th November over 350 aircraft were crammed wing-to-wing in all the available parking-space surrounding the runway, presenting an ideal target to an enemy.

The extension of the landing strip on the North Front at Gibraltar had been begun in 1941 to facilitate its use by British aircraft in transit between the U.K. and Egypt, and American aircraft between West Africa and the U.K. In March 1942 during the heavy bombing of Malta the work was speeded up to enable Wellingtons to take off with enough petrol to fly non-stop to Egypt. By 8th November 1942 the new runway, 150 yards wide, had been lengthened to 1,350 yards. The central width of 50 yards was for taking-off and landing; the remainder was designed for taxiing, but for the 'Torch' operations it provided invaluable space for assembly and parking of squadrons. Already the runway projected nearly 400 yards into Algeciras Bay, and work was in progress to extend it to 1,800 yards. The material used was scree from the north face of the Rock and spoil from the tunnels.[1] By the time 'Torch' began, every square yard of available space on the British part of the isthmus had been made ready to take dispersed aircraft.

But that was not the sum of Gibraltar's contributions to 'Torch'. Algeciras Bay had become the anchorage, none too secure, for all the various auxiliaries and small craft which had to be assembled before the assault forces passed into the Mediterranean. Fuel and water and many miscellaneous services had to be provided for this assembly as well as for many of the warships and some of the transports which would presently pass through the Straits. Vice-Admiral Sir F. Edwards-Collins, Flag Officer Commanding North Atlantic Station, was responsible for these arrangements. Luckily for the water supplies October's rainfall had been double the monthly average of the previous twenty-five years.

---

[1] Tunnelling Companies of the Royal Engineers and Royal Canadian Engineers were carrying out a big scheme of excavation for accommodation, storage and installations of all kinds.

The British Government had accepted the principle of placing the Governor and Commander-in-Chief (Lieut.-General F. N. Mason-MacFarlane) and the Flag and Air Officers Commanding at Gibraltar under General Eisenhower's control, and all the naval and air facilities there at his disposal, for operation 'Torch'.[1] Thus, besides being the administrative centre for the early stages of the whole expedition, Gibraltar became also the operational headquarters. It can be imagined what problems of communications and accommodation were involved. On 5th November General Eisenhower himself arrived by air.

From the Middle East came good news: the 8th Army had broken through at El Alamein and Rommel was in full retreat.

In mid-October General Mark Clark had flown to Gibraltar on a special mission. Mr. Murphy, in Algiers, had become convinced that Frenchmen in North Africa who favoured the Allies would co-operate more effectively if an officer of high rank could come to Africa for a clandestine meeting. Accordingly on 22nd October General Clark landed from the British submarine *P.219* near Cherchel, fifty miles west of Algiers, where he met Major-General Charles Mast, Chief of Staff of the French 19th Corps. Mast told him that if given four days warning he could guarantee there would be little resistance by army or air forces to an attempted military landing. He could also guarantee free entry into Bône. For the French Navy he could not speak, but he thought resistance would end after successful landings had taken place.

No change of plan was made as a result of this contact, which took place at great hazard to both parties. The result was encouraging, however, and led to the agreement of the distinguished General Giraud, with whom Mast was in secret communication, to escape from southern France and co-operate with the Allies.[2] On the night of 6th November *P.219* embarked General Giraud near Toulon, and transferred him to an R.A.F. Catalina in which he arrived at Gibraltar on the eve of D day. It was hoped that his great influence would encourage the many divergent factions in Africa if not to help the Allies at least not to hinder them. At first the General was very difficult and flatly refused to take part except as Supreme Commander, which, through a misunderstanding, he believed he was to be. However, on 8th November, after the landings had been announced and President Roosevelt had sent a message of profound

---

[1] For a full description of the control of the R.A.F. at Gibraltar at this time see S. W. Roskill: *The War at Sea*, Volume II (1957), pp. 359/360.

[2] Since his escape from a German fortress earlier in 1942, Giraud had been living in Unoccupied France.

friendship with France, General Giraud broadcast an appeal for support for the Allies.

Meanwhile a last minute complication had occurred which threatened to spoil Mr. Murphy's patient work and destroy all hope of French co-operation. Admiral Darlan, Commander-in-Chief of the French Armed Forces, had returned to France on 30th October after a tour of inspection in North Africa.[1] He left his son in hospital in Algiers apparently past the danger point of an attack of infantile paralysis. On 4th November, receiving word of a relapse, Darlan flew back to Algiers. Mr. Murphy had pinned great hopes on General Juin, the Commander-in-Chief of French Forces in North Africa, with whom he was intimate, but the Admiral's authority far surpassed that of any other French official in North Africa. His unexpected presence altered dramatically, and, so far as could be judged, greatly for the worse, the chances of French collaboration with the approaching Allied expedition.

The merchant ships and their escorts now nearing the Straits of Gibraltar from the west amounted to some 140 ships, which, in the $32\frac{1}{2}$ hours from 7.30 p.m. on the 5th to 4 a.m. on 7th November, were to pass through into the Mediterranean in their correct sequence and to an exact time-table. Many of the warships had to fuel at Gibraltar on the way. It says much for the planning in London and the organization at the Rock that before daylight on the 7th, Force 'H' and the Assault Convoys for Algiers and Oran were all steaming east well inside the Mediterranean. On passing the meridian of 3° W. the Naval Task Force Commanders took over their separate responsibilities, Rear-Admiral Sir Harold Burrough for the Algiers (or Eastern), Commodore T. H. Troubridge for the Oran (or Central) Force.[2] Outside, in the Atlantic, the Western Naval Task Force under Rear-Admiral Hewitt was approaching the Moroccan coast, on which the surf was reported to be breaking heavily.

The Axis Powers too had frequently reviewed their policy towards French Africa. Since November 1941 Hitler had been allowing the French to keep more men and equipment in Africa than was permitted by the Armistice. This he did against the wishes of the

---

[1] Jean Louis Xavier François Darlan: March 1937, Chief of Staff of the Navy; June 1940, Minister of the Navy in Pétain's Government; February 1941, Chief of the Government under Pétain; April 1942, on Laval's return to power, C.-in-C. of the Armed Forces.
[2] The term Naval Task Force included the Fast and Slow Sections of the Assault Convoy and the warships to escort and support them during the landings.

8. Left to Right: Air Chief Marshal Sir William Sholto Douglas, Rt. Hon. Winston S. Churchill, General Sir Alan Brooke. Cairo 1943.

9. General the Hon. Sir Harold Alexander, General Dwight D. Eisenhower.

10. Left to Right: Air Chief Marshal Sir Arthur Tedder, Brigadier-General Auby C. Strickland, Air Marshal Sir Arthur Coningham.

11. Air Vice-Marshal Harry Broadhurst.

12. Air Marshal Sir Arthur Coningham, General Sir Bernard Montgomery.

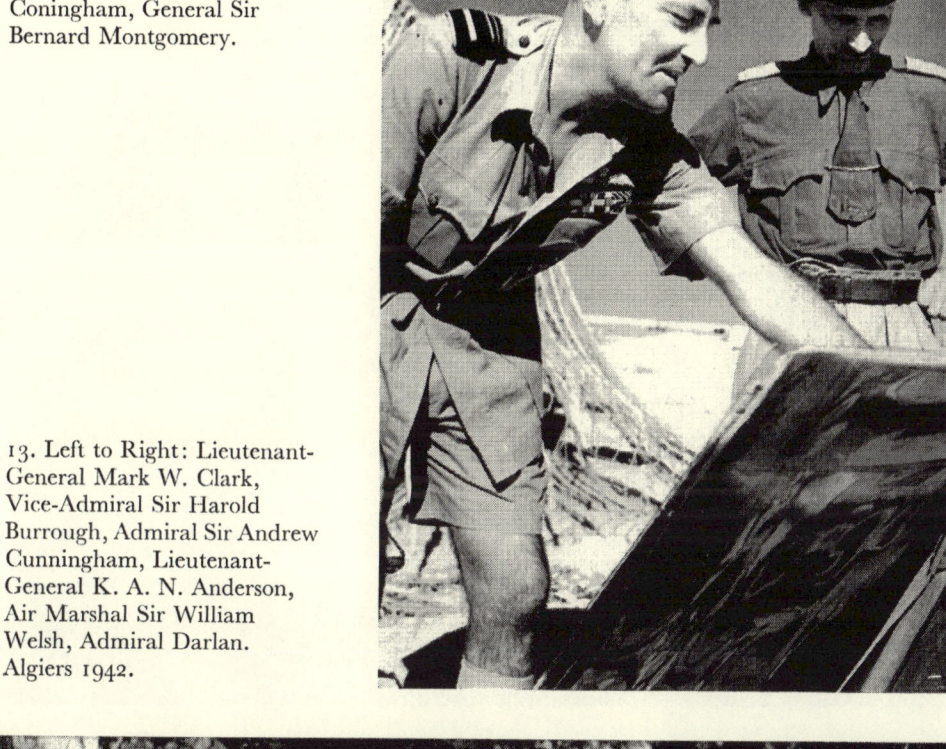

13. Left to Right: Lieutenant-General Mark W. Clark, Vice-Admiral Sir Harold Burrough, Admiral Sir Andrew Cunningham, Lieutenant-General K. A. N. Anderson, Air Marshal Sir William Welsh, Admiral Darlan. Algiers 1942.

14. Left to Right: Marshal Giovanni Messe, after surrender. Lieutenant-General Sir Bernard Freyberg, General Sir Bernard Montgomery.

15. Colonel-General Jürgen von Arnim, after surrender.

Italians, who had originally been given the right to determine the extent of the 'demilitarization, demobilization, and disarmament' in French colonial protectorates and mandated territories. Hitler hoped by these concessions to obtain the use of Tunisian harbours for the *Panzerarmee* and to enlist French help against the British. Right up to the day of the 'Torch' landings he seems to have clung to the belief that the French would vigorously resist any attempt by the Allies to occupy North Africa—a view certainly not held by the Italians—and he refused to take any counter-measures in advance for fear of setting up contrary reactions in the French. Nevertheless in April 1942 the Germans had discussed with the Italians the possibility of Allied landings being made in France, Spain, and north-west Africa, and Keitel warned Cavallero that Italy ought to have forces ready to advance into France in the event of a British invasion. At the same conference Hitler told Mussolini that if anything happened in Africa, Italy must be prepared to move not only into France but into Tunisia as well.

During October reports of Allied intentions to land in north-west Africa became more frequent and the Italians—not for the first time—pressed for counter-measures. They themselves had forces available in Italy, and also some small transports which had been held ready for the assault on Malta. But they would need the protection of the Italian Fleet, for which fuel was as short as ever. Nor was there enough aviation spirit for the large number of aircraft needed to hold down Malta and at the same time support a landing in Tunisia. On the 17th October *OKW's* view was that the Allies were preparing to land at Dakar. Landings in Morocco, especially on the Atlantic coast, were considered possible, in Algeria unlikely, and in Tunisia more unlikely still. *OKW* thought it a matter for the French, who would defend their colonial empire in their own nterests. It would be useful to hold Italian forces ready in western Libya, but they should not move into Tunisia until it was clear what the French intended to do, as it might, in *OKW's* opinion, drive the French 'into the arms of the Anglo-Saxons'. In view of the situation in other theatres no considerable reinforcements of German land, sea, or air forces in the Mediterranean could be expected, nor was it possible to supply the Italian Navy and Air Force with more fuel.

It seems that as late as 25th October the Germans interpreted information of an impending Allied operation in the Mediterranean as the preliminary to another Malta convoy. If, however, a landing were intended, Sardinia, Corsica, or even the south of France were looked upon as more likely objectives than North Africa. These views were based largely on the argument that the Allies would avoid a landing that would drive the French into Germany's arms.

On 4th November the exceptionally large concentrations of British naval forces and shipping reported at Gibraltar were still interpreted as a Malta convoy, especially as only a few landing-craft and not more than two transports had been reported.

In short, the Allies had successfully spread a number of false plans and kept their real intentions secret. Hitler, misled into expecting possible landings elsewhere and obsessed by his views on probable French reactions, took no precautionary measures in North Africa and dissuaded the Italians from taking any.

CHAPTER VI

'TORCH'—THE LANDINGS

(8th—13th November)

See Map 16

DURING daylight on 7th November, the Naval Task Forces in the Mediterranean (now numbering some 220 ships of all types) continued to steam eastward, the several groups adjusting position and making rendezvous to a rigid timetable. To preserve the appearance of being Malta-bound, the Fast and Slow Sections of the Oran Force remained as one convoy until, almost due north of their beaches, they split into nine groups for the final approach. In the case of the Algiers Force the run of the coastline enabled the Slow Section to make its approach independently and still appear to be making for Malta. Catalinas from Gibraltar and Fleet Air Arm fighters from the carriers provided anti-submarine patrols and fighter cover but could not entirely prevent enemy aircraft from shadowing, although these can have gleaned nothing about the expedition's destination.

About 5.30 a.m., some fifty miles east of Cartagena, the first casualty of operation 'Torch' occurred when the U.S. Combat Loaded Transport, *Thomas Stone*, in the Algiers Fast Section, was torpedoed and stopped.[1] There was just a chance that the troops she carried (2nd Battalion, 39th Regimental Combat Team) could still take part in the initial landings, so Captain O. R. Bennehoff U.S.N. disembarked 800 of them into his ship's landing-craft. There were delays, and it was dusk before they set off for Algiers, 155 miles away, led by the *Thomas Stone's* only escort—the British corvette *Spey*. This left the *Thomas Stone* unprotected until the destroyers *Wishart* and *Velox* arrived several hours later.

Force H, with the fuelling force under its lee, cruised to the south of the Balearics during the day, much as it was wont to do when covering a genuine Malta convoy. During the afternoon, while within sight of the Algiers Fast Assault Section, it came under bombing and torpedo attack from Ju.88s; the destroyer *Panther* was damaged by a near miss and had to return to Gibraltar. Warning of any movement of the Italian Fleet or of the French warships in

---

[1] It is not known whether the torpedo came from an aircraft or a U-boat.

Toulon could be expected from air reconnaissance or submarine reports. Malta was responsible for an air patrol between Sardinia and Sicily and for watching the Italian ports; Gibraltar for a patrol between the Spanish coast and the Straits of Bonifacio; and reconnaissance of Toulon was to be flown from the United Kingdom. In addition, three submarines of the 8th (Gibraltar) Flotilla were off Toulon with orders to report—but not to attack—French warships if they put to sea. Five submarines of this flotilla—three off Algiers and two off Oran—were acting as navigational beacons for the Assault Forces as they approached the coast. Submarines of the 10th (Malta) Flotilla, augmented by boats from the 1st Flotilla, were stationed north and south of the Messina Straits and on a patrol line stretching north-west from the western end of Sicily. Orders for the action to be taken if French ships were encountered had to be most carefully framed. Allied policy was to take no offensive action against French forces on land, sea, or air unless they had first taken definite hostile action. This had however to be modified to reduce the risk of being caught at a disadvantage.

Provided that his first duty of protecting the Assault Forces against attack by heavy surface ships permitted, Vice-Admiral Syfret was to bring Force H south to within some twenty miles of Algiers by daylight on D day. Here he would rendezvous with Force O, the cruisers *Sheffield* (Flag of Rear-Admiral C. H. J. Harcourt), *Scylla* and *Charybdis* and the carriers *Argus* and *Avenger* and five destroyers. Rear-Admiral A. L. St. G. Lyster, from his flagship *Victorious*, would then assume operational control of the carriers in both Forces in giving air support to the Algiers landings.

The warships and other vessels comprising the three Naval Task Forces and Force H are shown in the following table:

Footnotes for table on opposite page.

   (a) All the U.S. Combat Loaders, 8 of the British L.S.I., and the 3 L.S.T. were commissioned ships U.S.N. or R.N.
     (b) Detached to C.N.T.F.
     (c) Detached to E.N.T.F.
     (d) Designated Force O after Algiers Slow Section had arrived off the beaches.
     (e) Fuelling Force.

AIR AND SUBMARINE COVER

Operation 'Torch'—Maritime Forces Engaged

	Eastern Naval Task Force for Algiers (Vice-Admiral Burrough)	Central Naval Task Force for Oran (Commodore Troubridge)	Force H and fuelling force (Vice-Admiral Syfret)	Western Naval Task Force for Morocco (Rear-Admiral Hewitt, U.S.N.)
H.Q. Ships	Bulolo (Flag)	Largs (Broad Pennant)	—	—
Landing Ships Infantry (a)	11	15	—	—
Combat Loaders (a)	4	—	—	23
Landing Ships Tank (a)	—	3	—	—
Landing Ships Gantry	2	1	—	—
Mechanical Transport and other ships	16	28	—	8
Battleships and Battlecruisers	—	—	Duke of York (Flag) Renown Rodney (b)	Massachusetts Texas New York
Aircraft Carriers	Argus	—	Victorious (Flag) Formidable Furious (b)	Ranger
Escort Carriers	Avenger	Biter Dasher	—	Santee Sangamon Chenango Suwanee
	(d)			
Cruisers	Sheffield (Flag, Force O) Scylla Charybdis	Aurora Jamaica	Bermuda (c) Argonaut Sirius	Augusta (Flag) Wichita Tuscaloosa Philadelphia Savannah Brooklyn Cleveland
Monitors	1	—	—	—
A.A. Ships	3	2	—	—
Destroyers	13 (1 Polish)	13	17 (1 Dutch)	38
Cutters	—	2	—	—
Fleet Minesweepers	7	8	—	8
Sloops	3	2	—	—
Corvettes	4	6	1(e)	—
Trawlers (A/S and M/S)	8	8	4(e)	—
Minelayers	—	—	—	3
Seaplane Tender	—	—	—	1
Motor Launches	8	10	—	—
Submarines	3	2	—	4
Tankers	—	—	2(e)	5

Fleet Air Arm Aircraft Embarked

FORCE H

	Squadron		Aircraft
Victorious (R.A.A.):	No. 809	(6)	Fulmar P.R.
	No. 817	(9)	Albacore
	No. 832	(12)	Albacore
	No. 882	(11)	Martlet IV
	No. 884	(9)	Seafire IIC
Formidable:	No. 820	(6)	Albacore
	No. 885	(6)	Seafire IIC
	No. 888	(12)	Martlet II/IV
	No. 893	(12)	Martlet IV

CENTRAL TASK FORCE—ORAN AREA

	Squadron		Aircraft
Furious:	No. 801	(12)	Seafire IB/IIC
	No. 807	(12)	Seafire IB/IIC
	No. 822	(8)	Albacore
		(1)	Fulmar P.R.
Biter:	No. 800	(15)	Sea Hurricane IIC
	No. 833	(3)	Swordfish*
Dasher:	No. 804	(6)	Sea Hurricane IIB/C
	No. 891	(6)	Sea Hurricane IIB/C

EASTERN TASK FORCE—ALGIERS AREA

	Squadron		Aircraft
Argus:	No. 880	(12)	Seafire IIC
Avenger:	No. 802	(6)	Sea Hurricane IIC
	No. 833	(3)	Swordfish*
	No. 883	(6)	Sea Hurricane IIC

* Swordfish disembarked at Gibraltar for A/S patrols.

See Map 18

The troops forming the Eastern Assault Force were of the American 34th Infantry Division (Major-General Charles W. Ryder), comprising the 39th and 168th Regimental Combat Teams (R.C.T.) and the 11th and 36th Infantry Brigade Groups of the British 78th Division. The allotment of troops to Sectors is shown on Map 18.[1] Under command of 39th R.C.T. were five troops of the 1st Commando, and under command of 168th R.C.T. were the rest of

---

[1] One Sector was usually allotted to each assaulting formation, such as a brigade group or a regimental combat team. Each Sector was given a letter and a name. Individual beaches were designated by the Sector letter or name followed by a colour. For example, at Algiers there were two beaches in A Sector—Apples Green and Apples White.

Map 18

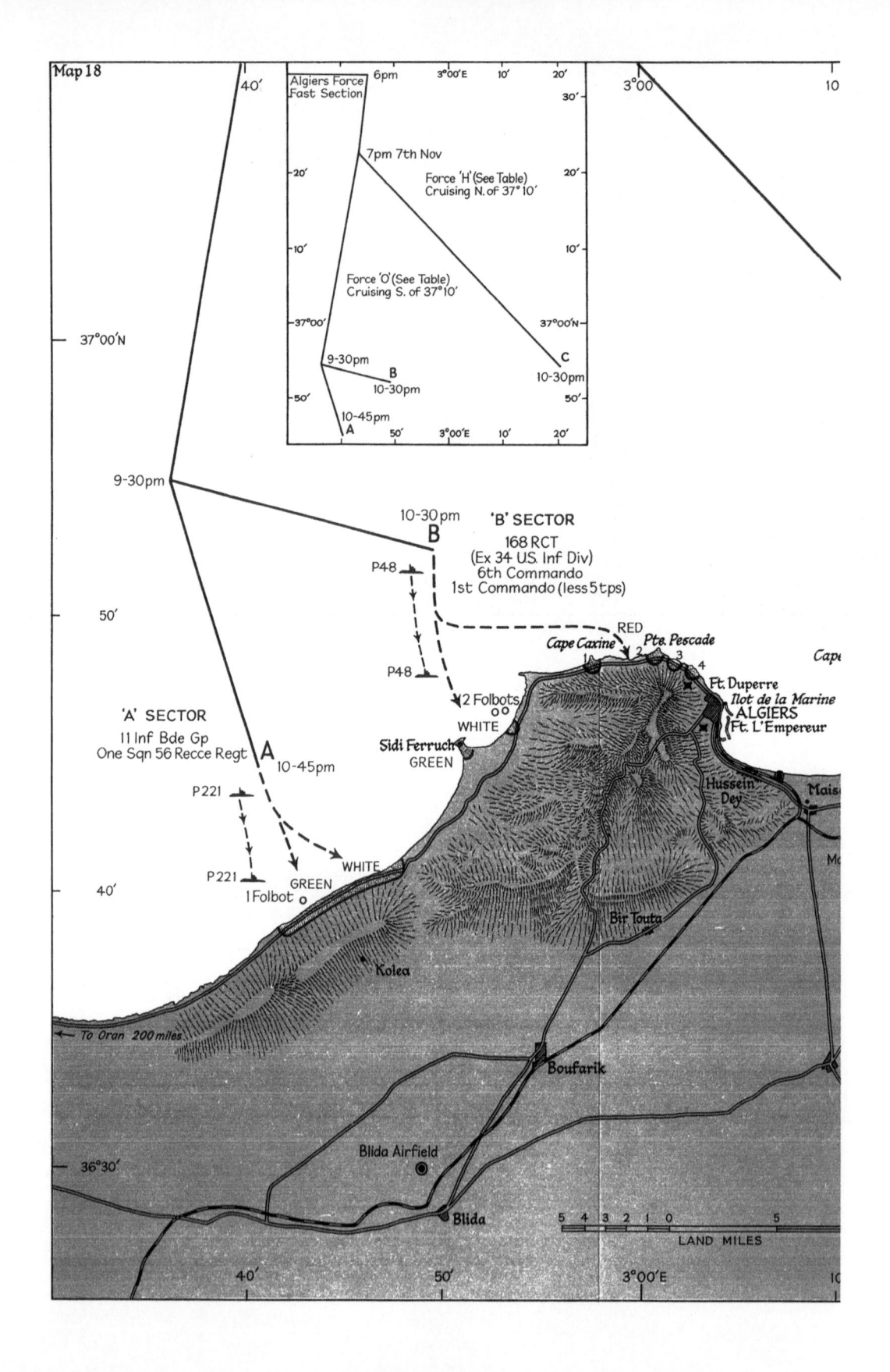

OPERATION 'TORCH'
The Assault on Algiers
Landings as intended....... ⇢
Inset shows tracks from 6pm 7th Nov.

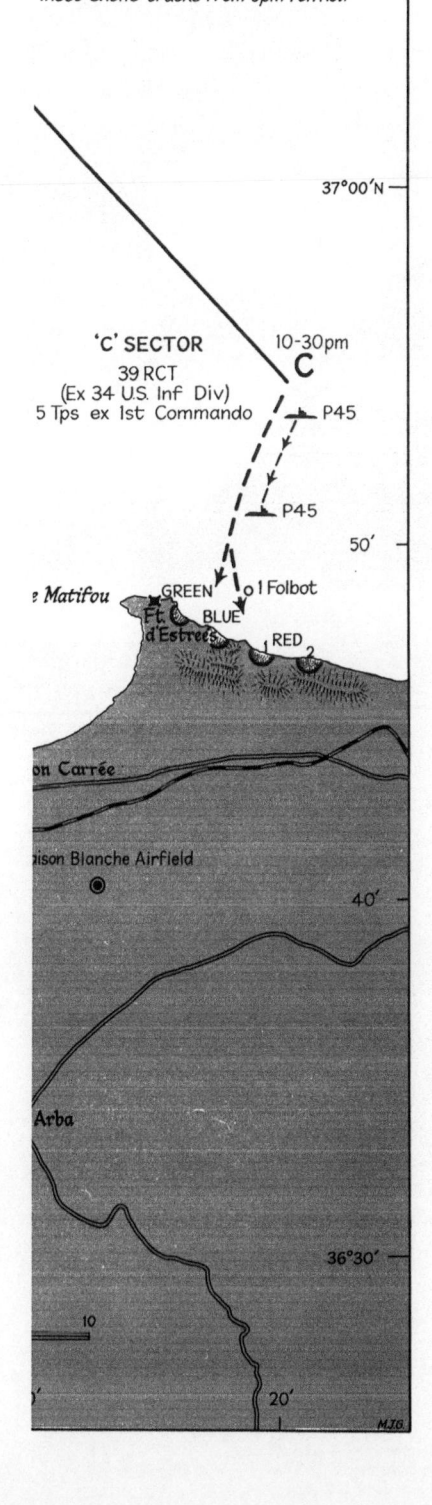

'C' SECTOR
39 RCT
(Ex 34 U.S. Inf Div)
5 Tps ex 1st Commando

10-30pm
C
P45
P45

Matifou GREEN o 1 Folbot
Ft. BLUE
d'Estrees RED

on Carrée

aison Blanche Airfield

Arba

LANDING GROUPS AND ESCORTS

'A' SECTOR

Landing Group	Escort
3 L.S.I.'s	1 A.A. Ship
1 L.S.G.	2 Sloops
4 M/T Ships	2 Corvettes
	3 Trawlers
	3 ML's

'B' SECTOR

Landing Group	Escort
1 H.Q. Ship	4 Destroyers
7 L.S.I.'s	1 A.A. Ship
9 M/T Ships	1 Sloop ✴
1 L.S.G	2 Corvettes ✴
	3 Minesweepers
	3 Trawlers
	3 ML's

'C' SECTOR

Landing Group	Escort
3 Combat Loaders (US)	1 A A Ship
1 L.S.I.	2 Destroyers
1 M/T Ship	4 Minesweepers
	2 Trawlers
	2 M.L.'s

✴ Also used with 'C' SECTOR

the 1st and the whole of the 6th Commando.[1] All these formations and units were to make the assault landings, except 36th Brigade Group (Brigadier A. L. Kent-Lemon) which formed the Floating Reserve. The Division was assault-stowed in L.S.I. or Combat Loaders, from which landing-craft would carry the troops ashore. The assault was to be controlled from the headquarter ship H.M.S. *Bulolo*, which carried Vice-Admiral Sir Harold Burrough, Major-General Ryder, and Air Commodore G. M. Lawson. Major-General V. Evelegh, of the 78th Division, whose operational command was not to begin until later, was also on board.

The plan for the assault was briefly as follows. On the right 11th Infantry Brigade Group (Brigadier E. E. E. Cass) was to land on two beaches in A Sector. After consolidating a beach-head it was to capture the airfield at Blida, and then secure the Bir Touta area, from which several roads could be controlled. In the centre, in B Sector, the 168th R.C.T. was to land on White beach, a few miles from the Sidi Ferruch promontory. Simultaneously 1st Commando was to land on the promontory itself (Green beach) and seize Fort Sidi Ferruch. The 168th R.C.T. was to advance east and capture Fort L'Empereur, overlooking Algiers, and the town itself. To guard the left flank of this advance the 6th Commando was to scramble ashore at four points, scarcely to be described as beaches, between Cape Caxine and Algiers, and seize, to begin with, certain of the coast defences. In C Sector the 39th R.C.T. and five troops of 1st Commando were to land near Cape Matifou. Their main tasks were to seize the airfields at Maison Blanche and Hussein Dey, and the locality named Maison Carrée. Until some airfields were captured the whole burden of air cover and air support would fall on the few carrier-borne aircraft of the Fleet Air Arm.

On the afternoon of 7th November General Ryder repeated the earlier forecasts that French army and air units would resist only slightly but that the naval forces would fight. Landings on the beaches were to continue only until the port of Algiers had been captured or had surrendered—one or the other was expected within twenty-four hours. The assault-force was equipped at 'assault scale'—that is, it landed with everything needed to enable it to fight up to a distance of about ten miles from its beach maintenance area. The next administrative step would be to land additional equipment and supplies to bring the force to 'light scale'—that is, roughly, everything needed for operating at a distance of thirty miles from the maintenance area for a period of three weeks. It has been seen that when 'Torch' was being planned no one knew whether the expedition would meet a friendly, neutral, or hostile reception. The Allied

---

[1] These Commandos were *ad hoc* units of British and American troops; each had about 620 British and 230 American officers and men.

force was therefore organized, equipped, and stowed with the main purposes of landing, seizing the principal ports and airfields, and setting up secure bases even if the French fought hard. The result was to handicap the execution of any but these main purposes.

At 6 p.m. on 7th November, one hour after sunset, Admiral Burrough wheeled the Fast Section of the Algiers Force to due south.[1] An hour later the ships for C Sector—three U.S. Combat Loaders, one Dutch L.S.I., one M.T. Ship, and their escorts—parted company to make for the disembarking positions off C beaches. Soon afterwards the remaining ships formed into two columns until at 9.30 p.m. these too diverged, three L.S.I. carrying the 11th Infantry Brigade Group making for A Sector, and seven L. S. I. (168th R.C.T., Commandos, and Floating Reserve) with the *Bulolo* in company, altering 90 degrees to port for B Sector. In each Sector contact was made with the beacon submarine and within a few minutes of the appointed times the three groups stopped. Each was six or seven miles off shore and two miles to seaward of its beacon submarine. There was a moderate north-east breeze, slight sea, clear sky, and good visibility. The moon was new, and the coast lights were burning. Escorts now began an endless chain anti-submarine patrol to seaward of the ships and craft. While landing-craft were being lowered, manned, and assembled, a westerly set caused ships to drift as much as five miles in the first hour and a half.

The composition of 11th Infantry Brigade Group was typical of a British assault formation.[2] The assaulting battalions were the 1st Surreys and the Northamptons, accompanied by artillery observation parties. The assault flights comprised 45 landing-craft of various

---

[1] Times (G.M.T.) on night 7th/8th November, 7th: Sunset 1702; 8th: H hour 0100, Sunrise 0632, Moon New, High Water 0158.

[2] 11th Infantry Brigade Group: Brigade H.Q. (including Signals, Defence Platoon, Light Aid Detachment); 2nd Bn Lancashire Fusiliers; Ist Bn East Surrey Regiment; 5th Bn Northamptonshire Regiment; B Squadron, 56th Reconnaissance Regiment; 132nd Field Regiment R.A.; 84th Light A.A. Battery R.A.; 237th Field Company R.E.; 11th Field Ambulance; Recovery Section 11th Brigade Ordnance Company; Platoon 11th Brigade Company R.A.S.C.; Section 78th Divisional Provost Company; Detachment 78th Divisional Signals; Detachment 78th Division Field Hygiene Section.

(It is interesting here to recall that the Lancashire Fusiliers had played a famous part in the landing at Gallipoli in the First World War, and that the East Surreys in their very early history had served as Marines.)

The following also landed with the assault flights: Assistant Beachmaster and party, naval and army beach signals parties, detachments of a Dock Operating Company, a Mechanical Equipment Company and an Army Field Company (all of the R.E.), and parties concerned with engineer stores and general transport.

The 'Landing Table' of 11th Infantry Brigade Group is an example of the detail in which a landing was arranged in advance. The document is the army part of the 'working programme' of the landing. It consists of 28 typed pages listing 422 'serials'. Each serial specifies a party of troops and equipment, and the list is arranged in the order in which each serial was expected to be required on shore.

Broadly speaking, arrangements of this sort governed the loading and landing of every man and item of equipment and stores from those in the assault formations right through to the build-up formations.

types. Loading and assembling them began shortly after 10.45 p.m. and at 11.50 p.m. they set out for the beaches, led by motor-launches in which were special pilot officers from the beacon submarine, who had, for security reasons, been able to do no more than survey the coast through the submarine's periscope. A folbot, whose crew had had one clandestine rehearsal inshore, was stationed a few hundred yards off Apples Green beach as a final check on the accuracy of the landfall. Support Landing Craft accompanied the assault waves, and destroyers crept up behind to add their fire if needed. The assault waves touched down almost exactly at the appointed time—1 a.m. on 8th November. Then began the ferry service. Brigadier Cass and his staff landed at 2.30 a.m. and the whole programme went well, though on Apples White beach it was delayed by heavy surf.

In B Sector things did not go so smoothly. A pilot officer was not transferred from the submarine to the pilot launch, and there were other avoidable mistakes; perhaps the westerly set caused more confusion than in A Sector. As a result a part of 168th R.C.T. bound for B beaches was set ashore on Apples White and on other beaches south-west of Sidi Ferruch. The Commandos were very late in getting away from their ship because of difficulties in assembling the landing-craft. Some of these lost touch with their escorting motor launch and many landed their troops on the wrong beaches. Six landing-craft came under fire from Ilot de la Marine and four were sunk.

In C Sector there was some confusion about the beaches to be used owing to delay in receiving an amending order. As a result men for Blue and Red beaches all landed on Blue beach. Part of the 1st Commando, which was to attack the batteries on Cape Matifou, was landed on the correct beach, but nearly two hours late.

Fortunately there was almost no opposition except from Ilot de la Marine, and mistakes were soon made good. Ships of the Slow Section joined the L.S.I. in all three sectors around 1 a.m., and well before 4.30 a.m. the several groups moved in closer to the beaches and anchored. Minesweepers, sweeping ahead of the merchantmen, found no mines, and the ferry service was soon working satisfactorily. Twice before daylight Cape Matifou battery opened fire but was subdued by H.M.S. *Zetland*, the destroyer supporting C Sector.

Meanwhile, at 1.30 a.m., Admiral Burrough had released the destroyers *Broke* and *Malcolm*, carrying a landing-party of the American 135th Infantry, to make the frontal attack on Algiers which it was hoped would prevent scuttling and sabotage within the port. At 3.45 *Broke*, followed by *Malcolm*, approached the southern entrance but could not distinguish it with certainty against the black background of hills and the dazzle of searchlights and gun flashes. At the third attempt *Malcolm* was heavily hit and had to withdraw. Dawn was breaking when *Broke* at last found the entrance right ahead, clove through the boom at high speed, swung to port, and disembarked her landing-party on a nearby quay. The landing-party soon secured the power station and oil installations but were then pinned down by machine-gun fire. Twice during the next few hours *Broke* shifted berth to shelter from fire of field guns and harbour batteries. Eventually, around 9.20, having been more than four hours in the harbour, she came under accurate fire from a battery to which she was unable to reply. She had to withdraw hurriedly, leaving 250 of the landing-party ashore. On the way out she was hit repeatedly. Unhappily the extent of her damage was under-estimated, and next day, in tow in a rising sea, she sank at a time when she might have been safely berthed in Algiers harbour.

Shortly after midnight R.A.F. aircraft began taking off from Gibraltar to add to the anti-submarine protection in the areas of the landings. By 6 a.m. Fleet Air Arm aircraft from the carriers *Argus* and *Avenger* were patrolling the beaches, while others, reinforced by aircraft from the Fleet carriers *Victorious* and *Formidable*, patrolled above the airfields at Maison Blanche and Blida. At 7.30 a.m. the pre-arranged signal to be sent when the airfield at Maison Blanche had been captured had not been received at Gibraltar, but Air Marshal Welsh decided to accept the risk of despatching his land-based fighters although they had not enough fuel to return. At 8 a.m. the first squadron—Hurricanes of No. 43 Squadron R.A.F.—took off for Maison Blanche followed two hours later by the Spitfires of No. 81. Shortly after 10 a.m. the Hurricanes landed at Maison Blanche. By this time it was known at Gibraltar that the airfield was in American hands, which meant that R.A.F. Servicing Commandos and squadrons of the R.A.F. Regiment accompanying the American troops would soon be available to maintain the fighter squadrons on patrol and provide some A.A. protection for the airfield for the rest of the day. More Spitfires (of Nos. 154 and 242 Squadrons) were ordered off from Gibraltar to join Nos. 43 and 81 Squadrons, and the first R.A.F. Wings (Nos. 322 and 323) arrived at Maison Blanche that day. It had not been possible to land the W/T or mobile radar sets as quickly as intended and a Fleet Air Arm Walrus was therefore flown to Maison Blanche and used as a W/T Station for communication with Gibraltar via the Headquarters Ship *Bulolo*, which also provided early warning and the main fighter control facilities. An R/T pack-set mounted on the roof of the airfield headquarters provided local control, and Verey light signals were used in the absence of an airfield telephone system.

Operations on land had gone smoothly on the whole. The 1st Surreys and the Northamptons met no opposition and the rest of 11th Infantry Brigade Group completed its landing shortly before noon. Part of 1st Commando had landed in B Sector as planned, and had occupied Fort Sidi Ferruch where General Mast welcomed them and formally surrendered the fort to Lieut-Colonel T. H. Trevor, but warned him that the French at Blida might fight. As it happened an odd situation came about at Blida. Colonel Trevor with three Commando troops went there in French transport, and at about 8 a.m. began to parley with the local French commander. At 9.30 a.m. a detachment of the Lancashire Fusiliers arrived, just as Lieutenant B. H. C. Nation R.N., leader of a flight of Martlets from H.M.S. *Victorious*, who had seen white handkerchiefs fluttering on the ground, landed and accepted from the French air commander a written agreement that Allied aircraft might land. Later some detachments of American troops also arrived. Some of the French troops in the neighbourhood were friendly, but not all, and the possibility of a clash lasted until the 10th. By nightfall on the 8th the positions of the other main units of 11th Infantry Brigade Group were: 1st Surreys and C Squadron, 56th Reconnaissance Regiment at Kolea; Northamptons and 132nd Field Regiment at and to the north-east of Bir Touta. In the late afternoon the 6th Battalion The Royal West Kent Regiment from the Floating Reserve landed as a reinforcement, but proved to be unwanted owing to good progress in the negotiations with the French. The battalion re-embarked on the morning of the 9th.

In B Sector there were some troubles. The 6th Commando had a difficult landing, as has been mentioned, and one of its objectives, Fort Duperré, showed fight. However the garrison, after a bombing by naval Albacores, surrendered to three troops of Commandos in the early afternoon. The 168th R.C.T. landed successfully and advanced to the high ground overlooking Algiers. But Fort L'Empereur stood in the way, the garrison seemed obdurate, and a battle appeared likely.

In C Sector events were rather similar. Fort d'Estrées and the adjacent Batterie de Lazaret resisted persuasion and light attack, and at 2 p.m. were bombarded by H.M.S. *Bermuda* and naval aircraft. Later the battery surrendered but the fort did not. The 39th R.C.T. occupied the airfields at Maison Blanche and Hussein Dey and the area of Maison Carrée without difficulty.

Meanwhile General Ryder had been negotiating in Algiers with General Juin, who represented Admiral Darlan. During the afternoon they agreed that a cease fire should be declared at Algiers and the near neighbourhood, and that the Allies should occupy the town at 7 p.m. American troops entered Algiers as agreed, but it was not known whether French troops elsewhere would receive General Juin's orders nor whether all—especially naval units—would obey them. The situation remained rather anxious until Darlan's general cease fire order was received on the morning of 10th November.

At dusk on the 8th German bombers and torpedo-bombers attacked ships of C Sector. The destroyer *Cowdray* and the U.S. Combat Loader *Leedstown* were seriously damaged and another U.S. transport received minor damage.[1] The cruisers *Sheffield* and *Bermuda* were heavily attacked but came to no harm. Of three German aircraft destroyed that day, two fell in the Algiers area, probably during this raid.

At 9 p.m. H.M.S. *Spey* had arrived with the American troops from the *Thomas Stone*, which she disembarked next morning in Algiers harbour. Weather and breakdowns had necessitated abandoning the landing-craft on passage and put an end to this laudable attempt to take part in the assault. Three days later the *Thomas Stone* herself arrived after a very difficult tow by the destroyer H.M.S. *Wishart* and the tug *St. Day*.

During the night of the 8th/9th a heavy swell and rising wind stopped all unloading at the beaches and caused many casualties to landing-craft. It was therefore all the more fortunate that Algiers harbour was now available. H.M.S. *Bulolo* entered and berthed alongside early next morning and Admiral Burrough ordered all shipping into Algiers Bay. At 4.30 p.m. this concentration of ships was attacked by about 30 Ju. 88s and He. 111s. They did no damage and at least four were shot down by Spitfires and one by A.A. fire, but it was evident that air attacks were to be expected in increasing strength and frequency.

See Map 19

At Oran, too, it was planned to land in three Sectors—X, Y and Z. Of these, Z was given much the strongest force in order to gain early use of the small port of Arzeu. The 18th R.C.T. from Z Green beach was to capture the coast defences and port of Arzeu, and advance on Oran from the east. The 16th R.C.T. was to secure a beach-head on Z White and Red beaches for the main part of Armoured Combat Command B, cover the eastern flank of 18th R.C.T., and take part in the attack on Oran. From Z Red beach a column of Combat Command B was to capture Tafaraoui and La Senia airfields. A part of the 1st Ranger Battalion landing on R beach was to capture the batteries at Fort de la Pointe; the remainder of the Rangers would land in Arzeu harbour. From Y beaches, near Les Andalouses, the 26th R.C.T. was to secure the Djebel Murjajo heights and attack Oran from the west. A second column from Combat Command B was to land on X beaches, capture the landing ground at Lourmel, block the roads leading to it, advance south of the salt lake known

---

[1] *Leedstown* sank next day after further air attacks.

LANDING GROUPS AND ESCORTS

'X' SECTOR

Landing Group	Escort
3 L.S.I.'s	1 Cruiser
4 M/T. Ships	1 Destroyer
1 L.S.T.	2 Corvettes
	1 M.L.
	1 Trawler

'Y' SECTOR

Landing Group	Escort
3 L.S.I.'s	2 Destroyers
2 M/T. Ships	4 Trawlers
	5 M.L.'s

'Z' SECTOR

Landing Group	Escort
1 H.Q. Ship	1 Cruiser
9 L.S.I.'s	1 A.A. Ship
2 L.S.T.'s	3 Destroyers
1 L.S.G.	5 Corvettes
22 M.T. & M.V.	1 Sloop
	2 Cutters
	8 Minesweepers
	3 Trawlers
	4 M.L.'s

Map 19

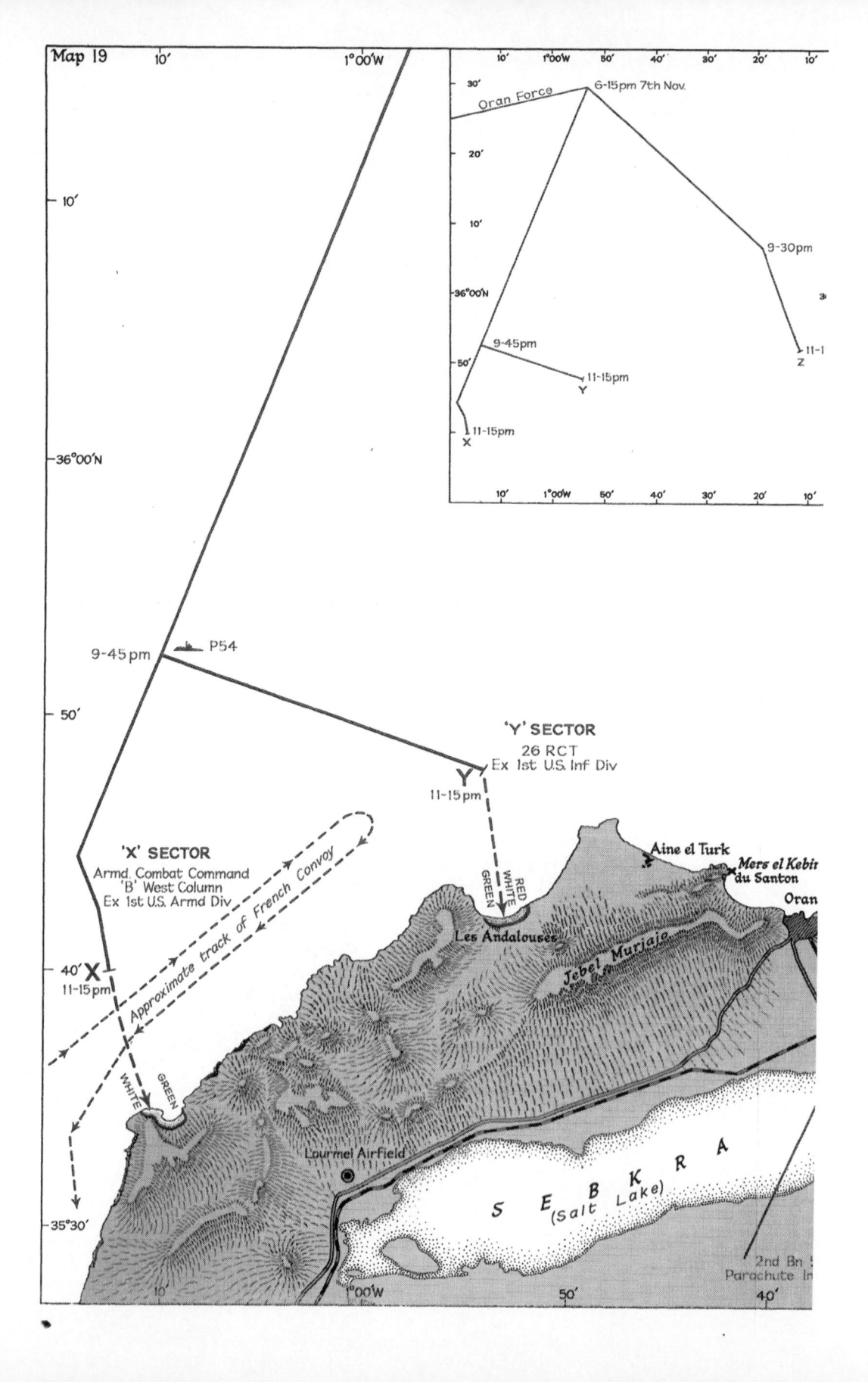

OPERATION 'TORCH'
The Assault on Oran

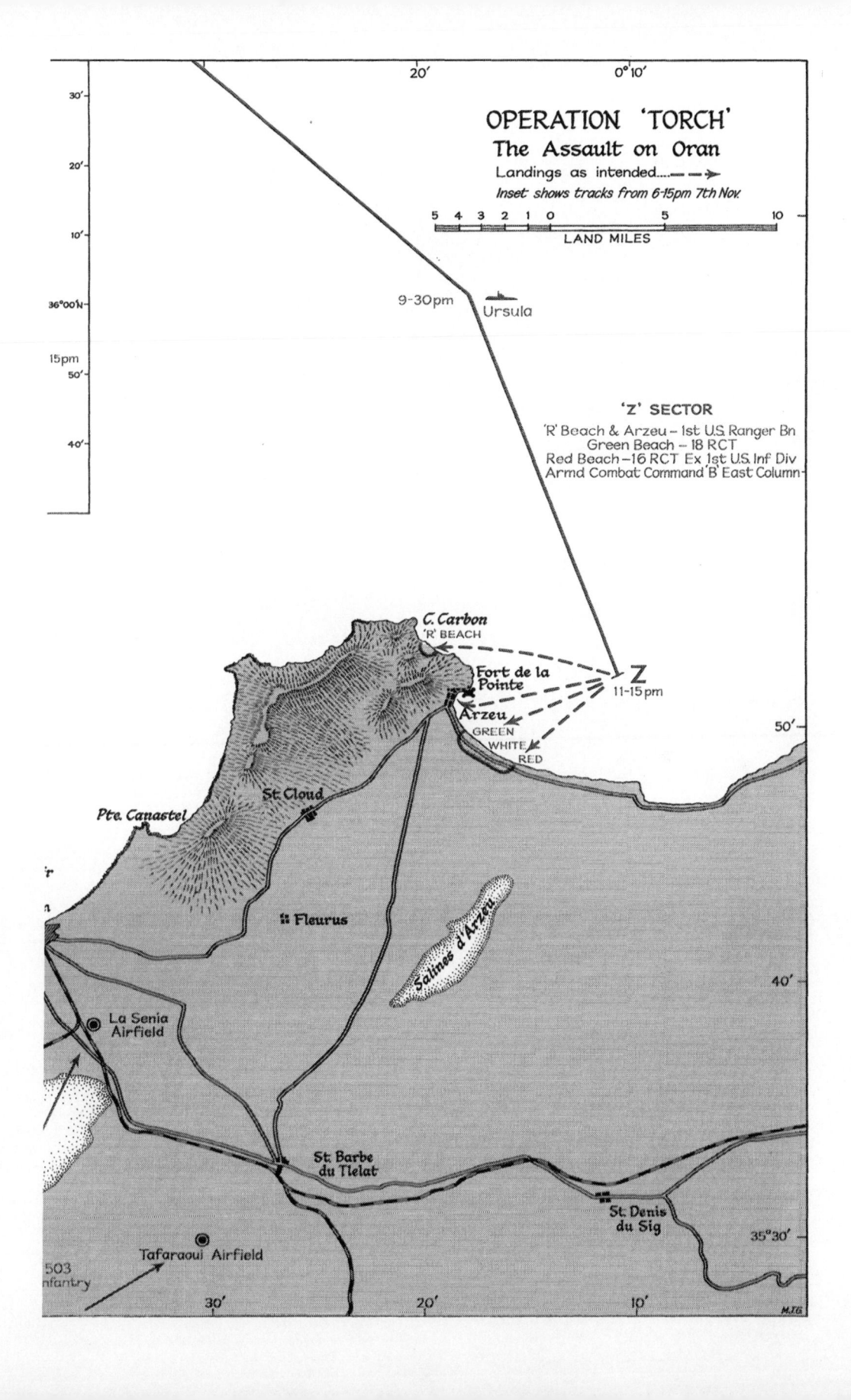

Landings as intended.....━━▶
Inset shows tracks from 6-15pm 7th Nov.

LAND MILES

9-30pm Ursula

'Z' SECTOR
'R' Beach & Arzeu – 1st U.S. Ranger Bn
Green Beach – 18 RCT
Red Beach – 16 RCT Ex 1st U.S. Inf Div
Armd Combat Command 'B' East Column

C. Carbon
'R' BEACH
Fort de la Pointe
Arzeu
GREEN
WHITE
RED

Z
11-15pm

Pte. Canastel
St. Cloud
Fleurus
Salines d'Arzeu
La Senia Airfield
St. Barbe du Tlelat
St. Denis du Sig
Tafaraoui Airfield
503 Infantry

in Arabic as the Sebkra, and help the Column from Z Red beach to capture the Tafaraoui and La Senia airfields. The paratroop battalion flying in from the United Kingdom had been added with the object of ensuring the early capture of these important airfields. The whole assault was to be controlled from the Headquarters Ship *Largs* carrying Commodore T. H. Troubridge, R.N., Major-General Lloyd R. Fredendall, U.S. Army, and the Commanding General of the U.S. Twelfth Air Force, Major-General James H. Doolittle.

By the afternoon of the 7th, Commodore Troubridge had collected the Fast and Slow Sections of his Force and various miscellaneous groups into one great assembly of about one hundred ships. These were now disposed in a number of columns ready to peel off after dark towards Oran as their turn came to make for their allotted beaches. In the meantime course was maintained as if for Malta. At 6.15 p.m. the ships for X and Y beaches, led by H.M.S. *Aurora*, broke away, made their rendezvous with the beacon submarine and then separated again for their respective Sectors. As they approached their anchorage the ships for X beaches were obliged to slow down to avoid a small French convoy which straggled across their course, and were further delayed through overrunning their own minesweepers, which had also been delayed by the French convoy. As a result, the landing-craft for X beaches touched down at 1.30 a.m. instead of 1 a.m. At Y beaches, too, most flights were half an hour late. Here an unexpected check was caused by an off-shore sand bar on which landing-craft grounded, with damage to rudders and propellers. Some troops had to swim ashore, and jeeps and guns disappeared under water before reaching dry ground.

As soon as the ships for X and Y Sectors were clear, H.M.S. *Jamaica*, with the *Largs* in company, led away the ships for Z beaches, and H.M.S. *Delhi* the ships carrying the Rangers for R beach. The Rangers were ashore punctually, and Fort de la Pointe and Arzeu harbour were soon in their hands. The landings on Z Green, White, and Red beaches also went well. There was, in fact, initially no opposition to any of the Oran beach landings, but between 2.30 and 3 a.m. tracer bullets were seen inshore from Arzeu and searchlights and gun-flashes from the direction of Oran. These last were the French resisting the frontal assault on the port.

As at Algiers this frontal assault had the object of preventing sabotage and the scuttling of ships within the port. But the chances of success were even less. Oran was used by the French Navy as a terminal port for coastal convoys, and several French destroyers were berthed in the harbour. Moreover, the nearby naval base of Mers-el-Kebir had been the scene of the Royal Navy's attack on the French Fleet in July 1940. Unless complete surprise could be effected resistance would be indeed bitter if the British appeared to be taking a hand. Two ex-U.S. coastguard cutters, renamed *Walney* and *Hartland*, and manned by the Royal Navy, were chosen for the task and they flew large American flags as well as the White Ensign. The landing party comprised predominantly American Rangers. The commander of the assault and the man largely responsible for the detailed planning was Captain F. T. Peters, Royal Navy, a retired officer.

At 2.45 a.m., as the *Walney* and *Hartland* approached, the port was alerted, searchlights were exposed, and fire was opened on the *Walney*, at first mostly with automatic weapons. An announcement in French by loud-hailer from the *Walney* did nothing to reduce the hostility of her reception. At 3.10, partly screened by smoke laid by accompanying motor launches, the *Walney* broke through the boom. Inside the harbour she nearly rammed, and was raked at point blank range by, the French sloop *La Surprise* which was under way. The *Walney's* engines were wrecked, and drifting up harbour she came under cross fire from submarines moored to the north and from the *Epervier*, the destroyer she had actually intended to board, berthed alongside to the south. A blazing hulk, her decks a shambles, she drifted round the harbour out of control until, at some time between 9 and 10 a.m., she rolled over and sank.[1] Her few survivors, including Captain Peters, were taken prisoner.

The *Hartland* had already been heavily hit before groping her way through the harbour entrance. Once inside, she came under point blank fire from the destroyer *Typhon* and was brought to a standstill. Attempts to berth alongside a trawler having failed, she drifted into the centre of the harbour and anchored, on fire from stem to stern, with hardly a man not killed or wounded. Those who survived left the ship by one means or another shortly after 4 a.m. It was daylight before she blew up.

The timing of the direct assaults on the ports of Algiers and Oran had been difficult to decide. At Oran the assault had been originally planned to take place just before H hour—the moment of touch-down on the beaches. This had been changed to H+2 hours to allow time for Commodore Troubridge to cancel the operation if the French were found to be alert and were resisting on the beaches or if they were found to be friendly. As it happened neither real resistance nor friendliness was met on the beaches, and so the direct assault was allowed to proceed—only to find the port very much on the alert.

The survivors of this gallant failure were not prisoners for long, but by a sad turn of fate Captain Peters, the sole survivor from *Walney's* bridge, was killed in an air accident a few days later. He

---

[1] According to some accounts she blew up before sinking.

was awarded posthumously the Victoria Cross and the American Distinguished Service Cross.

After giving such support as she could to *Walney* and *Hartland*, the cruiser *Aurora*, on patrol five miles to the north of Oran, was soon engaged in the distasteful task of intercepting French destroyers which began to come out of harbour as soon as the alarm was raised. Aided by two British destroyers, *Aurora*, veteran of Malta's Force K, sank the *Tramontane* and *Tornade* and forced the *Typhon* to withdraw into harbour again. The sloop *La Surprise*, attempting to attack ships off Y beaches, was sunk by the destroyer *Brilliant* at about the same time. French submarines also put to sea unobserved and attacked *Rodney* and *Aurora*, but without success.

At first light a field battery behind Arzeu opened fire on the ships off Z beaches as they moved inshore, and hit a large transport, the *Reina del Pacifico*, but withdrew on the arrival of the destroyer *Vansittart*. At 9 a.m. the Du Santon coast defence battery, above Mers-el-Kebir, opened fire on the ships off Y beaches and scored several hits. *Rodney* replied and the battery ceased fire. Thereafter *Rodney* was frequently engaged with Du Santon at extreme range, and her fire, though it did not knock out the battery, was sufficiently accurate to silence it.

Unloading at all beaches was in full swing by 7 a.m. Many landing-craft had become unserviceable, particularly at Y beaches where the sand bar had been encountered. The three Maracaibo oilers had certainly proved their worth. The *Misoa* and *Tasajera*, after first landing tanks on Z beaches with the help of their bridging equipment, had later used the seaplane ramp inside Arzeu harbour for discharging cargo from M.T. ships. The third Maracaibo, the *Bachaquero*, most skilfully handled, had been equally useful on X beaches.

As soon as it had become clear that the French were resisting, Albacores from H.M.S. *Furious*, escorted by her own Seafires and the Sea Hurricanes from the escort carriers *Biter* and *Dasher*, attacked the airfields at La Senia and Tafaraoui. The attacks were most effective. At La Senia about 70 French aircraft were destroyed on the ground or seriously damaged for the loss of one Albacore and one Sea Hurricane. Later inspection showed the French aircraft to have been fully armed and ready to attack at short notice. The American paratroops entrusted with the capture of both the La Senia and Tafaraoui airfields were to have flown from Cornwall in time to land at dawn. But bad weather over Spain broke up the formations, special aids to navigation failed to work, and poor visibility in the Oran area made it hard to see the ground. In consequence thirty of the thirty-nine aircraft were forced to put down on the dry bed of the large salt lake; seven landed elsewhere in North West Africa or at Gibraltar, and two were missing. By noon, however, the Armoured

Columns from Z and X beaches had captured Tafaraoui airfield, and during the late afternoon twenty-four Spitfires of the 308th and 309th Squadrons of the U.S. Twelfth Air Force flew in from Gibraltar. As the last four aircraft approached to land they were attacked by French Dw. 520s; one Spitfire was shot down and three Dw.520s were shot down in return. La Senia was not finally under American control until 4 p.m. next day. In addition to attacking La Senia and Tafaraoui, Fleet Air Arm aircraft machine-gunned four other landing grounds in the area, carried out continuous patrols over the beaches throughout the day, and were much used for tactical reconnaissance. A Spitfire from Gibraltar carried out photographic reconnaissance.

The 16th and 18th R.C.T.s, advancing from Arzeu towards Oran, met resistance as they neared the town, but by nightfall on the 8th they had gone forward between fifteen and twenty miles. The 26th R.C.T. had moved steadily forward from Y beaches overcoming all opposition and capturing Aine-el-Turk on the way.

During the 9th unloading was slowed down by a rising swell, and it was fortunate that Z beaches could be abandoned in favour of Arzeu harbour. Two more French destroyers, the *Epervier* and *Typhon*, which came out of Oran were engaged by *Aurora* and *Jamaica*. The *Epervier* was driven ashore in flames and the *Typhon* forced back into harbour where she beached herself. H.M.S. *Rodney*, when called upon, continued to engage the Du Santon battery, and other warships and Fleet Air Arm Albacores gave support to the American Army at a number of points along the coast. After the arrival of further U.S. Spitfires the aircraft carriers were ordered to return to Gibraltar.

Fighting ashore continued throughout the 9th November. The 1st U.S. Infantry Division after meeting stiff resistance at St. Cloud had made progress towards Oran. In the capture of La Senia airfield in the afternoon American Spitfires from Tafaraoui helped to break up French counter-attacks, and also attacked isolated French units. It was claimed that ten tanks and twenty-five lorries laden with troops were destroyed. At 8 a.m. on the 10th a general assault was launched in which *Rodney*, *Aurora* and *Jamaica* joined by bombarding Du Santon and Pointe Canastel batteries. American Spitfires provided tactical reconnaissance and air support. By noon Oran had surrendered. As had been feared, the port was found to be encumbered by scuttled ships, and the first follow-up convoy, due next day, was ordered to berth in Mers-el-Kebir harbour and Arzeu Bay.

See Map 16

Meanwhile, on the exposed Atlantic coast, the Western (all-American) Force had met stronger opposition. The story is told elsewhere in these histories, and will only be given in outline here.[1] In each of the three landing areas on the morning of D day the sea was calm but a long swell gave rise to considerable surf, which increased during the day. Losses in landing-craft were heavy. There were delays and mistakes similar to those at Algiers and Oran, and troops were late in being put ashore.[2] As soon as it was light enough for the shore batteries to see, they opened fire on the beaches and on inshore craft, and at Fedala and Port Lyautey there were attacks by French aircraft as well. Success came quickest at Safi, after two old destroyers had rushed the harbour. By 2.30 p.m. the town was in American hands, and half an hour later Sherman tanks were rolling ashore ready to advance on Casablanca. At Fedala and Port Lyautey several shore batteries had to be captured before they were finally silenced. The town of Fedala fell by 3 p.m. but the Americans met stiff resistance on the way to Casablanca, and at Port Lyautey the the airfield was still in French hands at nightfall.

In the meantime French warships had made several gallant sorties from Casablanca in vain attempts to interfere with the landings at Fedala; the heavy cruiser *Primauguet* was severely damaged and six destroyers were sunk or driven ashore. Shortly before the first of these sorties the uncompleted battleship *Jean Bart* was hit at her berth in Casablanca harbour by 16-inch shell from the battleship *Massachusetts* and later, on the afternoon of the 10th, by bombs from American aircraft. Bombs also further damaged the *Primauguet* at anchor outside the harbour. Four out of eight French submarines which put to sea were lost, and three others sunk in Casablanca harbour.

In spite of American attempts to bring about a cease fire, fighting continued on 9th and 10th November. Early on the 11th, when the Americans were about to launch a heavy attack on the town of Casablanca, the French capitulated—acting on the order issued by Admiral Darlan from Algiers.

During the planning of 'Torch' it had been fully realized that as soon as the Allies landed in French Africa, if not before, the enemy

---

[1] S. W. Roskill: *The War at Sea, Volume II*. Also Samuel E. Morison: *Operations in North African Waters. History of U.S. Naval Operations in World War II*, and George F. Howe: *Northwest Africa: Seizing the Initiative in the West* (a volume in the series *United States Army in World War II*).

[2] Of the landing-craft stranded, swamped, or otherwise made unserviceable during operations at Algiers, Oran and on the Moroccan coast, many were later salved and repaired, but in most cases not until Algiers, Oran and Casablanca had been opened to Allied shipping, by which time landing-craft were no longer a vital need. Of some 400 British landing-craft used at Algiers and Oran 106 became total losses. On the Moroccan coast, where surf and French opposition were heavier, the corresponding figures for American landing-craft were 629 and 216.

would probably send forces by air and sea to Tunisia, primarily to secure the ports and airfields of Bizerta and Tunis. It was clearly most important to try to be there first ourselves. Admiral Cunningham was one of those who had advocated a landing at Bizerta, and later wrote in his Despatch that he always regretted that this bolder conception was not implemented.

> 'Had we been prepared to throw even a small force into the eastward ports, the Axis would have been forestalled in their first token occupation and success would have been complete. They were surprised and off their balance. We failed to give the final push which would have tipped the scales.'

But the Allies had decided that they could not land on D day anywhere east of Algiers, for the reasons given on pages 123–25 of Chapter V. Moreover, any force landed at Bizerta, which was a naval zone, would certainly have to be British, and it was against the British that the French Navy were known to feel such strong resentment.

These arguments are impressive, and to the Allied High Command they were conclusive. Even a small force could not be provided to land as far east as Bougie on D day. Not that 'Torch' was a timid enterprise—it was in many ways an extremely bold one, and this boldness paid. The story of the first few days, however, leaves a feeling of disappointment. For although the immediate fly-in of German forces to Tunis and Bizerta had been expected, and its supreme importance realized, the Allies found it impossible to make any attempt by sea or air to forestall it at either place. As General Anderson later wrote, our one chance of winning the race for Bizerta and Tunis was to land troops as far east as possible on D or at latest D+1 day. If the first troops to reach Tunis and Bizerta had been British or American, however small in number, there is little doubt in his opinion 'that the French would have swung to our side.' Having decided however against this course, which would have entailed great risks, 'we really had no right to expect success.' As it turned out, Bizerta and Tunis were not captured until six months later.

The Germans made the most of their opportunity, for on 9th November came a report that about forty German aircraft had landed at El Aouina (Tunis) that morning. On the 10th British photographic reconnaissance of the airfield disclosed about a hundred German aircraft of various types—bombers, fighters, and air transports.[1] Twenty M.C. 202 Italian fighters were also reported to be there, and it was confirmed that Sidi Ahmed (Bizerta) was in

---

[1] 42 Ju. 52s, 24 Ju. 87s, 23 Me. 109s, 3 He. 111s, 2 Ju. 90s (transports) and 3 freight-carrying gliders.

German hands. At this moment expeditions for Bougie, Djidjelli and Bône were about to sail from Algiers.

On the evening of 9th November General Anderson arrived at Algiers and assumed command of the Eastern Task Force, now called the 1st Army. A plan had been made with the immediate intention of securing the ports of Bougie and Bône and the airfields at Djidjelli and near Bône, to enable an advance overland into Tunisia to be supported; at present there was no Allied airfield east of Maison Blanche—120 miles from Bougie.

On the evening of 10th November the 36th Infantry Brigade Group, now assault-stowed, sailed from Algiers for Bougie in the Infantry Landing Ships *Marnix* and *Cathay*.[1] They were preceded by a slow convoy carrying motor transport, equipment and supplies. Soon after 11 p.m. another L.S.I.—the *Awatea*—sailed for Djidjelli carrying R.A.F. Servicing Commandos, petrol and stores.[2] The Naval Officer in charge of the landings, Captain N. V. Dickinson, and the Military Commander, Brigadier A. L. Kent-Lemon, accompanied the fast Bougie convoy in the L.S.I. *Karanja*, whose landing-craft were to help ferry the troops ashore. The Naval escorts and covering force for the expedition were commanded by Rear-Admiral C. H. J. Harcourt, flying his flag in the cruiser *Sheffield*.

Although there was as yet no general armistice, there were grounds for expecting a friendly reception from the French at Bougie and Djidjelli. After the convoys had sailed, however, information was received that there might be opposition at Bougie and Captain Dickinson ordered all landings to take place to the east of the port beyond the range of the shore batteries. Meanwhile the despatch of a small mobile column (Hart Force, a detachment of 5th Northamptons, 11th Infantry Brigade) overland to Bône was delayed until the attitude of the French became clear.

In the event the landings at Bougie, which began at 6.15 in the morning of 11th November, were unopposed, and Hart Force set out by road from Algiers. At Djidjelli the swell was raising a heavy surf: the idea of landing there was therefore abandoned and the *Awatea* joined the ships off Bougie. Here friendly signals had been

---

[1] 36th Infantry Brigade Group: 5th Battalion The Buffs; 6th Battalion Royal West Kent Regiment; 8th Battalion Argyll and Sutherland Highlanders; 138th Field Regiment R.A.; 256th Field Company R.E.; and detachments R.A.M.C., R.A.S.C., and R.E.M.E.

[2] R.A.F. Servicing Commandos were being used for the first time, their purpose being to occupy advanced landing grounds immediately after capture by the Army. They were to undertake the daily servicing, refuelling and re-arming of the squadrons which used newly-occupied landing grounds until the regular maintenance crews arrived.

received from the shore, and, after contact had been made with local French officials, three ships from the slow convoy entered the port and began to unload.

Since dawn fighter cover had been provided from H.M.S. *Argus*, supplemented by other F.A.A. fighters flown to *Argus* from the escort carrier *Avenger* off Algiers. It was undesirable to expose the *Argus*—already damaged by bombing the previous evening—so far east after noon on the 11th, but by this time it was hoped that Spitfires would be operating from Djidjelli. Failure to land at Djidjelli, however, resulted in petrol not reaching the airfield until the 13th, and between noon on the 11th and the morning of the 13th ships and troops at Bougie had no air cover other than that provided by the Hurricanes and Spitfires from Maison Blanche—over 100 miles away.

The first enemy air attacks, between 1.30 and 1.50 p.m. on the 11th, did no harm, but at dusk a heavy attack was made in which 30 Ju. 88s were followed by He. 111 torpedo aircraft. The *Awatea* and *Cathay* were hit and sunk, and the monitor H.M.S. *Roberts* was damaged. Shortly before dawn next morning the anti-aircraft ship *Tynwald* was damaged by mines or torpedoes and quickly sank, and soon afterwards the *Karanja* was set on fire in a bomb attack and also sank. Spitfires of No. 154 Squadron, which had been grounded for lack of petrol at Djidjelli during the 12th, brought relief on the 13th, and, although minor damage occurred in further air attacks, it was not done without loss to the enemy. Altogether, in the three days 11th to 13th November, the Germans lost four and the Italians two aircraft in the Bougie area, one of the German aircraft probably being brought down by A.A. gunfire. Two R.A.F. Spitfires were shot down by the Royal Navy, and a Hurricane failed to return to base.[1]

The swift arrival of Axis forces at Bizerta and Tunis (dealt with more fully in the next chapter) ruled out the use of Allied airborne troops at either of these places. Instead, two companies of the British 3rd Parachute Battalion, flown out from the U.K. to replace the paratroops who had attempted to reach Tafaraoui on D day, dropped at Bône on 12th November, just as detachments of the 6th Commando landed from the destroyers *Lammerton* and *Wheatland*. The port and airfield were quickly seized. During the next two days the Spitfires of Nos. 81 and 111 Squadrons arrived, and maintenance crews, petrol, ammunition and A.A. equipment were flown in. The Axis air forces reacted vigorously, and in one of their frequent raids on Bône airfield on the 14th four Spitfires were destroyed on the ground.

---

[1] These losses brought the total in the 'Torch' area since the landing to: R.A.F. at least 12 in an estimated 540 sorties; F.A.A. 34 in 702 sorties; U.S.A.A.F. at least 8, including 3 interned air transports; German 23; and Italian at least 4.

British Army and Air casualties during the 'Torch' landings and up to and including 13th November were light. American casualties over the same period were much heavier, partly as a result of French resistance encountered in Morocco and partly because of losses sustained in *Walney* and *Hartland* in the direct assault on Oran. The Royal Navy's casualties given in the following table are those incurred in ships and Fleet Air Arm aircraft off and over Algiers, Oran and Bougie during these six days.

Allied casualties during the first six days of operation 'Torch': 8th–13th November 1942

	Killed	Wounded	Missing	Total
British				
Army	4	50	11	65
Air (approx.)	—	2	22	24
Navy (incl. F.A.A.)	536	126	—	662
American				
Army and Air	526	837	41	1,404
Navy	17	53	—	70
Total, British and American	1,083	1,068	74	2,225
Dutch				
Destroyer				
Isaac Sweers	98 (killed and missing)	19	—	117

At 6.30 a.m. on 8th November the German U-boat Command heard of the North African landings. Fifteen submarines operating between the Bay of Biscay and the Cape Verde Islands were ordered at high speed towards the Moroccan coast. Later, all boats to the west of Ireland with sufficient fuel were told to head for Gibraltar. None could arrive in time to interfere with the first landings, but it was hoped they might intercept follow-up convoys. The first of these boats reached the coast of Morocco on the 9th, but failed to penetrate the American anti-submarine screen. On 11th November other U-boats arrived in the area and on that day *U. 173* sank a U.S. transport. She herself survived only five days. On the 12th *U. 130* sank three transports off Fedala and other ships were damaged. Thereafter shipping off the Moroccan coast was able to move inside the ports to unload, and targets for submarines became much fewer.

In the western approaches to the Mediterranean the valuable submarine depot ship H.M.S. *Hecla* was sunk on the 11th November by *U. 515*. Three days later the 20,000-ton *Warwick Castle*, in a homeward-bound convoy, fell a victim to *U. 415*. On the 15th another homeward-bound convoy was attacked by *U. 155*; the American Combat Loader *Almack*, the P. and O. *Ettrick*, of 11,200 tons, and the escort carrier, H.M.S. *Avenger*, were torpedoed in that order. The *Avenger* blew up and sank within two minutes, with the loss of all but twelve of her company; the *Ettrick* sank later and the *Almack* reached Gibraltar in tow.

The nine German U-boats available for operations in the Mediterranean at the beginning of November had been stationed to meet the expected Allied expedition east of the line Cartagena-Oran. Reconnaissance by Axis aircraft of the whole Western Basin was not possible, and the Allied convoys bound for Oran were not discovered at all. So numerous were the Allied surface and air escorts that although both the Algiers convoys passed over the German U-boat line only two boats reached positions for firing torpedoes and they obtained no hits. Allied air patrols prevented the U-boats from shadowing, but the course being steered by the Algiers Fast Convoy deepened the impression that the expedition was bound for destinations east of that port. The U-boats were ordered to proceed east, and so missed the opportunity to attack the Allied transports at their most vulnerable—when they were disembarking their troops. Not until the 8th, when the B.B.C. announced that landings had taken place in French North Africa, were the U-boats ordered to reverse their course.

Early in November the Italians had stationed twelve submarines south of Sardinia and another six in the Central Mediterranean—all disposed to counter an Allied passage of the Sicilian Narrows. Only two boats were operating further west, near the Balearic Islands. When the first news of the landings came through, the submarines south of Sardinia were moved only slightly westward as the Italians expected other landings near Philippeville and Bône. It was midday on the 8th before it was known for certain that no landings had been made east of Algiers and no Malta convoy was at sea.

Once the enemy realized the scope and purpose of the Allied expedition, U-boats began to take their toll. On the 11th *U.407* sank the 19,600-ton *Viceroy of India* north of Oran, and *U.380* the 11,600-ton Dutch *Nieuw Zeeland* south-east of Gibraltar. These two fast troopships had been sailed independently for Gibraltar on their homeward journey as soon as they were empty. Admiral Cunningham had considered it an even chance whether they would be safer at sea at high speed or anchored in a mass of shipping off Oran or Algiers awaiting escorts. The luck went against them and Admiral Cunningham ordered ships to wait for escorts in future. The escorts themselves had had their losses, too. On the 10th, *U.431* sank the destroyer *Martin* north-east of Algiers and three days later the destroyer *Isaac Sweers*, which had given such long and good service in the Mediterranean and was the only Dutch warship taking part in 'Torch'. The same day another U-boat sank the 6,500-ton m.v. *Maron* north of Oran.

Although some Axis aircraft had been transferred from Sicily to the Western Desert to counter the desperate situation arising at El Alamein, only fighters had so far been involved. Towards the end of October there were still some 415 Italian and 300 German aircraft based in Sicily. In Sardinia the Italians had 159 or so aircraft of which a third or more were bombers and torpedo-bombers, and, together with 115 German (Sicilian-based) bombers operating from advanced bases there, they awaited whatever Allied operations were impending. They first attacked shipping off Algiers on the evening of the 8th November with moderate success, as already recounted. On the 10th, ten miles north of Algiers, they sank the destroyer *Ibis* with a torpedo, and slightly damaged *Argus* with bombs at about the same time. More successes followed on the 11th and 12th in the attacks off Bougie. To these were added, on the 14th, the sinking of the 16,600-ton P. and O. *Narkunda* shortly after she had left Bougie for Algiers. These losses illustrated once again the importance of establishing properly directed fighter protection at the earliest moment.

Surface ships of the Italian Fleet made no attempt to interfere with the Allied landings and for this they can hardly be criticised. To retain a Fleet in being appears to have been the proper strategy for the Italians, for even had they possessed fuel to send the whole of their Fleet to sea, an attempt to challenge Force H could only have led to disaster. For one thing, Force H possessed a powerful air striking force and adequate air cover, whereas the Italian Fleet would have had to operate at perhaps 300 miles from the nearest Italian air bases.

However, the Allied operations caused movements of some big Italian ships. On 11th November the three *Littorio* class battleships moved to Naples from Taranto[1] and three cruisers which had recently arrived at Augusta from Navarino went north to Messina on 9th November.

The general cease fire arranged with the French in North Africa released more Allied warships and aircraft for war on the U-boats, and successes mounted. In the Western Basin, between 9th and 17th November, five German and two Italian submarines were sunk, three by escort vessels, three by aircraft, and one by submarine. Among the German losses was *U.331*, which, almost exactly a year before, had so daringly sunk H.M.S. *Barham*. Her captain, Tiessenhausen, was among the survivors. In the western approaches to the Straits of Gibraltar two German submarines were sunk, one on

---

[1] The *Littorio*, *Vittorio Veneto*, and recently completed *Roma*.

the 15th by a destroyer and one on the 19th by an air patrol. To these can be added *U.173*, already referred to as sunk by U.S. forces off the Moroccan coast. Several other U-boats were damaged, among them *U.431*. Those in the western approaches to the Mediterranean were now withdrawn farther west, where they had little fortune.

Among the major factors which the Allies had to take into account before committing themselves to operation 'Torch' was the probable attitude of the military forces and the civil population in North Africa, not only to the initial landings, but, if the Axis won the race for Tunisia, to prolonged military operations as well. In the planning not a little hope was pinned on the Americans being favourably received; serious opposition, or even non-cooperation, might have disastrous consequences. In the event, forecasts of French reactions were shown to have been wide of the mark in several respects, but this is hardly surprising—indeed, it seems unlikely that either British or Americans will ever clearly understand what was going on in the minds of Frenchmen during the years of their country's occupation. Nor is it any criticism of Mr. Murphy's work and advice, for up to the last moment he believed that French reactions to the landings in North Africa would be a matter of chance.

Ever since the collapse of 1940 Frenchmen had been ranged in every shade of opinion from General de Gaulle's 'Free French' at one extreme to fanatical anglophobes and convinced—as opposed to opportunist—collaborators with Germany at the other. Between these extremes stood large numbers who were stunned and confused, or apathetic and anxious for peace at any price. Even after the United States entered the war many Frenchmen who had previously looked upon Britain's defeat as certain believed that even if Germany could no longer win she would still be able to make a peace which would leave her the dominant power in Europe. And this might be one way of bringing about a United States of Europe and of destroying Communism. Other Frenchmen who did not accept and even strongly disliked de Gaullism, desired to re-enter the war against Germany as quickly as possible and in the meantime to prepare for that happy day. But many who held this view wished to be led back into the war only by those whom they recognized as their legitimate rulers—Marshal Pétain and his government. This outlook towards legitimacy prevailed among government servants both civil and military.

The French attitude towards obedience and military honour was strict; there was great respect for the chain of command.

Moreover, although it could be argued that an oath given to one who was himself not a free agent is not binding, military officers and civil servants had in fact taken an oath of loyalty to the Marshal. Weighty problems of conscience confronted anyone who contemplated independent action. And the fact remained that in 1940 Armistice terms had been drawn up and agreed to: both honour and common sense required that they should be observed, at least unless flagrantly violated by the Axis Powers. In the Navy these perplexing issues were aggravated by hatred of the British, which sprang from Mers-el-Kebir, Dakar, Syria and Madagascar, and from the seizure of French warships in British ports.

There were, of course, Frenchmen in all walks of life with wider views on patriotism, and it was with these that Mr. Murphy and his vice-consuls had been attempting to consort in North Africa since 1941. At length, in the spring of 1942, the long awaited American expedition, which would free French Africa from Armistice Commissions and threats of Axis occupation, seemed to be taking definite shape. It was time, the patriots felt, to find a leader with the necessary prestige to rally Frenchmen of all shades of opinion. This man was certainly not de Gaulle, whom some of the most ardent patriots regarded as a traitor. Weygand had been sounded but had declined. Opportunely, the distinguished General, Henri Giraud, escaped from German captivity in April 1942, and in May agreed to accept the role of Algerian liberator. But the importance of legitimacy in the eyes of many Frenchmen, and of loyalty to Marshal Pétain, had been much underestimated by the Allies, and by the French patriot movement, including Giraud himself. In the event, the situation in early November 1942 was complicated, or simplified—according to the point of view—by the fortuitous presence of Admiral Darlan.

Nevertheless the steps taken by General Mast and his civilian colleagues to neutralize possible opposition to the landings at Algiers worked well at first. Early in the night 7th/8th, key positions within the town, including most of the communications centres, were taken over by young men of the patriot movement, and many of the principal French authorities, other than proven sympathizers, were placed under house arrest. These steps were more easily taken than might be supposed, because the authentic defence scheme for Algiers laid down that in an emergency civilians should relieve military guards and so release soldiers for more active tasks. Each group of patriots now presented an order signed by General Mast that such an emergency existed.

It is probable that if the Americans had known of this success they would have entered the town earlier. As it was, the orthodox French authorities were given time to recover most of their lost hold inside the town and cause the civilian patriots increasing anxiety. As might be expected there were many rumours; no one quite knew what was going on, so no one was very sure of what to do. This confusion and the element of surprise no doubt helped General Mast's plans. There was very little opposition to the Allies on or near the beaches, and later opposition to their advance towards the town and the airfields was only sporadic. It was the French Navy which manned the coastal batteries, and it was from them that most of the opposition came. General Mast himself went to the key point of Sidi Ferruch, where, as already related, he was able to contact and help the Americans. Later in the day, by order of General Juin, he was relieved of his authority.

On a higher level also there had been much activity during the night. At 10 p.m. on the 7th Mr. Murphy interviewed General Mast and other leaders of the patriot movement before they dispersed to their various tasks. Shortly after midnight he called on General Juin to tell him that the Americans were about to land. Much taken aback—for he was unprepared for the expedition to arrive while his superior, Admiral Darlan, was present in North Africa—Juin agreed to telephone the Admiral. Around 2 a.m. Darlan arrived. Informed in his turn—by now the landings were actually taking place—he became furious. (It is said that his first coherent words were to the effect that the Americans seemed just as great fools as their friends the British.) Under open arrest, he was permitted to report to Vichy not only what Mr. Murphy had told him, but his own reply, which was that France had signed an armistice with Germany and must defend French territory. Meanwhile the orthodox authorities in Algiers were recovering from their surprise and gradually re-establishing their control. At 6 a.m. on the 8th the young French patriots surrounding General Juin's house were dispersed by the police. Admiral Darlan and General Juin departed for Fort L'Empereur, overlooking the harbour, and Mr. Murphy found himself in his turn under restraint.

Presently a reply came from Pétain acknowledging Darlan's signal and expressing confidence in him. And when informed by Vichy that the Germans had inquired how German aircraft in Sardinia and Sicily could best help the French to repel the aggressors, Darlan suggested that they should attack Allied transports off Algiers. He appears to have been playing for time and trying to gauge the strength of the Allied expedition.

In two further signals to Pétain, Darlan warned the Marshal of the worsening situation and prepared him for the fall of Algiers. In the early evening, as already related, he authorized General Juin to negotiate the surrender of the town. During the night it was learnt that Vichy had rejected President Roosevelt's messages of assurance and goodwill and had broken off diplomatic relations with the United States.

For some days the political situation remained confused—complicated by rigid tradition and mutual suspicion, and, so far as the general public was concerned, by dislike of being dragged into the war. These uncertainties inevitably affected the military situation also.

General Giraud arrived at Algiers by air early on 9th November. He was very coldly received. Quickly realizing that his usefulness had been vastly overestimated he went into virtual retreat for the time being. General Mark Clark arrived the same evening and he and Mr. Murphy met Darlan and Juin next morning, 10th November. This conference ended with Darlan signing an order for a general cease fire throughout French North Africa. On learning of this, Pétain officially disavowed Darlan, but there is reason to believe that, a few hours later, he retracted his disavowal, using for the purpose a personal cypher held only by Darlan and Auphan, the Minister of Marine.

Be that as it may, Darlan, who was at first much depressed by the public disavowal, rallied. Perhaps the private message encouraged him, certainly his confidence was restored when, on the 11th, the occupation of Unoccupied France by the Germans enabled him to assert, and no doubt to believe, that the Armistice had been broken and that the Marshal was not a free agent. It was not, however, until the 13th that the principal French authorities in Algeria and Morocco arrived at a working agreement. Darlan was to remain in control of civil and political matters as High Commissioner; Giraud was to become Commander of all French forces in North Africa with Juin serving under him in command of the land forces; Noguès was to continue as Resident-General in Morocco and Chatel as Governor of Algeria. This agreement coincided, happily, with the arrival of General Eisenhower, who, accompanied by Admiral Cunningham, was paying his first visit to Algiers to inform himself of General Clark's progress in these difficult political negotiations as well as in military matters.

Next day, 14th November, back at Gibraltar, General Eisenhower was confronted with the first wave of official doubt and public indignation from Washington and London. The idea of making a deal with the notorious Vichyite, Darlan, had been very badly received. The Allied Commander-in-Chief promptly justified his decision on military grounds. French sentiment in North Africa had been completely misjudged. Pétain's name was one to be conjured with. Giraud was impotent and acknowledged it. Darlan was the only representative generally acceptable; without him the Allies' hopes for a quick conquest of Tunisia could not be realized and a military occupation of French Africa, with all its delays, would be necessary. The effect on Spain might be serious. With these arguments official opinion was largely satisfied, but public clamour continued for some time.[1]

Meanwhile the Allied landings in French North Africa gave grounds—or at least an excuse—for the Germans to move into Vichy France and for the Italians to occupy Corsica. For this task the Italian Special Naval Force, which had earlier been trained for the attack on Malta, was available, and landed troops at Bastia during the night of 11th/12th November after an agreement had been negotiated with the French Commander. Other troops disembarked at Ajaccio and Porto Vecchio.

On 14th November Pétain again publicly repudiated Darlan; he had already appointed Noguès, he said, to be his sole representative in North Africa. But Noguès by this time had fallen into line with Darlan, and, in general, less attention was now being paid to communications from Vichy.

The part played by the patriots at Algiers has already been related. At Oran and in Morocco the action by the local patriot movements had little or no effect in reducing opposition to the American landings—indeed it seems that premature action caused some authorities to be particularly alert. At Oran the surrender took place on the 10th shortly before Darlan's order for the general cease fire was received. In Morocco the order was not received until early on the 11th—fortunately just in time for a strong American attack on Casablanca to be called off, and many lives probably saved.

In Tunisia the conditions were quite different. Early Allied support could not be counted upon and Axis forces were much nearer. Neither Admiral Estéva, the Resident General, nor Admiral Derrien, the Naval Commander, had any love for Germans, but orders from Vichy and Algiers were contradictory, and if Vichy was under pressure from Germans, so was Algiers under pressure from Americans. If Estéva and Derrien ever contemplated independent action they left it too late. On 9th November, after an ultimatum had encouraged Vichy to acquiesce, German aircraft had begun to land at El Aouina (Tunis) airfield and by next day the German invasion of Tunisia was under way. General Barré, the French military commander, showed more independence. He did not oppose these landings, but withdrew his forces westward into the hills and astutely played for time before rejecting the German ultimatum of 21st November. To most French people in North Africa the Allied landings had come as a complete surprise, and time was needed for

---

[1] This was the subject, in a secret session of the House of Commons, on 10th December, of one of Mr. Churchill's most telling speeches. See *The Hinge of Fate*: pages 573–576.

all and sundry to adjust themselves and decide on their future attitude. General Barré's decision to fight on the side of the Allies soon caused Anglo-American relations with the French armed forces and civilians to improve. Indeed it might be said that whereas Darlan had caused active opposition to the Allies to cease, Barré's action encouraged widespread co-operation with them to begin.

On 22nd November General Clark and Admiral Darlan signed an agreement defining responsibilities in North Africa in such a way as to give the Americans and their Allies the security and help they wanted, without wounding French administrative pride. On the 23rd Darlan was able to announce that French West Africa (Governor-General Boisson) had placed itself under his orders, thereby making available to the Allies, for use in the Battle of the Atlantic, the port of Dakar and many valuable airfields.

One of the great prizes for which the Allies had hoped as a sequel to the landings in North Africa was the French Fleet, the main part of which was at Toulon under Admiral de Laborde. Prompted by Mr. Murphy and General Clark, Admiral Darlan made three appeals, or 'reasoned invitations', between 10th and 12th November to the Toulon Fleet to sail. He himself evidently doubted whether it would come, and if it did, whether its coming would be friendly. On 18th November the Germans, who had announced on occupying Vichy France that they would not move into the fortified area of Toulon, suddenly demanded the withdrawal of all French troops from this zone, which, they said, could be garrisoned only by naval units. Their intentions were of course suspect, and early on the morning of the 27th, when they tried to seize the Fleet, the French Navy was ready. One battleship, two battle-cruisers, four heavy and three light cruisers, twenty-four destroyers, sixteen submarines and a number of smaller craft were sunk or seriously damaged by their own crews. There remained some half-dozen destroyers and the like number of submarines only slightly damaged. From all the French warships at Toulon only three submarines succeeded in reaching Allied ports.

Thus the Allies' hope that the French Fleet would join them had not been realized. That it would happen had never been very likely and became less likely with the resignation on 15th November of Auphan as Minister of Marine and Pétain's further delegation of power to Laval. Nor was there any good reason to hope that Admiral de Laborde would act independently of the government he served, for his hatred of the British appears to have been even more intense than Darlan's. If his feelings underwent a change, when, early on the 27th, he learnt that German tanks were battering their way into his dockyard, it was then too late. His ships were not ready for sea and the Germans could have made his departure extremely hazardous. Scuttling was the sole alternative, and for this he was prepared. In this tragic way Darlan's promise, made in June 1940, that the French Fleet would never fall into enemy hands was fulfilled, and the Allies were freed from an anxiety which had been with them for two and a half years.

Neither Darlan's collaboration with the Americans in North Africa nor the self-destruction of the Fleet at Toulon was enough to bring Admiral Godfroy at Alexandria over to the Allies.[1] Concerned as to his duty to Marshal Pétain, whose real views were patently unobtainable, uncertain as to the Allies' ability to liberate Tunisia—let alone metropolitan France—and fearful lest the government of North Africa should fall into the hands of de Gaullists or other groups whom he mistrusted, Admiral Godfroy continued to pursue a policy of what at times seemed to be studied vacillation. It made a great many people understandably impatient, Mr. Churchill most of all.

Taking everything into account, the Allies could congratulate themselves on the success of the landings and regard themselves as fortunate. Secrecy had been well guarded, cover plans cleverly baited, and a large measure of surprise achieved. Tactically the operation on 7th/8th November had gone with great precision up to the time when the assault convoys reached the disembarkation points. Such preventable mistakes as occurred later were nearly all caused by lack of training, and this the Allies had been obliged to accept in order to mount the expedition as quickly as possible. In particular, lack of experience in handling landing craft had resulted in unnecessary losses. (It was just as well that the landings were made on the lightly defended beaches of North Africa, and not on those of German-held Northern France!). In an operation of such complexity and on such a scale, it would have been surprising if minor inter-Service and inter-Allied criticisms had never arisen, but there is no doubt that the teamwork in 'Torch', both in its planning and execution, had been excellent and that the mainspring of this co-operation and the man who had inspired it was General Eisenhower.

Having secured the footholds, the next step—and an urgent one—was to drive ahead and occupy Tunisia.

---

[1] Admiral Godfroy had at Alexandria one battleship, three 8-inch cruisers, one 6-inch cruiser, and three destroyers. For his relations with Admiral Cunningham see Volume I.

Map 20

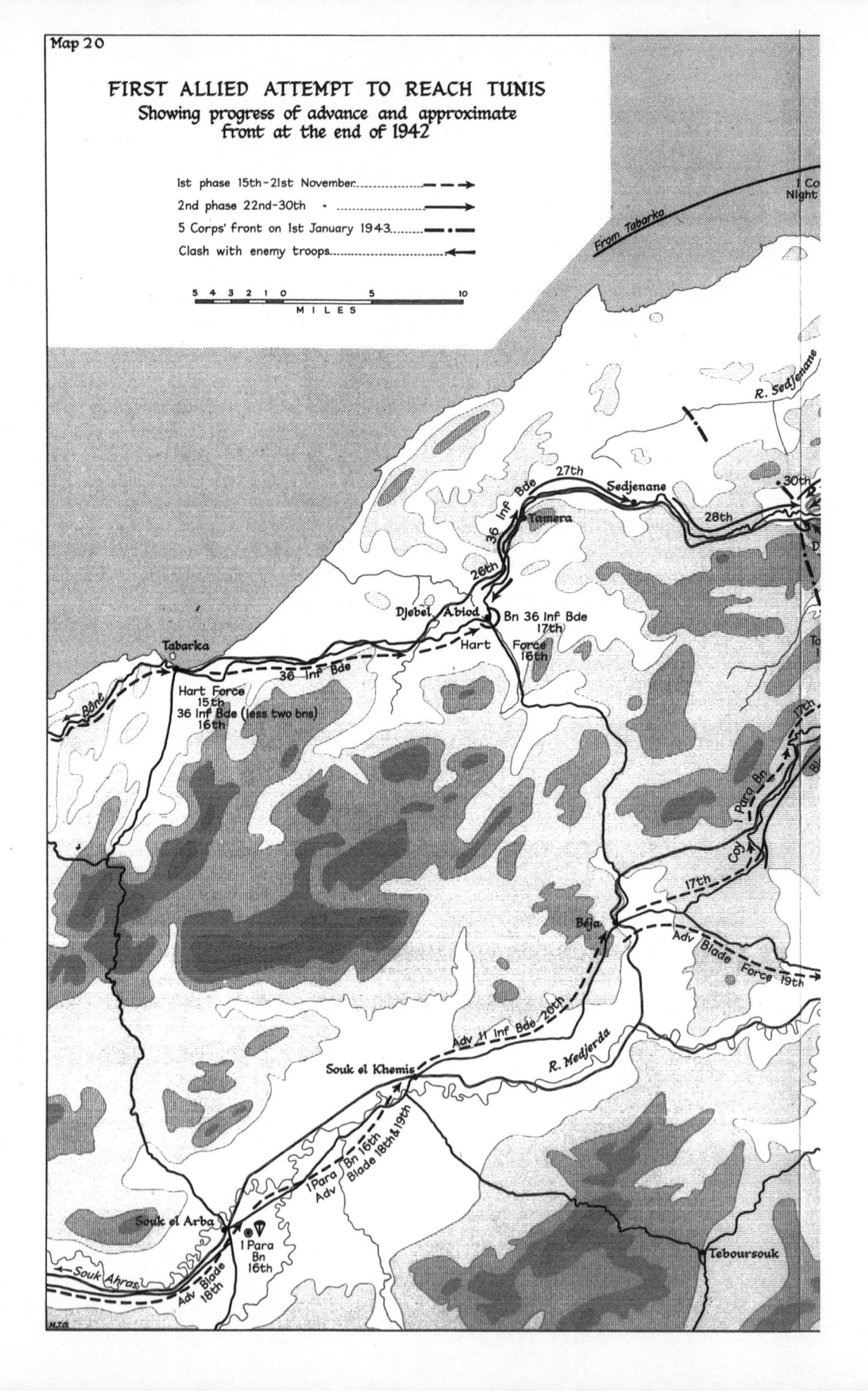

FIRST ALLIED ATTEMPT TO REACH TUNIS
Showing progress of advance and approximate front at the end of 1942

1st phase 15th–21st November .... – – →
2nd phase 22nd–30th " .... ⎯⎯→
5 Corps' front on 1st January 1943 .... – · – · –
Clash with enemy troops .... ←

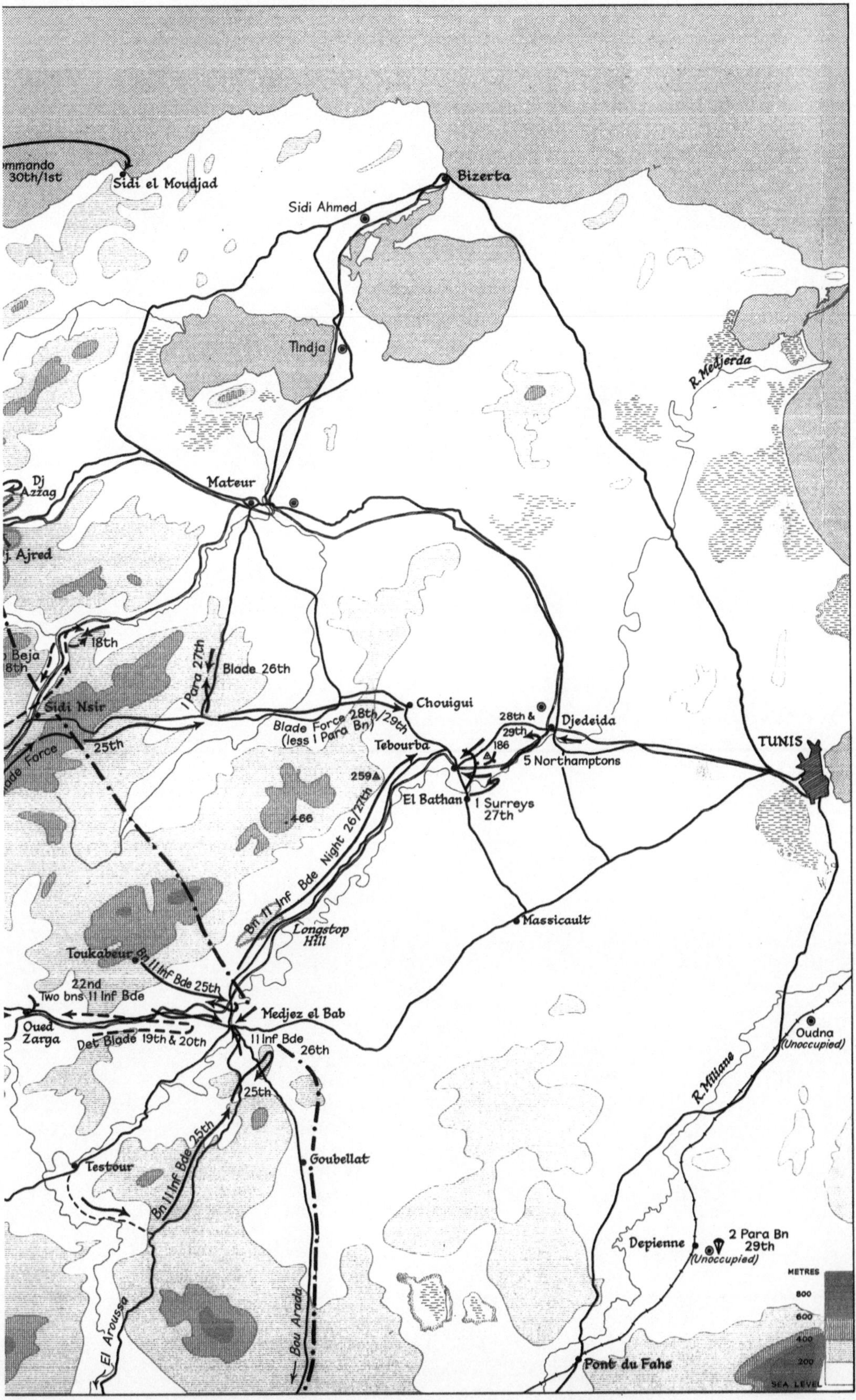

ommando
30th/1st
Sidi el Moudjad
Bizerta
Sidi Ahmed
Tindja
R. Medjerda
Dj
Azzag
Mateur
Dj. Ajred
18th
Beja
8th
Blade 26th
1 Para 27th
Sidi Nsir
Chouigui
Blade Force 28th/29th
(less 1 Para Bn)
25th
ade Force
28th &
29th
Djedeida
186
Tebourba
5 Northamptons
TUNIS
259
466
El Bathan
1 Surreys
27th
Bn 11 Inf Bde Night 26/27th
Massicault
Longstop
Hill
Toukabeur
Bn 11 Inf Bde 25th
22nd
Two bns 11 Inf Bde
Medjez el Bab
Oued
Zarga
Det Blade 19th & 20th
11 Inf Bde
26th
Oudna
(Unoccupied)
25th
R. Miliane
Testour
Goubellat
Bn 11 Inf Bde 25th
Depienne
2 Para Bn
29th
(Unoccupied)
METRES
800
600
400
200
SEA LEVEL
El Aroussa
Bou Arada
Pont du Fahs

CHAPTER VII

'TORCH' — THE EXPLOITATION EASTWARDS

(November and December)

See Maps 20 *and* 21

IN their directive to General Eisenhower the Combined Chiefs of Staff had laid down that when firm and mutually supporting lodgements had been made on the north and north-west coasts of Africa, the next phase would consist of vigorous and rapid exploitation to gain complete control of French Morocco, Algeria and Tunisia, and, if necessary, of Spanish Morocco as well.[1]

After the Eastern Assault Force had occupied Algiers and the adjacent airfields—Blida and Maison Blanche—General Eisenhower's orders to General Anderson required the 1st Army to 'build up rapidly a striking force through Algiers and adjacent ports' and 'occupy Tunisia at the earliest possible date'. An essential step would be to establish airfields at intervals along the coast and give air protection to shipping plying between Algiers and ports to the east. A start was made by occupying Bougie and Bône and the airfields at Djidjelli and Bône, as related in the previous chapter. Fortunately the 36th Infantry Brigade Group, which had been the floating reserve at Algiers, was available for these further landings.

It should here be pointed out that until early in 1943 the British 1st Army was an army in name only. In fact for some weeks it consisted of one incomplete division and part of an armoured division, which, in due course, together with a parachute brigade, an A.A. brigade and two commandos, formed the 5th Corps.[2] Most of the troops were basically well trained, but were without practical experience of war and did not have the great advantage (given by circumstance to the 8th Army) of being as a whole eased into battle. Nor were they trained for fighting in the type of country they were to find in northern Tunisia. How the 1st Army was to be built up will now be briefly described.

---

[1] This directive is summarized on p. 114, Chapter V.
[2] The Order of Battle on 6th December 1942, when the 5th Corps (Lieut.-General C. W. Allfrey) first became committed as a Corps, is given in Appendix 7.

It will be remembered that the way in which the assault and follow-up convoys were loaded had been dictated by the need to be prepared to overcome French opposition; if there were strong opposition the Allies might take perhaps three months to secure the necessary bases and lines of communication. But everything went so well with the landings that on 13th November the Chiefs of Staff were asking whether the flow of convoys could not be speeded up. The answer was that although from the purely naval point of view some speeding-up could be managed, the planned schedule would make the best possible use of the ports. Such changes in loading as became desirable were therefore confined to what could be done without interfering with the existing programme of sailings. The inevitable conflict of claims for shipping space is well illustrated by two comments in General Eisenhower's Despatch. In the assault phase the administrative backing had to be cut down to, and even below, the barest essentials in order to 'retain the minimum necessary striking power and mobility for the assaulting forces'. And then, writing of the expedition as a whole, he considers that the attacking Force, particularly at Algiers, included 'too great a proportion of troops equipped merely to seize and hold a harbour and base'. Truly, as Clausewitz has said, everything in war is simple, but to perform the simple is very difficult.

The convoy programme deserves a word of explanation. As regards the British, the assault convoy for Algiers carried the 78th Division (less one brigade group) with some anti-aircraft units and Army troops, and the Advanced H.Q. of two R.A.F. Wings. The 'follow-up' convoy arrived at Algiers on 12th November (D+4), by which time ships were able to discharge in the harbour. They brought the 1st Army's Advanced H.Q. and those of Eastern Air Command and two more R.A.F. Wings; the elements to set up two base sub-areas and a L. of C. area with one sub-area; an armoured regimental group of the 6th Armoured Division, called 'Blade Force'; a parachute brigade less two companies; men and equipment to bring the two infantry brigades up to light scale; and some more A.A. units.

As regards the Americans, arrivals in the assault and follow-up convoys included: at Algiers, the 34th Infantry Division (two Regimental Combat Teams) and some detachments of light anti-aircraft artillery; at Oran, 1st Infantry Division (three R.C.Ts), and Combat Command B of 1st Armoured Division. These will be met again because they were soon sent forward, wholly or in part, to operate with the British 1st Army.

A steady sequence of alternate fast and slow 'build-up' convoys now began, with one fast convoy arriving every fourteen days, followed four days later by a slow. This pattern was dictated by many considerations, of which the most important was probably the capacity of the ports to receive and handle cargoes. (A fast convoy took from three to five days to unload.) After some initial delays caused by bad weather and congestion at Algiers, the 'returned empties' began to be despatched westward with reasonable speed. Congestion was further relieved when, towards the end of November, after tedious negotiations, the first French vessels left Algiers for ports in West Africa—the best compromise that the French could be persuaded to accept.

On 22nd November (D+14) would arrive Rear H.Q. of 1st Army, Advanced H.Q. of 5th Corps and that of another Fighter Wing, and men and equipment to put fighting formations on the following footing:

78th Division:	two brigade groups at 'light' scale, and one at 'assault' scale.
6th Armoured Division:	two armoured regimental groups and one infantry brigade (less one battalion).

With the arrival of the fast convoy due on 6th December (D+28) the picture would become: 78th Division as above; 6th Armoured Division nearly complete on a reduced establishment; H.Q. 5th Corps nearly complete; H.Q. 1st Army complete; Allied Force H.Q. partly complete. By this date, too, over 10,000 reinforcements would have landed. The next fast convoy, due on 20th December (D+42), would almost complete H.Q. 5th Corps and both Divisions, but there would be many Army and Corps troops still to come. In block figures the totals brought by fast convoys by 20th December would be about 189,000 British troops and airmen and 23,000 vehicles.

Meanwhile the slow convoys were to deliver vast quantities of material of all kinds. A few examples will give some idea of the scale of the logistic problems. By about mid-December there would have been put on shore 8 million rations; 8 million gallons of petrol; 5½ million gallons of aviation spirit; maintenance transport vehicles with a lift of 6,600 tons; 463,000 rounds of artillery ammunition (apart from anti-aircraft); 23 million rounds of small arms ammunition; large quantities of bombs for the R.A.F.; hospital equipment and supplies for nearly 10,000 patients—to say nothing of a mountain of other things great and small, including 20,000 tons of coal for the railway.

The ultimate strength of the British 1st Army was to be from four to six divisions, landed at Algiers and ports to the east; that of the U.S. Forces seven divisions, landed in Morocco and at Oran.

The planned strength of Eastern Air Command was given on page 128 as 454 aircraft of all types by seven weeks after D day, that is, towards the end of December. This represented about 27 squadrons; actually the number of R.A.F. squadrons which reached Algeria was 31. The maximum strength of Western Air Command was to be 1,244 aircraft, including 282 in reserve.

Four Wing Headquarters R.A.F., including three of those which had arrived in the first two convoys, were to support the advance eastwards to Bizerta and Tunis. Three of the four wings were to be mobile; in all these consisted of eleven single-engine day-fighter, two twin-engine night-fighter, and two army co-operation squadrons (Tac. R/fighter-bombers). The fourth wing comprised two day-bomber and two bomber reconnaissance squadrons—also equipped with day-bombers. In addition there was one Air Observation Post (Air O.P.) squadron.[1] Transport aircraft for use in airborne operations were to be called forward from the United Kingdom as soon as airfields were available for them, but initially General Eisenhower had hoped to use the transport aircraft which were to land in the Oran area.[2] Another new type of R.A.F. unit making its first appearance in the Mediterranean theatre was the field squadron of the R.A.F. Regiment. Each squadron contained one armoured, one support (anti-tank guns) and three rifle flights, and had the primary role of defending airfields against airborne attack.

During the first five days of the campaign (8th to 12th November) it was reasonable that air defence of the convoys using Algiers, of the port itself, and of its airfields, should have first call on the available fighters. Accordingly five fighter squadrons were at first allotted to the Algiers area, mostly at Maison Blanche. One army co-operation squadron, one photographic reconnaissance flight, and one day-bomber squadron were to be established ashore at the same time. By the end of the third week it was hoped that all the remaining squadrons of Eastern Air Command would have arrived. In the event many squadrons were brought in well ahead of schedule. A few were delayed, but only for a matter of days, and several more were added to the force as the campaign went on.

The Hurricanes of No. 225 Army Co-operation Squadron were to work with 78th Division; No. 4 P.R.U., under the control of Air H.Q., was to provide strategic photographic reconnaissance, and No. 651 (Air O.P.) Squadron the artillery reconnaissance.

---

[1] A flight of Taylorcraft had been sent to France in 1940 in this role but was withdrawn when the German offensive began. Towards the end of 1941, however, Air O.P. squadrons began to form in the U.K. The Auster aircraft and maintenance crews were provided by the Royal Air Force and the pilots and remainder of the squadron personnel by the Royal Artillery. Air O.P. squadrons were allotted on the basis of one squadron to each Corps.

[2] See pp. 129–30 and pp. 147, 149.

Demands for all forms of air support were to be made through an Air Support Control at H.Q. 78th Division. When the Control moved eastwards beyond direct communication with the rearward airfields, calls for air support were to be sent by a wireless link, if possible; alternatively, by re-transmission through 1st Army Command Post (which would have a small R.A.F. Command Post alongside), to Air H.Q. at Algiers who would in turn contact the airfields. Not an ideal arrangement by any means, but another example of having to make do.

A repair and salvage unit would be established in each Wing together with an air stores park (A.S.P.), and each squadron was to carry an initial seven days' supply of aircraft spares to tide over until the A.S.Ps came into full operation. Replacement aircraft were to come from the United Kingdom via Gibraltar, where single-engine fighters would be erected and then flown to North Africa. Initially a pool of aircraft replacements equal to one month's fighter wastage was to be built up at Gibraltar.

On 14th November General Anderson decided upon a move eastward by all his available forces, hoping to be able to attack Bizerta and Tunis in about a week's time. Accordingly on the 15th advanced parties of the 11th Infantry Brigade Group and 'Blade Force' were directed on Souk el Arba through Souk Ahras; 'Hart Force' on Djebel Abiod; and the 36th Infantry Brigade Group on Tabarka, being joined by its detachments from Bougie, Djidjelli and Sétif which were replaced by units of 34th U.S. Infantry Division. Bearing in mind that Darlan's cease fire order was not signed until the 10th November and that the minimum follow-up force did not finish disembarking until the 14th at Algiers or grow beyond the minimum until the 27th, and that Algiers is over 500 miles distant from Tunis, it is clear that General Anderson was not allowing the many difficulties to deter him, and was determined to set a fast pace.

Meanwhile the Royal Air Force was establishing its fighters on forward airfields from which to give support to the land, cover at sea and over the ports and airfields, and escorts for its own and U.S. Bombers. By 14th November the Spitfires of Nos. 154 and 242 Squadrons were at Djidjelli, and those of Nos. 81 and 111 Squadrons at Bône. No. 225 Squadron—one of the two army co-operation squadrons—was just receiving its Hurricanes at Maison Blanche. From Blida, operating mostly by night, Bisleys in increasing numbers bombed the principal Tunisian airfields and the port of Bizerta, where Axis reinforcements were arriving by sea. From Malta, Wellingtons took El Aouina as their principal target, with occasional visits to Sidi Ahmed, in which, from the 16th, U.S. Fortresses from Maison Blanche began to take part.

It was now clearly important to broaden the basis of air operations by gaining the use of airfields farther inland. Accordingly on 15th November part of the 509th U.S. Parachute Regiment in American transports escorted by R.A.F. fighters dropped unopposed at Youks les Bains, near Tebessa. Two days later an American detachment penetrated to Gafsa—a first modest step in opening up the central Tunisian area of operations.[1] On the 16th, after a day's postponement for bad weather, the 1st (British) Parachute Battalion in American transports escorted by American fighters dropped on the airfield at Souk el Arba, where they found the local French troops friendly and helpful.

The small 'Hart Force' reached Djebel Abiod during the night 15th/16th November. On the 15th a liaison officer from 36th Brigade met General Barré (Commandant Supérieur des Troupes de Tunisie) at Béja. The French force was in several scattered groups and amounted in all to about 10,000 men with half a dozen guns but no anti-tank guns. Until 13th November Barré had had no orders, other than one from Darlan to resist the Americans, and therefore temporized with the Axis while withdrawing his troops to Teboursouk—Medjez el Bab—Sidi Nsir. On the 13th General Giraud ordered him to cover the British concentrations from Teboursouk northwards, while General Koeltz did the same from Souk el Arba southwards.[2] Barré, knowing his own weakness and not knowing what British help to expect, thought it best to temporize for a little longer, and did so with great success.

A glance must now be taken at the Axis side. General Warlimont (Deputy Chief of Operations at *OKW*) has admitted that on 8th November the Germans were taken by surprise. There had been no planning for any operations in Tunisia, and no guiding principles had been laid down on which to base immediate action. This, he wrote, was mainly because of uncertainty about the attitude of the French.

On 8th November Captain Schürmeyer of the *Luftwaffe*, who had been appointed by Kesselring (C.-in-C. South) to be 'Air Liaison Officer in North Africa', arrived at Tunis. His task was to prepare for the landing of *Luftwaffe* units in Tunisia. On the 9th the Vichy Government placed their Tunisian bases at the disposal of the Axis, and next day Hitler announced his policy in the new situation.

---

[1] A plan existed for creating a diversion and denying the port of Sousse to the Axis by landing there a brigade group of the Malta Garrison. On 19th November, however, the idea was dropped as being impracticable with the resources available.

[2] At this time General Giraud commanded all the French armed forces; under him General Juin commanded the army, and Koeltz the 19th Corps (of the Algiers and Constantine Divisions). All these, like Barré's force, were very poorly equipped.

Briefly, a bridgehead was to be gained and held in Tunisia in a race with the Allied forces; Kesselring was to subordinate all other activities in the Mediterranean to this task. Colonel Harlinghausen, appointed *Fliegerführer* Tunisia, would command the bridgehead at first. The front was to be short, on defensible terrain, and an adequate distance from the main supply ports in Tunisia. Relations with the French were to be close and friendly, on the basis that the French Government had asked for occupation by Axis forces, but if Barré's Tunisian Division was suspect it was to be disarmed. Harlinghausen was made subordinate to *Fliegerkorps II* and was to be responsible for air support to 90th Corps—as the first German command in Tunisia would be called.

The primary aim of the *Luftwaffe* was to slow down the Allied advance and so enable the Axis land forces to be built up in preparation for an offensive. Secondly it was to safeguard Axis supplies. A vigorous offensive would be adopted, so as to gain the necessary local air superiority. In October the Germans had steadily reinforced their air force in the Mediterranean area, mainly because of the critical situation in the Western Desert, but also because of disturbing reports of increased shipping and air activity at Gibraltar. The Allied landings in 'Torch' gave a strong impetus to the policy of reinforcement, and by 10th November the operational strength of *Fliegerkorps II* had risen to 445 aircraft from the 283 of a month earlier. Even more striking was the expansion of the German air transport fleet from 205 to 673 aircraft in the same period.

On 9th November some 27 German fighters and 24 Stukas flew in to El Aouina (Tunis). These were the first arrivals of the *Luftwaffe* and were unopposed by the French but hampered at the outset for want of a proper ground organization. More German aircraft and a handful of *Luftwaffe* troops arrived on the next and subsequent days. By 15th November it is estimated that *Fliegerführer* Tunisia had under his command 81 fighters (F.W. 190s and Me. 109s) of which 52 were serviceable, and 28 dive-bombers of which 20 were ready for immediate operations.[1]

On 11th November Colonel Lederer, of the Army, arrived to take command on land. On the 12th came two companies of the 5th Parachute Regiment and one of the 104th Panzer Grenadier Regiment, and two days later 11th Parachute Engineer Battalion, a weak Reconnaissance Company, and some motor-cyclists and one company of tanks.

---

[1] The arrival of the fighter F.W. 190 was an important event. Its performance was comparable with the Me. 109G, but its armament and armour were heavier. Its large radial engine in front and the heavy armour behind the cockpit made it difficult for an attacking fighter to get at the pilot, and its compactness made it highly manoeuvrable. Altogether a formidable aircraft, superior generally to anything the Allies possessed in North Africa at that time. Probably fourteen had arrived by 15th November.

In this fashion, on no prearranged plan, troops came tumbling in—among the first being men from the pool of reinforcements held in Italy for Rommel's *Deutsch-Italienische Panzerarmee*. The Germans were fortunate in having a strong force of transport aircraft, which at once began to ferry German troops at an average rate of 750 a day, or about 15,000 by the end of November. During the same period nearly 1,900 came over by sea, together with large quantities of weapons, equipment and ammunition. In terms of German units, there had arrived towards the end of November, in addition to those already named, two battalions of 5th Parachute Regiment and two and a half of the Barenthin Glider Regiment; three '*Marsch*' (or draft-holding) battalions; a signals battalion; a battery of field guns; twenty 8·8-cm dual-purpose guns; parts of an anti-tank and of a motor-cycle battalion. Mobile and armoured units included two Reconnaissance Companies; detachments of 190th and 501st Panzer Battalions; two companies of 7th Panzer Regiment of 10th Panzer Division.[1] The controlling Headquarters, which was to be called 90th Corps, was set up in Tunisia on 16th November in the persons of General Nehring and one staff officer.[2] It is recorded that their transport was a French taxi-cab, and that they had no clerks or typewriters; '... commands are at present in a state of complete confusion. No one can be found to say what units have arrived or where they are. No means of communication other than the French postal network.' The sole complete German formation due to arrive fairly soon was the 10th Panzer Division (Major-General Wolfgang Fischer).

On 12th November the Italians began to send over the Superga Division (General Lorenzelli), and the move was still going on during December. In addition, they sent the 10th Bersaglieri and two battalions of the San Marco Regiment of Marines. These Italian troops were *de facto* under German command, but not until 2nd December was Lorenzelli formally made responsible to Nehring. *Comando Supremo* appointed General Imperiali to command a (weak) Italian Group called 50th Special Brigade.

Colonel Lederer had decided that he could do little more than defend Bizerta. Nehring, on arrival, promptly dismissed him, adopted a more robust policy, and began to throw out the familiar battle-groups which the Germans always seemed to handle so easily

---

[1] *Tank Strengths*
Det. 190th Panzer Battalion: 13 Pzkw III and IV Specials. Det. 501st Panzer Battalion: 4 'Tigers', 2 Pzkw III. 7th Panzer Regiment: 32 Pzkw III, 2 Pzkw IV Specials. The monster Pzkw VI or Henschel Tiger I was a newcomer to Africa; it weighed 56 tons and was armed with a 8·8-cm Kwk 36 gun—the same as the dual purpose weapon so famous in the Western Desert. The Tigers had not overcome teething troubles and were proving unreliable; the British did not bag their first until 31st January 1943.

[2] Nehring had succeeded Crüwell (captured at Gazala in June 1942) in command of the *D.A.K.* He was wounded on 31st August at Alam el Halfa.

and effectively. It was just as well for them that they could, for units and detachments were arriving in bits and pieces and there were no prepared defences to occupy. The immediate framework was a Bizerta bridgehead under Colonel von Broich and a Tunis bridgehead under Colonel Stolz. Detailed reconnaissance was obstructed by the French in various ways, but Nehring rightly expected the British to advance against these places by the two principal roads, and judged that they would set particular store by the early capture of Bizerta. He also thought that the Allies would make a drive through Tebessa towards the east coast to cut what might later become a vital supply line for Rommel. He decided first to try to prevent the British from reaching Bizerta and Tunis, and that the best way would be to attack them. For this purpose Battle Group Witzig, named after the Commander of the 11th Parachute Engineer Battalion, was sent on 17th November from Mateur towards Tabarka with orders to drive the enemy back to Bône. Their place was taken at Mateur and Bizerta by Battle Group Stolz. During the next few days the Axis occupied Sousse, Sfax and Gabes, and raided Gafsa.

The Tunis bridgehead soon took firmer shape in two sectors—North under Stolz, and South under Lorenzelli. Gradually all units in the Bizerta bridgehead coalesced to form the Division von Broich, and at the end of the month the 10th Panzer Division became the parent formation of Tunis North. In this way the Germans built up their organization to receive the hotchpotch of reinforcements which continued to arrive by sea and air.

The fighting in Northern Tunisia during November and December 1942 falls into four phases. First, until 21st November, there is the period of making contact on the ground. The second phase, from the 22nd to the 30th, covers the unsuccessful attempt by the 1st Army to capture Tunis or Bizerta by *coup de main*. Then follows a period during which the enemy counter-attacked successfully and gained some ground. Lastly, from 12th December, the Allies were preparing to renew their advance, but continually worsening weather compelled them to postpone it and towards the end of the month to call it off altogether.

The first clash on the ground was caused by General Nehring's order to Witzig on 17th November to make for Tabarka and drive the enemy back to Bône. It occurred near Djebel Abiod after a patrol of Hart Force had reported tanks and lorried infantry approaching from Mateur. These were engaged and stopped by the foremost troops of 36th Infantry Brigade with appreciable losses on both sides. Elsewhere there was no contact. The leading troops of

Blade Force reached Souk Ahras, having covered 400 miles by rail and road from Algiers.

Next day a patrol of the 1st Parachute Battalion (now under Blade Force) ambushed and destroyed a German patrol on the road near Sidi Nsir, halfway between Béja and Mateur. Farther south troops of General Barré's Tunisian Division held the important road centre and bridge at Medjez el Bab, situated where the Medjerda river begins to open to the Tunisian plain. An ultimatum from General Nehring, demanding free passage early on the 19th, was ignored by General Barré. Two light attacks by German troops from Tunis North were then beaten off by the French, who withdrew from Medjez el Bab that night, having seen that the British could not support them as strongly as they wished. The Germans then occupied the town, which they were lucky to get so easily. But the fact that Barré had begun to fight on the side of the Allies was of much greater consequence.

On 19th November General Anderson moved his Headquarters forward from Algiers to near Philippeville, and the R.A.F. established a Command Post under Air Commodore Lawson alongside the Army Commander. But the results were disappointing owing to the poor communications. However the Eastern Air Command continued to build up its fighter strength on the few quite well-situated airfields in eastern Algeria. Arrivals since the 14th were: at Bône, No. 225 Squadron (Hurricanes, Tac R. and fighter-bomber); at Philippeville, No. 253 (Hurricanes); at Souk el Arba, Nos. 72 and 93 (Spitfires); and at Youks les Bains, one squadron (Lightnings) of U.S. 14th Fighter Group. Now that a front was beginning to form on the ground, calls for air support were increasing and in the week the fighters flew nearly 1,500 sorties mainly on reconnaissance and protective tasks. Bisleys from Blida and Fortresses from Maison Blanche continued to attack the ports and airfields of Tunis and Bizerta.

The *Luftwaffe*, too, was active, and attacked mainly troop and transport movement on the roads and railway and the harbours, especially Bône. Long-range bombers began to attack Allied airfields by night, particularly Bône and Maison Blanche. On one occasion thirteen Allied aircraft were destroyed and many damaged at Maison Blanche.[1] For greater safety the U.S. Fortresses moved back to Oran, whence they could still reach Tunis although the round trip was some twelve hundred miles! These enemy raids repeated a lesson learnt at home and in Egypt that unless night-

---

[1] On the 20th/21st about thirty enemy aircraft took part. Three Beaufighters, two Lightnings, one Fortress, four Spitfire fighters and three P.R.U. Spitfires were destroyed. Among aircraft damaged were nine Beaufighters. The entire ground equipment of a Photographic Reconnaissance Unit was destroyed.

fighters were equipped with Airborne Interception (A.I.) and operated under Ground Controlled Interception (G.C.I.) they could not be expected to do much harm to the attacking bombers.[1] But no G.C.I. station was in action at Algiers and no fighters had A.I. equipment: the Beaufighters had been stripped of theirs for reasons of security before leaving England.

The general eastward move of the 78th Division and its many attached units continued as rapidly as possible in spite of difficulties and shortages. But the attack on Tunis which General Anderson had hoped to stage for the 21st or 22nd had to be postponed a few days. He warned General Evelegh not to become committed piecemeal in the meantime, but to wait until he had concentrated the greater part of his force in the forward area.

Every available means—sea, road, rail and air—was used for these moves and for establishing the L. of C. Much improvisation was necessary. Road traffic was limited by the great lack of transport, which also affected the clearing of cargoes from the docks. The sea link was invaluable. Occasional ships from the United Kingdom went straight through to Bône, but usually men and cargoes were transferred at Algiers into smaller ships or landing-craft.[2] From Bône, where Commodore G. N. Oliver was installed as S.N.O. Inshore Squadron, landing-craft moved cargoes further east to the small ports of La Calle and Tabarka. Bougie and Philippeville were also used to capacity. Neither surface escorts nor fighter cover could be provided in adequate strength for these coastal convoys, which were frequently attacked from the air and sometimes by submarine; casualties at sea, however, were not high. Of the ports, Bône was attacked the most often by bombers and torpedo-bombers, and mines were laid by aircraft in the approaches.

A base sub-area was set up at Bône on 18th November, nearly 190 miles from the front by road, and 120 by rail from the advanced railhead at Souk el Arba—which opened (in name) on 20th November. Trains were slow and irregular, and took from four to six days to reach Souk el Arba from Algiers. The railway was still under French control, as British operating units had not yet arrived. The French railway staff, though helpful, knew little about British methods and needs; moreover, the French themselves, military and

---

[1] Ground Controlled Interception had its core in a radar device on the ground which showed in plan form the positions of the night-fighter and its quarry in the air. Airborne Interception enabled the night-fighter equipped with it to detect neighbouring aircraft. G.C.Is had been established in Egypt since August 1942, and A.I. had been in operation since December 1941.

[2] Troops were mostly carried forward in the small infantry landing ships *Queen Emma*, *Princess Beatrix*, *Royal Ulsterman* and *Royal Scotsman*, well known to peace-time passengers on the Harwich-Hook and Stranraer—Larne runs. Every third or fourth night they carried between them some 3,300 men.

civil, had to have their share of trains. Losses through pilfering were serious and very hard to prevent.

Relations with the French Army soon became good, and even cordial. At first General Giraud refused to allow French troops to serve under British commanders (there were more than forty French units in the forward area) but on 24th November it was agreed that French troops north of a line Kairouan—Le Kef should be controlled by the British, and British and American troops south of this line by the French. This did not settle the matter once and for all, indeed the system of command of the land front was to be a recurring problem for General Eisenhower, and General Anderson.

On 24th November General Anderson considered the 78th Division, though not complete, to be sufficiently ready, and ordered General Evelegh to gain 'the line Tebourba—Mateur, thence north-west to the coast'; this done, he was to advance on Tunis and Bizerta at the earliest possible moment. General Evelegh then ordered 11th Infantry Brigade to take Medjez el Bab on the 25th. Blade Force was to operate on the left and capture El Bathan and Djedeida from the north-west; if all went well, it was to attack Mateur. The 36th Brigade was to resume its advance towards Mateur.

The 11th Infantry Brigade's attack did not succeed, but Blade Force met little opposition and Stuart tanks of 1st Battalion U.S. 1st Armoured Regiment (under command since 21st November) raided Djedeida landing ground and destroyed seventeen Stuka aircraft and did other considerable damage. This encounter took place only ten miles from Tunis, and the threat caused Nehring to draw in his forces. Next day both British brigades made progress. The 11th occupied Medjez el Bab, and that night the 1st Surreys pushed on to Tebourba. To the south of Mateur, Blade Force had a brush with a small detachment which finally withdrew; meanwhile the 36th Infantry Brigade advanced a short way to Tamera. In his orders for the next day (27th) General Evelegh reversed the roles of 11th Infantry Brigade and Blade Force: the former, supported by the medium tanks of 2/13th U.S. Armoured Regiment, was to take Djedeida and Mateur; the latter, with all the armour, was then to strike at Tunis. The 36th Infantry Brigade was to press on again in the north.

Early on the 27th the 1st Surreys, widely extended in front of Tebourba, were attacked by the hastily formed Battle Group Lüder.[1] In the sharp fighting of that day the Surreys had many casualties and all eight guns of 322nd Field Battery R.A., supporting

---

[1] 190th Panzer Battalion with about 13 runners and two out of the four Tigers of 501st Panzer Battalion; 190th Signals Battalion.

them, were knocked out. Lüder reported eight of his tanks destroyed and four damaged. Brigadier Cass ordered up 5th Northamptons, with 19 medium (Grant) tanks in support, to take Djedeida on the 28th, hoping to continue the advance on Mateur the same day. Blade Force was to move to Chouigui, ready for the drive on Tunis.

General Evelegh now made two additions to his plan; the 2nd Parachute Battalion was to drop at Depienne on the 29th, attack the landing ground at Oudna, and later link with Blade Force. On the other flank the 1st Commando was to land from the sea near Sidi el Moudjad and harass the rear of the enemy opposing 36th Infantry Brigade, now at Sedjenane. The results were disappointing. On the 28th and 29th the 5th Northamptons failed to take Djedeida, and on the 28th the leading troops of 36th Infantry Brigade were ambushed between Djebel Ajred and Djebel Azzag. An attack by night on the 29th/30th November failed to eject the enemy. The parachute and commando operations also achieved little.[1] In the face of stiffening opposition General Evelegh decided on the 30th to pause for two or three days to await more air support, which General Anderson reported as being 'insufficient for the scale of enemy attack'.

The fighter aircraft of Eastern Air Command were going through a very trying time. Their rate of serviceability in the forward area was low—on the average nine aircraft in a Spitfire squadron. Squadrons were still working on a commando basis, and until maintenance crews and repair and salvage units arrived no improvement was likely. Wastage was very heavy—nearly 100 per cent of initial aircraft. In spite of all this more and more was required of the fighters. Cover for shipping and airfields was as important as ever, more escorts for bombers were wanted, and there was now a need for intensive air support for the advance of the 1st Army. But of the airfields in the forward area, only Bône was 'all-weather', and the rain of 24th and 25th November gave a foretaste of what would happen to grass or earth runways in the rainy season just beginning.[2] Another serious disadvantage was the distance of the airfields from the front—for example, to Tebourba was 60 miles from Souk el Arba airfield, 120 from Bône and 140 from Youks les Bains, but only 20 from Tunis. So the Axis had a double advantage, of which they made good use, for German fighter-bombers and

---

[1] By 28th November casualties in the two Infantry Brigades amounted to about 580 killed, wounded and missing. The 2nd Parachute Battalion's operation resulted in 23 killed and wounded, and 266 missing, though many later came in. Oudna landing ground was not in use and the advance of Blade Force, with which the Battalion was to have co-operated, did not take place.

[2] To surface a single runway might need 2,000 tons of steel mat, which at this time would have taken up the whole lift of the railway for two days.

Map 21

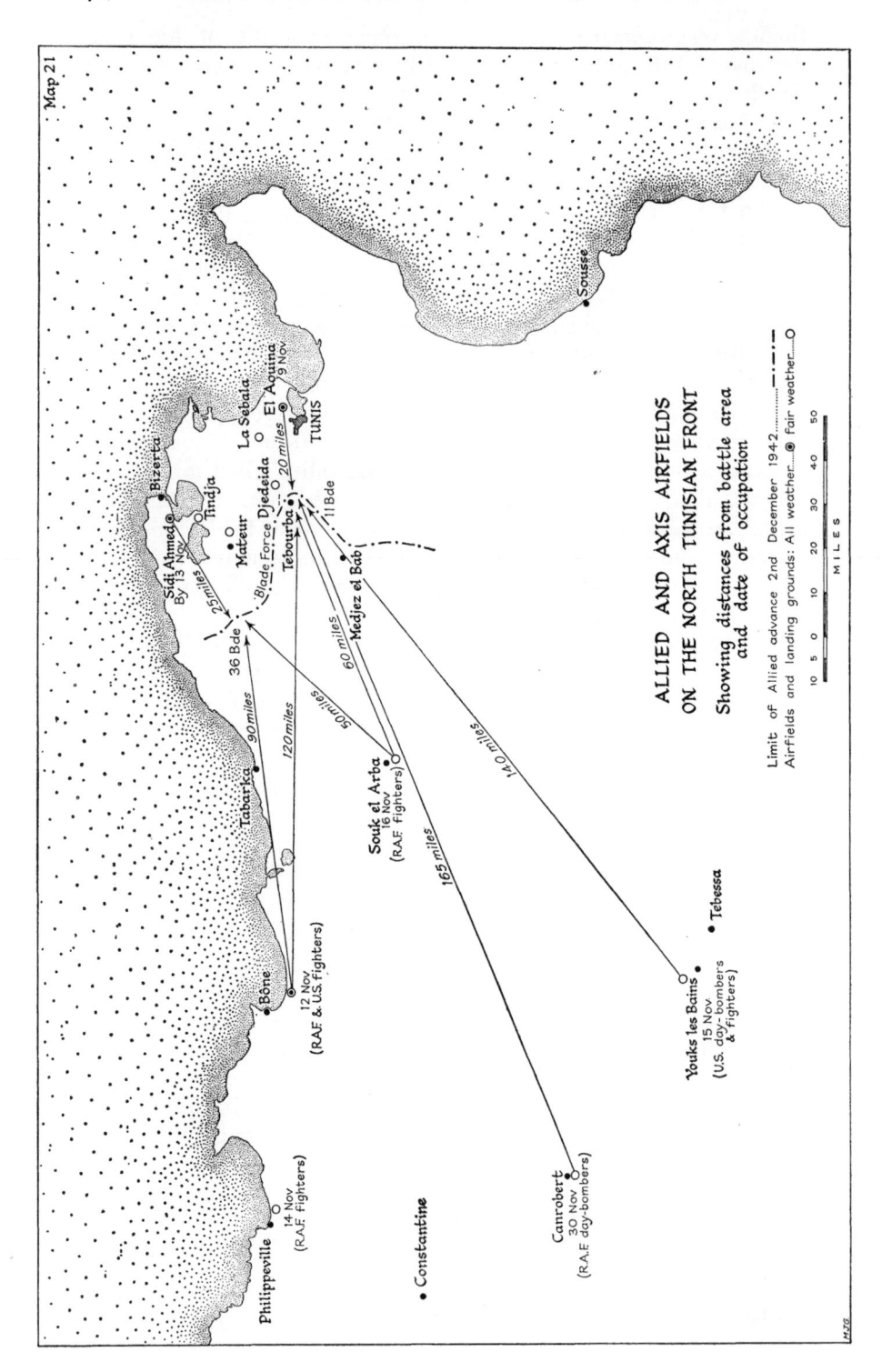

ALLIED AND AXIS AIRFIELDS ON THE NORTH TUNISIAN FRONT

Showing distances from battle area and date of occupation

Limit of Allied advance 2nd December 1942 ....
Airfields and landing grounds: All weather ⊙ fair weather ○

Stukas, working from their conveniently close and all-weather airfields, certainly seem to have supported their troops effectively. Although the Allied bombing was now getting into its stride and helping to delay the build-up and supply of the Axis troops facing the 1st Army, General Anderson felt the need of more direct support in the land battle.

The ports and airfields of Bizerta and Tunis were now being attacked nearly every night and sometimes by day; the working of the ports was impeded and many Axis aircraft were destroyed on the ground. The Allies also suffered in this respect: for example, on the 22nd Souk el Arba was dive-bombed several times and eleven Spitfires were lost, in the air and on the ground, and on the 28th seven were lost at Bône. Night attacks on Algiers continued without any interceptions until on the 27th a flight of Beaufighters went into action equipped with A.I. for the first time and shot down three German bombers. The enemy's losses in night attacks soon began to mount.

During the period 22nd–30th November, in direct and indirect support of the advance, Eastern Air Command flew an estimated total of 1,710 sorties and lost at least forty-five aircraft, ten of them on the ground. The U.S. Twelfth Air Force flew about 180 sorties and lost at least seven aircraft. The *Luftwaffe* in Tunisia flew some 1,084 sorties and lost sixty-three aircraft (excluding those destroyed by Malta's aircraft), including twenty-one on the ground and three to A.A. guns. The recorded Italian losses amounted to four aircraft.

All this time Southern Tunisia had been in the minds of the high command of both sides. The Allies, for their part, saw a danger of destructive raids from the south-east against the right rear and communications of the 78th Division. Some distant protection was given by the U.S. 2nd/509th Parachute Battalion, which, reinforced by a few infantry and anti-tank guns and named the Tunisian Task Force, watched the gaps and passes in the large area Tebessa—Kasserine—Sbeitla—Gafsa, while the French promised to co-operate, closer in, from their posts at Tebessa, Le Kef, and Teboursouk.[1] On the Axis side Nehring was anxious about a possible Allied thrust towards Sfax and Gabes, and, although Southern Tunisia was the special concern of General Imperiali, German reconnaissance units also patrolled widely throughout the area. In short, both sides were watchful and patrols quite often clashed.

At this stage the east coast Tunisian ports of Sousse, Sfax and Gabes began to receive attention from Allied aircraft—first

---

[1] It must always be remembered that the French troops were very poorly equipped.

U.S. Lightnings, joined later at Youks les Bains by U.S. Bostons. Marauders, recently arrived at Maison Blanche, and Beaufighter fighter-bombers from Malta added their weight to these attacks. A new feature of this period was the minelaying in the approaches to the more important Axis ports by Beauforts and F.A.A. Albacores from Malta.

See Map 22

General Evelegh's wish for a few days' pause was thwarted by the enemy, for Kesselring had not approved of Nehring's withdrawals and on the 28th ordered him to push the British back and so enlarge the Tunis bridgehead. Major-General W. Fischer, part of whose 10th Panzer Division was just arriving at Tunis, was appointed by Nehring to command the operation.[1] He was given the Stolz Group and four 'Marsch' battalions of low grade troops, and formed from his own Division and various odd units four small groups called 'Hudel', 'Lüder', 'Koch', and (in reserve) 'Djedeida'. The plan was for an enveloping attack. 'Hudel' with 40 tanks was to destroy the British at Chouigui, and then, joined by 'Lüder' with 20 tanks, attack Tebourba from the north-west; 'Koch' was to attack El Bathan from the south-east and then make for the British administrative area three miles west, known as 'Tebourba Gap'. The attack was fixed for 1st December.

The units of the 11th Infantry Brigade were disposed roughly in the areas reached in the advance of the 29th, the only change being the relief of the Northamptons by the 2nd Hampshires in the foremost position facing Djedeida. The 1st Surreys were stretched over a large area which included the prominent Djebel Maiana (Pt 186) and the river bridge at El Bathan. Blade Force, which still included 1st Battalion 1st U.S. Armoured Regiment, lay mostly around or to the south of Chouigui. The 17th/21st Lancers, less one squadron, had moved back to Tebourba Gap for maintenance early in the morning of 1st December.

Towards 8 a.m. the Hudel and Lüder Groups, led by General Fischer in person, advanced on Chouigui from two directions and caused Blade Force to disperse, part making for Tebourba and part for Tebourba Gap. Enemy tanks came dangerously near to the main road at the point where it enters the Gap, but worse confusion seems to have been averted largely by the steady shooting of the artillery, which caused the tanks to draw away. The enemy's

---

[1] The units of 10th Panzer Division available were: two companies of 7th Panzer Regiment with 40 tanks, most of them Pzkw IIIs; two companies of 10th Motor Cycle Bn; part of 90th Panzerjäger Bn with eight 7·5-cm and 7·62-cm Pak S.P. and eight 7·5-cm Pak guns. The Division's two Panzer Grenadier Regiments were yet to come.

Map 22

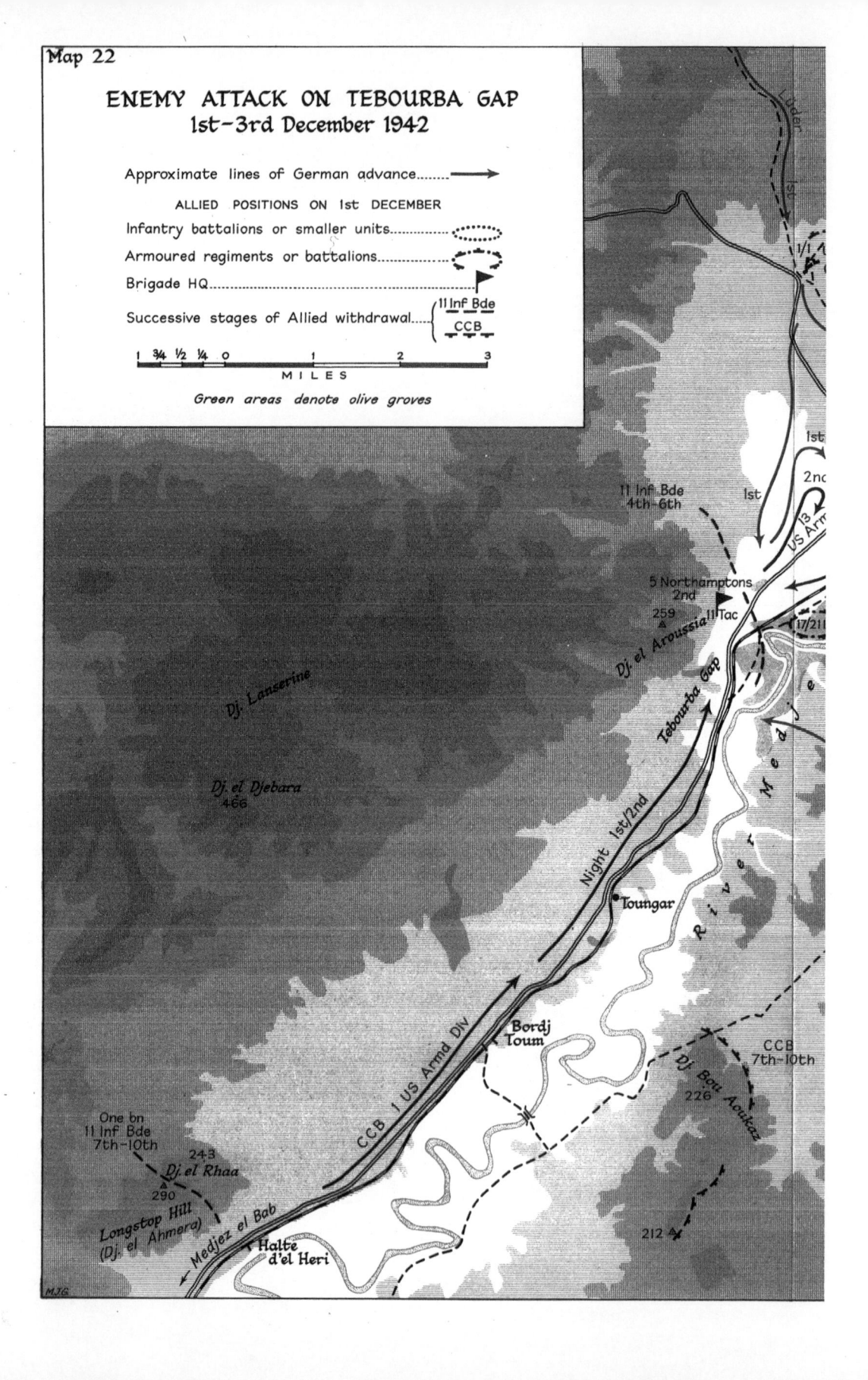

ENEMY ATTACK ON TEBOURBA GAP
1st–3rd December 1942

Approximate lines of German advance........ →

ALLIED POSITIONS ON 1st DECEMBER

Infantry battalions or smaller units............
Armoured regiments or battalions............
Brigade HQ....................
Successive stages of Allied withdrawal..... { 11 Inf Bde / CCB }

MILES

Green areas denote olive groves

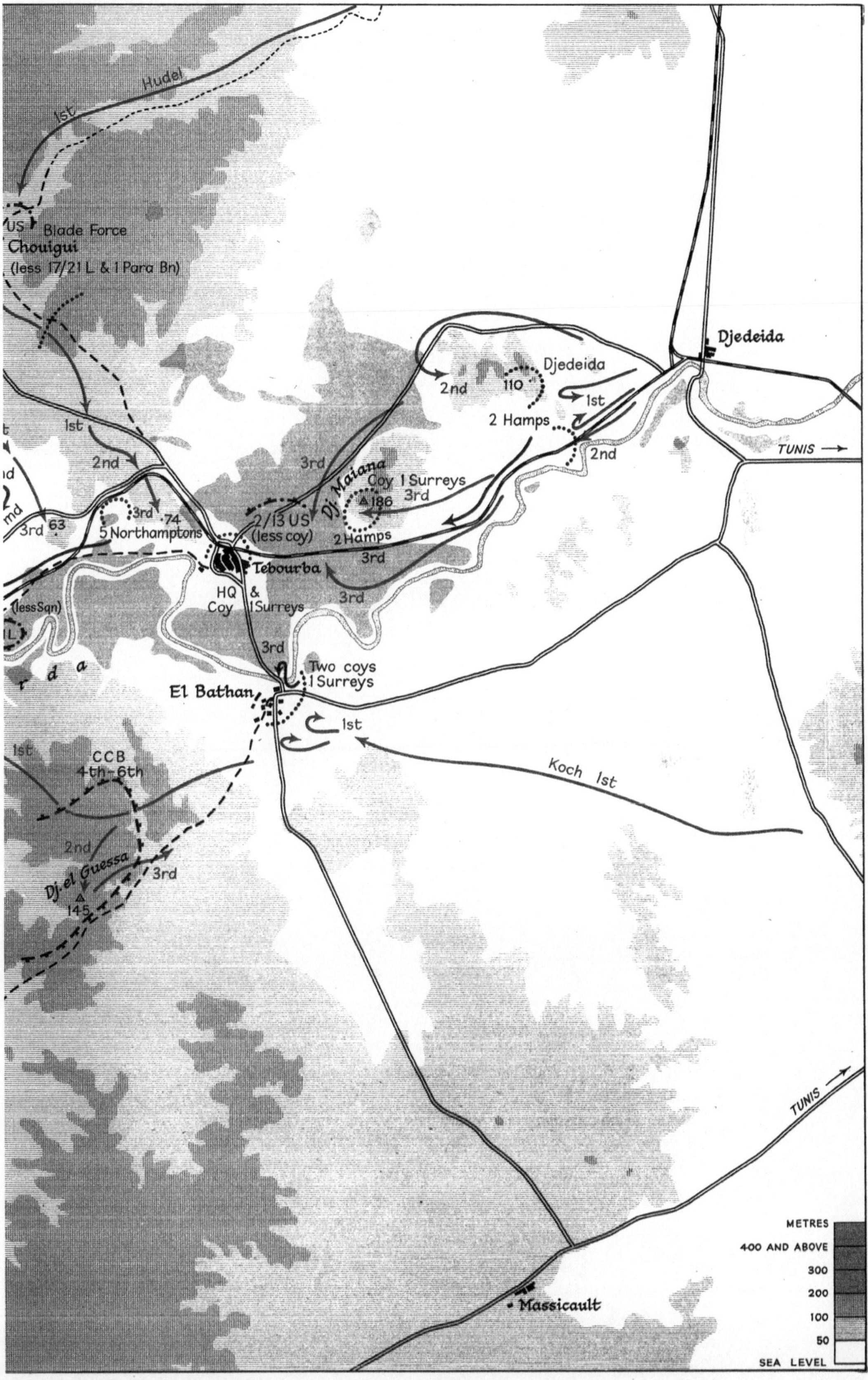

Hudel
1st
US
Blade Force
Chouigui
(less 17/21 L & 1 Para Bn)
Djedeida
Djedeida
110
2nd
1st
2 Hamps
2nd
TUNIS
1st
2nd
3rd
Dj. Maiana
Coy 1 Surreys
186
3rd
3rd
74
63
3rd
5 Northamptons
2/13 US
(less coy)
2 Hamps
3rd
Tebourba
3rd
HQ
Coy
&
1 Surreys
(less Sqn)
3rd
Two coys
1 Surreys
El Bathan
1st
1st
CCB
4th–6th
Koch 1st
2nd
Dj. el Guessa
145
3rd
TUNIS
Massicault
METRES
400 AND ABOVE
300
200
100
50
SEA LEVEL

ACTION AT TEBOURBA GAP

air was very active. Meanwhile, the Hampshires barred the way from Djedeida and the Surreys beat off Koch's infantry making for El Bathan bridge. The day ended with 11th Infantry Brigade holding all its forward positions, though its northern flank was exposed and some of Koch's troops had trickled west and established themselves between El Guessa and the river. General Evelegh decided to replace Blade Force next evening by U.S. Combat Command B, which he would use to counter-attack.[1]

On 2nd December Hudel and Lüder Groups, with 45 tanks, intended to attack Tebourba from the west, but were themselves attacked by part of the U.S. 13th Armoured Regiment. The Americans lost heavily, but their action and more good shooting by the artillery completely contained the German groups. Meanwhile Fischer's reserve group had stubbornly attacked the Hampshires and had been as stubbornly resisted.

But Brigadier Cass saw the risk in trying to hold too large an area with the enemy working round both flanks, and drew back the Hampshires level with Djebel Maiana. Next morning—the 3rd —Fischer's reserve group drove the company of 1st Surreys off Pt 186. The nearest company of the Hampshires counter-attacked repeatedly, inspired and led by their commander, Major H. W. Le Patourel, who was awarded the Victoria Cross for his conduct this day. Later, in a more deliberate counter-attack, the 1st Surreys regained the hill only to be driven off again. Finally the Hampshires, isolated and almost without ammunition, broke out to Tebourba which they found deserted. For General Evelegh had ordered the 11th Infantry Brigade to withdraw to a line running north-west through the Tebourba Gap from El Guessa, which had been cleared of enemy by 1/6th U.S. Armoured Infantry.

The honours of the three days' fighting lay with Fischer for his good plan and his strong personal leadership; his groups, too, deserve praise for their energy and persistence; their losses are not known. The Hampshires now numbered some 200 all ranks and the Surreys 343; and in the withdrawal 8 field guns, 14 anti-tank guns and 10 light A.A. guns had been lost.

On 2nd December General Anderson reported that the army and air forces were stretched to the limit; their communications were precarious and they had no reserve supplies forward. Unless he could reach Tunis very soon he would be obliged to act

---

[1] By 6 a.m. on 2nd December the following U.S. units had reached Tebourba Gap in support of 11th Infantry Brigade: 1st Bn, light tanks, and 2nd Bn, mediums, of 13th Armoured Regiment; 1st and 2nd Bns 6th Armoured Infantry; one Battery 27th Armoured Field Artillery Bn.

defensively for a while. Next day General Eisenhower reported to the C.C.O.S. that a short breathing space was essential, but that he hoped to resume the advance on about the 9th: an important condition for success would be fine weather. Commenting on the recent Allied advance he thought that although the air forces had been 'working at maximum pace' they could not 'keep down the hostile strafing and dive-bombing that is largely responsible for breaking up all attempted advances by ground forces'. On 5th December, in response to a request by the British C.O.S. to keep them better informed, Eisenhower sent them an admirable summary of the campaign: this is printed in full in Appendix 11 and reiterates the statement about the effect of the enemy's air attacks. A word of comment is called for.

General Anderson and General Evelegh had been impressed by the support given by the *Luftwaffe* with dive-bombers, fighter-bombers, and machine-gun attacks by low-flying fighters—known as ground strafing. Anderson even observed that unless the scale of these could be reduced he would have to withdraw to positions over which an air umbrella could be held with less strain. Some of the great difficulties facing Eastern Air Command were mentioned on page 177 above—airfields too far back, and runways made unserviceable by rain: the lack of landline communication was obviously a further great handicap.

The idea of an air umbrella was not new, and it had attracted notice in the Western Desert the previous year. On that occasion, in sending out 250 light A.A. guns for use 'in the best possible way', Mr. Churchill had laid down that 'Nevermore must the troops expect, as a matter of course, to be protected against the air by aircraft.'[1] The principle was clear—the army must defend itself; this meant meeting a low-flying attack with fire from every kind of available weapon. But the 'Torch' expedition had been able to bring out only the bare minimum of equipment, light A.A. weapons included, and the moral effect of heavy air attacks on inexperienced troops could be very great. The *Luftwaffe*'s figures indicate that during the eighteen days from 25th November to 12th December the average daily sorties against all targets were 18 by dive-bombers and 25 by fighter and fighter-bombers, while over the three days 1st–3rd December sorties by these types totalled 54 and 108 respectively. The term 'all targets' includes, for the dive-bombers, troops, tanks, vehicles, and guns; for the fighters and fighter-bombers it includes road convoys, troop concentrations, tanks, guns and airfields. Thus both types of attack were spread over many

---

[1] Extract from the Instruction by the Minister of Defence for the guidance of the Army and Air Commanders-in-Chief in the coming operation 'Crusader'. It is printed in full in *The Mediterranean and Middle East*, Volume II, pp. 287–8.

different targets in a large area, but if concentrated for a particular purpose they could be temporarily and locally heavy.

Other factors combined to deprive the troops of the satisfaction of seeing and hearing the enemy getting as good as he gave. Eastern Air Command had of course no dive-bombers, their fighters did very little ground strafing, and there was no fighter-bombing by the R.A.F. until 15th December. (There had been a few ground strafing and fighter-bombing sorties by U.S. Lightnings from Youks les Bains, 120 or more miles away). Moreover, it was not long before the Bisleys, which had been brought out as day-bombers, came to be used mainly for attacking airfields at Tunis and Bizerta by night— a highly important task. So what the troops saw of their own aircraft was chiefly the sweeps by Spitfires and Hurricanes, and less frequently by Lightnings, and very encouraging they were. References in units' diaries to being themselves attacked are usually factual and made without comment.

It is evident that General Anderson and Air Marshal Welsh had each a feeling of acute frustration. If they had been together this feeling might perhaps have been alleviated, but even so they would still be faced by many problems which derived from material shortages, or from the weather.

On 6th December Lieut.-General C. W. Allfrey and his 5th Corps took over command of the British front with Headquarters at Souk el Khemis. The Order of Battle at this date is given in Appendix 7.

There was a large number of attached units, but the principal formations were:

> 6th Armoured Division, of one armoured and one infantry brigade; arriving in the Teboursouk area.
> 78th Division, of three infantry brigades.
> Combat Command B from 1st U.S. Armoured Division (the rough equivalent of half a British armoured division).
> 1st (British) Parachute Brigade, of three battalions.
> 1st and 6th Commandos.

The same day No. 242 Group R.A.F. came into being with Air Commodore G. M. Lawson as A.O.C. A few days later he went forward to 5th Corps' Headquarters to be with General Allfrey.

The Axis had still not worked out, separately or together, a strategical plan for North Africa. The Germans, however, took steps early in December to strengthen their own command organization. For several reasons an army commander was needed in Tunisia. On 4th December Hitler announced that he would be

Colonel-General Jürgen von Arnim with Lieut.-General Heinz Ziegler as his Chief of Staff. General von Arnim was whisked from Russia, where he was commanding a Corps, to Hitler's headquarters, where the Führer told him that he was to command three armoured and three motorized divisions in North Africa. He was to be under the Italian *Comando Supremo* but would deal directly with Kesselring. With these instructions and an exposition of the political and geographical conditions in Tunisia, von Arnim was sent off to Rome. Mussolini spoke no more to the point than Hitler, and on 8th December von Arnim and Zeigler arrived at Tunis and sought out Nehring, who was not expecting them and who was thus superseded. In this way the 5th Panzer Army—*Pz AOK 5* for short—was created.

When von Arnim arrived General Fischer was still trying to lever the Allies out of the positions to which they had withdrawn after losing Tebourba. This had led to a sharp engagement on 6th December between part of 10th Panzer Division and Combat Command B at El Guessa. The result was damaging to both sides and although the enemy was checked Evelegh ordered Combat Command B to withdraw to Djebel Bou Aoukaz and the 11th Infantry Brigade to Longstop Gap. This was done during the night 6th/7th in heavy rain which continued throughout the 7th and 8th and part of the 9th. General Eisenhower was not having the luck with weather that he wanted so badly. And luck is the word, for early December normally marks the start of the rainy season in Northern Tunisia.

Late on the 7th General Allfrey reported that he proposed to withdraw a little farther in order to economize in troops deployed for defence. This withdrawal was to begin on the evening of 10th December. The 6th Armoured Division would then operate widely to eastward from Teboursouk, and the Corps would prepare to resume the offensive as quickly as possible. During the 10th, however, the enemy struck again south of the river against U.S. Combat Command B which was holding Djebel Bou Aoukaz. In fighting lasting all day Brigadier-General Lunsford E. Oliver and his Command repulsed the enemy's attacks and by evening was ready to withdraw in accordance with 5th Corps' plan. Misfortune was in store. Combat Command B was to have crossed the river at Bordj Toum and then moved along the main Medjez el Bab road. A detachment of tanks leading the American column joined in a fire fight near the bridge, and the noise and some misleading reports caused the foremost unit commander to jump to the conclusion that the bridge was uncovered and an attack imminent. He diverted the route of withdrawal to an earth track which ran along the eastern bank of the river. The result was that the force became mired, unable to move forward or back, and was compelled to abandon 18 tanks, 41 guns and 150 vehicles. Naturally it was temporarily useless as a fighting formation. No other incident marked the withdrawal, and the front settled down.

In the first half of December the scale of air operations by both sides did not increase as it undoubtedly would have done if the weather and state of the airfields had been better. In support of the Army the Eastern Air Command carried out mostly fighter sweeps and attacks by fighters, and occasionally by Bisleys, on concentrations of enemy vehicles and troops by day. On the 4th a day attack on the landing ground ten miles north of Chouigui ended tragically when, in the late afternoon, fifty or sixty Me. 109s caught nine unescorted Bisleys of No. 18 Squadron. All nine were shot down and only three crews survived. The leader of the formation, Wing Commander H. G. Malcolm, was awarded a posthumous Victoria Cross for most conspicuous bravery on this occasion.

The Bisleys' principal role, however, was to attack Tunis and Bizerta by night, but the four Bisley Squadrons were now thirty aircraft short, and in reporting this Air Marshal Welsh asked for a more modern type of replacement, since in his opinion the Bisleys were unsuitable for their tasks by day and were only suitable for night operations when conditions were very favourable.

To reduce the distance to be flown in reaching the front an attempt was made to bring into use an advanced landing ground at Medjez el Bab, which would have made a saving of forty miles from Souk el Arba. On 5th December six Spitfires flew there and were just about to land when they were heavily attacked by Me. 109s: two Spitfires were shot down and the other four badly damaged. The attempt had to be abandoned.

The Wellingtons from Malta, where they were hardly affected by rain or enemy action, were the most regular visitors to Tunis and Bizerta. They and the Eastern Air Command's Bisleys attacked Tunis and Bizerta incessantly by night, though it was the day-bombers—the American Fortresses—which delivered the heaviest blows on the ports and airfields, and in doing so they were now met by much heavier 'Flak'. Mitchells, Marauders and Bostons added their weight to the attacks on El Aouina and Sidi Ahmed, and also bombed Djedeida landing ground on several occasions. Railway buildings and tracks and port installations were much damaged in these raids and the movement of troops and supplies impeded. During the first two weeks of December a number of Axis ships in harbour were severely damaged by bombs.

Away to the south-east the smaller ports of Sousse, Sfax and Gabes were now under more frequent attack and the railways in particular suffered much damage. These attacks were made chiefly by Beaufighter fighter-bombers from Malta, by U.S. Lightnings and Kittyhawks from Youks les Bains, and by the newly arrived American Mitchells. On 11th December a Wellington from Cyrenaica bombed the Gabes area—the first recorded operation against a land target in the 'Torch' area by an aircraft based in Cyrenaica.

Between 1st and 12th December, in direct and indirect support of the advance, Eastern Air Command flew 2,225 sorties and lost at least 37 aircraft. The U.S. Twelfth Air Force flew 523 sorties and lost 17 aircraft. The *Luftwaffe* in Tunisia flew just over 1,000 sorties and lost 37 aircraft (excluding those destroyed by Malta's aircraft), 9 of them on the ground. The recorded Italian losses amounted to 10 aircraft.

On 12th December General Eisenhower reported to the C.C.O.S. that continual attacks by the enemy and bad weather had prevented him resuming the advance. Nevertheless he wrote '... While the difficulties, as presented to me by the air, the ground, and the supply organizations, are tremendous, and undoubtedly definite risks are assumed, I still insist that, if we can only be fortunate to get a spell of good weather, we can do the job.' He proposed to reinforce the 1st Army and attack again on about the 20th December, the objectives being the airfields at Tunis.[1] In General Anderson's view it would be right to make this attack, because the situation did not permit of passive acceptance of a strong German bridgehead. Complete success in December was doubtful, but the prospect, he thought, would improve with four or five days' delay and thereafter diminish until the end of January. He recommended starting preliminary operations on the night of 22nd December 'unless the rain or some other new factor clearly makes it out of the question.' Because 5th Corps would fight the battle he was giving General Allfrey a free hand in planning it.

By 9th December the Axis high command had a fair idea of the strength of the Allies in North Africa as a whole, and judged the slowness of their advance to have been caused mainly by administrative difficulties. *OKH* did not expect an immediate offensive but reckoned with action of some sort to coincide with a move by the British 8th Army against Rommel at Mersa Brega, which they forecast for about 15th December. On the 13th von Arnim

---

[1] Combat Command B was to remain with 5th Corps and have its losses made good as far as possible by A.F.H.Q. The U.S. 36th Field Artillery Battalion (with 155-mm guns) and 18th Regimental Combat Team were to join 5th Corps forthwith.

announced that the Allied forces in the area Tebourba—Mateur had been more or less destroyed, and that the 5th Panzer Army would now go over to the defensive. Broich would hold the right, 10th Panzer Division the centre (formerly Tunis North), and Superga the left (formerly Tunis South). In the south General Imperiali was to prepare to move west to occupy positions on the approaches to the coastal plain and could expect the (German) 47th Grenadier Regiment as a reinforcement.[1]

On the 17th Kesselring told von Arnim to expect three regiments (of 334th Division) and some transport, and authorized him to use any anti-tank guns which might reach Tunis for Rommel, if they could not be immediately sent on to him.[2] Kesselring also ordered airborne raids to be undertaken against the Allied L. of C., but these were prevented by bad weather.

General Anderson estimated that by 22nd December he would have ready the largest force that could be maintained in the forward area, and that there would be reserve stocks at railhead for between seven and nine days' hard fighting. General Allfrey's plan was for the 6th Armoured Division to make the main thrust to Tunis by way of Massicault, while the 78th Division protected its left flank by securing a number of tactical localities in succession, starting with Longstop Hill and the height El Aroussia (Pt 259) above the Tebourba Gap. The 1st Guards Brigade (Brigadier R. A. V. Copland-Griffiths) was given the first of these tasks, to begin on 22nd December, and the 5th Northamptons the second, one day later. The 6th Armoured Division was to advance on the 24th.

On the afternoon of the 22nd it began to rain heavily. That night the 2nd Coldstream Guards overcame stiff opposition at the small railway station Halte d'el Heri but lost it to a quick counter-attack.[3] They took Longstop Hill itself and the 1st Battalion U.S. 18th Infantry came up to replace them. The Coldstream then went back to prepare for the 1st Guards Brigade's next task. Early on the 23rd the Americans lost heavily in trying to retake the Halte, and shortly afterwards the enemy regained the top of Longstop Hill. An American counter-attack failed, whereupon Brigadier

---

[1] von Arnim had not been appointed to command Italian troops in Tunisia, but at this stage appears to have given them orders as a matter of course, without causing any protests.

[2] In *Krieg Ohne Hass*, (Heidenheim, Brenz, 2nd Ed. 1950), p. 318, Rommel mentions that he was not very pleased when it came out that Kesselring had diverted to Tunis 8·8-cm guns of the latest type (Flak 41) which had been promised to him by the Führer and which he urgently required.

[3] The Germans realized the importance of Longstop Hill and included it in the sector commanded by Colonel Rudolf Lang (69th Panzer Grenadier Regt) who had one bn of his own regiment, one bn 754th Grenadier Regt, and one bn 7th Panzer Regt with an unknown number of tanks.

Copland-Griffiths recalled the Coldstream Guards and learnt from 5th Corps that although the main attack on Tunis had been postponed 48 hours the operation to secure Longstop Hill was to continue. At about 5 p.m. on the 24th the Guards again recaptured the hill, only to realize that the enemy's main positions were on Djebel el Rhaa, which they were unable to take. On Christmas morning the Germans recaptured the upper part of Longstop Hill. That afternoon General Allfrey decided not to try again and ordered the operation to be broken off. It had cost the Coldstream Guards 178 killed, wounded, and missing and the Americans 356.

Early on 23rd December the 5th Northamptons, with a small improvised mule-train, had set off for El Aroussia by cross-country march from Toukabeur. Moving only by night they captured a German post thought to be on the objective, and withstood several counter-attacks.[1] Meanwhile, Corps and Division had been trying by every means to recall the battalion. Lieut.-Colonel A. A. Crook however, guessed (correctly) that the general offensive was not taking place, and withdrew to Toukabeur where the battalion arrived late on the 26th after an arduous adventure.

By now the rain, which fell in 'torrential buckets for three days' and was expected to continue in spasms for six to eight weeks, was making it practically impossible for wheels to move off the roads; any manoeuvre was out of the question. On 24th December General Eisenhower and General Anderson visited the front and Eisenhower signalled to the C.C.O.S. '... Due to continual rain there will be no hope of immediate attack on Tunis. May be possible later by methodical infantry advance. Am attempting [to] organize and maintain a force to operate aggressively on Southern Flank.' This was the end of the attempt to capture Tunis and Bizerta before the rains set in.

The middle of December saw a marked increase in the weight and scope of Allied air attacks in Tunisia. The ports and airfields of Tunis and Bizerta continued to be the principal objectives and were being bombed round the clock. By night, Wellingtons from Malta were now concentrating upon Tunis, and Eastern Air Command's Bisleys upon Bizerta. By day, U.S. Fortresses attacked both these places and were joined on 13th December by Liberators

---

[1] The 10th Panzer Division recorded that two companies of 754th Grenadier Regiment had driven the enemy off Pt 466, a hill some seven miles west of Colonel Lang's command post at Toungar. He had been warned by Arabs of what he took to be an outflanking move by Allied troops.

doing their first operation in the 'Torch' area. The scale of attack on targets on the east coast of Tunisia was also increasing, just when Rommel was withdrawing from El Agheila and was becoming more and more concerned about future Axis strategy for North Africa. He realized well enough that before long his Army might be dependent upon a line of communication running south from Tunis and through the east coast Tunisian ports. The Allies knew this too, and their aircraft, mostly American, from Tebessa, Thelepte, and Telergma (near Constantine) made frequent attacks on targets in central and eastern Tunisia, which served two purposes—hampering the build-up of Axis forces in that part of the theatre and weakening Rommel's probable life-line. On the 15th December U.S. Liberators flew from Cyrenaica to add their weight to the attack of railway targets around Sfax. The same day three U.S. Liberator squadrons moved from Oran to Gambut in exchange for one squadron of Middle East's Fortresses, for the reason that suitable airfields for Liberators in Algeria were scarce, and the great range of these aircraft could be best exploited from bases in Cyrenaica. A welcome event (on the 18th and 19th) was the arrival from the U.K. of two Wellington squadrons at Blida (Algiers), making an invaluable addition to the night-bomber force. That night R.A.F. Liberators from Cyrenaica marked their first appearance in Tunisia by bombing Sousse. U.S. aircraft from Cyrenaica were now often attacking east coast targets by day and night, and Beaufighter fighter-bombers from Malta were bombing Sousse and Sfax during darkness. In fact a remarkable amount of co-operation was being achieved, none the less useful through having been caused by force of circumstances.

Between the 13th and 26th December, in direct and indirect support of the advance, Eastern Air Command flew an estimated 1,940 sorties and lost at least twenty aircraft. The U.S. Twelfth Air Force flew about 720 sorties and lost sixteen aircraft. The *Luftwaffe* in Tunisia flew some 1,030 sorties and lost seventeen aircraft exclusive of those destroyed by Malta's aircraft. The Italians lost three.

By the time that the advance of the 1st Army had been halted by the mud, the Axis ports and lines of communication were under such frequent air attack from French North Africa, Libya and Malta that results were beginning to show. For example, the damage to the railway system meant that access by rail to any of the main ports was often cut and the stations rendered useless. Normal rail services had long since ceased. Repair shops and fuel tanks were all destroyed or severely damaged. An important result was the effect on the port labour; during air raids stevedores refused to work and locally recruited civilians would vanish, which meant that at a 'round the clock' target no sooner had they recovered from one raid than it was time to vanish again. German troops arriving by sea were therefore used for a day's unloading or other similar work in the port.

In the field of army/air co-operation the lack of co-ordination in the 'Torch' area between the tasks of the R.A.F. and U.S.A.A.F. was the principal air problem not yet satisfactorily solved. In the strategical field it was already clear that great advantages would be gained by bringing under a single command the long-range air forces based in French North Africa, Libya and Malta. In maritime air operations the need for co-ordination in both the Western and Central areas of the Mediterranean could also be seen and is discussed in the following chapter. At the end of the year, therefore, the stage was set for the creation of a combined Air Command in the 'Torch' area, and for overhauling the command structure for all the Allied air forces in North Africa from Casablanca to Suez.

It remains to turn again for a moment to the French political scene. Admiral Darlan, whatever his innermost feelings, continued during December to collaborate effectively with the Allied authorities in North Africa, in spite of President Roosevelt's announcement—made to soothe public indignation—that the Admiral was being used as a temporary expedient. Darlan ruefully referred to himself as a lemon which the Americans would drop when they had squeezed it dry. Other French authorities, military and civil, had fallen gradually into line, except, of course, those like Admirals Estéva and Derrien who had the misfortune to be in Axis hands in Tunisia. The French forces led by Barré and Koeltz were giving a good account of themselves as far as their lack of modern equipment permitted.

Notwithstanding its immediate practical value to the Allied leaders on the spot, the political system under Darlan, covertly at least, had many opponents among Frenchmen, particularly those who were anxious about the future government of France. Difficulties with de Gaulle loomed ahead. In this setting on 24th December Darlan was assassinated at Algiers by a young man who was quickly brought to trial by the French and shot. Whether the assassin had been encouraged in his fanaticism by one or other of the French political groups, or had acted on his own impulse, is not known. Anyhow there were no incidents nor was there any disorder. Darlan was succeeded as High Commissioner by Giraud and this too was taken quite calmly.

It is not the province of this history to pass judgement on Jean François Darlan, either as the man responsible for forging so fine a weapon as the French Navy of 1939 or as one of the principal characters of the French political drama from the fall of France

16. Landing drinking-water during 8th Army's advance.

17. Discharging cargo from a Tank Landing Craft (L.C.T.) at Benghazi during 8th Army's advance.

18. A Landing Craft Infantry (Large).

19. 'Torch'. Beaches near Algiers. British weapons and equipment being landed from Landing Craft Mechanized (L.C.M.).

20. 'Torch'. L.C.M. approaching beaches. Other landing craft manoeuvring in the surf.

21. 'Torch'. Destroyer lays smoke-screen around transport off Oran. Landing Craft Assault (L.C.A.) in foreground.

22. 'Stoneage' convoy to Malta. November 1942.

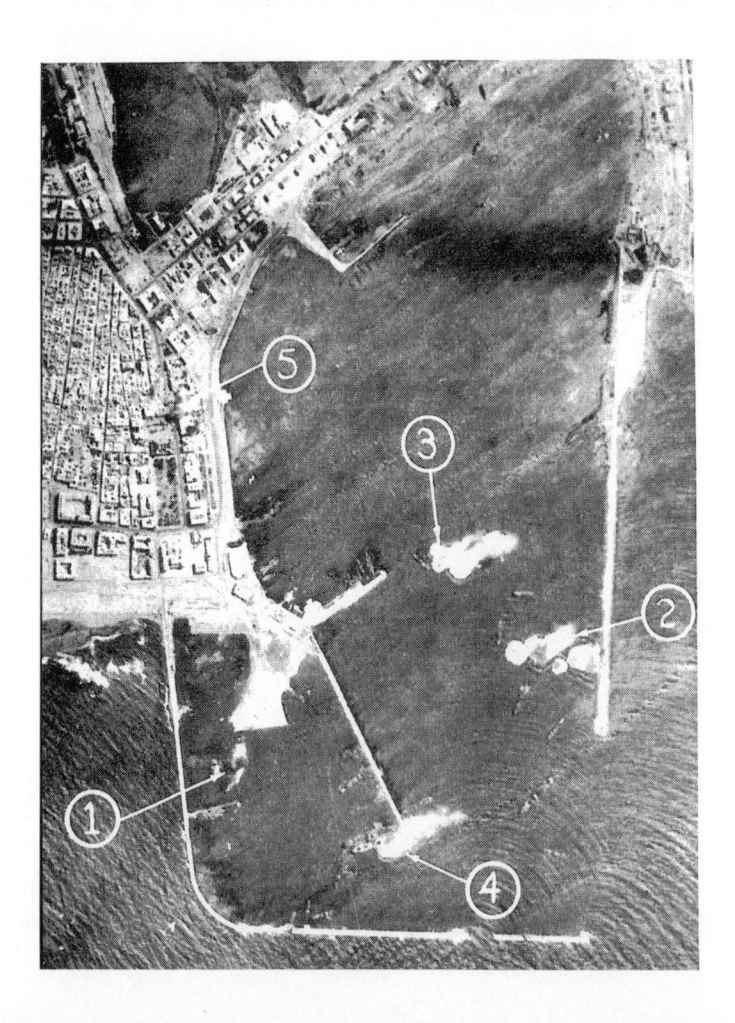

23. A Royal Air Force attack on Benghazi, September 1942. Photograph marked later to indicate bomb hits on targets.

until his death two and a half years later. Mention was made in Volume I of his control of the movements of French warships immediately before and after the French armistice, and of his assurances that no French warship would be allowed to fall into Axis hands—and few did. In the present volume we have seen him, after some hesitation, cast in his lot with the Allies, and both General Eisenhower and Admiral Cunningham have recorded that, having once taken this decision, Darlan never to their knowledge failed to live up to his promise. It so happened then, that this enigmatic French Admiral, politician, and anglophobe came to make a unique contribution to the Allied cause. For there can be little doubt that, at this time of great confusion of thought and heart-searching throughout French North Africa, Darlan alone possessed the authority which almost all could recognize with a sense of legitimate relief. Without him, internal conflict might easily have produced widespread chaos. His fortuitous presence in Algeria, far from being the calamity it appeared, turned out to be for the Allies the best thing that could have happened.

Map 23

AXIS SEA AND AIR TRANSPORT ROUTES TO NORTH AFRICA
October 1942 – May 1943

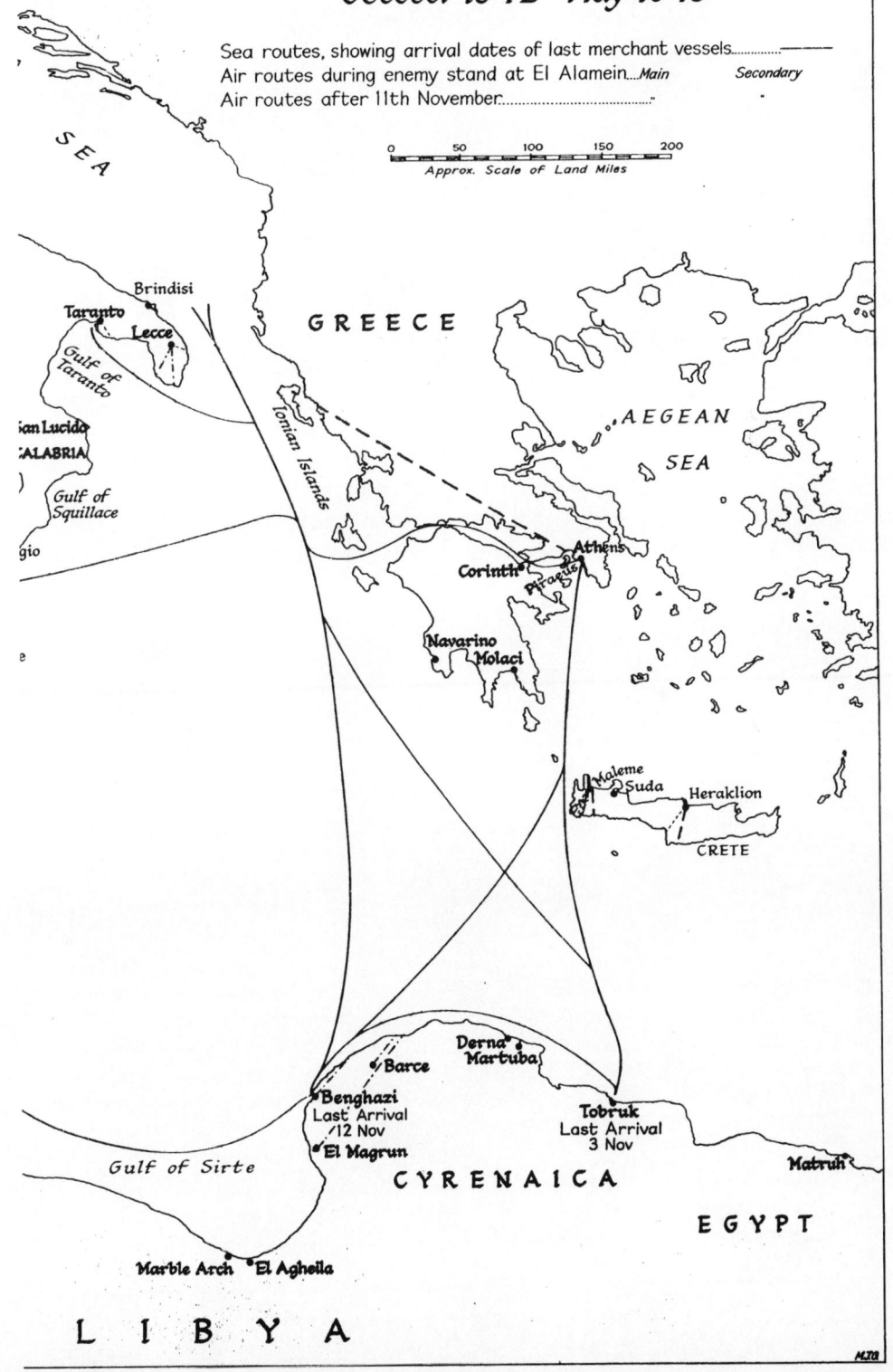

Sea routes, showing arrival dates of last merchant vessels..............
Air routes during enemy stand at El Alamein....Main   Secondary
Air routes after 11th November................................

CHAPTER VIII

MALTA AND THE WAR AT SEA

(October—December 1942)

See Maps 15, 23, 24.

SET beside the momentous happenings at both ends of the Mediterranean related in the preceding chapters, Malta may seem to have lost much of its earlier importance. In fact, at this decisive moment in Allied fortunes the island's value as a potential base for offensive operations was greater than ever. Its power to strike at shipping on passage to Tripoli had repeatedly affected the course of the Desert campaign, and by mid-November Tripoli had again become Rommel's only considerable port. But even more urgent targets were now to claim attention—the ships and aircraft hurrying men and material across the straits between Sicily and the ports and airfields of Tunisia. This route was short, well protected by minefields, and much more difficult to attack.

In Volume III the story of Malta was carried to the end of September 1942. By then the threat of invasion had receded, the island had partly recovered from the severe bombing of the previous April, and her submarines and aircraft were again causing loss and damage to the enemy's shipping, although strikes by aircraft were limited by shortage of aviation spirit. But Malta, though able to give quite a good account of herself both in defence and attack, was on starvation rations. The Governor reported that the food brought in during August by the remnants of the 'Pedestal' convoy had only extended to mid-December the date to which stocks would last. For practical reasons, connected with unloading and distribution, this meant that the next convoy must arrive at the latest by the third week in November, and even this date was subject to the proviso that in the interval 300 tons of certain foodstuffs would have to be sent in by special means. The margin, it will be noted, was fine; plans for the passage of convoys from east and west counted upon the capture of Cyrenaican or Tunisian airfields by mid-November, although, rather than that Malta should be allowed to fall through starvation, relief would no doubt have been effected at almost any cost.

Early in October the Chiefs of Staff announced their plans. In the Eastern Mediterranean four 14-knot merchantmen would be ready to sail for Malta during the November dark period (5th–10th) and ten others at various dates in December. In the Western Mediterranean four ships carrying between them 17,000 tons of food and 4,000 tons of aviation spirit would be ready by 13th November; another twelve were being prepared. It was intended to run in the special foodstuffs in fast minelayers, *Welshman* from the west and *Manxman* from the east. In addition attempts would be made to sneak through several unescorted merchant ships in disguise, and submarines would continue to carry in aviation spirit and such special foodstuffs as their limited stowage permitted. The Chiefs of Staff did not consider the use of aircraft for transporting food and aviation spirit justifiable.

If it proved impossible to get a convoy through in November, Malta would have to hold out until the dark period in early December, and the Chiefs of Staff believed this could be done by enforcing more rigorously the policy decided upon in August, but not yet fulfilled, for slaughtering livestock. To the livestock, in the last resort, could be added the draught animals.

It was fully realized by now that to be sure of bringing food and munitions to the people and garrison of Malta there must be no weak links in the chain. On this occasion food was the immediate and vital need, yet should even one of the components of success be lacking—whether fighters or fuel, minesweepers, anti-aircraft ammunition or motor transport—the food might never reach safe storage. Moreover, before a convoy could sail the Allied Armies must advance and capture the airfields necessary to its safe passage. Before that, aircraft and submarines should have been whittling away the enemy's means of resistance. Past experience of this tightly-knit interdependence had been well heeded: more fighters were to be flown in to replace casualties, and the greatest possible quantity of bombs and aviation spirit was to be sent in with the food—in anticipation of which some easing of the restrictions on the use of existing stocks became possible.

On 11th October, before these plans had got very far, the enemy's bombing of Malta was once more stepped up to what could be described as 'blitz' level, although it was not comparable with the peak reached in the previous April. It had not come without warning, for reconnaissance had revealed more and more aircraft on the Sicilian airfields. It was the enemy's response to his rising loss and damage at sea—a consequence of abandoning the plan to capture Malta in favour of advancing into Egypt. Not that Malta-based submarines, bombers, and torpedo-bombers were alone responsible for these shipping casualties, but Malta was a tangible target, unlike No. 201 Naval Co-operation Group or submarines of the 1st Flotilla based far away in the Eastern Mediterranean. That it

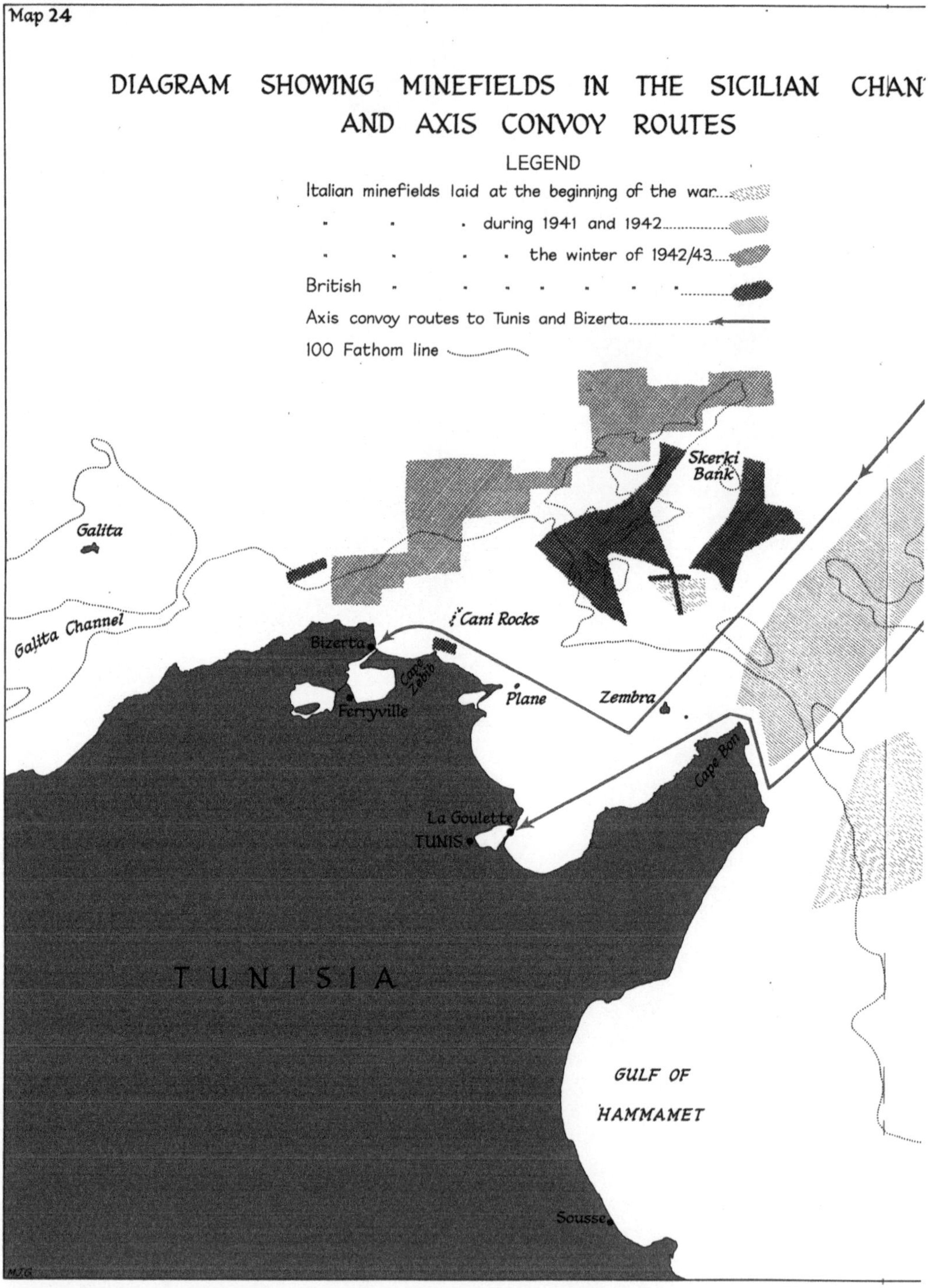

Map 24

DIAGRAM SHOWING MINEFIELDS IN THE SICILIAN CHAN[NEL] AND AXIS CONVOY ROUTES

LEGEND
Italian minefields laid at the beginning of the war
"   "   " during 1941 and 1942
"   "   " the winter of 1942/43
British "   "   "
Axis convoy routes to Tunis and Bizerta
100 Fathom line

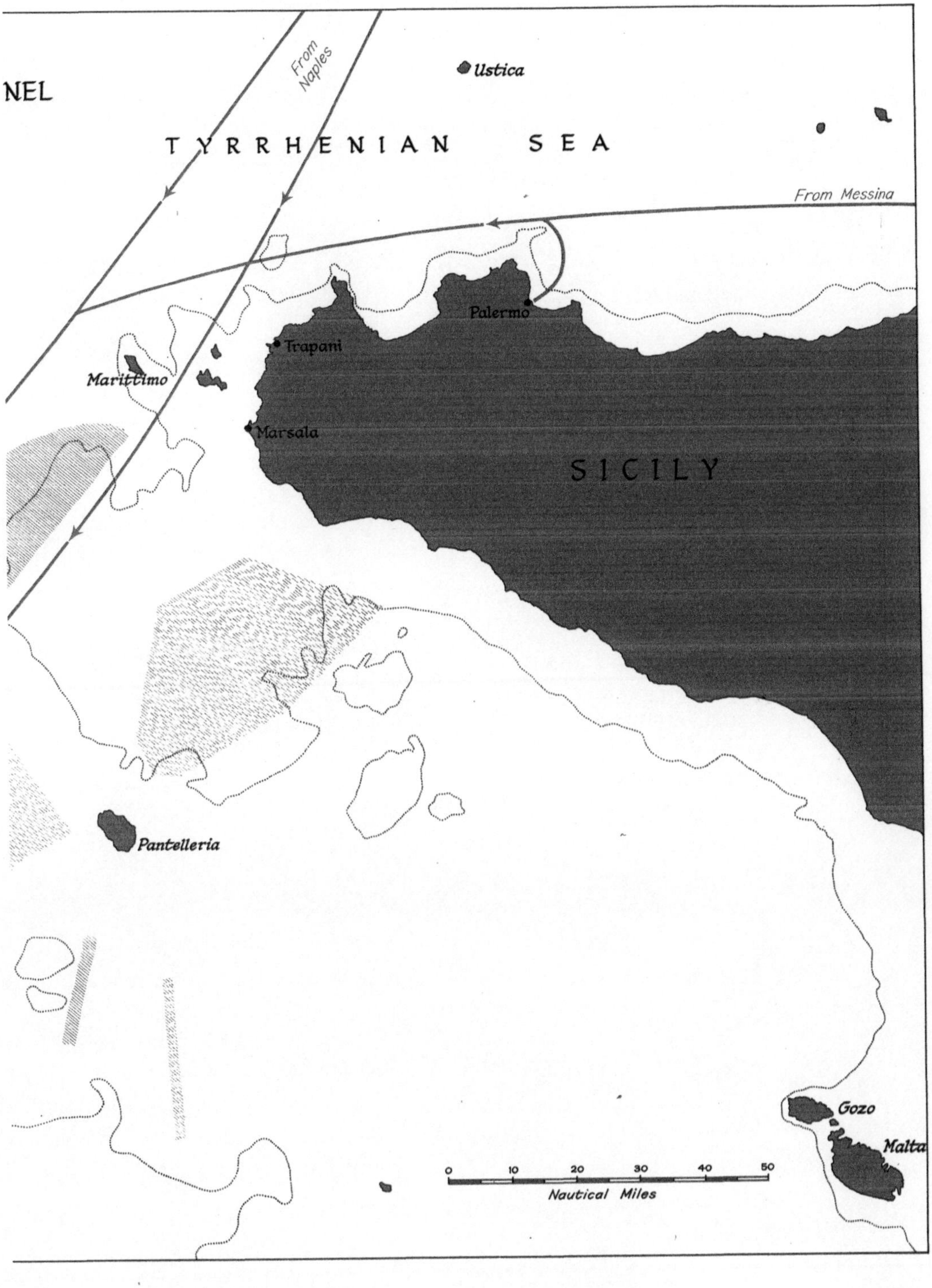

NEL
From Naples
Ustica
TYRRHENIAN SEA
From Messina
Palermo
Trapani
Marittimo
Marsala
SICILY
Pantelleria
Gozo
Malta
0 10 20 30 40 50
Nautical Miles

was hoped once again to neutralize Malta is shown by Kesselring's orders and later by those of Göring himself.

The new blitz, however, was soon defeated, raids usually being met and broken up over the sea north of the island. British radar could detect hostile aircraft as they formed up over their bases before setting out for Malta—a serious disadvantage of which the enemy was now well aware. At first some of his formations consisted of as many as 80 Ju. 88s escorted by nearly double that number of fighters, but by 15th October as few as 14 bombers were being escorted by nearly 100 fighters. By the 18th, after heavy losses in bombers, the enemy had given up using his Ju. 88s altogether in favour of Me. 109 fighter-bombers. By the 19th the blitz had patently failed and heavy attacks had come to an end. Though the estimated number of enemy sorties during the nine-day battle was close on 2,400, the total weight of bombs dropped on the island was only 440 tons—clear evidence of how the heavy losses forced the enemy to conserve his bombers and increase the ratio of fighters to bombers, until the latter were withdrawn altogether. The chief target had been Luqa airfield, but neither Luqa nor any other of Malta's airfields was ever out of action for more than half an hour at a time. Malta was not a popular target with German aircrews and there is evidence to show that on occasions the Italians fought with more spirit than the Germans.

The Germans started with 214 serviceable aircraft, of which 156 were bombers. The Italians had 163 serviceable aircraft, including 67 bombers, in Sicily at the time. Although it is known that a great many M.C. 202 fighters were employed, it is not known what part Italian bombers played in these attacks. At the outset the British serviceable fighter force numbered 113 Spitfires and 11 Beaufighters, but there were only 100 effective pilots. These fighters flew 1,115 sorties—a daily rate of 124, by an average for the nine days of 74 serviceable Spitfires and 8 Beaufighters—a remarkable achievement. At one time only 40 Spitfires were serviceable.[1] The British lost 30 Spitfires in the air, from which seventeen pilots survived, and only two aircraft—one Beaufighter and one Spitfire—on the ground. German records disclose the loss of 9 fighters and 35 bombers, some of which fell to the guns; the Italian losses were probably not far short of the German. This was a big price to pay, especially at a time when the Germans were being forced to divert bombers to fighter escort of shipping to and from North Africa. And for such small gains, for so effective were the air defences of Malta that strikes against Axis shipping were carried out every night except one, on which no enemy ship came within range of the island.

---

[1] During certain days of the blitz of April, 1942 there were only six fighters serviceable, and on occasions the figure was lower still.

The blitz of October 1942 marked the last serious attempt to neutralize Malta. There were a few nuisance raids by fighter-bombers towards the end of the month, and on the 29th the enemy made a half-hearted and unsuccessful attempt to intercept 29 reinforcing Spitfires flying to Malta from H.M.S. *Furious*, all of which landed safely. Thereafter the Axis air forces were fully occupied by the fighting in Libya and French North Africa. The only serious bombing attack on Malta during the remainder of 1942 was on the night of 18th December, when Luqa airfield was attacked by about 40 bombers, and 9 Wellingtons and 4 Spitfires were destroyed on the ground.

Not all the Chiefs of Staff's plans for replenishing Malta were successful, but attempts were made to carry out all of them. During October submarines made four store-carrying trips to Malta— *Parthian* and *Clyde* one each from Gibraltar, and *Rorqual* two from Beirut. They carried aviation spirit, special foodstuffs, diesel and lubricating oils, and torpedoes. On the 29th the reinforcement of Spitfires arrived. In the first three days of November *Parthian* and *Clyde* again arrived with important stores including aviation spirit and torpedoes. Two attempts to send in unescorted and disguised merchant vessels failed. The *Empire Patrol*, a 15-knot ship carrying 1,200 tons of aviation spirit and 300 tons of benzine, was routed west of Cyprus to Turkish territorial waters and thence north of Crete. On 2nd November, north-west of Cyprus, she was photographed by a Dornier 215 and later put into Famagusta with engine defects. As it seemed that the enemy was alert and suspicious the attempt was abandoned. From the west two small ships carrying foodstuffs— the *Ardeola* and *Tadorna*—entered the Mediterranean with the slow portion of the Algiers assault convoy. On 9th November they were stopped by shore batteries when off Bizerta and were interned by the French. The last few trips with special stores made in fast minelayers were completely successful. On 12th November *Manxman* reached Malta from Alexandria with 350 tons of powdered milk, dried cereals and preserved meat. She was followed on the 18th by *Welshman* from Gibraltar with similar stores and between 27th November and 4th December *Welshman* made a trip at high speed to Haifa and back to fetch torpedoes urgently needed by the Malta-based submarines.

Meanwhile preparations had been going ahead in the Eastern Mediterranean to sail the first four ships in convoy for Malta. It was planned to route the convoy —'Stoneage'—within some forty miles of the Cyrenaican coast, to reach the longitude of Benghazi around dusk some forty-eight hours after leaving Port Said. As in the previous

June it was the Italian Fleet which presented the most serious threat. This time the British would have no reinforcements from the Eastern Fleet, and the disparity between the Italian Fleet and the British surface escort might even be greater. The total Italian strength was 6 battleships (including 3 *Littorios*), 2 heavy and 5 light cruisers, and more than 20 destroyers. On 11th November the *Littorios* moved to Naples, but this would not have prevented them from striking at convoys bound for Malta. Five cruisers were at Messina.

The British escort consisted of two 6-inch cruisers, *Orion* and *Arethusa*, three 5·25-inch cruisers, *Cleopatra*, *Dido* and *Euryalus*, seven Fleet and ten Hunt class destroyers. This force could not hope to hold off the Italian Fleet for long in daylight, but the passage of the convoy was timed so that the first half of the 350 mile stretch across the Central Basin between the hump of Cyrenaica and Malta would be covered in the dark. If the Italian Fleet attempted to approach before dark, while the convoy was still off the Cyrenaican coast, it would be heavily attacked by air from Gambut; if it waited until the following morning it would be within easy range of Malta's dangerous air striking forces. It was unlikely that the Italian Fleet would attempt a night attack; if it did, it would present the light British warships with a welcome opportunity to demonstrate their superior night-fighting training and equipment.

The convoy had to be defended not only from the enemy Fleet but also from air attack from Crete and, later, from Sicily. Fortunately conditions in Cyrenaica were very different from those of the previous June, for although the enemy was still established on air bases in Cyrenaica he was in full retreat and his air forces were short of fuel and were for ever changing airfields. Moreover the convoy would not sail before the 8th Army had captured, at least, the Tobruk airfields, and it was hoped to be able to use airfields even further west.[1] Before dawn on the third day the convoy should be within range of Malta-based fighters.

The Royal Navy and Royal Air Force set up a Combined Operations Room in Headquarters No. 201 Naval Co-operation Group to conduct operation 'Stoneage'. In No. 201 Group there were available three squadrons for general reconnaissance, three for anti-submarine patrols (including one equipped with A.S.V.), four torpedo-bomber squadrons (including one with A.S.V.) for attacks on any enemy naval forces attempting to intercept the convoy, and one long-range twin-engine squadron for fighter protection. A.H.Q. Egypt and the Desert Air Force were to provide short-range fighter cover as far

---

[1] It was hoped that the Martuba landing grounds would be in operation by 17th November. In the event, owing to heavy rain, they did not become serviceable until the 19th. On the 17th, however, it had been possible to use the landing grounds at Gazala.

as forty miles west of the longitude of Benghazi. From here Malta would take over. American Liberators were to be made available at Gambut to support the striking force from No. 201 Group. At Malta there was one special composite squadron for photographic, general and A.S.V. reconnaissance, one squadron and two flights of torpedo-bombers provided a striking force, and three longe-range twin-engine fighter squadrons and the equivalent of five short-range single-engine fighter squadrons would give fighter protection. Malta's night bombers (the equivalent of one squadron) were to attack enemy landing grounds in Sicily on the night of the 19th/20th to give indirect support to the convoy.

So, in spite of the lightness of the escort, the chances of being able to defend the convoy from either surface or air attack appeared much better than in June, and at Malta there was confidence that the vital cargoes could be successfully protected during unloading.

For greater secrecy the four ships of the 'Stoneage' convoy, the British *Denbighshire*, the American *Mormacmoon* and *Robin Locksley*, and the Dutch *Bantam* were loaded at Port Sudan. They passed into the Mediterranean from the Canal in the evening of 16th November escorted by *Euryalus* and seven Fleet destroyers. Next day the Fleets entered Alexandria to refuel, and were relieved by the Hunts. At 7 a.m. on the 18th *Cleopatra*, *Dido*, *Arethusa* and *Orion* and the seven Fleets joined the escort to the north of Tobruk. Rear-Admiral A. J. Power, flying his flag in *Cleopatra*, was in command of the operation.

Day and night anti-submarine patrols were provided by Bisleys of No. 15 Squadron S.A.A.F., Hudsons of No. 459 Squadron R.A.A.F. and Swordfish of No. 815 Squadron, Fleet Air Arm. On the 18th shore-based fighters covering the convoy were reinforced at dawn and dusk by the Beaufighters of No. 252 Squadron R.A.F. During the forenoon a small force of enemy aircraft, reported as Ju. 88s, attempted to bomb the convoy but were driven off by Kittyhawks of No. 450 Squadron R.A.A.F., and thereafter the passage was without incident until dusk. The cruisers—less *Euryalus* —and the Fleets had just disengaged from the convoy to the north-ward for the night when torpedo-bombers attacked both forces. The convoy escaped damage but *Arethusa* was hit forward. Heavily on fire, she was ordered to make for Alexandria escorted by two destroyers. About an hour later two torpedo aircraft attacked the convoy but did no damage.

At dawn on the 19th Admiral Power brought his night striking force again into close company with the convoy, which was making excellent progress. Beaufighters and Spitfires from Malta gave continuous cover and from Gambut six Baltimores of No. 203 Squadron swept the waters to northward of the convoy. Throughout the passage there was a marked improvement in communications between ships and fighter aircraft, resulting from the use of V.H.F. radio-telephone sets and no doubt also from persistent combined training.[1]

At 2 p.m., leaving *Euryalus* and the Hunts to escort the merchantmen on to Malta, then eighty miles distant, Admiral Power turned his remaining warships back for Alexandria. By 3 o'clock next morning, 20th November, the convoy was safely berthed in Malta harbour. On the same day the 8th Army entered Benghazi, and in Tunisia the 1st Army was building up its strength for a further advance from a front about forty miles west of Bizerta.

In a jubilant Malta unloading beat all previous records. There was scarcely any attempt at interruption by enemy aircraft, nor were there any attacks worthy of note on Admiral Power's ships, or later on *Euryalus* and the Hunts, as they returned eastward. The damaged *Arethusa*, however, in tow stern-first and fighting dangerous fires and a rising gale, did not enter Alexandria until the evening of the 21st more than twelve hours after her squadron mates. She had had 155 killed, and among the seriously burned was Captain A. C. Chapman, who had remained on his bridge until a few hours before entering harbour. The Royal Air Force had lost five aircraft, including three Spitfires from unknown causes.

Two weeks later, on 5th December, another convoy (operation 'Portcullis') of five cargo vessels and one tanker arrived at Malta from the east, with no interference by the enemy either on passage or while unloading. The Axis air forces were fully extended in Tripolitania and Tunisia, and Malta had become an unprofitable target.

'Stoneage' and 'Portcullis' had together brought in 56,000 tons of cargo, apart from heavy oils. After 'Portcullis' had been unloaded Lord Gort reported that flour would last until mid-May 1943, other foodstuffs and fodder until March, benzine and kerosene until mid-April. These estimates took into account some small increases now being made in the rations. 'Portcullis' was followed by a succession of ships in pairs, which arrived on 11th, 13th and 21st December and 2nd January and among which were two tankers. This arrangement had several advantages: each pair could accompany one of the military supply convoys as far as Benghazi and be picked up in that neighbourhood by escorts from Malta. Not only was this method less conspicuous but it was economical in warships, which were consequently made available in greater numbers as a surface striking force at Malta. On 1st January Lord Gort signalled that to complete reserves to seven months' stock and two months' working margin would need a further 112,000 tons, which could be accepted during

---

[1] During 1942 the fighter squadrons and sector headquarters of the Desert Air Force had been progressively equipped with V.H.F. (very high frequency) radio-telephone sets on a large scale, affording them greater range of control and much better reception.

January at the rate of four ships a week. But the Commanders-in-Chief Middle East replied that it would not be possible to build up at this rate 'without detriment to 8th Army supplies which are vital at this stage. Nor is shipping readily available.'

In mid-December, there being no immediate prospect of sending a convoy from the west, the Chiefs of Staff agreed to Admiral Cunningham's proposal that the ships still waiting at Gibraltar should be unloaded either there or in French North African ports. Until further notice Malta would have to rely solely upon supply from the east, but certain important items, such as seed potatoes, unloaded from the ships at Gibraltar, were to be retained for shipment later. In the event 175 tons of them were brought to Malta on 4th January by the fast minelayer *Welshman*.

With the raising of the siege and the virtual disappearance of any likelihood of invasion, the Chiefs of Staff had accepted on 1st December a suggestion of Lord Gort's that the Commanders-in-Chief Middle East should once again assume responsibility for offensive operations by forces based on Malta.[1] It had already become clear that the build-up of the Axis forces in Tunisia was going ahead faster than that of the Allies, so that if Tunis and Bizerta were to be captured quickly the 'Torch' and Middle East Commands would have to combine in finding more effective means of stopping Axis ships and aircraft carrying men and stores across the Sicilian Narrows. Lord Gort's suggestion was therefore timely, for it was from Malta that much of the increased effort would have to come.

See Map 23

The story of the Allied—mainly British—warfare against Axis shipping in the Mediterranean during the last three months of 1942 is here told as one, in spite of the fact that in November and December the Mediterranean area was divided into two naval commands.[2]

In the following pages the reader will find a catalogue of enemy ships attacked and sunk and of air sorties flown, and in Chapters X and XVI he will find again similar facts for the months covered. Many readers will find these lists and figures dull but we feel that they are necessary in the text if the progressive influence of the enemy's shipping losses on the land campaign is to be made clear.

---

[1] On 15th May 1942, when Malta was fighting for survival and had no striking forces left, Lord Gort had been made Supreme Commander of the Fighting Services and of the Civil Administration. See Volume III, p. 186.

[2] For clarity, Axis maritime reactions to the 'Torch' landings and Allied shipping losses arising therefrom are included in Chapter VI.

Wherever possible we have related them to specific operations ashore. Such losses not only affected the ability of the Axis Armies to fight but seriously handicapped the Commanders who had to plan operations without knowing whether the supplies to sustain them would be available.

In October 1942 the 10th (Malta) Submarine Flotilla operating off the African coast from Cape Bon right round to the Gulf of Sirte, and the 1st Flotilla from Beirut patrolling in the Aegean and off Cyrenaica, had a successful month. The most notable success was scored between the 18th and 20th when reports from aircraft brought about a concentration of five submarines of the Malta Flotilla against a convoy of four ships bound for Tripoli. Near Lampedusa two large cargo ships and one of the escort, the destroyer *Da Verazzano*, were sunk and a tanker badly damaged. Fleet Air Arm aircraft from Malta shared in destroying the larger of the two cargo ships. Then on the 23rd *P.35* sank in Homs roads the 8,700-ton *Amsterdam*, which the Fleet Air Arm had damaged a week earlier, fifty miles farther east. So far as the 8th Flotilla from Gibraltar was concerned there was, of course, during October no 'Torch' Command and no enemy supply route to Tunisia, but submarines of this Flotilla were already occupied in reconnaissance patrols in preparation for the landings. In the second half of the month *P.219* carried General Mark Clark to his clandestine meeting with General Mast, and early in November the same submarine, nominally commanded by an American Naval Officer, picked up General Giraud off the south of France.[1]

Although less fortunate than the submarines in their total bag for October, it was aircraft of No. 201 Naval Co-operation Group who scored the successes most damaging to the enemy.[2] These came at the very end of the month and extended into November, just as the land and air battle in the Western Desert was reaching its climax. Rommel depended to a great extent upon the arrival of fuel; Kesselring's promise of supply by air was producing little more than a trickle. On 26th October the 4,870-ton tanker *Proserpina* was sunk in broad daylight off Tobruk after a most determined attack by Bisleys of No. 15 Squadron S.A.A.F. and Beauforts of No. 47 Squadron (one of whose torpedoes sank the ship) escorted by Beaufighters of Nos. 252 and 272 Squadrons; six aircraft from a total of

---

[1] See p. 133
[2] At this time Air Chief Marshal Tedder was feeling the lack of Beaufort IIs. The Beaufort Is, being some 25 m.p.h. slower, forced the indispensable Beaufighter escorts to fly at less than economical cruising speed, thus reducing the range of the strikes by 15% and leaving a considerable gap between the range of the Beaufort strikes from Malta and that of the Wellington torpedo-bomber strikes from Egypt. By the middle of September only twenty Beaufort IIs had been sent to the Middle East and only the Mk. Is would be supplied for the next six months.

twenty-two did not return. The enemy now sailed a tanker and supply ship, carrying cased petrol, for Tobruk. On the 28th the tanker was sunk and the supply ship turned back damaged off Navarino, this time by R.A.F. aircraft from Malta. No. 201 Group and American Liberators dealt with two further attempts. Early on 1st November Wellingtons sank the *Tripolino* by the light of flares to north-west of Tobruk, and Beauforts dealt with her small companion the *Ostia* four hours later at dawn. Next morning, also at dawn, Beauforts found the *Zara* from Piraeus sixty miles north of Tobruk and sank her. Her companion, the *Brioni*, managed to enter harbour but was sunk by U.S.A.A.F. bombs before she had time to unload. These last four victims all carried cased petrol and ammunition and made up the total to six ships sunk in seven days, five by aircraft torpedoes and one by bombs. During the same seven days two merchant vessels and six destroyers arrived at Tobruk and unloaded small quantities of stores but the petrol carried seems to have been less than 500 tons.

British submarines, it will be remembered, were so disposed for the 'Torch' landings as to counter any challenge from the Italian Fleet. None came, but *P.46*, off the western tip of Sicily, torpedoed the newly completed cruiser *Attilio Regolo* returning, on 8th November, with six destroyers from a minelaying task in the Sicilian Narrows. The damaged cruiser reached Palermo in tow stern first. On the 11th, Captain (S) 10—whose own submarines had been reinforced by boats from the 1st Flotilla[1]—was ordered to redispose his forces in the best way for attacking enemy ships making for Bizerta and Tunis and ports on the east coast of Tunisia. Four days later several boats of the 8th Flotilla were placed under his orders to operate to the north of Sicily and this arrangement remained in force until 20th January, 1943, by which time Captain (S) 8 had moved from Gibraltar to Algiers.

On 21st November, in response to a request from Admiral Cunningham, the Admiralty extended the 'sink at sight' zone to include the whole Mediterranean except Turkish territorial waters and the area to the west of a line running from the Franco-Spanish frontier, passing east of the Balearics, and thence due south to the Algerian coast.

Sinkings by submarines during November, however, were disappointing. There were some successes in the Gulf of Sirte and off the east coast of Tunisia, among them the Italian *Scillin*, which proved tragically, to be carrying over 800 British prisoners of war of whom only 26 were saved. But no ships bound for Bizerta or Tunis

---

[1] Captain (S) 10, an abbreviation for the Captain commanding the 10th Submarine Flotilla.

were sunk. The shortness of the route was a main cause—from Trapani to Tunis is only 130 sea miles—and Axis supply ships in the long nights of winter could cover much of this distance in darkness. There were plenty of other difficulties for the attackers to overcome. Submarines found these narrow waters extremely hazardous. German and Italian aircraft, fitted with A.S.V., and Italian surface patrols were very alert. Moreover, in such confined and heavily mined waters submarine commanders had to occupy themselves to an unusual degree with navigation, and the quality of their attacks suffered. Bad weather was another handicap.

The R.A.F. by contrast sank many ships during November, but these too were almost all off Tobruk or Benghazi or the coasts of Tripolitania and eastern Tunisia. Welcome as these further sinkings of Rommel's supply ships were, it was now the interruption of supplies to Bizerta and Tunis that was crucial. Some damage was done to ships in harbour during bombings of Bizerta and Tunis, described in the previous chapter, but again no ship bound for these ports was sunk. As with the submarines it was the shortness of the route which made it so difficult to attack from the air, coupled with the ease with which enemy ships making the passage could be provided with strong air escorts. The F.A.A. had a disappointing month, sinking only one ship; she, however, was a big one, the 10,500-ton *Giulio Giordani* sunk off Misurata. The U.S.A.A.F. from Egypt was now taking a hand, and sank two ships off Benghazi and one in Tobruk. On the 4th the Italian torpedo boat *Centauro* was sunk at Benghazi by bombs.

Although Malta's aircraft did not fare well against shipping in the Sicily—Tunisia—Sardinia triangle they achieved excellent results against the German air forces in the same area. They directed their attacks principally against air transport bases in Sicily, using Wellingtons by night and Beaufighters and Spitfire fighter-bombers (appearing for the first time in the Middle East) by day. Between 8th and 30th November at least fifteen German transport aircraft were destroyed, including one six-engine aircraft (a Me. 323 destroyed on the ground at El Aouina by Beaufighters of No. 272 Squadron); twenty-three bombers and dive-bombers; about twelve fighters; and one three-engine and one six-engine flying boat (a BV. 222, also shot down by No. 272 Squadron).[1] A further eleven aircraft lost by the Germans may well have been destroyed by Malta's fighters, too. Precise Italian losses are not known.

Emphasis has been placed on the exploits of Malta-based aircraft because the island faced both ways, so to speak. It was a part of the

---

[1] The Me. 323 transport aircraft normally carried 100–120 men or 10 tons of freight, but it was capable of lifting a maximum freight load of 20 tons. The BV. 222 flying boat could carry at least 10 tons of freight.

Middle East Command, but it had been arranged that aircraft from Malta should operate against ports and ships in the 'Torch' as well as in the Middle East area. And, whereas R.A.F. and U.S.A.A.F. aircraft from Egypt contributed largely to the attacks on enemy ships attempting to keep Rommel's forces supplied, it was left almost entirely to Malta to do what she could against ships bound for Tunisia. Quite simply the 'Torch' Command, in the early stages, had no air/sea striking force, British or American, with the exception of a few F.A.A. Swordfish based on Algiers, 450 miles from the route it was so important to attack. The 'Torch' Command were also desperately short of aircrews for reconnaissance over the sea and for anti-submarine patrols. Moreover, the Eastern Air Command and the U.S. Twelfth Air Force were fully extended in supporting General Anderson's attenuated forces and as has been seen were operating on a hand-to-mouth basis from airfields of poor quality.

There were limits, however, to what Malta could do. The island had recently defeated another attempt to neutralize it, and much of its airfield capacity was still required for fighters; the rest had to be shared between reconnaissance and striking force aircraft, and these were in just as great demand for seeking out and destroying ships supplying Rommel's Army as for like duties against ships supplying the new Axis forces in Tunisia. Moreover, aviation spirit for strikes was still rationed, and such attacks as were made, whether against enemy ships or transport aircraft, had to contend with strong escorts of single-engine fighters.

These difficulties had to be overcome. Soon after the 'Torch' landings the Chiefs of Staff were exchanging proposals with the 'Torch' and Middle East Commands for increasing effectively and speedily the effort against the enemy's supply line to Tunis and Bizerta. Early in December the various proposals for reinforcing Malta began to take effect.[1] The 22 Wellingtons already sent to

---

[1] The squadrons at Malta on the 24th November 1942 were as follows:

Squadrons	Role	Aircraft
Nos. 126, 185, 249 and No. 1435 Flight	Single-engine fighter	Spitfire
No. 229	Single-engine fighter	Hurricane and Spitfire
No. 272 (Det.)*	Twin-engine fighter	Beaufighter
No. 227†	Twin-engine fighter and shipping strike	Fighter and coastal versions of Beaufighter
No. 89 (Det.)	Twin-engine night-fighter	Beaufighter
No. 69	General, A.S.V. and photographic reconnaissance	Wellington, A.S.V. Wellington, Baltimore and Spitfire
No. 39*	Torpedo-bomber	Beaufort I and II
No. 828 ('Y' Flight), F.A.A.	Torpedo-bomber	Albacore
No. 830 ('X' Flight), F.A.A.	Torpedo-bomber	Swordfish
Nos. 40 (Det.) and 104 (Det.)	Medium bomber	Wellington

* Transferred from No. 201 Group that month.

† No. 227 Squadron (less its aircraft) was transferred to Malta in August 1942, and took over the coastal Beaufighters and aircrews of No. 235 Squadron Detachment (from U.K.) and the day-fighter Beaufighters of No. 248 Squadron whose aircrews returned to the U.K.

Malta were increased to 34 on 8th December. This left only 32 Wellingtons in No. 205 Group and of these the A.O.C.-in-C. Middle East was prepared to lend Air Vice-Marshal Sir Keith Park one squadron as a further addition to his striking power. As, however, it was intended to operate all the remaining Middle East Wellingtons from Benghazi after 12th December, Tedder retained the right to recall this squadron from Malta at short notice. Headquarters No. 248 Wing (of No. 201 Group) moved to Malta during December to control the naval co-operation squadrons. By the end of the month No. 23 Squadron (Mosquito IIs) from the United Kingdom, No. 821 Squadron F.A.A. (Albacores) and a detachment of No. 46 Squadron (Beaufighters), both from Egypt, had moved to Malta.[1] In Algeria there were now the two recently arrived Wellington squadrons and further units of the U.S. Twelfth Air Force had already been moved east in support of General Anderson and to assist in attacking the enemy's sea communications.

So far as the Navy was concerned, Admiral Harwood readily lent some more submarines to operate off Naples and against the Tunisian route as a whole, and sent M.T.Bs to Malta some of which presently moved to Bône for inshore operations. The safe arrival of the 'Stoneage' convoy had eased the pressure on the cruisers and destroyers of the Mediterranean Fleet and, on 27th November, Force K, under Rear-Admiral A. J. Power's command, was reconstituted at Malta with the cruisers *Cleopatra, Euryalus* and *Dido* and four destroyers. On 30th November, fighter protection over Bône having become strong enough, Admiral Cunningham was able to base Force Q—the cruisers *Aurora, Argonaut* and *Sirius* and the destroyers *Quiberon* and *Quentin*—on that port.

On the night of the 1st/2nd December, Force Q had its first and most spectacular success while sweeping the waters between the western end of Sicily and the north Tunisian coast. Around 12.30 a.m., guided skilfully by aircraft reports and flares, the British ships made contact by radar with an enemy convoy some sixty miles north-east of Bizerta. An hour later the ships of the convoy comprising three merchant vessels and the German war transport *K.T.1* —totalling 7,800 tons—had all been sunk. Of the escort of three destroyers and two torpedo-boats, one destroyer, the *Folgore*, was sunk after having put up what appears to have been a spirited resistance. Force Q received no damage during this one-sided engagement but

---

[1] The Mosquito, in this instance the fighter-reconnaissance version, first appeared in the Middle East on the night of the 29th/30th December when intruder operations were carried out from Malta.

Mosquitos from No. 1 P.R.U. in the U.K. had, however, landed previously at Malta after photographing ports, an outstanding example being the photographic reconnaissance on the 23rd December of all the principal Adriatic ports including the first cover ever obtained of Ancona.

on the return passage to Bône the *Quentin* was sunk by a torpedo-bomber shortly after daybreak.

On the following night to the east of the Kerkenah Islands the destroyers *Jervis, Nubian, Javelin* and *Kelvin* of Force K finished off the remnants of a convoy which had already been partly destroyed shortly after dark by F.A.A. aircraft from Malta. The destroyers also sank one of the escort, the torpedo-boat *Lupo*. A few days later the cruiser *Dido* was transferred from Force K to Force Q to bring the Bône force up to a strength of four cruisers and thus enable it to send two cruisers and two destroyers on sweeps every night. On the 14th however, the cruiser *Argonaut* was hit by aircraft torpedoes as she was returning to Bône from one of these sweeps, and, for the time being, the cruisers were reduced to three. *Argonaut's* bow and stern were severely damaged but two of her four propellers were still in working order and she reached Algiers under her own power.

On the night of 20th/21st December Wellingtons from Malta led *Jervis* and *Nubian* to an enemy merchant vessel off Djerba island near Gabes and illuminated the target while the destroyers sank her. Force Q's early success, however, was not repeated; the reappearance of surface striking forces had caused the enemy to discontinue or much reduce, for the time being, night passages across the Sicilian Narrows and to substitute day passages under strong air escort. This move drew the Allies' attention all the more upon the air effort possible from Malta, and from Algeria too.

Naturally the enemy was not content to go on risking his ships in daylight between Sicily and Tunisia if he could find a way of reducing appreciably the dangers of a night passage. He already had a barrier of minefields between Cape Bon and Sicily which made the passage through the Narrows hazardous for Allied warships, unless they hugged the Sicilian coast or that of Cape Bon. At the end of November the enemy had begun to lay another barrier fifty miles farther west, roughly from just west of Bizerta north-eastward to the Skerki Bank, beyond which the water was too deep for moored mines. Force Q, sailing from Bône, would be severely hampered in reaching the Axis' shipping route round the end of this new barrier without exposing itself to air attack by day, either on its outward or homeward passage, for which adequate fighter cover could not yet be given. The new barrier, but for its north-eastern extremities, was completed by mid-December and the enemy then felt able to revert to night sailings. Further developments in these moves and counter-moves occurred early in the new year, and will be related in their proper time.

At the end of November and again in mid-December Air Chief Marshal Tedder visited General Eisenhower at Algiers. He was not impressed by what he saw of the co-ordination of the 'Torch' air forces, nor did he regard as satisfactory the arrangements for the control of the air in the Mediterranean area as a whole. His visit occurred as a result of proposals which the Chiefs of Staff were examining for reorganizing the Mediterranean Commands, on which they had called for the views of the Commanders-in-Chief Middle East. In Air Chief Marshal Tedder's opinion it was necessary to set up one air command for the whole Mediterranean, at once, under an Air Commander-in-Chief who would be subordinate to General Eisenhower for operations in Algeria and Tunisia, and would co-operate with him in operations over the rest of the Mediterranean. This matter was not resolved until the Casablanca Conference at the end of January. In the meantime, Major-General Carl Spaatz of the U.S.A.A.F. was appointed to the staff of A.E.F. to advise General Eisenhower on allied air co-ordination.

Gradually, although not markedly until mid-December, results against enemy ships bound for Tunisia improved. During December, Allied submarines, aircraft, surface warships and mines accounted for some 23 per cent. of Axis cargoes embarked for Tunisia. In the Mediterranean as a whole the month was a highly successful one for submarines and aircraft and, as already related, Forces Q and K also contributed substantially to the total sinkings, although after their early successes their role was deterrent rather than destructive. Among the submarines, *Safari* and *Umbra* created havoc during their patrols off the east coast of Tunisia and along the Tripolitanian shore. *Safari* sank one supply ship, a small tanker and three petrol-carrying schooners and *Umbra* three supply ships, one of which was heavily laden with motor transport. For three other submarines the 14th December was a lucky day: three supply ships ranging between 5,000 and 7,000 tons, the *Castelverde*, *Honestas* and *Sant Antioco*, were sunk to the north-west of Cape Bon by *Unruffled*, *Sahib* and *Splendid* respectively. The first two were bound for Tunis, the *Sant Antioco* for Bizerta. Three days later *Splendid* sank the Italian destroyer *Aviere* north of Bizerta.

December was also a great month for the F.A.A. from Malta. They sank five ships and shared in the sinking of a further three—in all 24,000 tons. R.A.F. Wellingtons from Malta concentrated on shipping in the Tunisian ports with good effect, dropping more than 500 tons of bombs; of the 17 aircraft lost from Malta that month seven failed to return from these operations. As has been seen in the previous chapter some heavy attacks on Tunisian ports were also made by Wellingtons and American Fortresses from Algeria and by British and American Liberators from Cyrenaica.

Against the enemy's principal air bases and aircraft in flight in the Sicily—Tunisia—Sardinia area, Malta's air forces again had a successful month. The Spitfire fighter-bombers extended their activities to include Lampedusa and airfields in southern Italy, and Spitfire escorts were given to the Beaufighters in their attacks on fighter-escorted air transport formations.[1] In addition to the employment of Me. 323s and BV. 222s the enemy pressed into service a number of FW. 200s, each capable of carrying 10,800 lbs of freight or twenty-five to thirty troops, a few Ju. 90s, each of which could carry 9,000 lbs of freight or seventy troops, and a few Ju. 290s capable of carrying 19,000 lbs of freight or ninety troops each. Considerable use was also made of German He. 111s, Ju. 88s, Ju. 86s and, as in November, of a variety of Italian bombers for air transport purposes. In all, during December, Malta's aircraft accounted for at least seventeen air transports, about seventeen bombers and dive-bombers, eight fighters and three flying boats (including another BV. 222). A further nine aircraft lost by the Germans may well have fallen to Malta's fighters. Thus, in less than two months, Malta's aircraft had destroyed at least 97 German aircraft, and quite likely a further 20 of which complete details are not available, as well as an unspecified number of Italian aircraft in that area.[2] In contrast Malta lost seventeen aircraft on operations of all kinds during December, making a total of forty-three for the two months.

British minelaying also began to pay modest dividends. During November and December aircraft laid magnetic mines on several occasions in and about the harbours of Bizerta, Tunis, Sousse and Palermo. On 29th November the fast minelayer *Manxman* laid 156 moored mines in the neighbourhood of Cani Rocks which lie twelve miles to the east-north-east of Bizerta, and on 8th December the submarine *Rorqual* laid 36 in the same area. As a direct result of these lays the enemy lost during November and December two large merchant ships totalling 11,000 tons and a number of smaller vessels, but on the 1st December the *Manxman* was torpedoed by *U.375* and had to be taken to Gibraltar for repairs.

Although the Allies were still far from satisfied with their attempts to cut off the enemy's supplies, particularly those to Tunisia, the Axis were equally dissatisfied with their own attempts to maintain them. Their task was made more difficult by changes in the ports of departure and unloading, brought about by Rommel's retreat and by the need to build up forces as speedily as possible through Bizerta and Tunis. In October 46 ships left Italy and Greece for Africa and

---

[1] According to prisoners of war, the principal air route was Naples—Trapani—El Aouina (Tunis) or Sidi Ahmed (Bizerta), the Ju. 52 formations (with fighter escort) flying straight through from Naples to Tunisia and refuelling at Palermo on the return flight to avoid drawing on fuel stocks in Tunisia.

[2] Italian records show that in the last quarter of 1942 23 aircraft, operating from Sicily, were lost in combat or destroyed by A.A. fire. It is likely that most of these aircraft fell to Malta's fighters or A.A. guns. No figures are available of Italian aircraft destroyed on the ground.

during October and early November twenty of these arrived at Tripoli, six at Benghazi, six at Tobruk, twelve were sunk on the outward passage and two turned back damaged. In November, after the 'Torch' landings, Axis traffic to Tunisian ports increased rapidly and, as one consequence, Naples and Palermo became the principal ports of departure. During the month, 64 ships left Italy and Greece and of the 56 which in due course arrived in Africa, 39 unloaded at Bizerta or Tunis. But the seven ships of over 500 G.R.T. lost were all bound for Libyan ports. The last ship to unload at Tobruk had been the *Etiopia*, sunk there by American bombs on 6th November, and the last at Benghazi the *Foscolo* which arrived on 12th November. Eastern routes to Libya were then abandoned and ships bound for Tripoli all passed west of Sicily and down the east coast of Tunisia. In December sinkings rose. Forty-five ships left Italy for Africa but only 29 arrived. Of these 26 went to Bizerta or Tunis; only two merchant vessels and some store-carrying submarines unloaded at Tripoli. In December, Palermo became the principal port of departure and Naples dropped for the time being into second place.[1]

This traffic to and from Africa, so vital to the Axis, was hindered by the slowness of most of the voyages. In at least one out of every three outward passages calls were made at intermediate ports—Trapani, Pantelleria, and earlier Piraeus and Suda Bay—to adjust escorts, make good damage, or obtain respite from Allied attacks. There were, however, some notable exceptions, particularly on the run to Bizerta or Tunis, in which certain ships repeatedly made good speed and a rapid turn-round. Warships were used increasingly, destroyers for carrying troops, and submarines for small quantities of urgently needed material—chiefly fuel and ammunition. In December Italian destroyers ran 45 trips to Bizerta or Tunis from Palermo or Trapani.

The military cargoes disembarked in Libya and Tunisia and the percentage lost to the Axis on the way are shown in the following table:

---

[1] The shipping figures in this paragraph are compiled from records kindly provided by the Italian Naval Historical Division and from German war records.

Cargoes disembarked in North Africa and percentage lost on passage
(From figures given by the Italian Official Naval Historian)†

Month 1942	Type	Cargo disembarked in North Africa (tons)	Percentage lost on the way
Oct.	General Military Cargo / Fuel	33,390 / 12,308	44
Nov.	General Military Cargo / Fuel } to Libya	42,005 / 21,731	26
	General Military Cargo and Fuel to Tunisia	30,309	No loss
Dec.	General Military Cargo / Fuel } to Libya	4,093 / 2,058	52
	General Military Cargo and Fuel to Tunisia	58,763	23

†Bragadin: *Che ha fatto la Marina?*

The losses of ships mentioned so far refer to those engaged in carrying supplies to Africa. The losses in the whole Mediterranean during these three months were, of course, greater and are shown in the following table. During the same period the enemy lost from service for varying lengths of time many ships which had been damaged, but not sunk, by Allied attack.

Numbers and tonnage of Italian and German Merchant ships of over 500 G.R.T. sunk at sea or in port in the Mediterranean

October—December 1942

(Compiled from Italian post-war and German war records)

Month	By surface ships	By submarine	By aircraft	By mine	Shared	From other causes	Total
Oct.	—	11–30,524	4–18,276	—	1– 5,397*	1–2,747	17– 56,944
Nov.	—	4– 6,517	12–42,649	1– 5,418	—	—	17– 54,584
Dec.	3–8,058	10–37,055	14–28,631	1– 5,609	3–10,761†	1– 616	32– 90,730
	3–8,058	25–74,096	30–89,556	2–11,027	4–16,158	2–3,363	66–202,258

*F.A.A. and Submarine.
†Two F.A.A. and surface, one F.A.A. and Submarine.

During these three months some 50 vessels of less than 500 G.R.T. totalling 9,000 tons were also sunk. The figure for tonnage sunk by aircraft was double that reached during July, August and September, yet the total of 3,500 sorties flown in searching for and attacking enemy shipping was not much higher than in the earlier period.

Certain other aspects of the maritime war in the Mediterranean theatre during November and December now claim attention. After covering the initial landing operations at Algiers and Oran Force H returned to Gibraltar, where Admiral Syfret transferred his flag on 14th November to the newly arrived *Nelson*, and the *Duke of York* and *Victorious* (carrying Admiral Lyster) returned to the United Kingdom. During the remainder of November and during December, Force H carried out frequent sweeps round the Balearic Islands alternating with spells of showing the flag at Mers el Kebir and Gibraltar. Between 26th and 30th November Force H was at sea to give support to the French Fleet should it leave Toulon. There was still a chance that the Italian Fleet might attempt a raid, but a heavy bombing attack made on Naples on 4th December by American Liberators from Egypt sank the *Attendolo*[1] and severely damaged two other cruisers, the *Montecuccoli* and the *Eugenio*. This caused the three *Littorio* battleships and remaining cruisers at Naples to move to Spezia and the 3rd Division of cruisers from Messina to Maddalena, leaving only the 8th Cruiser Division in southern waters—at Messina. The likelihood of any offensive operation by the Italian Fleet was thus greatly reduced. In fact the Italians would have been hard put to it to find the fuel for even a few cruisers on active operations.

Fresh arrivals of German U-boats during November and December kept the total in the Mediterranean slightly above twenty in spite of losses. In December they had no losses, but the Italians had four—two to escort vessels, one to air and one to submarine attack. By the end of the year only three German U-boats were on patrol; three were returning to base and seventeen were in dockyard hands. Casualties to British merchant ships during December were not high, but among them were the 23,700-ton *Strathallan* (the last P. and O. of her class to be built before the war) sunk by *U.562* off Oran, and the 16,300-ton *Cameronia* damaged by aircraft torpedo north-east of Bougie.

Early in the morning of 12th December the Italian Tenth Light Flotilla attacked merchant ships in Algiers Bay with human torpedoes and limpets. They succeeded in sinking one vessel and

---

[1] Still under repair after being torpedoed during convoy operation 'Pedestal'.

damaging three others. The sixteen Italians taking part were all captured. Four days earlier three human torpedoes had set out from the interned Italian merchant ship *Olterra*, moored alongside at Algeciras, to attack Force H at Gibraltar, across the bay. The attack failed. Three of the six Italians lost their lives and two were taken prisoner. One succeeded in returning to the *Olterra*, which had just been secretly converted into a much more effective base ship than before. Workshops had been built into one of her holds and a door cut underwater through which human torpedoes could be launched unseen.[1]

Four British submarines and one Greek were lost during these three months in the Mediterranean. Four succumbed to depth charge attacks by small surface craft; the Greek *Triton* on 16th November in the Aegean; *Utmost* on 24th November north of Marittimo Island; *P.222* on 12th December near Naples, and *P.48* on 25th December in the Gulf of Tunis. H.M.S. *Traveller* is presumed to have been mined in the Gulf of Taranto on about 4th December, while she was examining the chances of attacking the Italian battleships at Taranto with 'Chariots'—the name given to the British human torpedoes.

During the last two months of 1942 events at both ends of the Mediterranean and in Russia, around Stalingrad, had changed the aspect of the war. In each of these areas the Axis was on the defensive and the effect of this on waiting neutrals and Axis-occupied countries must have been considerable. In the remaining two great areas of conflict, the Japanese were losing the long drawn out battle in the Pacific for the Solomon Islands and New Guinea, while in the Atlantic the outcome of the whole war was still quite undecided, depending upon the defeat or victory of the German submarines. During October and November 1942 German submarines had also been active off the Cape of Good Hope and up the east coast of Africa; ships carrying military cargoes for the Middle East had been among their victims.

Early in the new year the 8th Army, already half way across Tripolitania, faced the enemy at Buerat and the last vestiges of Italy's African Empire were about to disappear. In French North Africa there had been a disappointing check to the Allied attempt to prevent the Axis from getting a firm hold in Tunisia, but there was confidence that it was only a check. Malta appeared at long last to be secure, and conditions on the island were improving. A Christmas

---

[1] Previous reference to the *Olterra* is made in Volume III.

greeting from President Roosevelt gave pleasure and inspiration to Malta's indomitable garrison and people.

The Allies could now look forward to reopening the Mediterranean before long for through traffic and being able to conduct operations across the sea against southern Europe under Axis domination. The Italian Fleet was no longer a cause for anxiety to the Royal Navy. It had made no attempt to challenge the Allies' operations within the 'Torch' command nor even Admiral Harwood's small forces covering Malta convoys and the supply of the advancing 8th Army. Nor were Axis submarines a serious menace. The only serious opposition to the Allied war on merchant shipping, related in this chapter, came from the strong concentration of Axis air forces operating in the vital triangle Sicily—Tunisia—Sardinia. Before describing how this opposition was worn down and finally overcome, it will be convenient to turn once again to Libya, and follow the exploits of the 8th Army and the Western Desert Air Force as they made for Tripoli on their way to close the ring in Tunisia.

Map 25

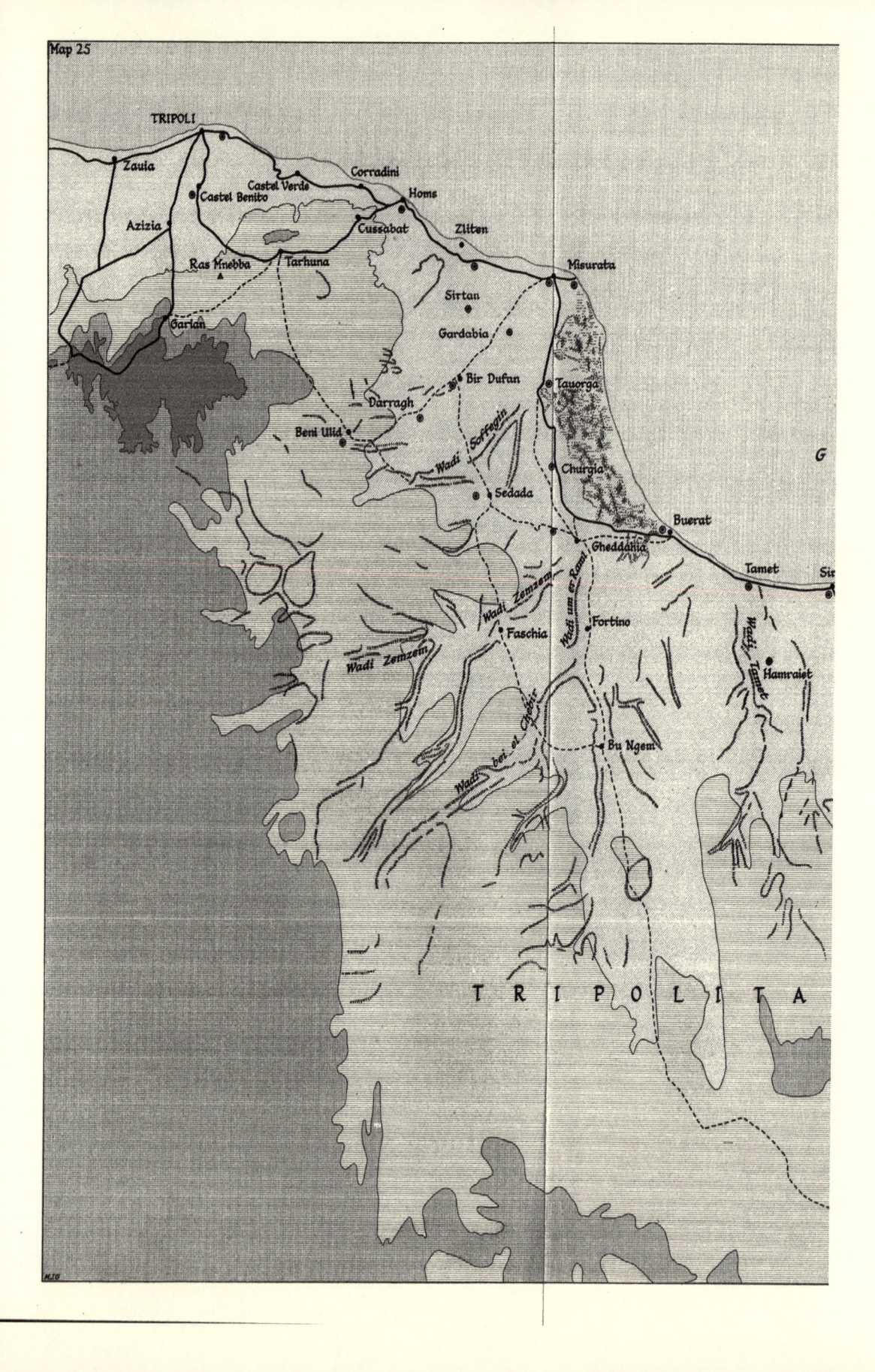

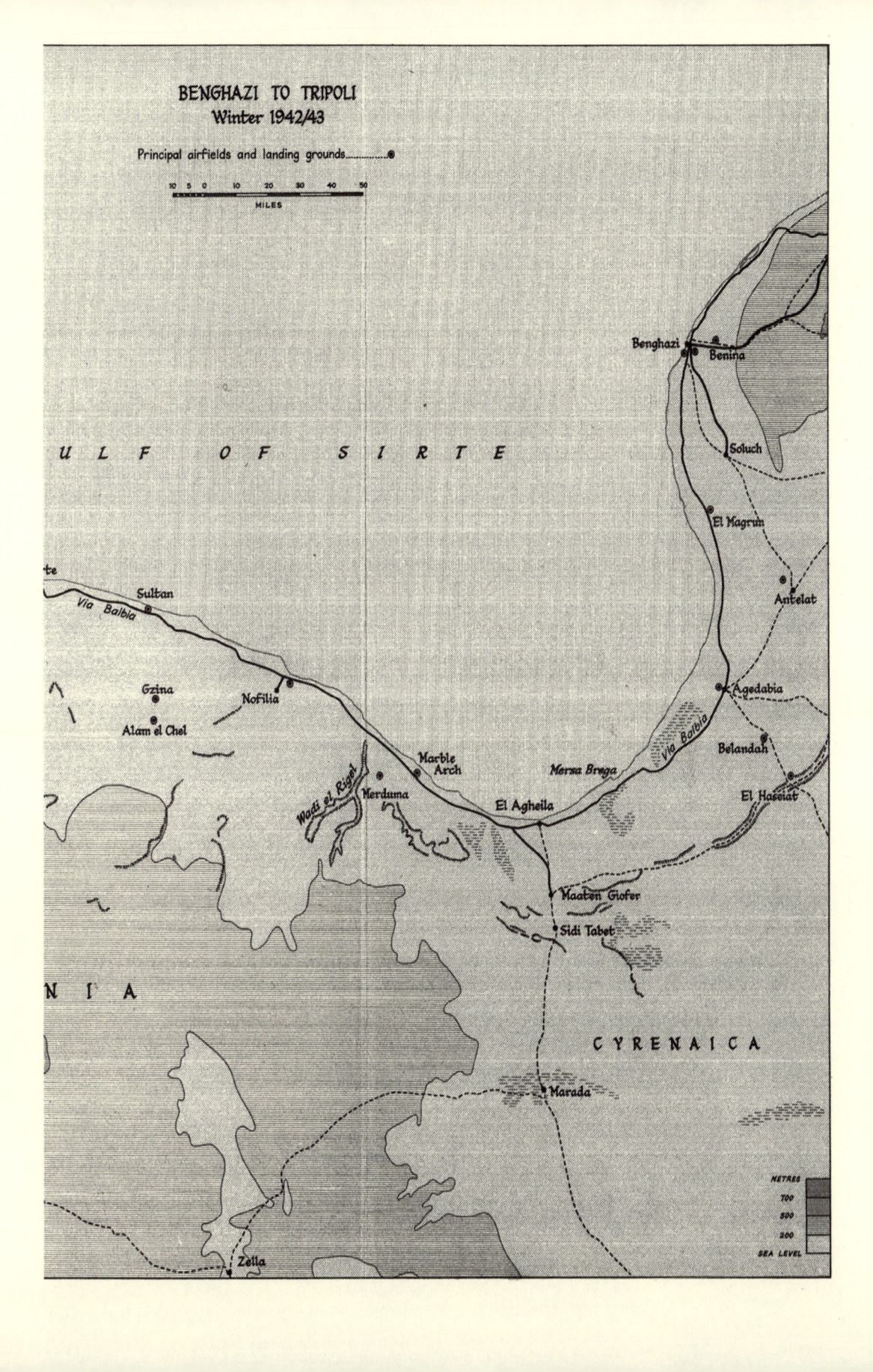

BENGHAZI TO TRIPOLI
Winter 1942/43

CHAPTER IX

FROM EL AGHEILA TO TRIPOLI
(12th November 1942 to 23rd January 1943)

See Maps 25 and 26.

WE left the 8th Army and the Desert Air Force near Benghazi (entered on 20th November 1942), and the leading troops moving towards the defences at El Agheila into which Rommel had withdrawn his defeated *Panzerarmee* by the night of 23rd/24th November.[1] Another phase of the British advance now begins, which will take the 8th Army and the Desert Air Force from Benghazi to Tripoli—675 miles by land, and 1,415 miles from Alexandria's administrative establishments.[2] The 8th Army attacked the Agheila position on 13th December 1942 and entered Tripoli on 23rd January 1943. The Axis leaders, whose policy shifted like a weathercock, decided not to fight hard at Agheila or Tripoli or at an intermediate position loosely named the Buerat line. But the British could not foreknow their enemies' wavering. General Montgomery made Tripoli his goal and was determined that Rommel should not rebound as he had successfully done in April 1941 and in January 1942.[3] Therefore he prepared for deliberate battles at the Agheila position and the Buerat Line.

The vast advance set G.H.Q. Middle East, 8th Army's Headquarters, and the other Services in their own and often overlapping fields, a prodigious administrative problem. Distances ran into hundreds of miles. The railway ended at Tobruk. There was no seaport which deserved the name between Benghazi and Tripoli (although small ships could discharge at Buerat), and supply across the beaches proved to be generally impracticable because almost everywhere the landward exits were too difficult for wheels without an amount of improvement which would need too much time,

---

[1] The defences in the neighbourhood of El Agheila will hereafter be called the Agheila position.

[2] Some distances by sea are interesting:
Alexandria to Tobruk—300 sea miles or 1½ days' voyage.
Alexandria to Benghazi—540 sea miles or 2½ days' voyage.
Alexandria to Tripoli—865 sea miles or 4 days' voyage.

[3] Lieut.-General Montgomery was promoted General and created a K.C.B. on 11th November 1942.

labour, stores and transport.[1] Moreover shipping off shore had to face the hazard of the Mediterranean's often tempestuous weather. Therefore in the end the burden of delivering supplies beyond Benghazi fell upon the motor-lorry. Failure in the administrative task would have meant failure in the advance, or delays that would have upset the high strategical plans now being made, that were clinched at the Casablanca Conference in January 1943, and which we describe in a later chapter. But there was no failure, and between August 1942 and May 1943 over a million tons were carried west from Egypt by rail, road, and sea.[2]

The Royal Air Force provided for special requirements of its own. Amongst these petrol was enormously important, and carrying it by air (to supplement the usual land convoys or to replace them when airfields were difficult for vehicles to reach) had passed the experimental stage which included overcoming snags. One of these was that R.A.F. Hudsons were unable to load 40–44 gallon steel drums, and 'flimsy' tins of high octane petrol were too dangerous to carry. Fortunately the Dakotas of U.S. 316th Troop Carrier Command could load drums, and—for the attack on the Agheila position—39 of these aircraft lifted over 130,000 gallons for the Desert Air Force from El Adem to Benina, El Magrun, and Agedabia. This solution of the problem was to be repeated on several occasions.[3] Another novel arrangement arose from the policy of putting squadrons of fighters on to landing grounds immediately that these were captured, or newly made by the engineers and the R.A.F. advanced airfield parties (see Chapter IV, page 98). This arrangement was to fly in ground crews and essential supplies in transport aircraft which flew with, and were protected by, the fighters whom they were to supply and maintain. Water and urgently needed spares and equipment for squadrons and Air Stores Parks (A.S.Ps) were also flown forward.

Immediate repair and salvage of aircraft was another vastly important need, and for this additional Forward Salvage Units (F.S.Us) were formed in Tripolitania.[4] They kept in touch with the advanced squadrons, the R.S.Us behind then holding the reserve aircraft as well as carrying out their normal functions. The F.S.Us, R.S.Us and A.S.Ps were all highly mobile; the A.S.Ps, for example,

---

[1] Where practicable beaches existed, they were used. For example, at Ras el Ali (between El Agheila and Marble Arch) 2,692 tons were discharged in the period 21st December to 3rd January.

[2] The air carried about 600 tons of emergency supplies.

[3] Marble Arch landing ground, for example, received by air 153,000 gallons of petrol and 9,500 gallons of oil during December 1942 and January 1943. This quantity of high octane petrol was equal to the total tank capacity of 1,575 Hurricane fighters or 1,240 Kittyhawk fighters, or 355 Boston day-bombers.

[4] To meet the immediate repair and salvage requirements for the pursuit from El Alamein an Advanced Salvage Unit (A.S.U.) had been formed by combining the forward salvage sections of the Repair and Salvage Units (R.S.Us) (see Chapter I, page 17). The lengthening L. of C. made the retention of the A.S.U. imperative and it became the first (No. 1) F.S.U.

could move with two hours' notice and be ready to issue spares and consumable stores within half an hour of reaching a new site. There was an excellent flow of repaired aircraft from the Delta, where the output of repaired airframes reached a total of nearly 1,600 and that of engines over 2,400 during November 1942—January 1943. As a consequence the Desert Air Force became less dependent on new aircraft, which were thus available in greater numbers for the Middle East air force as a whole.

So far, so good, but in spite of all the pains taken and skill applied there were difficulties and crises. As an example there was the usual container for petrol, the grossly inefficient 4-gallon commercial tin (or 'flimsy'), which could not stand rough handling or travel. A batch might leak up to 30 per cent., threatening fire in ships, asphyxiation in depots, or maddeningly drenching lorries and the desert.[1] There were not nearly enough good steel containers (the German 'Jerrican', American 'Merrican', Middle East's 'Tucan', and the 40–44 gallon drum) to oust the 'flimsies'. By 2nd January the shortage of returnable containers of all sorts was alarming.

The defended area which we have called the Agheila position and into which Rommel withdrew was very strong naturally because it was almost surrounded by salt marshes, soft sand, or ground too broken and rough to give tracked or wheeled vehicles freedom to manoeuvre. Defended localities and minefields stretched in a bold though not continuous sweep from the small anchorage of Mersa Brega for some forty miles to Maaten Giofer, on the track which runs south to the oasis of Marada. The line then followed this track for ten miles to Sidi Tabet. At Marada, forty-five miles farther south, there was a detached post. Round El Agheila itself there was a chain of minefields touching the shore on east and west. About seventeen miles west of Agheila an anti-tank ditch, protected by minefields, blocked a narrow passage between the sea and a large salt marsh.[2] From the British point of view the whole Agheila position was difficult to attack. The opinions of Axis leaders differed sharply whether to defend it or not.

Rommel, on 23rd November, reported that he could probably hold the British for a few days but that one of their full-dress attacks

---

[1] '... The British Army has for some years been going to war while carrying around its petrol in a paper bag or something which is very nearly the same thing. The 4-gallon flimsy container is enough to wreck any campaign in which long distances are involved.' (Brigadier Sir Brian Robertson).
It is fair to add that necessity more than choice had led to the original introduction of the 'flimsy'. The reader may see *The Story of the Royal Army Service Corps* 1939–1945 (London 1955) pp. 43–45, 482, and s.v. *Petroleum*.

[2] The Germans named this spot the 'El Mugtaa Narrows'.

THE NEW ZEALAND LEFT HOOK AT EL AGHEILA

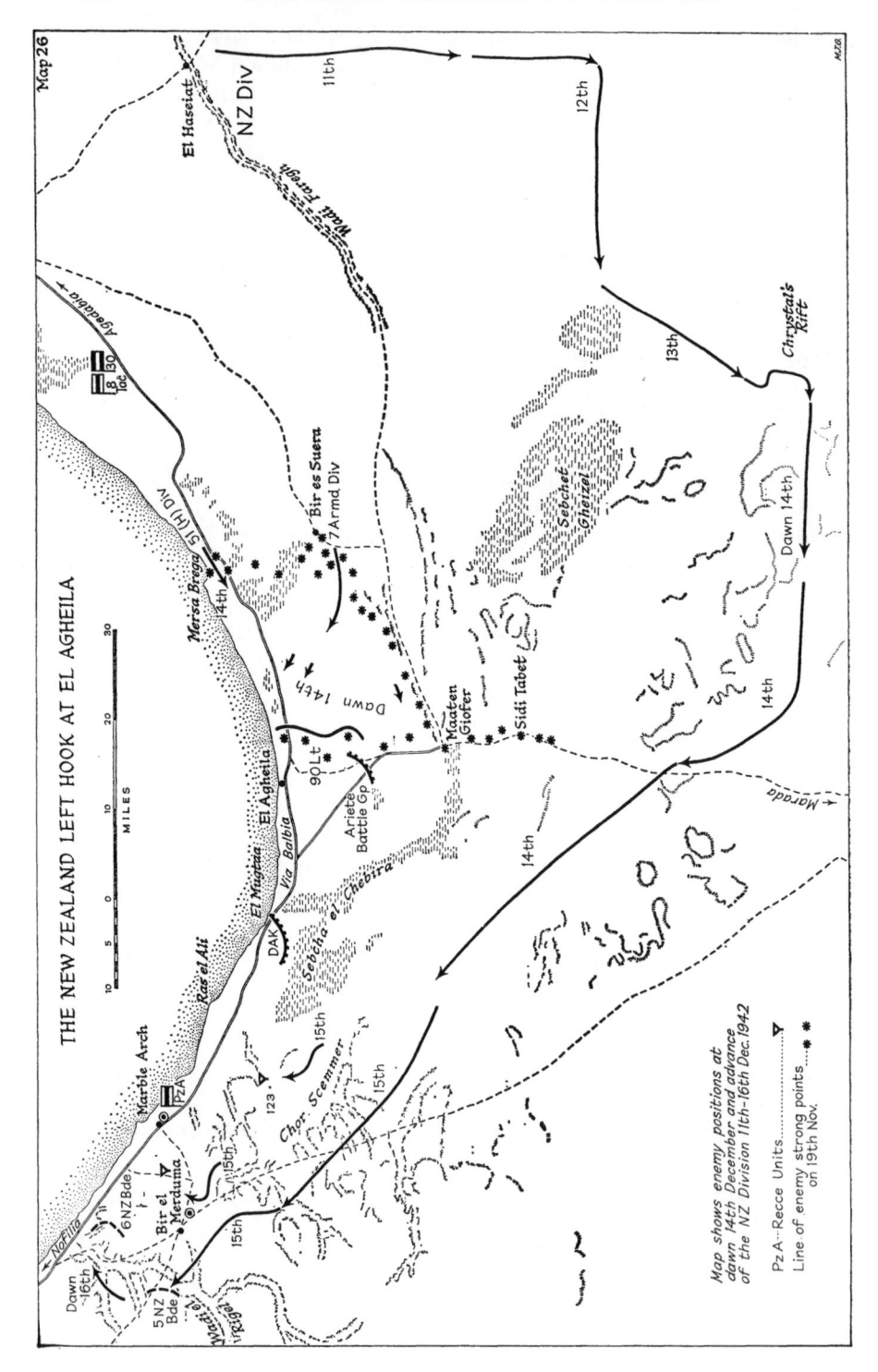

Map shows enemy positions at dawn 14th December and advance of the NZ Division 11th–16th Dec. 1942

Pz A – Recce Units
Line of enemy strong points on 19th Nov.

would destroy him because he had not enough troops to defend the position in depth, nor the transport and fuel to fight a battle of manoeuvre. The Axis High Command was finding it difficult to make up its mind. Hitler's eyes were on Russia and he still regarded the war in the Mediterranean theatre as mainly the Italians' business. But the Allied landings in French North Africa on 8th November forced him to attend to this new front. When he decided to give preference to Tunisia instead of to Libya he ensured that Rommel, who was short of almost everything, would go shorter still.

Mussolini had to show some fight for the remains of the Italian African Empire. The dictators decided between them that the Agheila position must be defended to uphold prestige and as an eastern outwork of Tunisia. Meanwhile the Italian military delegation *Delease* was absorbed by *Superlibia* under Marshal Bastico who on 22nd November became Rommel's immediate superior once more.[1] On 24th November Cavallero, Kesselring and von Rintelen conferred with Rommel at Marble Arch. Rommel repeated his views, and after discussing a possible 'half-way house' at Buerat between El Agheila and Tripoli, they grasped at least that Rommel might not be able to hold on at El Agheila for long. On the 25th Cavallero directed Bastico that the Agheila position must be held 'as long as possible' but if the British attacked in greatly superior force Bastico and Rommel might propose to withdraw to Buerat, and fix the date, which would have to be approved by Mussolini unless the emergency was extreme. Rommel (to summarize) reported that he could defend the Agheila position with his entire strength and risk total destruction, or retreat at once and save something. He thought that there was no master-plan for the campaign in North Africa as a whole, and that nobody in the High Command understood the condition of his army. Therefore on the 28th November he left Africa to explain his views to Hitler. He was disappointed by Hitler's failure to discuss a withdrawal of any sort, disgusted by Göring's attitude and meddling, and irritated by the indecision of Mussolini to whom he was sent by the *Führer*. Yet a few days later Mussolini, apparently with Hitler's approval, agreed that the first preparations for a possible retreat to Buerat would be made. Rommel and Bastico looked into the problem, paying special attention to the amount of transport and fuel likely to be at their disposal. They concluded that the first troops to go back (the Italians of 21st Corps now consisting of La Spezia, Trieste, and Pistoia Divisions) could probably begin to move on 5th or 6th December. It is clear that Rommel did not

---

[1] *Delease* (short for *Delegazione del Comando Supremo in Africa Settentrionale*) under General Barbasetti di Prun, had been created in August as a link between *Comando Supremo* and Rommel, who had been made directly subordinate to *Comando Supremo* for operations. See Volume III, p. 378.

intend to allow his army to be destroyed in the Agheila position if he could help it.

General Montgomery held the initiative and had the superior force. Perhaps his principal problem was to maintain administratively a part of his army strong enough to make certain that no reverse could possibly happen while his tactical plans to polish off Rommel were being perfected. Administration was none the easier because the 8th Army was being put in trim after the disorganization which had been caused by the twelve days' battle of El Alamein and the advance of some 800 miles which had immediately followed. Rommel's main problem, in contrast, was to persuade his superiors to allow him to withdraw before he was pinned down.

Administrative forecasts at first suggested that the end of December was the earliest time at which the attack on the Agheila position could begin. But Benghazi port proved to be less damaged than had been feared, and good organization and hard work caused the amount of supplies unloaded there to beat estimates. Improvement in traffic control and the arrangements for loading and unloading convoys of lorries raised the quantities delivered by road. Petrol was severely rationed and ammunition-dumps, abandoned in the retreat from Cyrenaica in January, were successfully searched for. As a result the date of administrative readiness was brought forward, and when General Montgomery issued his plan of attack, on 29th November, he was able to direct that the operation would begin on the night 16th/17th December.

Meanwhile the 8th Army, stretched across several hundred miles of desert, was regrouped. The Corps were reduced to two: 30th, and 10th of which General Horrocks took command in place of General Lumsden. 13th Corps passed to the control of G.H.Q., and its main components were distributed as follows:

50th Division and 4th Indian Division—to join 30th Corps, but not at once.

44th Division—disbanded, but most of its units remained in 8th Army.

1st South African Division—to return to the Union to become an armoured division.

9th Australian Division—to return to Australia.[1]

On 26th November General Leese and his 30th Corps H.Q. took over command in the forward area from 10th Corps. 30th Corps was

---

[1] After several months of discussion between H.M.G. and the Australian Government the Australian wish to recall the Division prevailed. Under General Morshead it had given distinguished service in the Middle East, especially through the siege in Tobruk in 1941, and at El Alamein. It was to win further distinction in fighting the Japanese.

to include 7th Armoured, 51st (Highland), and New Zealand Divisions.¹ 10th Corps was to collect itself afresh near Benghazi as a guard against any attempt by Rommel to lash out.

In the Royal Air Force the organization of the fighter force underwent changes throughout the Middle East, mainly because Air H.Q. Egypt ensured that the Desert Air Force could attend wholly to the offensive by relieving it of responsibility for defensive fighter tasks in the rearward areas, principally the protection of coastal shipping. On 25th November Air H.Q. Egypt took over No. 212 Group. This formation's H.Q. was at Benina and it was the fighter defence group responsible for Cyrenaica. Air H.Q. Western Desert was empowered to extend this area of responsibility westwards. On 6th December No. 219 Group was formed for the fighter defence of Egypt, and on the 15th No. 209 Group for the Levant including Cyprus. Some of the Desert Air Force's fighters were transferred to these new Groups.

To give all the direct support possible to the 8th Army's approaching attack on the Agheila position Sir Arthur Coningham deployed Nos. 239 and 244 Fighter Wings R.A.F.; U.S. 57th Fighter Group; No. 3 Day-Bomber Wing S.A.A.F.; and U.S. 12th Medium Bombardment Group.² He also had No. 73 Squadron with its night-flying Hurricanes; the resources of No. 285 Reconnaissance Wing; and Wellingtons of No. 205 Group, and possibly of No. 201 Group, which he hoped might together be capable of 100 sorties each night. Two squadrons (fighters) of No. 243 Wing protected the L. of C., and No. 233 Wing formed the Fighter Reserve.

General Montgomery, by 29th November, had decided to trap the enemy by turning his inland (southern) flank while pinning him down by a frontal attack near the coast. 30th Corps was to fight the battle and General Leese was to make the detailed plans. The New Zealand Division was to pass quickly and widely round Rommel's flank to cut the Via Balbia well west of El Agheila while 51st (Highland) Division attacked in the neighbourhood of Mersa Brega, and 7th Armoured Division farther inland at Bir es Suera. The main operation was to begin on the night 16th/17th December, but the New Zealand Division's preliminary moves were fixed for 11th–14th December because it had to drive in all for over 200 miles

---

¹ *7th Armoured Division:* 8th Armoured Brigade; 131st Lorried Infantry Brigade.
51st (Highland) Division: 152nd, 153rd, 154th Infantry Brigades; and temporarily 1st Greek Infantry Brigade.
New Zealand Division: 4th (U.K.) Light Armoured Brigade; 5th and 6th N.Z. Infantry Brigades.
7th Armoured Division's 8th Armoured Brigade had joined from 10th Armoured Division which returned to the Delta.

² Air Vice-Marshal Coningham was created K.C.B. on 27th November 1942.
On 29th November Air Commodore H. Broadhurst became S.A.S.O. at Air H.Q. Western Desert.

through a tract of desert which was not very well known and was expected to prove difficult 'going'. Sir Arthur Coningham believed that Rommel was unlikely to stand in the Agheila position and looked on his own plans to support the Army's attack as a phase of a larger air plan covering the whole advance to Tripoli.[1]

While the Army was preparing to attack, the Royal Air Force aimed at giving it fighter protection, and also at forcing the hostile air force on to the defensive and driving it from its most advanced landing grounds at Marble Arch.[2] When the airfields at Antelat, Agedabia, El Haseiat and Belandah came into use in the first week of December the Allied fighters and fighter-bombers reached westward and, with the help of the night-flying Wellingtons, drove most of the enemy's aircraft from Marble Arch to Nofilia, Tauorga, and Churgia. The heavy bombers of No. 205 Group attacked Tripoli and Naples by night, and those of the U.S. Ninth Air Force followed suit by day. It was during the heavy raids on Tripoli on the night of 28th/29th November, and next day, that the *Sirio* of 5,222 tons was sunk and the *Giulia* of 5,921 tons badly damaged. The R.A.F. Liberators attacked smaller Tripolitanian ports, and Wellingtons and Halifaxes bombed Heraklion airfield in Crete. Air reconnaissance of the Agheila position and as far as Tripoli was continual. Air activity between 25th/26th November and 12th/13th December (roughly the period of the Army's preparations for its attack on the Agheila position) can be measured in terms of sorties as 3,201 by the R.A.F. (which excludes those flown from Malta and against shipping) and 300 by the American Ninth Air Force. The British lost eight aircraft; the Americans at least eleven; the Germans fifteen and the Italians at least four. But from El Alamein to the Agheila positions 408 German aircraft and 111 Italian (and three of French origin), in various states of repair, were found abandoned. These numbers were additional to those which had been found in earlier advances.

On the ground the principal activities were building up supplies of all sorts for the approaching attack, and reconnaissance of the hostile position and the New Zealand Division's route to outflank it. We have already mentioned that railhead opened at Tobruk Road on 1st December, and this meant that some eight and a half General Transport Companies could be added to the 20 which were already at work between the port of Tobruk and Benghazi.[3]

---

[1] The Army made detailed plans to meet several courses which Rommel might adopt, for example an earlier retreat than seemed likely to the British. As things turned out none of these plans proved to be necessary.

[2] By 25th November the Germans had about 85 serviceable aircraft on airfields at, Marble Arch, Tamet, and between these places. The Italian air force was moving to distant airfields in Tripolitania, and even to Italy.

[3] Chapter IV, page 104.

Sea transport to Benghazi and the discharge of cargo there went on outstripping the estimates: indeed during the first half of December by twice the number of tons expected. The administrative machine upon which the prospect of fighting depended was working well.

A very useful ground reconnaissance was made by Captain P. D. Chrystal and a small patrol of his regiment (1st King's Dragoon Guards) to find a route to the Marble Arch for the New Zealand Division. After difficulties they found 'going' that was fair and sometimes good all the way, except for a rift about eight miles across with steep or precipitous sides.[1] The Long Range Desert Group kept a road-watch near far-distant Misurata, looked into Marada and Jalo, and provided the New Zealand Division with navigators.[2]

General Leese's final plan was, briefly, that 51st (Highland) Division (less one brigade) should capture the enemy's positions in, and south-west of Mersa Brega. One Brigade of the Division (that selected by the Divisional Commander was the 153rd, composed of 1st and 5/7th Gordon Highlanders and 5th Black Watch), under command of 7th Armoured Division, was to make a gap near Bir es Suera through which the armoured division would then pass westwards. Orders for the New Zealand Division covered only the beginning of the battle: the Division was to make a firm base on the track north of Marada; to destroy hostile posts as far as Maaten Giofer (inclusive); to patrol towards Marble Arch and Zella; to contain or occupy Marada.[3] General Freyberg intended to reach the Marada track during the night 15th/16th December and a point some ten miles west of it the next night. During the preparatory period from 9th December he was steadily being given the supplies required for his move. 4th Light Armoured Brigade was filled with petrol for 450 miles, and the rest of the Division for 410 miles; rations were enough for nine days and water for ten, and a special R.A.S.C. convoy was to dump a supply for a further two days west of Chrystal's Rift. There were some last minute difficulties in 4th Light Armoured Brigade.[4] The Brigade had arrived in the Division's concentration area two days in advance. But the Greys had just received a fresh issue of tanks including some Shermans which were new to the regiment and had to be 'learned', while all types required

---

[1] This obstacle was, and is, often called Chrystal's Drift. But it was a rift and Chrystal's report correctly described it as one.

[2] Captain L. H. Browne, a New Zealand officer of the L.R.D.G. and a detachment of R. 1 (New Zealand) Patrol.

[3] The orders concerning Marada and Zella were needless because a patrol of the K.D.G. had reported Marada to be unoccupied and that it was going on to Zella.

[4] *4th Light Armoured Brigade* (Brigadier C. B. Harvey); 1st The King's Dragoon Guards, 1st The Royal Dragoons (armoured car regiments); The Royal Scots Greys.
3rd Regt R.H.A.; one troop 64th Medium Regt R.A.; one troop 41st Light A.A. Battery R.A.
1st Battalion, King's Royal Rifle Corps. One troop, 21st Field Squadron R.E.

adjustments to machinery, wireless sets and so on.[1] The Regiment's 21 heavy tanks seemed far too few to Freyberg who argued his view with Corps and Army H.Q. but got no larger reinforcement than 'A' Squadron, The Staffordshire Yeomanry (of 8th Armoured Brigade) with 9 Shermans.

30th Corps' patrols, mainly found by 51st Division, had begun from about 9th December to detect signs of shakiness in Rommel's front and by the 12th it seemed unlikely that he would await attack. Montgomery advanced his starting-time by 48 hours to the night 14th/15th December. By the evening of the 12th it was certain that the enemy were getting out, and on the 13th the 51st and 7th Armoured Divisions advanced, and 30th Corps ordered General Freyberg (who had crossed Chrystal's Rift and was preparing to head for the Marada track) to move faster—in a signal which took nearly nine hours to reach him! 51st Division's advance down the Via Balbia was reduced to a crawl (at times one mile an hour) by the great numbers of mines and booby-traps which had been cleverly laid in the road and its verges, in likely turning-off points and in tracks and parking-places. 7th Armoured Division was delayed by mines and on the 14th the 8th Armoured Brigade was fought sharply by the Ariete Division, acting as a rearguard, whose flash of pugnacity won unusual praise from Rommel. Nevertheless 7th Armoured Division entered El Agheila from the south on the 15th. Rommel however had long suspected that the British would try to outflank him and on the 14th (at 5 p.m.) his reconnaissance aircraft spotted a large hostile force including tanks moving west and north-west at a point south of Maaten Giofer. The force was not identified (it was the New Zealand Division) but the information confirmed Rommel's suspicions. He hankered to launch his two German armoured divisions against the out-flanking force but had not enough petrol, and instead, within minutes, confirmed orders which he had earlier given provisionally that all troops would at once begin to withdraw west of the El Mugtaa Narrows.

Freyberg meanwhile had been travelling well in spite of some friction: for example, the Greys because of their earlier troubles were behind their brigade, and on the 14th everyone had to take on petrol because the amounts which had been used in patches of poor going had exceeded the estimates. On the 14th one petrol convoy did not catch up until 5 p.m., another did not find the Division, and a third which was quickly called forward could not finish its issues until 11 p.m. Nevertheless lost time was nearly made up by travelling

---

[1] Royal Scots Greys. Fit tanks on 12th December 1942: Sherman 17, Grant 4, Stuart 15.

late into the night, and Freyberg signalled to Corps that he hoped to be at Bir el Merduma by 11 a.m. on the 15th. He explained, before daybreak on the 15th, that he meant to cut in on the 'high' ground a little west of Marble Arch. On the 15th, however, the Greys were still behind, in need of high octane petrol, and because the long fast march since 12th December had caused some of the tanks to limp. It was mid-morning before they could move and Freyberg insisted that they should be with their brigade because contact with the enemy now seemed imminent. The 6th New Zealand Brigade meanwhile had to 'mark time'. There had also occurred an irritating mix-up about bomb-lines.

Air Support Control H.Q. had asked Divisional H.Q. to fix a bomb-line for the Desert Air Force. Divisional H.Q. delegated this task to 4th Light Armoured Brigade and 6th N.Z. Brigade, and the result was requests that there should be no bombing at Marble Arch or south-east of it, thus putting the coast road hereabouts out of bounds to the bombers, although Freyberg himself had earlier given this as a target. The consequent short temper between the army and air staffs may at least have polished some of the rust off the machinery for calling for air support for mobile forces.

When the leading units of 4th Light Armoured Brigade approached the high ground south-east of Marble Arch, they found 15th Panzer Division already there. The armoured cars then reconnoitred towards Bir el Merduma only to discover that the enemy held the escarpment which guarded the coast road. The rest of the Brigade slowly closed up to its foremost troops. The Greys were now down to seventeen 'runner' tanks, which was a worry to Freyberg who liked to have plenty of them if hostile armour was knocking about.

The 6th New Zealand Brigade missed Bir el Merduma and ended its day's march a little west of Wadi el Rigel.[1] It was about 5 p.m. and darkness was falling when Freyberg ordered the brigade north to cut the coast road. He ordered the 5th New Zealand Brigade, which brought up the rear, to deploy, facing east, because it was imperative to protect the mass of 'soft' divisional vehicles which had arrived. Moreover if, as he hoped, the 5th Brigade could link up with the 6th, a good block stretching inland from the coast road would be formed.

The 6th Brigade struggled towards the coast road across difficult country, struck and dispersed a flank-guard, and in the small hours of the 16th took up positions which seemed likely to overlook the road. The tantalising sound of traffic moving steadily westward was heard through the dark. In fact by evening of the 15th Rommel had

---

[1] Bir el Merduma had no special tactical importance. It was marked on the map, and might be recognizable on the ground, and was a likely spot at which to turn north to cut the coast road.

decided to break contact during the night 15th/16th and withdraw to Nofilia. Just enough petrol for this move had reached him.

Daylight revealed that the 6th Brigade was two miles from the road and some six miles separated it from the 5th Brigade. Through these small gaps scraped the last enemy units. 'Enemy in small columns including tanks passed through at high speed and wide dispersion,' ran Freyberg's candid report to 30th Corps. 'Most difficult to intercept. Majority escaped around our flanks . . .' This went out shortly after midday on the 16th. In the afternoon 8th Armoured Brigade reached Bir el Merduma and made contact with the New Zealand Division.

The New Zealand official historian admirably sums up the outflanking move in these words:

> '. . . The high hopes of cutting off even some of the retreating enemy had come to nothing, partly because greater speed was possible along the road than across the desert, partly because the enemy was well seasoned and adopted the orthodox safeguards of flank and rear guards, and partly because of the difficulties of deploying by night in unknown country at the end of a long and tiring move . . .'[1]

The British estimated the total bag, between 13th and 17th December, as 450 prisoners, 25 guns, and 18 tanks.

Other events must be glanced at. By midnight 16th/17th the much-tried Sappers of 30th Corps had cleared the Via Balbia as far as Agheila, though in stretches only one-way. The day-bombers had been grounded on water-logged airfields on the 13th, and on the 14th were not called on by the Army. The fighter-bombers had been fairly busy though without spectacular results. On the 15th the day-bombers joined in, and again on the 16th, when about a quarter of their number was damaged by heavy 'flak' while bombing scattered and hardly worth-while targets. By this date too the enemy was getting beyond the reach of fighters except those fitted with long-range fuel tanks. By the morning of the 17th, 8th Army believed the enemy's rearguards to be at Nofilia and the New Zealand Division, led by 4th Light Armoured Brigade, was heading towards them. 8th Army's main object at this moment was to bring new forward landing grounds into use, and General Montgomery intended that 30th Corps as a whole should advance to contact west of Nofilia on 7th January.

To keep within range of the most advanced troops of the New Zealand Division, preparations had been made to maintain by air a fighter wing as far forward as possible. On 18th December, within

---

[1] W. G. Stevens: *Bardia to Enfidaville* (Wellington 1962) page 57.

two hours of the Royal Engineers clearing the landing ground of mines, transport aircraft of No. 216 Group R.A.F. and the U.S. 316th Troop Carrier Wing, both operating from Belandah, began to land at Marble Arch. In 78 sorties the 61 transport aircraft carried a total payload of 160 tons which included maintenance crews and equipment. Fighters of No. 239 Wing escorted the transport aircraft and themselves took off later to carry out fighter-bomber attacks amounting to 60 sorties on targets which earlier had been well out of range.

During the lull which followed the enemy's retreat to the Buerat position, 7th Armoured Division took over the front from the New Zealand Division and on Christmas Eve gained touch with the hostile rear-guards south of Sirte. The engineers were heavily burdened by such tasks as clearing the airfields and main roads of mines, booby traps and obstacles, and finding and providing water.[1] The general advance of the Army was to halt until enough supplies had been accumulated to enable 30th Corps to reach Tripoli in a ten-day operation, to begin probably on 15th January. 10th Corps was to reassemble near Agheila by 20th January.[2] The building and clearing of forward airfields were to be tackled most urgently.

From the enemy's point of view at the turn of the year *Fliegerführer Afrika* was finding it very difficult to maintain his effort against the 8th Army. For example, on one occasion no aircraft were available for reconnaissance at all and the *Panzerarmee* remained in ignorance of British movements. And even when considerable air reinforcements arrived in the last week of December, lack of fuel continued seriously to hamper air operations.

At the same season some senior commanders in the Royal Air Force changed. On 22nd December, 1942 Air Commodore Ritchie left No. 205 Group for an appointment in England and was succeeded by Air Commodore O. R. Gayford. This group passed under the operational control of the Desert Air Force on 7th January, 1943. On 11th January Air Chief Marshal Sir Sholto Douglas became A.O.C.-in-C. Royal Air Force, Middle East in succession to Tedder.

Tedder was appointed A.O.C.-in-C. Mediterranean Air Command in February.[3]

Until about 8th January scarce advanced landing grounds, bad weather, and the enemy's retreat towards Buerat reduced the British

---

[1] Between 14th December, 1942 and 8th January, 1943 the engineers of 30th Corps suffered 170 casualties while clearing mines.
[2] The order of battle, in outline, was forecast as:
30th Corps: 7th Armoured, 50th, 51st and New Zealand Divisions.
10th Corps: 1st Armoured, 4th Indian Divisions.
Army Reserve: 22nd Armoured Brigade.
[3] See page 265

fighter effort. Protecting ships, intercepting occasional enemy air attacks and attacking his landing grounds were the main tasks. British and American bombers flew against distant targets, for example, Crete, Syracuse, Marsala, Naples, Sousse, Tripoli, Tunis, Bizerta and Sfax.[1] From 13th December until 11th/12th January, including air operations in support of the 8th Army at El Agheila, the British Middle East air force flew 4,950 sorties and the American Ninth Air Force 698.[2] The British lost 22 aircraft, the Americans about 6, the Germans 22, and the Italians an estimated 10.

From Nofilia to Buerat by the coast road was 140 miles, from Buerat to Misurata 100 miles, and from Misurata to Tripoli 130 miles: a total distance from Nofilia to Tripoli of some 370 miles. Tracks, which at Tarhuna became a road, led from Gheddahia through Beni Ulid to Tripoli—nearly 200 miles. The country was desert, and the 'going' was a patchwork, in places very fair and in others bad. Even the coast road was often built on a low embankment. Wadis seamed the desert and the Wadi Bei el Chebir and the Wadi Tamet, between Sirte and Buerat, were not easy to cross except near the coast.[3] Water was scarce. Near Buerat salt marshes extended almost to Misurata on the seaward side of the road. At Misurata the coast road turned westwards to Homs and Tripoli and ran through a narrow cultivated and wooded belt, puckered by wadis, between sea and hills. The inland route to Tripoli was from Gheddahia and crossed obstacles at the Wadis Zemzem and Soffegin. At Beni Ulid this route entered a difficult tract of hills 600 feet or more high before descending sharply to Castel Benito in the plain of Tripoli. There was a lateral road through these hills from Homs to Cussabat and Tarhuna from where it ran to Castel Benito and Tripoli. There were airfields at Sirte, Homs, Castel Benito and Tripoli, and landing grounds at Sultan, Tamet, Bir Dufan, and in the area Misurata—Zliten. In sum the country between Nofilia and Tripoli did not favour the movement of large forces of all arms.

[1] 13th December, 1942 to 11th January, 1943:

	Targets in Africa Sorties	Targets outside Africa Sorties
Royal Air Force Liberators	14	32
Bostons and Baltimores	99	36
Wellingtons	109	48
U.S.A.A.F.:		
Liberators	70	69
Mitchells	42	12

[2] These figures represent about 170 British sorties and 21 American, daily. The British figures exclude sorties from Malta and against the enemy's shipping.

[3] A wadi may be quite easy for a few vehicles to cross but becomes a nasty obstacle to large numbers for many reasons. For example, there may be one or two good crossings yet if a large number of vehicles must use them, at once true 'bottle-necks' are formed which cause jams, delay, exposure to air attack and so on.

By mid-December the *Panzerarmee* was preparing for defence at Buerat, which after the withdrawal from El Agheila, became the next position which the Axis High Commands decreed was to be held 'to the last'. Neither Bastico nor Rommel felt that this would be possible, and although the Italian commander was not prepared to agree with all of Rommel's arguments, he concurred in their submission to *OKW* and *Comando Supremo*. Accordingly on 17th December Rommel reported that his army's fitness to fight was extraordinarily low, and that want of fuel, which was likely to continue, made mobile defence impossible. He expected to be attacked about 20th December, and thought that his army would probably be destroyed, Tripolitania lost, and the road to Tunisia thrown open to the enemy.[1] The only way to avoid these disasters was to fall back, fighting, to positions near Gabes which he believed were more defensible than the French-built Mareth Line—'a line of antiquated French blockhouses which in no way measured up to the standards required by modern warfare . . .' as he later wrote. As a stop-gap, withdrawal from Buerat to the hilly country between Homs and Garian should be considered.

All the Axis theatres of war were discussed at conferences which were held at Hitler's H.Q. in East Prussia between 18th and 20th December, 1942. Mussolini did not feel well enough to travel and sent Ciano to argue that an armistice should be made with Russia, or at least a defensive policy and positions should be adopted in order to free Axis divisions for other fronts. Hitler rejected these proposals. He maintained that Allied operations in 1943 would depend upon shipping. Therefore the Axis must aim, in the Mediterranean, at consolidating its gains in Tunisia which was an area essential to future developments, at cutting the Allied lines of communication, and at causing the Allies to lose as much shipping as possible. Hitler's military entourage had rather more sensible views because they admitted that the state of Rommel's affairs in Libya was critical. But any proposal to abandon Tripolitania was ruled out because that would compromise the Tunisian front which Hitler had decreed to be essential. Rommel must therefore be reinforced to enable him to hold out and gain the time which was needed to consolidate the bridgehead in Tunisia.[2] The Italians agreed but emphasized that it was important to hold Libya for as long as possible because its loss would be a grievous blow to their country.

As a result of this conference Mussolini signalled Bastico on the 19th 'Resistance to the uttermost, I repeat resistance to the uttermost, with all troops of the *Panzerarmee* in the Buerat line'. After

---

[1] It is possible that Rommel was designedly putting the worst case in his appreciation.
[2] On 13th December the 5*th Panzerarmee* in Tunisia had gone over to a defensive policy See Chapter VII.

much argument from Rommel this directive was superseded, on 31st December, by an order from *Comando Supremo* which told Bastico that if the army were threatened by a powerful offensive it might retreat when he thought fit. Cavallero came himself to Africa on 6th January to announce that as it had proved impossible to keep both the Tunisian and Libyan theatres supplied, the Duce had decided that Tripolitania must be evacuated, for Tunisia was the more important to the Axis war effort. In accordance with orders already given to Bastico on 2nd January the withdrawal must however take at least six weeks, and 8th Army must be kept at bay by counter-attacks. Rommel, who had already ordered 20th and 21st Corps to begin moving their non-motorized troops back to Tarhuna, maintained that offensive operations were ruled out by the fuel shortage and that he could not be tied to fixed defence positions. He therefore kept his German formations forward at Buerat but at the same time issued preliminary orders for their retreat. His own High Command, worried about the inadequacy of the Axis defences in southern Tunisia, supported *Comando Supremo* in requesting that these should be reinforced by the *Panzerarmee*. Rommel chose 21st Panzer Division, which moved off to Sfax on 14th January—minus its tanks and most of its artillery, which Cavallero decreed were to be left behind to reinforce 15th Panzer Division. By mid-January, therefore, the sixty-mile Buerat/Bu Ngem front was held by a predominantly German force and the bulk of the Italian troops were streaming back to Tarhuna.[1] Constantly reminded from Rome that two months must elapse before his Army reached Mareth, Rommel invariably replied that he would do his best but he doubted that 8th Army could be held off for so long. As a result of these discussions he settled the lay-out of the *Panzerarmee* between Buerat and Bu Ngem, but also planned his retreat.

To occupy advanced landing grounds was a principal part of preparing the British attacks. The staffs had foreseen that landing

---

[1] In the Buerat position by 10th January, 1943:
At Buerat: H.Q. 20th Corps; Nizza Reconnaissance Battalion.
Between Buerat and Gheddahia: One-third each of La Spezia, Young Fascist, and Pistoia Divisions; Ramcke Parachute Brigade; 19th Flak Division.
Near Gheddahia: H.Q. D.A.K.; 21st Panzer Division; 90th Light Division.
South of Gheddahia: 164th Light Division; Panzer Grenadier Regiment Africa; Centauro Battle Group.
North West of Fortino: 15th Panzer Division; 3rd Reconnaissance Unit.
West and North-West of Bu Ngem: 33rd and 580th Reconnaissance Units.
By the night 9th/10th January, 1943 the following were in position between Homs and Tarhuna:
H.Q. 21st Corps with Trieste Division, two-thirds of Pistoia Division and some miscellaneous units.
Two-thirds of each of the Spezia and Young Fascist Divisions were on their way to Tarhuna. There were small reserves at Misurata and Tripoli, but the troops on the 'Buerat front' held petrol for 150 miles, two-thirds of an 'issue' of ammunition, and five days' rations.

grounds were likely to be usable by aircraft much sooner than vehicles could carry equipment to them over mine-strewn approaches. Marble Arch had been cleared on 18th December, and Merduma, Gzina and Hamraiet thereafter.[1] Coningham's aim was to continue to move his squadrons forward as quickly as the enemy was driven back. He believed that it would be quicker to make new landing grounds than to restore captured ones which the enemy would be sure to have ploughed and mined. Reconnaissance had disclosed likely sites near Sedada, Bir Dufan and Tarhuna and special R.A.F. airfield detachments were to accompany the attacking formations, whose engineers had prepared to give them their utmost help. No. 239 Wing and British and American transport aircraft were earmarked to fly on to new landing grounds as they had done at Marble Arch.

Altogether, in support of the 8th Army, there were to be three fighter wings and a fourth in reserve; two day-bomber wings; and a reconnaissance wing.[2] Owing partly to the continued air lift, already described, to Marble Arch, which supplemented vehicle convoys, the air force administrative situation was satisfactory.

General Montgomery's plan to break the Buerat position (issued on 7th January) was that 30th Corps should attack and then advance on two widely separated lines: 50th and 51st Divisions along the main road and near the coast; 7th Armoured and the New Zealand Divisions in the direction Beni Ulid—Tarhuna, that is well inland. The advance on the coastal road was to be deliberate, aiming to contain the enemy and to clear the road for supply columns. 22nd Armoured Brigade, in Army Reserve, was to link the coastal and inland forces. 30th Corps had 23rd Armoured Brigade (Valentines) but these superannuated tanks were thought fit for one major action and no more. On the 3rd and 4th January a storm raged at Benghazi with consequences that at first seemed ruinous to the administrative preparations. General Montgomery however did not alter his plan except to withdraw 50th Division, and to order 30th Corps not to labour its attack in the coast sector if the enemy fought hard. He decided not to bring forward 10th Corps.[3]

---

[1] 21st Field Squadron R.E. removed 500 anti-tank and 360 anti-personnel mines from Marble Arch. 2nd Field Squadron R.E. and 6th N.Z. Field Company removed 269 anti-tank and 261 anti-personnel mines from Merduma. New Zealand working-parties made Gzina and Hamraiet, the second of these in face of persistent air attacks.

[2] *Fighters*
No. 239, 244 Wings R.A.F., 57th Fighter Group U.S.A.A.F. on three landing grounds at Hamraiet.
Day-Bombers
No. 3 S.A.A.F. Wing at Gzina.
12th Medium Bombardment Group U.S.A.A.F. at Alam el Chel.
Reconnaissance
No. 285 Wing R.A.F. at Tamet—where also was advanced Air H.Q. Western Desert.

[3] All the transport of 10th Corps was used to carry supplies to offset the interruptions in the port of Benghazi caused by the storm.

The 30th Corps intended 'to capture Tripoli destroying any enemy forces encountered'. 51st Division was to make a deliberate infantry attack and then clear the main coastal road for supplies. 7th Armoured and the New Zealand Divisions, moving abreast, were to head fast for Tripoli via Sedada, Beni Ulid, and Tarhuna.[1]

The success of the plan depended on the success of the administrative backing.[2] We have already said that there was no port that deserved the name between Benghazi and Tripoli, and that supply across the beaches was not generally practicable. The distance by land from Benghazi to Tripoli was 675 miles, and though the 8th Army's General Transport companies now stood at about 52 this was not enough transport to give an unbroken flow of supplies across this great distance. Sea transport from Egypt and Tobruk under the auspices of the Royal Navy, and protected by the Navy and Royal Air Force, was discharging a splendid quantity of cargo at the new Advanced Base at Benghazi. Road transport west of Tobruk and Benghazi had been increased.[3] Although Tobruk was now fading out as an importing sea-port for other than local purposes, it was still important because it re-exported by sea and road the supplies which had been accumulated there. Towards the end of December the plan was to put about 2,380 tons a day by sea into Benghazi, and about 2,200 tons a day by rail into Tobruk mostly for re-export to Benghazi. West of Benghazi, roadheads were to be set up at El Agheila, Nofilia, and Misurata to fill the now well-tried F.M.Cs which would be placed where needed close behind the advancing ground and air forces. To carry the traffic two desert tracks were built from Agheila to Nofilia, and from there four to the Wadi Bei el Chebir.

---

[1] 7th Armoured Division comprised 8th Armoured Brigade and 4th Light Armoured Brigade. 8th Armoured Brigade had 57 Shermans, 27 Grants, 58 Crusaders, and 4 Stuarts. 4th Light Armoured Brigade's sole tank regiment, the Royal Scots Greys, was under command of the N.Z. Division, and the Brigade's main units were the Royal Dragoons and 1st K.D.G. (armoured car regiments); 2nd K.R.R.C.

[2] '... On it the General will frame his plan in more detail and give his ideas as to the date and weight of the attack. Having said what he is going to do, a Commander must not cheat. He must not beat the pistol, nor wangle up additional troops, nor sneak his troops further forward than he said he would. A good administrative staff does not over-insure and cannot be cheated without unfortunate consequences. Some Generals have no morals. Fortunately, General Montgomery does not cheat—whether that is due to his innate honesty or to the fact that I watch him like a cat does does not matter—and moreover he doesn't let other people cheat ...'
(Brigadier Sir Brian Robertson on 14th February 1943).

[3] The General Transport Companies were distributed roughly as follows:

30th Corps	$6\frac{1}{2}$
10th Corps	$1\frac{3}{4}$
Miscellaneous duties	$4\frac{1}{2}$
Under Army H.Q.	40.

The general tasks of Army H.Q.'s companies were:
Carrying supplies from Tobruk to Benghazi: $12\frac{1}{2}$—13 companies.
Stocking roadheads west of Benghazi: 27 companies.

On 3rd January the weather caused a crisis, which seemed likely to ruin every plan. The gale at Benghazi on the 3rd January which had seemed to threaten administrative preparations had raised heavy seas which breached the already damaged mole. Five merchant ships and three landing-craft sank, three merchant vessels were severely damaged, and others, and harbour craft, less badly. One ship was lost outside the harbour, and two—running for shelter at Tobruk—were sunk by a submarine. Lighter-berths at Benghazi were destroyed and several administrative depots were flooded. On 4th and 5th January nothing was landed; on the 6th 859 tons were landed and on the 8th about 2,000 tons. In spite of this quick recovery, the damage had been so great that Benghazi could now be looked on as only a fair-weather harbour, and in fact more gales between 13th and 16th January interrupted work, and over the whole month the rate of discharge of cargo fell to about 1,800 tons a day.[1] This occurrence at a time when every day and every ton was being counted was almost a disaster. Yet the administrative staff had foreseen this risk and had a plan. General Montgomery therefore was not taken aback but made the instant decisions described on page 231, the most important administratively being to 'ground' 10th Corps and set all its vehicles to carry supplies, mainly P.O.L., from Tobruk to Benghazi and beyond.[2] 10th Corps at once skilfully organised a 'Carter Paterson' operation which produced the equivalent of fifteen G.T. companies to add to the road-lift from Tobruk. These 10th Corps' convoys went on until 14th February. By a great all-round effort by everyone the crippling effects of the damage at Benghazi were offset. The Inshore Squadron from the beginning of November 1942 until 23rd January 1943 landed no less than 157,000 tons in the various ports, and over beaches where possible.

When everything was taken into account the administrative side of the plan (always as important as the tactical) fixed 15th January as the earliest date on which the advance to Tripoli could begin. The administrative arrangements were splendid but the problem was relentless. Once the Army and air forces moved they *had* to reach Tripoli without pause in a set time or withdraw for want of supplies. The sea was now the sole practical means of continuously supplying the vast quantities of stores of all sorts which were needed, and Tripoli was the next port where it could be used.

On 12th January the Desert Air Force began its preparatory air operations. By day escorted Bostons, Baltimores and American

---

[1] Delay in discharging cargo could be caused by ships in the harbour putting to sea as a result of gale warnings.

[2] e.g. between 8th and 25th January, 10,786 tons P.O.L. (or about 2,700,000 gallons) were carried by road from Tobruk to Benghazi.

Mitchells attacked enemy forward landing grounds and targets and M.T. in the battle area. The enemy's fighters strongly opposed them and the British losses were particularly heavy. By night the Bostons attacked the landing grounds at Tauorga and Bir Dufan and No. 205 Group's Wellingtons, helped by flare-dropping Albacores, bombed roads and traffic in the neighbourhood of Churgia, Tauorga and Gheddahia. A few British and American Liberators attacked Tripoli and Sousse. In the 72 hours the British flew 650 and the Americans 120 sorties. The British lost 18 aircraft, the Americans 2, the Germans 9 and the Italians 2.

The 30th Corps' advance on 15th January was not spectacular. Continuously protected by fighters and helped by the fighter-bombers' various missions, the N.Z. Division crossed the Wadi Um er Raml near Fortino, and 8th Armoured Brigade did the same five miles northwards. 4th Light Armoured Brigade's Royal Dragoons slipped round south of the New Zealanders and neared Faschia. By Army and 30th Corps Orders 51st Division was not to attack until the night 15th/16th. Rommel however expected an all-out attack on the night of 15th/16th or next day. He judged that his troops had too little fuel and ammunition to accept battle. He therefore withdrew them during the night 15th/16th to a temporary line which ran from Sedada to where the Gheddahia road joined the Via Balbia. He intended to delay the British with rearguards on a broad front. The Highlanders' attack consequently met little more than a deep minefield.[1] The careful British preparations bore fruit when on the 17th by 11.30 a.m. the Advanced Party of No 239 Wing flew to a new landing ground south-east of Sedada in four Hudsons and eight Dakotas. Ninety minutes later more Hudsons and Kittyhawks followed, and four A.A. batteries by road—a neat combined operation accomplished almost under the noses of ten German fighter-bombers. From the night 15th/16th January the day-bombers switched to night attacks in an attempt to thwart the enemy's policy of moving mainly at night. For the rest the Royal Air Force continued to be aggressive and apparently everywhere at once.

At first on the ground things were sluggish. The British advanced slowly, treating the enemy's rearguards with respect, and were greatly impeded by mines and demolitions on the coast road and by bad 'going' inland. On the night 17th/18th Montgomery sent for Wimberley (commanding 51st Highland Division) and told him that he must now press on at his best speed. This Wimberley was eager to do, but his efforts were grievously hampered by the fact that only two companies of troop-carrying transport had been given him

---

[1] The minefield seemed deeper than it in fact was owing to one of those curious incidents which occur in battle, though seldom in history books: some Scorpions struck a dog-leg and for a time swept down it instead of to their front.

in the original plan and that his petrol had been and continued to be doled out.[1] Montgomery also decided to move by day *and* night as Wimberley, before receiving Montgomery's summons, had already ordered his leading brigade, the 152nd, to do that night. Rommel, who had pulled his troops out of their positions near Sedada and put them into the Homs—Tarhuna line by noon on the 18th, was alarmed by the threat of encirclement by the British inland force, and was constantly preoccupied with the uncertain state of his supplies. On the 19th the 51st Division began to enter Homs; 7th Armoured Division was not yet at Tarhuna some twenty miles from Garian.[2]

On the same evening *Panzerarmee's* Intelligence (including a captured document) led Rommel to suspect a British threat from Garian towards Zauia (west of Tripoli), a main attack at Tarhuna, and a lesser one along the Via Balbia. He therefore decided that it was time to quit his line from Tarhuna to Homs and to begin to destroy the port of Tripoli. 90th Light Division was to make a 'fighting retreat' on the Via Balbia, and *D.A.K.* was to act as rearguard just west of Tarhuna and to prevent the enemy from reaching the road Castel Benito—Tripoli.[3] Everyone else was to get away to Tripoli and west of it. Rommel's orders angered the Italian High Command which had ordained that he should hold fast, and he was sharply taken to task.

Meanwhile, because P.R.U. Spitfires on the 17th had reported the bulk of the enemy air forces withdrawn to Castel Benito (nearly 200 aircraft were seen on the ground), all available Bostons, Baltimores and Wellingtons, numbering 50, bombed the airfield that night, followed on the 18th by 13 Lightning-escorted Fortresses from the 'Torch' area and on the night of the 18th/19th by 43 more Bostons, Baltimores and Mitchells. On the 18th the Desert Air Force had brought one of three new landing grounds at Darragh into use, and the other two on the 19th. On the 19th air reconnaissance of Tripoli (constant since the 12th) suggested that the enemy was getting ready to leave. In spite of low cloud, fighters and fighter-bombers by day and bombers by night were active over the whole area.

On the 20th Montgomery made decisions exactly contrary to Rommel's suspicions: to make his main thrust along the coast road

---

[1] For example on the 18th no petrol arrived at all, on the 19th only a part of the amount asked for, and on the 22nd —the day before reaching Tripoli—a portion was obtained only by personal discussions between administrative staffs.

[2] On the 17th the N.Z. Division had given way to 7th Armoured Division because the 'going' did not permit two divisions to follow the same axis side by side. On the 19th Major-General A. F. Harding, Commander of 7th Armoured Division, was wounded. He was succeeded on the 20th by Brigadier G. P. B. Roberts from 22nd Armoured Brigade.

[3] *D.A.K.* included 164th Light Division, the Ramcke Parachute Brigade, and the Army artillery.

with 51st Division and 22nd Armoured Brigade. 7th Armoured Division was directed on Tarhuna, Castel Benito, and Tripoli. The 51st Division, weary, strung-out, very short of petrol and of troop-carrying transport, and cleverly opposed by 90th Light Division, pressed on.[1] On the night 20th/21st and the morning of the 21st two battalions of the Black Watch, two of the Seaforth Highlanders, and one of the Argyll and Sutherland Highlanders sharply fought 90th Light Division near Corradini, and took prisoners and guns. Mines and demolitions were a bugbear—109 craters between Buerat and Homs, and near Corradini three enormous craters which occupied every available resource to fill.[2] On the 21st, very early, 4th Light Armoured Brigade emerged from a tangle of hills on to the plain fifteen miles south-east of Azizia, but the rest of 7th Armoured Division on another route was held up by rearguards. On the 22nd the 51st Division's leading troops entered Castel Verde and 22nd Armoured Brigade, by General Montgomery's order, was coming along pell-mell to take the lead. By that evening the New Zealand Division was through the hills via Ras Mnebba with orders to press on to Tripoli from the south. 7th Armoured Division was to guard the west flank from a possible riposte from the direction of Azizia. The whole situation was exciting because the goal, Tripoli, was in sight: 'the Devil take the hindmost' roughly describes the advance. Rommel had decided to abandon Tripoli on the night 22nd/23rd. Rearguards, however, continued to cover the evacuation until it was complete. Early on 23rd January British troops entered Tripoli unopposed. The distinction of entering first was won deservedly, though by a narrow margin, by 'B' Squadron 11th Hussars.[3] A close second was 'C' Squadron 50th R.T.R. (23rd Armoured Brigade), carrying 'A' and 'C' Companies 1st Gordon Highlanders (51st Highland Division).[4] At noon General Montgomery formally received the surrender of the city from the Italian Vice-Governor of Tripolitania.

The city was in a fairly good state and the people were on the whole orderly. There was a stock of food for two months, but there was very little fuel, and no cash in the banks. The wells were intact although damaged equipment lessened their output. The main electric power

---

[1] 51st Division had been allotted only two companies of troop-carrying transport by higher formations. In consequence the infantry had to move by a combination of marching and 'ferrying' in M.T.

[2] The sizes of these craters were, in feet:
    i. $180 \times 40 \times 14$
    ii. $165 \times 40 \times 18$
    iii. $240 \times 45 \times 16$

[3] On the night 11th/12th June 1940 the first shots of the Desert War were exchanged with Italian posts at Sidi Omar by patrols of 'A' and 'B' Squadrons, 11th Hussars.

[4] 'C' Squadron joined 51st Highland Division on 21st January. The rest of 50th R.T.R. was unloading landing-craft at Buerat. H.Q. 23rd Armoured Brigade and 40th Royal Tanks had been under command of 51st Division throughout the advance from Buerat.

station was unharmed but some of its machinery was in bad condition. The telephone exchange was undamaged but the wireless station had been dismantled. The sewage works was not damaged. Large quantities of useful engineer's stores were found. This short stocktaking of Tripoli leaves out the port and harbour—the great administrative prizes—but these will be mentioned again.

The Prime Minister's directive, dated 10th August 1942, had been obeyed in so far that Rommel's army had been driven out of Egypt, Cyrenaica, Libya, and Tripolitania.

The Royal Air Force could take credit for its sustained support to the 8th Army in achieving this. The most remarkable of its feats were undoubtedly the very quick action from new airfields. These had a crowning touch on 21st January when Kittyhawks of Nos. 250 and 260 Squadrons, in the face of heavy 'flak', completely prevented the enemy from ploughing the important airfield at Castel Benito by destroying all the 'ploughs' at work. A word is due to 12th A.A. Brigade which showed great perseverance and skill in getting forward and into action during the advance.

The British and American strategic bombers had given heavy support to the Desert Air Force, devoting most of their 200 sorties to this end. Bomber attacks of all kinds on targets in Tripolitania were:

12th–23rd January (sorties flown)	Tactical support targets	Castel Benito airfield	Tripoli	Other targets in Tripolitania
R.A.F.				
Liberators	2	3	6	3
Wellingtons	45	28	2	9
Bostons and Baltimores	275	61	—	—
U.S.A.A.F.				
Liberators	—	13	66	—
Mitchells	35	9	—	—

In December 1942 the heavy bombers in the Middle East had begun to attack targets in Tunisia (see Chapter VII, pages 188–89). On the eve of the fall of Tripoli, the Desert Air Force also turned its attentions to Tunisia, Medenine being attacked by the bombers that night.

Between the 12th and 23rd January the Royal Air Force in the Middle East flew 3,359 sorties and the U.S. Ninth Air Force 660.[1] The British lost 31 aircraft, the Americans 2, the Germans 40, and

---

[1] These figures exclude sorties flown from Malta and against ships, but a considerable proportion of the fighter sorties included in the totals were expended on protecting coastwise shipping.

the Italians at least 7. During the advance from the Agheila position to Tripoli, 114 German and 327 Italian aircraft in various stages of repair were found abandoned, bringing the total since the advance from El Alamein to nearly 1,000 Axis aircraft captured in this way. Perhaps the total would not have been so big had the spare parts not been at the bottom of the sea: just one result of British naval and air power.

Since the battle of El Alamein the purely fighting side of the 8th Army had travelled far rather than fought much. The laurels belong to the administrative side which, with the invaluable contributions of the Navy and Air Forces, had accomplished a magnificent task. If one singles out the names of Sir Wilfrid Lindsell, Lieut.-General in charge of Administration at G.H.Q. Middle East, and Brigadier Sir Brian Robertson, the administrative head of the 8th Army, one must not praise them alone but also the officers and men who toiled upon the whole L. of C. A senior officer of G.H.Q's administrative staff has well written:

> '... In the rear services let tribute first be paid to troops in their tens of thousands—to the driver trundling his truck through hundreds of miles of nothingness day after day, cursing his "V" cigarette, consoled by his brief "brew-up" of tea; to the private cockily controlling a gang of skilled Egyptians in a workshop; to the sergeant confidently carrying out a charge which in England would have been given to an officer assisted by senior non-commissioned officers.
> Let tribute also go to team-work at all levels, a main ingredient of success...'[1]

These words, written about the men of the Army, can as well be translated into praise of those of the Royal Navy and Royal Air Force who were essential members of the whole administrative team.

Although the British plan had succeeded, the *Panzerarmee* had not been routed. Rommel, in spite of being ill, depressed, and at loggerheads with his superiors, had kept his army in being by timely retreats. He was far from hopeful of defending the Mareth line, which was to be his next task, but the end of his retreat temporarily eased his administrative problems because his L. of C. had become much shorter. Yet his day in Africa was nearing its end.

---

[1] Major-General G. Surtees, *The Royal United Service Institution Journal*. August 1962. p. 236.

CHAPTER X

THE WAR AT SEA
(January and February 1943)

See Map 23

THE Anglo-American strategy which had given rise to 'Torch' aimed at clearing the Axis forces out of Africa and opening the Mediterranean to through traffic. The previous chapter described how in carrying out this strategy the 8th Army advanced 1,350 miles from El Alamein in three months and entered Tripoli on 23rd January 1943. Meanwhile, Malta, relieved in the nick of time, was recovering rapidly and was again among the foremost in attacking Axis communications to Africa. But in Tunisia the Allies' plans had been checked. The Germans had reacted vigorously to the 'Torch' landings and Hitler himself was taking an active, if spasmodic, interest in the situation in the Mediterranean. Heavy rains and inferior airfields had tipped the scales against the British 1st Army—thinly deployed 300 miles east of its main base—when within sight of its goal, and the Royal Navy and Allied Air Forces had been unable during the first two months of the campaign to delay the enemy's build-up sufficiently to alter the balance.

The Allies had realized that an attempt to reach Tunis and Bizerta overland before the Axis forces could establish themselves was a gamble with the odds in the enemy's favour. The immediate consequences of the Allies' landings in French North Africa favoured the Axis in a number of ways. The Germans had been intriguing off and on with the French for two and a half years for a foothold in Tunisia which would give them a much shorter sea passage to Africa than the routes to Tobruk, Benghazi and Tripoli. Now they had got one which gave them the shortest possible crossing. Bizerta and Tunis are only 120 sea miles from the ports and airfields of western Sicily, 180 from Palermo, and scarcely more than 300 from Naples. The passage across the Narrows was ringed by Axis airfields and a large fleet of transport aircraft was available. To challenge this strong position the Allies had to cross thousands of miles of ocean. Even in the Mediterranean, the 865 miles' coastal passage from Alexandria to Tripoli and that of 700 miles between Gibraltar and the 1st Army's front looked much more vulnerable than a well-timed dart across the Sicilian Narrows. The Desert campaigns had shown that success on land depended as much on the lines of supply as upon operations in the field. At the beginning of 1943 the Allies had still to find out whether their maritime strength could overcome the enemy's new geographical advantages.

During January 1943 approximately 15,000 Germans and 70,000 tons of equipment and supplies arrived in Tunisia by sea and 14,250 Germans and 4,000 tons by air. By one means or the other, some 12,000 Italians also arrived. The bulk of the cargo carried by sea was loaded in merchant ships in Naples and Palermo, or on to ferries at Palermo and Trapani.[1] Palermo and Trapani were also the ports from which most of the men who went by sea were transported to Bizerta or Tunis, usually in destroyers under cover of darkness.

Two merchant vessels in every three were loaded at Naples and from there moved to one of the neighbouring assembly anchorages for convoys where they were joined by ships from other mainland ports such as Leghorn. Less than half the convoys made the passage to Tunisia direct—the majority put in at Palermo on the way. A call at Palermo increased the total distance from Naples to 360 miles but gave more freedom in timing, and providing surface and air escorts.

In practice, it was difficult to adhere to any system in timing passages, for so many factors were conflicting or unpredictable. Moreover, irregularity had its merits. After Force Q's destruction of a convoy on the night of 1st/2nd December the Italians had tried to restrict passage of the Narrows to daylight until they had completed a new mine barrier as an obstacle to Force Q's approach. In fact, convoys continued to cross both by day and night, which indeed was inevitable because the speeds made good were usually so low that a voyage from Palermo, or even from Trapani, to Bizerta or Tunis was seldom completed in less than twenty-four hours, and in heavy weather often more. The risk of attack by surface warships was, it is true, greater by night, but the risk from air attack was much the same in daylight or dark; Wellington, Beaufort and Albacore

---

[1] The ferries frequently referred to in the text were of various types of which the most common were:

Kriegstransporter (K.T. with number)—1,200 tons, 14½ knots. It was a small ship, constructed in sections, rather than a ferry and could be used either as a transport for men and stores or for A/S duties. Armament—one 8·8-cm, one 3·7-cm A.A. twin, one 2-cm A.A. quadruple, three 2-cm A.A. single, depth charge rails and throwers.

Naval ferry barge (M.F.P. Marinefährprahm)—150–250 tons, 10 knots. For transport and landing of troops and equipment, escort duties and minelaying. Armament—one 8·8-cm, one 3·7-cm A.A. twin, one 2-cm A.A. quadruple, one 2-cm A.A. twin, two rocket dischargers.

Siebel Ferry—137–170 tons, 7½ knots. For transport and landing of troops and equipment; minelaying. Armament—one 4-cm A.A., one 2-cm A.A. twin, two rocket dischargers.

torpedo-bombers from Malta usually attacked by night and Marauders and Mitchells of the U.S. XII Bomber Command by day.

Many other factors affected the loading, routeing and timing of Axis convoys. A series of heavy air raids sometimes caused Palermo to become the principal loading port instead of Naples. Such a change did not last long. Palermo's nearness to Tunisia was offset by its nearness to Allied airfields, and still more because its rail and road communications were vulnerable to air attack and to gunfire and sabotage by parties landed from submarines. Again, because of losses in the Tyrrhenian Sea, several Axis convoys at the end of January were routed near the coast from Naples to Messina and thence to Palermo, a detour which added 130 miles to the voyage but little or nothing to security. Winter weather and shortage of escorts introduced further complications.

Much of the information about Axis shipping movements came from photographs of Italian and African ports brought back to Malta by P.R.U. Spitfires, and from the results of searches for ships already at sea carried out day and night by Malta's Wellingtons and Baltimores, and from reports of African-based Hudsons and Swordfish engaged on anti-submarine and other patrols.[1] If enemy ships suspected that they had been sighted they were likely to alter or even reverse course, consequently it was essential for a reconnaissance aircraft to avoid being spotted itself and to withhold its report either until well clear of the ships, or even until it returned to base. Daylight reconnaissances were chiefly of value to Malta's torpedo-bombers which operated at night, setting off at dusk and using A.S.V. Wellingtons to pick up the targets already reported. Conversely, the American Marauder and Mitchell day-bombers, based near Constantine, relied on the British night reconnaissances and swept the following day for targets reported during the previous hours of darkness. The Americans flew many of their anti-shipping sweeps in very low visibility and bombs were dropped from less than 200 feet by aircraft moving at high speed.

Nearly 1,700 R.A.F. and at least 180 U.S.A.A.F. sorties are recorded as spent by the 'Torch', Malta, and Middle East air forces in searching for and attacking shipping during January; yet, largely because of bad weather, the first air success of any note on the Tunisian route was long in coming. It was not until the 20th that six U.S. Mitchells escorted by twelve Lightnings sank the 5,000-ton German tanker *Saturno*, north of Tunis. Two days later, also in

---

[1] The Wellingtons, Hudsons and Swordfish were equipped with A.S.V.—Air to Surface Vessel radar.

daylight, and in the face of an escort of six German and four Italian fighters, the R.A.F. torpedoed and the F.A.A. bombed another German ship, the *Ruhr* of 6,000 tons. She sank north-west of Cape Bon carrying to the bottom tanks, M.T., and a Giant Wuerzburg radar equipment urgently needed to improve Tunisian defences. The sinking to the north of the island of Ustica on the night 23rd/24th of two ex-French ships on their maiden voyage, the *Verona* by a Wellington of No. 221 Squadron, and the *Pistoia* by a Wellington of the same squadron and two Beauforts of No. 39 Squadron, was the first success in the Tyrrhenian Sea against ships bound for Tunisian ports. The event caused the temporary diversion of convoys to the coastal route Naples—Messina—Palermo already referred to. On the 29th, U.S. Mitchells sank the 3,100-ton *Vercelli* north-east of Bizerta.

The most decisive way of destroying a ship is to sink her at sea in deep water, but ships at sea are targets of opportunity. If the full power of the aircraft at the Allies' disposal in the Mediterranean by January 1943 was to be directed against Axis communications, a planned programme of attack on less fleeting targets was necessary. Therefore during January the Allies for the most part bombed enemy ports. It was owing to the initiative of the Commanders concerned that, despite difficult communications and lack of a comprehensive air command, there was no serious overlap, nor were any opportunities wasted on account of observing too rigidly the boundaries of the several Commands.

In January, 395 British and 573 American bomber and fighter-bomber sorties were flown against ports of arrival and 113 British and 70 American against ports of departure. The Wellingtons of Nos. 142 and 150 Squadrons of Eastern Air Command, operating by night, flew nearly 150 sorties over Bizerta, dropping 250 and 500 lb bombs, a number of 1,000 and 4,000 lb, and a great many incendiaries. On the nights of the 10th/11th and 18th/19th they attacked Ferryville. In daylight, U.S. Fortresses, with Lightning escort, also attacked Bizerta and Ferryville. They flew more than 180 sorties. Unloading at both ports was seriously affected and the Fortresses sank the 7,960-ton *Spolete* at Bizerta and the 3,168-ton *Noto* at Ferryville. Fortresses and Mitchells, American and British Middle East Liberators and Malta's Wellingtons, Mosquitoes and Beaufighters all attacked the east coast of Tunisia, damaging the ports of Sfax and Sousse and the airfield at Gabes. Their efforts denied the enemy the full use of his eastern seaboard. As almost no shipping from Europe had docked in Tripolitania since the beginning of the year, the supplies required by Rommel's Army, as well as the stores and equipment he was bringing out of Tripolitania, had all to be sent along this strip of coast. It was clearly desirable that Sousse and

Sfax should be worked to the limit—but Sousse, capable of receiving 800 tons a day, handled only eight small ships from Europe throughout January, and in February three. Sfax was used by coastal vessels, but heavy air raids at the end of December had greatly damaged the port and a sunken dredger was still obstructing the entrance a month later. Aircraft from Malta laid many mines down this coast. The Middle East bombers took the lead in a concentrated effort against Tripoli, the Liberators of the U.S. Ninth Air Force playing the principal part. On 15th January the *Agostino Bertani* of 8,329 tons sank in Tripoli harbour as a result of daylight attacks by the Liberators and night attacks by Malta's Wellingtons. From Malta, too, Spitfire fighter-bombers, Mosquitoes, and Beaufighters made daily attacks on ground targets in southern Sicily. Later they attacked the toe of Italy. Targets included factories, road convoys, railways, airfields and power stations. In addition, Spitfires and Beaufighters attacked ships with cannon and machine-guns.

By January, because of the enemy's persistent air and surface anti-submarine patrols and the hazards of navigating in heavily mined and shoal waters, the submarines of the 10th and 8th Flotillas were leaving the attack on enemy ships in the Sicilian Narrows almost entirely to the Allied air forces. Submarines found more profitable patrol grounds off the west coast of Italy, the north coast of Sicily, and the east coast of Tunisia. But this wider spread of the net meant that the submarines' prey was not so likely to be Tunisian-bound as that sighted by aircraft. In January, submarines sank five medium-sized ships off the east Tunisian coast and *Unbroken* shared with the Fleet Air Arm the sinking of the 6,107-ton *Edda* off Djerba on the 19th. (As luck would have it these six ships were homeward bound.) The submarines' larger victims were found further afield and, with one exception, chanced not to be supplying the North African forces. The exception was the *Emma*, of 6,070 tons, sunk by *Splendid* on the 16th south of Ischia, outward bound from Naples with 10 tanks and 118 vehicles. Every ship, however, was grist to the mill. Italy could not neglect such tasks as carrying grain and coal to Sicily and essential supplies to her Aegean garrisons. Ships sunk on these and kindred services had to be replaced even at the expense of the Tunisian traffic.

The submarines, seeking always to harm the enemy's communications, used spare moments on patrol to upset rail and road traffic and destroy military targets within reach of the sea. Thus on 11th January, *Turbulent* shelled and wrecked a train near San Lucido on the west Calabrian coast; on the 29th *Rorqual* bombarded a railway bridge from the Gulf of Squillace; in the Gulf of Genoa a seaplane hanger was set ablaze by *P.212*. And now another method of attack was ready for certain of the Allies' submarines to use. By the end of

1942 plans for launching the first British human torpedo attacks were complete. Crews had been training in the Shetland Islands for many months, and the submarines *Trooper*, *Thunderbolt* and *P.311* had been fitted with special containers on deck in which to carry the torpedoes, which the British had named 'Chariots'. Several crews under the command of Captain G. M. S. Sladen, a submarine officer, had arrived at Malta.

The original intention had been to attack the Italian battleships in Taranto and it was when seeking information to further this plan that *Traveller* had been lost (Chapter VIII). When it was learnt that the *Littorios* had moved to Naples it was decided that the Chariots from *P.311* should attack two 8-inch cruisers, the *Trieste* and *Bolzano*, located at Maddalena, while those from *Trooper* and *Thunderbolt* dealt with Palermo. The attacks were arranged for the night of 1st/2nd January, but were postponed for twenty-four hours because the enemy in the Narrows was alert.

Trooper and *Thunderbolt* launched five Chariots off Palermo just before midnight on 2nd/3rd and withdrew, leaving *Unruffled* to act as recovery ship. Three of the Chariots had bad luck, either through mishap to members of their crews or mechanical failure, and did not get into the harbour. Of the others, one attached her explosive head to the recently completed cruiser *Ulpio Traiano* and split her in two, and one placed hers under the 8,500-ton liner *Viminale* where it exploded, causing damage that could not be repaired in Palermo's yards. The *Viminale* was later sunk by air and surface attack while being towed to Naples. The crews of these two Chariots with the survivors from the others were taken prisoner. Nothing is known of the attack on Maddalena. It appears likely that *P.311* struck a mine in the approaches before launching her Chariots.

Destroyers of Force K and M.T.Bs from Malta carried out numerous sweeps down the east coast of Tunisia during January and seldom returned without some adventurous encounter to report. On the night of the 15th/16th *Paladin* and *Javelin* sank the 4,500-ton *D'Annunzio* east of the Kerkenah Islands and the following night the same two destroyers found and sank the Italian Naval Store Carrier *Tanaro* in the Gulf of Gabes. Early on the 19th, *Pakenham*, *Nubian* and the Greek *Olga* sank the *Stromboli*, another Naval Auxiliary, northwest of Lampedusa. The *Stromboli* was carrying cased petrol. Vessels which were not earmarked to block the harbour at Tripoli were now trying to escape. On the night 19th/20th, *Kelvin* and *Javelin* sank a number of these which were making for temporary sanctuary in Zuara, among them the small tanker *Irma*. Early on the 23rd Zuara itself was bombarded by the cruisers *Cleopatra* and *Euryalus* and four destroyers of Force K. In order to delay the departure of enemy shipping before the Naval attack, a large force of Kittyhawk fighter-bombers escorted by Spitfires of the Desert Air Force had bombed the harbour several times during the previous afternoon.

At Bône ships of Force Q appeared to be the favourite target for enemy aircraft in their frequent raids on the harbour. The powerful anti-aircraft armaments of these ships were, however, a great help in defending the port and the other ships present, and on 18th January No. 985 Balloon Squadron R.A.F. arrived to supplement the air defences.[1] On 1st January the cruiser *Ajax* was seriously damaged in one of these attacks but reached Gibraltar under her own steam after temporary repairs. Until *Penelope* arrived, the cruisers *Aurora*, *Dido* and *Sirius* and the destroyers *Laforey*, *Lightning*, *Loyal* and *Lookout* composed Force Q. Force Q had little fortune during January. *Lightning* and *Loyal* sank the 1,320-ton merchant ship *Favor* on the 18th but in spite of repeated sweeps to the eastward, including several as diversionary cover to minelaying, this was the only target Force Q found during the month. M.T.Bs, which had been sent to establish a base at Bône, were even less fortunate; they drew a blank.

See also Map 24

The minelaying just referred to was the British countermove to the enemy's placing mine-barriers, between which he hoped to run his ships to Tunis and Bizerta in reasonable security from surface attack from either east or west. The British lays have been aptly described by Admiral Cunningham as like fitting rungs into a ladder of which the two enemy fields formed the uprights. A beginning was made in January when *Welshman* carried out two and *Abdiel* one of these extremely hazardous operations which had of necessity to take place without escort. Between them these two fast minelayers laid 442 mines in the waters around the Skerki Bank during the month. The submarine *Rorqual* added her contribution of 48 off the Cani Rocks, and it was one or more of these mines which caused the loss, on the 18th, of the 4,700-ton German *Ankara*. This well-found ship had made twenty-one crossings to Africa, usually carrying tanks, as she was fitted with especially powerful derricks. Her loss had a considerable moral effect because she was regarded as an emblem of German endurance and reliability. She was, in fact, the counterpart of the British *Breconshire*. Hitler promptly gave orders that tanks were in future to be loaded in shallow-draught ferries. On this last voyage

---

[1] There had been balloon squadrons in the Egyptian Delta and Canal zones since the spring of 1941 but, beset by technical and other difficulties and forced to operate with poor equipment, they had been scarcely more than scarecrows. By the end of 1942, balloon squadrons were established at ports along the Cyrenaican coast; by the end of January 1943 at Tripoli; and in February at Malta.

the *Ankara* had been carrying 700 tons of ammunition, sorely needed by von Arnim as his troops had that same day launched an offensive in the mountains south of Pont du Fahs. By 22nd January they were so short of ammunition that the Army Commander, who had already reported officially to Kesselring that the situation was bad, followed this up with a personal letter on the same subject. He wrote bluntly that announcements from Rome that (say) 700 tons of ammunition were 'loaded and on the way' meant little to the troops in the field if nothing arrived.

The results of this combined effort of the Royal Navy and Allied air forces against Axis shipping plying to and from Africa during January were, as might be expected, in proportion to the opportunities open to each form of attack. Aircraft accounted for nine ships of over 500 G.R.T. (six at sea and three in harbour), submarines for four, surface warships for four, and mines for three. In addition, the Axis scuttled five ships, totalling 17,450 tons, in Tripoli before evacuating the port. Of the six ships sunk by aircraft at sea, three were sunk by night and three by day. Three Italian destroyers were sunk during the month, the *Bersagliere* by bombs in Palermo, the *Corsaro* by a mine near Bizerta, and the *Bombardiere* by the submarine *P.44*. Two Italian torpedo-boats and one corvette were lost on mines and a dozen lesser vessels, comprising motor ferries, auxiliary powered sailing vessels and lighters, were destroyed at sea, mostly by gunfire from surface warships and submarines or cannon and machine-gun fire from fighter aircraft. Many more were destroyed in harbour by bombing.

During February some 16,000 Germans and 59,000 tons of equipment and supplies arrived in Tunisia by sea and 12,800 Germans and over 4,000 tons by air. Most of the 7,000 Italians arriving during the month came by air. There was little change in the methods of carrying men and supplies, though sailings from Naples were fewer than in January. In general, ferries carried most of the tanks, guns and vehicles and Marsala was used as an additional loading port for them. On account of their shallow draught the ferries were looked upon as less vulnerable than ships to torpedoes and mines and near-misses by bombs. They had the further advantage that anything wheeled or tracked could be driven on board and ashore instead of being hoisted. Some of the Siebel ferries carried a powerful anti-aircraft armament, which discouraged low flying attack. For much of February the destroyers hitherto employed as troop carriers were diverted to minelaying and patrolling, while most of the troops crossing by sea were put aboard ferries. The most direct route to Tunis and Bizerta lay between the two mine barriers giving partial protection from Forces Q and K. New British minefields were, however, making this channel more dangerous, and a route outside the eastern barrier and then through a swept passage close under Cape Bon now came into use as an alternative. Such diversions complicated still further the problem of finding escorts; the average numbers available during February were only one destroyer, eight torpedo-boats and two corvettes.

The R.A.F. flew well over 1,300 sorties and the U.S.A.A.F. at least 110 during February in searching for and attacking ships at sea.[1] Six Axis merchant ships ranging from 1,700 to 10,000 G.R.T. and totalling 33,000 tons were sunk, five of them at night by torpedoes fired from Malta's Wellingtons and Beauforts and one in daylight by bombs from U.S. Mitchells. The first three were all caught within twenty-five miles of Marittimo Island. They were the *Pozzuoli*, sunk on the first night of the month, the *Capo Orso*, carrying petrol and 500 Italian soldiers, on 15th/16th and, two nights later, the *Col di Lana* homeward bound. On the 22nd, U.S.Mitchells sank the German *Gerd* half way across the Narrows north-east of Bizerta and, on the 24th/25th, the *Alcamo* was sunk by Wellingtons and Beauforts in the middle of the Tyrrhenian Sea while returning to Naples from Bizerta. But the biggest air success during February was the sinking of the 9,955-ton tanker *Thorsheimer*. She was first sighted on the morning of the 20th in a convoy south of Naples by a Baltimore on reconnaissance from Malta. That night she was found by Wellingtons, Beauforts and Albacores forty miles north of Trapani. They hit her with several torpedoes which probably caused her to postpone an attempt to cross the Narrows until the following night. Four Beauforts of No. 39 Squadron picked her up again, shortly after 8 p.m. on the 21st, midway between Trapani and Cape Bon, and here four more torpedoes hit her. She sank, carrying with her 5,400 tons of fuel, that is between one-third and one-half of all the fuel loaded for Africa during February. In a characteristically unreasonable outburst at his Situation Conference on 4th March, Hitler exclaimed that valuable fuel had been lost entirely because of the slovenliness of Field-Marshal Kesselring's Air Force and the casual way in which the Navy had operated shipping.

During February, 126 British and 150 American bomber and fighter-bomber sorties were flown against the enemy's ports of arrival and 198 British and 254 American against those of departure.

---

[1] On 3rd February Air Commodore J. R. Scarlett-Streatfeild, C.B.E., took over command of No. 201 (Naval Co-operation) Group, Middle East, from Air Vice-Marshal Sir Leonard Slatter.

The bombing greatly dislocated labour, and damaged cranes and quays and lengthened the list of ships sunk and damaged. Harbour craft to replace casualties could no longer be dribbled from unimportant small ports—these barrels were running dry. Bizerta remained the chief target for the Wellingtons from E.A.C., although there were occasional visits to the airfields at Trapani, Elmas and Villacidro. Tunis was Malta's particular responsibility. The U.S. Fortresses turned their attention to Gabes, Sousse and Palermo and most of these attacks were heavy. During the last week of February, after the Northwest African Air Forces had absorbed E.A.C. and the U.S. Twelfth Air Force, the newly formed Strategic Air Force attacked Cagliari twice. The second of these raids, carried out by American aircraft, accounted for one of the four ships sunk in port during February, the 3,800-ton *Paolo*. The 5,000-ton *Santa Rita* was damaged in the same raid. The other three big ships sunk in harbour were all in Naples, two by American and one by R.A.F. Liberators from the Middle East, and this in spite of low cloud which hampered attacks on Naples during the month. The Middle East bombers attacked Palermo, making over 100 sorties on the port, and increased their attacks on Messina in the belief that the enemy was making more use of Sicilian ports. Malta's Spitfires continued to attack targets in Sicily and also attacked Lampedusa and Pantelleria. Beauforts and F.A.A. Albacores from Malta were busy minelaying during the first half of the month, chiefly in ports on the east coast of Tunisia and in Trapani.

In February sorties both against shipping at sea and over the ports were fewer than in January. Over ports of departure sorties actually rose but were more than offset by a heavy fall in those over ports of arrival. The great effort during February in support of the land campaign, including many attacks on Axis airfields, principally in Sardinia and Tunisia, accounted for much of this fall. Nevertheless the figures for the numbers and total tonnage of ships sunk by air attack were slightly higher than in January, a result probably attributable more to chance than to a particular cause, although improved reconnaissance and greater experience no doubt helped.

Allied submarines did rather better than in January. They were still handicapped in comparison with aircraft because they could not operate within the Sicily—Tunisia—Sardinia triangle where targets converged. The best hunting grounds for submarines were still those off the north coast of Sicily, off Naples, off the toe of Italy and in the Gulf of Genoa. After the fall of Tripoli only small fry were to be found along the east coast of Tunisia.

On the 2nd February *Safari* sank the 5,733-ton *Valsavoia* and the 1,176-ton *Salemi* near Capri. Two days later *Unseen* operating in the

Gulf of Taranto added the *Le Tre Marie* of 1,086 tons, and on the 5th *Turbulent* caught the 5,300-ton tanker *Utilitas* just before she reached Palermo with 5,000 tons of fuel to replenish stocks for convoy escorts. *Unbending*, *Una* and *Unrivalled* operating in the south Adriatic and off the toe of Italy sank two ships apiece between 9th and 16th. Then on the 17th *Splendid* sank the 4,787-ton *XXI Aprile* north-west of Palermo, and on the 21st the *Baalbeck* of 2,114 tons was sunk by *Unruffled* east of Cape Bon. Right at the end of February *Torbay* spent a lively three days in the Gulf of Genoa where her sinkings included the 3,651-ton *Juan di Estigarraja* and the 5,101-ton *Ischia*. It was no fault of the submarines that only four of these ships were carrying supplies to North Africa, and the loss of the *Utilitas* reduced the oil reserves of the Italian Fleet to 5,000 tons and left none at all in Sicily.

Surface warships, Forces K and Q and the M.T.Bs. based on Malta and Bône, although a constant source of anxiety to the enemy, did not find any merchant ships of over 500 tons during their sweeps in February, nor were any sunk by mines. Mines in the neighbourhood of Bizerta, however, accounted for the Italian destroyer *Saetta*, two torpedo-boats and one corvette. The loss of *Welshman*, referred to in this chapter, curtailed the February programme of minelaying. Nevertheless her sister ship the *Abdiel* laid nearly 500 mines in three separate fields, two designed to catch ships passing through the channel between the enemy's mine barriers and the third north-west of Bizerta. The submarine *Rorqual* added fifty mines off Marittimo Island and M.T.Bs made their first contribution with a lay near Plane Island on the 22nd/23rd and further lays off Plane Island and Cape Zebib at the end of the month.

In January there had been a big increase in the number of air transports landing at Tunis from Sicily and Italy, and the daily average rose to seventy. In February the numbers were still greater and an Allied air operation ('Flax') was planned to disorganize the enemy's air transport system completely. The Kasserine battle caused 'Flax' to be postponed until early in April.

In attacks on Axis transport aircraft during January and February the 'Torch' and Middle East air forces destroyed twenty-eight Ju. 52s, one Me. 323 and one DFS 230 (Gotha) glider; Malta's aircraft accounted for six Ju. 52s and one Me. 323. During the same period Malta's aircraft also destroyed thirteen German bombers and four fighters in the air and on the ground, and of a further eighteen bombers lost by the Germans during that time but unaccounted for, some may well have fallen to Malta's fighters. Italian losses are not known. Malta's losses on operations of all kinds amounted to forty-nine aircraft.

In February, the tonnage of Axis shipping sunk by Allied submarines and aircraft was much the same as in January, but, because surface warships and mines took no toll and no Axis ships of over 500 G.R.T. were scuttled, the total tonnage sunk from all causes during the month was less. Yet the enemy was feeling the effects. In February 14 per cent. fewer men and 16 per cent. less material than in January reached Tunisia by sea and air. A number of the enemy's best supply ships had been sunk or severely damaged and those that remained needed refitting. Escort vessels were in the same plight. More ferries were being used, but more were being sunk. British minefields were adding to the delays and difficulties of navigating in the Narrows. In Tunisia both von Arnim and Rommel made clear to *OKW*, in appreciations written at the end of February, that their campaign depended upon a sufficient and secure flow of supplies across the Mediterranean. Hitler angrily criticized their views, but General Warlimont, Deputy Chief of the Operations Branch at *OKW*, stated after a visit to Tunisia in early February that it was a 'house of cards' and that the supply situation was the key factor, which should dominate all strategic and tactical decisions. The Chief of *OKW*, Field-Marshal Keitel, wrote on 23rd February that 'nothing would be of any use [in Tunisia] unless the transfer of supplies could be guaranteed', so it is clear that by the end of this month many highly placed German officers were far from complacent about the chances in Africa.

TABLE I

Axis cargoes disembarked in Tunisia and

percentage lost on passage

(from figures given by the Italian Official Naval Historian)*

Month 1943	Type	Cargo disembarked in Tunisia (Tons)	Percentage lost on the way
Jan.	General Military Cargo and fuel	69,908	23
Feb.	General Military Cargo and fuel	59,016	

* Bragadin: *Che ha fatto la Marina?* (Milan 1950, 2nd ed.).

AXIS LOSSES

TABLE II

Number and tonnage of Italian and German merchant ships of over 500 G.R.T. sunk at sea or in port in the Mediterranean January and February 1943

(Compiled from Italian post-war and German war records)

The upper line in each case gives the figures for the whole Mediterranean. The lower figures are the losses in ships engaged in supplying Tunisia.

Month	By surface ships	By submarine	By aircraft	By mine	Shared	From other causes	Total
Jan.	4–7,757	11–28,561	9–41,088	3–12,502	1–6,107*	6–21,881	34–117,896
	4–7,757	6–13,969	9–41,088	3–12,502	1–6,107*	5–17,452	28– 98,875
Feb.	—	15–45,090	11–44,790	1– 674	—	3– 4,211	30– 94,765
	—	4–17,976	10–43,357	—	—	1– 3,078	15– 64,411
	4–7,757	26–73,651	20–85,878	4–13,176	1–6,107	9–26,092	64–212,661
	4–7,757	10–31,945	19–84,445	3–12,502	1–6,107	6–20,530	43–163,286

* F.A.A. and submarine.

Over the same period some 85 vessels of less than 500 G.R.T., totalling 7,100 tons, were also sunk.

For interest rather than as matter for comparison, Allied shipping losses are shown in the following table.

TABLE III

Number and tonnage of Allied merchant ships of over 500 G.R.T. sunk at sea or in port in the Mediterranean January and February 1943

Figures in brackets in the 'By submarine' column are included in the figures immediately above them and show the losses in the Eastern Basin. All other losses were in the 'Torch' area.

Month	By surface ships	By submarine	By aircraft	By mine	Shared	From other causes	Total
Jan.	—	9–27,773 (2–6,186)	4–21,858	—	—	2– 8,750	12– 58,381
Feb.	—	4–13,803 (2–4,614)	—	3–14,064*	1–6,640†	1– 7,176	9– 41,683
		10–41,576 (4–10,800)	4–21,858	3–14,064	1–6,640	3–15,926	21–100,064

* Just west of the Straits of Gibraltar.
† U-boat and torpedo-bomber.

See Map 16

While the scurrying to and fro between Italy and Tunisia grew more desperate, the vastly greater undertakings of maintaining and building up the 'Torch' forces and the 8th Army, and of continuing to run the ocean convoys to Suez, went steadily on.

In the west, fast convoys carrying men from the United Kingdom (KMF) and from the United States (UGF) continued to arrive at the rate of two a month. They were followed after an interval of about four days by slow convoys (KMS and UGS) carrying supplies. As in November and December, most of the men and cargoes arriving in convoys from the United Kingdom were transhipped into smaller vessels at Algiers before being carried forward the further 230 miles to Bône. The *Princess Beatrix* maintained a ferry service for the men and carried 36,000 forward during January without loss. The Americans had similar arrangements between Oran and Philippeville. For the tanks, guns, and vehicles, the three Maracaiboes proved most useful. The first Sherman tanks arrived at Oran in a fast convoy (UGF 4) on 27th January and more were due on 3rd February. From Bône and Philippeville men and material were carried to their destinations by road and rail, and from Bône by the extra means of a ferry service of L.C.M. and L.C.T., which plied the twenty and thirty miles eastward to La Calle and Tabarka.

The U.S. Twelfth Air Force was responsible for providing air cover for convoys from Gibraltar eastward as far as Cape Tenes, and E.A.C. took over beyond that point. E.A.C. could only spare Hurricanes and these were little faster than Ju. 88s. Nevertheless their presence over a convoy often turned hostile aircraft away. Early in January, after many hundreds of miles of land-line had been laid, it became possible to divide the French North African coast into fighter sectors each with its own radar equipment for giving early warning.

Anti-submarine patrols in the 'Torch' area had at first been the responsibility of the Royal Air Force at Gibraltar. As 'Torch' progressed general reconnaissance and anti-submarine squadrons were moved to Oran and Algiers where they came under the command of E.A.C. When the air commands were reorganized in February responsibility for air cover and A/S patrols passed to the Northwest African Coastal Air Force.

On 10th January there were 213 German bombers in Sicily and Sardinia—124 serviceable—and about 170 Italian (110). These figures did not change much during February. Axis air attacks in the Western Basin against ships at sea were made by German torpedo-bombers and those against African ports such as Algiers and Bône mostly by German long-range bombers. All these aircraft operated from Sicily but used airfields in Sardinia as advanced bases.

Both the German torpedo and long-range bomber forces—particularly the former—suffered heavily. Their losses were owing in part to the natural hazards of such operations and in part to the cumulative effects of too little rest for men and machines and to lack of trained crews as replacements. A rapid decline in operational efficiency set in at the end of February as a consequence.

Some twelve Italian submarines were usually on patrol at this time in the Western Mediterranean, but they achieved little. German submarines were rather more successful, although the Senior Officer of the Mediterranean U-boats complained bitterly at the end of 1942 of the Allied mastery of the air in the Western Basin, which deprived U-boats of mobility and vision and stopped the *Luftwaffe* from providing good reconnaissance. There were twenty-three German boats in the Mediterranean at the end of 1942. In January 1943, one, outward bound from Germany, got through the Straits of Gibraltar, but two were sunk during the month and three more in February, leaving nineteen by the beginning of March. For practical purposes the figure was much lower, as it became harder and harder to keep the boats fit to fight. The Italians lost three submarines in January and three in February.

In January there were no losses during the ocean passages of the KM and UG convoys from the United Kingdom and United States. Very serious losses, however, occurred in a tanker convoy (TM 1) carrying oil from Venezuela for the 'Torch' Command. Spotted off the Azores and set upon by a U-boat pack, seven of its nine ships were sunk. In the Mediterranean, KMS 6 lost two ships torpedoed by aircraft and KMS 7 one, and UGS 4 three from submarine attack. In addition a number of merchant ships were sunk or damaged in harbour by air raids on Algiers and Bône. Losses in local convoys and ferry services were slight, and the escorts suffered more than their charges. The anti-aircraft auxiliary cruiser *Pozarica* and the Hunt class destroyer *Avon Vale* were both torpedoed in a heavy air attack on a coastal convoy on 29th January and towed to Bougie, where the *Pozarica* subsequently capsized during salvage operations and became a total loss. On 30th January the corvette *Samphire* was sunk off Bougie by a submarine, probably the Italian *Platino*.

During February the pattern of events at sea was much the same. Axis air attacks against ships at sea persisted much as before but over the harbours they were lighter. KMF 8 and 9 arrived, followed at the customary interval by KMS 8 and 9. Two ships were lost from KMS 8 between Oran and Algiers, one by U-boat attack and one by U-boat followed by T/B attack, and the Canadian corvette, *Louisburg*, escorting this convoy, was sunk by air attack. Just west of the Straits of Gibraltar in the homeward bound MKS 7 three merchant ships were lost on 7th February on mines laid by *U.118* five days earlier, and on 22nd another Canadian corvette, *Weyburn*, was lost on the same minefield.

Force H remained very much on the alert, covering in particular the ocean convoys on their passages from the Straits of Gibraltar to Algiers and Oran and always ready to move further east at a hint of surface attack on Allied shipping between Algiers and Bône. On 23rd January, Vice-Admiral Sir Neville Syfret, who had commanded this famous force since January 1942 in so many notable operations in and outside the Mediterranean, developed acute appendicitis. Vice-Admiral Sir Harold Burrough, also experienced in Malta convoy operations, and recently Naval Commander of the Algiers landings, was flown out to relieve him temporarily.

In mid-February the changes in Naval, Military and Air Force Commands in the Mediterranean, agreed upon at the Casablanca Conference and described in the next chapter, came into force. For the Royal Navy this meant that Admiral Sir Andrew Cunningham—promoted to Admiral of the Fleet on 21st January—relinquished the title of N.C.X.F. and became Commander-in-Chief Mediterranean once again and Admiral Harwood, until now C.-in-C. Mediterranean, became C.-in-C. Levant.

A change of a different kind had just taken place in Germany when on 30th January, Admiral Raeder, unable to stomach any longer Hitler's ideas on Naval strategy and his insistence on paying off all the larger German surface warships, resigned and was replaced by Admiral Dönitz, until now Flag Officer Commanding U-boats.

The contribution of the Royal Navy and Merchant Navy to the vital task of supplying the 8th Army during its advance from El Alamein to Tripoli has been told in earlier chapters of this volume. At Tobruk and Benghazi, and at lesser ports, the planned rate of discharge was exceeded and seems to have met the needs. General Montgomery expressed his thanks to the Navy on 12th November, and later to the small party which moved forward around the Gulf of Sirte and landed urgently needed stores on the beaches close behind the front lines.

During the third week of January the bombing of Tripoli by Middle East and Malta-based aircraft was intensified in the hope that it might hinder the enemy's attempts to block the entrance to the harbour and demolish the port's facilities.[1] Several Naval operations were staged from Malta for the same purpose. On the night of 18th/19th January, two chariots were launched from the submarine

---

[1] See page 242

Thunderbolt with the object of sinking or damaging potential blockships. One chariot succeeded in reaching the harbour entrance, but only in time to hear the scuttling charges in the blockships being blown. The crew became prisoners of war. The other chariot had to be destroyed because of damage to its hydroplanes. Its crew also were captured but later escaped and reached the advancing 8th Army. A second enterprise on the night of 20th/21st was an attack on the mole by M.T.Bs. During this the M.T.Bs encountered and torpedoed the Italian submarine *Santarosa*, which tugs were trying to rescue from a point of land on which she had grounded five days earlier. In the next few nights British surface warships, sweeping along the coast, sank numerous small craft attempting to escape to Zuara and to Tunisian ports.

On 10th January the Naval Base Party destined for Tripoli moved forward from Benghazi to join the 8th Army and, on the 23rd, the Naval Officer-in-Charge designate, with a small Naval contingent, entered Tripoli five hours after the leading troops of the Army. The entrance to the harbour was found to be completely blocked by six merchant ships, a sheerlegs, a rock-crusher and several barges filled with concrete blocks. Demolition on both moles had been thorough and effective and warehouses and installations had been heavily damaged as a result of the Allied air attacks. Numerous wrecks and burnt out ships strewed the harbour but four tugs and some fifty lighters were fit for use. That day specially equipped Wellingtons swept the harbour and its approaches and exploded one magnetic mine. At dusk, Captain Wauchope, the S.N.O. Inshore Squadron, arrived by air from Benghazi, but unfortunately the Fleet Salvage Officer had to come by sea as few air passages were given because of suspected mining of Castel Benito airfield. Commodore Dundas, C.O.S. to Admiral Harwood, was delayed in his flight from Alexandria by a defective aircraft and did not arrive until early on the 25th.

The salvage vessel *Gamtoos*, a mine clearing force, and a supply convoy of L.C.T., all of which had been waiting at Benghazi, also arrived on the 25th. The *Gamtoos* began work next day. The first convoy, of five merchant ships and a tug, which had left Alexandria on the 21st and had been held at Tobruk awaiting the progress of the 8th Army, arrived at 2 p.m. on the 26th and anchored outside the harbour in an area already cleared of mines. Unloading began at once, using L.C.T. as lighters, and 370 tons were discharged. Bad weather held up operations on the 27th, only 230 tons being discharged. By the 28th a 30-foot gap with a depth of 9 feet had been made in the centre of the blockships and six of the L.C.T. entered the harbour and began unloading. On the 30th, 1,000 tons were discharged. The Prime Minister with General Alexander visited Tripoli on 4th February and was able to see the first two large merchant ships enter harbour through a 100-foot gap with a depth of 24 feet.

Mr. Churchill and General Montgomery have both paid tribute in their writings to the speed with which Tripoli was reopened, and the plans for the further advance of the 8th Army do not appear to have been delayed through lack of supplies coming through that port. Nevertheless, on the 26th—three days after the 8th Army's occupation of Tripoli—General Montgomery criticised severely the Navy's preparations for the task in front of them. Basing, so it would appear, his statement principally upon the impressions of his Chief Engineer, General Montgomery told Commodore Dundas on 26th January that the Navy's arrangements 'for uncorking the harbour were totally inadequate both as regards personnel and equipment'. Next day, in Cairo, the Prime Minister interviewed Admiral Harwood in the presence of the C.I.G.S., who had received complaints from General Montgomery, and told him of the Army's dissatisfaction and surprise that an estimate of fourteen days had been given for clearing the harbour. Back in London a few days later the C.I.G.S., when questioned by Admiral Pound, informed him that the Army in the Middle East had lost confidence that the Navy would in all circumstances give them the necessary support.

As highly satisfactory unloading figures were already reaching London from Tripoli, this sorry disturbance of the happy relations between Army and Navy, which had been sustained through all the wear and tear of the Mediterranean campaigns, might perhaps have subsided without further consequences. Other incidents, however, had caused Mr. Churchill to doubt whether Admiral Harwood was suited to his present appointment. On a recent visit to London Mr. Casey, Minister of State in Cairo, had stated his opinion that the Navy's representation on the Middle East Defence Committee was not so strong as that of the Army and Royal Air Force. In Admiral Harwood's own opinion much of the Prime Minister's loss of confidence in him arose from impatience over Admiral Godfroy's intransigence and Admiral Harwood's policy in handling the French squadron at Alexandria.

The Admiralty decided to relieve Admiral Harwood and to offer him the sea-going appointment of Second in Command of the Eastern Fleet. In a letter to Admiral Harwood explaining this decision Admiral Pound wrote, 'I am afraid that the arrangements for the clearance of Tripoli harbour are largely responsible for this'. The First Sea Lord went on to make clear that the Admiralty considered that the work of the *Gamtoos* and the salvage party had been admirable but that not enough supervision had been given on the highest level to ensure that an operation so vital to the Army, and on which everyone's attention was focussed, had behind it all the drive and forethought which it demanded.

Admiral Harwood's health at this time was already beginning to show signs of breaking down and he had to be relieved even before the date intended. On 27th March, Vice-Admiral Sir Ralph Leatham, who had been succeeded as Vice-Admiral Malta on 29th January by Vice-Admiral Sir Stuart Bonham-Carter, took over C.-in-C. Levant, until the arrival of the new C.-in-C. designate, Admiral Sir J. H. D. Cunningham, on 5th June.[1]

It may fairly be asked whether the First Sea Lord's summing up was right and the Admiralty's decision was just. Our evidence does not provide satisfying confirmation of the summing up. It is a fact that the Navy in this affair gave an unfortunate first impression, yet one which arose almost entirely out of a series of incidents, none of which was foreseeable. The most unfortunate were the delayed arrival of the Naval Chief of Staff and the Fleet Salvage Officer, and the consequence that neither was master of the problem when they first discussed it with the 8th Army's Chief Engineer. Yet the Navy cannot be exonerated from all blame. It failed to make its readiness abundantly plain to military commanders and staffs who looked upon supply by sea through Tripoli as all-important in the next phase of the 8th Army's fight. In this the Navy's fault was that it did not make a powerful and convincing display of competence and drive. General Montgomery's impetuous outburst, although understandable, does not excuse his complaint, over the head of General Alexander, to the C.I.G.S. in Cairo. There never was a trouble that could better have been settled by the Commanders-in-Chief.

As to Admiral Harwood's relief we conclude that he would have been too harshly treated had the matter of Tripoli been the sole cause. But, as has been seen, Tripoli served only to bring to a head the Prime Minister's and First Sea Lord's earlier doubts whether he was suitable in his appointment.

Meanwhile the restocking of Malta had been going on steadily. Convoys from Alexandria ran in company with those for the 8th Army until their routes diverged off Benghazi. Here cruisers and destroyers from Malta took over the Malta-bound ships. During January two convoys carrying between them 34,600 tons of general cargo and 16,000 tons of furnace oil were unloaded, and during February a further two with 59,224 tons, including 4,000 tons of kerosene and 6,000 tons of aviation spirit.

---

[1] Between 31st December 1942 and 15th March 1943 Admiral Leatham acted as Governor of Malta during Lord Gort's absence on sick leave.

Air cover for the Malta and 8th Army convoys was given by fighters under command of Air Headquarters Egypt, from airfields along the coastline from Port Said to Benghazi. No. 219 Group covered the convoys as far as the Egyptian frontier, where No. 212 Group took over.[1] Air attacks from Crete and Sicily were still thought likely, for besides the German and Italian bombers in Sicily already referred to, there were in Greece and Crete 155 German bombers (of which 72 were serviceable) in January, dropping to 52 (36) in February, and in the Aegean between 40 and 55 Italian bombers of which 20 to 30 were probably serviceable.

Attacks on Allied convoys by surface warships were now unlikely; nevertheless an air striking force was always kept ready. As the 8th Army advanced westwards, naval co-operation wings of No. 201 Group followed close behind. By the beginning of 1943 a chain of naval co-operation squadrons covered the sea route from the Levant to the Gulf of Sirte, and Malta's anti-shipping force had been augmented from Nos. 201 and 205 Groups.

In the event, no ships of over 500 G.R.T. were lost by air attack in the Eastern or Central Mediterranean during January and February, but one Greek and three Norwegian ships were all sunk by one submarine—the *U.617*. This boat was responsible for a more serious loss, when on 1st February she torpedoed the fast minelayer *Welshman*, about forty miles east of Tobruk. At dusk *Welshman*, bound for Alexandria and steaming at high speed, unescorted, was hit by two, if not three, torpedoes. Three hours later she unexpectedly heeled over and sank. Rescue vessels were unable to arrive before midnight and the losses were heavy—152 Naval officers and men, besides a number of soldiers and airmen. Like *Breconshire*, *Welshman* was a name to conjure with at Malta. Unescorted she had made five trips at high speed to succour the Island and was shortly to have returned there to begin again the hazardous task of laying mines in the Sicilian Narrows.

To complete the story of the Eastern and Central Basins during January and February 1943 mention must be made of the activities of the 1st Submarine Flotilla and of the Marauders from No. 201 (Naval Co-operation) Group in the Aegean. These activities, together with the move of 4,000 troops from Syria to Cyprus (carried out by *Welshman* in six trips during January) were part of a plan to mislead

---

[1] In January, 1943, No. 243 Wing of the Desert Air Force was transferred to No. 212 Group and made responsible for the protection of the ports at Tripoli and Misurata and of convoys in the area. In February No. 243 Wing was replaced by a new fighter Group (No. 210) which became responsible for the protection of convoys and shipping west of the Cyrenaica border, initially to longitude 13° East and thereafter progressively farther westwards keeping abreast of the Desert Air Force in its advance into Tunisia.

the enemy's intelligence about Allied strategy in the Mediterranean. This will be referred to when preparations for the invasion of Sicily are described.

Down in the Gulf of Suez the 9th Australian Division was embarked during the last two weeks of January to return home. The monsters, *Queen Elizabeth*, *Aquitania*, *Ile de France* and *Nieuw Amsterdam* and the Armed Merchant Cruiser *Queen of Bermuda*, each called at Suez for their quota, and early in February the convoy of great ships was escorted clear of the Gulf of Aden by destroyers of the Mediterranean Fleet. The cruiser *Devonshire* formed the escort for the passage through the Indian Ocean, which was safely completed.

In late January the minelayer *Teviot Bank* left the Mediterranean Command to rejoin the Eastern Fleet, after finishing the laying of a deep minefield in the Straits of Bab-el-Mandeb, near Aden, as a defence against Japanese submarines.

The two months covered by this chapter were critical ones in the struggle to stop the Axis supplies to Tunisia. During November and December the result had been in doubt. The Allies' attacks on ships at sea, and in harbour had been disappointing in November and, although more successful in December, it had seemed possible that the Axis would be able to build up and maintain enough forces in Africa to hold their own for a long time. By the end of February, however, it was clear that the Allies had gained the upper hand in the battle over supplies. Every means of attack by sea and air was being used and every means was needed, but it was the Allies' increasing domination of the air that was making decisive their attack on the enemy's communications and the defence of their own.

CHAPTER XI

THE CASABLANCA CONFERENCE AND THE FIGHTING IN TUNISIA IN JANUARY 1943

THE Anglo-American decision of July 1942 to occupy French North Africa had been made because this was the most practicable operation to undertake in 1942 with the resources then available to the Allies.[1] But few Americans had accepted 'Torch' whole-heartedly, and a result had been to throw the rest of the Allied strategic plans into uncertainty. In December the President and the Prime Minister, expecting an early and successful end to the whole African campaign, agreed it was time to arrange another meeting at which ideas could be clarified and decisions made on what to do next. At first it was hoped to make the conference tripartite, but Marshal Stalin regretted that he could not leave Russia and so Mr. Roosevelt and Mr. Churchill chose Casablanca, geographically convenient, as their meeting point, finding accommodation a few miles off at Anfa. The conference was to be primarily military. At the President's express wish 'no Foreign Affairs people' were to attend. The principals were to bring their Chiefs of Staff, and Field-Marshal Sir John Dill would come from Washington to represent the British Joint Staff Mission. Admiral Leahy, the President's representative on the American C.O.S's committee and its chairman, was taken ill on passage to the conference and did not attend. Among others summoned from Algiers to attend were Mr. Robert Murphy and his recently appointed British colleague, Mr. Harold Macmillan, who were relieving General Eisenhower of some of his political burdens.[2] Mr. Churchill arrived at Casablanca during the morning of 13th January and Mr. Roosevelt in the afternoon of the following day.

The Americans, with the notable exception of the President, came to the conference strongly opposed to further peripheral military ventures in the European theatre. They wanted no more dissipation of force from the agreed main purpose, the cross-Channel invasion of Europe. And, because the hearts of many Americans

---
[1] See Chapter V.
[2] Mr. Macmillan's appointment was Minister Resident at Allied Force Headquarters.

were really in the Pacific War, some even questioned the policy of 'Germany first', while others could easily swing that way should they become convinced that the British were bent on postponing indefinitely, if not dodging altogether, a direct attack on Germany, which seemed to most Americans so obviously the quickest way to win the war.

However, even before the conference opened, it had become plain to nearly all the participants that no cross-Channel operation was practicable until the spring of 1944. Neither the men nor the equipment, on the scale now appreciated to be necessary, could be ready earlier. It was soon agreed that in the interval a full-scale war would be continued against the U-boats and that the Allied air forces should concentrate on the bombing of German industry. What to do on land after North Africa had been cleared of the enemy was a more difficult question.

The task of the C.I.G.S. (General Sir Alan Brooke), as chairman of the British C.O.S., was to persuade the Americans to exploit 'Torch' within the Mediterranean by invading Sicily or Sardinia.[1] He explained that the British thought that this policy would compel Germany to disperse her forces, and perhaps knock Italy out of the war, and bring Turkey in. Such an enforced dispersal of German forces along the whole Mediterranean coastal area from the Pyrenees to the Aegean would ease the pressure on Russia and was an essential preliminary to a cross-Channel assault. Such a dispersal committed the troops concerned most effectively, for whereas good east and west communications enabled the Germans to switch seven divisions simultaneously from the Russian front to France in ten to fourteen days, only one division could be moved at a time from Italy, Yugoslavia and Greece. The Chief of the Air Staff (Air Chief Marshal Sir Charles Portal) added that it would be much more advantageous to the Germans if we built up against France and left the Mediterranean alone. The Germans would learn our intention and be able to withdraw large numbers of aircraft from the Mediterranean and reinforce the Russian front, relying on the strong defences of Northern France to resist an invasion.

Unpalatable facts persuaded the Americans, who at the outset criticized the idea of assaults on Sicily and Sardinia as opportunist, without relevance to an integrated plan to win the war, to accept a Mediterranean strategy. General Marshall's agreement, however, came about more on logistic grounds. A new estimate of General Eisenhower's, that twelve instead of the six divisions

---

[1] This volume is concerned only with decisions affecting the campaign in the Mediterranean and Middle East. For a complete account of the momentous decisions taken at Casablanca affecting Allied strategy all over the world see *Grand Strategy*, Volume IV (*August* 1942–*August* 1943), Michael Howard (in preparation).

previously thought necessary would be needed for the most modest assault on northern France, had deflected him from the idea of a 1943 'Round-up', and he was won over to support 'Husky' (code name for the assault on Sicily) when he learnt that many of the troops could be found from those already in North Africa and that the reopening of the Mediterranean would mean a saving in shipping of 225 merchantmen in the Allies' world-wide requirements. General Marshall made it clear, however, that to accept 'Husky' did not imply assent to interminable operations in the Mediterranean.

The Combined Chiefs of Staff chose Sicily rather than Sardinia because it was a greater political and military prize—which commended it to the President and the Prime Minister—and because the Americans were impressed with the contribution it would make towards completely opening the Mediterranean. The practicability of the operation had not been discussed. Now, a detailed discussion of ways and means took place. Timing presented the crucial problem. It was desirable to invade either Sicily or Sardinia as soon as possible after the end of the North African campaign to forestall reinforcement by the enemy and take advantage of the summer weather. The Tunisian battle, it was hoped, would be over by the end of April.

In British discussions, however, doubts were expressed whether 'Husky' could be launched before the end of August. It appeared that neither the British or American troops nor the landing-craft could be ready earlier. By comparison, the forces required for 'Brimstone', the capture of Sardinia, would be few, and could be ready in June. Moreover, the capture of Sardinia, it was argued, would be as effective in forcing Italy out of the war as the capture of Sicily and the collapse of Italy meant possession of Sicily. The C.I.G.S., however, thought that Sicily was the better operation. He believed that the enemy could reinforce Sardinia more rapidly than Sicily and consequently he foresaw a long and difficult campaign to master the island by which time the chance of taking Corsica easily would be gone. Besides, having persuaded the Americans to adopt his Mediterranean strategy in the shape of 'Husky', he was unwilling to weaken his position by asking them to change over to 'Brimstone'. But he conceded that if by the 1st March it was clear that the American portion of the assault could not possibly be ready in time, we should then decide to proceed with 'Brimstone' as a predominantly British operation with American air and naval support.

The Americans killed this compromise at the C.C.S. meeting on 22nd January. For them it was Sicily or nothing. They regarded 'Brimstone' as a minor operation which would jeopardize the prospects of either 'Husky' or a cross-Channel assault whilst yielding no very valuable return. The Americans did not attach the same importance as the British to eliminating Italy from the war. Even the Sardinian airfields, they said, had a very small capacity and would have to be developed. They thought the United States forces assigned to 'Husky' could be ready by 1st August. To assist the British in advancing their target date, it was agreed that they could train at Bougie and in ports on the east coast of Tunisia, and load in the Tunis area. (It had previously been thought that the Americans might need all Tunisia to mount their part of the invasion.) So the target date was fixed for the favourable July moon.

At the final plenary meeting next day, the Prime Minister, true to form, sought to bring this date forward to June.[1] He and the President expressed uneasiness at the prospect of four (sic) summer months when no Allied troops would be fighting Germans. Indeed Mr. Churchill still hankered after a landing in Northern France as well as in Sicily during 1943, mindful that his promises to Stalin were falling far short of fulfilment. General Marshall explained that the limiting factor was the provision of landing-craft and crews and pointed out the danger of launching such an operation with inadequate preparations. Mr. Churchill agreed but said every possibility of advancing the date should be rigorously examined. He thought that training might be started earlier if some of the landing-craft used to maintain 8th Army could be at once recovered and that loading could perhaps be accelerated. The President likewise remarked that the proposals of the C.C.S. were as yet based on estimates which might or might not prove correct. It was therefore decided to let the July date stand but to instruct General Eisenhower to explore rapidly every device which might make an assault in June possible.

Sir Alan Brooke had begun to arrange the movement of forces. Having decided to mount the major part of the expedition in North Africa the C.O.S. selected for the British assault force two divisions from P.A.I.C. and one from Tunisia, rather than vice versa, because training could thereby begin earlier. The divisions from P.A.I.C. were the 5th and 56th, and the 78th was chosen from 1st Army. An outline plan proposed a landing by these three divisions on the south-east of the island on D day with the object of securing Syracuse, Augusta and the nearby airfields. A fourth division was to be assembled in the United Kingdom for an assault on Catania

---

[1] The news that 8th Army had entered Tripoli was received a few hours before the final meeting: a happy contrast to the previous meeting of the President and Prime Minister in Washington just seven months earlier when the news of the loss of Tobruk had come through.

on D plus 3 and a fifth in Tripolitania for the follow up. An assault on the south-west of the island to take the airfields in that area and then, on D plus 2, Palermo, was envisaged for the American divisions taking part in the operation.

General Eisenhower was appointed Supreme Commander, and General Alexander Deputy Commander-in-Chief. The question of the dividing line between the North African and Middle East theatres was raised and the British suggestion of the Tunisian/ Tripolitanian frontier to Corfu accepted.[1]

At the same meeting the British recommendations to co-ordinate all operational air forces in the Mediterranean were agreed to in principle. Air Chief Marshal Tedder had been the chief advocate for the unity of air command, not only for North West Africa but for the Mediterranean theatre as a whole. The problem here was how to combine a single air command with two land commands (i.e. French North Africa and Middle East), and an independent British air Service with one which formed part of the United States Army. The British proposed to circumvent these difficulties by bringing the C.-in-C. A.A.F., the A.O.C.-in-C. M.E. and the A.O.C. Malta under an Air C.-in-C. for the whole Mediterranean area and making him subordinate to the C.-in-C. A.E.F. for all air forces and their operations in the North West African theatre.[2] This device provided, on the highest level, for the American principle of army control of the U.S.A.A.F. but did not affect the independence of the R.A.F. nor its freedom of action in Malta, Tripolitania or the Middle East. Within the North West African air organization there were to be three main operational sub-commands; one for bombers and their escort fighters, one for general reconnaissance and fighter protection of shipping, ports and rearward areas and the third for the support of the armies. The structure of the proposed air support system was carefully outlined. Its commander was to share an advanced headquarters with the Deputy C.-in-C. and co-ordinate air operations through Army Support Wings attached to each of the three armies.[3]

After the meeting the Americans stated that the appointment of Air Chief Marshal Tedder as Air C.-inC. would be agreeable to them. They also welcomed the appointment of Admiral Cunningham, whom they esteemed highly, to command the naval forces for 'Husky' as he had done for 'Torch' with responsibility for a correspondingly larger portion of the Mediterranean. The new dividing

---

[1] The line chosen ran from the Tunisian/Tripolitanian frontier through position 35° N 16° E to Cape Spartivento (Calabria). See Map 16.
[2] Major-General Spaatz was appointed Commander-in-Chief of the Allied Air Force in North West Africa on 5th January 1943.
[3] The organization and Order of Battle of the Mediterranean Air Command as at mid-April 1943 are shown at Appendix 8.

line would bring Malta into Admiral Cunningham's command. Admiral Harwood was to remain responsible for the waters to the eastward with the title of C.-in-C. Levant, but Admiral Cunningham was to control the distribution of forces and co-ordinate all movements throughout the Mediterranean.

Among other matters it was hoped to clear up while the President and Prime Minister were together was the delicate one of French authority beyond the frontiers of Metropolitan France. Darlan's assassination at the end of December seemed to present an opportunity for bringing together Frenchmen in North Africa now supporting the Allied cause and de Gaulle's 'Fighting French'. Giraud, who succeeded Darlan, was a soldier and openly professed his dislike for political responsibility, which must inevitably bring him into contact with the intrigues, jealousies and suspicions of the various French political groups. de Gaulle, on the other hand, who had political ability, wished to build a government in exile capable of undertaking the reconstruction of France when the Germans had been driven out and one which the Allies would recognize without delay as the authentic voice of France. The day after Darlan's death he suggested to Giraud that they should meet and was understandably incensed when he learnt that Washington had intervened to delay such a meeting until it could take place in an Anglo/American setting during the Casablanca conference. Under pressure from Mr. Churchill, however, he arrived at Anfa on 22nd January and he and General Giraud exchanged views. Although encouraged by the President to give an impression of accord for purposes of publicity, this meeting did little to narrow the differences between the leaders themselves nor between the Frenchmen they represented.

After the conference was over Mr. Churchill flew to Cairo accompanied by the C.I.G.S. Their main purpose was to secure a meeting with the Turks.[1] But they also hoped to settle on the spot questions arising from the changes in command. General Wilson had already been chosen to succeed General Alexander as C.-in-C. Middle East and was subsequently charged with the following four tasks in order:
(*a*) to maintain Eighth Army;
(*b*) to train and mount the Middle East portion of 'Husky';
(*c*) to prepare to support Turkey;

---

[1] For earlier Anglo/Turkish meetings see Volumes I–III under index heading 'Turkey'.

(*d*) to plan for amphibious operations in the Eastern Mediterranean.

At first the Prime Minister did not consider filling the command in Persia and Iraq because he had it in mind to include both countries once more in the Middle East Command. But the C.I.G.S. and General Wilson opposed this idea on the ground that G.H.Q. P.A.I.C. was still needed to handle the large administrative problems connected with supplies to Russia. So P.A.I.C. continued although in February its strength was scaled down to that required for Internal Security only. When the new C.-in-C., General Sir Henry Pownall, took over in March the dispersal of his forces had begun.

From Cairo the Prime Minister flew to Adana on 30th January 1943 accompanied by the C.I.G.S. and by Sir Alexander Cadogan from the Foreign Office. Friendly meetings took place with the Turkish President, Mr. Inönü; the Prime Minister, Mr. Saracoglu; and Marshal Chakmak. Arrangements were made to increase supplies of British and American equipment to Turkey and Mr. Churchill was able to assure the Turkish authorities of the readiness of anti-aircraft and anti-tank units and of divisions of the 9th Army to come to Turkey's help, particularly now that the German threat from the north was much less. But the Turks, conscious that Russian and British successes might lead to a desperate venture by the Germans to reach oil by the middle road through Turkey, were not prepared to risk encouraging such action by actively joining the Allies or by granting them the use of airfields from which to attack the Rumanian oilfields.

On 31st January Mr. Churchill began his homeward journey, calling at Cairo and Tripoli, where he reviewed units of the 8th Army, and at Algiers on the way.

By January 1943 the Axis were within sight of losing the war, not only in Africa but perhaps throughout the whole Mediterranean area as well. The combined bomber offensive against Germany coupled with unfavourable events in far-off Russia were beginning to exert a disastrous influence on events in Tunisia; and in Italy, the main base of African operations, difficulties multiplied. And there is evidence of confusion and dangerous strain in the Axis war-machine in the Mediterranean which appears constantly until the end in May.

Policy was uncertain. The Duce after his decision to withdraw from Tripolitania successively contemplated containing the Allied offensives; thrusts towards Algeria and Morocco and the reconquest of Libya; and plain defence. Hitler on the other hand, on 16th February, could only spare Africa half a page of a long letter to Mussolini and left next day for the Russian front. Nevertheless he considered the campaign in Africa to be among the decisive factors of the war because it compelled the Allies to use an enormous amount of shipping. In March however Hitler, moved by the pessimistic appreciations of Rommel, von Arnim and Messe, looked more closely at the African theatre and gave some directions, sensible, but too late. Mussolini meanwhile sought from everyone assurance that all was well whatever the truth.

There were changes in the Axis higher command. Hitler on 28th January expanded the functions of Kesselring, the Commander-in-Chief South.[1] He was to present to Mussolini and *Comando Supremo* Hitler's views on the conduct of operations in the Central Mediterranean; to assert German influence in the affairs of the armies in Tunisia; to be in authority over the C.-in-C. of the 'Central German Command Headquarters' in Tunisia (which did not yet exist). He was to administer all supplies for German troops in the Central Mediterranean, and to put before *OKW* and *OKH* any proposals concerning organization made by Rommel or von Arnim or by *Comando Supremo*.[2] Kesselring at once began to try to behave as C.-in-C. of the armies in Tunisia. General Vittorio Ambrosio replaced Cavallero as Chief of Staff of the Italian Armed Forces on 4th February. There can be little doubt that Cavallero was a victim of the growing defeatist element in the Italian hierarchy who considered him too pro-German. On the 15th Bastico, Commander-in-Chief North Africa and Governor of Libya since July 1941, returned to Italy. With the Allied occupation of Libya, and with the appointment of Messe and the imminent setting-up of an Army Group in Tunisia, Bastico's appointments lapsed.

It had been evident since December that two German-Italian armies would be fighting in Tunisia, and on 3rd January 1943 Hitler had agreed that some kind of Italian Army Command should be formed. This measure became entangled with intrigues to get rid of Rommel. The Italians had for long resented him and now blamed him for abandoning Tripoli so soon. If Ciano's evidence is to be trusted, Kesselring bore Rommel a grudge and constantly hinted to Mussolini that the Field-Marshal should be recalled or

---

[1] For Kesselring's earlier functions see Chapter I, page 24.
[2] *OKH* is the abbreviation for *Oberkommando des Heeres*, the High Command of the German Army. *OKW* is the abbreviation for *Oberkommando der Wehrmacht*, the High Command of the German Armed Forces. (See Volume II).

sent on sick-leave. On 21st January Cavallero proposed to Mussolini that General Messe should be appointed to command the 'German-Italian Panzer Army' and on the 25th Mussolini made this appointment, to take effect when this army reached the Mareth Line. Rommel, depressed and distressed by the tactical situation and the intrigues, asked the Italian command to send Messe to Tunisia at once because he himself could not carry on much longer for reasons of health. On the 28th Hitler intervened formally for the first time by directing that von Arnim's *Pz AOK 5* would be subordinate to *Comando Supremo*. Further he directed that there was to be a single German command in Tunisia to be held by von Arnim because Rommel had applied to go on sick-leave; von Arnim was to arrange his relations with *Comando Supremo*. On the same day Mussolini proposed that an Army Group Headquarters under von Arnim should be set up and that a new commander should be sent to the *Pz AOK 5*. OKW agreed but took no action. On the 30th Cavallero dissolved '*Superlibia*' and directed that the 'German-Italian Panzer Army' should be renamed First Army.[1] On 2nd February Messe, commander-designate of *AOK 1*, arrived at Rommel's H.Q. but refused to take up his appointment, probably because of the uncertain state of operations. Rommel, moreover, had now decided that he would not relinquish his command until ordered to do so. Ambrosio repeatedly pressed Kesselring to find a solution of the problem, but on 18th February *OKW* directed, on Hitler's instructions, that the system of command would not be reorganized until operations in progress had been successfully ended.[2] *OKW* also directed that when an Italian commander took over *AOK 1* his German Chief of Staff was not to be subordinate to him but to a German Commander-in-Chief and would control all German troops in *AOK 1*. On the 23rd February Ambrosio reported to Mussolini that he had, in agreement with Kesselring, decided that an Army Group command (Army Group Africa) should be formed at once in Tunisia, under Rommel who was to be superseded by von Arnim as soon as possible. The reluctant Messe had been ordered, on Rommel's demand, to take over *AOK 1* on the 20th.[3] Even now the tangle was not unravelled. Rommel left Tunisia on 9th March hoping to return after interviews with Mussolini and Hitler, but the latter ordered him to take the sick-leave which served to explain his departure. The Italians feared his return, but Rommel's two-year ascendancy in the African theatre was at an end.

General von Arnim assumed command of Army Group Africa

---

[1] The new title of the 'German-Italian Panzer Army' was Italian First Army. To the Germans: *Italian AOK 1*, in short: *AOK 1*.
[2] Operation '*Morgenluft*' which is described in Chapter XII.
[3] On this date the title 'German-Italian Panzer Army' lapsed.

and General von Vaerst took his place at the head of the *Pz AOK 5*. Colonel Fritz Bayerlein was appointed German Chief of Staff at *AOK 1*. Thus the chain of command in Tunisia at last became clear and satisfactory to the Germans. Both Kesselring and von Arnim continued to pay lip service to *Comando Supremo* while at the same time dealing direct with *OKW*. In the circumstances, it is not surprising that German-Italian relations grew no smoother.

The machinery of command on the British-American-French front in Tunisia was creaking although the Allied Chiefs on 18th January had decided to create an Army Group Headquarters. On 24th November 1942 a rough and ready arrangement had been made that the British should control French troops north of the line Le Kef—Kairouan and that the French should control British and American troops south of that line, but this was not a formal chain of command. On 17th December Giraud proposed to Eisenhower a single command in Tunisia and himself as commander, but the proposal was gently shelved. On 1st January 1943 Allied Force Headquarters took up its functions of command in Algeria and Tunisia, and the Eastern Task Force was abolished. But Eisenhower and A.F.H.Q., at Algiers, were too distant and too exalted to control day to day operations. Giraud refused to place French troops under British command, and the 2nd U.S. Corps was concentrating on 1st Army's southern flank, but not under its command. On 15th January Eisenhower opened a Command Post at Constantine where he was represented by a staff officer, Major-General Lucian K. Truscott—but this was simply a 'post-office'.[1] On 21st January Eisenhower decided that Anderson should co-ordinate British and United States forces in Tunisia but did not authorize him to move American formations about. As regards French forces, Anderson was to request Juin's co-operation. This arrangement merely forced Anderson to scour 'more than 1,000 miles of Tunisian roads in order to confer with independent commanders and guide them towards decisions conforming to a general plan of action.'[2] However the pressure of events, the absence of Giraud at Algiers, and co-operation between Anderson and Juin led Eisenhower to give Anderson a fresh directive on 26th January. The relevant passage ran:

> '. . . you are given command of all Allied forces on the Tunisian front, including, in addition to the troops presently assigned to

---

[1] General Anderson describes Truscott as 'a kind of resident deputy', and says of the Command Post 'This was admittedly far from a satisfactory solution. It broke down at the first test.'

[2] George F. Howe: *U.S. Army in World War II* (*Northwest Africa: Seizing the Initiative in the West*) (1957). page 384.

the First Army, the II Corps (U.S.), and a Composite Corps (French and U.S.). The Composite Corps will consist ultimately of the 34th Division (less detachments) and certain French elements now in the Ousseltia area, all under a French corps commander...'[1]

The decision of the Allied Chiefs of Staff on 20th January to reorganize the air forces in the Mediterranean area was implemented on 17th February when the Mediterranean Air Command came into being.[2] For the Allied air forces in North West Africa this introduced a major shuffle of all the British and American air staffs and formations to form integrated functional commands. Strategic bombers together with the American escort fighters were placed under the Northwest African Strategic Air Force commanded by Major-General H. Doolittle, U.S.A.A.F.; general reconnaissance aircraft and fighters for the protection of shipping, ports and rearward areas under the Northwest African Coastal Air Force commanded by Group Captain G. G. Barrett until relieved by Air Vice-Marshal Sir Hugh P. Lloyd; photographic reconnaissance aircraft under the Northwest African Photographic Reconnaissance Wing commanded by Colonel E. Roosevelt, U.S.A.A.F.; and aircraft maintenance and air training resources under two further sub-commands. On 17th February Air Marshal Sir Arthur Coningham (he had been promoted on the 8th) had taken over command from Brigadier-General L. S. Kuter of the Allied Air Support Command, which had been formed hastily on 22nd January to co-ordinate the activities of the American XII Air Support Command and No. 242 Group R.A.F. because of the critical situation on the ground.[3] On 18th February it became the Northwest African Tactical Air Force, and on the 23rd the Desert Air Force, which since 1st February had been commanded by Air Vice-Marshal H. Broadhurst, Coningham's successor, came under its operational control. On 22nd February Air Commodore K. B. B. Cross took over No. 242 Group from Air Commodore Lawson who was to

---

[1] General Giraud agreed to this directive before its issue.
[2] *Mediterranean Air Command*
 (Air Chief Marshal Sir Arthur Tedder):
 Middle East Air Command
 (Air Chief Marshal Sir Sholto Douglas)
 Malta Air Command (established 18th February. Formerly A.H.Q. Malta)
 (Air Vice-Marshal Sir Keith Park)
 Northwest African Air Forces (established 18th February)
 (Major-General Carl Spaatz, U.S.A.A.F.)
[3] The Allied Air Support Command began to function on 25th January. It should not be confused with 'Army Air Support Control' (ASC), a purely British organization for laying-on and controlling air support.

command another Group. On 1st March Air Commodore G. R. Beamish rejoined Coningham as his S.A.S.O.[1]

When, on 24th January, American fighter-bombers drove the enemy off their last air base in Tripolitania, at Zuara, all the German and Italian air formations in Africa became based in Tunisia, facing one front in the north and another in the south. On the northern front there were approximately 118 German and 40 Italian aircraft; on the southern front the numbers were approximately 180 German and 60 Italian. It was not long before the Axis air forces were also forced by the pressure of events to reorganize their commands, but unlike the Allies the German and Italian air forces remained independent of one another, except for interchange of operational control of air formations 'in particular circumstances'. On 11th February a new German Air Command, *Fliegerkorps Tunis*, which was directly subordinate to *Luftflotte 2*, was introduced with Tactical Headquarters at La Fauconnerie: General Seidemann was appointed A.O.C.-in-C. Subordinate to *Fliegerkorps Tunis* were: *Fliegerführer 2*, replacing *Fliegerführer Tunisia*, with Tactical Headquarters at Tunis—Colonel Benno Kosch in command; *Fliegerführer 3* replacing *Fliegerführer Afrika*, with Tactical Headquarters at Gabes—Colonel Walter Hagen in command.[2] On 6th January a new Italian Air Command, *Comando Aeronautica Tunisia* with headquarters at Tunis, had been formed with Brigadier-General G. Gaeta, who had commanded all Italian air units in Tunisia from the beginning of operations, in command. Under him three subordinate commands had been set up: *Settore Aeronautico*

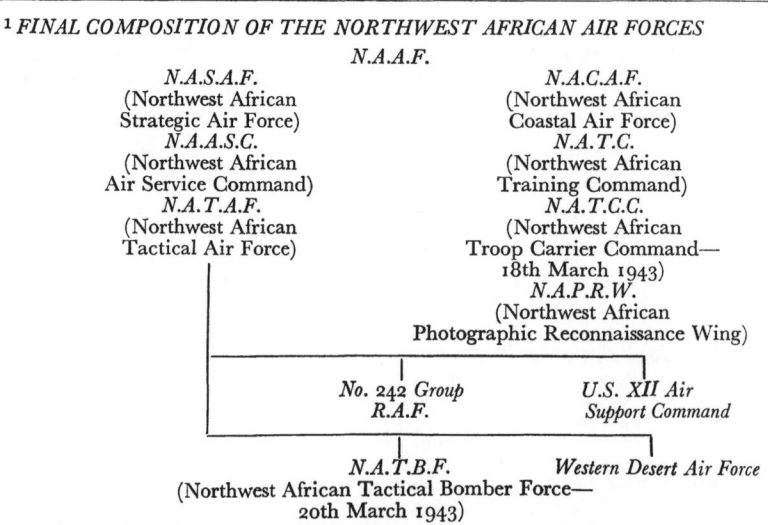

---

[1] *FINAL COMPOSITION OF THE NORTHWEST AFRICAN AIR FORCES*
N.A.A.F.

N.A.S.A.F. (Northwest African Strategic Air Force)	*N.A.C.A.F.* (Northwest African Coastal Air Force)
N.A.A.S.C. (Northwest African Air Service Command)	*N.A.T.C.* (Northwest African Training Command)
N.A.T.A.F. (Northwest African Tactical Air Force)	*N.A.T.C.C.* (Northwest African Troop Carrier Command—18th March 1943)
	N.A.P.R.W. (Northwest African Photographic Reconnaissance Wing)

No. 242 Group R.A.F.   *U.S. XII Air Support Command*

N.A.T.B.F. (Northwest African Tactical Bomber Force—20th March 1943)   *Western Desert Air Force*

[2] *Kommando Gabes* had been dissolved in late January and its units divided between the then existing *Fliegerführer Tunisia* and *Fliegerführer Afrika*.

Est—Colonel Carlo Drago in command; *Settore Aeronautico Ovest*—Brigadier-General Ruggero Bonomi in command; *Settore Aeronautico Centrale*—Colonel Augusto Bacchiani in command. Brigadier-General Gaeta was responsible to the Axis Armed Forces Command in Tunisia for operations. On the 15th February *Comando Aeronautica Tunisia* was absorbed by *5th Squadra*, formerly in the desert, which by then had its headquarters at El Hamma. General Mario Bernasconi, who had succeeded General Marchese as Commander of *5th Squadra* on 1st October 1942, continued in command. Under him two subordinate Commands were set up: *Settore Aeronautico Nord*, to operate north of the 34th parallel in co-operation with *Fliegerführer 2*—Colonel Augusto Bacchiani in command; *Settore Aeronautico Sud*, to operate south of the 34th parallel in co-operation with *Fliegerführer 3*—Colonel Carlo Drago in command. The original three subordinate commands were disbanded.

A short summary of the administrative situation of the opposing forces is appropriate at this point. To the Allies the stalemate in Tunisia at the end of December 1942 and the subsequent generally defensive policy gave a breathing space during which to build up the base and lines of communication, and reserves in the forward area. From 1st January 1943 A.F.H.Q. took control of general administration and relieved H.Q. 1st Army of many burdens. The sea convoys arrived at their regular intervals, equipment and stores accumulated at the ports, and the means of sending them forward steadily improved. The 1st Army received the new British Infantry tank, the Churchill (58 to a regiment). The Churchill with its good 6-pdr gun and excellent cross-country performance quickly earned the confidence of its crews. It was the only form of transport other than mules to get up certain difficult hills in the 'Longstop' area. Also in early February Sherman tanks—urgently diverted from the Middle East allotment—came forward to replace the Valentines and Crusaders of 6th Armoured Division. And by the middle of the month twenty-four of the new 17-pdr anti-tank guns had reached the front, as well as the first regiment of heavy artillery to go abroad since the B.E.F. had gone to France, the 56th Heavy Regiment R.A., equipped with sixteen 7·2-inch howitzers. The 1st Army Group Royal Artillery (three field and three medium regiments, and one heavy regiment) came into action in February on 19th Corps front; another important step had been taken in the British development of massed artillery fire.[1]

By contrast the Axis forces in Africa were dying administratively although until the end they rallied just sufficiently to meet each

---

[1] At Bardia in January 1942 and at El Alamein groups of medium artillery had been improvised. On 26th November the Army Group R.A. and its commander (C.A.G.R.A.) were officially sanctioned for the Royal Artillery.

crisis. Rommel, von Arnim, and also Warlimont who had been sent over to look into things, were convinced that whether Tunisia could be held depended on whether the volume of supplies could be increased beyond the needs of mere existence. They were pessimistic; Kesselring was optimistic. *Comando Supremo* carefully estimated what could be done, which was not enough. Mussolini temporized. Hitler, when he attended to the situation, grasped it at once, but by then no one could apply the remedies which were obvious to all: extra supplies and shipping and increased naval and air protection.

On the 8th January Rommel's and von Arnim's administrative officers had estimated that to supply all troops in Tunisia approximately 150,000 tons per month must be delivered. On the 12th Kesselring informed Hitler that 60,000 tons per month could be delivered, but he did not, it seems, compare this figure with demand, and neither did the *Führer*. The German policy was that the Russian front was to have first claim but that the present needs of the troops in Tunisia were not to suffer. By the 22nd von Arnim was complaining to Kesselring that the situation was catastrophic. Shortage of ammunition was a single symptom, and promises that ammunition was on the way were useless because 'The Army could not fight with shells which were at the bottom of the Mediterranean . . .' On 7th February Warlimont arrived in Tunisia and to him von Arnim reported that *Pz AOK 5* was unfit for large offensive operations because of want of ammunition, fuel and transport. He repeated that *Pz AOK 5* and *AOK 1* required for daily maintenance and reserves a guaranteed delivery of 150,000 tons per month for the next four months. On the 9th Rommel made similar points to Warlimont and repeated them to *Comando Supremo* adding that the defence of the Mareth Line depended upon shortages being made good. On the 12th Ambrosio said that to deliver 150,000 tons was impossible; *Comando Supremo's* estimate was a maximum of 80,000 tons per month to be sent, of which—after allowing for loss by enemy action—60,000 tons per month would actually arrive. These figures remained basic although minor variations were recorded in later discussions at all levels. During these it emerged that the minimum monthly requirement for both armies for subsistence alone was 70,000 tons. Here was the long-term dilemma recognized by all, except perhaps by Hitler who refused to pay serious attention until early in March when he reacted with fury. He bitterly reminded Rommel that he had promised that there would be no more crises once the Mareth Line had been reached, and Kesselring that he had promised that by the end of 1942 it would be possible to send over sufficient supplies to ensure success in the field. He accused his Navy and *Luftwaffe* of mismanagement and failure to co-operate.

Apart from supplies the long-term policy for reinforcements was

Map 27

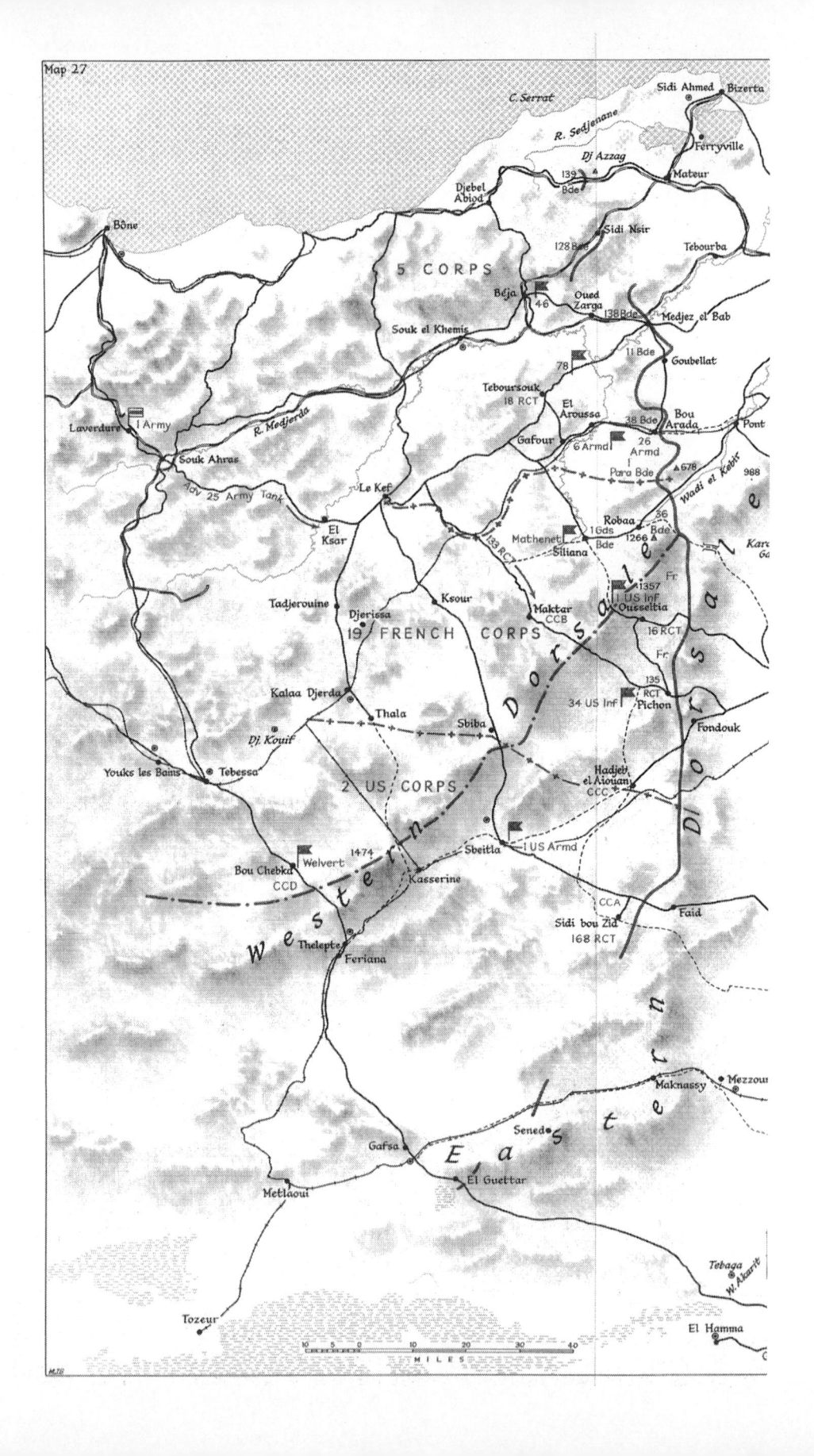

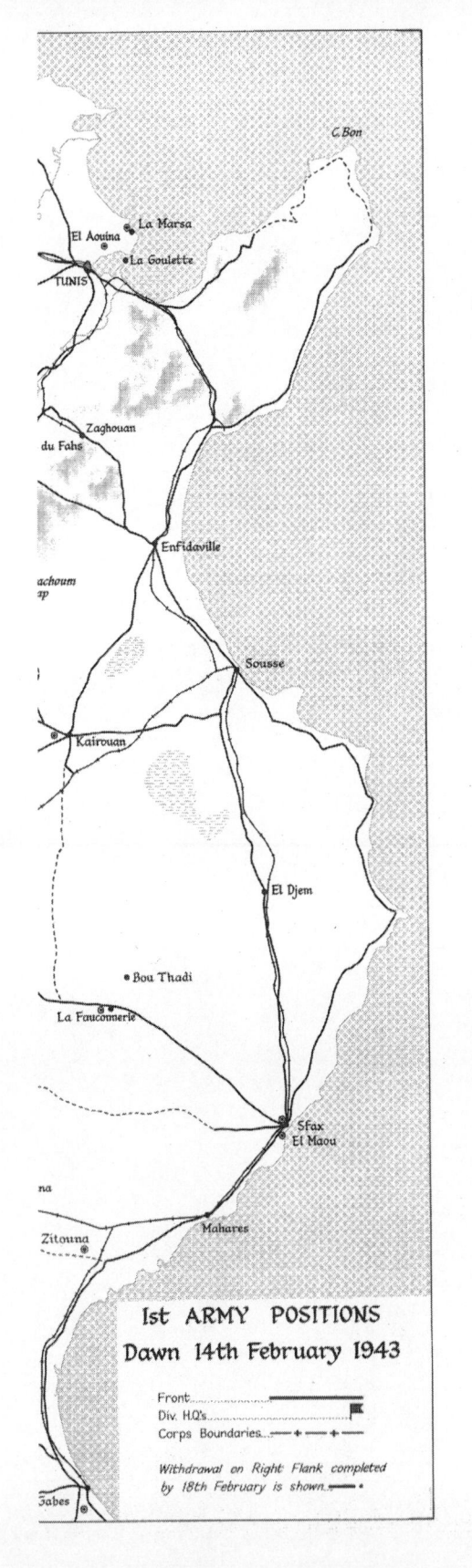

1st ARMY FRONT 14th FEBRUARY 1943
(Reading North to South)

5 Corps

    46 Div
        139 Bde
        128 Bde
        1 Commando
        Two French bns

    78 Div
        138 Bde (with French Group of five bns)
        11 Bde
        6 Commando

    6 Armd Div
        38 Bde
        26 Armd Bde (less 16/5 L)
        1 Para Bde (with three French bns)

Reserve: 18 RCT (less 2/18) about to rejoin 1 US Inf Div.

19 French Corps (As far as known)

    Mathenet Div
        36 Bde (with four French bns)
        Dets French Inf and Arty

    1 US Inf Div
        16 RCT
        French Group (five bns)

    34 US Inf Div (took over from Deligne Div as attack started)
        135 RCT
        133 RCT moving up

Army Reserve: 1 Gds Bde : 25 Army Tank Bde moving up
Corps Reserve: CCB

2 US Corps

    1 US Armd Div
        CCC
        CCA
        168 RCT (less 1/168)

    26 RCT (less 2/26)

    Welvert Div

Reserve: CCD

1st ARMY POSITIONS Dawn 14th February 1943

Front ....
Div. H.Q's ....
Corps Boundaries ....

Withdrawal on Right Flank completed by 18th February is shown

bleak. Early in January Kesselring rightly informed *OKW* that two more mobile formations at least were required by *Pz AOK 5* because to switch troops between von Arnim's and Rommel's armies was not practical. *OKW* replied that it could not send complete formations quickly. The only reinforcements available were 999 Africa Brigade and the Hermann Göring Division of which a part was already in Tunisia. In the event 999 Africa Brigade, which received divisional status in February, began to arrive in March. By the end of April about half its troops had reached Tunisia.[1] By then, two-thirds of the Hermann Göring Division and a few of its tanks were in Africa, but its commander remained in Europe. Other reinforcements consisted of 'Marsch' Battalions and drafts. The reasons why complete formations were not available were, shortly, the demands of the Russian front and the earmarking of formations which might have been sent to Tunisia for other tasks such as defence of the West Front and Italian islands, or for possible intervention in Spain. *Comando Supremo* sent no more complete Italian formations to Africa but kept up a fairly constant supply of drafts.

See Map 27

After the attempt to reach Tunis and Bizerta had failed in December 1942, General Eisenhower decided to hold his front as far east as possible. To withdraw some distance would make administration and air support easier, yet it was very important to prevent the enemy from increasing the depth of the defences, which the Allies must later pierce, by pushing his bridgehead into the mountains of western Tunisia or eastern Algeria. Moreover to withdraw would be taken by the French and the natives as a sign of weakness, and would hardly be tolerated in America and England. But Eisenhower wanted to do more than merely build up the 1st Army for, if that were all, the enemy would be left with the initiative on that army's weak southern flank. A plan was therefore made to launch the 2nd U.S. Corps at Sfax from the area of Tebessa in order to cut communications between the Axis armies and also the German-Italian Panzer Army's supply line. The drier weather of central Tunisia favoured the plan. The 23rd of January was fixed as starting-day, and motor transport was taken from work in the Tunisian ports and base area to collect supplies for maintenance (some 20,000 tons) at Tebessa. The

---

[1] 999 Africa Division was mainly recruited from those 'unworthy of military service' which meant broadly men of 42 years or less who had served or were serving long sentences of imprisonment but who were not habitual criminals. Officers and N.C.Os were hand-picked from the Army. 999 Africa Division was to consist of Africa Schützen Regiments 961, 962, 963; artillery regiment; signals, reconnaissance and engineer battalions, and an anti-tank company. This strangely composed formation was probably a symptom of growing shortage of man-power. Its troops fought well.

project and objections to it were discussed at Casablanca, and General Eisenhower dropped it because of the forecast of the 8th Army's advance which he there received. A real risk in the Sfax project was of defeat in detail. This risk would be slight if the project were to coincide with the 8th Army's attack at Mareth, and the chances of real gain vastly improved. But the 8th Army could not be ready to attack at Mareth before mid-February, if then. It was clearly undesirable to delay the Sfax project for so long—in view of the estimated rate of the enemy's reinforcement, to give but one reason. The British Chiefs of Staff believed (29th December) that the initiative was passing to the enemy and that 'far more intensive measures are necessary if the Germans are to be driven out of Tunisia, and if, indeed, we are to avoid defeat'. They believed that Eisenhower's immediate object should be to concentrate more forces east of Algiers and to plan for an earlier attack.[1] The measures which they had in mind were obvious: accumulation of greater reserves east of Algiers; rapid improvement of the maintenance system in the forward area by providing more road transport; an increase in transport aircraft (from the United States); and speeding up the building of airfields. They offered another armoured division from the U.K. but Eisenhower held this offer open and five weeks later asked for 'an old model infantry division' instead. The first need, in his eyes, was transport.

Meanwhile General Anderson, on 1st January, 1943, had ordered 5th Corps in the near future to keep the enemy fully occupied by constant pressure and limited attacks; to hold ground required for present defence and for jumping-off points for the future offensive; to reorganize, re-equip and train for this renewed attack on Tunis and Bizerta; to help the French as much as possible as far south as the Pont du Fahs sector. The enemy was thought to have not enough armour, artillery and motor-transport to mount a large attack.

The first of the limited attacks—by 36th Infantry Brigade—on the Djebel Azzag was a failure.[2] Evidence accumulated of offensive preparations by the enemy in the Pont du Fahs area. French troops under Generals Barré and Mathenet advanced through the 'Karachoum Gap' to help the expected (so far as was then known) American operations against Sfax. But small attacks by 6th Armoured Division on the 11th and 13th January to turn the enemy

---

[1] It is interesting that on 18th January Kesselring issued a directive to von Arnim in view of a possible American thrust to Sfax and Gabes. *Pz AOK 5* was to hold its ground and organize for further operations a mobile force consisting of 10th and 21st Panzer Divisions and the Hermann Göring Division. von Arnim paid small attention to the directive.

[2] 5th–7th January. 5th Buffs; 6th Commando; detachments of 3rd Parachute Battalion; successfully opposed by detachments of the Barenthin Regiment and Witzig's Parachute Engineer Battalion.

off a hill east of the road Bou Arada—Goubellat failed, the first one with heavy loss in the 6th Inniskilling Fusiliers. Something was in the wind and this we now know to be the German attack known as '*Eilbote*'.

Between the 27th December 1942 and 17th January 1943 (eve of '*Eilbote*') the total effort of the 'Torch' air forces was only moderate. The British fighters flew on average about 136 sorties daily, mainly on providing patrols over shipping, harbours and airfields, cover to troops and escorts to tactical reconnaissance aircraft and fighter-bombers. There were many encounters with German fighters, frequently when the latter were acting as escorts to fighter-bombers and Stuka dive-bombers, and the R.A.F. gave a good account of itself in spite of the great use that the enemy was making of his F.W. 190s. Attacks on ground targets were few because only two fighter-bomber squadrons were available and these had to provide the tactical reconnaissances as well.

The Bisleys, now confined to night bombing, were out on seven occasions, flying 53 sorties in all. Targets were mostly roads radiating from Tunis, but Sfax was visited once. The Beaufighters were on patrol every night, often in strength, and one Ju. 88 was destroyed and most likely two Italian bombers for the loss of two aircraft—a second Ju. 88 was brought down by A.A. fire in the Bône area.

The American fighters and day-bombers between them flew on average some 90 sorties daily, so far as is recorded. Marauders, Bostons and Mitchells took part in a widely dispersed series of attacks which included airfields at Tunis and Gabes, the ports at Sousse and Gabes, and railway track and junctions and other targets among which Kairouan was prominent. On 9th January Marauders joined the Fortresses in a series of attacks on Tripolitanian airfields, in co-operation with the Middle East air forces, by bombing the airfield at Castel Benito. On the 16th they supported the Middle East bombers' highly organized offensive against Tripoli harbour.

The German Air Force in Tunisia flew on average about 109 sorties daily, but the Italians appeared only to be operating single-engine fighters of which few were believed to be serviceable, and they were seldom seen.

The American Fortresses, operating by day, paid considerable attention to the Tunisian ports as did the British and American Liberators from the Middle East and Malta's Wellingtons. (See Chapters VIII and X). This was part of the continuous harrying of the Axis administrative machine by the Allied strategic bombers throughout the Mediterranean area. German records attest the cumulative though unspectacular results of the bombing which was gathering momentum by day and night. After the Fortresses' attacks they reported much damage on land at Gabes and also at Sfax where the power station was completely destroyed. At La Goulette heavy damage to civilian property was reported and at Ferryville a supply depot and W/T station were destroyed. Sousse railway station was also demolished. Sidi Ahmed airfield was attacked twice and Castel Benito (Tripoli) once, where a Ju. 52 and a fighter were destroyed. On 11th January twenty-three Fortresses attacked tactical targets, such as a bridge over the Wadi Akarit, roads and bridges on the approaches to the battle area, and a Libyan fort at Gadames in support of Le Clerc's column. In all these attacks the Fortresses flew an estimated 315 sorties.

By night, the Wellingtons of Nos. 142 and 150 Squadrons made their North African debut on 28th/29th December by bombing Bizerta docks. This was the first of a long series of raids on the port, and by mid-January ten had been flown (see Chapter X). The airfield at Sidi Ahmed was also attacked twice. During a total of 120 sorties four Wellingtons were lost.

Altogether, from the 27th December 1942 to 17th January 1943, and excluding operations against shipping, the British flew 3,160 sorties of all kinds and lost 38 aircraft. The Americans flew an estimated 3,200 or so (including 694 by their invaluable air transport aircraft) for the loss of 36, so far as is recorded. Forty-seven German aircraft were destroyed, but total Italian losses are unknown.

See also Map 28

On 2nd January Kesselring had set *Pz AOK 5* a wide range of tasks, namely: to discover whether the Allies were regrouping for a decisive attack in southern Tunisia; to ensure the defence of the Tunis—Bizerta bridgehead by capturing Medjez el Bab and the passes west and north-west of Kairouan; to reach Maknassy—El Guettar and later Sidi Bou Zid—Gafsa—Tozeur. Practical impediments soon appeared, namely shortage of reinforcements and of transport; the heavy rain which clogged movement with mud; and the air forces' commitments to protect sea convoys. Then came the French successes noticed above, against Superga Division's sector. von Arnim feared that if the Italians lost more ground, the Allies might thrust, north of Kairouan, to the coast between Enfidaville and Sousse, thereby cutting Rommel's L. of C. to Tunis and Bizerta. On the 14th he therefore ordered a limited attack to restore the situation, to begin on the 18th with code-name '*Eilbote*'. A battle-group of Weber's 334th Infantry Division was to advance as far as Robaa, and then turning east to attack in rear the enemy in the Djebel Belloute—Karachoum area. Simultaneously Battle Group

Map 28

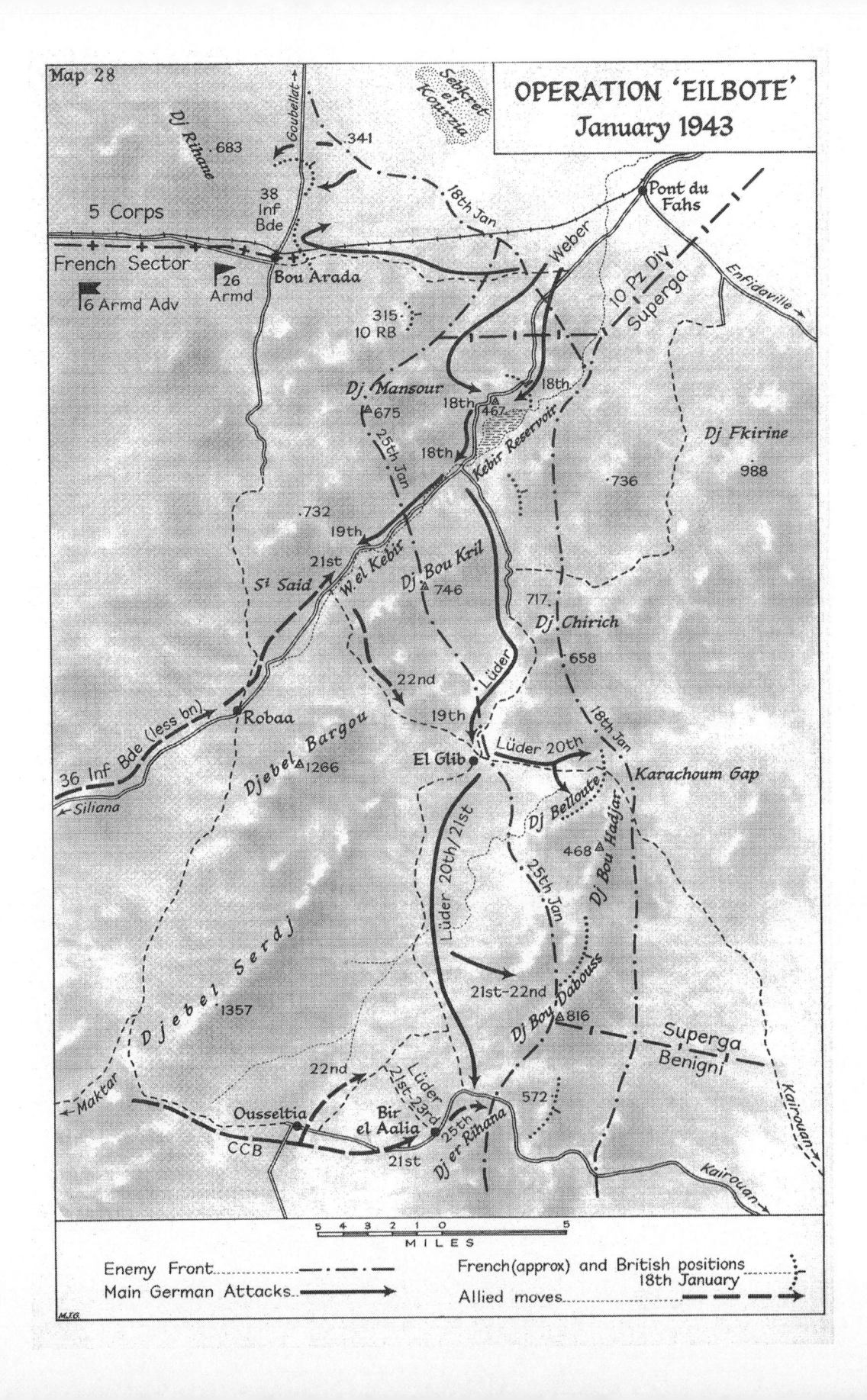

OPERATION 'EILBOTE'
January 1943

- Enemy Front —·—·—
- Main German Attacks ⟶
- French (approx) and British positions 18th January ·······
- Allied moves ╌╌╌▶

Mickley was to advance westwards between Djebel Mansour and El Glib. These operations were to be covered on the west by a holding attack by part of 10th Panzer Division in the area Bou Arada. Superga Division was to hold on and at a suitable moment attack to regain its lost positions.[1]

The German plans for '*Eilbote*' were hardly more ambitious than those of the Allies during the first half of January. Nor did the sense of urgency seem much more marked. And though resulting in gains for the enemy, the fighting which followed was equally uninspiring.

On the 18th, 10th Panzer Division's diversionary attacks towards Bou Arada were easily dealt with by 6th Armoured Division, and some anti-tank guns were sent south to Robaa to help the French. Weber and Lüder, however, pushing down the Wadi el Kebir, struck the junction of Barré's and Mathenet's troops near the Kebir Reservoir.[2] The French resisted well in spite of their scanty equipment but by the morning of the 19th the Germans were west of the reservoir and on the Djebel Mansour, while Stolz's groups had advanced almost to the Djebel Chirich. On the 19th Weber pressed on towards Robaa, and Lüder to clear the Karachoum Gap before moving south to the Kairouan—Ousseltia road. By the evening General Juin reported the situation to be serious and was asking for reinforcements. An American force from 1st Armoured Division (Combat Command 'B') under Brigadier-General Paul McD. Robinett moved from Sbeitla to Maktar and certain units of 5th Corps began to move southwards.[3] By the 21st Weber was still some miles from Robaa severely hampered by want of transport. Lüder on the other hand had advanced as far as the area of Bir el Aalia. The Allies decided to try to cut the German communications with Pont du Fahs, to attack northwards from Ousseltia with Combat

---

[1] (a) *Battle Group Weber*: H.Q. 334 Inf Div; 756 Mountain Regiment; II/Panzer Grenadier Regiment 69; Panzer Abteilung 501; two troops/334 Artillery Regiment; det. Flak Div. 20.
Battle Group Mickley: Marsch Battalion A.25; 3/Panzer Abteilung 190.
10th Panzer Division:
Battle Group Koch: 5 Parachute Regt; Marsch Battalion A.24; Infantry Gun Coy, Panzer Grenadier Regiment 69; 5½ Troops Artillery Regiment 90; 6/Flak Regiment 52.
Battle Group Burk: Three Coys Panzer Regiment 7; detachments Light Flak and Engineers.
(b) Battle Group Weber as above was sub-divided into: Weber Group: 756 Mountain Regiment (two battalions); Det. Panzer Abteilung 501 (4 Pzkw VI; 4 Pzkw III); two troops 334 Artillery Regiment; detachments engineers and flak.
Lüder Group: One Coy Panzer Abteilung 501 (5 Pzkw VI; 10 Pzkw III); II/Panzer Grenadier Regiment 69; detachments engineers and flak.
(c) Colonel Stolz commanded a mixed force of Germans and Italians which in the end included the Mickley Group and troops of the Superga Division.

[2] The French 19th Corps was not constituted until 3rd February. Its H.Q. (General Koeltz) opened at Djerissa on 9th February.

[3] Combat Command 'B' included 2nd/13th Armoured Regiment; 2nd/6th Armoured Infantry; 27th Field Artillery Battalion; 601st Tank Destroyer Battalion (less one company).

Command 'B' and to launch a further American attack near Fondouk. But the Allies had not yet a command able to make a quick counterstroke; and the Germans thought that '*Eilbote*' had done what was necessary, and moreover, *Pz AOK* 5 was undergoing a minor administrative crisis. During the night 23rd/24th January the German troops withdrew and settled down on their much improved sector running roughly from the Djebel Mansour—Djebel Bou Kril—Djebel Bou Dabousse—Djebel er Rihana.[1]

The German report on '*Eilbote*' records that the Allies had put up large numbers of aircraft throughout the operation and caused much damage to supply movements and M/T. This helps to interpret the statistics of British and American air activity. In opposing '*Eilbote*' between 18th January and dusk on the 24th, the British day fighters flew 1,066 sorties or a little better than 150 daily. As usual at this time the tasks were defensive patrols of all kinds, a few sweeps, cover to troops and escorts to fighter-bombers and Tac/R. Only the few available fighter-bombers were employed in direct support to the army, and altogether 65 sorties were flown against strong points, road bridges, troops and M/T and a fuel-laden train which was almost completely destroyed. The Bisleys, operating each night, paid most attention to roads in the Tunis, Tebourba, Pont du Fahs and Sousse areas and attacked the airfield at Kairouan once—79 sorties were flown in all. Meanwhile the Beaufighters patrolled ceaselessly, and in considerable strength. They destroyed two German and most likely two Italian bombers for the loss of one Beaufighter. Another German bomber was destroyed, probably by A.A., and two more recorded as lost might well have fallen to the guns.

The American fighters and tactical day-bombers between them flew an estimated 1,340 or so sorties, an average of about 190 daily. A variety of targets were attacked, including Medenine town, an airfield west of it, M/T in the same area and targets at Pont du Fahs. On the 21st support was given to General Koeltz's French counter-attack from Ousseltia. Next day Marauders and Mitchells joined the Fortresses in a successful attack on El Aouina airfield, which will be described later. The Fortresses also gave tactical support, attacking targets in the Djebel Djelloud area on the 19th and a camp and barracks at Gabes the following day.

In support of '*Eilbote*' the German Tunisian-based air force was

---

[1] The main gains claimed by the enemy from 18th to 24th January were:

	Weber Group	*10th Panzer Division*
P.O.W.	4,000	119
Tanks	9	15
Guns	46	6
Anti-tank guns	24	3
Vehicles	201	27
Aircraft	4	3

24. Before Mareth. A patrol of the Gordon Highlanders.

25. Wadi Akarit. Part of the battlefield. An anti-tank ditch in foreground. Tapes mark a gap swept clear of mines.

26. Tunisia. British Infantry tanks, Churchill.

27. Tunisia. Left, a German 'Tiger' tank (Pzkw VI); the first to be knocked out. On right, a damaged British Valentine.

28. British 17-pdr anti-tank gun.

29. Tunisia. Djebel Bargou area. 25-pdr gun in action.

30. Tunisia. Heidous area. British shells falling on ridge in middle distance

31. Medjez el Bab. Bridge over R. Medjerda. Royal Engineers at work on a ford.

ALLIED COUNTER-ATTACKS

employed mainly in the Bou Arada area, fighter-bombers and Stukas taking Allied concentrations, tanks, artillery positions and A.A. guns as their principal targets. On the 20th, however, some of the Stukas focused their attentions on countering an Allied attack in the Bou Arada area. Other targets attacked were at El Aroussa, Robaa and M/T at Hadjeb el Aioun. The total sorties flown amounted to 721, so far as is known, which means an average of 103 daily as against that of 109 for the previous three weeks. The German Army was displeased with the 'inadequate' support given by the *Luftwaffe*, but on the morning of the 21st General Seidemann had made it quite clear that more air support could only be made available if all the fighters covering the ports were withdrawn from that task. That this was a step to which the Army could not and dare not agree illustrates the dilemma facing the German forces in Tunisia. It was to have disastrous consequences, but not for some time yet.

Allied counter-attacks continued until the 28th without endangering the enemy's positions on the passes through the Eastern Dorsale. There were post-mortems on both sides. *Pz AOK 5* reported faults in training, equipment, and supplies. On the Allied side it appeared that the French 19th Corps, though it had fought well and earned German praise, was a very weak link in the chain because of its poor equipment. Yet French *amour propre* had to be studied, and therefore British and American reinforcements had to pass under French command in a French sector, thus creating a complicated organization. From the first General Anderson saw the difficulties of mingling British, American and French troops, but events persistently prevented him from creating 'national' sectors. Nor apparently could General Eisenhower, as C.-in-C., do anything to help this very desirable reorganization.[1] Meanwhile 1st Army's formal task became first to re-establish itself on the general line Bou Arada—Ousseltia—Fondouk; second to seize and hold the eastern exits of the passes through the Eastern Dorsale on the line Fondouk—Faid—Maknassy—El Guettar. General Anderson directed General Lloyd R. Fredendall (2nd U.S. Corps) to command ground troops of all nationalities south of the line Thala—Sbiba—Fondouk, and north of the line Tozeur—Gabes. The task of the 2nd U.S. Corps was to protect the right flank of the Allied Forces in Tunisia. Anderson hoped to withdraw most of the 19th Corps by stages to rearm. This measure caused Eisenhower (on 11th February) somewhat to alter 1st Army's instructions. These became: to protect the airfields at Souk el Khemis, Tebessa and Thelepte in order that the air forces might continuously operate from them; and to secure the defiles at Medjez el Bab and Bou Arada which would be needed when the offensive

---

[1] General Eisenhower's improvement of the chain of command on 26th January has been referred to on pages 270–71.

was renewed. Without prejudicing these main tasks, General Anderson was to take other defiles held by the enemy which would be advantageous to the Allied offensive, and to interfere with the enemy's L. of C. in the Tunisian coastal plain. General Eisenhower urged that the mobile striking forces in the south (i.e. 2nd U.S. Corps) should be held well concentrated. In his view (9th February) the build-up of the Allied force in Tunisia depended almost wholly on transport. He expected the enemy to make a series of limited attacks to gain ground which would protect his L. of C. in the coastal plain. He believed that the enemy recognized the French sector between Pichon and Gafsa as a soft spot and he had ordered Anderson to support it. He hoped to maintain the present position in Tunisia, but could not ignore the possibility of being forced back to the area Sbeitla—Feriana. The 1st U.S. Armoured Division was now mainly responsible (under 2nd U.S. Corps) for the southern flank of the Allied line, Combat Command 'A' being at Sbeitla, 'B' at Bou Chebka, and 'C' at Gafsa. Roughly, Anderson had set up three sectors:

North. British 5th Corps. To develop and defend its sector as a springboard for a future offensive against Tunis and Bizerta.

Centre. French Force (19th Corps designate). To form a firm central base, allowing for offensive operations on both flanks.

South. 2nd U.S. Corps. To protect the right flank of the Allied Forces in Tunisia.

This arrangement was tidier on paper than on the ground, but on 31st January General Eisenhower informed Anderson that the Casablanca Conference had decided to form 18th Army Group about 10th February. This new H.Q. was to plan future operations and meanwhile Anderson's main object was to press on with building up reserves.

On the 30th, 21st Panzer Division captured the Faid Pass from a small French garrison, and on 1st February 1st Army ordered 2nd U.S. Corps to regain this position. Next day however it was decided to suspend operations in this area in order to concentrate 1st Armoured Division to form a reserve of sorts. Between 3rd and 5th February troops of the 1st Guards Brigade and 1st Parachute Brigade tried without success to dislodge the enemy from Djebel Mansour and its neighbour feature overlooking the Kebir reservoir.[1]

---

[1] On the night 4th/5th February another method was tried for the first time by the British in this war, when a battery of 70th Field Regiment fired shell filled with propaganda leaflets on Djebel Azzag.

In the interval following the end of '*Eilbote*' until the Germans launched their next attack the Allied tactical air forces were fully occupied, despite the variable weather between the 6th and 13th February, and their activity increased still more as further units, particularly American, moved into the forward area. The British fighters continued to be employed on protective patrols of all kinds but there were several sweeps, mainly in the Mateur, Tebourba, Medjez el Bab and Pont du Fahs areas. Their daily average was about 170 sorties—an indication of at least some general improvement in the weather. A welcome event was the arrival towards the end of January of No. 243 Squadron at Souk el Khemis with its Spitfire IX aircraft. This was the only aircraft in operation at that time which could deal adequately with the German F.W. 190.[1] Fighter-bomber activity had again been very slight, less than an average of three sorties per day. The Bisleys, too, were rarely employed but mainly because of the moonless period during the first half of February when they were stood down. Despite the limited resources available tactical reconnaissance aircraft ranged over a large area of Northern Tunisia, and P.R.U. aircraft were operating on most days mainly on strategic tasks. Meanwhile the night-flying Beaufighters carried on their nightly patrols, most probably destroying three Italian bombers. Two German bombers were brought down by the A.A. guns.

The American fighters and tactical day-bombers were also more active. It was noticcable that their fighters took more and more to ground strafing. The day-bombers attacked targets, including tanks and M/T, principally at Bou Thadi and in the area east of Maknassy, and also airfields at Sfax and Gabes. Together with the fighters they vigorously opposed 21st Panzer Division's attack on Faid on the 30th January and the following day flew offensive patrols in support of U.S. troops attacking Maknassy. In countering the *Luftwaffe's* attacks on their troops the American fighter casualties were heavy, eleven for example being lost on the 2nd February and nine on the 4th.

Principal targets for the German fighter-bombers were M/T concentrations, gun positions, ports and airfields. The Stukas confined themselves mainly to gun positions, though on a very small scale. During the fighting in the Robaa area the fighters strafed tanks and M/T, otherwise they appear to have been employed mainly on defensive tasks. The Germans recorded that the standard of army/air co-operation had much improved since '*Eilbote*' and Kesselring, writing later, that 'The German airmen still ruled supreme'. But the facts reveal a different picture. Their air losses, which they could ill

---

[1] A number of Spitfire IXs had been lying idle at Gibraltar since December 1942, and their tardy release by the Air Ministry had unnecessarily prolonged the advantage the *Luftwaffe* in North West Africa enjoyed with its F.W. 190s.

afford, had continued to mount and their daily rate of effort to show little improvement. It would be truer to say that the balance was in fact tipping more sharply in the air than on the ground in favour of the Allies.

On the 30th January action was taken to forestall one of the problems which was bound to arise as the 8th Army and the Desert Air Force approached Medenine. A.F.H.Q. signalled 8th Army of the urgent need for E.A.C. and the U.S. Twelfth Air Force to be told of the boundary east and south beyond which they must not engage targets without positive identification. This was a temporary measure until tactical air force boundaries could be properly established.

Since mid-January the Allied strategic air forces in the Mediterranean had been devoting most of their attentions to ports, the Middle East concentrating mainly on Sicily and Italy, and Malta and the 'Torch' air forces on Tunisia (see Chapter X). But the American Fortresses also carried out daylight attacks on airfields. Castel Benito (Tripoli) received one visit, and in an attack on El Aouina on 22nd January, in which 40 Fortresses accompanied by 30 Marauders and Mitchells took part, 31 German aircraft were destroyed and many casualties caused among military and civilian personnel. Another successful attack was against Elmas (Sardinia) where six German bombers were destroyed. On 19th January the Fortresses were called upon to attack an important rail junction on the outskirts of Tunis. By night the Wellingtons also attacked airfields, one visit being made to Sidi Ahmed and three to Elmas where a total of six German bombers were destroyed and several Italian aircraft set on fire. The main landing ground at Medenine was also raided.

In all these operations between 18th January and 13th February, including air support in opposing *Eilbote* but omitting air action against shipping, the British in North West Africa flew close on 5,000 sorties and the Americans an estimated 6,250 or so. The loss of 34 British aircraft was modest, but that of 85 American and 100 German particularly heavy. Italian losses are unknown.

In February the main preoccupation of 1st Army became the arrival of reinforcements, the accumulation of reserves and the organization of a cohesive front. By midnight on 13th/14th February some progress had been made. Between the coast and roughly Bou Arada the 5th British Corps had in the line from north to south, 46th Division, most of 78th Division, and 6th Armoured Division.[1] Then from Bou Arada to Hadjeb el Aioun came the French sector of 19th Corps holding, piecemeal, the Mathenet Division, 36th British

---

[1] General Anderson's most urgent reorganization was to try to draw 6th Armoured Division into a much needed Army Reserve and to exchange its Valentines for Shermans. By 11th February one regiment, 16th/5th Lancers, was beginning this change.

Infantry Brigade (78th Division), Combat Command 'B' (1st U.S. Armoured Division) and part of 34th U.S. Infantry Division. South of the French sector an enormous area was the responsibility of 2nd U.S. Corps—in fact of 1st U.S. Armoured Division less one Combat Command. General Anderson however had directed the Americans not to try to hold Gafsa against a heavy attack. The whole front was a sprawl produced by circumstances, and H.Q. 1st Army at Laverdure in the north was badly placed to control it, mainly because its Signals had never been intended to cover so great an area held by troops of three nations.

Such were the conditions in 1st Army when the enemy launched the series of heavy attacks described in the next chapter. And it is against this background, particularly as it affected 2nd U.S. Corps, that the fighting should be judged.

Map 29

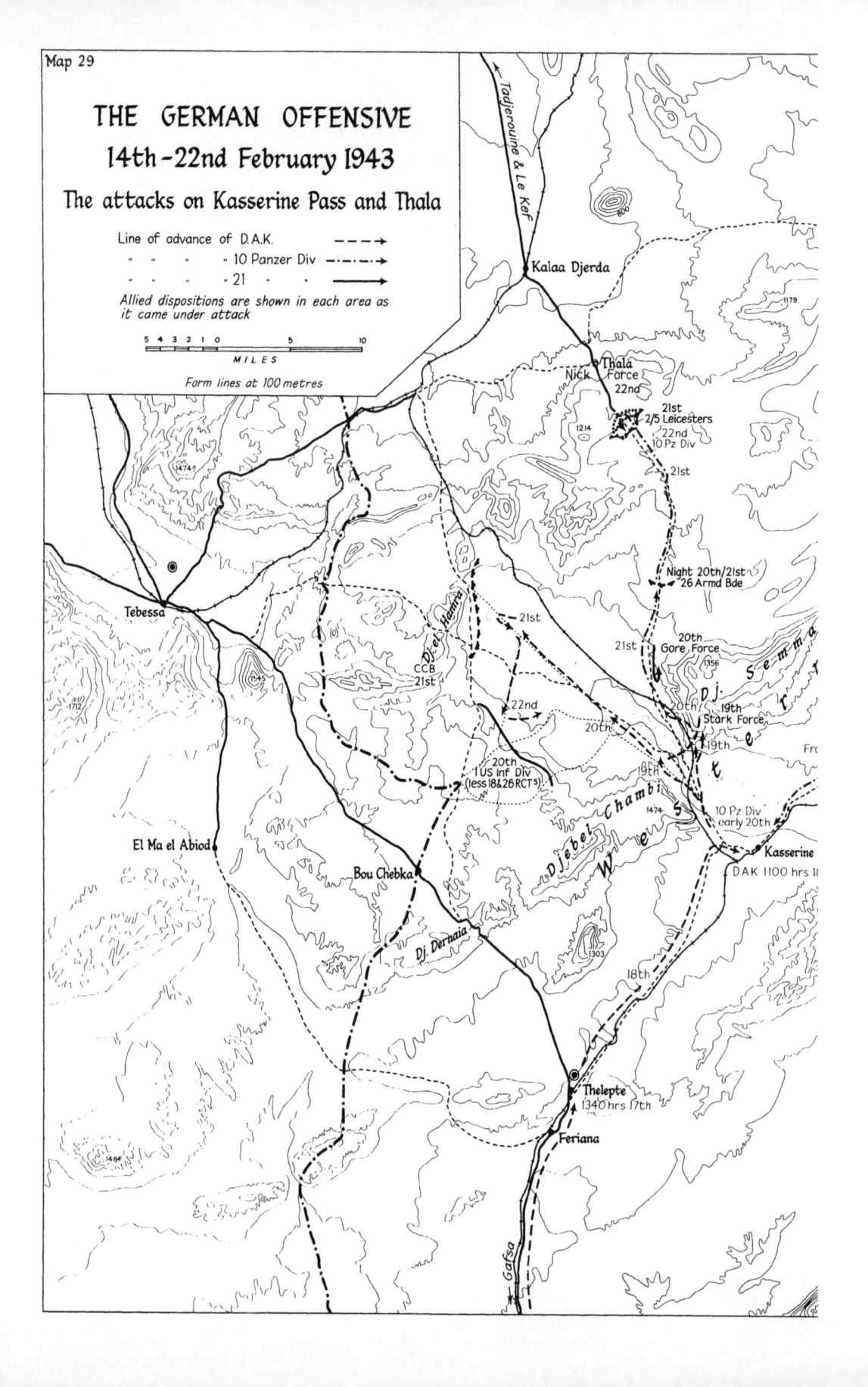

THE GERMAN OFFENSIVE
14th–22nd February 1943
The attacks on Kasserine Pass and Thala

Line of advance of D.A.K. ------>
" " " 10 Panzer Div -·-·->
" " " 21 ———>

Allied dispositions are shown in each area as it came under attack

5 4 3 2 1 0 5 10
MILES

Form lines at 100 metres

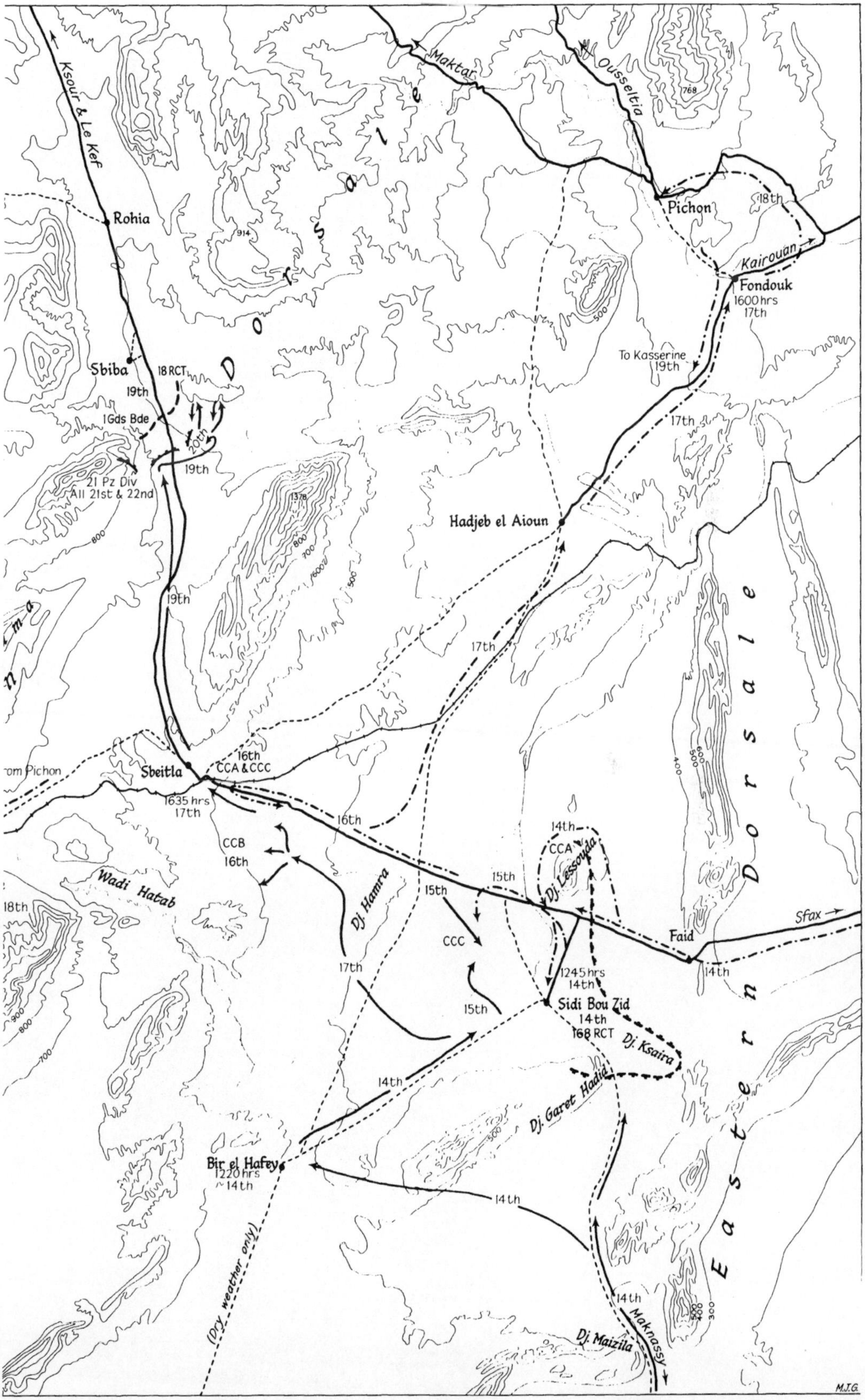

Ksour & Le Kef
Maktar
Ousseltia
768
Dorsale
Rohia
914
Pichon
18th
Kairouan
Fondouk
1600 hrs
17th
500
To Kasserine
19th
Sbiba
18 RCT
19th
1 Gds Bde
20th
19th
21 Pz Div
All 21st & 22nd
1378
800
700
600
500
17th
Hadjeb el Aioun
19th
17th
Eastern Dorsale
From Pichon
Sbeitla
16th
CCA & CCC
1635 hrs
17th
16th
CCB
16th
Wadi Hatab
18th
Dj. Hamra
15th
15th
CCC
17th
15th
14th
CCA
Dj. Lessouda
15th
Faid
Sfax
14th
1245 hrs
14th
Sidi Bou Zid
14th
168 RCT
Dj. Ksaira
14th
Dj. Garet Hadid
Bir el Hafey
1220 hrs
14th
14th
(Dry weather only)
14th
Maknassy
Dj. Maizila
M.J.G.

CHAPTER XII

THE FIGHTING IN TUNISIA IN FEBRUARY 1943: SIDI BOU ZID AND KASSERINE

See Maps 27 and 29

AT the end of January and during the first fortnight of February there were marked divisions and uncertainties in the Axis Command. By the beginning of February most of Rommel's German-Italian Panzer Army was back in the Mareth Line, and the boundary between it and von Arnim's *Pz AOK 5* was an east-west line just north of Gabes.[1] Since 24th January von Arnim had been planning an attack in the Faid area to forestall any American advance towards Sfax or Gabes. On the 25th Kesselring told von Arnim that the zone Mareth—Gabes was decisive for defence and that Rommel's army must be protected while refitting there; von Arnim's first task therefore was to create a mobile force to operate south or west from Mareth. On 28th January *Comando Supremo* issued its first directive to von Arnim. His main task was to advance his army's left wing to areas more favourable for defence against expected Allied attack. He was to prepare to destroy the American forces at Tebessa as a sequel to his attack in the Faid area; later the 'Gafsa basin' was to be seized. *Comando Supremo* informed him that two armoured divisions would be required for the operations. von Arnim replied curtly that the Faid operation was in train; two armoured divisions were not enough to attack Tebessa and were not available because 10th Panzer Division was required in his northern sector, and 21st Panzer Division was not yet fit for operations.

On the 3rd February Rommel told *Comando Supremo* that a fortnight's lull might be expected at Mareth. But he expected the Allies to strike strongly from Gafsa towards the coast. The best, if risky, counter was a spoiling attack by a group from *Pz AOK 5* and one from the German-Italian Panzer Army under a single commander. von Arnim should provide the mobile troops (i.e. from 10th and 21st Panzer Divisions) because he (Rommel) could not spare 15th

---

[1] On the 12th February the German-Italian Panzer Army's boundary was fixed to include Gafsa—Sened—Sfax.

Panzer Division. On 5th February Ambrosio told both Army Commanders that there was a favourable opportunity to attack the Allied flank from El Guettar provided that Mareth was not denuded. Nothing happened immediately, however, because Rommel and von Arnim were each determined to hang on to his own mobile formations. On the 8th Ambrosio tried again. Most of the mobile troops of both armies were to be collected for a stroke through Gafsa and north of it to gain space for manoeuvre and to hit the Americans before they were ready. Successive objectives were to be the 'Gafsa basin', the American troops in open country, and the hills west of Gafsa. Rommel was to command and the force was to include part of 10th Panzer Division, and other formations of *Pz AOK 5* near the proposed scene of operations, 15th Panzer Division (Rommel's), and mobile units of both armies which were not indispensable elsewhere. Rommel refused 15th Panzer Division but promised a small battle group.[1] On the 9th Kesselring met Rommel, von Arnim, and Messe who told him that the enemy was leaving Gafsa and that Ambrosio's plan was out of date.[2] It was decided that von Arnim should attack in the Sidi Bou Zid area between 12th–14th February. After this 21st Panzer Division, but not the 10th, would be available for the Gafsa operation.

On 11th February *Comando Supremo* issued another directive to Rommel. The Americans, it said, had probably given up the idea of a thrust to the coast, and had withdrawn to the area Sbeitla-Tebessa. Rommel was to follow von Arnim's attack at Sidi Bou Zid by an encircling attack on Gafsa and an advance to Tozeur. Rommel agreed half-heartedly, pointing out that he doubted whether he could hold both Gafsa and Tozeur because his mobile troops could not remain in these places since they would soon be required at Mareth. He was sure that he would be strongly opposed at Gafsa and again asked von Arnim for 10th Panzer Division. von Arnim

---

[1] This was the origin of the *D.A.K.* Assault Group which appears often in the following pages.
The succession of G.O.Cs of *D.A.K.* and of Commanders of *D.A.K.* Assault Group is somewhat confusing. The main figures were:

G.O.C. *D.A.K.*	*Commander D.A.K. Assault Group*
General Gustav Fehn, wounded 14th January.	—
Major-General Freiherr Kurt von Liebenstein (acting).	Who also commanded the above group from 14th February until wounded on 17th.
General Hans Cramer appointed 13th February, but assumed command 5th March.	Major-General Buelowius from 17th–25th February.
Lieut.-General Heinz Ziegler (acting) from 23rd February–3rd March.	Appointment lapsed.

[2] In fact on the 5th Anderson had ordered that Gafsa was not to be held against a heavy attack, in deference apparently to Fredendall's report of 28th January that he was only just strong enough to hold on.

refused because he wanted the division for his own operation, now fixed to begin on the 14th and named '*Frühlingswind*'.

von Arnim intended to push through Faid to Sidi Bou Zid to complete his hold on the Eastern Dorsale. If he succeeded in destroying the American forces west of Faid—his first objective—he hoped to drive further, northwards to Pichon. Rommel's plan was to strike at Gafsa—Tozeur, destroying the American 2nd Corps (operation '*Morgenluft*'), and possibly to exploit to Tebessa. He would use D.A.K. Assault Group and a yet unspecified force from *Pz AOK 5*. von Arnim was to move first and as soon as he had cleared the Faid area was (in theory) to send 21st Panzer Division to Rommel. But in the outcome the Axis' plans were badly concerted and the commanders helped each other very little. Their forces' present administrative needs could be supplied but there were no reserves.[1]

On 13th February the last of Rommel's army entered Tunisia and the campaign in Libya ended. On the same day, though the front of 2nd U.S. Corps was quiet, air reconnaissance observed enemy transport moving east and south from Faid and east from Maknassy. The Intelligence Staffs at A.F.H.Q. and 1st Army at this time believed the enemy to be over-stretched, that he would improve his defensive positions, and at present husband his few mobile reserves. The Intelligence Officer of 2nd U.S. Corps however gave warning of a stiff attack on Gafsa with a strong diversion in the areas of Pichon or Pont du Fahs. Air Intelligence held much the same view. On the 13th Anderson visited Fredendall, repeated that Gafsa was not to be held against a major attack and directed that the main defence line was to be on the hills east and west of Feriana.[2] General Eisenhower met Anderson the same day and judged that his dispositions were 'as good as could be made pending the development of an actual attack and in view of the great value of holding the forward regions, if it could possibly be done.'

Lieut.-General Lloyd R. Fredendall, Commander of the American 2nd Corps, could in fact dispose of not more than the slightly reinforced U.S. 1st Armoured Division under Major-General Orlando Ward to meet an attack. Its Combat Command 'B' which included 110 medium tanks and 69 guns was near Maktar and subject to some strings attached to its use by 1st Army. South of it was Combat

---

[1] A report exists dated 13th February. The troops and reserve stocks held between $1\frac{1}{2}$–2 issues of ammunition. Fuel amounted to $3\frac{1}{2}$ consumption units. Transport was in bad shape—30% usually off the road and spares scarce. Field and anti-tank guns and ordnance spares were fewer than requirements.

[2] With General Anderson was Major-General McCreery, C.O.S. of 18th Army Group H.Q. then forming. Up-to-date information of the 1st Army's situation was therefore available to General Alexander—a point of interest when General Alexander's impressions on taking command of 18th Army Group are described.

Command 'C', and south of this again Combat Command 'A' and 168th Regimental Combat Team (of 34th Infantry Division). The last two formations were destined to meet the first onslaught launched at Sidi Bou Zid. Combat Command 'A's (Brigadier-General Raymond E. McQuillin) dispositions in the Sidi Bou Zid area were somewhat scattered. North of the village the Djebel Lessouda was held by 'Lessouda Force' (Lieutenant-Colonel John K. Waters).[1] East of the village, on Djebel Ksaira and Djebel Garet Hadid, was most of 168th Regimental Combat Team (Colonel Thomas D. Drake). Near the village was 3rd Battalion 1st Armoured Regiment (some forty medium tanks) and the remainder of the Combat Command.

General Ziegler (von Arnim's Chief of Staff) went south to take command of 10th and 21st Panzer Divisions for the attack. The 10th Panzer Division was in three battle-groups: Reimann, Gerhardt and Lang.[2] Reimann was to lead straight along the road from Faid towards Sbeitla. Gerhardt was to follow, swing north round Djebel Lessouda, and then cut the Faid-Sbeitla road well to the west. 21st Panzer Division was in two battle-groups: Schütte and Stenckhoff.[3] Schütte was to take and secure the Maizila Pass (twenty miles south of Sidi Bou Zid) then detach his battalion of tanks to Stenckhoff, and turn north with the remainder of his group to Sidi Bou Zid. Stenckhoff was to move west from the Maizila Pass twenty-five miles to Bir el Hafey, and thence turn north-east and drive on Sidi Bou Zid from the rear. The plan therefore comprised one direct attack and three flank approaches.

The exact strength of 10th Panzer Division is not known. Probably besides 5 heavy Pzkw VI under command, they held over 50 medium tanks (Pzkw IIIs and IV Specials); for anti-tank work they held the S.P. 7.62-cm Pak 36 and the 7·5-cm Pak 40—excellent guns. The best equipped of the German formations was 21st Panzer Division with 64 Pzkw III and 21 Pzkw IV Specials; eight 8·8-cm Flak 36 and, 'for ground operations', 13 of the powerful new 8·8-cm Flak 41. The weakest group was *D.A.K.* with 16 Pzkw III and 10 Pzkw IV

---

[1] 2nd Bn 168th Infantry; G and Recce Coys 1st Armd Regiment; B Bty 91st Field Artillery; one platoon 701st Tank Destroyer Battalion. The infantry held the hill, the tanks and artillery were below in the plain.

[2] Reimann: II/Panzer Grenadier Regiment 86; one Company Pz. Abt. 501 (Tiger tanks); 1/Pz. Jäg. Abt. 90 (anti-tank); one Troop assault guns; detachments of Engineers and Flak.

Gerhardt: I/Pz. Regiment 7; II/Panzer Grenadier Regiment 69; 3/Pz. Jäg. Abt. 90; Detachment Light Howitzers and Engineers.

Lang (Reserve): Motorcycle Bn 10; Panzer Engineer Bn 49 (less one company); one Platoon Pz. Jäg. Abt. 90; Detachment of Flak.

[3] Schütte: IV/Panzer Grenadier Regiment 104 (less detachments); I/Panzer Regiment 5; I/Artillery Regiment 155; an Anti-Tank Company; a Section of 8.8-cm Flak. Stenckhoff: II/Panzer Regiment 5; I and III/Panzer Grenadier Regiment 104; II/Artillery Regiment 155; Detachments Heavy and Light Flak.

Specials and 23 outdated Italian tanks of the Centauro Division; eight 7·5-cm Pak 40 were backed by about fifteen 8·8-cm Flak. An interesting forecast of things to come, however, was their troop of 15-cm Nebelwerfer (rocket projectors) which were going into action for the first time in the Mediterranean theatre. Rommel was to be delighted with their performance and signalled urgently for more. He had an eye for a new weapon and tried hard to wrest control of the re-equipped 21st Panzer Division and the 'Tiger' Abt. 501 from von Arnim—who as steadily resisted![1] None of the formations had much artillery and ammunition.

The German plan worked smoothly. By 6 a.m. on the 14th Reimann's infantry were five miles west of the Faid Pass. He, and Gerhardt circling Djebel Lessouda, were opposed mainly by Waters' tanks, for a failure in American communications had spoiled the prepared artillery fire plan. The German Air Force attacked the Sidi Bou Zid area in strength at 7.15 a.m., and sent in its dive-bombers and fighter-bombers against troop targets on several later occasions. A reinforcement of two companies of 1st Armoured Regiment and some anti-tank guns could not prevent Reimann and Gerhardt uniting north of Sidi Bou Zid by about 10 a.m. Schütte's tanks, from the Maizila Pass, were delayed by soft sand and Ziegler ordered 10th Panzer Division to attack Sidi Bou Zid from the north-east. The American tanks and artillery were driven back south-west and west. Stenckhoff's battle-group came up during the afternoon and harassed the American mobile troops. By 5 p.m. Stenckhoff and 10th Panzer Division had made contact. Combat Command 'A' had been driven west to Djebel Hamra with a loss of 44 tanks and many guns.[2] The infantry of Lessouda Force and 168th Regimental Combat Team were marooned on Djebel Lessouda, Djebel Ksaira and Djebel Garet Hadid.

The opposing tactical air forces had hurled all they had into the battle, the American effort rising to 391 sorties and the German to 360–375, though with negligible losses on either side. While the American bombers had attempted to stem the main enemy advance by attacking tanks in the Faid Pass, their fighters had been unable to prevent the German dive-bombers and fighter-bombers causing considerable damage among the American army units. German Tac/R appears to have been very alert, taking back valuable information of American army movements.

When he heard that '*Frühlingswind*' was going well Rommel ordered the *D.A.K.* Assault Group to prepare to attack Gafsa on the 15th. Ziegler was at this stage ready to send 21st Panzer Division to support

---

[1] Further discussion of equipment will be found in Appendix 9.
[2] 10th Panzer Division claimed 40 tanks, 15 field-guns, and one anti-tank gun, and a number of prisoners.

this attack. In fact American and French troops left Gafsa for Feriana during the night 14th/15th February in obedience to 1st Army's orders. General Ward was planning to counter-attack Sidi Bou Zid on 15th February and ordered up Combat Command 'C' (Colonel Robert I. Stack) from Hadjeb el Aioun and 2nd/1st Armoured Regiment (of Brigadier-General Robinett's Combat Command 'B'). He could not form a stronger force because 1st Army would not yet release all Combat Command 'B' from Maktar.

Combat Command 'C's counter-attack was an attempt to push straight through from Djebel Hamra to Sidi Bou Zid—about thirteen miles over flat country, cut by a number of wadis. The troops were bombed and strafed early in the advance, suffering some casualties to guns, and later found themselves within the jaws of a pincer attack launched by 10th and 21st Panzer Divisions. The Americans began a hurried withdrawal, but out of the battalion of tanks which had headed the advance (and now brought up the rear) only four managed to escape the gauntlet of anti-tank fire. The remainder of Combat Command 'C' just escaped to Djebel Hamra.[1]

Combat Command 'A's infantry therefore remained isolated, and were ordered to withdraw during the night 16th/17th February. A number from Djebel Lessouda succeeded, but those from Djebel Ksaira and Djebel Garet Hadid were hunted down on the plain and some 1,400 were captured. The battle at Sidi Bou Zid had indeed been unfortunate for 1st Armoured Division.

The pace set by the opposing tactical air forces the previous day could not be maintained, but both were very active throughout the 16th. The American fighters concentrated on patrolling and strafing in the Sidi Bou Zid area, while some of the Mitchells and Marauders made two attacks on the busy German airfield at Kairouan destroying at least five F.W. 190s, four of them on the ground. Altogether the Germans lost six fighters and a Stuka and the Americans two fighters and a bomber in these operations.

Meanwhile there were important shifts of policy on both sides. On the 15th Anderson concluded that his whole force was in danger of being outflanked from the south. An evident counter-measure was to concentrate a force, strong in armour, in the area Sbiba–Sbeitla. But Anderson had not this force, and he therefore decided on the 15th to withdraw completely from the Eastern Dorsale to the general line of the Western Dorsale as far south as Feriana. General Eisenhower approved, and Anderson gave the order at 10.40 a.m. on the 16th. 2nd Corps was told to counter-attack no more but to hold the areas Feriana, Kasserine, and Sbeitla. General Anderson's decision

---

[1] 1st Armoured Division reported the loss of 46 medium tanks (2nd/1st Armoured Regiment), 130 vehicles and 9 S.P. guns.

set going many complicated troop movements but the general pattern was a shift southward, ending at Sbiba, of 1st Army units to cover the westward withdrawal of the French and Americans.

The enemy acted raggedly. Rommel's troops entered Gafsa on the evening of the 15th and reconnaissance detachments went towards Feriana. Ziegler did not send 21st Panzer Division south because he and von Arnim saw no need since Gafsa had been captured, and moreover the division was still engaged near Sidi Bou Zid. They decided to mop up this area on the 16th and move on Sbeitla on the 17th. Rommel appeared to waver. He told *D.A.K.* Assault Group, on the morning of the 16th, that he could advance to Feriana only if 10th and 21st Panzer Divisions attacked Sbeitla and Kasserine; and also that he might have to send a strong detachment of the Group back to Mareth to reinforce his rearguard there. However von Arnim's and Ziegler's intention to move on Sbeitla decided him and by the end of the 16th he ordered *D.A.K.* Assault Group to strike at Feriana on the 17th but not to engage in heavy fighting. *Comando Supremo* during the night of the 16th/17th directed von Arnim to exploit the success at Sidi Bou Zid in any way that supplies and the need to keep a mobile reserve permitted. Rommel was to consolidate the line Gafsa–Metlaoui–Tozeur. von Arnim replied that 21st Panzer Division would secure Sbeitla, and that 10th Panzer Division would attack towards Fondouk: all that the administrative situation allowed. von Arnim's orders to Ziegler were to strike a quick, powerful blow at Sbeitla to destroy allied supply dumps and then to turn north against Fondouk. In this area, on the night of 15th/16th, the R.A.F. Bisleys began operating again by bombing a bridge.

On the 15th 1st Army released Combat Command 'B' which moved to Sbeitla late on the 16th. Combat Commands 'A' and 'C' were covering Sbeitla on the line of Djebel Hamra but were preparing to withdraw. In the afternoon of the 16th Group Gerhardt and Group Pfeiffer (21st Panzer Division) advanced and, though checked for a time, closely followed the American rearguards.[1] These groups reached Sbeitla in the darkness and scattered part of Combat Command 'C' but the situation of the Americans improved when the German force was ordered to stand fast until daylight on the 17th, and 10th Panzer Division was sent on a wild-goose chase to Hadjeb el Aioun and Pichon to catch Allied forces who were already safely on their way to the Western Dorsale. The German tactical air effort was about the same as on the day before, but their Tac/R appears to have suffered from the spirited defence of the American fighters. Combat Command 'A' most probably bore the brunt of the Stuka

---

[1] Group Pfeiffer comprised a battalion of tanks; a battalion of infantry; and two troops of light artillery. It was temporarily under command of 10th Panzer Division.

attacks and U.S. XII Air Support Command did what it could to give fighter cover. The American bombers, in support of their hard-pressed troops, attacked M.T., tanks and gun positions over a wide area silencing some howitzers near Sidi Bou Zid, and bombing enemy concentrations north-west of Gafsa. Airacobras were used to strafe targets in the general Kairouan—Sidi Bou Zid—Gafsa area. Each side lost one aircraft. That night the weather prevented the R.A.F. Bisleys from supporting the Americans in the central sector.

Early on the 17th Anderson permitted Fredendall to withdraw from Feriana and Sbeitla, although Combat Command 'B' was not to quit Sbeitla until particularly ordered. The remains of Combat Command 'A' began to leave at about 11.30 a.m., and were dive-bombed soon afterwards. At noon 21st Panzer Division again attacked Sbeitla and at 1.30 p.m. Fredendall ordered Combat Commands 'B' and 'C' to withdraw. They disengaged by 5.30 p.m., and the enemy did not follow, though their air force had inflicted damage on the American 1st Armoured Division throughout the day. By the night 18th/19th February 1st Armoured Division was settling in south-east of Tebessa which it was ordered to defend. The enemy reported heavy American losses, yet Combat Command 'B' at least was in shape to fight again; Combat Commands 'A' and 'C' had been roughly handled. General Alexander was somewhat concerned about the trials and training of the American troops.

On the 17th bad weather set in which damped Allied tactical air operations on that day and the 18th. Yet on the night of the 17th/18th, in the teeth of the weather, R.A.F. Bisleys attacked enemy M.T. in the Fondouk—Faid—Sbeitla—Gafsa area. On the 18th the evacuation of Thelepte airfield, the main air base in 1st Army's southern sector, was a further bad set-back to Allied tactical air support and also meant that 34 unserviceable aircraft had to be destroyed. Counting in this calamity, 42 American aircraft had been lost in two days.

Rommel's troops held Feriana and Thelepte by the afternoon of 17th February and as they already had Gafsa and Tozeur, '*Morgenluft's* objectives had been gained. Ziegler's forces had Sidi Bou Zid and Sbeitla and '*Frühlingswind*' therefore had paid.[1] The Allies completed withdrawal to the Western Dorsale during the night of the 17th/18th. In sum the Axis armies had ended a phase and held the initiative although their commanders were still not in harmony. Rommel by the morning of the 17th had begun to set his sights on Tebessa, but when he asked von Arnim if he too would advance as far as that he received the discouraging answer that 21st Panzer Division was to operate in the Sbeitla area and the 10th at Fondouk—

---

[1] 10th and 21st Panzer Divisions claimed 2,866 prisoners, 169 tanks, 44 field guns and 19 anti-tank guns.

Pichon and that, in general, no troops would go forward of the crest of the Eastern Dorsale because of difficulties in maintaining them. Rommel received von Arnim's answer at midnight on the 17th/18th but had by then cooled to the point of thinking of pulling back his forward troops to Gafsa. However air reports that the Allies were withdrawing encouraged him to signal (at 2.30 p.m. 18th February) to *Comando Supremo* a proposal to advance immediately to Tebessa and the area north of it, provided that *Pz AOK 5* had sufficient supplies. He asked that 10th and 21st Panzer Divisions should be placed under his own command.

In the early hours of the 19th a directive from *Comando Supremo* reached Rommel and von Arnim. In short, it said that the Axis armies in Tunisia now had a unique opportunity to exploit northwards because of the proven low fighting quality of the enemy. The object must be to attack the rear of 5th Corps and if possible to cut off the British troops or at least drive them to the Algerian frontier. 'With all available mobile troops of the G.I. Pz Army and 10 and 21 Pz Divs under command, F-M Rommel, concentrating his forces and strongly protecting his west flank, is to advance from the general line [sic] Sbeitla–Tebessa–Maktar–Tadjerouine, with Le Kef as his first objective. Weak forces will be adequate for protection of the line Tebessa–Tozeur'. Rommel was to remain responsible for the Mareth front also. *Pz AOK 5* was to harass and pin down the Allies between Pont du Fahs and the coast and to prepare to attack later on a broad front.

This directive pleased neither commander. Rommel thought that to make his first objective Le Kef instead of Tebessa was tactically unsound because to advance in this direction was likely to lead him where the Allied reserves (as he estimated) were strongest. von Arnim disapproved of even the mention of Tebessa and told Kesselring that the armoured divisions should move on Le Kef from Sbeitla and Pichon, and that a later attack to roll up the enemy should begin up the Medjerda river and aim at Béja.

Kesselring rejected von Arnim's idea, and Rommel felt that time was more valuable than objections. On 19th February at 4.50 a.m. he ordered *D.A.K.* Assault Group to capture the Kasserine Pass and then await more orders. 21st Panzer Division was to advance through Sbiba to Ksour and 10th Panzer Division was to concentrate at Sbeitla, ready to exploit the success of 21st Panzer Division or of *D.A.K.* Assault Group. General Buelowius, temporarily commanding *D.A.K.* Assault Group, decided to try to surprise the Kasserine Pass at once with 33rd Reconnaissance Unit; Panzer Grenadier Regiment Africa to follow if necessary; I/8 Panzer Regiment was to make a firm base near Thelepte.

The Allied arrangements for command in the sector of operations were confused, to say no more. On the 19th February, Sbiba was in the sector of General Koeltz's French 19th Corps and H.Q. 6th Armoured Division was responsible to him but was in fact directly controlled by 1st Army. In the Sbiba area were 1st Guards Brigade (78th Division), 18th Regimental Combat Team (1st U.S. Division, Major-General Terry Allen) and three infantry battalions of 34th U.S. Division (Major-General Charles W. Ryder), 16th/5th Lancers (6th Armoured Division), 2nd Hampshires, three American Field Artillery Battalions, parts of 72nd and 93rd Anti-Tank Regiments R.A., and some French detachments. 26th Armoured Brigade (Brigadier C. A. L. Dunphie) less 16th/5th Lancers had just arrived at Thala. 1st U.S. Armoured Division was reorganizing near Tebessa. Its tasks were to protect Tebessa against attack from south and southwest; to lay, and cover with fire, mines in the passes at Kasserine, Dernaia, and El Ma el Abiod; and be ready to counter-attack at Dernaia. These orders amounted only to good intentions because 2nd Corps' area was in fact held by scattered detachments. In the Kasserine Pass under Lieut.-Colonel Anderson T. W. Moore were 1st/26th Infantry, 19th Combat Engineers Regiment, 33rd Field Artillery Battalion, 805th Tank Destroyer Battalion, and a battery of French 75-mm guns. In the Dernaia area under General Welvert were the American 1st Ranger Battalion, 1st/168th Infantry, 36th and 175th Field Artillery Battalions, engineer and A.A. detachments, three French battalions and four French batteries. At El Ma el Abiod was 3rd Battalion 26th Combat Team, known as Bowen Force.

Hostile reconnaissance of the Kasserine Pass on the evening of 18th February convinced General Fredendall that an attack there was imminent. He ordered Colonel Alexander N. Stark (Commanding Officer 26th Infantry) to take over Colonel Moore's miscellaneous units as Stark Force. These orders were again good intentions only, since the defence in the Pass was sketchy. About 2,000 men were strung across three miles of difficult country; on each side of the pass an infantry company had been given the almost impossible task of stopping virtually certain infiltration on the large and important tactical features Djebel Semmama and Djebel Chambi; mine-laying had been hasty. The main reinforcing formation was 26th Armoured Brigade which General Fredendall could not commit without 1st Army's approval.[1] The 3rd/39th Infantry (9th U.S. Division) was on its way up and a company of 13th Armoured Regiment was available.

33rd Reconnaissance Unit lost its gamble on surprising the Kasserine Pass, and the two battalions of Panzer Grenadier Regiment Africa

---

[1] This string had been attached by 1st Army because 26th Armoured Brigade was Anderson's sole immediate armoured reserve.

moved up, one beginning to climb the eastern flanking hill Djebel Semmama, the other sticking mainly to the floor of the pass. Defensive artillery fire slowed them and shortly after noon Buelowius committed 1/8th Panzer Regiment. 21st Panzer Division at Sbiba was also moving slowly. At 1 p.m. Rommel arrived at *D.A.K.* Assault Group. He directed that the main thrust was to be made by 10th and 21st Panzer Divisions; the Assault Group was simply to capture and seal the Kasserine Pass. Buelowius attacked again at about 3.20 p.m. and advanced slowly and persistently, getting a grip on Djebel Semmama. Brigadier Dunphie, reconnoitring, decided that he should intervene but Army H.Q., which felt that he might be needed at Sbiba, allowed him only to send forward a small detachment—'Gore Force'.[1] At Sbiba 21st Panzer Division was not getting on, was losing tanks (ten in all), and was using much ammunition. 10th Panzer Division was arriving slowly at Sbeitla and was at half-strength because *Pz AOK 5* was holding on to units which had not fought in '*Frühlingswind*'. On the evening of the 19th Rommel decided to switch 10th Panzer Division's thrust on the 20th to follow *D.A.K.* Assault Group through the Kasserine Pass and then to push north-west to Kalaa Djerda. Buelowius, after clearing the Pass, was to head also north-west to Djebel el Hamra. A battle-group from Centauro Division was to force the smaller passes at Djebel Dernaia.

The full story of the events of the night of 19th/20th February in Stark Force is not recoverable. Clearly, the enemy gained Djebel Semmama and on the opposite side of the Pass dispersed 19th Combat Engineers Regiment. At 8.30 a.m. on the 20th Panzer Grenadier Regiment Africa and 5th Bersaglieri began to attack again. They were not quick, and 3/6th Armoured Infantry counter-attacked successfully on Djebel Semmama. Nevertheless Brigadier Dunphie, reconnoitring, judged that by 10 a.m. Stark Force was about to collapse. Gore Force was ordered forward on the Thala side of the Pass. At about 1 p.m. Rommel committed two battalions of 10th Panzer Division and chased on Panzer Grenadier Regiment Africa and the Bersaglieri. Under this pressure the American defence fell to bits, and wholesale withdrawal ensued to the neighbourhood of Djebel el Hamra where Combat Command 'B' was arriving from El Ma el Abiod. In the American Official Historian's words the enemy 'was amazed at the quantity and quality of the American equipment captured more or less intact.' Gore Force leapfrogged slowly back towards Thala, losing all its tanks in the fighting, and in

---

[1] Lieut.-Colonel A. C. Gore, 10th Rifle Brigade: C Coy 10th Rifle Brigade, 'C' Sqdn. 2nd Lothians (7 Valentines, 4 Crusaders), 'F' Bty R.H.A., Troop 93rd Anti-Tank Regiment R.A.

the evening rejoined 26th Armoured Brigade. 2/5th Leicestershires, newly arrived, were hastily digging in astride the road some four miles south of Thala.

The weather for flying on the 19th was so bad that the enemy had no air support in their fight in the Kasserine Pass, though some Tac/R aircraft managed to fly. American air support was negligible, which relieved Rommel whose forces lay vulnerable 'in the deep, ravine-like valleys . . .' But that night, even though the Beaufighters had to be stood down for the first time since early December, 26 R.A.F. Bisleys faced the weather to attack roads in the Gafsa–Feriana—Kasserine–Sbeitla area. On the 20th the weather was even worse, but that night the Bisleys were out again in strength attacking the same roads as on the previous night, and the Beaufighters resumed their vigil for enemy night flying aircraft.[1]

Since the 19th General Fredendall had had confused information or none. A personal reconnaissance on the morning of the 20th made him think that the enemy had broken through towards Tebessa. Therefore he decided to try to cover Tebessa with an American force and Thala with a British one. Elements of 1st U.S. Division were moved into the area Djebel Chambi–El Ma el Abiod, and Brigadier Dunphie was given the task of combining the action of his own 26th Armoured Brigade, Combat Command 'B' and the remains of Stark Force, but not the staff or signals to do so. At 8.30 p.m. 1st Army, thoroughly alarmed by the situation in the Kasserine Pass, appointed Brigadier C. G. G. Nicholson (2nd in Command of 6th Armoured Division) to take command of the whole allied force north-west of the Kasserine Pass under the name of 'Nick Force'. Too many, and confused, arrangements for command had been a great weakness in the fighting. Under the remote presidency of General Fredendall, whose freedom to act was in many ways restricted by 1st Army, General Ward (1st U.S. Armoured Division), Colonel Moore, Colonel Stark, Brigadier Dunphie, Brigadier-General Robinett (Combat Command 'B') and now Brigadier Nicholson all had fingers in the pie.

In the small hours of 21st February Rommel ordered *D.A.K.* Assault Group to 'defend the passes west of the Kasserine–Thala road. Send a Battle Group forward to reconnoitre Djebel el Hamra.' Dunphie and Robinett had decided to await attack, hoping for a chance to counter-attack. Brigadier Nicholson decided to fight a defensive battle. North-west for some fifteen miles to Thala there stretched open, heath country, crossed from east to west by low

---

[1] By the 20th General Spaatz had placed most of his strategic bomber force, including the Wellingtons, at Coningham's disposal and this arrangement lasted throughout the critical fighting. Regrettably, the weather prevented full advantage being taken of it. The same day a *Luftflotte 2* order exhorted the German Air Force to greater efforts 'In this situation, where as yet unimagined success could be achieved . . .'

ridges a mile or so apart. Behind one of these ridges were 17/21st Lancers, 2nd Lothians (less a squadron), and a company (later, all) of 10th Rifle Brigade supported by 'F' Battery R.H.A. and 450th Field Battery (71st Field Regiment R.A.). Fifteen miles to the west at Djebel el Hamra was Combat Command 'B'. Four miles south of Thala 2/5th Leicestershires (from 46th Division) and 86th Chemical Warfare Company R.E. (4·2 inch mortars) were occupying a defensive position supported by 90th/100th Field Battery (23rd Army Field Regiment R.A.) and 229th Anti-Tank Battery (58th Anti-Tank Regiment R.A.).

On the 21st 10th Panzer Division's forward troops were making little ground against 26th Armoured Brigade. Rommel ordered *D.A.K.* Assault Group to seize Djebel el Hamra and 10th Panzer Division to go for Thala. Combat Command 'B' successfully resisted *D.A.K.* which by evening was four miles short of its objective. 10th Panzer Division however pushed 26th Armoured Brigade slowly back from ridge to ridge until at about 4 p.m. the British formation was about nine miles from Thala, and had lost fifteen tanks. At 5.45 p.m. Dunphie ordered his armoured regiments back to a position about two miles short of those of the Leicestershires. His unarmoured troops were already on the way back. Brigadier Nicholson approved.

Behind the Leicestershires' position was a handful of British artillery.[1] There was expected during the night the artillery of 9th U.S. Division which in four days had driven 800 miles from Tlemcen in Morocco. Reinforcement from Sbiba could not be quick because rain had made the direct track impassable, and a long detour had to be made through Le Kef. As the British tanks towards dusk on the 21st withdrew through the Leicestershires, enemy tanks followed unsuspected on their tails and into the position. Once inside, the hostile tanks opened fire, machine-gun teams followed them, and very quickly the Leicestershires' position with many of the anti-tank guns ceased to exist. 17/21st Lancers at once hurried back to this confused and dangerous situation from their leaguer, which indeed they had scarcely reached, and 'F' and 450th Batteries turned themselves into anti-tank guns. Fighting lasted by the light of burning vehicles until about 10 p.m. when the enemy tanks retired, although machine guns and some S.P. guns remained overlooking the British gun areas at close range. Brigadier Nicholson gave orders that no one would withdraw, and every man capable of fighting as an infantryman was collected and took post. Brigadier Parham, B.R.A. 1st Army, who was on the scene, reconnoitred positions, which he caused to be

---

[1] 450th Bty 71st Fd Regt R.A., 90th/100th Bty 23rd Army Fd Regt R.A., 'F' Bty R.H.A., 229th Bty 58th A/Tk Regt R.A. (less troop); Det 93rd A/Tk Regt R.A. (one gun), American A/Tk Company of six 37-mm guns. In addition there were two sections of 4·2-inch mortars of 86th C.W. Company R.E.

hastily surveyed, for the American artillery. Between 9 p.m. and 2 a.m. on 22nd February three field artillery battalions and two cannon companies were led straight into action, darkness, unfamiliar terrain, and a confused situation notwithstanding.[1] American and British guns were hastily grouped as a single fire-unit under the American artillery commander, Brigadier-General J. Le Roy Irwin. Brigadier Nicholson decided to counter-attack somehow or other, early on 22nd February.

There were signs of improvement in the weather on the 21st in the north, but rain and fog in the central sector made a strong recovery by the American tactical air force of little effect. German Stukas, however, found and dive-bombed the U.S. 27th Armoured Field Artillery which was opposing General Buelowius's main force in the Pass, and German Tac/R succeeded in covering the Allied positions east of the Kasserine-Thala road and facing 21st Panzer Division. The same day Tebessa airfield had to be evacuated because of the mud and the American squadrons there moved to Youks les Bains and Le Kouif[2]. That night the R.A.F. Bisleys were stood down but the Beaufighters, out in strength, destroyed two Ju. 88s for the loss of one of themselves.

To Allied eyes the situation in the Kasserine area seemed extremely dangerous. On 20th February General Anderson had issued a special order forbidding withdrawal. This he repeated on the 22nd: 'It is absolutely essential that all individuals, units and formations stand fast to their posts and do not withdraw when being attacked directly or outflanked or threatened with outflanking. There is to be NO further withdrawal under any excuse...' But in fact the enemy's offensive was at an end. On the 20th February Kesselring had told von Arnim that Rommel's operations might have to be stopped unless they achieved a decisive success, and on the 22nd this result was not in sight. D.A.K. Assault Group was not getting on below Djebel el Hamra; 10th Panzer Division at Thala, far from pressing its advantage, was inexplicably awaiting counter-attack; von Arnim was as aloof as ever; the field formations had fuel for about 180 miles and not much ammunition; and reserves for Rommel Group were low.[3] During the afternoon Rommel and Kesselring again conferred near Kasserine. Rommel said that there was no chance of success in continuing the offensive. The enemy was heavily reinforcing his southern sector, but apparently not at the expense of his northern

---

[1] 34th Field Artillery Battalion (twelve 155-mm howitzers); 60th and 84th Field Artillery Battalions (each twelve 105-mm howitzers); 47th and 60th Cannon Companies (each six 75-mm howitzers).

[2] Tebessa was the fourth airfield to be abandoned in eight days, i.e. Gafsa—14th; Sbeitla—15th; Thelepte—17th/18th; Tebessa—21st.

[3] Fuel for about 120 miles, a little more than a day's supply of ammunition, rations for six days.

sector. The Kasserine area was unsuitable for mobile operations and made worse by the weather. There had been much rain during the past four days. However he believed that heavy losses had been inflicted upon the Allies, and their concentrations in the area Gafsa–Sbeitla had been destroyed. Now was the time to break off the offensive and concentrate in Southern Tunisia for a blow at 8th Army which could be caught off balance while still assembling its forces.[1] Kesselring went on to see von Arnim, who persuaded him that he could not help Rommel and gained Kesselring's agreement to pursue his own plans. The same evening *Comando Supremo* ordered that the offensive was to be broken off and that formations were to return to the sectors where they had been at the start. The withdrawal began at once and the retreating formations were slowly followed by the British and Americans.

The low cloud had dispersed by mid-morning on the 22nd, and in drier weather tactical air operations once more got into full swing. British fighter-bombers of No. 225 Squadron escorted by Spitfires of Nos. 111 and 152 Squadrons attacked armoured vehicles and M.T. approaching Thala, and set several on fire. American tactical aircraft, now forced to operate from the one over-crowded forward airfield at Youks les Bains, were further handicapped by being confined to a single steel plank runway.[2] At 11.35 a.m. the first bombers took off and from then on all that were available attacked targets in the area south of Thala and east of Djebel el Hamra, flying a total of 114 sorties. The American fighter-bombers joined in these attacks and Airacobras strafed Axis traffic in the Pass, but attempts by the Fortresses to give tactical support failed because cloud obscured the ground. Despite the late start, the American tactical air effort amounted to 304 sorties of all kinds but losses (four bombers and seven fighters) were heavy. The Germans, because their Tac/R led them to expect an imminent Allied counter-attack, expended most of their available air support in attempting to halt the arrival of Allied reinforcements at Thala by striking at columns north and north-west of the town, but some Stukas also operated over the Tebessa–Kasserine road and fighters covered the Pass. The same night, though low cloud returned and visibility was poor, every available R.A.F. Bisley (most of them flying two sorties each) attacked roads in the Sbeitla–Kasserine area, a tank harbour, and the Kasserine gateway. Fog prevented more than a total of 56 sorties being flown.

---

[1] Kesselring, after the war, described Rommel at this meeting as mentally and physically exhausted, displeased with his role and by some of his troops, irritated by von Arnim's attitude, and anxious to return to Mareth.

[2] The Americans evacuated Le Kouif and Kalaa Djerda airfields that day in the belief that Thala was still in danger, whereas the Germans were in fact leaving Thelepte and Sbeitla.

By the morning of 24th February the Kasserine Pass was again in Allied hands. The Axis had won no ground but had inflicted considerable losses in men and material upon the Allies. The 1st U.S. Armoured Division had lost about 1,400 men, and the 2nd and 3rd Battalions of the 1st Armoured Regiment had to be combined in a single unit. Losses in the 168th Infantry (34th Division) were very high. British losses were mainly in tanks but there were Shermans ready to replace the lost Valentines and Crusaders.[1]

The main adverse results of the fighting since 14th February were summed up by A.F.H.Q. as the loss of about half the armoured strength of 1st U.S. Armoured Division together with a large amount of other equipment; delay in the re-equipment of 6th Armoured Division; and the loss of Thelepte airfield. German material losses were comparable with those of the Allies and could be less well afforded.

In opposing the enemy's attacks in the central sector, from 14th February to the start of his retreat on the 22nd, the Americans had flown little more than an average of 200 sorties daily, because the bad weather had seriously disrupted air support. They lost 58 aircraft including the 34 they themselves destroyed at Thelepte to avoid capture. The R.A.F. contributed a modest 170 sorties all told for the loss of two Bisleys and a fighter. In support of 'Frühlingswind' and 'Morgenluft' the German losses were two Stukas and eight fighters.

While the Kasserine operations had been spreading, the fronts of 5th Corps and the French 19th Corps remained rather quiet, but for No. 242 Group there had been the usual routine tasks in addition to providing some air support in the central sector.

During the 23rd and 24th, in pursuit of the retreating ground forces, U.S. XII Air Support Command got back into its stride and Fortesses added a heavy attack on Kasserine on the 23rd and on Kairouan airfield the next day. Rommel, referring to the 23rd, later recorded that 'The bad weather now ended and from midday onward we were subjected to hammer-blow air attacks by the U.S. air force in the Feriana–Kasserine area, of a weight and concentration hardly surpassed by those we had suffered at Alamein.'

Meanwhile the strategic bombers in North West Africa had had a lean time, the bad weather no doubt being the main cause. Between the 14th and 22nd February there were only three raids of significance, two of them by Fortresses and Wellingtons against ports (described in Chapter X) and one by Fortresses on the airfield at

---

[1] The total number of prisoners taken between 16th and 24th February was stated by the enemy to be 4,026, and equipment claims (other than those made by 10th and 21st Panzer Divisions) amounted to: Guns 20; anti-tank guns 2; tanks 3; miscellaneous armoured vehicles 44; transport vehicles 174. German losses are recorded as casualties 989; guns 20; anti-tank guns 5; tanks 20; miscellaneous armoured vehicles 5; transport vehicles 60. Italian casualties are not recorded.

Elmas. Marauders also attacked airfields at Villacidro and Decimomannu. Three U.S. bombers were lost in these operations.

Altogether, on each of these nine days, but omitting anti-shipping operations, the British in North West Africa flew an average of only 135 sorties of all kinds for the loss of five aircraft; the American figure was an estimated 230 for the loss of 61 aircraft. German losses all told amounted to 20.

By coincidence the armies on both sides during the February battles reorganized their arrangements for the higher command. At the Casablanca Conference it had been decided that General Alexander was to become Deputy Commander-in-Chief of the Allied forces in French North Africa and commander of a group of armies, to be called 18th Army Group, operating in Tunisia.

The gist of General Eisenhower's directive, dated 17th February 1943, to General Alexander was:

> '1. . . . You are appointed Deputy Commander-in-Chief of the Allied Forces in French North Africa. Further you are appointed Commander of the Group of Armies operating in Tunisia.
> 2. This appointment takes effect on 20th February 1943, on which date you will take command of all Allied forward forces engaged in operations in Tunisia. These consist of the British 1st Army, which exercises command over the United States and French forces operating in Tunisia, the British 8th Army, and such reserve formations as may be placed under your command.
> 3. Your mission is the early destruction of all Axis forces in Tunisia. . . .'

A naval officer from the staff of the Commander-in-Chief Mediterranean was appointed to General Alexander's staff as adviser on naval matters. The Air Officer Commanding the Tactical Air Force was to share Alexander's H.Q. and direct the air forces assigned for the direct support of his armies to the best advantage of the land operations prescribed by him. A.F.H.Q. was to be responsible for the supply and maintenance of the 1st Army including all American and French forces under its command, and for that of any reserve and air forces found by A.F.H.Q. G.H.Q. Middle East was to be responsible for the supply and maintenance of the 8th Army, and of air forces found by R.A.F. Middle East.

The frontier between Tripolitania and Tunisia was made the boundary between the Middle East and North African Commands. Malta remained under the direction of the Middle East Defence Committee except for its air forces which became part of the Mediterranean Air Command.

General Alexander's Chief of Staff was Major-General R. L McCreery. A small administrative staff whose main functions were to advise and inform the Commander on logistic matters arising from two Lines of Communications, and to co-ordinate operational administrative arrangements within 1st and 8th Armies, was headed by Major-General C. H. Miller.

General Alexander took command on 19th February and did not like what he found. To the C.I.G.S. on that day, he reported 'General situation is far from satisfactory. British, American and French units are all mixed up on the front, especially in the south. Formations have been split up. There is no policy and no plan of campaign. The air is much the same. This is the result of no firm direction or centralized control from above . . . We have quite definitely lost the initiative . . .' On the 22nd he signalled 'Situation on battle front is critical and the next day or two should decide issue . . . My main anxiety is the poor fighting value of Americans . . . .' On the 27th he reported to the Prime Minister and C.I.G.S.

> . . . I am frankly shocked at whole situation as I found it. Although Anderson should have been quicker to realize true state of affairs and to have started what I am now doing he was only put in command of whole front on 24th January [sic]. Real fault has been lack of direction from above from very beginning resulting in no policy and no plan. Am doubtful if Anderson is big enough for job although he has some good qualities. . . . Hate to disappoint you but final victory in North Africa is not just around the corner. A very great deal requires to be done both on land and in the air. General Eisenhower could not be more helpful. . . .'

In these reports General Alexander is too hard on General Anderson. First, General Eisenhower was the C.-in-C. of an expeditionary force in the field and if there was no policy and no plan of campaign the responsibility was his, though it is true that he was swamped with quasi-diplomatic, political and economic cares as General Wavell had been for so long in the Middle East. Then until 26th January Anderson had been in command only of his own wholly British 1st Army. That Army, since 27th December, had been working on a policy, laid down by Eisenhower, of preparing to resume the attack on Tunis and Bizerta in March or April. When on 26th January and 11th February Anderson had received fresh directives from Eisenhower he had done a great deal to carry them out in most difficult circumstances. Since taking command of all troops on the front, Anderson's aim had been to create national 'sectors' of command and to form a reserve. Moreover Eisenhower, on 31st January, had told him that plans for future operations were to be prepared, and directives issued by 18th Army Group, and that his main task was to press on with creating a reserve.

On taking up his appointment Alexander asked Anderson for his plans to restore the situation on 1st Army's front in preparation for an offensive on Tunis. Most of Anderson's points (which were obvious enough) appeared in Alexander's Operation Instruction No. 1 dated 20th February. This gave Anderson as immediate tasks: to stabilize the front in the southern sector; to reorganize and regroup the army in British, American, and French sectors; to form a general reserve; to regain the initiative at the first possible opportunity and to keep it. He was to hold positions to cover certain vital areas: the landing-grounds near Tebessa; the plain between Le Kef and Thala with its landing grounds; the 'gap' between Sbiba and Maktar; the Bou Arada valley; Medjez el Bab and the Medjerda valley. On the 24th General Anderson issued orders to carry out these instructions. The development of General Alexander's policy for 18th Army Group and its operations belong to later chapters.

On the Axis side we have seen how Army Group Africa came into being on 23rd February on the initiative of Ambrosio and Kesselring. On the same day *Comando Supremo* issued a directive to Rommel to the following effect. The offensive had been successful but it was to be broken off because the Allies had strongly reinforced the Tebessa area, and because it was now vital to mount an offensive against the 8th Army. Mobile troops were to defend the area Gafsa–Metlaoui–Tozeur but the bulk of the Assault Group was to return to *AOK 1*. 10th Panzer Division, which had pulled back from Thala to the Kasserine Pass by the morning of 23rd February, and 21st Panzer Division, which abandoned its fruitless attempts to take Sbiba the next day, were both to refit and then to join *AOK 1* in readiness for an attack on 8th Army during the first days of March. *Pz AOK 5* was to cover the retreat from Kasserine by making raids and sorties, and was also to prepare an offensive to advance its front in northern Tunisia. Rommel immediately ordered Messe to make by the 26th a plan to destroy the enemy south of Mareth, using two or three Panzer divisions. von Arnim as quickly declared that if 10th and 21st Panzer Divisions were taken from him he could only hold his present line. von Arnim was privately eager to attack on his own account and on the 24th went to Rome (without the knowledge of his new superior, Rommel) to gain Kesselring's backing. Kesselring, always open to new ideas, supported him, and told Ambrosio that the time was now ripe for an offensive against Béja. Ambrosio was non-committal, but on the 25th von Arnim issued the orders for his operation '*Ochsenkopf*', to begin on 26th February.

The underlying assumption of this plan was that the Allies had greatly weakened their front in Northern Tunisia by removing troops to oppose Rommel's forces.[1]

See Map 33.

The broad plan was that Weber's 'Corps' should advance in three main groups: one, strong in armour, on Béja from the north-east; a second group from Goubellat towards Sloughia and Oued Zarga to encircle and destroy the British positions at Medjez el Bab; a third group to carry out a pincer movement in the Bou Arada valley and then advance by way of El Aroussa to Gafour. General Weber, who was to command the whole operation, had a 'Corps' including 334th Infantry Division, the units of the Hermann Göring Division which had arrived in Africa, and those of 10th Panzer Division which had not been engaged in '*Frühlingswind*'. In the north the patchwork (though good) division, formerly von Broich's and now commanded by Colonel von Manteuffel, was to destroy the British positions in the Sedjenane valley and to cut their L. of C. leading from Jefna to Djebel Abiod and to cover Weber's northern flank.

The Axis commanders were trying to keep the initiative but in fact Rommel, von Arnim, and Messe had separately formed very unhopeful views of the prospects in Tunisia.

This is an opportune moment to see how the creation of the Mediterranean Air Command affected the Allied Air forces, particularly those opposing the enemy in northern Tunisia.

Operationally, the Malta and Middle East air forces were not greatly affected. Malta became an independent air command under M.A.C. and operational control of the Desert Air Force passed from H.Q., R.A.F., M.E. to Northwest African Tactical Air Force (N.A.T.A.F.). Otherwise they experienced no great change with the important exception that co-ordination of all their operations with those of Northwest African Air Forces (N.A.A.F.) could now be achieved through properly established channels of command, and no longer rested solely on the personal initiative of the various air commanders. Administratively there was no change at all, H.Q.,

---

[1] In very general terms the following formations and units had been sent into the southern sector and central sector:

British	American
One armoured brigade.	One regimental combat team.
Two infantry brigades.	Two infantry regiments.
One armoured regiment (less squadron).	Three field artillery battalions.
Two infantry battalions.	
One medium regiment R.A.	
Three field regiments R.A.	
Six anti-tank batteries R.A.	

R.A.F., M.E. continuing to be responsible for both Malta and the Desert Air Force.

In N.A.A.F., however, the effect on both operations and administration was marked. An A.O.C.-in-C. for all the 'Torch' air forces, exercising full powers of operational control, solved the problem of unified air command in North West Africa, which had plagued Allied air operations from the start (see Chapter V, page 113). Full co-ordination of the Allied air effort followed the sub-division of N.A.A.F. into inter-Allied functional commands, resulting in much greater economy of effort and concentration of force. An attempt was made to gain like benefits in the administrative field by creating the Northwest African Air Service Command. In principle it absorbed the British and American maintenance organizations to form a central unit for maintenance and supply, but it did not immediately affect their activities. Indeed, both the British and the Americans appear to have worked in obedience to their own doctrines until as late as mid-April when some combination was achieved in the forward area.

Of the air formations which made up the subordinate commands in N.A.A.F., those in Northwest African Strategic Air Force (N.A.S.A.F.) were least affected by the reorganization. Hitherto strategic bombing had been carried out by the U.S. XII Bomber Command with its Fortresses and Lightnings by day and by the two R.A.F. Wellington squadrons by night, and this continued but with the Wellingtons now directly under command of N.A.S.A.F. In Northwest African Coastal Air Force (N.A.C.A.F.) the effect was rather more marked. No. 328 Wing, responsible for naval co-operation, continued to function as a smooth working organization and to share an operations room with Admiral Cunningham's staff. But the establishment within N.A.C.A.F. of a fighter force for the defence of shipping, ports and rearward areas relieved N.A.T.A.F. from having to look all round the compass: and the day-to-day loan from N.A.S.A.F. of two U.S. Mitchell bomber squadrons provided a much needed anti-shipping strike force. In N.A.T.A.F. the effect of reorganization was great and the results remarkable. To understand why, we must look at the planning and early development of tactical air operations in 'Torch'.

The Americans had not been at all clear how they would support the advance eastwards, and it fell to Eastern Air Command (E.A.C.) to provide the initial air support to the armies. Unfortunately almost every approach E.A.C. made to the operational problems of air support was obsolete by Desert standards. It had been planned that air support for the Eastern Task Force would be arranged by the A.O.C., E.A.C., and G.O.C. 1st Army together, and that a R.A.F. officer experienced in army/air co-operation, with a small staff, would be attached to 78th Division and later to 5th Corps. When General Anderson moved forward with the 1st Army Command Post he had hoped that Air Marshal Welsh would accompany him, but Welsh did not, on the grounds that his total responsibilities required him to stay in Algiers, although an Air Vice-Marshal had already been appointed Assistant Chief of Staff (Air) at A.F.H.Q. as Welsh's representative, and as Air Adviser to General Eisenhower. Instead Air Commodore Lawson became the senior R.A.F. officer at the small R.A.F. Command Post which accompanied Anderson. At 78th Division's Advance H.Q. the senior R.A.F. representative was a wing commander—much too junior in the circumstances. Not until No. 242 Group was formed, with Lawson in command, and its H.Q. placed alongside that of 5th Corps in mid-December 1942 was the system somewhat improved, but only at Corps level, because Anderson now had no direct touch whatsoever with the Royal Air Force. For that matter there was no close liaison between E.A.C., H.Q. and No. 242 Group.

For air support operations (see Chapter VII, pages 168–69) it had been planned that the four tactical bomber and bomber reconaissance squadrons, all equipped with Bisleys, were to carry out their tasks in daylight. In the Desert, as early as May 1941, it had been found that the Blenheim IV (which was faster than the Blenheim V/Bisley) needed such heavy escort by day that its use was virtually limited to dusk and night attacks. E.A.C., clearly ignorant of Desert experience, used the Bisleys by day (as well as by night) until the loss of an entire formation on 4th December 1942 forced them to turn wholly to night-bombing. The two army co-operation squadrons included in the plan were first for tactical reconnaissance and second for fighter-bombing. In the Desert experience had shown that a tactical reconnaissance squadron had to be a highly skilled unit concentrating on that one role. In the circumstances it is not surprising that Welsh found himself unable even to operate more than the equivalent of one fighter-bomber squadron in support of the army, and that at times no fighter-bombers were available at all. The role of the fighter force was planned to be almost wholly defensive. During the third week of November when 78th Division first came under enemy air attack only one army co-operation and two fighter squadrons were available to the A.S.C. (Army Air Support Control) with the Division, and because the primary fighter task had been laid down as the defence of the port of Bône and convoys in that area, they were often unavailable for air support. On the 20th and 21st, however, two more fighter squadrons were moved forward to Souk el Arba. To help the Army more effectively Lawson turned these fighters on to ground strafing on his own initiative until, on 3rd January, Welsh stopped him on the grounds that 'The primary role of the fighter is to destroy enemy aircraft. It should only be used as a long range gun on ground targets in exceptional circumstances'. Lawson was then back to where he had started—with just a handful of fighter-bombers to meet all the daylight air support operations required of him.

Poor communications had afflicted all the forces in the forward area from the start of the advance. Unfortunately E.A.C. had not a suitable W/T organization nor sufficiently experienced Signals personnel. An apparent omission, surprisingly enough, was the centralised control of fighters and radar in the forward area. In the Desert this control had long been the hub of fighter operations.

The principal features of E.A.C's maintenance and supply arrangements for the Wings (see Chapter VII, page 169) were, however, similar in outline to those in the Desert. But they had not the all-important simplicity which the Desert Air Force had achieved by concentrating on highly mobile salvage sections and reducing maintenance, supply and repair in the forward area to the minimum, daily servicing, refuelling and rearming having first claim. A striking contrast to Desert practice was that the Army was made responsible for holding and distributing on behalf of the R.A.F. all petrol, oil and lubricants, small arms ammunition, bombs and pyrotechnics. (See Chapter IV, page 101). For several reasons, but principally because it was thought that the whole of Morocco, Algeria and Tunisia would fall into Allied hands by D plus 46 (24th December), E.A.C. made no plans for bases in the rear to deal with repairs beyond the power of the forward R.S.Us. Thus the ability of E.A.C. to maintain its front line aircraft strength depended, in theory, on the campaign ending in forty-seven days.

From the beginning of 'Torch' many things went wrong. In the assault stage there were bad packing, wrong or sketchy marking of crates, wrong priorities in loading, deliveries to the wrong beach or port, delays on the beaches because of soft sand and through lack of M.T.—most were understandable in this first attempt at a big amphibious landing. When the advance eastwards began, the bad rail and road communications, and scarce and unreliable motor transport, added to and prolonged the difficulties. Shortage of experienced officers and men in the maintenance and supply units did not help, and premature calling forward of some squadrons, notably the Bisleys, without thought of the maintenance difficulties made matters worse. But by one means or another supplies never quite ran out, and the aircraft were kept serviceable thanks largely to the R.A.F. Servicing Commandos. The air and ground crews of British and American squadrons did sterling work in spite of difficulties and weather at times appalling.

By January, however, it was understood that the R.A.F. maintenance and supply organization fell short of requirements. Three maintenance areas were therefore created—forward, intermediate (L. of C.) and base. The forward maintenance, supply and repair units including the A.S.Ps were to be simplified to enable them to move at short notice and the personnel and resources thus thrown up were to be absorbed by units in the rear. This was a good move and some headway had been made before M.A.C. was created in mid-February 1943. But it was not enough to prevent Air Marshal Sir Arthur Coningham expressing surprise on finding on his arrival to command N.A.T.A.F. that the arrangements in Tunisia were the same as those which he had found in the Western Desert in the summer of 1941, or to dispel his view that no attempt had been made to apply the lessons of warfare learned in the Desert, though conditions in Tunisia were often similar. E.A.C. had awakened too late to the fact that its whole maintenance system needed modernizing to be able to correct it before N.A.T.A.F. came into being.

The U.S. XII A.S.C. also lacked experience on operations but had been employed less defensively than No. 242 Group, though its tactics were unwise. Sorties were often carried out in unsuitable weather, and all kinds of targets were accepted without discrimination, including tanks heavily screened by flak. American tactical reconnaissance aircraft spent more time on strafing than on Tac/R. Tactical bombers were misused in low level daylight attacks and in small numbers, often in pairs and even singly. And, like No. 242 Group, the U.S. XII A.S.C. had no centralized fighter control nor adequate forward radar to deal with enemy ground strafing. Of its administrative problems nothing is known except that its daily rate of aircraft serviceability was falling alarmingly by mid-February.

It had not been possible to plan to co-ordinate British and American tactical air operations. The American air planners had thought that in the early stages of 'Torch' their air operations would have little in common with those of the British because the R.A.F. and U.S.A.A.F. would be operating in separate and clearly defined areas. It will also be recalled that the American air planners had no firm policy about the part the U.S.A.A.F. was to play in the subsequent advance eastwards. Nor is there any evidence of vigorous effort by the British towards co-ordination. They and the Americans therefore planned for 'Torch' in isolation. Had an Allied A.O.C.-in-C. been appointed for 'Torch' he would undoubtedly have encouraged Allied air co-ordination, in planning and execution, not least between the tactical air forces, where its absence was to be most keenly felt. The creation of the Allied Air Force on 5th January 1943, with General Spaatz in command, made some amends but even this arrangement did not solve the co-ordination problem for tactical air forces. On 22nd January, because of the critical land fighting,

General Spaatz prematurely implemented one of the Casablanca decisions by placing No. 242 Group and the U.S. XII A.S.C. under a single command. On the 25th this new organization, known as the Allied Air Support Command, began to function and requests for bomber support could be passed back as a matter of drill to the units of E.A.C. and the U.S. Twelfth Air Force based in the rearward areas. Co-ordination had at last begun in a small way and little more could have been expected in the circumstances. What was required was that No. 242 Group and the U.S. XII A.S.C. should be subordinated to a commander experienced in up-to-date air support operations and organization and exercising full powers of co-ordination, reorganization and training. This subordination was equally desirable in administrative matters.

The arrival of Coningham as A.O.C.-in-C. N.A.T.A.F. solved the operational side of the problem. He quickly grasped that almost all the fighter effort was defensive. No. 242 Group's squadrons, for example, were split between the forward landing grounds and those in the Bône area and distracted by coastal fighter defence. This last task was soon handed over to N.A.C.A.F., and control of all the British fighters was immediately centralized under the Group. The use of 'air umbrellas' over the troops unless specially authorized by N.A.T.A.F. was forbidden, because Coningham was convinced that an offensive air force automatically protected the troops. Air support by aircraft in 'penny packets' was to cease and No. 242 Group and the U.S. XII A.S.C. were to liaise closely to help each other. Tanks were to be left alone because enemy concentrations and thin skinned vehicles were much better targets. The British and American tactical bomber forces were to be centralized and trained in formation flying with fighter escort, and in medium-level daylight bombing against targets such as landing grounds and troop concentrations.[1]

At this time critical land fighting was going on, and not until the pressure eased could some of the new measures be put into force. On the 2nd March Coningham issued his first directive. The first requirement was air superiority so that the Army would suffer little interference from the air, and the Allied air forces enjoy greater freedom in attacks on targets in the battle area and beyond. To this end a continuous offensive was to be waged against the enemy air forces in the air and on his main airfields, the tactical bombers operating by day and night and supported by N.A.S.A.F. To obtain increased warning of enemy air attacks, radar cover and signal

---

[1] In February and March some American Bostons were loaned to No. 18 Squadron for training purposes. At the end of March Boston III aircraft began to arrive for both Nos. 18 and 114 Squadrons.

The British and American tactical bomber forces began functioning as an operational entity on 1st March, No. 326 Wing R.A.F. acting as the headquarters. On the 20th the Northwest African Tactical Bomber Force was formed under N.A.T.A.F.

communications throughout the N.A.T.A.F. area were to be expanded and improved. The use of N.A.T.A.F. landing grounds was to be flexible so that squadrons could move from one sector to another at short notice. Training for the fighters was to be begun immediately, including 'shadow firing' (see Volume III, page 207). In areas where the enemy operated in small numbers, Coningham preferred a greater number of small well-drilled fighter formations rather than fewer large ones for offensive patrols. In bomber escort he stressed the importance of fighters keeping to their proper role—'It is a point of honour that the bombers should not be attacked by enemy fighters'—and of good communication between fighter escorts and bombers. The responsibility for abandoning a fighter escort mission owing to weather or casualties would rest with the fighter leader.[1]

Air Vice-Marshal G. G. Dawson, who took up his appointment as Director of Maintenance and Supply, M.A.C., on 19th February, applied his characteristic drive to the R.A.F. maintenance reorganisation and considerably enlarged its scope.[2] He immediately entered into agreements with the French aircraft firms in North Africa for the overhaul and repair of airframes and engines. An aircraft repair depot was set up in Algiers and aircraft repair units at Sétif and Blida by using personnel of three of the five existing R.S.Us and the maintenance elements of two wings. An aircraft erection unit was set up at Casablanca to assemble Spitfires and Hurricanes sent by sea from the U.K. Responsibility for the storage of explosives and fuel for the squadrons was taken over from the Army, and an air ammunition park and three dump sections were formed in the forward area. Of the six A.S.Ps in existence, three remained in the forward area and a fourth was converted into an advance equipment park. The fifth was moved to Algiers to serve Maison Blanche and Blida and the last one to Sétif to serve No. 325 Wing which was responsible for static fighter defence in the rearward areas. A salvage unit was formed to cover all units of No. 242 Group in the forward area. It was divided into eight highly mobile sections taken from R.S.Us, which were now reduced to three, and made responsible only for light repair and urgent salvage from airfields. The M.T. maintenance organization was reshaped on the desert pattern, the chief feature being the withdrawal of M.T. salvage and repair sections from the forward R.S.Us to form an M.T. light repair unit. By these means Dawson was able to simplify and get the most

---

[1] On 12th March H.Q. 18th Army Group took action to educate the 'Torch' armies, too, in Army/Air co-operation. Special emphasis was placed on: full use being made of the Air Support Control system; the passing back of information of enemy air attacks and of the results of Allied air attacks; clear marking of vehicles with the star or roundel; and the display of landmarks to assist the tactical air forces.

[2] Air Vice-Marshal Dawson had played a prominent part in the reorganization of R.A.F. maintenance in the Middle East in 1941. See Volume II, Chapter XV.

out of the maintenance, supply, repair and salvage arrangements in the forward area and build up a sufficient supporting organization in the rear.

All these measures were soon vastly to change for the better the quality and quantity of air support on the whole of the northern Tunisian front. The unhappy fact is that much that was done to bring the tactical air forces in North West Africa, and No. 242 Group in particular, up-to-date in the latest techniques in air support operations and organisation as practised in the desert could have been embodied in the original 'Torch' air planning for the asking.

Map 30

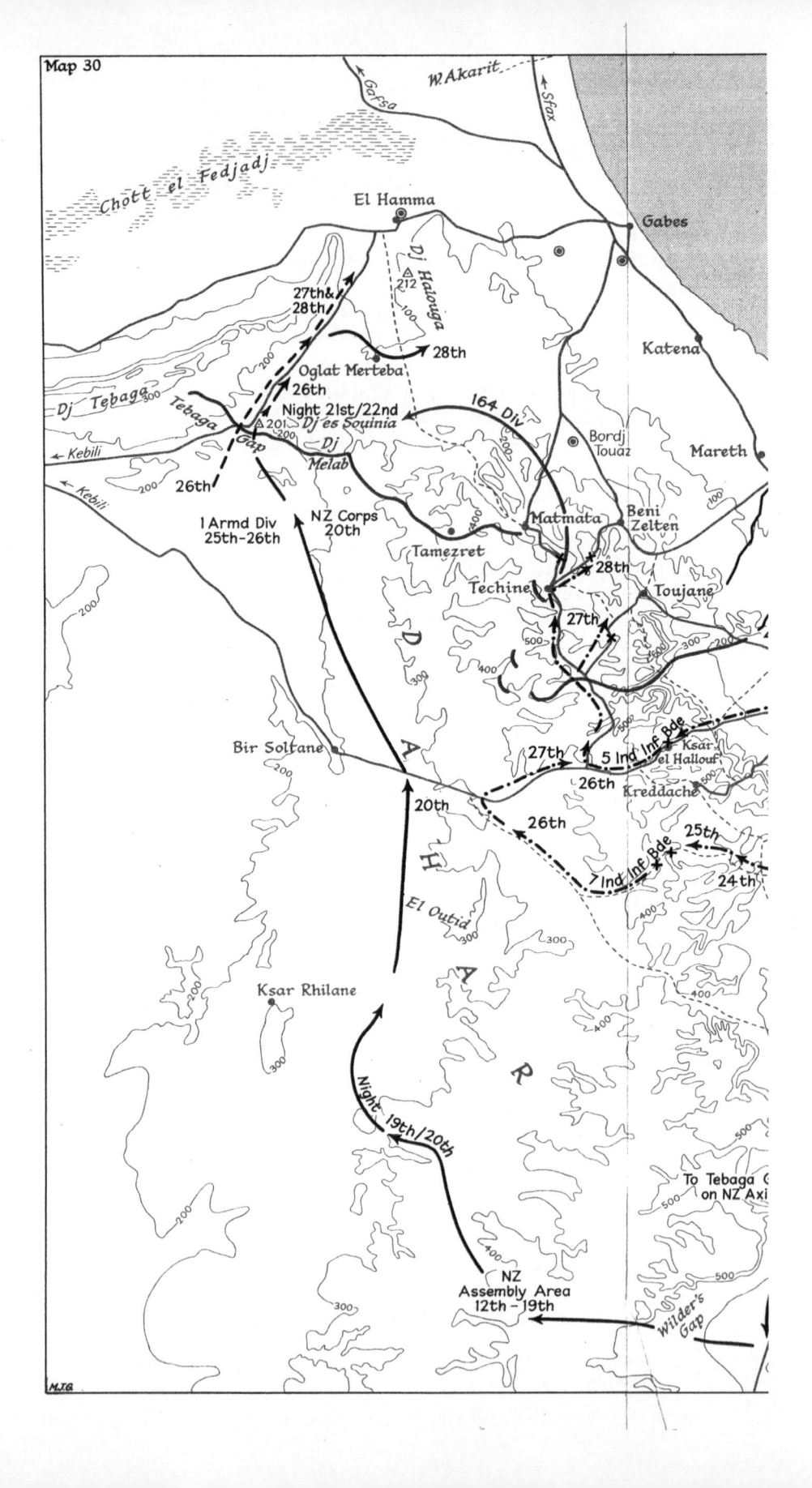

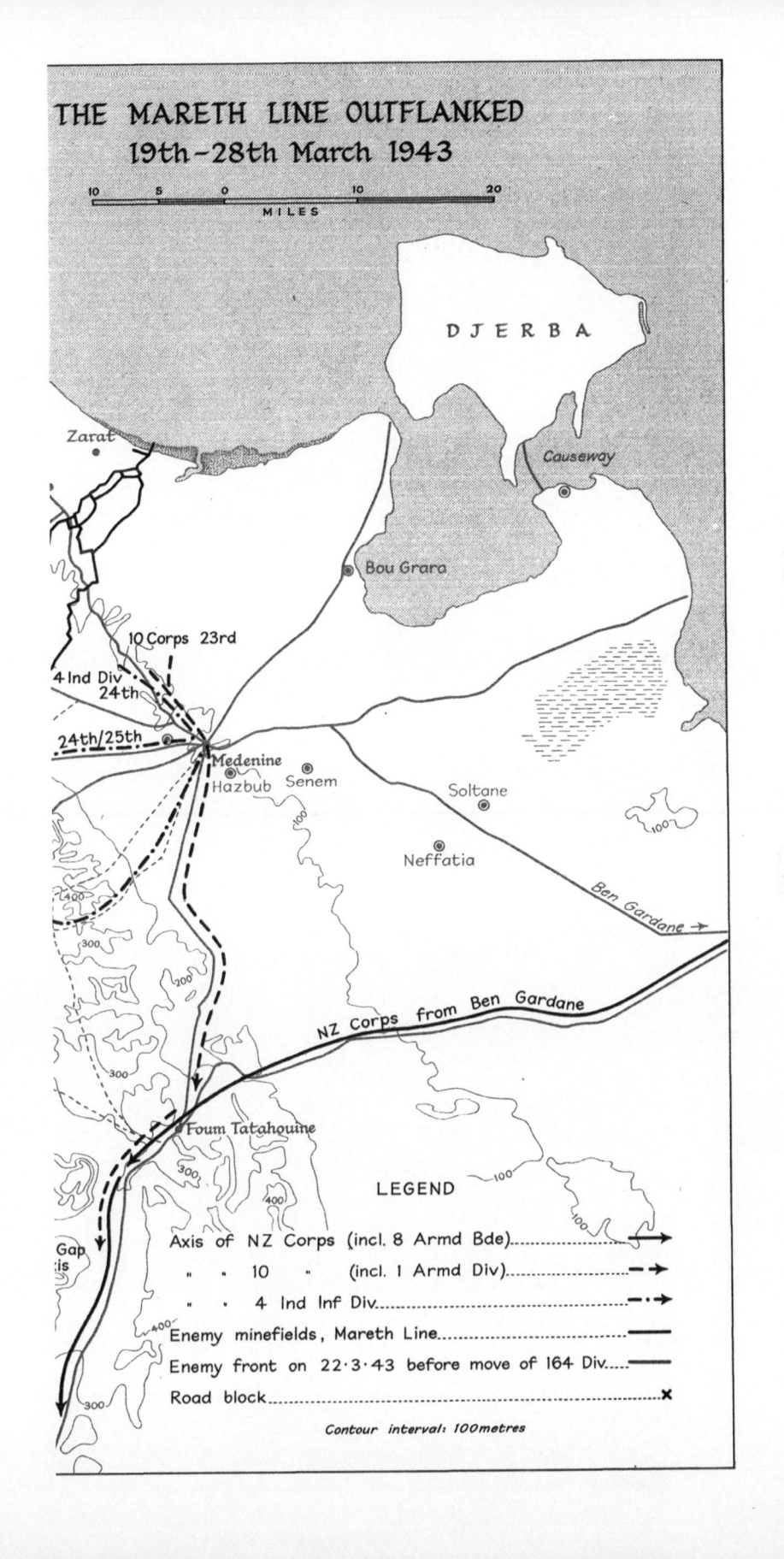

THE MARETH LINE OUTFLANKED
19th–28th March 1943

DJERBA

Zarat

Causeway

Bou Grara

10 Corps 23rd
4 Ind Div
24th
24th/25th
Medenine
Hazbub Senem
Soltane
Neffatia
Ben Gardane →
NZ Corps from Ben Gardane
Foum Tatahouine
Gap

LEGEND

Axis of NZ Corps (incl. 8 Armd Bde).................. →
" " 10 " (incl. 1 Armd Div)..................... –→
" " 4 Ind Inf Div.................................. –·→
Enemy minefields, Mareth Line.........................
Enemy front on 22·3·43 before move of 164 Div......
Road block.. ×

Contour interval: 100 metres

CHAPTER XIII

THE AXIS AT BAY

(26th February—30th March, 1943)

See Map 30

BY 12th February 1943 General Anderson had told his army that he intended to regain the initiative which had been temporarily lost. Four main measures of reorganization were indispensable. To create national sectors held by British, American and French troops under their own commanders whom he, as Army Commander, would direct. To form an Army Reserve because without one there could be no end to dancing to the enemy's tune. To restore scattered units and formations to their proper parents. To equip the French troops in up-to-date style. The boundaries between the new national sectors would come into force at midnight 25th/26th February, and the 1st Army, when remodelled, would be:

5th Corps:	78th, 46th, 1st (British) Infantry Divisions.
19th Corps:	Two French Infantry Divisions.
2nd (U.S.) Corps:	1st (U.S.) Armoured Division; 9th, 34th Infantry Divisions.
Army Reserve:	6th Armoured Division, 1st (U.S.) Infantry Division.

The Army would wear down the enemy and eventually defeat him by assault in co-operation with 8th Army.

General Alexander, on 21st February, declared that his object was to destroy the entire enemy force in Tunisia and that the key was to capture Tunis. The campaign would have two phases, the first to pass the 8th Army north of the Gabes gap.[1] In this phase the 1st Army would help the 8th Army by mounting carefully prepared, timed, and controlled attacks to secure dominating areas from which further advances could be made and by forcing the enemy to react and draw off reserves which otherwise he could use against the 8th Army. In the second phase both armies would direct their efforts to gaining airfields from which the ever-growing strength of the Allied

---

[1] 'The Gabes gap' is a portmanteau topographical description. We define it as the narrow strip of land extending from Gabes to the Wadi Akarit, and lying between the sea and the Chott el Fedjadj, and the northwards-running ridges and humps which end in the crags of Djebel Tebaga Fatnassa.

air force could be applied. When this phase had been accomplished the Allies would be able to co-ordinate fully the striking power of the three Services to draw a tight net round the Axis's position in Tunisia.

General Alexander had to remember always the decision of the Casablanca Conference, that the campaign in Africa must end by the 30th April in order that the invasion of Sicily should be launched before August, that is while the weather in the Mediterranean was still likely to allow small craft to make the passage.

General Montgomery, when thinking about the Mareth Line, had ordered the Long Range Desert Group to reconnoitre the inland flank of this position early in January 1943.[1] He had also been ordered by Alexander, on 21st February 1943, to create as powerful a threat as possible on the enemy's southern flank in order to help General Anderson who was having his hands full with the Kasserine battle. The 8th Army's administrative position was not strong enough to permit Montgomery to do anything forceful at once, but by 25th February parts of 7th Armoured and 51st Highland Division were at and beyond Medenine, and Leclerc's 'L' Force was at Ksar Rhilane, fifty miles south-west of Medenine. In the autumn of 1942 General Leclerc (commander of French forces in the district of French Equatorial Africa called Chad) had collected 555 French and 2,713 Colonial and African troops comprising camel and horsed cavalry, motorized infantry and a few guns—all equipped on a shoestring. He cleared the Fezzan of Italians, and with part of his force reached Tripoli on 26th January 1943. He was welcomed, as he deserved, by Alexander and Montgomery into the 8th Army as 'L' Force.[2]

G.H.Q. Middle East and H.Q. 8th Army had early understood that when Tripoli was captured the administrative problem would change. At Tripoli the 8th Army and the air forces would be 1,400 miles distant from G.H.Q. and the Main Base in the Delta, and about 1,000 miles by road from the nearest railhead at Tobruk. It was taken as an axiom that supplies of all natures for the further westward advance would come to Tripoli by sea.[3] At these distances efficient maintenance on a day-to-day method by direct contact between G.H.Q. and the 8th Army H.Q. would no longer be possible. In fact, at about this time, maintenance demands on G.H.Q. by 8th Army had to be prepared by the Army staff some thirty days

---

[1] Montgomery: *Memoirs* p. 157.
Stevens: *Bardia to Enfidaville* p. 157.
[2] The Fighting French Flying Column, which had been with 8th Army all the way from Alamein, was a small mixed force of armoured cars, tanks, infantry, A.A. and a/tk guns.
[3] There were some exceptions, e.g. vehicles might be sent by rail to Tobruk, and would then travel onwards by road.

before a sea-convoy was due to arrive at Tripoli. The length of notice, though necessary, practically ruled out adjustments of demands to meet changing circumstances. For though adjustments could be signalled, they could in practice be made only if the loading of the ships in the Egyptian ports had not reached a point at which an alteration would have meant a re-stowage and upheaval unacceptable to common sense. Major decisions about maintenance, taken hitherto by G.H.Q., would in future have to be taken by Army H.Q. G.H.Q. would have to look on the forces advancing through Tripolitania as an overseas expeditionary force, and maintain and control them in much the same way that the War Office controlled land forces in the Middle East in general. But to relieve the Army commander and his administrative staff from care of general maintenance and to free them to concentrate on operational maintenance, it was decided to create a complete Base and L. of C. Staff at Tripoli under the direct control of the Army commander. Tripolitania Base and L. of C. Area ('Tripbase' for short) had as its main role to ensure that the maintenance demands of the 8th Army were met, and secondly to administer the many units and installations of all kinds which were required in the Base Areas and upon the L. of C. at large. 'Tripbase', under a Major-General, included sections of the three branches of the Staff, 'G', 'A', and 'Q', and deputy-Directors of the main services.[1] It was wise to place the new organization in subordination to the 8th Army's commander because he and his staff best knew their own needs and local circumstances. 'Tripbase' began to form in Cairo on 28th January 1943, and on 28th February Brigadier Sir Brian Robertson, D.A. and Q.M.G. of 8th Army, was appointed to command it. 'Tripbase' took control of the Base Area and installations on 3rd March.

Since the capture of Tripoli on 23rd January no important fighting had occurred on 8th Army's front, but the air had tried to fulfil varied tasks though bad weather and regrouping had seriously reduced flying.

Within twenty-four hours of his losing Tripoli, American fighter-bombers of the Desert Air Force drove the enemy from his last air base (at Zuara) in Tripolitania. That same night the day-bombers (in use temporarily as night-bombers), after attacking M.T. convoys on the coast road near Ben Gardane, were stood down until the fourth week in February. For the rest of the month the fighter-

---

[1] The services represented were: Movements and Transportation; Supplies; Medical; Ordnance; R.E.M.E.; Pay; Provost; Postal; Printing; Judge-Advocate; Welfare; Chaplains; Pioneer and Labour; Salvage; Claims and Hirings; Catering. Tripbase was to play an important part in administration during the campaigns in Sicily and Italy.
Lieutenant-Colonel Miles Graham, A.Q.M.G. 8th Army, became its D.A. and Q.M.G. in succession to Sir Brian Robertson, and Lieutenant-Colonel R. M. Lymer R.A.S.C. became A.Q.M.G. 8th Army.

bombers alone provided air support, the airfield at Medenine, targets at Zuara, and roads and tracks between Medenine and the Tripolitanian frontier being the main attractions. Thereafter tactical air operations followed a regular course, with special attention to reconnaissance of all kinds. Reconnaissance of the Mareth area had begun in earnest at the end of January. It included photographic survey, mapping of the Mareth line, and producing photographic strips of surrounding areas, as well as normal tactical reconnaissance. This work continued at a steady pace whenever the weather was suitable and on 13th March it resulted in a first-class map of the Mareth line showing the terrain and defences in detail. Thereafter reconnaissance was intensified, and photographs of the Mareth area were still being taken at the height of the battle on 21st March.

The retreating enemy forces presented few worthwhile targets, but on the 8th and 11th February, during a break in the weather, the fighter-bombers attacked them in the Ben Gardane area. On the 14th the airfield at El Assa (35 miles south-east of Ben Gardane) became available, enabling the fighter-bombers to move some 100 miles nearer their targets. Next day, the enemy evacuated Ben Gardane, the centre of a vital group of airfields.

On the 17th February the bad weather returned and prevented a large group of enemy M.T. just west of Medenine from being attacked. On the night of the 23rd/24th the day-bombers, still as night-bombers, began operating again. Together with No. 205 Group's Wellingtons, and in support of 8th Army's preparations, they bombed targets in the Mareth area on three successive nights—150 or so British and American sorties were flown all told. On the 24th the fighter-bombers also were able to attack the enemy's forward landing ground at Bordj Touaz. Next day it was the turn of Gabes West airfield. From the 24th January to the 25th February, the daily British tactical air effort was, on average, only about 142 sorties of which nearly half were flown by the fighters of A.H.Q. Egypt protecting coastal shipping. The American average, so far as is recorded, was less than 10 sorties.

Throughout this period German air activity also appears to have been very small, but the enemy's reconnaissance aircraft were busy and closely watched the 8th Army. At night the Germans confined their air attacks mostly to the ports at Tripoli and Tobruk. At Tripoli they found the A.A. defences intense, and towards the end of February they replaced low-level attacks by bombing from medium altitude. There was a heavy raid on Tripoli on the night of 21st/22nd February by 15 Ju. 88s, two of which were destroyed by Beaufighters of No. 89 Squadron. Another Ju. 88 had been destroyed over Tobruk the previous night.

The British and American Middle East strategic bombers were

mainly occupied against embarkation ports in Sicily, Italy and Crete (See Chapter X). But the targets for the Wellingtons and Halifaxes, when they began a series of operations on the night of 23rd/24th February in support of the 8th Army's preparations, were the Gabes airfields. The sorties amounted to 89 in four consecutive nights.

Altogether, from dusk on the 23rd January to the night of the 25th/26th February, but excluding Malta's and the anti-shipping operations, the Royal Air Force flew 4,917 sorties and the U.S. Ninth Air Force 411, so far as is recorded. The British losses were 18 aircraft, the American 6 and the German 28. Italian losses are unknown.

It had been a rather dull time for the Middle East air forces. Operations of all kinds suffered from the weather and the Desert Air Force had few landing grounds beyond Tripoli. Those in the Tripoli area became congested and the enemy's ploughing and mining tactics, and the poor quality of the airfields themselves, made things worse. When El Assa airfield came into use on 14th February it was a big step forward, for though targets were by then widely dispersed and difficult to pinpoint, it brought the Desert Air Force fighter-bombers within easy striking distance of Medenine.

This period saw changes in command and deployment. On 25th January Advance A.H.Q. of the Desert Air Force was established near Castel Benito. The same day, the photographic reconnaissance resources of the Desert Air Force were combined in a new squadron, No. 680. On the 8th, No. 210 Group was formed under A.H.Q. Egypt to relieve the Desert Air Force of responsibility for the defence of Tripolitania. During the next two weeks the South African day-bombers moved forward to Sirtan and the Halifaxes and Wellingtons of No. 205 Group to Gardabia. The American Liberators quickly followed and were dispersed on a semi-circle of airfields around Benghazi, and the R.A.F. Liberators of No. 178 Squadron (formerly No. 160) moved into Hosc Raui airfield on the Tripoli road a little more than 20 miles south of Benghazi.[1] During the last week of the month Baltimores of No. 232 Wing and the Mitchells of the U.S. 12th (Medium Bombardment) Group arrived in the Tripoli area, completing the forward move of the Desert Air Force day-bombers for future air support operations. In conjunction with 8th Army's demonstrations to relieve enemy pressure on 1st Army, some of the Desert Air Force fighters moved to the Medenine area, No. 244 Wing going to Hazbub and No. 7 (S.A.A.F.) Wing to Neffatia—all under the control of an advanced H.Q. of No. 211 Group. Also in

---

[1] The 93rd U.S. (Heavy Bombardment) Group, which was the one transferred from the 'Torch' area to the Middle East in exchange for Fortresses, was not included. It returned to the U.S. Eighth Air Force (in the U.K.) later in February.

February the American squadrons operating with the Desert Air Force became 'Desert Air Task Force, Ninth Air Force.'

See also Map 31

By the 26th February the 8th Army was facing the Mareth position—which Alexander thought nearly as strong as Alamein, and only to be overcome by a deliberate and well-organized attack by as strong a force as could be maintained. That day Montgomery issued his plan for the attack. In outline his object was to destroy the enemy in the Mareth position, believed to be 90th and 164th Light Divisions, 15th Panzer Division, and the Spezia, Pistoia, Young Fascist, and Trieste Divisions, and then to advance and capture Sfax. He had to take the French-built defences between the sea and the Matmata hills, and based on the Wadi Zigzaou; and a less elaborate system between the Djebel Tebaga and Djebel Melab at the north-west end of the Matmata range. Montgomery had three Corps: 30th, comprising 50th, 51st, 4th Indian Divisions, 201st Guards Brigade; New Zealand, comprising New Zealand Division, 8th Armoured Brigade and Leclerc's 'L' Force; 10th, made up of 1st and 7th Armoured Divisions and the Fighting French Flying Column. 30th Corps was to deliver the main attack against the eastern flank of the Mareth line proper to break in, roll it up from east and north, destroy or prevent the escape of the garrison, and then to advance and capture Gabes. The New Zealand Corps was to move round the enemy's western flank by Ksar Rhilane, break through the secondary line and try to establish itself astride the Gabes—Matmata road in order to cut off fugitives from the whole Mareth position. 10th Corps was the 8th Army's Reserve. It was to protect the left flank and rear of 30th Corps, and to be ready to exploit success towards Gabes and Sfax. Montgomery gave the night 20th/21st March as the beginning of 30th Corps' main attack. This date was fixed mainly for administrative reasons, and because of the move of 10th Corps from Benghazi and Tmimi to an area south-west of Tripoli—1,300 miles for some units, accomplished between 27th February and 14th March, and in itself a great operational and administrative feat.[1] Alexander accepted this date, and he later directed 2nd U.S. Corps to help 8th Army by capturing Gafsa, exploiting towards Maknassy, and also by trying to capture El Guettar—beginning on 15th March.[2] The American Corps was to dump petrol at Gafsa for 8th Army.

---

[1] On 26th February Montgomery estimated that Tripoli held two days' reserves for the 8th Army. He required at least fourteen days' reserves.

Two administrative illustrations of 10th Corps' move must suffice. 1st Armoured Division's tanks were carried on 289 tank-transporters for which over 100,000 gallons of special fuel had to be placed at nine staging points. For the whole Corps, 1,198,750 gallons of fuel (4,795 tons) had to be placed at the right points along the route.

[2] Alexander issued his formal directive to 8th and 1st Armies for Mareth and later operations in Tunisia on 14th March.

Map 31

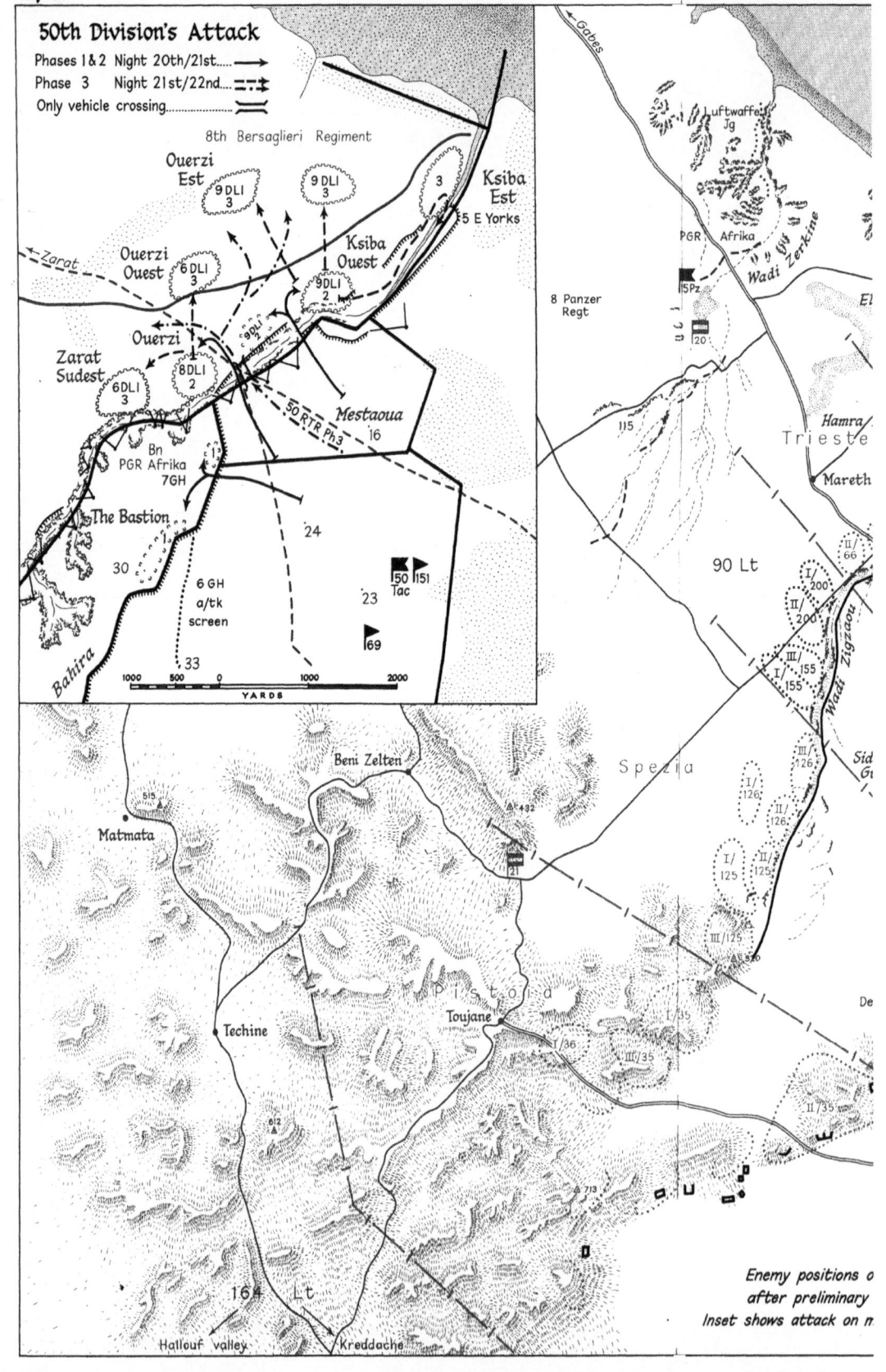

50th Division's Attack

Phases 1 & 2 Night 20th/21st........ →
Phase 3 Night 21st/22nd....... ⇢
Only vehicle crossing.................. ═

Enemy positions o
after preliminary
Inset shows attack on m

BATTLE OF MARETH

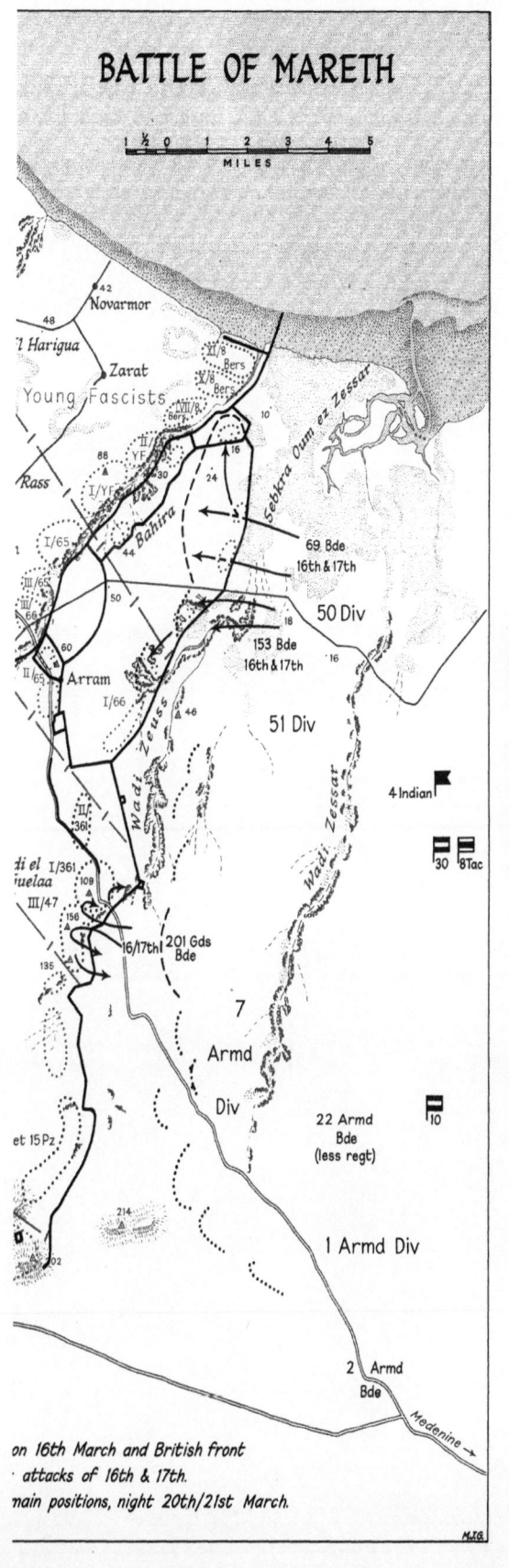

BATTLE OF MARETH
16th – 23rd March 1943

British troops are shown in red, German in blue and Italian in Green

	Headquarters of Armies
🏳 8	8th (Montgomery)
	AOK 1 (Messe) *(Southwest of Gabes)*
	Headquarters of Corps
🏳 10	10th (Horrocks)
🏳 30	30th (Leese)
🏳 20	20th (Orlando)
🏳 21	21st (Berardi)
🏳 🏳 🏳	Headquarters of Divisions
🏳	Headquarters of Brigades
(69) (115)	Brigades or Panzergrenadier Regiments
(8) (5)	Armoured Brigades and Panzer Regiments
(6H) (II/361) (I/65)	Other units and detachments
(⌒)	Armoured (British) Regiments
⊢—⊢—⊢	Inter Divisional boundary
▬▬▬	Enemy minefields, main alignment
▒▒▒▒	Anti-tank ditch
>	Wadi bank impassable to all vehicles

on 16th March and British front
attacks of 16th & 17th.
main positions, night 20th/21st March.

On 11th March N.A.T.A.F. issued an outline plan to cover tactical air operations until the end of the campaign in Africa. The points relevant at this stage in our narrative follow. Administratively, it was foreseen that first No. 242 Group R.A.F. and U.S. XII A.S.C. would move generally eastward, and that later the Desert Air Force would follow northwards. Existing airfields would have to be improved and new ones acquired, and sufficient stocks laid down so that the Desert Air Force would find everything ready. The general trend thereafter would be both eastwards and north-eastwards, and more airfields, radar stations, and all kinds of stores would be needed.

Operationally, the Desert Air Force was, first, to support the 8th Army while No. 242 Group and U.S. XII A.S.C. brought the enemy to battle in the air and attacked his airfields. Then, when the enemy air forces began their retreat northwards, U.S. XII A.S.C. and the Desert Air Force together were to harry them while No. 242 Group, this time assisted by N.A.S.A.F., attacked his main airfields.

Air Marshal Coningham was determined that there should be no doubt about his intentions, and that the organization and preparation to carry them out should be complete. The immediate problem, however, was air support for the Battle of Mareth, and on 12th March Coningham conferred at Canrobert with his subordinate tactical air force commanders, and made further decisions. Before D day No. 242 Group and U.S. XII A.S.C. would attack the enemy's airfields on all fronts, and enemy army concentrations reported by Desert Air Force reconnaissance aircraft in the south. When the battle began they were to try to bomb, round-the-clock, the enemy's airfields, including those in the Gabes area, to divert his attention from 8th Army's front. The Desert Air Force would, in consequence, be free to keep command of the air over the battle area and to support the 8th Army. In the second task the Desert Air Force day-bombers were to attack enemy army concentrations and landing grounds in the forward area, and at night also if not fully employed by day. The fighters would give cover to the troops and escort the bombers, but up to a third of the fighter force was cast for a fighter-bomber role against targets in the battle area. At night the Hurricanes of No. 73 Squadron were to supplement the fighter-bomber attacks by ground strafing, protecting the forward troops and covering the Desert Air Force's landing grounds. Meanwhile, during the moon period, No. 205 Group was to attack the enemy's landing grounds, and targets in the battle area to deprive the Axis troops of sleep.

It was obvious that the Axis might try a spoiling attack: '... exactly what we would like;' wrote General Montgomery in his plan, 'it would give us a great opportunity to take heavy toll of the enemy as a first step and then to put in our own *heavy attack* when he was disorganized ...'

His self-confidence was admirable, but he later wrote that the first days of March were anxious. There was indeed much at stake because a successful Axis attack might wreck the Forward Maintenance Area which was growing up at Ben Gardane, and set back the 8th Army's time-table, and the timing fixed by the Casablanca Conference for the whole campaign.

The Axis commanders were, in fact, planning offensives in north and south Tunisia but scarcely in accord. As noticed in Chapter XII, on 23rd February Ambrosio had directed Rommel to attack the 8th Army south of Gabes but von Arnim the next day flew to Rome and persuaded Kesselring to back his plans for an independent offensive in the north. This began on the 26th and petered out by the beginning of March—soon after Rommel had accepted from his subordinates a plan for the attack south of Gabes, which he did not like, and which failed.

The senior commanders in the Army Group were pessimistic as well as pugnacious. On 26th February von Arnim gave an appreciation to Rommel, and Messe, who was now in command of the Axis forces in the south renamed 'Italian First Army' or *AOK 1*, followed suit. The pith of von Arnim's was that the Axis forces were too weak in every way to withstand the attempt which he believed that the two Allied armies would make to drive a wedge between the two Axis armies. If he were in Eisenhower's shoes, he would not bother to mount a land offensive but would set himself to pulverising the Axis L. of C. and air forces, because '. . . if no supplies reach us, all will be up in Tunisia by 1st July . . .' The only thing to do was to concentrate both Axis armies, and to supply them sufficiently to enable them together to defeat first one Allied Army, and then the other. Messe, on the 27th, wrote that he was too weak to hold the attacks which he expected the Allies to make on the Mareth Line proper, on its secondary position at Djebel Tebaga—Djebel Melab, and on Maknassy and Sfax. His main suggestion was to retreat to the Wadi Akarit while there was yet time.

On 1st March Rommel sent these papers to *Comando Supremo*, *OKW*, and Kesselring, with his own observations. The gist of these was that his Army Group was far too weak for its long front and that his administrative situation was nearly desperate. He would do what he could with spoiling attacks but the Allies would certainly put their entire forces into a simultaneous offensive probably at the next full moon, and would drive an irremovable wedge between his two armies. The only remedy was to retreat to a line running from *Pz AOK 5's* positions on the northern Tunisian coast through the area of Djebel Mansour to Enfidaville. This short front, which presented many severe natural obstacles to an assailant, could be held for a fair time. The main disadvantages of the policy were that it would allow the 1st and 8th Armies unhindered contact, and would give up airfields which were very valuable to the German Air Force. But any other policy would lead to the Axis Armies being crushed in turn, and to the certain loss of the bridgehead in Africa.

On 6th March Kesselring let Rommel know that Hitler and *Comando Supremo* rejected his views. Kesselring himself opposed Rommel's policy because he thought that it would sterilize the Axis air force in the African theatre. He told *OKW* that only extreme emergency, as yet absent, could justify shortening the front. To concentrate the armies was to risk losing Tunisia. Instead widely-ranging mobile formations should check the Allies and gain time for reinforcements and equipment to arrive with which to extend and strengthen the front. Hitler, whose attention to the Tunisian theatre had been unpleasantly sharpened by the field commanders' reports, criticized Kesselring's handling of its administration. The Army Group was told that supplies to Tunisia must be doubled if not tripled, but not how.

Meanwhile, on 28th February, Rommel discussed with Messe, Ziegler, and the commanders of the German armoured divisions, the attack which was now to be directed at Medenine, an important junction of roads and tracks.[1] These subordinates advised attacking on three axes: the Hallouf Pass—Medenine; Toujane—Metameur; and a third roughly equidistant between. Rommel disagreed and suggested that the 10th and 21st Panzer Divisions should advance from Bou Grara (near the coast) upon Medenine; 15th Panzer Division and part of 164th Light Division from Toujane via the Hallouf Pass on Metameur; and 90th Light, Spezia and Trieste Divisions astride the road Mareth—Medenine. This plan gave two armoured divisions a chance of cutting in from an unlikely direction, but the subordinate commanders objected to the risks.

Messe and Ziegler, as spokesmen, said that the approaches from the coast were very difficult, perhaps impassable, heavily mined and covered by many guns.[2] If two armoured divisions were committed here they would have no elbow-room and would be an easy target for the British aircraft and artillery. Rommel did not impose his own plan and agreed to further reconnaissance before a decision. In fact he gave no more suggestions, and the final plan was made by Messe and Ziegler. On 3rd March Army Group Africa noted that the attack would not begin until the 6th to allow time to replace the

---

[1] Ziegler was acting as commander of *D.A.K.* until its new commander, Lieutenant-General Hans Cramer took over on 5th March.
[2] This information came from reconnaissance by 15th Panzer and 90th and 164th Light Divisions; and Ziegler, when commanding *D.A.K.*

casualties which the mobile formations had suffered during '*Morgenluft*', and to regroup.

See Map 32

Messe's orders trickled out between 2nd and 5th March. His object was to envelop and destroy the British deployed between the Mareth Line and Medenine—but privately he thought the British would accept battle without interrupting their plans. He formed two main groups: *D.A.K.* (Cramer) and Column Bari (von Sponeck).[1] *D.A.K.'s* task was to capture the line Hir en Nraa—Ksar Rebounten (in fact held by 7th Armoured Division and 154th Infantry Brigade) and then make an enveloping move north or north-eastwards. More explicitly, 10th Panzer Division was to debouch from the Hallouf valley and take Metameur. 21st Panzer Division, emerging from the southern Djebel Tebaga, was to go for Hir Ksar Koutine. 15th Panzer Division from Djebel er Remtsia was to make for Hir en Nraa, their infantry was to follow and mop up. The Reconnaissance Units were to block the road Foum Tatahouine—Medenine to prevent the arrival of reinforcements. Column Bari was to attack frontally Zemlet el Lebene with Spezia Battle Group on the right, Panzer Grenadier Regiment 200 in the centre, and Trieste Battle Group on the left. The mobile formations had three consumption units of fuel and the entire force had about one 'issue' of ammunition. The artillery's shell was not well proportioned among its various types of gun. It was a scrappy plan. It seems that Rommel took no interest in the details, although he gave a 'pep talk' to divisional commanders on the 5th. His former fiery spirit was burning low.

On 5th March the Axis air force was to bomb Allied airfields and also protect the assembly of the Axis formations. On the 6th it was to strafe the British guns east of Zemlet el Lebene, to neutralize the forward Allied airfields, to give fighter cover to the assaulting troops, and to reconnoitre south of Foum Tatahouine and to Ben Gardane. It seems that the German Air Force had about 100 serviceable aircraft, and we estimate serviceable Italian fighters, fighter-bombers, and dive-bombers at about 60.

General Montgomery had by 5th March reinforced 30th Corps with the N.Z. Division and 8th Armoured and 201st Guards

---

[1] *Main formations*

D.A.K.: 10th, 15th, 21st Panzer Divisions; 3rd and 33rd Reconnaissance Units, one bn 164th Light Division; one parachute battalion; seven German field batteries; two divisional A.A. bns. *Column Bari.*: Panzer Grenadier Regiment 200 (two bns); Panzer Grenadier Regiment 361 (two bns); Spezia Battle Group (two bns); Trieste Battle Group (two bns); one battery German field artillery with some attached Nebelwerfers; seven Italian field batteries; detachments of three A.A. batteries.

D.A.K. and Column Bari both included anti-tank and engineer units.

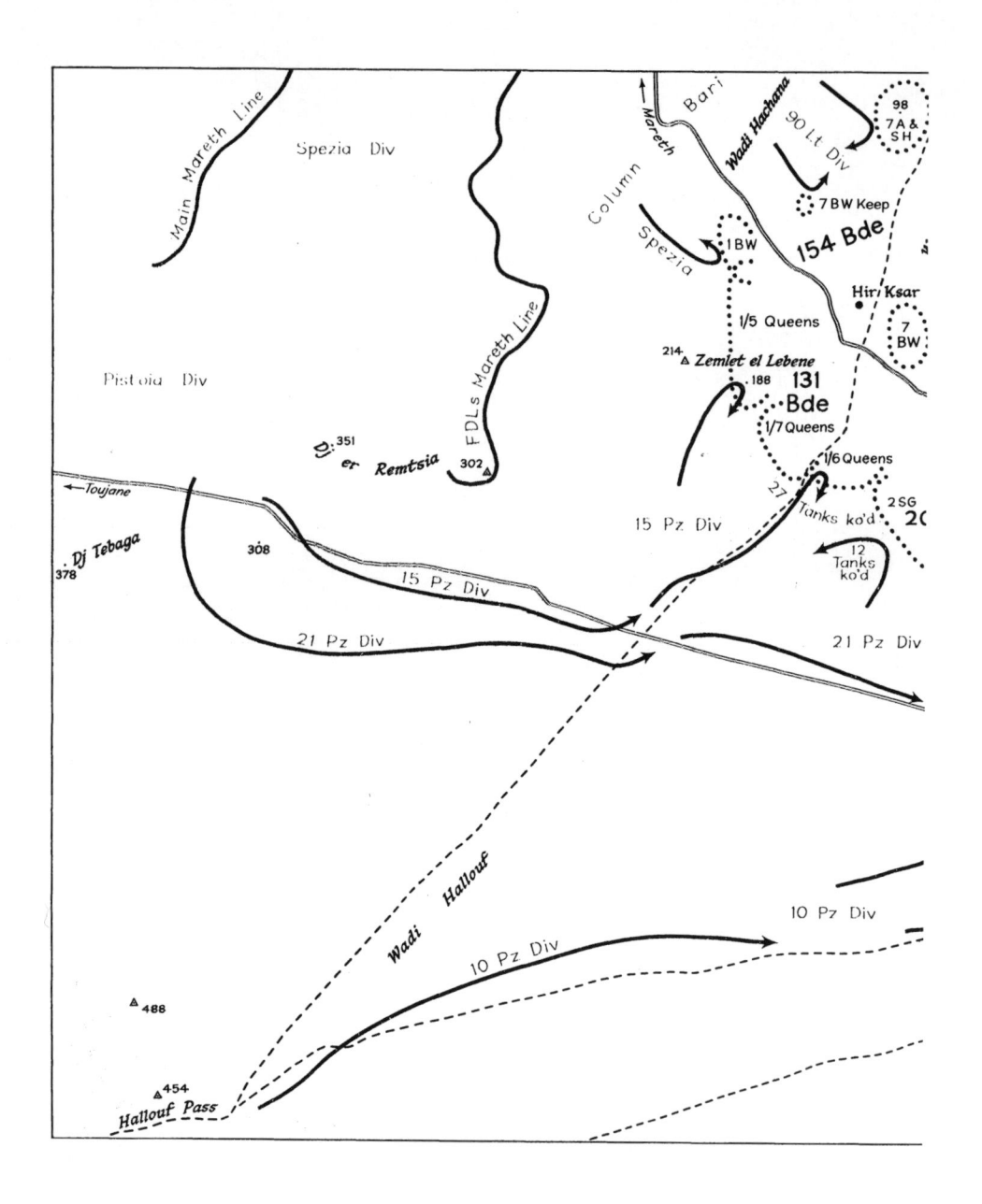

Map 32
BATTLE OF MEDENINE
6th March 1943

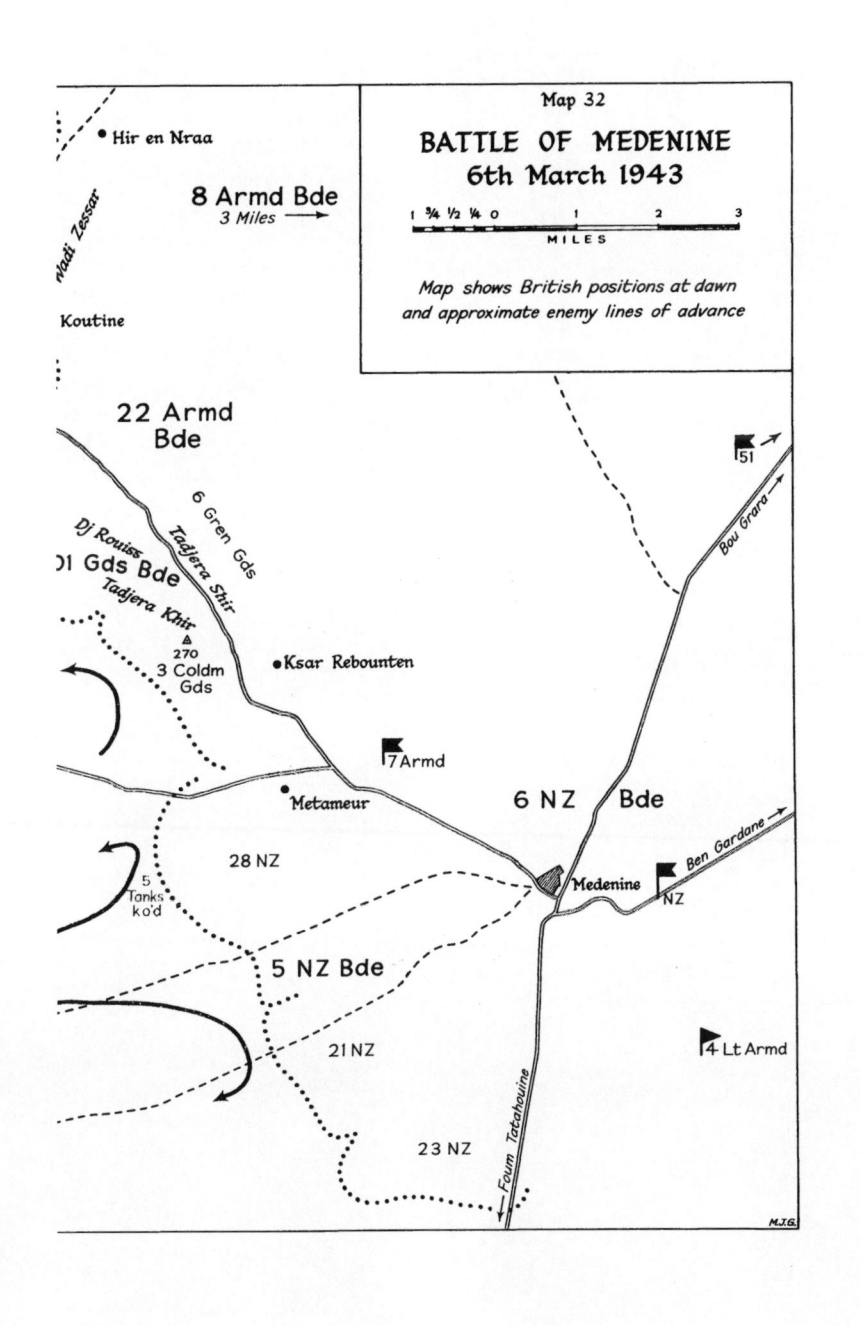

Map shows British positions at dawn and approximate enemy lines of advance

Brigades. The Corps held a front of about 43,000 yards and the defence was admirably thought out. The anti-tank guns had at last been sited to kill tanks and not to 'protect' infantry, field guns, or anything else. Some 3·7″ A.A. guns had been added to the anti-tank guns, and no 25-pdrs had been saddled with an anti-tank task. 51st Division on the right held about 20,000 yards along the Wadi Zessar, a natural anti-tank ditch strengthened by 70,000 mines.[1] 130 anti-tank guns were in position; six regiments of 25-pdrs and 43 medium guns were in support. Somewhat left of the Division's centre stood 22nd Armoured Brigade. 7th Armoured Division occupied the area which in fact was to be Messe's main objective. 131st Infantry Brigade occupied the Zemlet el Lebene ridge, and 201st Guards Brigade the small hill Tadjera Khir which overlooked the whole Corps' position.[2] In the rear of 131st Infantry Brigade were 22nd and 8th Armoured Brigades in depth. The Division disposed of about 100 field guns and 200 anti-tank guns. New Zealand Division was in the Medenine area with 4th Light Armoured Brigade, three field and two anti-tank regiments.

The Corps had, in round numbers, 350 25-pdr and medium guns, 460 anti-tank guns, 300 tanks, and plenty of shells. The incomplete Axis records which survive suggest that Messe's German formations had 124 assorted field guns, and possibly 33 8·8-cm A.A./A-tk guns and 58 anti-tank guns of calibres from 5-cm to 7·62-cm. On 4th March 10th Panzer Division held 35 'fit' tanks, 15th Panzer Division 60, and 21st Panzer Division 46.[3]

The Desert Air Force, too, was ready to scotch a spoiling attack in this Medenine area. For days Tac/R and Strat/R aircraft had closely watched what the enemy was doing. The bad weather had not saved his columns from being bombed during their approach march, and attacks on his airfields had included Bordj Touaz, situated well forward and therefore vital to him.

On 6th March the Panzer Regiments set off towards their objectives but once across the plain were quickly in trouble. 10th Panzer Division seems to have taken hardly the loss of five tanks, mainly at the hands of 73rd Anti-Tank Regiment R.A. (temporarily under command of the New Zealand Division). 21st Panzer Division's leading tanks crossed a ridge clumsily and 'got shot' while the rest 'wandered rather vaguely', as observers in 201st Guards Brigade reported. 15th Panzer Division alone closed with the British positions, and was smitten by 131st Infantry Brigade and 2nd Scots

---

[1] Montgomery's statement ('*Alamein to the Sangro*', pages 46, 55) that he had no mines may be a slip. Alternatively 30th Corps may have diverted transport from carrying mines to dumping shells with the result that not every formation had received mines.

[2] 201st Guards Brigade was temporarily under command of 7th Armoured Division.

[3] Messe gives Trieste Division 48 field guns and Spezia 54, but not their distribution to the troops in battle and in the Mareth defences.

Guards.[1] The British anti-tank gunners distinguished themselves in a way neatly described by a New Zealander—'a truly grand victory for the Tommy (English) gunners ... The way in which they held their fire was an example to us all.' The Axis attacked again in the afternoon with infantry as well as armour but by about 5.30 p.m. had come almost to a standstill. The artillery of 30th Corps fired about 30,000 rounds with fine effect. At an unrecorded time Messe, who does not seem to have been on the battlefield at all, suggested calling off the battle and at 8.30 p.m. Rommel gave the order to end what was to prove to be his last battle in Africa. He explained to von Sponeck that *AOK 1* could not punch a way through except at the cost of losses which would jeopardize its defence of the Mareth position.

The British losses were trifling. The Axis had 635 casualties, two-thirds German, and lost between 44 and 56 tanks. Heavy mist spoiled the British air plans but the German Air Force was unusually active. It attacked the Desert Air Force's airfields and damaged several fighters. It had no success against the British troops, and Stukas had a rough reception from the A.A. when they attacked artillery positions. Reconnaissance aircraft however did quite well. The 8th Army and supporting air forces scored a complete and well-deserved success at Medenine and were justifiably proud and elated.

See Map 33

Ambrosio's directive of 23rd February had been based on the false belief that the Kasserine battles had inflicted heavy land and air losses on the Allies, supported by assertions that the Axis had broken off these operations simply because the Allies had robbed northern Tunisia to reinforce central Tunisia heavily, and that the Axis Command now gave first place to attacking the 8th Army. He therefore directed *Pz AOK 5* to launch harassing raids and sorties and to prepare to advance its main line in the north. von Arnim skipped the raids and, with Kesselring's approval but without consulting Rommel, staged a strong thrust by Weber towards Gafour, Teboursouk and Béja, and a weaker one by von Manteuffel aimed at Djebel Abiod.[2] von Arnim in fact was resurrecting his plan

---

[1] Main units of:
131st Infantry Brigade (Brigadier L. G. Whistler): 1st Bn/5th The Queen's Royal Regiment; 1st Bn/6th The Queen's Royal Regiment; 1st Bn/7th The Queen's Royal Regiment.
201st Guards Brigade (Brigadier J. A. Gascoigne): 6th Bn The Grenadier Guards, 3rd Bn The Coldstream Guards; 2nd Bn The Scots Guards.
5th N.Z. Infantry Brigade (Brigadier H. K. Kippenberger): 21st., 23rd, 28th (Maori) Bns; 5th N.Z. Field Regiment; 'A' Battery, 73rd Anti-Tank Regiment R.A.
1st Bn The Black Watch and 7th Bn The Argyll and Sutherland Highlanders of the Highland Division's 154th Infantry Brigade (Brigadier J. E. Stirling), on the right of 131st Infantry Brigade, repulsed certain attacks.

[2] Weber's operation was named '*Ochsenkopf*' and von Manteuffel's '*Ausladung*', but '*Ochsenkopf*' was used by Axis higher commanders to describe both together.

Map 33

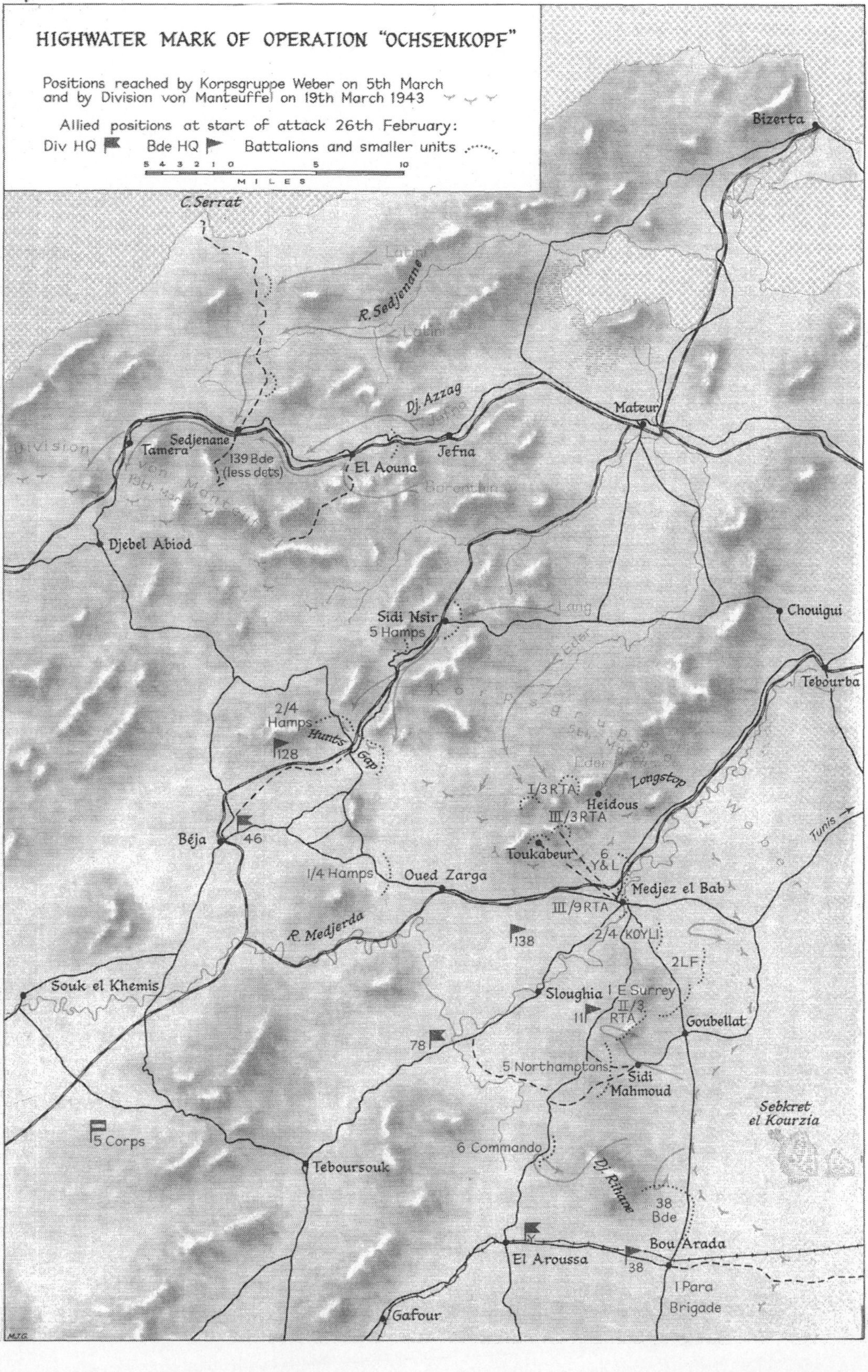
HIGHWATER MARK OF OPERATION "OCHSENKOPF"
Positions reached by Korpsgruppe Weber on 5th March and by Division von Manteuffel on 19th March 1943
Allied positions at start of attack 26th February:
Div HQ
Bde HQ
Battalions and smaller units
5 4 3 2 1 0 5 10
MILES
C. Serrat
R. Sedjenane
Dj. Azzag
Bizerta
Mateur
Sedjenane
Tamera
139 Bde (less dets)
El Aouna
Jefna
Djebel Abiod
Sidi Nsir
5 Hamps
Chouigui
Tebourba
2/4 Hamps
Hunts Gap
128
I/3 RTA
Heidous
Longstop
III/3 RTA
Béja
46
Toukabeur
6 Y&L
Tunis
1/4 Hamps
Oued Zarga
Medjez el Bab
III/9 RTA
R. Medjerda
138
2/4 KOYLI
2LF
Souk el Khemis
Sloughia
1 E Surrey
II/3 RTA
11
Goubellat
78
5 Northamptons
Sidi Mahmoud
Sebkret el Kourzia
5 Corps
6 Commando
Dj. Rihane
Teboursouk
38 Bde
Bou Arada
El Aroussa
38
1 Para Brigade
Gafour
M.J.G.

to strike at Béja which had been killed, on 19th February, by '*Morgenluft*'. His idea was promising because success would deprive the Allies of the very good tank-run from Medjez el Bab towards Tunis.

'*Ochsenkopf*' began punctually on 26th February, by the end of the 27th showed no signs of the spectacular gains predicted by von Arnim, and then, on the 28th, Rommel directed that it must both succeed *and* stop. Nevertheless fighting by von Manteuffel against 46th Infantry Division on the extreme northern flank went on until 1st April, and by Weber's troops, also against 46th Infantry Division, in the Hunt's Gap area which covered Béja, bitterly and stubbornly until 5th March. In the Teboursouk—El Aroussa sector, held by 78th and 'Y' (this, a collection of detachments) Divisions, Weber made almost no impression.

The fighting during '*Ochsenkopf*' though rather scrappy, was often hard. As regards the Allies it fell mostly on 46th Division, newcomers who had much to learn and who, because of the general-post forced on the 1st Army by the Kasserine battles, were denied the advantage of fighting closely knit as a division. On the extreme northern flank 139th Infantry Brigade (Brigadier B. Howlett; later Brigadier R. E. H. Stott) was engaged with mixed German and Italian Battle Groups.[1] Matters did not at first go well for the British because they were elbowed out of El Aouna on 1st March, out of Sedjenane on the 4th, and out of Tamera on the 17th. But on the 29th they counter-attacked, and by 1st April had regained every position.

Harder fighting occurred between 128th Infantry Brigade (Brigadier M. A. James V.C.) and Weber's Battle Group Lang in the Hunt's Gap sector.[2] This began on 26th February at the patrol-

---

[1] (a) *139th Infantry Brigade*. Main units included: 6th Bn The Lincolnshire Regiment; 2nd/5th Bn The Sherwood Foresters; 16th Bn The Durham Light Infantry; 1st Commando; 70th Field Regiment R.A.; 15th/17th Medium Battery R.A.; 456th Light Battery R.A.
  (b) *Battle Group Latini*. 10th Bersaglieri Regiment; Field Battalion T.4; Marsch Battalion A 30; two companies 11th Parachute Engineer Battalion; troop Flak Regiment 52 (8·8-cm); troop light howitzers.
  (c) *Battle Group Jefna*. Field Battalion T.3; one company A/Tk guns; one company Light Flak artillery; one troop miscellaneous field guns.
  A reserve was formed by the Barenthin Regiment and 11th Parachute Engineer Battalion.

[2] (a) *128th Infantry Brigade*. Main units included:
    1st/4th Bn The Hampshire Regiment; 2nd/4th Bn The Hampshire Regiment; 5th Bn The Hampshire Regiment; 2nd/5th Battalion The Leicestershire Regiment; two squadrons North Irish Horse; 171st and 172nd Field Regiment R.A.; one battery 102nd Army Field Regiment R.A.; 457th Light Battery R.A.; 58th Anti-Tank Regiment R.A.; 5th Medium Regiment R.A.
    Reinforcements were received from 8th Bn The Argyll and Sutherland Highlanders (78th Infantry Division); 2nd Parachute Bn (1st Parachute Brigade).
  (b) *Battle Group Lang*
    Pz. Abt. 501 (14 Tigers, 12 Pzkw IV Special, 15 Pzkw III). II Panzer Regiment 7 less one company (8 Pzkw IV, 25 Pzkw III). I/Panzer Grenadier Regiment 86. Reconnaissance Bn 190. II/Artillery Regiment 22. Dets. of Light Flak and Engineers.
  (c) *138th Infantry Brigade* (Brigadier G. P. Harding)
    of 46th Division, under command of 78th Division, was in the area Medjez el Bab—Oued Zarga.

base of Sidi Nsir (twelve miles north-east of Hunt's Gap) when Lang's group fell upon a detachment consisting of 5th Hampshires and 155th Battery R.A. and overwhelmed it after a fight of twelve hours. 120 survivors of the Hampshires and nine of 155th Battery reached the main position after retreat had been ordered, but all the field guns were knocked out by the enemy, or destroyed by the gunners when it became impossible to save those still in action. About 40 of Lang's tanks were destroyed or crippled, although many were repaired because his troops held the field. On the 27th and 28th Lang went on towards Hunt's Gap and met a hot reception. By 1st March he appeared to have only five tanks fit to fight, and by that evening Weber judged that he had small chance of success. He ordered him to go over to the defensive, to withdraw his tanks for repair, and to hand over command of his sector to Oberst Buhse of Grenadier Regiment 47 of the 'Corps' reserve. Next day Lang was given command of most of 334th Division's infantry which had been in action south of Hunt's Gap and on the 4th Weber ordered his whole Corps to take up defensive positions. Lang's defeat was caused mainly by the excellent British artillery fire, by the rain-soaked ground on which his tanks could not manoeuvre, and by well-staged infantry attacks during which the Sappers destroyed damaged tanks which the enemy might have pulled out of harm's way.[1]

The spot-light has been directed on Hunt's Gap as a sample of the fighting on the whole front. The Allied air forces took a full share in defeating von Arnim's plans although in northern and central Tunisia the weather was bad for flying on one day in three from 28th February for about a month. Under this handicap No. 242 Group R.A.F. and the U.S. XII A.S.C. (this formation mainly supporting 2nd U.S. Corps) carried on their usual tasks: fighter sweeps, attacks on ground targets, escorts to bombers and tactical reconnaissance aircraft, and so on.[2] The day and night-bombers maintained 'business as usual' unless the weather decisively interfered. Variation was given by the occasional use of Fortresses and Wellingtons against tactical targets. Newcomers were the Huitième Groupement of the Free French Air Force who operated LeO 45 night-bombers from Biskra in Algeria.

We have merely pointers to the results of air operations from enemy records. By 1st March movement of transport by day was becoming almost impossible. The middle of the month saw the Axis air forces beginning to be harried from one airfield to another. On

---

[1] The German tank casualties caused an official 'breeze' right up to Army Group H.Q.; and it is said that the troops nicknamed Lang 'Tank-Killer'.

[2] During the second week in March Nos. 225 and 241 Army Co-operation Squadrons were at length employed in accordance with up-to-date practice: No. 225 Squadron solely on tactical reconnaissance; No. 241 Squadron as fighter-bombers.

16th March the Germans began to use long-range bombers tactically to support ground troops—a sign that their dive-bombers and ground-attack aircraft were being forced out of the game. Lang writing postwar mentions 23rd March as the beginning of the 'suffocation' of the German air force. The reason was not excessive loss of aircraft but that aircrews were becoming worn out by too heavy and too varied duties.

The activities of the Allied strategic bombers from North West Africa up to the end of the third week in February have been described in previous chapters. From then until the end of March they were mainly employed against the Tunisian, Sicilian and Sardinian ports (see Chapters X and XVI). By day, however, the Fortresses also attacked the airfields at El Aouina; La Marsa, near Tunis; also Gabes and Kairouan—on the 10th and 11th March a total of 4 Ju. 52s were destroyed at El Aouina. After an attack on the marshalling yard at Sousse on the afternoon of 12th March the Germans recorded much damage to the railway, repair shop and water tanks, adding that these services were restored only in part by the end of the month. By night the Wellingtons attacked the marshalling yards at Bizerta and Tunis on a small scale. Throughout these five weeks the strategic bombers were plagued by bad weather by day and night.

General Alexander on 8th March took 2nd U.S. Corps under his direct command, while leaving 19th Corps under 1st Army. On 14th March he issued a directive more precise than that of 21st February. 8th Army was to capture the Mareth position and 2nd U.S. Corps to advance on Maknassy and Gabes to threaten the enemy's L. of C. north of Gabes. Then 8th Army was to exploit to Gabes while the American Corps kept up pressure, thus jointly forcing the enemy into defensive positions in central Tunisia. General preparations for the final assault to destroy the Axis in North Africa were to begin at once, but the detailed plan would depend upon the results of the operations which would follow the capture of Mareth.

The Axis leaders agreed that Tunisia must be held for strategic reasons; that the Tunisian 'bridgehead' must not be narrowed; and that supplies were all-important. Hitler sent Admiral Dönitz to Rome, with some good proposals to better the administrative system, (related in Chapter XVI) on 15th March: too late. There was no harmony between the German and Italian staffs. Ambrosio saw facts clearly, and was stronger in dealing with the Germans than Cavallero had been. Kesselring gave Mussolini doses of soothing-syrup which were effective and even tried some on von Arnim which had contrary effects.

von Arnim took command of the Army Group when Rommel left Africa on 9th March. The next day Kesselring and Westphal arrived to confer with von Arnim, Gause, Mancinelli (Messe's

Italian Chief of Staff) and Seidemann, the recently appointed Commander of *Fliegerkorps Tunis*. Kesselring said that the Army Group's task was to hold its positions from Cape Serrat to Mareth. von Arnim replied that *Comando Supremo* must bear the responsibility for refusing to shorten a front which could hold in the north, but was weak in the centre, and about to face a fierce assault in the south. Penetration somewhere was inevitable and the necessary counter-attacks would consume the Axis reserve. He emphasized the shortage of ammunition. Kesselring retorted that the troops' morale had not been improved by so often withdrawing them from positions which they had been ordered to hold, and that the cry of shortage of ammunition had been heard at Alamein, and yet 12,000 tons had been abandoned there.

After this angry conference von Arnim next day issued a directive for operations at Mareth. The forward defences, which were vital, must be held while a man remained alive. The British infantry would probably attack on both sides of, and north of, the road Medenine—Mareth, at night with heavy artillery support, and tanks would follow. If the attack went well, the enemy would aim at rolling up the position from north to south. The defence must meet the enemy's infantry with concentrated artillery fire, and must prevent mine-lifting. *AOK 1* must lay out a deep area on each side of Mareth in which counter-attacks could be made, probably by Army Group reserve which was likely to comprise 10th and 21st Panzer Divisions under command of *D.A.K*. Anti-tank defence was not to be provided by fixed guns in the advanced infantry positions but by mobile anti-tank groups held ready in each divisional sector.

On 12th March Rommel, after his interviews with the Dictators, wrote to von Arnim that although neither High Command would agree to shorten the front in Tunisia, Hitler would agree that *AOK*'s 'marching' formations should be allowed to withdraw to the Akarit positions, provided that the mobile formations were committed to a 'last ditch' defence at Mareth. Army Group therefore issued the necessary orders, with *OKW*'s sanction, on 14th March. When Ambrosio heard of this plan he angrily forbade it, and on the 16th ordered *AOK 1* to 'mass' for defence on the Mareth line, although he permitted some dispositions in depth if these were essential to secure mobility. Kesselring, back in Tunisia on the same day, defined the Mareth positions as including the French-built Mareth position proper, the secondary Matmata—Tebaga positions, and the Wadi Akarit. It is not surprising that von Arnim demanded written orders. On the 17th these arrived from *Comando Supremo*:

'... the task of the Army Group is to hold its ground in Tunisia. In west Tunisia [sic] the present front is to be held and if possible extended, particularly on the northern wing. Vis-a-vis Eighth

Army the Mareth Zone [Mareth and Schott Lines] is to be defended to the last.[1] For this purpose all forces of *AOK 1* are to be deployed in, and in rear of, the Mareth Line. The Schott Line, which is to be strengthened and consolidated with all speed, is for the time being to be occupied by holding detachments only. Enemy attempts to outflank the Mareth Zone are to be contained by offensive action, in so far as the supply situation permits . . .'

On the 17th von Arnim directed 21st Panzer Division to the area south-west of Gabes and held 10th Panzer Division south-west of Sousse. On the 18th he told Messe that 15th Panzer Division might be used to counter-attack when the British had committed their tanks at Mareth, but how 21st Panzer Division would be used must depend on events in the Gafsa area. Messe required further orders and on the 19th signalled to von Arnim that most of 8th Army was facing the Mareth Line proper but that locally superior forces were assembling south-west of it and at Gafsa. He intended to defend Mareth to the last, but must know von Arnim's views about the use of reserves if he had to withdraw *AOK 1* to the Wadi Akarit in order to escape complete destruction. Messe's position as a commander was not enviable. The German troops in *AOK 1* were nominally subordinate to him, but in fact took their orders from Bayerlein, their C.O.S. Moreover Bayerlein presented the Italian formations with 'faits accomplis'. If he had not done so, he said, decisions and orders would have been given too late for German troops to escape 'impossible' situations. Although some German formations were included in Italian corps, there was no 'sandwiching' as at Alamein. Bayerlein considered Messe to be 'haughty', verbose, and ignorant of commanding troops. On the 20th von Arnim replied. Messe's task was to defend the Mareth Zone to the uttermost as *Comando Supremo* had directed, but he must not count on any reinforcements for the moment, and the use of Army Group's reserve would depend on circumstances. If the British broke through at Mareth proper or the secondary Matmata—Tebaga line or at both, von Arnim expected that *AOK 1* would make a planned withdrawal to the Wadi Akarit. Messe however was not to prepare for this nor give up any ground without von Arnim's sanction.

See Maps 30 and 31

Much information about the Mareth Line proper was available to the 8th Army before the 26th February when General Montgomery issued his plan to breach it. From about 29th January No. 285 (Reconnaissance) Wing R.A.F. had been tireless in photographic reconnaissance. 30th Corps had been closing up to the outpost positions and patrolling had been constant. There had been the local

---

[1] In Axis documents the 'Schott' line or position means the Wadi Akarit area.

knowledge of French officers, in particular General Rime-Bruneau, a former Chief of Staff of French troops in Tunisia, and Captain Paul Mezan, Garrison Engineer of Mareth.

The country was unpleasant. From the seashore the plain tilted up to the Matmata hills. Gravel and sand were on the surface, and in the sandy tracts were salt-pans which a little rain made impassable to wheels. Many wadis ran from the hills to the sea, the most important being the Wadi Zeuss and the Wadi Zigzaou. All the wadis were steep and rocky near the hills but opened out towards the coast where they held water or were swampy, though there were places firm enough to allow light wheeled vehicles to cross.

The front between hills and coast was about twenty-two miles long. The Axis held outpost positions on the northern side of the Wadi Zeuss, which is about three and a half miles in front of the Wadi Zigzaou on which were the main defences. The enemy had excellent observation of every approach.

Between the Wadi Zeuss and the Wadi Zigzaou the enemy had built some strong field-works, in particular at Sidi el Guelaa south of Arram on the main Medenine—Mareth road, and at and north-east of Arram, and in the area of Bahira. The Wadi Zigzaou had been scarped into an anti-tank ditch, severest between Hamra Rass and the sea.[1] Wire obstacles covered about nineteen miles of the front, and some 100,000 anti-tank and 70,000 anti-personnel mines had been laid. The defensive works were mainly 'nests' of pill-boxes, and the largest could hold up to half a battalion. Deep and narrow trenches connected the various strongpoints. The works were well sited to cover the Wadi Zigzaou and its obstacles with fire from defiladed weapons. Nevertheless many of the best French anti-tank emplacements were too small to hold German guns of 50-mm and larger calibres, and therefore these had to accept worse positions. The heaviest defences were around Mareth, but those which chiefly interest us lay nearer the sea; to be noted are Zaret Sudest, Ouerzi, Ouerzi Ouest, Ouerzi Est, Ksiba Ouest and Ksiba Est.

Between Mareth and the Matmata hills the defences were weaker than between Mareth and the coast. The Matmata hills run northwards from near Foum Tatahouine and the important lateral road (Medenine—Ksar el Hallouf—Bir Soltane) through them was well known. Moreover air photographs had shown, and patrols from 4th Indian Division had confirmed, that from west of Ksar el Hallouf well-surfaced, though narrow, military roads led to Techine and Toujane, and that there was a good cart road from Techine to Beni Zelten. Thus there was a practicable route for good infantry and transport on the west of the main Mareth Line besides the route

---

[1] The perpendicular banks were from 8 to 20 feet high; the wadi was on average 60 feet wide, with a stream whose greatest width was about 30 feet and greatest depth about 8 feet.

chosen by General Montgomery for the New Zealand Corps' flanking manoeuvre.[1] At the secondary Tebaga—Djebel Melab position about 1,000 yards of anti-tank ditch and about 15,000 yards of wire obstacle had been completed and 12,000 anti-tank and 6,000 anti-personnel mines had been laid.

The British picture of the enemy troops in the Mareth Line was from east to west: the Young Fascist Division; then as far as the main Gabes—Mareth road Trieste Division; forward of Mareth between Arram and Sidi el Guelaa, blocking the main road and covering the Wadi Zeuss, were the Panzer Grenadier regiments of 90th Light Division with an attached battalion of Panzer Grenadier Regiment 47; then the Spezia Division. Near Kreddache (covering the Hallouf Pass) was 164th Light Division. At Toujane was the Pistoia Division. The armoured divisions were well in rear, widely separated. A fuller picture of the main formations from the enemy's records is given in footnote.[2]

---

[1] The route chosen for the New Zealanders was known to the enemy from the report of a reconnaissance made in 1938 by General Catroux and Colonel Gautsch. These officers reported that a force of three divisions could reach the area Ksar el Hallouf—Bir Soltane from the Tripolitanian frontier in six days. This force could next attack the gaps east and west of the Djebel Melab, and the gap between the Djebel Tebaga and the Matmata range. The report mentioned the gap which the L.R.D.G. in its turn was to find, and name Wilder's Gap.

The outflanking of the Mareth position was examined at a conference at *Panzerarmee* Battle H.Q. on 29th January.

[2] (a) From the coast
to beyond Zarat. — Young Fascist Division (five battalions) and fourteen troops of artillery.

Area Mareth and Arram. — Trieste Division (six battalions) and fifteen troops of artillery.

South of Trieste Division. — Seven battalions of 90th Light Division and about thirteen troops of artillery.

South of 90th Light Division. — Spezia Division (six battalions), 34 Recce Battalion, twenty-two troops of artillery, and three German batteries.

South of Spezia Division. — Pistoia Division (five battalions) and eighteen troops of artillery.

Area of Kreddache. — 164th Light Division (four battalions), three troops of artillery and one Italian battery.

Zerkine (5 miles N.W. of Mareth). — 15th Panzer Division ('Fit' tanks: Pzkw III 8, Pzkw III Special 10, Pzkw IV Special 14).

(b) 21st Panzer Division S.W. of Gabes.
10th Panzer Division S.W. of Sousse. } Total 'fit' tanks was 110.

(c) Djebel Tebaga—Djebel Melab line.
Raggrupamento Sahariano:
Infantry Regiment 350 (two battalions).
Novara Group (three companies).
One Battalion, Frontier Guards.
Savona Battalion.
One M.G. Battalion.
Four Saharan Companies.
Nine troops of artillery.

Enemy records (in particular of the artillery) allow us to form only an approximate comparison of strengths. The 8th Army had two armoured divisions, and forty-three battalions of infantry against the Axis's three armoured divisions and a little over forty-three infantry battalions. The 8th Army was much superior in equipment. Thus:

Tanks (other than light) 743 to approximately 142.

Field and medium guns 692 to perhaps 447.

Anti-tank guns 1,033 (at least 752 being 6-pdrs) to about 244 German and 408 Italian of calibres other than 8·8-cm. Some 76 8·8-cm AA/A.tk guns must be added. Of these at least 7 troops were sited for A.A. defence.

To support 8th Army the Desert Air Force, including the American squadrons, had: 535 fighters, fighter-bombers and tank-destroyers in the Hazbub, Medenine, Bou Grara and Soltane areas and on the Causeway; 140 day-bombers in the Zuara, El Assa and Ben Gardane areas; the equivalent of three air reconnaissance squadrons, Tac/R aircraft being at Bou Grara and the remainder in the Senem area with the Hurricane night-fighters; and all the Halifaxes and Wellingtons of No. 205 Group totalling up to 80 aircraft, split between Gardabia and Castel Benito.[1] In addition all the Mitchell and Marauder day-bombers of N.A.S.A.F. (less two Mitchell anti-shipping squadrons) were made available for the 20th and 21st. To oppose this formidable Allied air force, German records show that on the 20th there were 129 aircraft in southern Tunisia, of which 83 were serviceable. There seem to have been about 40 Italian aircraft fit for operations. The Axis had adequate landing grounds in the Gabes and El Hamma areas, and a very important advanced landing ground at Bordj Touaz south-west of and close to Mareth.

On 9th March 50th Division (from Tripoli) came under command of 30th Corps. On 15th March 30th Corps prepared to attack the outposts of the Mareth position, and the attacks went in on the night of the 16th/17th March. General Nichols (commander of 50th Division) was given the 30th Corps' outline plan on 4th March, and thereafter was left largely to his own devices.[2] He was directed to attack on a narrow front and cross the Wadi Zigzaou somewhere between Hamra Rass and the sea. He looked for the place where the defence works seemed thinnest, where water in the Wadi Zigzaou seemed most shallow, and where there were crossings of a sort. These

---

[1] No. 40 (S.A.A.F.) Squadron which was responsible for tactical reconnaissance had at last received Spitfires (modified Mark V Bs). These flew their first sorties on 7th March.

[2] H.Q. 30th Corps was at first entirely pre-occupied with the forthcoming battle of Medenine, and thereafter seems to have felt that the planning of the main attack was perhaps best left to the commander who had to carry it out.

considerations suggested the sector between the strong points at Ouerzi and Ksiba Ouest, but a drawback was that newly-made hostile positions overlooked the approaches from higher ground between Bahira and a point just south of Ouerzi. 30th Corps made some alterations in its outline plan. On the night 16th/17th, besides the attacks on the outposts to be made by 50th and 51st Divisions, 201st Guards Brigade (from 7th Armoured Division; Brigadier J. A. Gascoigne) was to capture the strong point at Sidi el Guelaa in order to puzzle the enemy about the sector chosen for the main attack. 4th Indian Division was to move to an area alongside 50th Division to be ready to exploit success or form a reserve in case of failure.

50th Division's attack on the Mareth outposts was made by 69th Infantry Brigade (Brigadier E. C. Cooke-Collis) supported by the whole divisional artillery.[1] The brigade captured all its objectives to a depth of a little over a mile beyond the Wadi Zeuss without much difficulty. 51st Division, on 50th Division's left, took its objectives against negligible opposition. 6th Grenadier Guards and 3rd Coldstream Guards (201st Guards Brigade) had heavy casualties from A.P. mines in an unsuspected minefield, and met strong resistance from nearly two battalions of 90th Light Africa Division. The Guards battalions nevertheless reached most of their objectives but were then very heavily shelled and mortared and could not get forward their supporting weapons. The diversion failed and the brigade therefore was withdrawn early on the 17th March.[2] On the 17th 50th Division pushed 5th Battalion, East Yorkshires two and a half miles further ahead, taking Mestaoua (Pt 16) which overlooked the sector between Ouerzi and Ksiba Ouest. Meanwhile the engineers made a track and crossing over the Wadi Zeuss. Two tracks were to be made on the divisional front but rain on the 15th had made their completion uncertain. Yet 50th Division had made a very good beginning and had added confidence to its ambition to win a good battle and once again 'to get into the news'. The Division had had no opportunity of winning attention since its break-out from the Gazala line in June 1942 which had taken the public's fancy as a dashing feat.

Messe's counter moves were slightly to reinforce the area of the Hallouf Pass with German infantry, and to put Panzer Grenadier Regiment Africa (attached to 15th Panzer Division) south-east of Zarat into the Young Fascist Division's sector. On the 18th the enemy was sure about the concentration of N.Z. Corps (to be des-

---

[1] 50th Division now comprised two infantry brigades—69th and 151st. Under its command also were 50th R.T.R. (Valentine tanks); 'B' Sqn 'T' Scorpion Regiment R.A.C.; 2nd Bn (M.G.) The Cheshire Regiment, less a company; 102nd (Northumberland Hussars) Anti-Tank Regt. R.A. less a battery.
[2] Casualties were:
    6th Grenadier Guards: 363 killed, wounded and missing, including 27 officers.
    3rd Coldstream Guards: 159 killed, wounded and missing, including 11 officers.

cribed) and discerned its purpose. Therefore on the 19th 164th Light Division began to move to the Tebaga—Djebel Melab position.

For more than a week before the battle of Mareth began, the Desert Air Force attacked the enemy's concentrations and gun positions in the battle area and his forward landing grounds. The Germans recorded that because, on the 17th, their aircraft were pinned down by the bombing, long-range bombers from Sicily had to be called in to give support in the south. Air reconnaissance aircraft were very active and it is clear that both sides were well informed of each other's movements. Unfortunately, on the 19th, bad weather upset Allied preliminary air operations against the *Luftwaffe* and the Mareth positions. The Tactical Air Force day-bombers from the north, with U.S. XII A.S.C. fighters as escort, attacked enemy airfields and landing grounds, but the N.A.S.A.F. bombers were grounded. In the south, low cloud interfered badly with the Spitfires' attempts to scotch the enemy's reconnaissance aircraft, and no other daylight offensive operations were possible. That night, however, the Bisleys succeeded in attacking the landing grounds at Tebaga and Gabes. The Wellingtons of Nos. 37, 40 and 70 Squadrons R.A.F., guided by Albacores of the Fleet Air Arm, dropped 62 tons of bombs on guns and troops from Mareth towards Gabes, and bombers of the Desert Air Force attacked targets in the Mareth line itself.[1] On the 20th March Marauders and Mitchells of N.A.S.A.F. twice attacked the landing grounds at Tebaga near the Wadi Akarit and were followed the same night by Bisleys of North West African Tactical Bomber Force. At Mareth itself the weather turned fine and clear. Bostons, Baltimores and American Mitchells of the Desert Air Force attacked the defences nine times, and American fighter-bombers attacked targets in the Mareth Line and at Gabes.[2] Air opposition was negligible but A.A. fire was intense and accurate. The same night 45 Wellingtons of Nos. 37, 40, and 104 Squadrons R.A.F. and 11 Halifaxes of No. 462 Squadron R.A.A.F., guided by two Albacores of No. 821 Squadron F.A.A., dropped 124 tons of bombs on the Mareth Line and on Katena.

On the 17th and 18th troops of the 2nd U.S. Corps occupied Gafsa and El Guettar, and on the 19th General Alexander ordered Fredendall to seize the hills east of Maknassy but to go no further until ordered.[3]

---

[1] The perversity of war led the enemy to interpret these attacks as a well-known sign that an offensive was imminent.

[2] Of the D.A.F. the British day-bombers flew 125 sorties, and the fighters 306. The Americans flew 36 day-bomber sorties, their fighters 64 and fighter-bombers 36.

[3] 2nd U.S. Corps was all American and comprised 1st Armoured Division, 1st, 9th, and 34th Infantry Divisions.

At midnight 11th/12th March the New Zealand Division (designated New Zealand Corps in Montgomery's orders of 26th February because of its special task) passed from the command of 30th Corps, and was assembling south-east of Foum Tatahouine.[1]

It will be remembered that in February General Montgomery had placed Leclerc's 'L' Force at Ksar Rhilane (which was to become a staging-area on the New Zealanders' outflanking route), and that the enemy had for some time had suspicions of being outflanked. On 10th March Major von Luck with a group of reconnaissance units reinforced by tanks investigated this area. Leclerc's Force, with air support, drove him off. The low-flying aircraft had destroyed seven assorted guns and nine machine-guns.

By 17th March the N.Z. Corps was concentrated in an assembly area about fifty miles from Foum Tatahouine and ten miles or so west of Wilder's Gap. Freyberg intended to 'capture the airfields West of Sfax destroying any enemy forces encountered'. On the night 19th/20th March a move of twenty to thirty miles would bring his leading troops to an area west of Ksar Rhilane where they would be covered by the French troops who were to have captured El Outid and Bir Soltane. On 20th/21st March an advance of forty miles would end ten miles short of Tebaga Gap. On 21st March the entrance to the gap ('Plum') was to be seized. Thereafter the objectives were El Hamma ('Peach') and some hills which overlooked the road a little north-west of Gabes ('Grape'). Then on to the Sfax airfields.

Everything was now in train for the attack on the Mareth position. 50th Division's 151st Infantry Brigade (Brigadier D. M. W. Beak

---

[1] New Zealand Divisional H.Q. was not augmented to that of a Corps, and there was no corps echelon of administrative troops (a fact which somewhat worried 8th Army's administrative staff) although extra R.A.S.C. units were provided.
    The Corps comprised in outline:
  (a) New Zealand Division: 5th and 6th N.Z. Infantry Brigades and complement of N.Z. supporting arms.
  (b) 1st King's Dragoon Guards (armoured cars).
  (c) 8th Armoured Brigade: 3rd Royal Tank Regiment; the Nottinghamshire Yeomanry; the Staffordshire Yeomanry.
    Total tanks in Brigade: Sherman 76; Grant 13; Crusader 62 = 151.
  (d) 111th Field Regiment R.A.; 64th Medium Regiment R.A.; 57th Anti-Tank Regiment R.A. (less battery); battery 53rd Light Anti-Aircraft Regiment R.A.
  (e) 'L' Force
    F.F. Column.
Approximate Total Strength of N.Z. Corps:
  Men 25,600.
  Tanks 151 (excluding Stuarts of N.Z. Divisional Cavalry Regiment, and some French tanks).
  Field guns 112.
  Anti-Tank guns 172.
General Freyberg commanded the whole directly, i.e. there was no acting divisional commander.

V.C.) was to begin it on the night 20th/21st. 9th D.L.I. was to capture Ksiba Ouest; 8th D.L.I. Ouerzi; 50th R.T.R. in the centre was to follow, cross the Wadi Zigzaou and then fan out; 6th D.L.I. was to mop up and consolidate. Thirteen field and three medium regiments of artillery were to provide the fire support, and up to 500 rounds of ammunition per gun had been dumped. A troop of Scorpions was to go ahead of each battalion to clear anti-personnel mines. To help in making crossings over the Wadi Zigzaou, 50th Division had made a large number of fascines to be dropped into place by the tanks and to be used by the engineers, scaling-ladders for the anti-tank ditches and so on. The division was ready to carry essential equipment forward on Jeeps and Bren carriers, but unfortunately as things turned out had not learned the trick of dismantling anti-tank guns for man-handling.[1] Half an hour before the main attack began, a battalion of 69th Infantry Brigade was to capture a position from which to guard 151st Infantry Brigade's left flank.

4th Indian Division (apart from detachments) was on the left rear of 50th Division to carry out any of the following tasks: to pass through 50th Division in the area Novarmor—el Harigua and turn west to the Mareth—Gabes road; (less ambitiously) to pass through between Zarat Sudest and the sea and capture the area Novarmor—el Harigua; (most ambitiously) to pass through in the areas given above and exploit to Gabes. 51st Division was to patrol, and if either of the other infantry divisions broke through, was to advance by the main road to Gabes and Sfax. 10th Corps had merely warning orders for a quick advance to Gabes on 21st March by whatever route might be opened.

At 9.45 on the night 20th/21st March 30th Corps artillery began its programme with a short deceptive shoot by three medium and three field regiments on Arram, and then nearly an hour's counter-battery fire. At 11.15 p.m. began the main programme of barrage and concentrations, and a machine-gun barrage by 2nd Cheshires. At the same hour 151st Brigade and its Scorpions advanced, and though the defensive fire was heavy and stiff close-quarter fighting occurred, 9th D.L.I. took Ksiba Ouest and 8th D.L.I. took Ouerzi. Meanwhile 7th Green Howards (69th Infantry Brigade), to secure 151st Infantry Brigade's left flank, took and cleared their objectives in fighting which was heavy notwithstanding very effective artillery support. In this action the valour of Lieut.-Colonel D. A. Seagrim won him the V.C.

---

[1] A trick possibly abhorrent to R.E.M.E. but at this time certainly practised by 4th Indian Division.

Following the infantry, 50th R.T.R. made for the chosen crossing place over the Wadi Zigzaou (nearly opposite Ouerzi Ouest)[1]. 9th Field Squadron R.E. cleared mines and blew in a section of the anti-tank ditch. But unfortunately many of the fascines, carried by the tanks to drop in the wadi to give their tracks a grip, had caught fire from the hot exhausts, and the leading tank stuck fast in three feet of water, blocking the crossing. The firing in the wadi (especially in enfilade) was severe, but the Sappers contrived a by-pass round the tank and three tanks crossed. Then another tank stuck, but four in all got over. Brigadier Beak then decided that a squadron at most might be able to cross during the remaining hours of darkness, and therefore ordered 50th R.T.R. (less the four tanks on the far side of the wadi) to return to its assembly area.

Two other crossings had been planned but heavy casualties among the Sappers delayed work, and it was not faint-hearted to expect that to continue in daylight would end in slaughter. No anti-tank guns were able to cross. General Nichols decided to wait for nightfall on the 21st, when all his engineers would work on the crossing used by 50th R.T.R., and 151st Infantry Brigade would attack again to bite out a big segment of ground, defined east to west by the strongpoints Ksiba Est, a nameless post west of it, Ouerzi Est and Ouest, and Zarat Sudest.

The enemy reinforced the Young Fascist Division with a battalion of 200th Panzer Grenadier Regiment, a troop of anti-tank guns, and 15th Panzer Division's artillery; and brought up a *Luftwaffe Jäger* battalion to Novarmor. Messe and Bayerlein foresaw that 50th Division would try to deepen its bridgehead during the night 21st/22nd and ordered 15th Panzer Division to be ready to counter-attack.

At 11.30 a.m. on 21st March Montgomery reported to Alexander that the N.Z. Corps was fifteen miles south-west of El Hamma and directed on Gabes.[2] The enemy clearly intended to fight 'and I am preparing a dog-fight battle in Mareth area which may last several days . . .' The N.Z. Corps was to work through Gabes and turn south to threaten the rear of the Mareth Line and a thrust by the Americans to east of Maknassy would be most useful.

During the day 30th Corps ordered 50th Division to complete its attack during the night 21st/22nd March and to ensure 'without fail' that one crossing place over the Wadi Zigzaou was completed of the three that were to be attempted. 4th Indian Division was warned to

---

[1] In 50th R.T.R. there were 51 'fit' tanks (Valentines) of which 43 mounted the 2-pdr and 8 the 6-pdr gun. Only the 6-pdr tanks could equal the range of Pzkw III Special; all were outranged by Pzkw IV Special.
[2] On the 21st the N.Z. Corps was about thirty-five miles from El Hamma and was beginning to contact the enemy in the Djebel Tebaga—Djebel Melab gap.

pass through 50th Division on the night 22nd/23rd and to consult it about clearing a route.

151st Infantry Brigade was reinforced by the 5th East Yorkshires from 69th Infantry Brigade, and was to attack at 11.30 p.m. on 21st March. General Nichols had received a report from his engineers that one crossing over the Wadi Zigzaou could be completed in two hours. He therefore banned all vehicles from trying to cross until 10 p.m., and tanks until midnight.

The 5th East Yorkshires took a part of Ksiba Est; 9th D.L.I. secured Ouerzi Est and the nameless post at very heavy cost to the two companies engaged; 6th D.L.I. captured Ouerzi Ouest and Zarat Sudest quite easily.[1] In the small hours of 22nd March 42 Valentines of 50th R.T.R. contrived to cross but so damaged the crossing that no anti-tank guns or other vehicles followed. By daylight a bridgehead had been made, but was not consolidated, and early on the 22nd a sharp shower deepened the water in the wadi. By noon there was confusion at the crossing and 50th Division's battered and much-taxed engineers were flagging. The troops were very tired and signal communications were failing as W/T batteries weakened and telephone cables were continually cut. Towards noon Nichols was ordered by General Leese to attack again on the night 22nd/23rd, but doubted whether his division was fit to do so.

At 11.45 a.m. on the 22nd Montgomery sent Alexander a confident signal:

> 'My operations progressing well. On left flank N.Z. Corps is about 10 miles south-west of el Hamma and is pushing on up road to that place . . . On right flank 50 Div had [sic] secured bridgehead through all organized defended localities Mareth position east and south-east of Zarat and this bridgehead is now being extended and operation will be developed from it. Enemy resisting strongly and operations in Zarat area are very like those at Alamein. . . . We are now through main minefields and prepared defended positions . . . Suggest you now announce that my operations are proceeding satisfactorily and according to plan. . . . Do not yet mention movement of N.Z. Corps in flank movement.'[2]

This confidence was possibly hopeful. At 1.40 p.m., 15th Panzer Division counter-attacked with great ferocity. No British anti-tank guns were in position, and the Valentines were out-gunned. The

---

[1] As an example of the 'nests' of pill-boxes mentioned on page 332 Ksiba Est turned out to be 1,200 yards long by 400 yards deep and capable of holding a battalion. Zarat Sudest was of the same type.

[2] The enemy had spotted the N.Z. Corps' move on the 18th, and 'trailed' it since then and was preparing to meet it.

Germans pressed 151st Brigade back to the lip of the wadi, retaking the Ouerzis and part of Zarat Sudest, and knocked out some 30 tanks.

Nevertheless at 9.15 p.m. on the 22nd 30th Corps gave orders that it was 'absolutely essential for the further development of operations to enlarge our present bridgehead to permit the construction of crossings over the Wadi Zigzaou'. 50th Division was to re-establish the bridgehead. 7th Armoured Division was to send one, and if possible two, squadrons of heavy tanks across the Wadi Zigzaou before daylight on 23rd March. The 4th Indian Division's engineers were to take over the wadi crossings, but C.R.E. of 50th Division was not informed, and C.R.E. 4th Indian Division, during thirty hours' work in support of 50th Division, received from it no orders or information.

During the afternoon General Nichols had been busy arranging a counter-attack for the same night: to be made by 69th Infantry Brigade, and 5th R.T.R. (Grants and Shermans) which had been allotted to him. Information was scarce and conflicting, and a constantly changing situation constantly interfered with preparations. An exception was that the 4th Field Company Bengal Sappers and Miners and 12th Field Company Madras Sappers and Miners of 4th Indian Division, working during the night 22nd/23rd in a hail of fire and led by their C.R.E., the heroic John Blundell, built two crossings over the Wadi Zigzaou by the small hours 22nd/23rd March. (The enemy were now fairly confident of holding the Mareth Line and were shifting their attention to the Djebel Tebaga—Djebel Melab sector, about which they were nervous.) In the event, 69th Infantry Brigade's counter-attacks were cancelled and General Nichols asked, and received, permission from General Leese to withdraw all troops from across the Wadi Zigzaou.

At about 2 a.m. on the night 22nd/23rd General Montgomery altered his plan. He realized that 30th Corps' attack (the main stroke) had failed. He therefore decided to change the New Zealand Corps' subsidiary flanking manoeuvre into the principal stroke and to reinforce General Freyberg as strongly as possible. 30th Corps was to try to prevent the enemy from likewise reinforcing the Djebel Tebaga—Djebel Melab sector. In the event 1st Armoured Division was ordered to join the N.Z. Corps by the route Medenine—Wilder's Gap—Bir Soltane. 4th Indian Division's 5th Brigade was to clear the road Medenine—Ksar el Hallouf, and its 7th Brigade the road Medenine—Kreddache, thus gaining a shorter lateral route between the separated formations of 8th Army. Thereafter 4th Indian Division was to strike northwards into the hills for Toujane, Techine, and Beni Zelten from where it could thrust into the rear of the Mareth Line or its subsidiary between Djebel Tebaga and Djebel Melab.

The air forces continued to help in the fight to break the main Mareth Line. On the 21st 125 day-bombers of the Desert Air Force and 54 American Mitchells attacked points in the main position and behind it, and found good targets, but about a quarter of the aircraft were damaged by flak. The British fighters flew 297 sorties and the Americans 60 on various missions. The enemy felt the blows because they recorded 19 bombing and four low-flying attacks by an estimated 600 aircraft in all. From the north, Lightning-escorted American Fortresses made two attacks in the morning, each with 18 aircraft, on the Tebaga landing grounds. In the afternoon a further raid by 46 Fortresses was upset by the weather, some of the aircraft bombing the El Hamma landing ground and targets in the Gabes area instead. Bostons, with Spitfires as escort, attacked landing-grounds elsewhere. *Fliegerkorps Tunis* recorded that American air attacks in northern Tunisia were diverting them from concentrating against the main danger points in the south—where, in fact, they were failing effectively to oppose the Allied air forces. The same night 61 Wellingtons and Halifaxes, guided by four Albacores, bombarded various targets in the area of battle from the Mareth Line as far as Gabes.

On the 22nd morning thick cloud three times frustrated the day-bombers' attempts to break up 15th Panzer Division when it was forming up to counter-attack 50th Division. However, late in the afternoon Bostons, Baltimores, and American Mitchells dropped 37 tons of bombs in the area of Zarat, and during the night 22nd/23rd the Halifaxes and Wellingtons, with guiding Albacores, dropped about 100 tons of bombs in the battle area. Allied aircraft from the north attacked landing grounds at Tebaga, Sfax el Maou and Mezzouna and that night a strong force of Bisleys and French LeO 45s continued the attacks on Sfax el Maou while Wellingtons from N.A.S.A.F. attacked a German army H.Q. in the same area. Next morning (23rd March) Bostons, Baltimores and American Mitchells of the Desert Air Force attacked Zarat and other areas and 31 Kittyhawk fighter-bombers (Nos. 2 and 5 Squadrons S.A.A.F., 450 Squadron R.A.A.F.) supported a small demonstration by 10th Corps. This was the busiest day for the Desert Air Force for many weeks. Nearly 620 sorties were flown in support of 8th Army during which four German fighters were destroyed. Day-bombers from N.A.T.B.F. continued to attack enemy landing grounds, including one at Tebaga. That night while Halifaxes and Wellingtons of No. 205 Group with Albacore pathfinders found targets in the Mareth and El Hamma areas and Desert Air Force bombers also were active, over 40 Bisleys and French LeO 45s from the north bombed the landing ground at Sfax el Maou and the Sfax—Sousse road.

While 30th Corps had been attacking in the coast sector the N.Z. Corps had been carrying out its 'left hook.' During the night 19th/20th March 8th Army told Freyberg that the enemy had spotted his move. Freyberg therefore decided to quicken his pace by some twelve hours and by last light on the 20th he was in sight of the Djebel Tebaga—Djebel Melab gap. By 1.45 p.m. on the 21st 8th Armoured Brigade were probing the hostile position, and Freyberg had had a signal from Montgomery that the enemy were going to fight for Mareth, and asking him to capture El Hamma as quickly as possible, and then be ready to move on 'Grape' and to turn mobile troops towards Mareth. Freyberg replied that he would take Djebel Tebaga—Djebel Melab during the night 21st/22nd March, and exploit towards El Hamma. On the night 21st/22nd the 6th N.Z. Infantry Brigade (Brigadier W. Gentry) took a strong outpost (Pt 201) to pave the way for 8th Armoured Brigade to break through. But the enemy had not been idle. During the night 19th/20th 164th Light Africa Division had begun to move to meet the N.Z. threat. 21st Panzer Division was ready to move to the same sector; and 10th Panzer Division was to move south to Mahares on 21st March, with the American 2nd Corps in mind. Gentry suggested to Freyberg at about midnight 21st/22nd March that 8th Armoured Brigade should break through at once instead of at first light but Freyberg allowed him only to consult Brigadier Harvey (8th Armoured Brigade). Though both brigadiers were willing, nothing resulted because Freyberg had not been enthusiastic. The New Zealand historian writes '... The 6 Brigade victory thus remained an isolated one in the midst of a lethargy in the rest of the Corps ... an opportunity was lost ...'. On the other hand Montgomery had not given Freyberg a clear picture of events on 30th Corps' front, particularly of the known or likely actions of the Axis reserves, and (to quote again the N.Z. historian) '... it must have seemed that he (Freyberg) was being asked to advance alone and absorb single-handed the thrust of all the mobile armour and infantry.' Two more factors which affected General Freyberg throughout the Mareth battle must be mentioned. From the first he had been doubtful of a quick success by 30th Corps. Then as G.O.C. 2nd N.Z. Expeditionary Force, he was very much worried about man-power. He had received one draft of reinforcements during the past fifteen months, and was still short of about an eighth of his establishment.

> 'This compared favourably enough with other divisions, both Allied and enemy, but the 2nd N.Z. Expeditionary Force was a national force whose fate had already trembled in the balance, and further serious losses could lead to its entire withdrawal from the Middle East theatre.[1]'

---

[1] Stevens *op. cit.* p. 249.

On 22nd March both sides sparred. 8th Armoured Brigade won toe-holds on the enemy's right and north of Pt 201, but nothing more because of artillery and anti-tank fire. 21st Panzer Division began a counter-attack but soon called it off because (it reported) of bad going and strong British reinforcement. However it was clear that the Axis meant to hold on. The artillery duelled and the opposing tanks played long bowls.

On the 23rd the N.Z. Corps continued to search for the enemy's flanks and tap at his front; its artillery was very lively, and the engineers steadily lifted mines. Freyberg was worried by conflicting reports from 8th Army of the movements of 10th Panzer Division and placed his 5th Infantry Brigade in a defensive position, facing south and south-west, some seven miles west by south from Pt 201. At 4.30 a.m. he had received a personal message from Montgomery giving the changed plan. 30th Corps was now to contain the enemy in the Mareth Line,

> '... [I] ... Will reinforce your thrust with 1 Armd Div and this increased strength should enable you to push on and reach Gabes. 15 Pz Div closely engaged on my front. 10 Pz Div engaged in Gafsa area. Troops available to oppose you are 21 Pz Div [less part en route to Gafsa]. Must also expect more of 164 Div to oppose you. For maintenance and other reasons essential have Corps HQ on your flank and am sending Horrocks to take charge. Am sure you will understand. You and he will work well together and should achieve decisive results. Horrocks and recce parties should reach you tomorrow about 12 noon. 10 Corps to take over when 1 Armd Div have arrived probably afternoon 25 March.'

General Montgomery thus created a dyarchy and, as the days passed, did not put Horrocks 'in charge'. Instead he yoked an ill-matched pair.[1] Horrocks was coldly received by Freyberg who '... was determined to make sure that no newcomer should intrude in the handling of 2nd N.Z. Division, and was grim, firm, and not at all forthcoming.' Horrocks felt embarrassed; and was annoyed too that his troops had to make a long, fast move for which 8th Army H.Q. Staff had not prepared nor given his own staff the chance to prepare. He was justified because a first-rate tangle resulted between 1st Armoured and 4th Indian Divisions at Medenine.

On the Axis side 164th Light Division was ordered into a defensive

---

[1] Freyberg: Major-General 24th August 1939; temporary Lieut.-General 1st March 1942.
Horrocks: Acting Major-General 27th June 1941; acting Lieut.-General 13th August 1942.
Freyberg was six years older than Horrocks. De Guingand and Horrocks arranged that all messages from Army H.Q. should be sent to both commanders, and Montgomery began certain personal letters with the salutation 'My dear Generals ...'

position astride the track Kebili—El Hamma and to help 21st Panzer Division in stopping a break-through. In the afternoon 21st Panzer Division attacked rather feebly and fruitlessly. The very able Major-General von Liebenstein (164th Light Africa Division) replaced Mannerini in command of the whole sector, and towards evening Bayerlein reported that the situation was under control but only for the time being. He and Messe expected attack again everywhere but thought that the battle would be decided on von Liebenstein's front.

At 7.30 p.m. on the 23rd 1st Armoured Division set out to join the N.Z. Corps. 4th Indian Division began to move at 6 p.m. and found the road blocked by 1st Armoured Division at Medenine, which could not be by-passed. Thus through bad staff-work at higher headquarters the Indian Division lost twelve valuable hours and, as things turned out, the chance of descending from the Matmata hills in rear of the Mareth Line in time to cut off retreating enemy.

On the 24th little happened on the N.Z. front but towards evening 15th Panzer Division and other reinforcements left the Mareth Line for positions about fifteen miles south-west of Gabes, where they were well placed as a 'lay-back' for the Mareth front or von Liebenstein's.[1] During the afternoon Freyberg received from Montgomery a proposal to blast a hole in the Djebel Tebaga—Djebel Melab position on the 25th and pass the armour through. Very heavy bombing and low-level air attacks were to precede this 'blitz' on the ground. At about the same time Horrocks arrived at Freyberg's H.Q. and the dyarchy debated Montgomery's proposal. A signal was sent at 3.30 p.m., to Montgomery 'From Generals Freyberg and Horrocks'. This described the Djebel Tebaga—Djebel Melab as a bottle-neck too narrow to allow armour to manoeuvre, and covered by 21st Panzer Division and anti-tank guns. It suggested three courses. First, to force a gap and pass 1st Armoured Division through, an operation which might take from five to seven days. Second, to send 1st Armoured Division right round the west end of the Djebel Tebaga and then east on El Hamma, while the N.Z. Division attacked frontally. This operation might be well under way by the night 27th/28th March. Third, to launch 8th Armoured Brigade head-on at the enemy with very heavy air and artillery support. The dyarchy recommended the second course—surprisingly, because it would put N.Z. Division and the 1st Armoured Division on opposite sides of an impassable range of hills, ensure (one of many objections) dispersion, and rule out concerted action.

Montgomery quickly replied '. . . I want to speed up your thrust as much as possible, and I think we can do a great deal to help you

---

[1] Messe and Bayerlein dispute the credit for this sound move.

by heavy air bombing all night and day. To take full advantage of this you would have to do an afternoon attack with the sun behind you. The plan would be as follows:

(a) Continuous bombing by Wellingtons and night-bombers on night D−1/D.
(b) Intensive artillery shelling for say one hour before Zero. Smoke, etc., on high ground on flanks and/or to cover mine lifting.
(c) Air cover and attacks by fighters on any movement to and from the battle area.

I do not believe that any enemy could stand up to such treatment, and you would, after it, burst through the defile quite easily and get to El Hamma and Gabes.

... we can lay it on if you agree you will accept it ... I would like D day to be tomorrow 25th March, 1 Armoured Division to be up by then, ready to exploit success on 26 March.

I think you would get surprise, as the enemy thinks we always attack at night ... The R.A.F. will play 100%. Let us call it Supercharge and give me a date for D Day.'

Montgomery added that he intended two other simultaneous attacks, by 7th Armoured Division on Mareth and by 4th Indian Division on Toujane, and that the German troops, already stretched, could not deal with all three.

The air plan originated with Air Vice-Marshal Broadhurst who, learning of the Army Commander's changed intentions, formed the idea of concentrating his aircraft in a degree hitherto unknown, on a narrow front, in order to paralyse the enemy for long enough to permit the ground forces to break through. Montgomery enthusiastically accepted Broadhurst's plan.

The air forces, of course, had been supporting the N.Z. Corps—at first, in accordance with the air master-plan, by attacking with North African formations the hostile airfields near Tebaga and Gabes. On the 22nd the tactical support became closer, No. 6 Squadron R.A.F. tank destroyers (of W.D. Air Force; Hurricane IIDs) assailing 21st Panzer Division.[1] On the 23rd Allied fighter-bombers greatly damaged 164th Light Division's scanty transport; and again on the 24th, when *AOK 1* recorded the loss of 32 vehicles of the division. That night, in brilliant moonlight, British and American Desert Air Force bombers together with Halifaxes and Wellingtons of No. 205 Group, guided by F.A.A. Albacores, heavily attacked targets in the battle area, and the Germans recorded that the troops were greatly exhausted by lack of sleep. The 143 sorties flown were preliminary to the detailed air plan for the 26th, described later.

---

[1] Unfortunately the claims of the squadron cannot be checked by enemy records.

Map 34

BATTLE OF TEBAGA GAP 26th MARCH 1943
Showing British plan of attack; and enemy dispositions (taken off captured map)

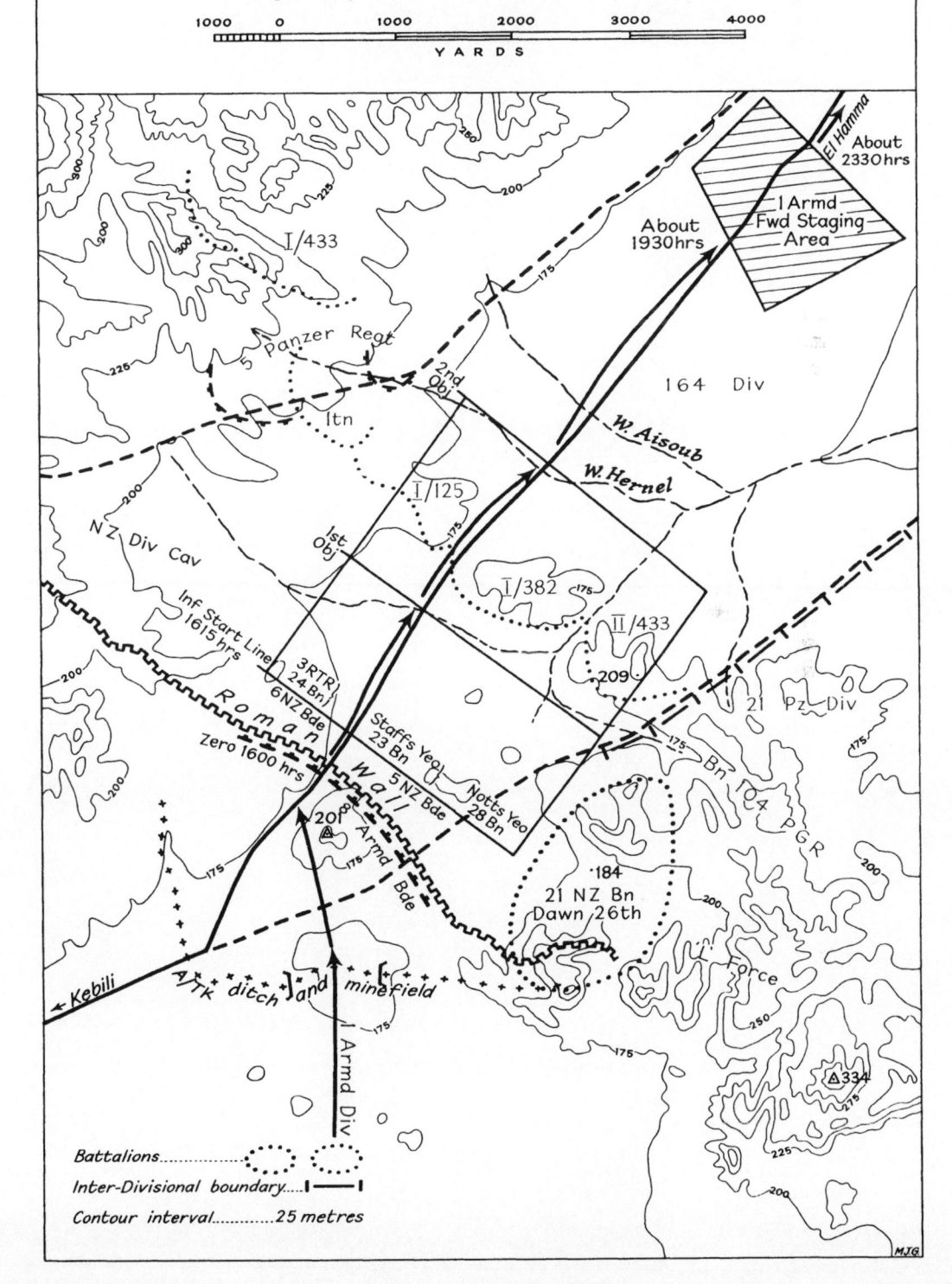

TEBAGA GAP: ARMY AND AIR PLAN

See also Map 34

Towards 8 p.m. on 24th March Freyberg and Horrocks answered Montgomery that they would carry out 'Supercharge', but asked for D day to be postponed until the 26th in order to allow 1st Armoured Division to arrive by a forced march rather than a frantic rush, and reinforcing artillery to get into position. Montgomery approved. Freyberg and Horrocks meanwhile began to plan together, Freyberg taking the break-in, and Horrocks the action of 1st Armoured Division. Wing-Commander J. Darwen represented Air Vice-Marshal Broadhurst.[1] The timing of 1st Armoured Division's advance was most important. Freyberg favoured an early start in full daylight and Horrocks at first agreed. But Major-General R. Briggs (1st Armoured Division) pointed out that if the infantry attack began at 4 p.m.—a time which gave the R.A.F's plans the greatest advantage and let the infantry go in when the sun was blinding the enemy's eyes—the armour could best advance at about 6 p.m. and still just reach its jumping-off place in daylight. Freyberg, a little reluctantly, agreed, and insisted on assurance that the armour would go through. (So long did the unhappy memories of 1942 linger.) Horrocks gave him the assurance without qualification.

The following plan resulted. The N.Z. Corps would attack and capture the hostile position between Djebel Tebaga and Djebel Melab on 26th March beginning at 4 p.m. A small operation to deprive the enemy of a particularly good observation point (Height 184) was to be staged on the night 25th/26th. As at Alamein, the troops were to get into their starting positions during the night, and lie concealed all next day. 5th N.Z. Infantry Brigade was to attack on the right, and 6th on the left, while 8th Armoured Brigade, in the lead, covered the whole front. The first objective was some high ground 2,000 yards from the start line, and the second was a wadi 2,500 yards beyond the first objective. The whole N.Z. Artillery with two field and one medium regiments added from 10th Corps was to fire a creeping barrage, mixed with timed concentrations on known hostile localities and artillery positions.

The 1st Armoured Division, with 2nd Armoured Brigade in the lead, was to pass through the New Zealanders at 6.15 p.m. to a forward staging area about 3,000 yards beyond the New Zealand Division's final objective. As soon as General Briggs decided that the moon gave enough light to make movement possible he would order his division straight to El Hamma. This would probably be between 11.15 and 11.30 p.m.

The Royal Air Force's plan was that during the nights 24th/25th

---

[1] Wing-Commander Darwen had led the R.A.F's adventurous stroke in November against the retreating enemy from LG 125. Chapter IV, pages 99-100.

and 25th/26th March the heavy bombers of No. 205 Group R.A.F. and bombers of the Desert Air Force were to attack targets in the battle area, in order to destroy motor transport and telephone lines and to deprive the enemy of sleep and rest. The air bombardment was to continue until 3.30 p.m. on the 26th. At this hour three day-bomber formations of the Desert Air Force were to attack from low level, dropping their bombs in pattern, to create disorganization and further to disrupt telephone lines. Then as the artillery opened and the troops rose from cover, the fighter-bombers were to arrive in relays every fifteen minutes, to fly continuously over the enemy and ahead of the New Zealanders, first bombing specified targets and then strafing. From first to last the day-bomber and fighter-bomber attacks were to go on for two and a half hours. Patrolling Spitfires were to protect the fighter-bombers from counter-attack by enemy aircraft; and to make doubly sure, there was a well-devised programme of attacks by the remainder of N.A.T.A.F. on hostile airfields. The feature of this plan (apart from concentrating a large number of aircraft against specific targets on a narrow front) was precise co-ordination between air and ground of a hitherto unknown standard, although the methods were well known to the Desert Forces. Examples were: briefing pilots by a R.A.F. officer (using a direct radio link) who observed the battle from a forward observation post; setting up unmistakable landmarks; marking the area to be attacked by red and blue smoke; most forward troops indicating their positions at set times by orange smoke; the artillery firing smoke for particular signals.

By 24th March von Arnim had decided that it was less probable that the 8th Army would renew its attempt to break the Mareth Line than that the Allies would strike elsewhere, perhaps in the Maknassy area which he always thought most vulnerable. Therefore, in spite of encouraging reports of the 8th Army's slow progress he determined that *AOK 1*, covered by von Liebenstein, must withdraw to the Wadi Akarit, beginning on 25th March and finishing in 72 hours. Messe objected for administrative reasons and was encouraged by Kesselring, who arrived at Messe's H.Q. on the afternoon of the 24th, and pronounced against withdrawal and for more counter-attacks by 15th Panzer Division.

On the 25th Kesselring visited the Tebaga sector and reported to von Arnim that von Liebenstein was not in immediate danger. Messe asked (in writing) for the withdrawal to the Wadi Akarit to be postponed, for the Tebaga sector to be reinforced, and for a counter-attack. von Arnim did not change his mind. He argued that von Liebenstein could not restore his situation because troops might

TEBAGA GAP: THE ATTACK

be taken from him to send to Maknassy. If the Americans cut in to Gabes it would mean the end of *AOK 1*. Therefore Messe must get out of Mareth, and then out of Tebaga.

On the 25th tactical day-bombers from the north and south converged on the Tebaga landing grounds, which suffered four raids in all. South-west of El Hamma Desert Air Force tank-destroyers struck at enemy tanks, and though eleven were believed destroyed six of the ten Hurricane IIDs were lost. That night No. 205 Group's and the Desert Air Force's bombers flew 133 sorties in the Tebaga battle area, and over El Hamma and Gabes.[1] 164th Light Africa Division recorded its dislike of the treatment. On the morning of the 26th Bostons and Mitchells from the north again attacked the Tebaga airfields. Unfortunately sandstorms on the airfields of the Desert Air Force stopped the proposed programme of bombing. However by the afternoon some of the airfields were clear, and the plan was then executed exactly. At 3.30 p.m. three formations of day-bombers from Nos. 12, 21, and 24 Squadrons (S.A.A.F.), No. 55 Squadron R.A.F. and the 83rd and 434th Squadrons U.S.A.A.F. attacked from low level, dropping their bombs in pattern. Then came the fighter-bombers beginning with the Kittyhawks of No. 250 Squadron R.A.F. and No. 3 Squadron R.A.A.F. Every fifteen minutes relays of about 30 aircraft came over. Spitfire patrols of squadron strength protected them, and the attack continued until 6 p.m. The Desert Air Force (including American squadrons) flew 412 sorties for a cost of eleven pilots and one bomber crew missing.[2]

The effects, according to German records, were heavy damage to guns and equipment, some casualties, destruction of communications between units, and interruption of those between H.Qs *AOK 1* and Army Group Africa, and a complete bar on movement to and from the front line. Various German commanders urgently appealed for protection by fighters, in vain. It is therefore rather surprising that Army Group stated that the *Luftwaffe* had given effective support to ground operations.[3]

By 2.50 a.m. on the 26th 21st N.Z. Infantry Battalion (5th N.Z.

---

[1] In all on the nights 24th/25th and 25th/26th March 400 tons of bombs were dropped.
[2] Total sorties flown by the Desert Air Force during the day, including those solely in support of 'Supercharge':
  British day-bombers: 30; American 24.
  British fighter-bombers: 87; American 91.
  British fighters: 207*.
  * Excluding sorties flown to protect shipping. Aircraft losses: British nine; American at least five; German one.
[3] The success of this Allied air attack caused both official and popular belief that some new technique had been used. In fact the technique had long been worked out by the Desert Air Force. The novelty lay in the large-scale application, and the splendid co-ordination of detail between air force and army.

Infantry Brigade) had captured Pt 184 on the right of the start-line. For everyone else in the N.Z. Corps the night 25th/26th was intensely busy: there was a good deal of shuffling of units and digging into camouflaged slit-trenches, mine-lifting by engineers, and deployment of artillery and dumping of ammunition. The artillery of 1st Armoured Division arrived, after dark on the 25th after a very fast march, and went straight into action. A 'khamsin' helped no one. Nevertheless by dawn on 26th March everyone and everything was hidden. This fine effort by staff and troops was rewarded by no increase of hostile shelling except on Pt 184 which had obviously changed hands.

At 4 p.m. the artillery began its programme and 8th Armoured Brigade emerged from cover near the Roman wall and was soon followed by the carriers of infantry battalions, and then the infantry. The sun shone in the faces of the enemy and a strong wind blew the dust kicked up by shells, tanks, and men into his eyes. The enemy did not at first seem to grasp the danger rushing upon him (the change from the 8th Army's habit of attacking by night may have been one cause), and showed little fight. 8th Armoured Brigade's regiments though technically 'in support' of the N.Z. Brigades had been ordered to get on as fast as possible and not to conform rigidly to infantry pace.[1] The Nottinghamshire Yeomanry on the right, the Staffordshire Yeomanry in the centre, and 3rd R.T.R. on the left dashed forward quickly to the first objective, closely followed by 28th (Maori) Battalion on the right, 23rd N.Z. Battalion in the centre (both from 5th N.Z. Brigade); and on the left 24th N.Z. Battalion (6th N.Z. Brigade).[2] There was no pause on the first objective, but then the enemy's resistance stiffened. On the right a strongpost on Pt 209 knocked out three Shermans of the Nottinghamshire Yeomanry and held up the regiment for a long time while it hunted for a way round. 28th (Maori) Battalion then attacked the feature and fought a hard and successful 'private war' for it, but this did not delay the general advance. The Staffordshire Yeomanry went straight through to Wadi Aisoub, beyond the second objective, at a cost of six Shermans, and behind them came 23rd N.Z. Battalion, knocking out post after post and never losing its drive. On the left 3rd R.T.R. struck a minefield covered by anti-tank guns. Some tanks swung left, and others right and the right-handed thrust reached the second objective close to the El Hamma—Kebili road. 24th N.Z. Battalion met difficulties in the minefield, with many hostile posts, and with

---

[1] In fact a fast pace had been set the infantry:
    100 yards in a minute to the first objective;
    100 yards in two minutes to the second.
[2] In 5th N.Z. Brigade 21st N.Z. Battalion had been committed to Pt 184. In 6th N.Z. Brigade 25th N.Z. Battalion was given a diversionary task far on the left flank, and 26th N.Z. Battalion was held in hand as reserve and 'moppers up'.

enemy prisoners who, because few guards could be spared, rearmed themselves, and were a nuisance. Nevertheless the battalion, following 3rd R.T.R's successful route, gained the second objective.[1] Although fighting on the Djebel Tebaga—Djebel Melab front was not over, the gap through which 1st Armoured Division could pass had been won by the appointed time.

Late in the afternoon von Liebenstein asked that 15th Panzer Division should come up on his left (near Djebel es Souinia) as a reserve for counter-attack, but owing to delays in communications Bayerlein did not give the order for nearly three hours. 21st Panzer Division's 5th Panzer Regiment had been broken through and I/125th Panzer Grenadier Regiment had been dispersed. At about 7.15 p.m. 5th Panzer Regiment began to retreat and about the same time Hildebrandt (21st Panzer Division) sent 3rd and 33rd Reconnaissance Units to make a 'lay-back' (although almost minus the help of 8·8-cm guns owing to another delayed order) some four miles south of El Hamma. At 9.15 p.m. *AOK 1* ordered von Liebenstein to go over to mobile defence in the area Oglat Merteba if possible until the evening of the 27th, but by the time he received the order the impact of 1st Armoured Division had made him think that he could do little more than disengage.

1st Armoured Division, with 2nd Armoured Brigade Group in the lead, had come pelting along and went straight into action. Brigadier Fisher, commanding the brigade, at 6 p.m. had ordered '... Speed up, straight through, no halting.'[2] The Brigade passed through 8th Armoured Brigade and at once engaged the enemy; by 7.30 p.m. it had reached the forward staging area and the rest of the division was arriving. Just after 11 p.m. the moon began to rise, but unluckily was almost hidden by clouds. Nevertheless at midnight

---

[1] 'A' Company made the final assault on the right, and had an interesting reinforcement of seven men of 3rd R.T.R. who had been 'unhorsed' but had decided that they were not going to miss anything—like the N.Z. A.S.C. drivers who joined 1st Battalion The Royal Fusiliers and 3/1st Punjab Regiment in the assault on Tummar West in 1940 (Volume I, page 268).

[2] i. 1st Armoured Division's outline composition was: 12th Lancers; 2nd, 4th, and 11th (H.A.C.) Regiments R.H.A.; 76th Anti-Tank Regiment R.A., 42nd Light A.A. Regiment R.A.; 1st Field Park Squadron, and 1st and 7th Field Squadrons R.E.; 2nd Armoured Brigade; 7th Motor Brigade (1st Bn K.R.R.C., 2nd and 7th Bns The Rifle Brigade).

ii. Tank State—last light 26th March.
2nd Armoured Brigade

	Sherman	Grant	Crusader III	Crusader II
Brigade H.Q.	—	1	—	2
Bays	26	—	1	19
9th Lancers	22	7	12	9
10th Hussars	19	5	9	8
	67	13	22	38

The Division was below its establishment of tanks by 14 'heavies' and 17 Crusaders of various marks. 10 tanks broke down during the march.

26th/27th General Briggs ordered the advance to El Hamma, and one minute later 2nd Armoured Brigade was off. At 2.10 a.m. von Liebenstein ordered all troops on his right flank to move to a position south-west of El Hamma and these withdrew parallel to, and even mixed up with, the British armour. Friend and enemy plunged through half darkness and bursts of fire. von Liebenstein, racing the British, at 3.15 a.m. scraped together an anti-tank screen of three 8·8-cm, four 5-cm anti-tank, and four 10-cm field guns at a point about three miles south of El Hamma. These, with oddments of 21st Panzer Division, checked the British armour which at dawn on the 27th found itself exposed on a ridge and therefore went into hull-down positions. At about the same time 15th Panzer Division attempted to attack the rear of 1st Armoured Division's column but was quickly repulsed by the 17-pdr anti-tank guns of 76th Anti-Tank Regiment R.A. and by 1st Northumberland Fusiliers and 8th Armoured Brigade. A Battalion of 7th Motor Brigade occupied high ground (Pt 212) on the right of the armour, while the remainder formed an anti-tank screen to protect 1st Armoured Division's south-east flank. Stalemate now occurred. 2nd Armoured Brigade could not pierce the hostile anti-tank screen, and could not find a way round the hills on its flanks. General Horrocks decided to give up the attempt to put the armour through to El Hamma, and to await the arrival of the N.Z. Division which might repeat the break-through of the 26th.

Meanwhile 28th (Maori) Battalion and II/433rd Panzer Grenadier Regiment fought fiercely for Pt 209 which fell towards evening—an action during which Second-Lieutenant Ngarimu won a Victoria Cross, posthumous, for he was shot dead in the last grapple. The remainder of the N.Z. Division was not held up by this fight, but owing to the uncertain information of what was happening at El Hamma, was delayed. At 4.30 p.m. General Freyberg was ordered by 8th Army to move by moonlight to join General Horrocks.[1] Shortly afterwards Horrocks asked Freyberg if he would stage another 'Supercharge' at El Hamma. Freyberg (at 6 p.m.) replied that he preferred to by-pass El Hamma, and strike east and north to Gabes. Horrocks was still considering the proposal when at 2 a.m. on the 28th Freyberg joined him. Horrocks then agreed, though he was doubtful how Montgomery would view the matter because he had told him to go first for El Hamma, to secure his L. of C., and to ensure that his force was 'collected and well-balanced'. Time had been lost by the British, and the Axis had gained it by abandoning

---

[1] At 9.45 a.m. Montgomery had told Horrocks and Freyberg to press on 'relentlessly' to El Hamma and Gabes, but changed his mind as less optimistic reports from Horrocks came in.

COMMENTS ON THE BATTLE OF MARETH

the whole Mareth position 24 hours earlier than in their original programme.[1] This haste underlined the success of 'Supercharge' but also showed that the enemy could still manoeuvre and with some luck would once more escape. Moreover during the 27th the enemy had the opportunity to recover somewhat from the effects of 'Supercharge'. 15th and 21st Panzer Division settled down again, and a couple of battalions were placed on Djebel Halouga, an awkward obstacle in the approach to El Hamma and Gabes.

The outcome of the discussions between Horrocks and Freyberg and their reports to Montgomery was something of an anti-climax. 30th Corps was to advance on the 28th to clear the Mareth Line. In fact the enemy was clearing it himself, and 4th Indian Division which had made great efforts to make good the delay which had been imposed on it at the beginning of its advance into the Matmata hills, and to overcome the physical obstacles to speed, was frustrated to see the last of the enemy slipping away in the plain below. The war diary of 90th Light Division recorded of the general situation 'the enemy does not follow, although he sees that the Mareth Line is being evacuated.'

On the afternoon of the 28th Horrocks gave orders (which apparently applied to the N.Z. Corps also) that 10th Corps would occupy the line Gabes to El Hamma, and later added '. . . . no major action or attack will be undertaken as the policy now is for us to conserve our resources of men and material. The enemy will be dislodged by manoeuvre and fire . . .'

There was a little fighting during the 28th March, but the battle of Mareth was over, and on the 29th the N.Z. Division was on its way through Gabes as was 51st Highland Division. Spirits were high in 8th Army. The British forces had indeed won a great battle, which had taken an interesting course. The first, and main, thrust had been aimed at the heart of the Mareth position where the defences were very strong. Yet a successful, quick thrust there would have split open the position, and crippled the defence, and so would have given the considerable forces of exploitation, and the outflanking New Zealand Corps, their opportunity. It was not to be. The main attack by the equivalent of a division failed against strong field defences. More troops could scarcely have been used, if one takes into account the ground and the artillery available. The available

---

[1] The original programme had been:
Night 26th/27th. Half of 90th Light Division and Trieste Division to Zerkine. Most of Spezia Division to Gabes.
Night 27th/28th. Half of Trieste, Young Fascist, and Pistoia Divisions to remain in Mareth Line; the remainder of these divisions to Gabes and Wadi Akarit.
28th March. Remainder of 90th Light Division and all troops under command of von Liebenstein, except 164th Light Division, to Gabes. All other troops to Wadi Akarit. 164th Light Division to be rearguard.

artillery in fact could not subdue the defence sufficiently to give the infantry more than an even chance, and an even chance is not good enough in a major battle. Poor flying weather weakened the air forces' support at important conjunctures. The Germans showed yet again their ability to counter-attack shrewdly and damagingly. General Montgomery then turned the New Zealand Corps' subsidiary flanking manoeuvre into a main operation. Freyberg, Horrocks, and Broadhurst acted with speed, and their forces gave a splendid demonstration, fruitful for the future as well as decisive at the time, of the power of land and air forces acting in the closest tactical union. The Tebaga Gap attack won the battle but could not make a victory of it. For the earlier failure of the main attack, and the mounting of the fresh one had given Messe and Bayerlein a little time. Though a platitude, it is a practical truth that in battle a gift of time is precious to anyone who is capable of using it. The enemy showed themselves to be thus capable, met the changing situation, and got themselves out of great danger. The British could take full credit for what they had achieved but, as at El Alamein, El Agheila, and Buerat, they had not produced the quality of being what pugilists call 'good finishers'.

On the night of the 26th/27th a strong force of 63 Halifaxes and Wellingtons dropped 110 tons of bombs on enemy M.T. concentrations in the Gabes area, and these attacks were followed up by the fighter-bombers on the 27th which covered the El Hamma—Gabes road and El Hamma itself. The hostile A.A. fire was so fierce that low-flying attacks were for the time being forbidden unless ordered by A.H.Q. Western Desert. On the 28th air operations during the morning were spoiled by sandstorms and low visibility: in the afternoon American fighter-bombers ranged over the El Hamma—Gabes area (12 sorties in all) and the British fighter-bombers flew 69 sorties in the areas of Gabes and Sfax. On the same night 48 Wellingtons and 4 Halifaxes led by 2 Albacores bombed the enemy as they were settling into the Wadi Akarit positions. The Germans, by 28th March, had withdrawn their aircraft from the Gabes group of airfields and had moved to fresh bases around Sfax—La Fauconnerie while they were preparing yet other bases further north. The Italian squadrons had withdrawn to the neighbourhood of Sfax but their will to fight had been so broken that they had scarcely to be reckoned with.

A remarkable feature of the air support given to 8th Army was that of No. 205 Group from 17th/18th March onwards under the operational control of A.H.Q. Western Desert. Close on 500 sorties were flown in a tactical role by R.A.F. Halifaxes, Wellingtons and F.A.A. Albacore pathfinders—almost the entire effort of the British Middle East strategic bomber force.

During the four to five weeks covered by this chapter, the Allies throughout north and north-west Africa flew on average about 705 sorties every day, a striking indication of the powerful air force being created within the Mediterranean Air Command. No less remarkable was the loss of only 156 Allied aircraft against the German figure of 136, since the air war was being waged almost entirely over enemy territory.[1]

From the enemy's point of view the situation in the air had continued to grow worse. The Axis air forces were being forced more and more on to the defensive, and on 27th March *O.B. Süd's* H.Q. informed *OKH* that

> 'It is no longer possible to put up an effective fight against the enemy's air force as our own aircraft and crews are so heavily strained by having to support the ground operations of Army Group Africa, by protecting our convoys and by attacking those of the enemy.'

The Allies were determined to increase the strain relentlessly. With the Mediterranean Air Command fully established, they had set about reorganizing their air defences. In early March N.A.C.A.F. assumed responsibility for the day-fighter defence of all north-west African ports, bases and inshore shipping westwards of a point fifty miles behind the front line, and for night-fighter defence of the whole area including northern Tunisia, thus enabling No. 242 Group R.A.F. and U.S. XII A.S.C. to concentrate on offensive operations (see Chapter XII). The like benefits which the Desert Air Force was already enjoying as the result of the creation of fighter defence groups in the Levant, Egypt, Cyrenaica and Tripolitania, were enhanced by the conversion on 4th March of A.H.Q. Egypt to A.H.Q. Air Defences, Eastern Mediterranean.

By the end of the month the Allied air forces were ready to give direct and indirect air support to the Allied armies of a quality and quantity never before possible. This was true also of the offensive against the Axis air forces in the air and on the ground—in Sicily, southern Italy and particularly in Tunisia. Behind N.A.T.A.F. was the powerful N.A.S.A.F. seeking hard to find the best pattern of day-bomber formation and the best type of bomb to neutralize airfields and landing grounds and to destroy aircraft; and already the 20-lb fragmentation bomb, dropped in great clusters among parked aircraft, was beginning to prove itself. The air forces were now about to reap a fine harvest from devastating attacks against the enemy's air transport fleets and on his airfields and landing grounds.

---

[1] Figures of sorties given exclude those flown against shipping and by aircraft based on Malta.
Italian losses are unknown, but according to Santoro 22 Italian aircraft were lost in Tunisia during February and March.

CHAPTER XIV

THE AXIS AT BAY:
THE BATTLE OF WADI AKARIT, AND THE ACTION AT FONDOUK, APRIL 1943

See Map 27

ON 29th March 1st Armoured Division and the New Zealand Division began to probe the defences of the Wadi Akarit.[1] Several possibilities lay ahead but Horrocks's present task was by close contact with the enemy's defences to determine whether 10th Corps could force them without heavy loss. Early on the 30th Montgomery received his report that he was making contact, and also that '... If Army Commander prepared for heavy casualties might be possible to carry out Blitz attack right through ...'. At a conference with Horrocks and Freyberg later in the morning, Montgomery decided against a blitz. It was possible that the enemy might withdraw if pressure were continued by 8th Army and 2nd U.S. Corps, or he might just as well stand fast. But it was certain that mobile operations would occur once the enemy had been forced from Akarit or had withdrawn, and therefore it was unwise to expose the mobile troops of 8th Army to the risk of heavy casualties. Montgomery ordered Horrocks to probe for twenty-four hours longer, and to decide by the 31st morning whether he could get through. If he could not, 30th Corps would be called forward.

On the 31st Horrocks reported that his Corps alone could not force Akarit. Montgomery then decided that 30th Corps would make a set-piece attack and that 10th Corps would exploit it. On 1st April he signalled to Alexander '... Am held up by strong resistance in the Wadi Akarit. Am preparing to break through enemy positions and will stage a strong attack on night 4/5th April and continuing on 5th April ...' He wished 2nd U.S. Corps to press on because '... if that Corps could come forward even a few miles it would make my task very simple ...'

---

[1] The New Zealand Division did not formally lose its status as a Corps until 31st March when it passed under command of 30th Corps for operations.

The date proposed by Montgomery gave Alexander time to co-ordinate 8th Army's offensive with two other thrusts which he had planned. On 3rd April he issued a scheme of operations which he had agreed with the commanders of 1st and 8th Armies. His object was still to prepare for the final assault on Tunis, which must necessarily be delivered by the land forces. But it was essential to use the Allies' great superiority in the air to make easier the land forces' rapid advance. Therefore he aimed at seizing and securing all airfields from which the weight of the air forces could be applied to paralysing the enemy's system of supply. It will be remembered that since 11th March the air forces had been giving a great deal of effort to precisely this purpose as an important part of their conduct of the whole air war. On the 5th April they launched operation 'Flax', the campaign to smash the enemy's air supply from Italy to Tunisia. This was to be immensely successful and to round off the whole task.[1] Success by 18th Army Group would help the Air Forces to their goal as surely as the Air Forces would help the Armies to theirs. It was a combination of means in two elements towards a common end—the destruction of the Axis forces in Africa. Allied maritime power was pursuing the same end at sea.

General Alexander's plan of the 3rd April had two phases. The first was to drive the enemy from the 'Gabes gap', whose northern limit was the Wadi Akarit, by a frontal attack by 8th Army and flanking pressure by 2nd U.S. Corps. When the enemy had been ejected, 8th Army would be loosed into the coastal plain where its superior armoured and motorized formations could have full play, and 2nd U.S. Corps could be transferred to the extreme northern flank, i.e. on the left of 1st Army. At this time General Alexander contemplated a rather subsidiary role for the 2nd U.S. Corps in the last stage of the campaign. General Eisenhower, however, stipulated that the whole Corps must be used in its own sector on the north because '... The largest issues were involved, some of them extending beyond the limits of our own theatre ...'. The second phase was to coincide with the 8th Army's advance towards Sousse and depend upon its progress, and would begin after 7th April. In this phase Alexander proposed to use the Army Group Reserve, which he was forming under the recently-arrived Headquarters 9th Corps (Lieut.-General J. T. Crocker) by appropriating (as was certainly expedient)

---

[1] On the 5th, the first day of operation 'Flax', U.S. Lightnings shot down 13 Ju.52 transport aircraft north-east of Cape Bon. Another eight were destroyed on Milo (Trapani) airfield by U.S. Fortresses which also attacked Bocca di Falco (Palermo), bombed by British and U.S. Liberators from the Middle East the previous night. Four more Ju.52s were destroyed as a result of all these attacks. Three Italian Savoias, most probably in use as air transports, were also destroyed by bombing in Tunisia. It was a thoroughly bad day for the Axis air transport organisation. See Chapter XVI.

formations from which General Anderson, since early February, had been trying to create a reserve for 1st Army.[1] 9th Corps was, when the time was ripe, to capture the Fondouk Gap in the Eastern Dorsale and send its armour through it towards Kairouan to threaten the rear of *AOK 1*. During both phases 1st Army's 5th and 19th (French) Corps were to tie down the enemy on their fronts by constant thrusts which might also win jumping-off places for the final assault on Tunis.

By the evening of 28th March almost all the Italian formations of *AOK 1* were in or on their way to the Akarit positions, and 15th and 21st Panzer Divisions, 164th Light Division and most of 90th Light Division were retiring thither, covered by rearguards. On the 29th the Desert Air Force had its busiest day since the battle of El Alamein. Nearly 800 sorties were flown and many targets in the traffic on the coast road were found. The German war diaries record heavy air attacks but seldom the losses caused by them.[2] Next day *AOK 1* reported that all formations were ready for defence in the Akarit positions. On 29th morning von Arnim had signalled to Jodl, sending a copy to Kesselring for *Comando Supremo*: 'Supplies shattering. Ammunition only available for 1–2 more days, no more stocks for some weapons such as medium field hows. Fuel situation similar, large-scale movement no longer possible . . .'[3] This signal, no doubt, referred to the Army Group in general, and the words were perhaps chosen to goad the High Command. But von Arnim was not a man who cried out before he was hurt.

In Rome discussions on policy continued. These were often angry because Ambrosio did not share Kesselring's optimistic moods, and

---

[1] H.Q. 9th Corps and Corps Troops were complete in Algiers (from the United Kingdom) on 5th March, and reached a concentration area at El Ksar on 24th March. 6th Armoured Division passed under its command on 12th March, and was completed with Sherman tanks by 15th March. Owing to the course of operations the Corps was not complete with 1st British Armoured Division, 6th Armoured Division, 46th Infantry Division until 15th April.

On 4th March No. 654 A.O.P. Squadron arrived in North Africa and was placed under command of 9th Corps temporarily until transfer at a later date to 8th Army.

[2] As an example: 21st Panzer Division reports that one attack killed five men, wounded four, and destroyed twelve motor vehicles; and also damaged nine motor-vehicles and two tanks. Formations whose vehicles had been depleted in the recent fighting would find losses on this scale serious in terms of transport, if not in life.

[3] On 30th/31st March *AOK 1*'s supply-return gave these figures:
AOK 1 (including *D.A.K.*):
Rations. 3 days with troops; 7 days in dumps.
P.O.L. 0·6 units in all (about 40 miles per vehicle); nothing at Sfax or Sousse.
Ammunition. About $\frac{2}{3}$ of an issue with troops; 1½ issues in dumps, the bulk at Sfax.
Pz. AOK 5's return gave:
Rations.   6 days with troops.
P.O.L.   0·3 units with troops; a minute reserve in dumps.
Ammunition. 1·2 issues with troops; 1·6 issues in dumps.

showed himself determined 'to be tough with the Germans' as he had earlier told the Duce he would be. Because of the Allies' increasingly severe pressure after Mareth, these high-level disputes were little relevant to what was going on in the field, yet the Axis leaders could not agree upon even general questions of future tactics.

On the 29th Ambrosio announced that he was about to direct von Arnim to hold the southern front stubbornly, but that in view of the present threat to the right wing and rear of *AOK 1* (by 2nd U.S. Corps thrusting eastward against *D.A.K.*) a withdrawal from the Akarit position to one at Djebel Mansour—Enfidaville might become necessary in order to save this army from complete destruction. Cautious preparations for this retreat were to be made but *Comando Supremo* reserved to itself the decision to retreat unless *AOK 1* was in immediate danger of destruction, when the C.-in-C. Army Group could give the order.

Kesselring argued that this directive might make von Arnim 'retreat minded' and that it was contrary to Hitler's pronouncement that the Akarit position was the final defence line. He produced his own directive which indeed mentioned a retreat to Enfidaville but guarded the point with orders to stand firm at Akarit and to meet the threat to the Maknassy–El Guettar front by armoured counter-strokes. Ambrosio triumphantly replied that the Duce had approved *his* directive which was at that moment in the hands of two senior Italian staff officers, to be taken to Tunisia next day. Kesselring could only suggest that Westphal too should go to 'explain' the document to von Arnim. Ambrosio agreed.

On the 30th Westphal had a preliminary meeting with von Arnim and his principal German staff officers before the Italians joined in. He found his hearers in a state of pugnacious gloom, and they did not like the idea of counter-strokes at Maknassy–El Guettar. There were hard words; for example Westphal said that the Army Group seemed always to be 'squinting over its shoulder', and von Arnim replied that he was squinting for ships, and closed with the remark that 'we are without bread and ammunition, as was Rommel's Army before. The consequences are inevitable.'

Later General Rossi (Chief of the Operations Branch of *Comando Supremo*) and General Mattioli (*Comando Supremo's* Liaison Officer to Army Group Africa) appeared. von Arnim repeated his gloomy forecasts, and said that the defences of Akarit were 'nothing special' and that the enemy would decide how long *AOK 1* could hold them. If pressure on *D.A.K.* increased he might have to withdraw part of it next evening and then *AOK 1* too would have to begin to move back. Rossi and Mattioli protested and demanded counter-attacks. von Arnim replied that it was no use 'butting at the mountains' with tanks, and that his forces were not strong enough (presumably in infantry) to dislodge the enemy. He was not thinking of counter-attacks unless the enemy broke through. In his opinion the High Command would be better occupied in getting supplies to Africa than in trying to conduct operations.

On the 31st von Arnim conferred with the administrative staffs on such preparations to withdraw to the 'bridge-head' positions as removing supplies and stores after a generous issue had been made to the troops, and withdrawing static units. Inessential officers and men of the administrative organizations were to be sent to Italy if transport could be provided, but no decision had been taken about a general evacuation of Tunis and Bizerta which was thought to be politically impossible. In short only completely motorized troops were to remain in the forward areas. von Arnim and his principal staff officers enjoined secrecy in all preparations, few orders, and no explanations.

In the small hours of 1st April von Arnim sent to Kesselring, for *Comando Supremo*, a message that he could not execute *Comando Supremo*'s directive unless he received 10,000 tons of ammunition and 8,000 tons of fuel by 6th April, excluding the Italians' needs. He asked also for '. . . instructions as to what is to happen if these conditions are not fulfilled.' Kesselring replied non-commitally, but Ambrosio replied sharply that Arnim's and the Italian troops' needs together amounted to 25,000 tons of ammunition and fuel—extremely high requirements. However he promised to meet them by 12th April 'provided that there were no unforeseen events': to do more was impossible.

Of this period Messe wrote at a later date that to combine an all-out defence in the Akarit positions with preparations for a retreat of almost 200 miles to Enfidaville was '. . . easier to express in an order than to carry out in reality.' In particular, preparation for retreat did not escape the troops and by 5th April *Comando Supremo* was sufficiently stirred by signs of 'retreat-mindedness' in Tunisia to warn *AOK 1* sternly that any idea that Akarit was merely a delaying position must be dismissed. However according to 90th Light Division's records, it was common knowledge that a final defence line was being prepared in northern Tunisia. The Axis commanders indeed were beginning to taste tribulations similar to those which the British had suffered when the 8th Army fell back to Alamein in June and July 1942. They even noted that the British powers of recovery were 'very different' from their own, perhaps owing to an exaggerated estimate of British losses.[1] On 31st March von Arnim wrote personally to Jodl, describing the state of the troops, and asking what was to be done if shortage of fuel and ammunition made it impossible

---

[1] See Volume III of this history, Chapter X–XII and XIV.

to go on fighting. He was not answered. Ten days later Jodl minuted that 'for the time being nothing was to be done about it'. von Arnim it seems, did not write again to *OKW*.

See also Map 35

The Akarit position was the last natural barrier against access to the coastal plain of Tunisia from the south. It was short, some 18 miles across from the sea to Djebel Haidoudi on the west. The eastern flank rested securely upon the sea, and the broad and deep Wadi Akarit was a difficult natural obstacle for a distance of some four miles inland from the coast. The western flank lay on the great salt marshes at the Chott el Fedjadj. These marshes were impassable to vehicles in winter, but in April were drying fast, and were not to be accounted a complete obstacle—a fact known to the Axis but not, it seems, to the British. Two features dominated the coastal part of the position. The eastern of these was Djebel Roumana, a bare ridge running roughly parallel to the coast road, about 500 feet high, steep-sided and impassable to tracks and wheels. Nearly 5,000 yards west of the western end of Djebel Roumana there sprang up Djebel Tebaga Fatnassa, nearly 900 feet high, a towering, horrible-looking labyrinth of pinnacles, chimneys, gullies, and escarpments. The approaches to that part of the position lying between Roumana and Fatnassa are across open and fairly level country which then becomes rolling. West of Fatnassa the remainder of the position was protected by a line of hills, about 500 feet high, running south-westward to where Djebel Haidoudi stood guard over the metalled road linking Gabes with El Guettar and Gafsa. The Akarit position had great natural advantages, vouched for by Rommel who would have preferred to stand there rather than at Mareth, but it had no depth, and the field works were not elaborate.

Comando Supremo had given priority to Mareth and Messe therefore seems to have done little to organize the Akarit position until 27th March. He then made 20th Corps responsible for work, and ordered the Army Engineer Commander to plan minefields and other obstacles. Near the coast the Wadi Akarit had been scarped, and this obstacle was continued to the Djebel Roumana by an anti-tank ditch. Another ditch extended from Roumana's western end to Djebel Tebaga Fatnassa; wire obstacles were thin; and about 4,000 mines had been laid, mostly between the coastal road and Roumana, and in small patches between Roumana and Fatnassa.

AOK 1 disposed the following force in the Akarit position. 20th Corps held the sector from the coast road to Fatnassa with (east to west) Young Fascist Division; two battalions of 90th Light Division

Map 35

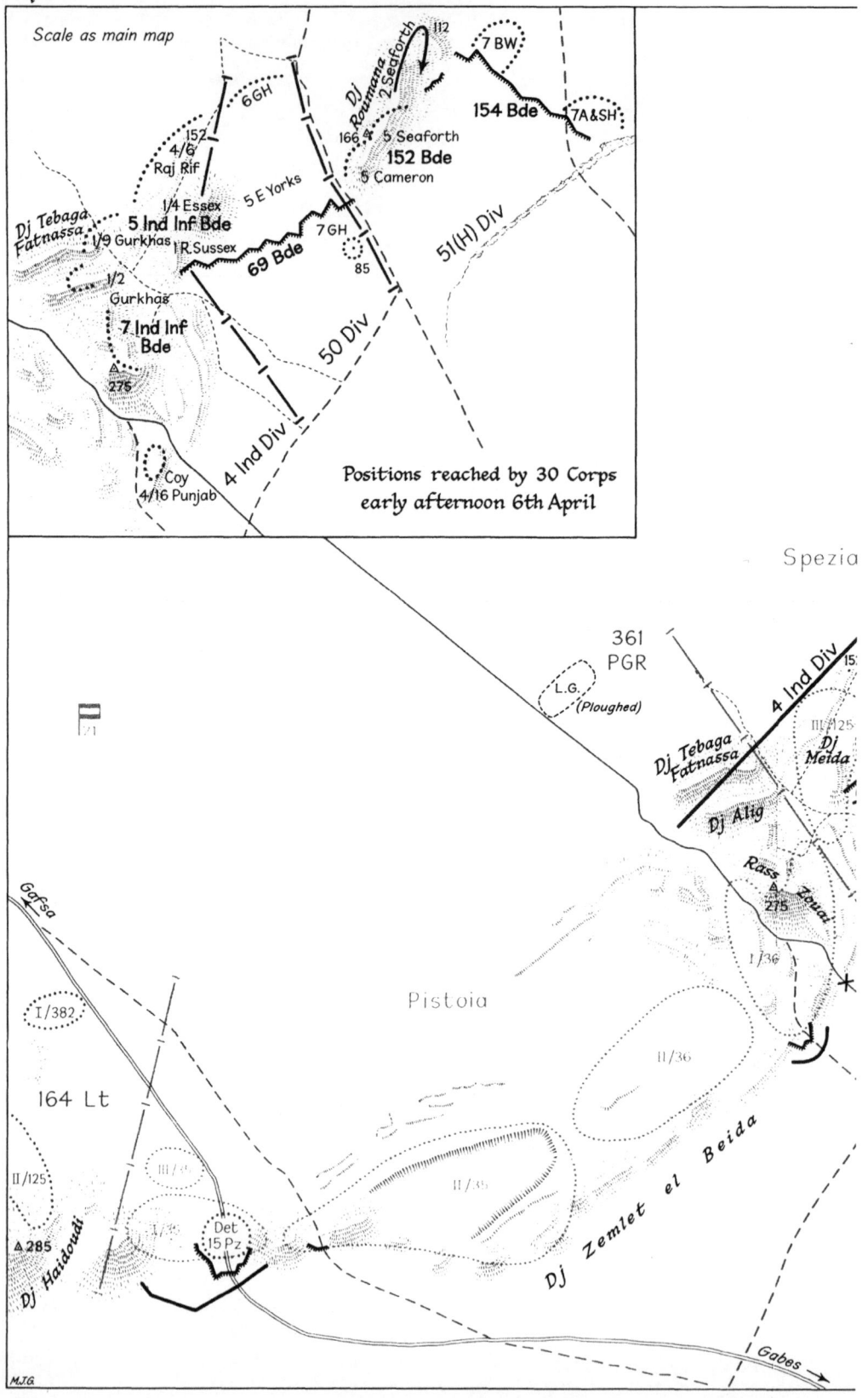

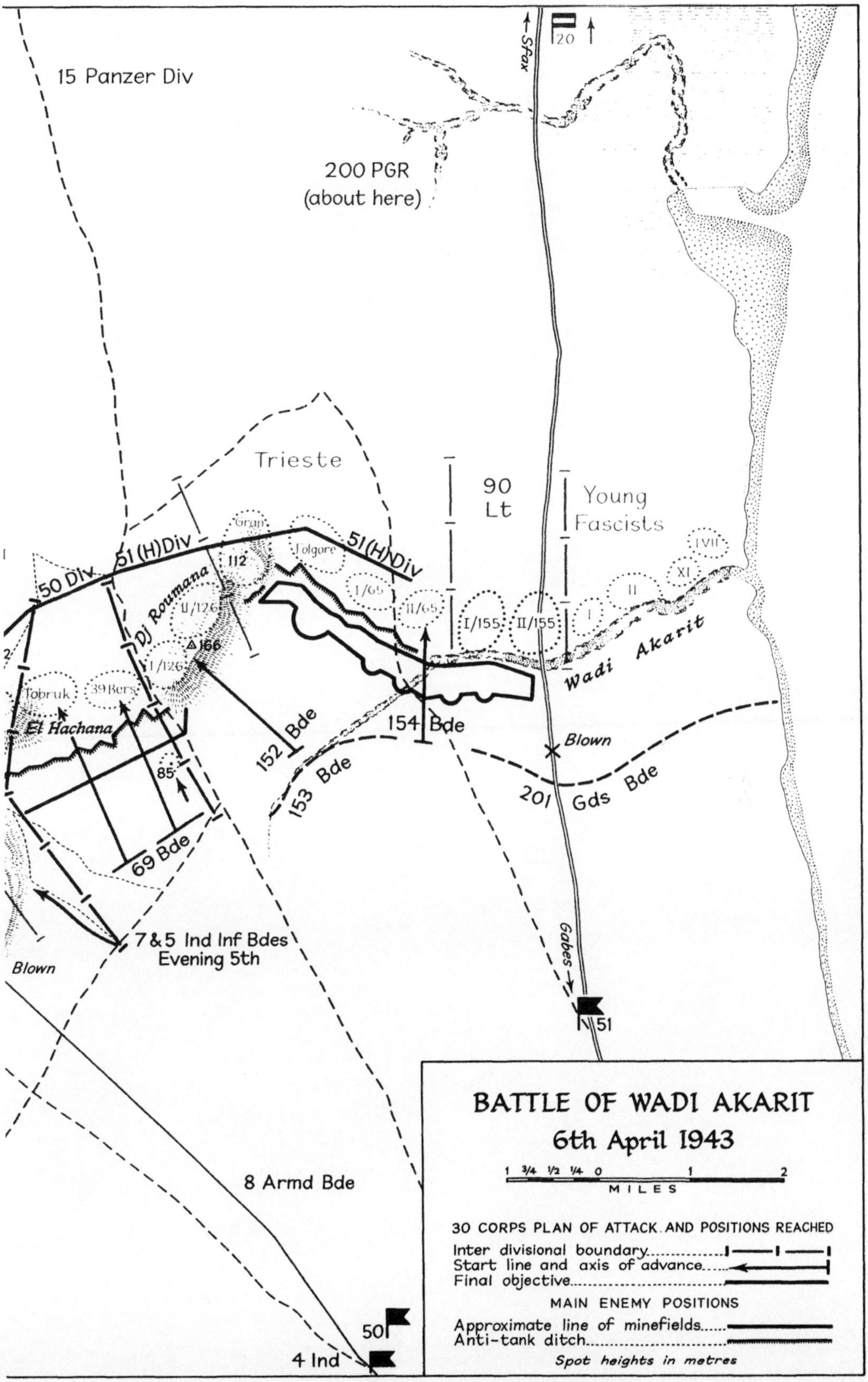

BATTLE OF WADI AKARIT
6th April 1943
1 3/4 1/2 1/4 0 1 2
MILES
30 CORPS PLAN OF ATTACK AND POSITIONS REACHED
Inter divisional boundary
Start line and axis of advance
Final objective
MAIN ENEMY POSITIONS
Approximate line of minefields
Anti-tank ditch
Spot heights in metres
15 Panzer Div
Sfax
20
200 PGR
(about here)
Trieste
90
Lt
Young
Fascists
Gran
112
Folgore
51 (H) Div
51 (H) Div
50 Div
Dj Roumana
II/126
I/126
166
I/65
II/65
I/155
II/155
I
II
XI
VII
Wadi Akarit
Tobruk
39 Bers
El Hachana
85
152 Bde
154 Bde
153 Bde
Blown
201 Gds Bde
69 Bde
7 & 5 Ind Inf Bdes
Evening 5th
Blown
Gabes
51
8 Armd Bde
50
4 Ind

astride the coast road; Trieste Division; Spezia Division. West of Fatnassa 21st Corps had (east to west) Pistoia Division covering the Fatnassa by-road and the Haidoudi Pass; a detachment of 15th Panzer Division in the mouth of the pass; on the hills to the north-west what remained of 164th Light Division (von Liebenstein, the commander, vainly protested that he was wasted there); the ragged Saharan Group. The reserves were 361st Panzer Grenadier Regiment and 190th Anti-Tank Unit of 90th Light Division for counter-attack in the Fatnassa area; and 15th Panzer Division (less detachment), and 200th Panzer Grenadier Regiment (90th Light Division) north of Roumana.

We are unable accurately to assess the enemy's strength from the incomplete records known to us. *AOK 1* had approximately 12 German and 26 Italian infantry battalions. 90th Light Division had six battalions, and 15th Panzer and 164th Light Divisions three each. The Young Fascist, Spezia, and Trieste Divisions each had six battalions, the Pistoia Division five, and the Saharan Group probably three. 55 German guns are accounted for on 4th April; and on the 13th 155 Italian, some 'glorious but decrepit'. 19th Flak Division held sixty-three dual purpose 8·8-cm guns of which 28 were sited in an anti-tank role, i.e. 8 covering the Haidoudi Pass, 4 the Fatnassa by-road, 10 the area west of Roumana, 6 the coast road. 15th Panzer Division on 6th April had 22 serviceable German tanks and 4 Italian, but the types are not known.[1] Motor transport had steadily been growing scarcer for several reasons. For example: replacements from Italy were not keeping pace with losses; spare parts and tyres were insufficient partly owing to the fact that some 200 types of vehicle were in use in Africa; Peter was robbed to pay Paul as when Gause on 2nd April ordered units not in the front line, and Headquarters everywhere, to surrender a quarter of their serviceable vehicles. On the other hand supplies of fuel and ammunition had grown a little because several small ships had arrived during the first week in April.[2]

On 20th March General Montgomery had told his Army that having destroyed the enemy at Mareth and burst through the Gabes Gap, it would drive north on Sfax, Sousse, and finally Tunis. On 31st March he conferred with his Corps Commanders and outlined his plan for forcing the Wadi Akarit. The enemy seemed to be holding the whole position with a single Corps, the 21st, with 15th and 21st Panzer Divisions (too weak in tanks to be much taken into account) on the western flank. The ground did not permit manoeuvre. Therefore Montgomery decided to breach the Akarit position with one division of 30th Corps, and then to send 10th Corps through, with

---

[1] There were in all Africa on 5th April the following serviceable tanks: German 121, Italian 12.

[2] The German divisions, at least of *AOK 1*, now had about 60 miles' worth of fuel; in general units of the Army held 1 issue of ammunition.

New Zealand Division leading and directed on Mezzouna airfields, 1st British Armoured Division following.[1] Reconnaissances then began at all levels, each giving birth to ideas, which may explain the overlapping of subsequent plans, and the welter of orders and instructions.

It soon became evident that the enemy was stronger than had been thought. Both 20th and 21st Corps were detected and their composition and dispositions were discovered fairly correctly. General Leese therefore decided to use two infantry divisions to breach their line by seizing Roumana, and the defences west of it, and including Rass Zouai. 10th Corps' role was unchanged, but it was not settled whether it would move on a two, or one-divisional front between Fatnassa and the sea, or through the passes of the Djebel Zemlet el Beida. Meanwhile General Tuker, commander of 4th Indian Division which, with 51st Highland Division, was to break in, had formed certain conclusions. The most important were that any attack between Roumana and Fatnassa would be overlooked, and caught between two fires. Secondly that the Fatnassa massif was the 'key' to the position. If this could be taken, the enemy's centre would be turned and his minefields and anti-tank ditch rendered useless. Then if a way could be made round the west end of these obstacles, 10th Corps could pour through and cut the enemy off where he stood. He did not like the proposed plan and neither did General Wimberley, commander of the Highland Division. In the end Tuker virtually guaranteed to take the whole Fatnassa massif by night before the attack in the Roumana area began. He reasoned that the enemy would not think that an attack of this sort was possible and he confirmed by small patrols that it was possible for mountain-trained troops like his two brigades.[2] Moreover his vastly experienced eye saw that to hold this big, tangled feature there would be needed a mass of infantry, which the enemy had not got. Therefore Fatnassa which seemed the strongest part of the position was in fact the weakest —for the right troops. Tuker and Wimberley put their views to Leese who agreed, and obtained Montgomery's agreement.

The final plan came out on 3rd April. 4th Indian Division to take Fatnassa during the night 5th/6th April and build a crossing over the anti-tank ditch at its foot; on 6th April 50th Division was to breach the anti-tank ditch and wadi in the centre; 51st Highland Division to take Djebel Roumana including Pt 112 and the defences at its south-western end, making some crossings over the ditch. As a

---

[1] The style 1st British Armoured Division is used here although the 18th Army Group Order thus designating it did not come into force until 4th April. To distinguish Allied formations bearing the same number, the following styles were then ordered: 1st British Armoured Division; 1st British Infantry Division; 1st U.S. Armoured Division; 1st U.S. Infantry Division. The three last-named were in 1st Army.

[2] 4th Indian Division's third Infantry Brigade, the 11th, had been lost in Tobruk in 1942 and no permanent replacement had been provided.

diversion, 1st British Armoured Division was to demonstrate against the Haidoudi Pass on the evening of the 5th (to the Indian Division's understandable annoyance) and 201st Guards Brigade in the coastal area on the morning of the 6th. For 10th Corps there was a curious arrangement. Its New Zealand Division was to pass through a gap to be made by 30th Corps, and therefore was under tactical command of that Corps at the outset, but at a suitable time when it was in or through the gap, it would revert to the tactical command of 10th Corps. The Division would go forward either east or west of Roumana and the rest of the Corps would probably follow it. The New Zealand Division's objective was a salt marsh twenty-five miles beyond the Wadi Akarit; 1st British Armoured Division's was on the New Zealanders' right, a ridge fifteen miles beyond the wadi. The direction of the Corps' thrust suggests that there was no intention of cutting the enemy off. Further plans, as was customary in British mobile formations, were apparently to depend upon which way the Axis cat jumped.

The date of the 8th Army's attack was governed by the shortest time required for preparations. Montgomery could not await the next moon, and there was a chance that the change from the usual assault by moonlight would win surprise. The enemy knew that he would be attacked, thought that the Roumana feature would receive the main blow, and expected several days of grace. The three-divisional attack in the dark, and especially the inclusion of Fatnassa, surprised him.

4th Indian Division's task was to capture or neutralize the whole of Djebel Tebaga Fatnassa by 8.30 a.m. on 6th April. The approach was to begin as soon as darkness fell on the 5th. 7th Indian Infantry Brigade was to lead, making first for Rass Zouai (Pt 275) and Djebel Alig, and then eastward to Djebel Meida. 5th Indian Infantry Brigade was to pass through the 7th on Rass Zouai and send one battalion across the Fatnassa ridge to clear and screen the north-west flank, and another battalion to exploit north-east to El Hachana. Here it was to consolidate, and be ready to advance along the spur to Pt 152 at 8.30 a.m. on the 6th, to look after 50th Division's left flank. Its third battalion, 1st/4th Essex, was to advance independently, behind 50th Division, and seize a passage over the anti-tank ditch leading on to El Hachana.[1] The Essex also had under their wing a field regiment and all the artillery parties necessary to enable all the

---

[1] *5th Indian Infantry Brigade*
(Brigadier D.R.E.R. Bateman): 4/6 Raj Rif, 1/9 G.R., M.G. Bn 6 Raj Rif less two coys, Bty 149 A/Tk Rgt R.A.
7th Indian Infantry Brigade
(Brigadier O. D. T. Lovett until wounded; then Lieut.-Colonel C. E. A. Firth): 1 R. Sussex, 4/16 Punjab, 1/2 G.R., Bty. 149 A/Tk Regt. R.A., 12 Fd Coy Madras S. & M., Coy M.G. Bn 6 Raj Rif.
1/4 Essex Group
149 A/Tk Regt R.A. less two btys, 4 Fd. Coy Bengal S. & M., Coy M.G. Bn 6 Raj Rif.

division's guns to get right forward at dawn, thus gaining much range.

Surprise was vital (hence the division's annoyance at the diversion ordered from 1st British Armoured Division) and the attack therefore was to begin 'silently', but all likely targets for artillery fire had been chosen and an artillery programme had been arranged. The troops were to approach on foot, the fewest possible vehicles were to be taken, and those anti-tank gunners whose guns were not in action performed the strenuous and vital role of porters. The plan demanded great boldness, stamina, and first-class training including that almost unconscious mountain-craft with which tradition and experience had endowed many Indian regiments.

The attacks by 50th and 51st Highland Divisions were to have two phases. The object of the first was to cross minefields and anti-tank ditches and get a good grip of the main hostile positions; of the second, to exploit by seizing tactical features beyond. The early part of the first phase was to be silent, and 4.15 a.m. on the 6th was set as the time for the guns to open fire. Fifteen field and four medium regiments were to support the three attacking divisions, and 300 rounds per gun for field, and 130 rounds per gun for medium guns were dumped. 50th and 51st Divisions chose concentrations and barrages, and one of the five barrages fired for the Highland Division had to end with a difficult change of direction. Armoured support was provided for 50th Division by a squadron of Valentines of 40th Royal Tank Regiment and a squadron of Shermans of 4th County of London Yeomanry; for 51st Division by 40th and 50th R.T.R. (Valentines) and a squadron of Shermans and Crusaders of 4th C.L.Y.[1] Some of the Valentines were told off to tow anti-tank guns (crews and ammunition on the back of the tank)—a lesson from Mareth.

50th Division was to tackle both phases with a single brigade, the 69th, because its remaining brigade and two field regiments had been left at Gabes. 7th Green Howards was to clear Pt 85, an enemy outpost which overlooked the approaches, in a preliminary operation.[2] In 51st Division, 154th Brigade was to punch a hole a little east of Roumana; and link up with 152nd Brigade which was to capture Roumana itself.[3] 153rd Brigade was to form a firm base.

---

[1] 40th and 50th R.T.R. belonged to 23rd Armoured Brigade; 4th C.L.Y. to 22nd Armoured Brigade. 4th C.L.Y. held in all 29 Shermans and 21 Crusaders.

[2] *69th Infantry Brigade*
(Brigadier E. C. Cooke Collis); 5 East York, 6 and 7 Green Howards, 40 R.T.R., 288 A/Tk Bty. N.H., B Coy and pl. A Coy 2 Cheshire (MG). In support: A Sqn 4 C.L.Y., 102 (Northumberland Hussars) A/Tk Regt. R.A., 42, 233, 505 Fd Coys R.E., 2 Cheshire (MG) less dets.

[3] *152nd Infantry Brigade*
(Brigadier G. Murray): 2 and 5 Seaforth, 5 Camerons, 50 R.T.R., 296 A/Tk Bty R.A., 275 Fd. Coy R.E., D Coy 1/7 Middlesex (MG). 5 Black Watch of 153rd Brigade came under command on afternoon 6th.

154th Infantry Brigade
(Brigadier J. E. Stirling): 1 and 7 Black Watch, 7 A. and S.H., 40 R.T.R. (less det.), det. Scorpion Regt, 274 Fd Coy and pl. 276 Fd Coy R.E., B Coy 1/7 Middlesex (MG).

50th and 51st Divisions were each to make four gaps and four crossings in the minefields and over the anti-tank ditch. The New Zealand Division was to make what gaps it needed.

The advance to 30th Corps' second objective was to begin at 8.30 a.m. behind a barrage, and was to end at 9.16 a.m. This phase aimed at extending the penetration to a final depth of about two miles, clearing the hostile gun-areas and reserve positions, and opening the way for 10th Corps.

In 10th Corps the New Zealand Division prepared a minefield task force to make and mark three gaps through the minefield in 50th Division's sector, and laid down the divisional 'order of march'. Briefly 8th Armoured Brigade, the New Zealand Divisional Cavalry, and the King's Dragoon Guards were to lead, and when through, were to reconnoitre to north and west while the main body of the division awaited developments.[1] The intention of 1st British Armoured Division was to assist 30th Corps' attack and pass through 30th Corps' bridgehead. It planned to move in rear of the N.Z. Division but an instruction said 'It is impossible to give detailed timings for the move of formations, as the move of 2nd N.Z. Div is unpredictable.'[2] 30th Corps was responsible for the movement of N.Z. Division within 30th Corps area—the division was to 'Be prepared on receipt of orders from HQ 30 Corps to advance through the bridgehead.'

In round numbers the two British Corps could bring against the enemy:

33 infantry, 6 motor or lorried, and 5 machine-gun battalions to 38.
400 field and medium guns to 200 (estimated).
462 tanks (including 210 Grants and Shermans) to 25.[3]

---

[1] *N.Z. Division 'Minefield Task Force'*
Comd. Lieut.-Colonel F. M. H. Hanson (C.R.E.): One Sqn Crusader tanks (8 Armd Bde), Pl. 8 Fd Coy, D Coy 26 N.Z. Bn, det. Provost Coy.
Order of March N.Z. Division
8 Armd Bde, N.Z. Div. Cav., K.D.G., Gun Group, 5 N.Z. Inf Bde., Div H.Q., Div. Reserve Group, 6 N.Z. Inf. Bde.

[2] *Order of March 1st British Armoured Division:*
2 Armd Bde and Sqn 12 L., 12 L. less sqn, Div. Arty, Div. H.Q., 7 Mot. Bde.

[3] The number of serviceable British tanks on 5th April was:

	Grant/Sherman	*Crusader*	*Crusader III*	*Valentine*
1 British Armd. Div.	70	31	26	—
8 Armd. Bde.	58	26	24	—
7 Armd. Div.	80	33	29	—
23 Armd. Bde.	—	—	—	71
Force 'L'	2	10	2	—
Total	210	100	81	71

No more reinforcements were to come from the Delta.

Administratively, the British forces were well found. Thus, for example, 30th Corps fired at the Wadi Akarit some 82,000 shells, field and medium, and large quantities of mortar and small-arms ammunition, and this expenditure was rapidly replaced. The troops were successfully maintained but not without anxious spells and continual toil on the L. of C. The 8th Army, based on Tripoli, depended on the single road between that place and its roadhead at Gabes, a distance of 220 miles, until the port of Sfax was captured. Petrol was plentiful in Tripoli but expenditure had to be carefully controlled very largely because barrels and jerricans were scarce owing to various malpractices by the troops. Besides, since October 1942 all transport vehicles and drivers had been relentlessly overworked. The mechanical condition of vehicles was growing worse, and the ever-increasing shortage of manpower meant that drivers sent as reinforcements were often of poor stamp, insufficiently trained, and inexperienced. The general transport situation was in fact very serious. These summarily-chosen illustrations indicate that for the administrative staffs and units from Egypt to front line there was 'no discharge in this war' if the troops in the line were not to be numbered in the legion of the lost ones and the cohort of the damned.

In early April the German Air Force in Africa mustered about 178 serviceable aircraft out of a total of 324, and the Italian Air Force about 65 in all. The Western Desert Air Force, which most concerns us at this point because most directly linked with 8th Army, numbered in its R.A.F. units five squadrons of bombers (Bostons and Baltimores), eight squadrons of fighter-bombers (Kittyhawks), five squadrons of fighters (Spitfires and Hurricanes), a tank-destroying squadron (Hurricanes IID) and upward of three squadrons of reconnaissance aircraft. In the American component there were two squadrons of bombers (Mitchells) and four of fighter-bombers and four of fighters (all Kittyhawks). In indirect tactical support of the Desert Air Force were the remaining British and American squadrons of N.A.T.A.F. numbering twenty fighter, two fighter-bomber, three tactical reconnaissance; and in N.A.T.B.F. 11 bomber squadrons besides. The Allied numerical superiority in tactical air support was formidable in itself, while aloof from the battlefield yet swaying the fortunes of the troops on it, were also the powerful strategic bomber and coastal forces of the Northwest African, Malta and Middle East air forces.

Air operations (other than those of the strategic bombers) between 29th March and 5th April which directly affected the battle at Wadi Akarit were of a familiar pattern. The elements in this pattern were constant near and distant reconnaissance; attacks by bombers, fighter-bombers, and fighters on hostile airfields; by fighter-bombers on troops, guns, and transport; and by widely-sweeping formations of fighters on anything hostile that flew, or lived and moved on the ground. An air 'blitz' upon the Akarit positions like that of 26th March ('Supercharge') was proposed but abandoned because the terrain and the nature of the enemy's positions did not favour it. Weather which was often unfavourable for flying reduced the sorties flown but those that were flown were, generally, effective. The airfields and landing grounds attacked were Zitouna, Mezzouna, those at La Fauconnerie, and Sfax to which the Desert Air Force and the Middle East Wellingtons paid special attention, forcing the enemy to abandon it on 1st April. Between 29th March and 5th April the Germans lost 51 aircraft in Tunisia, 21 of them in the south. This was a high casualty rate throwing a heavy burden on the maintenance organisation as did the damage to the airfields. The 8th Army enjoyed the fruits in almost complete freedom from aerial observation and attack. The sorties flown to achieve this result are at this point given for the Desert Air Force only and are a close approximation for the eight days 29th March to 5th April. A comprehensive enumeration of sorties over a longer period is given in a later chapter. The total sorties for our present purpose were some 2,630 and of these about 1,770 were flown by the fighters (excluding those flown to protect shipping), 470 by the fighter-bombers, 360 by the day bombers and the remainder by the tactical reconnaissance aircraft—all for a total loss of five R.A.F. and eight U.S. aircraft. The Middle East Wellingtons added a further 50 sorties or so against the Sfax landing ground, and lost one aircraft.

In early April Messe and Bayerlein thought that the attack would come at full moon, in the third week, but the troops expected it almost daily. *AOK 1* deduced from the actions of the British artillery that the sector between Djebel Roumana and the coast road would receive the main blow. von Sponeck suggested, and Bayerlein and Messe thought likewise, that Djebel Roumana was the 'key' to the position—a view exactly the opposite of Tuker's. Yet Messe and Bayerlein could spare no more than three small detachments of Panzer Grenadier Regiment 200 to reinforce the feature, in fact to protect observation posts. The enemy Intelligence assumed that 10th [sic] and 1st Armoured Divisions, New Zealand Division, and part of 4th Indian Division were arrayed against them.

At 1 a.m. on 6th April 7th Indian Infantry Brigade was 'creeping forward in the foothills' with 1/2nd Gurkhas leading. The Fatnassa massif was held by Italians, III Bn/125 Regiment (Spezia Division) on the east and I Bn/36 Regiment (Pistoia Division) on the west. It was on the last-named that the Gurkhas fell, taking Pt 275 on Zouai after a sharp and savage close-quarter fight. In this Subedar Lalbahadur Thapa won a Victoria Cross for leading, with almost superhuman dash and valour, a small party to clear machine-gun nests, and finishing off the enemy by himself when all his men had been struck down. Next Djebel Alig was taken, and then the Royal Sussex captured El Meida. 5th Indian Infantry Brigade passed through, part of 1/9th Gurkhas taking the Fatnassa ridge, and made for El Hachana. Sappers had already begun to make a track round the western edge of the anti-tank ditch.

By 8.30 a.m. General Tuker knew that his division had taken most of the Fatnassa 'massif', that 5th Brigade was advancing, and—for good measure—that a crossing on to Djebel Meida for tracks and wheels would soon be ready.[1] He ordered 5th Brigade to push on to Pt 152, north of Hachana.

The assembly and move forward of 50th and 51st Divisions were not simple, in the dark, because there were differences in the direction and distances of approach marches and in the locations of start lines. The intricate business went well and on time. What Messe colourfully describes as an 'apocalyptic hurricane of steel and fire' then began. 51st Highland Division's attack went like clockwork. Soon after six o'clock 5th Camerons and 5th Seaforth of 152nd Brigade were reported on top of Roumana, and 2nd Seaforth had passed through and was pressing along the ridge. The Italians began to surrender in numbers that were a nuisance. The capture of Pt 112 at the north-eastern end of the feature was reported an hour later, by which time two gaps in the obstacles on the brigade's front were open and the supporting Valentines of 50th R.T.R. were passing through. 154th Brigade, on the division's right had breached the enemy's defences—7th Argylls had found rope-ladders and prisoners' backs useful in escalading the anti-tank ditch's 10-foot side—and 7th Black Watch was going on to exploit.

For 50th Division the attack did not go quite as well. In 69th Brigade, 7th Green Howards took the outpost on Pt 85, but they and 5th East Yorkshires could not gain the anti-tank ditch in the face of severe artillery, mortar, and small-arms fire. Private E. Anderson, 5th East Yorkshires, here won a posthumous V.C. A stretcher-bearer, he had carried three wounded to safety, and was killed while rescuing a fourth. Casualties mounted, the two commanding officers were wounded and both battalions were pinned

---

[1] 12th Field Company, Madras Sappers and Miners record a story that rings true of a night action. Sapper No. 7322 (because of the similarity and difficulty of Madrassi names men of this Corps were, by old custom, always known by their Regimental numbers) appeared on the afternoon of the 6th, having 'wandered all night and all morning—it is believed in and out of the Italian lines—trying to find someone to understand him, and still clutching firmly his rifle, his pair of pliers, and his prepared charge'.

down. This check meant that 152nd Brigade might meet awkward opposition when it came down the north-western slopes of Roumana in the second phase of 30th Corps' plan. General Leese decided that the plan should continue unchanged, but it was arranged that 50th Division's squadron of 4th C.L.Y. and 6th Green Howards should, by using the gap which the Highland brigade had opened, cut in behind the enemy in this area.

The events which have been summarized occupied the period from the early hours of 6th April until about 9 a.m. The Axis seem first to have had their eyes on Trieste Division's left flank (51st Division's right), then to have concluded that the attack was general in the sectors of Trieste, Spezia, and Pistoia Divisions. By about 8 a.m. *AOK 1's* H.Q. knew that Roumana and Zouai had been lost. Panzer Grenadier Regiment 200 was ordered to regain Roumana, and Panzer Grenadier Regiment 361 and a battalion of Pistoia Division to counter-attack Zouai. 15th Panzer Division and two troops of 8·8-cm guns were ordered into Spezia Division's sector. This committed all *AOK 1's* reserves, but Army Group at Bayerlein's request placed *D.A.K's* tanks, about 80, under the Army's command. At about 10 a.m. these tanks were reported to be 'on the way' from El Guettar area.

Among the British commanders there began during the period which has been described a series of events about which evidence conflicts, but though the detail cannot with certainty be recovered, a clear trace of cross-purposes, arising from the differing view-points taken in battle and its always present 'fog', survives.[1] By about 7 a.m. General Tuker knew from reports that his brigades were highly successful. At 7.35 30th Corps received his message that Zouai, El Alig, and El Meida had been taken and that he was ready to go on; at 9.20 a.m. that there was a crossing for vehicles at the western end of the anti-tank ditch; at 9.50 that 4th Indian Division's infantry were on their final objective, and that its wheels were going forward. 10th Corps records that Horrocks left for the front at 7.10 a.m. but does not mention him again until noon. Tuker relates that Horrocks arrived at 4th Indian Division's H.Q. at 8.45 a.m. and states, quoting from an untraceable document, that he (Tuker) told him '. . . that we had broken the enemy; that the way was clear for 10th Corps to go through; that immediate offensive action would finish the campaign in North Africa . . .' He goes on to relate that Horrocks telephoned Montgomery for permission to put in 10th Corps to maintain the momentum of the attack, received permission, and then said that

---

[1] In 1839 the Duke of Wellington said to Stanhope '. . . about the various accounts and anecdotes of the battle of Waterloo, "I shall begin to doubt if I was really there myself".'
Stanhope: *Notes of Conversations with the Duke of Wellington 1831–1851*. (O.U.P. 1938) p. 150.

his armour was going through at once, using the Indian Division's crossing and one south-west of Roumana. Horrocks then alerted his Headquarters by radio telephone. Thus Tuker; there is no other record of the matter. According to the New Zealand historian, Freyberg, whose division was to lead 10th Corps, was at 11 a.m. undecided whether to move east or west of Djebel Roumana.

To return to the 51st Division. 152nd Brigade attacked westward at 9 a.m. but almost at once Panzer Grenadier Regiment 200 counter-attacked; dormant Italian positions awoke, and the Highlanders were pressed off their gains on Roumana ridge. They reorganized just below the crest. Here 5th Seaforth, unable to dig in on rocky ground, fought and held for three hours. 2nd Seaforth to the north-east fought for Pt 112 against 15th Panzer Division. On the division's right 154th Brigade had won its final objective but there was a 1500-yard gap between the Argylls and the Black Watch, and the whole area was under fire from three sides. The Valentines of 40th R.T.R. were engaged but were gradually picked off, and 4th C.L.Y's squadron was sent over; anti-tank guns reached 7th Argylls but not 7th Black Watch. During a hard-fought day the Highlanders held on and the deeds of all were in the Division's view recognized by the award of the V.C. to one, Lieut.-Colonel Lorne Campbell, 7th Argyll and Sutherland Highlanders, for day-long valour.

In 50th Division's sector the fight had taken a favourable turn. By 9.35 a.m. the first Shermans had passed through a minefield gap west of Roumana, the 6th Green Howards went forward and soon began to come to grips with the enemy on the far side of the anti-tank ditch, capturing about 400 Italians. In 4th Indian Division's sector 5th Indian Infantry Brigade thrust on. 4/6th Rajputana Rifles took the sprawling El Hachana hill and over 1,000 Italian prisoners. 5th East Yorkshires (50th Division) crossed over to help, while the Rajputana Rifles got ready to assault Pt 152. Meanwhile 6th Green Howards (50th Division) pressed on towards their final objective. Behind them the engineers made a way for anti-tank guns through the obstacles. At 12.25 p.m. General Nichols, looking out from Pt 85, reported to 30th Corps that resistance on 50th Division's front had 'definitely broken'. To the enemy the situation was not clear. 20th Corps had reported that Trieste Division had been deeply penetrated but that Spezia was holding its own. To Messe it appeared that Trieste had not suffered much but that Spezia's units on El Meida and El Hachana had been destroyed. The Germans were preoccupied with their fight in the Roumana area and commented harshly on the Italians' will to fight. Between noon and 3.30 p.m. von Arnim, Gause and Cramer (commanding *D.A.K.*) were at H.Q. *AOK 1*. Bayerlein told them that all reserves had been committed, that the German counter-attacks might enable *AOK 1* to hold on for a few days, but that the 8th Army's full weight had yet to be felt. Cramer said that he could not hold his El Guettar sector indefinitely. In this area, in fact, the leading units of 2nd U.S. Corps were on the move down the road to Gabes after a slow week.

At this point it is necessary to turn again to the higher British commanders, and to see how 10th Corps was faring. General Tuker at his H.Q. was consumed with impatience. At 10.45 a.m. General Leese ordered the N.Z. Division to move, using the gap between 51st and 50th Divisions. At 11.10 a.m. he placed the division under command of 10th Corps, and at noon General Horrocks conferred with General Freyberg, but what passed is not recorded in detail though it can be deduced that first orders were that a regiment of 8th Armoured Brigade was to pass the gap between 50th and 51st Divisions to turn the enemy out of the anti-tank ditch, and that another might follow as a 'pincer'. In fact by 1.30 p.m. the Staffordshire Yeomanry were passing into the gap below the western end of Roumana, and 3rd R.T.R. were at the other end below Fatnassa. The Staffordshire Yeomanry however soon ran into the fire of certainly two, and probably more, 8·8-cm guns which were concealed behind the lower slopes of Roumana and were firing in enfilade. The Staffordshire Yeomanry were checked, so were 3rd R.T.R., and so ended the projected advance of 10th Corps.

In the air, while Mitchells and Bostons from the north had kept the enemy air forces at La Fauconnerie occupied by bombing them, the Desert Air Force fighters swept the battlefield. They frustrated one attempt by the enemy to interfere from the air and the A.A. guns drove off a second attempt. To begin with, air support took the form of armed reconnaissance and fighter patrols, then the fighter-bombers and Hurricane tank-destroyers went into action and by 1 p.m. they had flown 160 sorties in attacking targets in the battle area. Unfortunately the only successes were against motor transport.

Montgomery had been too optimistic in a signal sent to Alexander at noon; '... all main objectives captured according to plan. 10 Corps now in movement to pass through hole blown by 30 Corps.' A hole of a sort certainly had been made, and 30th Corps settled down to hold it. 50th Division consolidated and mopped up. Up in the hills 4th Indian Division repelled until night-fall persistent attempts by 361st Panzer Grenadier Regiment to infiltrate. On the opposite flank 51st Highland Division fought stubbornly and successfully, in spite of mounting losses, with Germans nearly as stubborn as itself.

The irony of the situation is that from about 3.30 p.m. von Arnim, Messe, Bayerlein, Cramer, and others had been discussing how to scrape up reserves. 164th Light Division alone was possibly available, but order and counter-order produced confusion. von Arnim thought that the time to retreat had not yet come; Messe declared that he could hold on until the evening of the 7th, but longer only if he and von Arnim were ready to throw 'the last man into the furnace'; Bayerlein complained furiously about the slow and inadequate Italian methods of command which forced him to give orders to the troops without authority. von Arnim pacified him by authorizing him to give orders to German troops as from himself. All through the afternoon 15th Panzer and 90th Light Division fought, but their commanders had increasing misgivings. Forty of *D.A.K's* tanks arrived, and counter-attacked half-heartedly in the neighbourhood of Pt 152. Here indeed there were left, apart from these tanks, only some field and anti-tank guns to oppose a break-through. To meet these counter-attacks the Desert Air Force launched five waves of day-bombers of 18 aircraft each and sent in the Hurricane tank-destroyers and a large force of fighter-bombers. By 5 p.m. the German divisional commanders, and Bayerlein, and Messe agreed that on the 7th the game would be up. At 7 p.m. 90th Light Division summed up:

> 'The enemy has captured all the commanding features of the Akarit Line and thus brought about its collapse. All the troops have been thrown into the Italian Divisions' sectors and there are no more reserves. But the Army cannot make up its mind to retreat. By tomorrow this will be impossible.'

In fact Messe had already informed the Army Group (von Arnim had left after his conference) that *AOK 1* risked annihilation on the 7th, and at 8 p.m. Bayerlein received from Army Group orders that *AOK 1* was to retreat at nightfall, behind rearguards, to a line which was in fact almost the same as 10th Corps' objective.

Messe however had other ideas. He ordered the remains of Trieste and Spezia Divisions and his Army artillery straight back to Enfidaville, and Young Fascist Division to El Djem, midway between Sfax and Sousse, and collected transport for the move. Only Pistoia Division, the Saharan Group, and some guns were to share German fortunes. In the end most of the German troops, including those of *D.A.K.* facing 2nd U.S. Corps, withdrew on foot during the night 6th/7th April.

Throughout the 6th the Desert Air Force had flown some 830 sorties in direct support of 8th Army, 188 of them by the day-bombers and fighter-bombers over the battlefield, in which 80 tons of bombs had been dropped, and a further 34 sorties against targets immediately in rear. The Americans had lost four aircraft and the Germans five. That night 48 Wellingtons of No. 205 Group led by four Albacores of the Fleet Air Arm set out to bomb transport on the Sfax—Mahares road, but the retreating Axis forces were lucky enough to escape their notice and thus instead 70 tons of bombs were dropped on small groups of vehicles, and various camps and buildings. Yet

Messe wrote, after the war, that the 'constant day and night air attacks' had kept the troops in a continual state of tension.

At about the time that the Axis troops received permission to withdraw, 8th Army issued orders for a renewed attack next day, the 7th April. The whole artillery of 10th and 30th Corps were to saturate with shells the area behind Roumana in which the offending 8·8-cm guns lay hid. Then 8th Armoured Brigade and a New Zealand brigade were to break out further supported by an air 'blitz' on their immediate front and flanks. This proved to be unnecessary because by morning all the enemy who would and could move had gone. A great number of Italians took themselves into captivity, and by 10 p.m. on the 6th 125 Germans and 5,211 Italians had been counted in the cages, and the figure rose on the 7th. On the evening of the 6th, Mattioli reported to *Comando Supremo* that $AOK\ 1$ had lost 6 battalions and an unknown number of guns. Messe later amplified this report by stating that the infantry of Spezia Division was reduced to $1\frac{1}{2}$ companies, and of Trieste to three incomplete battalions, while Pistoia and 90th Light Divisions had had heavy casualties which increased during the retreat. Divisional, Corps, and Army artillery were much reduced. He later laconically summed up '. . . Non è stata una bella battaglia . . .' 'This was not a good battle'.

In this battle the 8th Army suffered approximately 1,289 casualties, the heaviest loss being in 51st Highland Division. Some 32 tanks were lost and damaged. One casualty must be mentioned by name—Brigadier Kisch, R.E., who, after continuous service in the Desert war from its early days, had become 8th Army's Chief Engineer, and who was killed by a mine when inspecting the battlefield on 7th April.[1]

Once again the 8th Army had won its battle and had given the enemy a severe mauling. Yet once again it had failed to finish the enemy off, and there are those who believe that at Akarit it had a fair opportunity to dispose of $AOK\ 1$ for ever. The argument turns on whether 30th Corps had made a sufficient opening for 10th Corps to exploit, and, if 30th Corps had in fact done this, whether 10th Corps made the most of the opportunity. It is a matter which soldiers can profitably discuss, but the military historian should not presume to settle because he cannot at his desk reproduce the uncertainties of battle. Two points he may perhaps make. Did the system of command provide for the moment, which invariably comes, when someone must push the battle or fight over the hump? Had tactical training yet really got to grips with the problem of dealing—quickly—with the anti-tank gun sited beyond an obstacle?

---

[1] Mr. Churchill sent a personal message of condolence to General Montgomery.

See Maps 27 and 36

The events which came thick and fast on fronts where the majority of troops were British have pushed from mid-scene the telling operations of the American 2nd Corps. It is necessary to return to this formation, which entered Gafsa on 17th March and El Guettar on the 18th, before describing the immediate aftermath of the battle at Wadi Akarit.[1] General Alexander's latest instruction to it included seizing the hills east of Maknassy and raiding Mezzouna but set the approximate line Maknassy—Faid—Fondouk as the eastern limit of operations. General Alexander's policy of limited operations and close control certainly hurt some ardent American spirits who interpreted it as prohibiting a thrust to the sea and as a sign that there was no confidence that the Corps could carry out ambitious operations on its own. In fact Alexander felt that the standard of training was not yet high enough (as he did of many British and French troops in his Army Group), and was taking account of administrative difficulties, and of likely hostile counter-strokes.

Maknassy was entered on 22nd March by 1st U.S. Armoured Division which was given a further task of seizing the hills just to the east. Resolute hostile resistance prevented this, and on the 25th 18th Army Group changed the plan in this area to containment.

Meanwhile 9th Division and 1st Division had been trying without much success to force a gap east of El Guettar for an armoured stroke towards the east. On the 29th Alexander again revised his directives to 2nd Corps, for the fourth time in all (details have been omitted): an armoured force was now to burst through on the Gabes road forthwith. This suited General Patton's thrusting spirit and he assigned to the operation a task force from 1st U.S. Armoured Division named after its commander, Colonel Clarence C. Benson of 13th Armoured Regiment.[2] This force struck eastward on the 30th afternoon but was held up next day. On 1st April therefore Alexander changed the bowling: Benson was to stand fast and the infantry were to open the way once more. 1st and 9th Divisions doggedly renewed their efforts, but without much success. Amongst other

---

[1] On 6th March Lieutenant-General George S. Patton took over command of 2nd Corps from Lieutenant-General Lloyd R. Fredendall. The Corps' main formations were:
    1st U.S. Armoured Division (Major-General Orlando Ward; then Major-General Ernest N. Harmon).
    1st U.S. Infantry Division (Major-General Terry Allen).
    9th Infantry Division (Major-General Manton S. Eddy).
    34th Infantry Division (Major-General Charles W. Ryder).
    13th Field Artillery Brigade.
    1st Tank Destroyer Group.

[2] *Main Units, Task Force Benson:*
    2nd/1st Armoured Regiment; 2nd/13th Armoured Regiment; 81st Reconnaissance Battalion; 899th Tank Destroyer Battalion; 65th and 68th Field Artillery Battalions; 3rd/39th Infantry; 2nd/6th Armoured Infantry.

Map 36

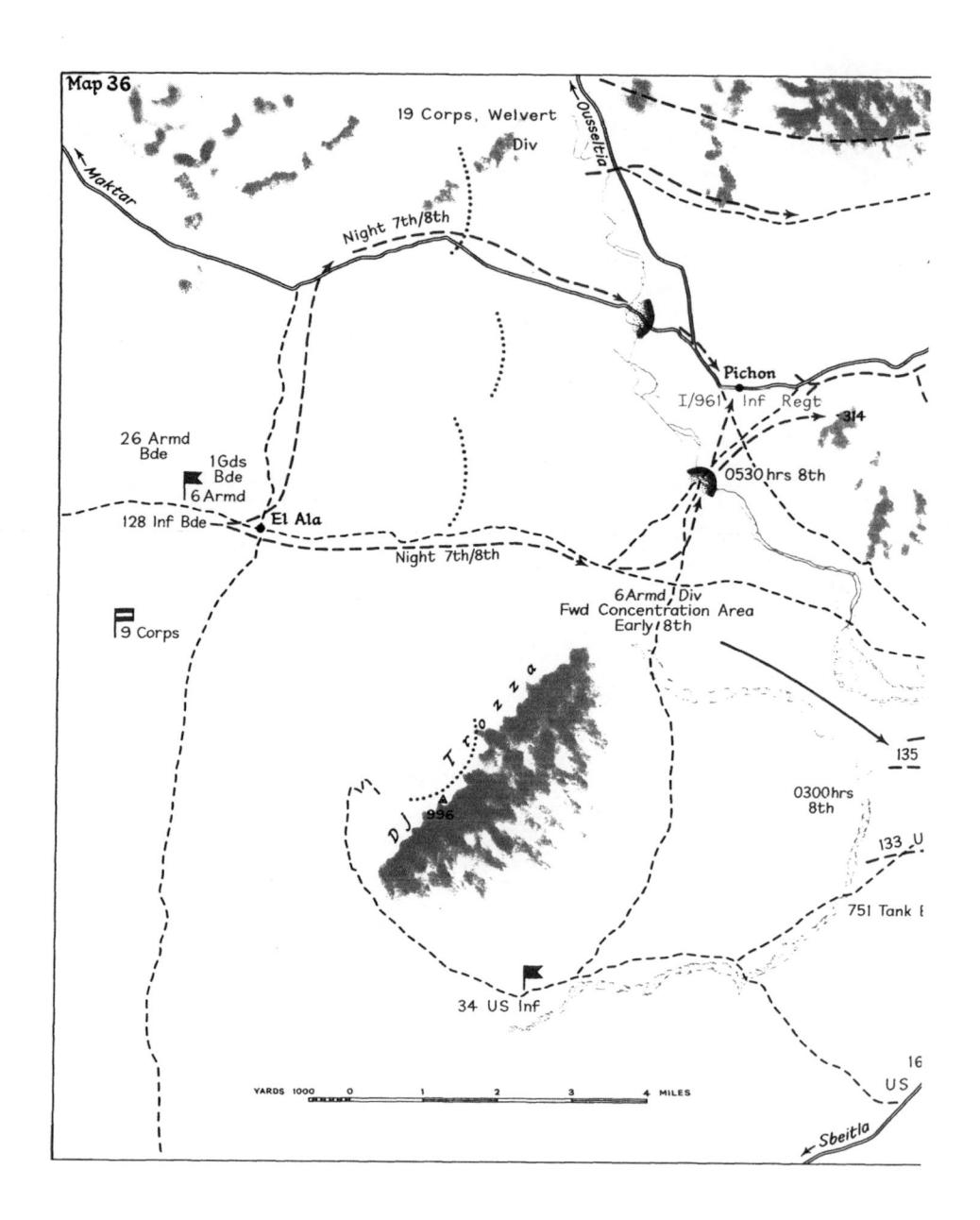

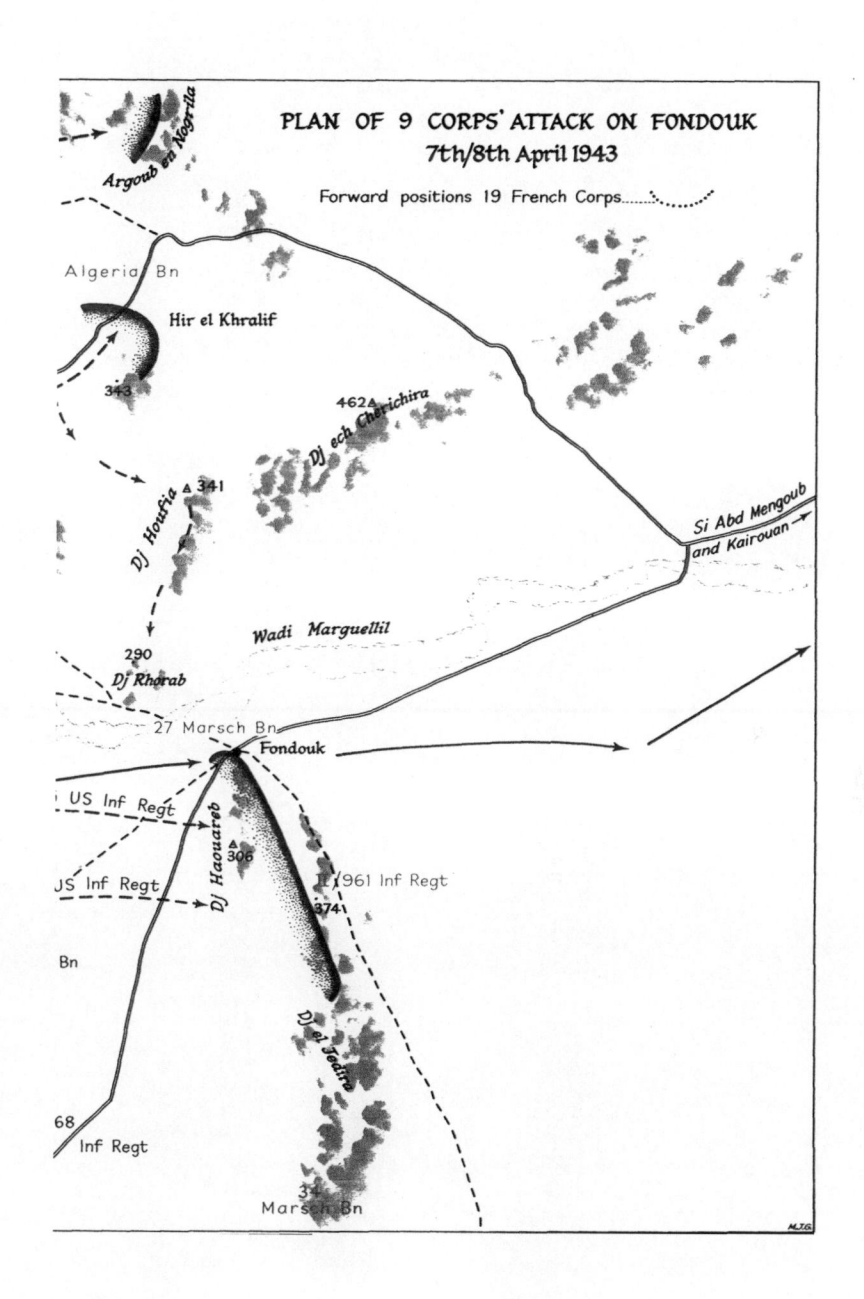

PLAN OF 9 CORPS' ATTACK ON FONDOUK
7th/8th April 1943

troubles it seemed to the Americans that they were receiving not enough air support, yet despite poor weather, particularly on the 2nd, U.S. XII A.S.C. together with N.A.T.B.F. had flown a daily average of about 300 sorties during the first week of April in support of 2nd U.S. Corps, losing 23 aircraft and destroying 18 of the enemy in the process. On 5th April Major-General Ernest N. Harmon took over command of 1st U.S. Armoured Division from Major-General Orlando Ward who returned to America to train troops and ultimately to command an armoured division in Europe. On the 7th Benson's force, much reduced, started eastward 'for a fight or a bath' as Patton crisply put it, and 2nd Corps prepared to follow. 2nd Corps may not have fulfilled its ambitions and at times felt that it was being hobbled, but the value of its operations is proved by the enemy's often expressed concern for the safety of his right flank.

The defeat of the enemy at Akarit sent 8th Army off again on a stern chase, but General Alexander had already started 9th Corps (in Army Group reserve) on an attempt to intercept. On 4th April he ordered 9th Corps to attack on the 7th to seize positions which would enable its 6th Armoured Division to get astride the Axis L. of C. in the neighbourhood of Kairouan, to dislocate Messe's withdrawal and to inflict the maximum losses. 9th Corps at Sbiba, some sixty miles distant from Kairouan, had been well placed for this stroke.

To return, however, to 8th Army. By 5.40 a.m. on 7th April air and ground reconnaissance confirmed that the enemy had abandoned his positions at Akarit, and those facing 2nd U.S. Corps. The scheme for the chase was—from east to west—30th Corps' 51st, and 7th Armoured Divisions to follow nearest the sea; then 10th Corps' New Zealand Division (including 8th Armoured Brigade) further inland, and inland again its 1st British Armoured Division. On the extreme right (or east) there was some delay caused by difficulty in crossing the anti-tank ditch east of Roumana. Elsewhere the obstacles were fewer, and the troops swept forward. The enemy, it is true, had mostly reached his appointed positions yet there were laggard units and stragglers to be picked up and *D.A.K.* was on the move to Mezzouna (east of Maknassy). Overhead the Allied air forces were busy. American Bostons, Mitchells, and Kittyhawks (all from the 'northern' front) attacked southeast of El Guettar, in the Akarit area, and at the Fauconnerie landing grounds. The Desert Air Force's day bombers, fighter-bombers, and fighters were out with good effect, and 90th Light Division's 361st Panzer Grenadier Regiment and *D.A.K.* suffered casualties and the loss of invaluable transport vehicles. The Hurricane tank-destroyers made their last important appearance in this role because Air Chief Marshal Tedder decided that the loss resulting from its peculiar hazards—26 highly specialized aircraft since 10th March—was too high.[1] By evening the British troops were in touch with the Axis main formations—*D.A.K.* (10th and 21st Panzer Divisions); 90th and 164th Light Divisions; 15th Panzer Division; Pistoia Division and the Saharan Group. 15th Panzer Division was exchanging long shots with the British tanks on the west-centre and flank, but the unhappy Pistoia Division had more or less ceased to exist. At 6.30 p.m. Army Group Africa ordered *AOK 1* to hold on for 24 hours more. Bayerlein replied that this was impossible and suggested retreat to a line running west from Sfax, but von Arnim relented to the extent only of allowing withdrawal during the night ahead to the line, approximately, of the railway between Mahares and Mezzouna. 49 Wellingtons set out to bomb this expected retreat during the night but unfortunately were unable to pick up good targets.

On this day a patrol of No. 5 Troop (Lieutenant J. H. D. Richardson) 'B' Squadron 12th Lancers met one from Benson's Force.

10th Corps' intention for the 8th was to exploit to the Sfax—Sbeitla road as fast as possible subject to a first task of destroying hostile equipment, tanks, and troops. The enemy had disengaged successfully during the previous night but was somewhat disconcerted by the quick British follow-up at daylight. 15th Panzer Division, with thirty-five 'fit' tanks including three Tigers, was forced a short way northward by 7th Armoured Division and 164th and 90th Light Divisions conformed. On the west flank 1st Armoured and New Zealand Divisions worried *D.A.K.* The country now provided little cover, and as a result the air force's targets were very good. Therefore the pilots were freed from restrictions on low-flying attack. Fighters and fighter-bombers made the most of it, and nine formations of R.A.F. and S.A.A.F. Bostons and Baltimores (139 aircraft in all) and 29 American Mitchells joined in.[2] Bayerlein recorded heavy casualties and shaken morale amongst the troops as a result of repeated air attacks and the *Luftwaffe's* almost complete failure to appear, but in fact the *Luftwaffe* had begun to evacuate the La Fauconnerie landing-grounds that day. At about 5.30 p.m. Messe ordered a withdrawal to a line about four miles north-east of Mahares and the British followed. That evening Bayerlein informed Army Group Africa

---

[1] The sorties flown by the Desert Air Force on 7th April were:

	British	American
Day-bombers	104	36
Fighter-bombers	141	64
Fighters	355	107

The R.A.F. lost one fighter, and six Hurricane IIDs.

[2] The day's sorties were:

	British	American
Day-bombers	139	29
Fighter-bombers	169	12
Fighters	356	272

that any positions which might be defended would almost certainly be out-flanked and the best course was to use mobile tactics so far as scarce fuel would allow, beginning with a backward jump of 40 miles by next evening. Messe said that his army was being worn down by 'milling on the retreat'—to translate him by a phrase from the Prize Ring—and submitted that the policy should be a long leap to the north. This, in fact, meant to Enfidaville.

During the night of the 8th/9th the Wellingtons looked for targets too far north between Sfax and Sousse, but the night-flying Hurricanes found some between Mahares and Sfax. On the 9th the weather was bad for flying, and during the day the enemy began to draw out of range of the Desert Air Force's tactical aircraft.

On the ground the scene had now changed from desert to a plain dotted with small white villages, olive groves, and patches of cultivation. The troops near the coast were delayed by cultivated ground and demolitions but those inland pressed on. By mid-morning *AOK 1* received Army Group's orders to retreat forty miles the same evening and permission to thin out earlier if need be. At 2 p.m. came orders for a longer jump to an area west of Sousse. This however had to be made more gradually, and not without difficulty, over the next thirty-six hours because some units needed fuel, and some valuable ammunition had to be cleared from Sfax. However the rearmost formations of *AOK 1* were now in quick retreat, albeit covered by rearguards, and the increased pace was, it seems, largely owing to the situation at Fondouk where 9th Corps had begun its main attack on the 8th.

For its intercepting stroke 9th Corps had been allotted, from 2nd U.S. Corps, 34th Infantry Division, and 1st Derby Yeomanry who had been with the Americans from early days in Tunisia. From 1st Army there came 128th Infantry Brigade (46th Division), 51st Royal Tanks (less a squadron), 2nd Field and 58th Medium Regiments of Artillery, and 586th and 751st Field Companies R.E.

Intelligence gauged the enemy's force in the Fondouk area, under Lieut.-Colonel Fullriede, fairly accurately but estimated 961st Infantry Regiment to be low grade—a mistaken judgment of the 'convicts.'[1]

The country was not easy. Near Fondouk the dry Wadi Marguellil narrows to a width of about two miles and is flanked on either side by high rocky ridges, Djebel ech Cherichira to the north, Djebel Haouareb to the south. On the north the high, rocky outcrop of

---

[1] *Axis troops—Fondouk Area:*
961st Infantry Regiment (999th Division); Marsch Battalions 27 and 34; Reconnaissance Unit 190; Mobile Detachment 334th Division (cyclists, with some 7·5-cm S.P. anti-tank guns); and the Italian II/91st Infantry Regiment and the locally raised Algeria Battalion. There were four troops of artillery: two German, two Italian.

Djebel Rhorab is, tactically, unpleasingly dominant. General Crocker's main infantry formations were rather inexperienced: two of 128th Brigade's battalions were classed by H.Q. 18th Army Group as not completely ready for battle while 34th Division's troops had been much on L. of C. duties and were short of training.[1]

On the night 7th/8th April 128th Infantry Brigade was to seize crossings over Wadi Marguellil just south-west of Pichon. Then at 5.30 a.m. on the 8th the brigade was to capture high ground near Hir el Khralif and then turn south to Djebel el Houfia. At the same time 34th Infantry Division was to take the high ground between Fondouk and Djebel el Jediri. When the infantry had breached the enemy's positions, 6th Armoured Division was to go through and seize a jumping-off place near Sidi Abdallah Mengoub, fourteen miles away, from which to attack the enemy in the Kairouan neighbourhood. This division's thrust might be made at any time from 1 p.m. on the 8th. General Ryder was not very satisfied with this plan. In his view Djebel Rhorab threatened his left flank and was not specifically included in 128th Brigade's objectives. This brigade therefore might or might not take the feature, and even if they did, probably not early enough to cover him. He thought that he could not extend his front of attack to include this objective, and, if he shelled it, he was restricted to using only smoke. General Keightley warned the commander of his Guards Brigade that if things did not go well he might have to tackle Djebel Rhorab to enable the Armoured Division to get through, but said that General Crocker wished to avoid this situation if possible. General Crocker thought that the enemy, who he believed to be thin on Djebel Rhorab, would not seriously threaten 34th Division's flank, and because he wished for a quick success and therefore was averse from possibly needless additions to his plan, saw no reason to change his orders. However General Ryder felt that he must now attack under cover of darkness and obtained Crocker's permission to begin at 3 a.m. 19th Corps was to prevent the enemy from interfering with 9th Corps' northern flank.

---

[1] *Main formations of 9th Corps:*
  6th Armoured Division (Major-General C. F. Keightley).
    26th Armoured Brigade (Brigadier G. P. B. Roberts).
      16th/5th Lancers, 17th/21st Lancers, 2nd Lothians, 10th Bn The Rifle Brigade.
    1st Infantry Brigade (Guards) (Brigadier S. A. Foster).
      3rd Grenadier Guards, 2nd Coldstream Guards, 3rd Welsh Guards.
    1st Derby Yeomanry. 51st R.T.R. less a squadron (Churchill tanks).
    12th R.H.A., 152nd Field Regt. R.A., 72nd A/Tk Regt R.A., 51st Lt. A.A. Regt R.A., 625th and 8th Field Squadrons R.E.
  128th Infantry Brigade (Brigadier M. A. James).
    1st/4th and 2nd/4th Bns The Hampshire Regt., 5th Hampshire Regt.
  34th Infantry Division (Major-General Charles W. Ryder).
    133rd Infantry, 135th Infantry, 168th Infantry. 125th, 175th, 185th Field Artillery Battalions. Detachments 751st and 813th Tank Destroyer Battalions. 751st Tank Battalion.

128th Infantry Brigade crossed the Wadi Marguellil during the night 7th/8th April and at 5.30 a.m. on the 8th began its main attack, supported by 72 field and 16 medium guns. It overcame not very strong resistance, was joined by 'C' Squadron 51st R.T.R., and by noon was on its objective. At about 3 p.m. 5th Hampshires and the squadron of tanks began to move south towards Djebel Rhorab some four miles distant. Fullriede's Algeria Battalion had collapsed but he plugged the hole with German and Italian reinforcements and contrived to hold up the British at a half-way point.

Meanwhile all had not gone well for 34th Division. Their 135th Infantry were attacking on the left and 133rd Infantry on the right. They were to pause some 1,500 yards from the objective to reorganize and then to advance again supported by six battalions of artillery. Unfortunately the troops made a slow start and fell about two and a half hours behind the time-table. The result was that they 'lost' their supporting artillery fire and, as the light grew, were caught on the flat by increasing fire from their front and left flank. There was more delay which led to hitches in the artillery fire plan, and which probably accounted for the failure of American direct support aircraft to make a pre-arranged strike. About 9.30 a.m. the attack was resumed but the hostile fire was galling and little by little the troops went to ground.

Just before 5th Hampshires moved south towards Djebel Rhorab General Crocker ordered 6th Armoured Division to reconnoitre vigorously to discover the nature of the opposition in the Fondouk area and to help 34th Division. 1st Guards Brigade was to come forward with a view to occupying Djebel Rhorab before the enemy could reinforce it. 17th/21st Lancers Regimental Group therefore moved towards Fondouk until stopped by well-concealed anti-tank guns. Unhappily, the British tanks passed through 34th Division, which was just renewing its attack supported by its own tanks, drew fire, and confused the Americans. The American effort again petered out. 3rd Welsh Guards, towards evening, set out for Djebel Rhorab but did not get far. However 9th Corps' attack had at least shaken Fullriede.

General Alexander meanwhile told Crocker to disregard 34th Division's situation and to launch 6th Armoured Division at the pass. Early on the morning of 9th April Crocker, nothing loth, gave orders that 26th Armoured Brigade must find or make a gap, and that Djebel Rhorab must be captured. At about 9 a.m. thirty-five American tanks made a bold sally on 34th Division's front which came to nothing for want of artillery and infantry support, and again two hours later with the same result. 26th Armoured Brigade soon found that the western end of the Fondouk Pass was mined and held hidden anti-tank guns, estimated at 30, whereas the enemy records say 13, which were protected by infantry on Djebel Rhorab. The Brigade continued to jab at the defences and to look for a way round. By 4 p.m. the Guards Brigade took Djebel Rhorab, the hardest fighting and the honours falling to 3rd Welsh Guards who had 108 casualties. Concurrently 16th/5th Lancers managed to get through the minefield and by dusk they and 2nd Lothians were just east of Fondouk. During the day, 17th/21st Lancers had 27 tanks damaged by anti-tank fire and mines, and the other two regiments 7. 34th Division too secured part of its objective. Fullriede had been badly worried and reported that his right wing did not exist while his left was very insecure. Army Group however ordered him to hold on for 24 hours longer to allow *DAK* to reach the area west of Kairouan which was to be held until all of Messe's troops had passed through.

By 10 a.m. on the 10th the whole of 26th Armoured Brigade was east of Fondouk. Crocker, three hours earlier, had ordered Keightley to press on to Sidi Abdallah Mengoub. 9th Corps then asked 18th Army Group for instructions because it rightly deduced that the enemy was escaping. The answer came towards evening: to exploit north and north-west from Kairouan to cut off the enemy on the Eastern Dorsale. During the day the tanks ploughed north-east through green standing corn agreeably splashed with marguerites and poppies (as a diarist records) and had two small brushes with rearguards, and just before 5 p.m. saw enemy tanks escaping, out of range. We need not take the story further. The operation made the enemy's higher command very anxious but failed to prevent his troops from successfully disengaging. Moreover bad flying conditions prevented Allied tactical aircraft from intervening effectively until about midday on the 10th when American Marauders and British and American fighter-bombers and fighters bombed and strafed the enemy retreating northwards, and a large number of M.T. were believed destroyed. Fortunately the enemy air forces were also seriously hampered by the weather. But though Kairouan was entered on the 11th, the enemy on 8th Army's front was to remain out of touch until Enfidaville. It was a pity that injudicious comment on the events of the past three days caused Anglo-American carping which had to be stilled by Eisenhower and Alexander. 'Faithful are the wounds of a friend . . ..'

Map 37

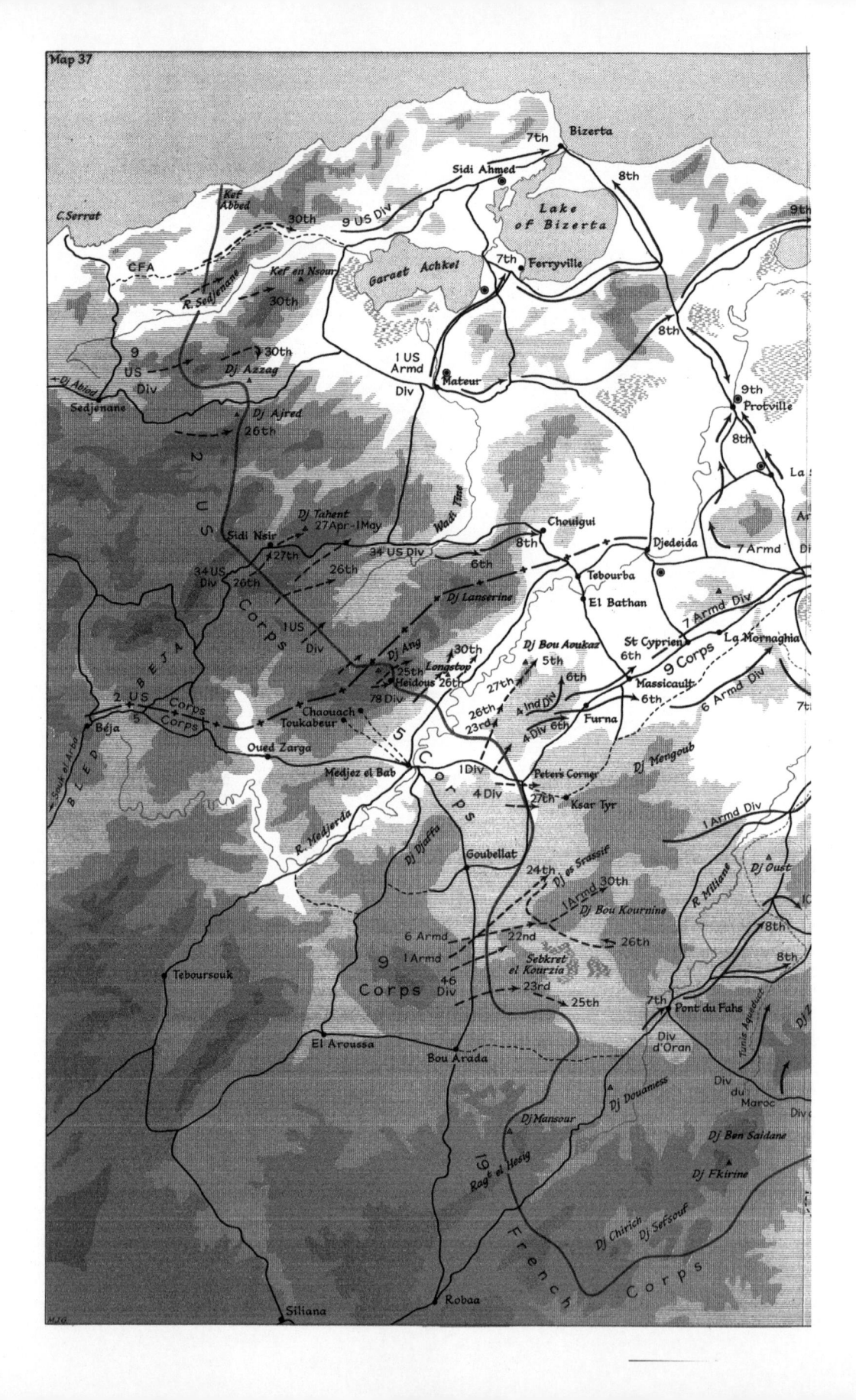

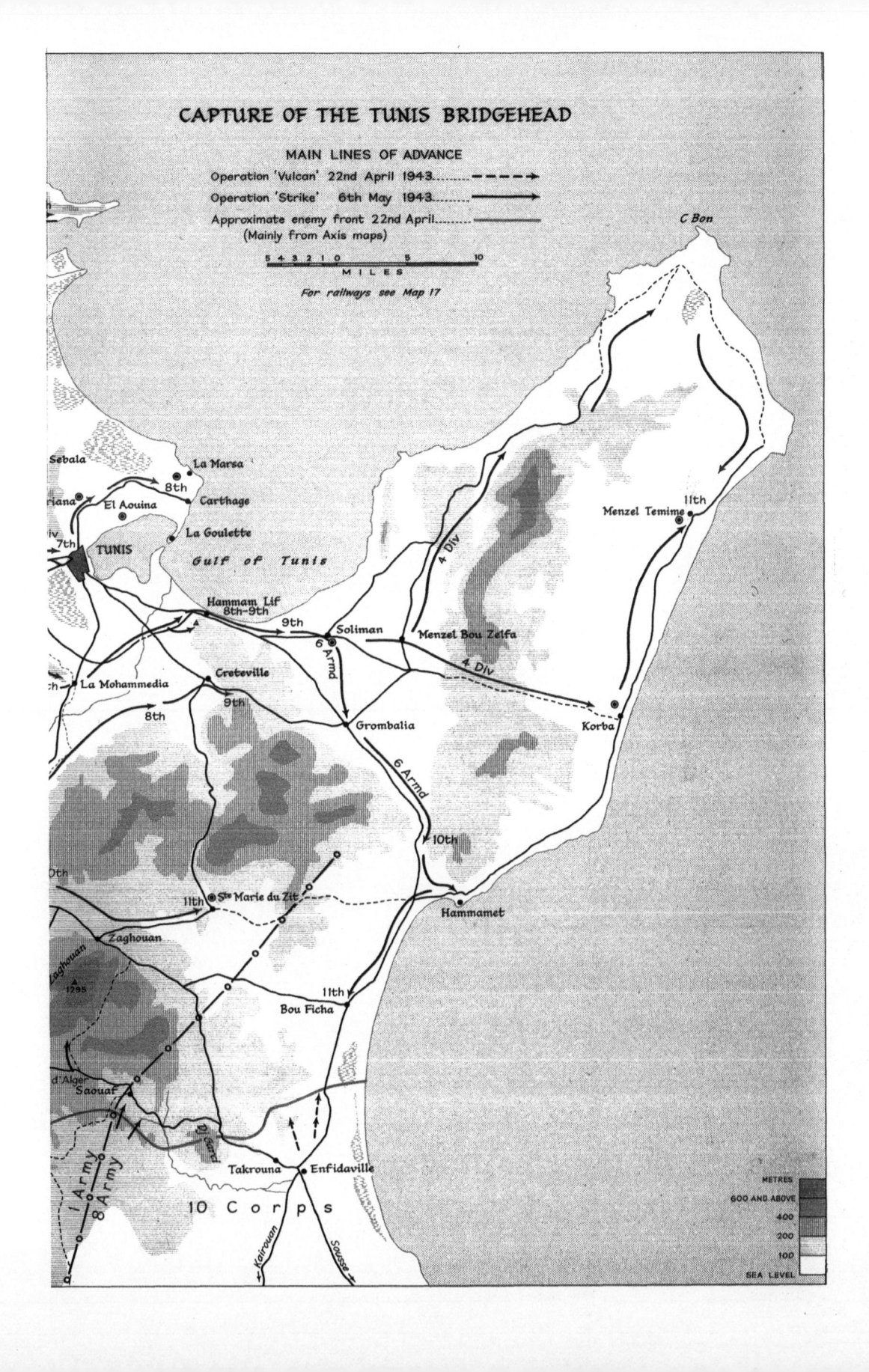

CAPTURE OF THE TUNIS BRIDGEHEAD

MAIN LINES OF ADVANCE
Operation 'Vulcan' 22nd April 1943......... ----->
Operation 'Strike' 6th May 1943......... ———>
Approximate enemy front 22nd April......... ———
(Mainly from Axis maps)

For railways see Map 17

CHAPTER XV

THE ALLIED FORCES FACE THE BRIDGEHEAD

(March—April 1943)

See Maps 33 and 37

IN Chapters XIII and XIV the 8th Army, and the air forces co-operating with it, occupied almost the whole stage, and we left them victorious at the Wadi Akarit on 6th April and 9th Corps successful at Fondouk. Now it is necessary to turn back a little and take up again the story of 1st Army, and the air forces in North and Central Tunisia, and of the strategic air forces of Mediterranean Air Command in general.

Early in March General Alexander told General Anderson that the enemy seemed to have removed most of his tanks from 1st Army's front and to have shifted much of his air force southward. 1st Army was to take advantage of this possible weakening of the enemy facing it, to regain the initiative by limited offensive operations. These were intended to win back Tamera and Sedjenane in the extreme north; to turn the enemy out of the commanding, hilly area between Toukabeur and Heidous; to capture tactically useful features in the neighbourhood of the Sebkret el Kourzia; and then to launch a small armoured raid into the plain of Tunis.[1] On 13th March Anderson wrote to Allfrey, commander of 5th Corps. He thought that the Corps would not be capable of undertaking major offensive operations before 20th March at earliest. 5th Corps then was to clear the area immediately to the east of Djebel Abiod; to drive the enemy from the high ground north of the road Béja—Medjez el Bab which was needed for administrative purposes; and finally to capture Longstop Hill (the Djebel el Ahmera and Djebel el Rhaa, which had been abandoned on Christmas Day 1942). As soon as was possible 19th (French) Corps was to advance northwards up the Western

---

[1] This programme was formally set out in 18th Army Group Operation Instruction No. 8 dated 25th March 1943. On this occasion, as so often, discussion and verbal, or informally written, instructions came earlier than instructions and orders in formal dress. This procedure was usual among commanders at every level and explains some chronological tangles.

Dorsale with the object of occupying the high ground which dominated the approaches to Pont du Fahs. All these operations were preliminaries of a main thrust at Tunis. General Anderson thus gave a glimpse of the future and added an interesting remark on the role of the 9th U.S. Division which he then understood was to relieve his 46th Division on the northern flank. The American division would protect the left flank of the main attack by 5th Corps and also help a cover-plan by suggesting to the enemy that the main effort was to be directed against Bizerta, not against Tunis.

On 23rd March the programme took clearer shape. As soon as might be (later settled as 28th March) 5th Corps was to retake Sedjenane, Toukabeur, Chaouach, and Djebel Ang and regain control of the area Hunt's Gap to Sidi Nsir. 19th (French) Corps was to capture Djebel Mansour and Ragoubet el Hesig. Thereafter 5th Corps was to take Longstop Hill, and 19th Corps was to clear the hills as far as Djebel Ben Saidane and Djebel Douamess which looked down on the lateral road running from Enfidaville to Pont du Fahs. For the main attack, at a later, as yet undecided date, the following objectives were given. To 5th Corps the high ground immediately west of the road from El Bathan to Massicault, and to 9th Corps the line Massicault—St. Cyprien by an axis which passed south of Ksar Tyr and by Djebel Mengoub. The left flank of this attack would be covered by 2nd U.S. Corps (for this whole Corps, and not just 9th Division, was now to be engaged) and the right flank by 19th (French) Corps. The 8th Army also had an important part to play which will be described later. Circumstances were to modify this outline plan but General Anderson's intentions were clear. He meant to annihilate the enemy's forces and to capture Tunis and La Goulette. He had chosen the ground on which he would force the enemy to fight and to commit his reserves, and at a suitable moment he intended to launch his armour to complete the enemy's destruction. The way to Tunis would then be open.

Armies and air forces can fight only with what the Lines of Communication succeed in delivering. We have described in earlier chapters the enemy's increasingly sore administrative need. This is shown in human terms, as a change from terms of tons, by the complaint of an Italian soldier-diarist on 14th March that his meals for the day were half a mess-tin of cold rice, a slice and a half of bread, and two potatoes. That the Allied forces in North Africa were in contrast well provided with the means to live and fight was owing to the fact that before the end of March a clear system of operational maintenance and general administrative responsibility, suitable to the circumstances of the campaign, had been evolved by the administrative staffs and was being put into practice by administrative units. This had been achieved in the face of dire difficulties some of which, in November and December 1942, have been noticed. At the end of December much of the lay-out of the 1st Army's Lines of Communication and of the eastern Advanced Base ports had been transformed from plans to facts and the process was continuing. This did not mean that the troops in the forward areas as yet had much more than bare, daily needs. In planning language, the 45 days' reserves for the theatre which were to be distributed in the right places in North Africa by D plus 90 were not near completion. This meant, to take a small example, that the soldier up in front had just received a second blanket to wrap round his chilled, and often soaked, body at night. Tents too were very scarce and the fact illustrates the large effect of a little stupidity. The sea-convoy which reached Africa in the third week of December carried quantities of tent-pegs, but the tents had been 'shut out'.

The failure at the end of December of the dash to seize Tunis disappointed many people but in the upshot was an administrative blessing, because the defensive period of January and February gave a breathing-space in which to develop the Bases and Lines of Communication, and to accumulate reserves in the forward area.

On 1st January Allied Force Headquarters took over general administrative control and relieved 1st Army H.Q. of the encumbrance of responsibility for Main Bases. By the end of January Algeria and Tunisia showed an administrative pattern of Main, Advanced, and Forward Base Areas. This was just the common-sense way of distributing administrative installations and stores along a L. of C. of over 500 miles. The Main Base held the largest installations and stores of all kinds for all troops in the theatre; the Advanced Base area held smaller quantities of the same kinds of stores, again for all troops but by so much nearer the front; and in the Forward Area were reserve and maintenance stocks for the troops in that area only. Rail and road systems could not handle much traffic by European standards, and it was fortunate therefore that the Advanced Base Area had its own ports at Bône and Philippeville to which cargoes could be transhipped from Algiers and Bougie, or sent direct.[1] Completing this administrative pattern, and within the general framework described above were L. of C. Areas and Sub-Areas, in each of which a commander with a small staff was

---

[1] The scale of reserves for the theatre was soon raised from 45 to 90 days'. Of this total holding 60 days' was the level below which stocks must not fall, and 30 days' was treated as working margin.
On 30th January the total holding was raised to 105 days'.

responsible that his section of the L. of C. properly fulfilled its functions.[1]

Algeria and Tunisia were regarded as a British Administrative area and were run on British principles which were altered as required to meet special circumstances, for example those arising from features of the American and French systems. In general there were fewer departures from orthodoxy than in the Middle East mainly because distances were shorter. From Algiers to Tunis was about 500 miles as the crow flies, a great distance, yet only as far as from Alexandria to Tobruk which was less than a third of the 8th Army's 1,800-mile L. of C. Again, when 1st Army was closing in on Tunis, its principal railhead, Souk el Arba, was but 130 miles behind it. The ports, too, were far enough to the east to bring supply by sea if not to the 1st Army's back-door at least to the lodge-gate. Movement by rail and road therefore developed on the normal pattern of pack-train to railhead and third- and second-line links of road transport working ahead of that. The Field Maintenance Centre, an essential part of Middle East's system, appeared towards the end, and then only in 9th Corps and in formations transferred from 8th Army.

When H.Q. 18th Army Group was formed in February, the inclusion in its H.Q. staff of a Major-General, Administration was a great step forward in operational maintenance.[2] The M.G.A., besides advising the Army Group Commander on all administrative questions, co-ordinated and supervised general operational maintenance within the Army Group's area of responsibility. As a central administrator in the operational area, he co-ordinated all the divergent requirements of operational maintenance and stock-piling and settled administrative priorities in conjunction with A.F.H.Q. A good example of his work may be taken from a meeting of senior administrative staff officers, British and American, of A.F.H.Q., 18th Army Group, 1st Army, 9th Corps, the Royal Air Force, and the American Third Service Area Command on 15th March.[3] General Miller outlined and explained 18th Army Group's present and future administrative policy and plans, heard the policies and plans of others, and co-ordinated results. These included the finding, after

---

[1] As an example taken at random, in one L. of C. Sub-Area on December 26th 1942 there were the following units performing L. of C. functions:
    R.E. 17   Provost 4
    R.A.S.C. 9   Pioneer 4
    R.A.O.C. 3   Field Security 1
    R.E.M.E. 3   Others 5.
In addition there were various R.A.F., American, and French units.

[2] Major-General C. H. Miller was appointed M.G.A. in February 1943.

[3] A Service Area Command had no precise British equivalent. It may be understood as an American administrative organization, responsible for the maintenance and supply of army and air forces.

examination of various 'customers' bids for tonnages of stores and placing them in priority, that 1st Army's build-up for the final phase could not be complete until 20th April, ten days later than the date first estimated. At the same meeting the senior administrative staff officer of 1st Army was asked to tell his brethren of the General Staff that their estimates for artillery ammunition were excessive.[1]

A most important administrative development was the creation in January of a combined American and British petroleum section at A.F.H.Q. to control and co-ordinate all problems of petroleum products. In February 1st Army, just one 'customer', was using about 1,000 tons of fuel a day. The effects of the immense demands for petrol, oils, and lubricants were felt everywhere; for example on sea, rail, and road transport because the life-blood of movement had itself to be moved; on space, tanks, and tins for storage and transport, on the supply of food and ammunition; even upon the endurance of a much-enduring R.A.S.C. driver who, or his counterpart, was one of the tiny but absolutely indispensable links in the huge administrative chain. Always the means of bringing forward a great volume of supplies and stores set one problem after another. At the beginning of December at the railhead of Souk el Arba no more than 40 wagons could be unloaded in a day because of crude lay-out and lack of equipment and motor lorries. At the end of the month the figure was 200 wagons per day, more indeed than the railway in rear could carry. The improvement of the railways exacted continuous technical work—as an example, track was shipped from Algiers to Bône. The first consignment was sunk on passage, a second got through. Heavy materials for the railways had of course to compete for scarce means of transport with other stores as urgently needed by other users. In war administration has daily to solve the riddle of whether the chicken or the egg comes first. As regards railways, 143 trains ran eastward in January, 220 in February, and roughly the same number in succeeding months.[2] In February A.F.H.Q. became responsible for railway policy and for carrying it out. Sea transport, without which nothing could have been accomplished, fulfilled and often exceeded expectations. In March Algiers, Bougie, Philippeville and Bône daily handled 11,803 tons of cargo, and in April 13,293.[3] By the middle of March stocks of most commodities were satisfactory.

---

[1] A most important duty of an M.G.A. or Chief Administrative Officer was to see that the administrative plan did not over-insure. Field-Marshal Montgomery has written "... The results of under-insurance inevitably become apparent to all, whereas the crime of over-insurance does not become apparent, and may, indeed, lead to a feeling of satisfaction that supplies of all sorts are plentiful and that the administrative arrangements are excellent..." *High Command in War. 21 Army Group, 1945.* p. 9.

[2] By 26th April the permanent way had been repaired as far as Medjez el Bab, and a test train had run to that place.

[3] The best figure for a day was 29,500 tons—on 17th April.

The foregoing and few examples may show how soundly the administrative staffs and units of 1st Army had laid the foundations upon which A.F.H.Q. and 18th Army Group built. It is not a criticism of 1st Army but a compliment to say that at times the more detailed administration had seemed chaotic because of its ceaseless, unavoidable, and brilliant improvisation. A slender organization had had to take on tasks seemingly beyond its powers in maintaining intermingled British, American, and French formations and doing much for growing British and American air forces. The problem we have been sketching may be likened to supplying the entire wants of a fairly populous area in the neighbourhood of Dundee from ports situated between Falmouth and Hastings, by railways of two gauges, and an insufficient number of lorries.

In March and early April 1st Army received reinforcements. 1st Infantry Division (Major-General W. E. Clutterbuck) landed between 5th–9th March and arrived in the forward area between 14th and 18th. 4th Infantry Division (Major-General J. L. I. Hawkesworth) landed between 23rd and 27th March and reached the forward area between 3rd and 6th April.[1] These divisions joined

---

[1] Main Formations and Units:
  1st Infantry Division
    2nd Infantry Brigade (Brigadier E. E. J. Moore)
      1st Bn The Loyal Regiment.
      2nd Bn The North Staffordshire Regiment.
      6th Bn The Gordon Highlanders.
    3rd Infantry Brigade (Brigadier J. G. James)
      1st Bn The Duke of Wellington's Regiment.
      2nd Bn The Sherwood Foresters.
      1st Bn The King's Shropshire Light Infantry.
    24th Infantry Brigade (Guards) (Brigadier R. B. R. Colvin)
      5th Bn Grenadier Guards.
      1st Bn Scots Guards.
      1st Bn Irish Guards.
    23rd, 248th, 238th Field Coys R.E.; 2nd, 19th, 67th Field Regiments R.A.; 81st Anti-tank Regiment R.A.
    90th L.A.A. Regiment R.A.; 1st Reconnaissance Regiment.
  4th Infantry Division
    10th Infantry Brigade (Brigadier J. H. Hogshaw)
      2nd Bn The Bedfordshire and Hertfordshire Regiment.
      1/6th The East Surrey Regiment.
      2nd Bn The Duke of Cornwall's Light Infantry.
    12th Infantry Brigade (Brigadier R. A. Hull)
      2nd Bn The Royal Fusiliers.
      6th Bn The Black Watch.
      1st Bn The Queen's Own Royal West Kent Regiment.
    21st Tank Brigade (Brigadier T. Ivor-Moore)
      12th Bn Royal Tank Regiment ⎫
      43rd Bn Royal Tank Regiment ⎬ Churchills Mk I and III
      145th Royal Armoured Corps ⎭
    7th, 59th, 225th Field Coys R.E.; 22nd, 30th, 77th Field Regiments R.A.; 14th Anti-Tank Regiment R.A.; 91st L.A.A. Regiment R.A.; 4th Reconnaissance Regiment.

5th Corps, respectively on 25th March and 2nd April. Interesting newcomers in February and March were 56th and 54th Heavy Regiments R.A. each with 16 7·2-inch howitzers, and a squadron of the Royal Air Force Regiment which entered the line in the Medjez area.[1] At a rather late stage some of the infantry received the Projector Infantry Anti-Tank, a shoulder-controlled weapon which looked rather like a piece of filleted gutter-pipe, and fired a high-explosive bomb to a range of 115 yards, sometimes with slightly disconcerting results.[2]

On 25th March 18th Army Group gave General Anderson formal orders to prepare a limited offensive to regain the initiative on the whole of 5th Corps' front. Late on 27th March 46th Division began this with an attack on the Tamera positions as a prelude to regaining Sedjenane. This meant turning the enemy out of the hills south-west of that place—1st Parachute Brigade, on the left, moving up the hills just north of the main road to draw the enemy's attention from 36th and 138th Infantry Brigades who were on the right, just south of the road. The country was not easy and the weather was wet but the enemy's resistance was patchy and on the afternoon of the 30th 46th Division entered Sedjenane.[3] It happened that on the same day the American 34th Infantry Division made an attack in the Fondouk area far to the south. This was not connected with 1st Army's operations but was designed as a demonstration to prevent the enemy from reinforcing his troops facing 8th Army in the south. This attack failed because to make an effective 'demonstration'—'to make a lot of noise but not to run risks merely to gain ground' in the words of the American official history—demands a degree of experience in battle which the troops had not had the opportunities to gain.

The first week of April was fairly quiet and General Alexander's forces on all fronts regrouped and prepared themselves. Then followed the battle of Akarit, 8th Army's chase to the north after *AOK 1*, and 9th Corps' failure to intercept it at Kairouan. 1st Army,

---

[1] The 7·2-inch howitzer had been accepted in November 1940 as the sole British heavy artillery weapon, although production was delayed by the greater need for field and anti-aircraft artillery. The American 155-mm gun did not become available to the British army in numbers until August 1943. The 7·2-inch howitzer weighed 10 tons 5 cwt. in action and could be towed on a road. The weight of the H.E. shell was 202 lbs and the maximum range was 16,900 yards. In the Tunisian campaign the carriage was that used in World War I for 6-inch gun or 8-inch howitzer, and which was later superceded by the 155-mm carriage.

[2] By coincidence the German army, in the autumn of 1943, introduced an infantry anti-tank weapon known, even officially, as *Ofenrohr* or "stove-pipe".

[3] In this operation 1st Parachute Brigade and 36th Infantry Brigade fought under command of 46th Division. This division's 138th Infantry Brigade was engaged, and its 128th Brigade was in reserve; its 139th Infantry Brigade elsewhere. There was still a good deal of unavoidable juggling with formations in 1st Army and details are purposely left out.

having regained the ground which Weber had taken during his offensive in North Tunisia ('*Ochsenkopf*'), made ready for 5th Corps' next stage i.e. clearing the high, almost mountainous and very difficult, country north of the road from Béja to Medjez el Bab.

In this area lies open rolling country, where the views are wide, and most hills big enough to swallow up a brigade of infantry. Westward in the Bled Béja lies some of the best farming land in Tunisia. It has long been cultivated, the Romans left their mark there, and it now held many European settlers. Eastward the ground becomes rougher and a chain of hills bars the cross-country approach to the Medjez-Tebourba road. In the hill country criss-crossing tracks skirt rocky summits, to link patches of cultivation and Berber villages such as Chaouach and Toukabeur. In the whole area the movement of guns and even tanks was very restricted.

From the hills the ground falls away south-eastward to the Medjerda valley where runs the Medjez-Tebourba road. Of all the approaches to Tunis, therefore, which were open to 1st Army this was the most easily defended and the least suitable for an armoured and mechanized force. Yet this flank had to be cleared before the other easier approaches could be used.

Between the lower Medjerda hills and the sharp crests and precipitous walls of Djebel Zaghouan, far to the south-east, stretches open and comparatively flat country, where the little hills and growing crops have an air of England. Communications are easy between a series of plains: Medjez, Goubellat, Bou Arada and Pont du Fahs, and these are linked in turn by a low-lying lateral road which runs via Zaghouan township to Bou Ficha and the coast—a back door to Enfidaville.

There were thus three ways by which 1st Army might gain access to the plain of Tunis—that area of crowded villages and small properties, cornfields, over a million olive trees, and flourishing vineyards. In the south the Bou Arada road ran through a strongly held defile at Pont du Fahs, and the Bou Arada plain itself, much ploughed and cut up by irrigation ditches, offered bad going for armour. In the centre, the Goubellat plain gave good going but fairly soon broke against a stretch of rough country stretching from the Sebkret el Kourzia north to Ksar Tyr. The outlying slopes of the hills might be passable to tanks, it was thought, but the dense scrub would make heavy work for the infantry. It was, therefore, the Medjez—Massicault—Tunis road to the north which presented both the most direct route and the best tank country.

Something has been said of the tactical air forces in the preceding chapters, and the strategic bombers now require attention. The operations of these aircraft, though directed to the common purpose, for the most part were carried on outside the fields of battle and were not necessarily linked closely in time with events on the ground. At this point it happens that the weeks 29th March to the night 21st/22nd April are a convenient period to consider.

The Northwest African Strategic Air Force included, in American squadrons, 8 (later 16) of Fortresses, 8 of Mitchells and 4 (later 8) of Marauders, and 2 of R.A.F. Wellingtons. In Middle East No. 205 Group R.A.F. had 4 squadrons of Wellingtons, 1 of Halifaxes, and a detachment of pathfinder Albacores of the Fleet Air Arm. The U.S. IX Bomber Command had 9 squadrons of Liberators, one of which was of the R.A.F. These squadrons whose number rose from 36 to 48 during this period flew, so far as is recorded, 997 sorties (excluding attacks on ports and anti-shipping operations), the Middle East contributing rather more than N.A.S.A.F. The approximate yardstick is about 40 aircraft in the air every twenty-four hours, although they did not of course fly with this mechanical regularity.[1]

Against airfields outside Africa N.A.S.A.F. divided its attentions between Sardinia and Sicily. In Sardinia the airfield at Decimomannu was the main target and in Sicily the one at Bocca di Falco (Palermo). It was against Bocca di Falco, on 5th April, that Middle East Air Command launched its only notable attack on airfields outside Africa. Yet within Tunisia it was No. 205 Group R.A.F. from the Middle East which played by far the greatest part with its Wellingtons and Halifaxes by night. Heavy attacks were made on Sfax on the night of 30th/31st March to support a three-day offensive by the tactical bombers to drive the enemy air forces from the landing-ground. This succeeded after 230 tons of bombs had been dropped and several aircraft had been destroyed or damaged. On 1st April the enemy aircraft were withdrawn to the La Fauconnerie area which was abandoned a week later. Except for that addition to the tactical bomber effort, all No. 205 Group's attacks were crowded in to ten consecutive nights beginning on 10th/11th April in support of the Desert Air Force's offensive against enemy airfields and landing

---

[1] *N.A.S.A.F.*

Total sorties (*400: or American 302, British 98*)
    Against airfields outside Africa   242
    Against airfields in Tunisia   130
    Against tactical targets   28

Middle East

Total sorties (*597: or American 42, British 555*)
    Against airfields outside Africa   34
    Against airfields in Tunisia   402
    Against tactical targets   150
    Against communication and other targets   11

grounds in the 'bridgehead', the landing ground at Ste. Marie du Zit being the main target.[1]

Against tactical targets in support of the land fighting in Tunisia all attacks, all by night, were made by the R.A.F. Wellingtons of N.A.S.A.F. and those of No. 205 Group with Albacore pathfinders. For example during the nights 6th/7th to 8th/9th April they flew 135 sorties against the enemy retreating from the Akarit positions during which they dropped 266 tons of bombs.

Strategic bomber operations were as much bedevilled by the weather as were those of the tactical air forces. Only the worst conditions are normally mentioned in reports, such as existed at the end of March and early in April throughout the Mediterranean and mid-April in North West Africa when aircraft were sometimes grounded. But often operations had to continue in weather almost as bad though not prohibitive, presenting yet another hazard to the bomber crews.

The Axis air forces had been forced on to a defensive which grew steadily weaker, and the enemy decided that if his land forces retreated into the last bridgehead, the fighters would remain with them but the bombers would go to Sicily and Sardinia. On 6th April Ambrosio issued a hortatory directive on the full use and reinforcement of the air forces but nothing indicates that it was attended to.

---

[1] The following examples of Axis aircraft destroyed and damaged in some of these attacks, apart from damage to airfields and airfield installations, will give some idea of the havoc.

		G.A.F. Destroyed	G.A.F. Damaged	I.A.F. Destroyed	I.A.F. Damaged
	Sardinia				
March 31/31, 31st	Decimomannu	—	2	5	40
April 10th	La Maddalena (port)	—	—	3 (seaplanes)	
	Sicily				
5th	Bocca di Falco (Palermo)	4	9	—	—
18th	,,	2	—	18	—
5th	Milo (Trapani)	13	11	8	30
13th	,,	4	11	5 (set on fire)	
13th	Castelvetrano	8	2	'Numerous' (I.A.F. Report)	
	Italy				
4th	Capodichino (Naples)	1	1	3	31
	Tunisia				
20th	Sidi Ahmed	10	1	—	—
20th	La Marsa	3	11	—	—

In contrast, on the 3rd, N.A.A.F. had issued a precise directive on dealing with the enemy if he tried to evacuate Tunisia. In the second week of April the enemy air force in Tunisia was falling back to airfields east and south-east of Tunis where it would be as badly placed in relation to the land-fronts as had been the Allied tactical air forces during the dash into Tunisia.[1] The Allied air forces had now established the same sort of supremacy as they had achieved on the Egyptian front by the time of Alamein. One may mention, of many reasons for this victory (a victory over a period), a fine fighting spirit, growing strength and steadily improving training and maintenance. The enemy credited the Allies with technical superiority in aircraft but this cannot yet be asserted as a general factor. For example the German Me. 109G and F.W.190 still outclassed their Allied counterparts other than the Spitfire IX and American Mustang II which were as yet few in number, and very slighty superior in performance.[2]

On 7th April Hitler and Mussolini met at the castle of Klessheim near Salzburg, and agreed that Tunisia must be held at whatever cost. The Duce's military entourage reckoned in the cost more German aid for Italian forces, and produced long shopping-lists. The Germans received these with a coldness which aggravated the bad feeling between the Axis partners. Hitler however felt that he had 'pushed Mussolini back on the rails', but betrayed uneasiness about possible derailment in the future by offering to supply him with German equipment for a new bodyguard. Indeed after Mussolini had been overthrown in July 1943 the German High Command divulged that it had long felt that a collapse in Tunisia would produce the worst consequences in Italy, and that for this reason the decision to hold on in Africa had been reaffirmed at Klessheim. On 12th April, in Rome, Mussolini told Kesselring that he did not expect the Allies to invade Europe until they had settled matters in Tunisia. Therefore Tunisia must be held until autumn to pin down the Allies there, and rob them of the summer months favourable for invasion. Kesselring said that the casualties at Akarit had been heavy, and that more men, guns, and ammunition were urgently needed in Africa. To move these to Africa however was acutely difficult because supply-ships were so vulnerable, and so many transport aircraft had of late been lost.

---

[1] On 15th April Seidemann took direct operational and administrative command of all *Luftwaffe* forces in Africa, *Fliegerführers 2 and 3* being transferred to Sicily or Sardinia. On that same day the equivalent Italian *Settore Aeronautico Nord* and *5th Squadra*, were disbanded and *Comando Aeronautica Tunisia* was reinstituted with Brigadier Mario Boschi in command.

[2] The North American Aviation Mustang II (designated P.51 by the U.S.A.A.F.) was capable of a speed of 402 m.p.h. at 12,000 feet. Its high speed at comparatively low altitudes made it ideal for tactical reconnaissance.

Kesselring sent Mussolini's views to von Arnim on the early morning of 13th April, a few hours after the Army Group Commander had received a directive from *Comando Supremo*. This told him that the Duce, in agreement with the Führer, had ordered that Tunisia was to be defended to the last. The Army Group would be reinforced —how and with what were not stated—and was to hold a line from the coast, at Kef Abbed, across Djebel Mansour to Enfidaville. It was to seize every opportunity of improving its positions by local offensives. *Supermarina* (the Italian Naval Command) would treat as its first task the safe passage oversea of Axis supplies, but would also attack Allied convoys and mine Allied ports. The Italian and German air forces were to give direct support to their own ground troops, and also to attack the enemy's reinforcements. Finally, surplus administrative troops who could fight or labour were to be set to do so, but absolutely 'useless mouths' were to be sent back to Italy.

This directive, with its visionary talk of offensive operations which the Axis Services in the theatre were incapable of making, added little to an Army Group instruction which von Arnim had issued on the 11th. This said that there would be no retreat from the final positions in Tunisia, which were to be laid out in depth, and held by *AOK 1* on the left and *Pz AOK 5* on the right, the boundary between them running from west of Bou Arada to the mouth of the River Miliane. When the front had been organized, all German and Italian tanks were to form an 'assault reserve' under *D.A.K's* command, and *AOK 1* would take over the Superga Division, and various Italian units until then under 30th Corps.[1]

See also Map 38

By 12th April all the main formations of *AOK 1* were back to the Enfidaville area, but von Arnim and Messe did not see eye to eye about the 'main line' that they were to defend. von Arnim in his directive defined it as running from south of Enfidaville through the open country south of Djebel Garci to Djebel Fkirine, but Messe and his senior German commanders were for once united in the criticism that this line gave bad observation, bad fields of fire, and bad natural protection against tanks. Artificial protection so far amounted to little more than 3,000 mines and an incomplete anti-tank ditch at Enfidaville. After much argument and a personal reconnaissance, von Arnim agreed on 14th April that his line should be treated as

---

[1] *D.A.K.* (10th and 21st Panzer Divisions) took command of Superga Division and attached troops on 13th April. *Pz AOK 5* included von Manteuffel, 334th, 999th, and Hermann Göring Divisions. *AOK 1* included 15th Panzer, 90th and 164th Light Divisions, and Pistoia, Trieste, Spezia, and Young Fascist Divisions.

Map 38

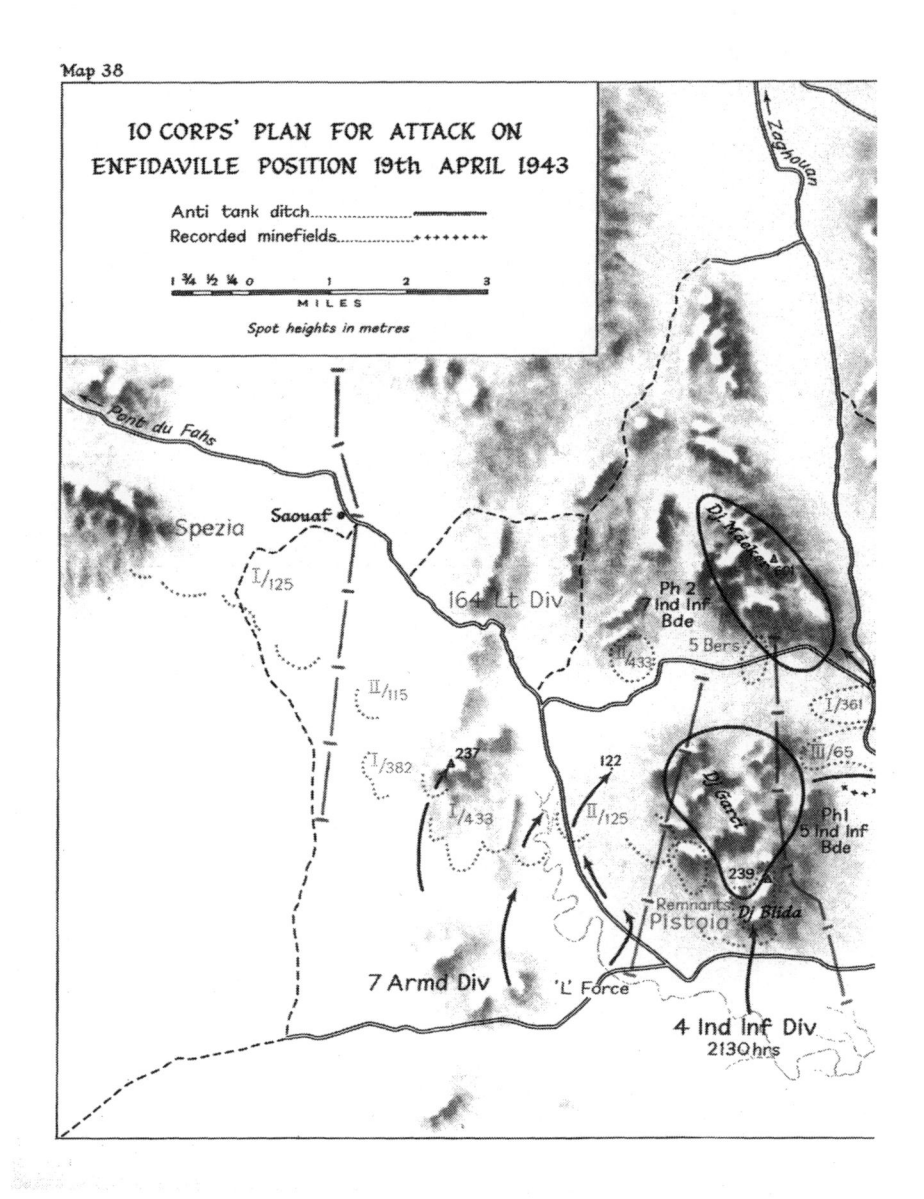

10 CORPS' PLAN FOR ATTACK ON ENFIDAVILLE POSITION 19th APRIL 1943

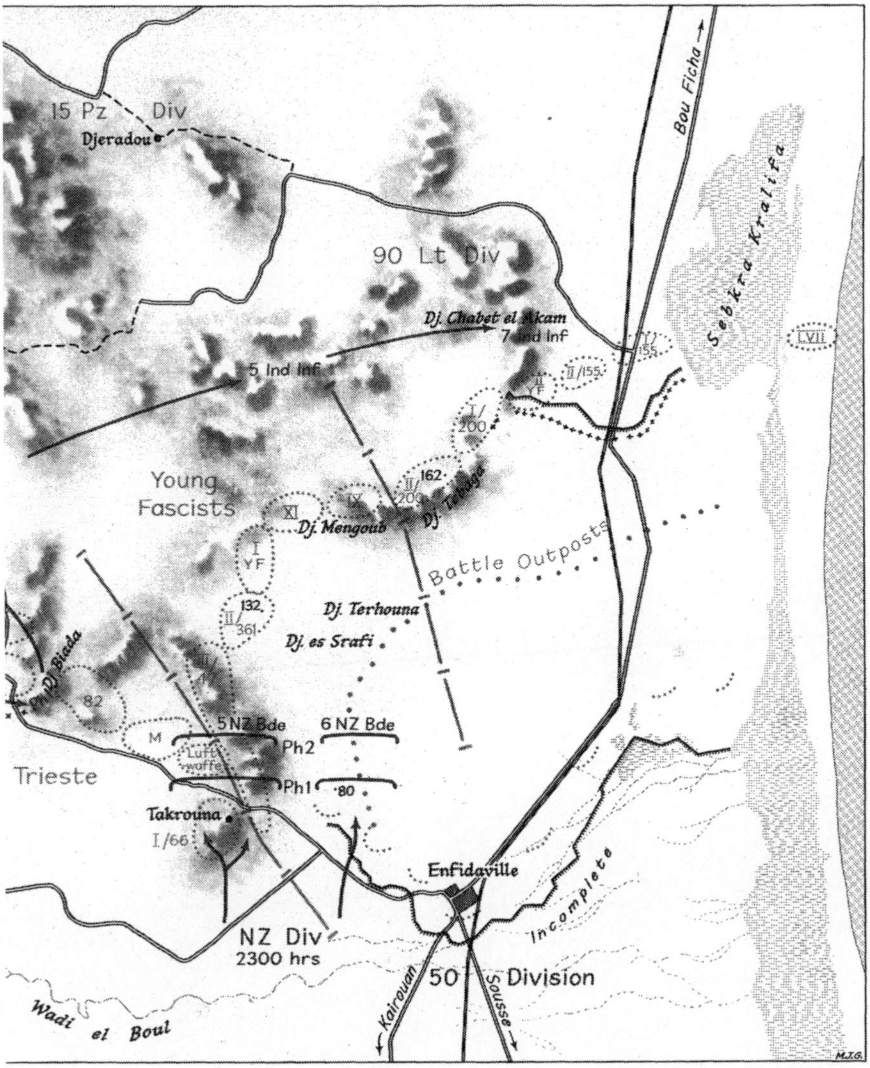

15 Pz Div
Djeradou
90 Lt Div
Dj. Chabet el Akam
7 Ind Inf
5 Ind Inf
Bou Ficha
Sebkra Kralifa
Young Fascists
Dj. Mengoub
Dj. Tebaga
Battle Outposts
Dj. Terhouna
Dj. es Srafi
Dj. Biada
5 NZ Bde
6 NZ Bde
Ph2
Ph1
Trieste
Takrouna
Enfidaville
Incomplete
NZ Div
2300 hrs
50 Division
Kairouan
Sousse
Wadi el Boul

outposts and advanced positions, and that a new 'main line' should run more to the north, from Sebkra Kralifa to Takrouna, Djebel Garci, and the mountains encircling Saouaf. Messe accordingly put 90th Light and the Young Fascist Divisions on his coastal (or left) wing, 164th Light, Pistoia, and Trieste Divisions in the centre, and Spezia Division on the extreme right wing. 15th Panzer Division and the German Reconnaissance Group were in reserve near Djeradou. Italian reserves elsewhere amounted to 5th Bersaglieri Regiment and eight scratch battalions.

Though he had conceded some tactical points von Arnim was displeased with the mood of his troops and on 12th and 14th April issued stern warnings against rumour-mongering and defeatist opinions. He also demanded from his senior officers a better understanding of the broad tactical position, and told *AOK 1* (which had three-fifths of the artillery and two-thirds of the infantry of the Army Group) that he would listen to no protests if he had to move any of its units northwards—for example to meet the threat of an attack at Medjez el Bab or Bou Arada by a reinforced British 1st Army. While the senior Axis commanders were thus wrangling, an officer of 999th Division (whose officers were carefully chosen) on 12th April wrote to a friend that the battle for the Tunisian bridgehead had entered its terminal stage. Defeat was simply a matter of time because of the Axis' want of supplies, and the Allies' overwhelming superiority in everything material.[1]

On the next day Kesselring gave von Arnim some reasons for the Dictators' decision to hold Tunisia to the end. Anglo-American naval, military, and air forces which were pinned down in Africa could not be used elsewhere. The blockade (*Sperrung*) of the Straits of Sicily coupled with the successful U-boat war compelled the Allies to use their shipping in a way that might have an important effect upon the sum total of operations. To hold Tunisia would make it difficult for the Allies directly to attack southern Europe. Kesselring may have been repeating a brief, or even agreeing with it: so experienced an observer as von Rintelen was of the opinion that optimism clouded his judgment, fair in other matters, of operations in Africa, though he had great energy, organizing ability, and was a careful and sympathetic commander. von Arnim for the moment said little and kept an eye on morale.

So much for the enemy. On 8th April 1st Army affirmed the tasks of formations to be as follows. 5th Corps was to secure ground

---

[1] After defeat it became almost the enemy's set form to assert that his will to fight had never been impaired and that he had surrendered only to gross material superiority; had not, in fact, been defeated in battle. However the Axis allies did not hold that this was exactly true of each other.

necessary to open the road Oued Zarga—Medjez, and to detect any sign that the enemy was thinning out or leaving his positions on the whole Corps front. Then when American troops had taken over the left sector the Corps was to place 1st, 4th, and 78th Divisions suitably for the capture of Longstop Hill and the high ground north-east of Bou Arada, and later for the big offensive towards Tunis on the axis Medjez el Bab—Massicault—St. Cyprien. General Koeltz's 19th Corps was to move into contact in the area Djebel Fkirine—Djebel Chirich—Djebel Mansour, and later capture the heights south of Pont du Fahs.

There now began for 5th Corps a period of fighting which in the outcome was to break the enemy's back before the final blows were delivered in May. The 1st Army—to take the title that embraces the most men, although it must not be forgotten that for a long time it had been courage and endurance rather than numbers that proved the title—was about to come into its own. The country north of the Medjez road was very hilly, though scarcely big enough to be called mountainous except by plainsmen. The heights ranged from about 1,000 to 3,000 feet, and the slopes were bare and crowned by battlement-like rocks and pitches. Tanks could move only in restricted areas, and the infantry often needed mules to carry heavy equipment and supplies.[1]

78th Division opened 5th Corps' new phase by attacking with its three brigades, the 11th, 36th and 38th, the foothills and slopes leading up to its final objectives the villages of Chaouach and Toukabeur.[2] Both heavy regiments, 54th and 56th, were included in the supporting artillery. Preliminary objectives were gained without much difficulty and Toukabeur was seized on the 8th and Chaouach

---

[1] There were only Nos. 10 and 11 Pack Transport Companies R.A.S.C. in 1st Army, and some pack transport on local animals was improvised. The wretched mules suffered and lost efficiency because of the ignorance of elementary care of animals among regimental officers and men. By April 1943 however the educative efforts of the R.A.S.C. officers and men were bearing some fruits, e.g. it was generally realized that animals must eat and drink, and cannot stand for hours under load.

[2] *Main units of Brigades*
11th Infantry Brigade (Brigadier E. E. E. Cass):
  2nd Bn The Lancashire Fusiliers,
  1st Bn The East Surrey Regiment,
  5th Bn The Northamptonshire Regiment.
36th Infantry Brigade (Brigadier B. Howlett):
  5th Bn The Buffs,
  8th Bn The Argyll and Sutherland Highlanders,
  6th Bn The Royal West Kent Regiment.
38th Infantry Brigade (Brigadier N. Russell):
  1st Bn The Royal Irish Fusiliers,
  6th Bn The Inniskilling Fusiliers,
  2nd Bn The Hampshire Regiment,
  16th Bn The Durham Ligh Infantry.
    38th Brigade's parent formation was 6th Armoured Division, from which it had been unavoidably parted in February to pass under command successively of 'Y', 78th, 46th Divisions before returning to 78th Division until May 10th.

next day. The attack had gained some ten miles of country, had fallen heavily on 334th Division and had drawn in most of the enemy's available reserves. von Arnim deduced that pressure would not abate in this area but that transport movements towards Medjez el Bab indicated a dangerous build-up for an assault on Tunis. This was correct. In a conference on the 10th Anderson gave 5th Corps its next tasks: to advance to the line Sidi Nsir—Heidous (Djebel Tanngoucha) by 17th April. 2nd U.S. Corps was beginning to relieve 46th Division on the northern flank. Plans for the offensive on Tunis were to be complete by the 25th. The watchword was no rest for the enemy. 78th Division continued to advance, and on the 11th 4th Division advanced about six miles towards Sidi Nsir.

On the 11th April Lieutenant Richardson and a patrol of his Troop, No. 5 of 'B' Squadron 12th Lancers, by a pleasing turn of events, again made a memorable meeting. At a point some twenty miles south of Kairouan his patrol fell in with one from 'C' Squadron, 1st Derby Yeomanry, and thus the 8th and 1st Armies touched hands. No heroics occurred, nor had they occurred when Richardson met Benson's Americans on the 7th. Yet each meeting is historic: that of the 11th meant that the Axis forces were besieged on the battlefield by troops who had travelled and fought across the stupendous distance which had separated them, for that sole, deadly, purpose. Seldom can so supreme a military ambition have been so exactly fulfilled, and symbolized by the oaths and jokes of two handfuls of troopers.

On 11th and 12th April General Alexander confirmed rather than announced the next stage in his policy, for on the 11th Montgomery told him, in a personal signal, that 10th Corps was advancing to Sousse and then to the Enfidaville position. He went on

> '... Consider it essential that operations between the mountains and sea should be directed by me. Will you put 6 Armd. Div under my operational command at once. This would enable me to leave 1 Armd. Div. in Sfax area which will greatly help my supply arrangements. Am moving [two infantry divisions] forward... 13th April as will require infantry to gain close contact on Enfidaville position. Am going to try and gate crash position this moon period...'

Alexander replied the same evening

> 'Main effort in next phase of operations will be by First Army. Preparations already well advanced for attack earliest date 22 April. Most suitable area for employment armour is in the plain West of Tunis so require 1 Armd. Div. and 1 Armd. C. Regt. to join 9 Corps from you as early as can be arranged. Hope you can develop maximum pressure possible against Enfidaville position to fit in with First Army attack...'

On the 12th Alexander gave Anderson preliminary instructions for the offensive to capture Tunis. These were affirmed on the 16th. The gist of the preliminary instructions was: 5th Corps and 9th Corps (under command of 1st Army) were to make the main attack on the front Bou Arada to Medjez el Bab; 2nd U.S. Corps was to attack towards Bizerta; French 19th Corps would advance towards Pont du Fahs; 8th Army would contain the enemy's left flank in the Enfidaville sector.

The ideas behind this plan were the following. The enemy's two fronts were at right angles facing west and south, the point projecting south from the tangled mountain-country between Djebel Mansour and Djebel Fkirine. General Alexander intended to thrust along the easiest 'going'—from the west—to Tunis; split the enemy in two; turn the greater part of his force south to drive the greater part of the enemy against the 8th Army, and to leave the smaller part of the enemy in the north to be mopped up by the Allied troops on the spot. He had rejected the idea of making the 8th Army deliver the main thrust for two reasons. It would, by its direction, knit the enemy forces together rather than split them. It would have to overcome a mountain-barrier through which the only good road (there were two others through narrow passes) was a defile between the coastal marshes and the inland montains.

General Alexander was anxious that the enemy should have no chance of planting himself in the Cape Bon peninsula where he might hold out for too long—in view of the invasion of Sicily for which detailed planning was now in full swing. Sicily indeed was a distracting claimant for attention. In this week Montgomery, commander-designate of the British land forces of invasion noted '. . . I myself, and my Army H.Q. Staff, know very little about the operation as a whole, and *nothing whatever* about the detailed planning that is going on . . .'[1] This was a great exaggeration.

Events began now to move into the final phases which inevitably overlap. First Army was regrouping and was also fighting to deny the enemy a lull. 4th Division was meeting stronger resistance to its move towards Sidi Nsir, and as an example the 6th Black Watch (12th Infantry Brigade) on 12th April in a sharp fight lost its Commanding Officer, Adjutant, six other officers and over fifty men, mainly to mortaring and shelling. The enemy had always used mortars well but it was in Tunisia that the true damaging effect of the mortar-bomb, silent in flight, dropping from above into well-covered positions, lethal in spread, was fully understood, and

---

[1] Extract from notes for a conference in Cairo to which Montgomery went on 19th April. He had made the same point to the C.G.S. 18th Army Group on the 14th.

that counter-measures began to get great attention. Next day 4th Division was held up and was to remain so for the three following days.

On 14th April 78th Division attacked the 2,000 foot ridge called Djebel Ang and the long rocky crest of Djebel Tanngoucha just above Heidous. These high features overlooked all others in this area, including Longstop Hill, and were held by I/Regiment 962 of 999th Division and the Brandenburg Battalion, reinforcing 334th Division.[1] The country was extremely broken and difficult and the British troops were, as far as possible, on pack-transport. The early stages of the attack, begun in the small hours, resulted in 1st East Surreys (11th Infantry Brigade) reaching the top of Djebel Ang. This was temporarily lost to counter-attack, and recaptured. 11th Brigade then went for Tanngoucha but could not carry it.

On the 15th the enemy on Tanngoucha counter-attacked and virtually eliminated one of the two companies of 5th Northamptons and a company of 2nd Lancashire Fusiliers who were furthest forward. The enemy also attacked Djebel Ang and fighting went on intermittently all day and until after dark. The East Surreys, the Lancashire Fusiliers, and 1st Royal Irish Fusiliers and 2nd London Irish Rifles (both of 38th Brigade) were all engaged. They inflicted heavy casualties on III/756 Mountain Regiment and I/Regiment 962 and drove them off. Shells, mortar-bombs, machine-gun bullets and grenades had flown about fairly thickly, whiffling, whispering, cracking and crashing, as these missiles variously do. That afternoon 38th Infantry Brigade relieved the 11th, and during the night the Royal Irish Fusiliers made more ground. All gains were extended and consolidated on the 16th. In the small hours of the 17th, 6th Inniskilling Fusiliers took the peak of Tanngoucha but the country mules bringing up tools and other stores were heavily fired on, the Arab drivers understandably bolted, and the battalion was withdrawn because it could not consolidate. However 78th Division was thought to have made satisfactory progress in 5th Corps' present tasks. But the Germans were still full of fight, though the fact that about 300 men of Mountain Regiment 756 had been taken prisoner drew a rebuke from Kesselring. Schmid, acting commander of the Hermann Göring Division, suggested a spoiling attack south-east of Medjez el Bab which was soon to involve 1st and 4th Divisions. All this time 19th French Corps had been moving steadily north-east from the area of Fondouk until on the 13th it made touch, near Djebel Sefsouf, with the left of 8th Army's 10th Corps. On the 10th General Welvert, commanding the Constantine Division, had been

---

[1] The Brandenburg Battalion was descended from the Lehrregiment Brandenburg Z.b.V.800 which had been intended for special operations, e.g. sabotage in uniform. By the date above the battalion mentioned was fighting as ordinary infantry.

killed and was succeeded by General Schwarz. However this division was withdrawn to re-equip and was replaced by General Boissau's Oran Division.

Meanwhile, as some earlier pages have indicated, the Allied air forces had been disproving the 18th century German writer Jean Paul Richter's remark that Providence had given to the Germans the empire of the air. In mere numbers the Mediterranean Air Command had a strength of 3,241 aircraft as against the German and Italian estimated at 900 each, but the proportion of serviceable aircraft in M.A.C.—approximately 80% as against about 58% for the Germans and 50% for the Italians—tells of excellent organization of maintenance without which the airman and his fighting spirit and skill stay grounded.[1] In contrast the almost daily and nightly attacks upon the enemy's airfields in Tunisia compelled the German Air Force to send, from 15th April, damaged aircraft to Sicily for repair.[2]

Circumstances somewhat affected Allied air operations as April went on. First, varying weather which was often bad for flying. Secondly, during the second and third weeks of April the Desert Air Force was moving forward to airfields in the area Kairouan—Sousse whence it could operate over the Cape Bon peninsula and Tunis. And during the third week the Desert Air Force's fighters were engaged on sweeps against the German air transport traffic. The 8th Army's advance put 22 airfields and landing grounds into the Desert Air Force's hands—a fulfilment of part of Alexander's directive of 21st February, that is '. . . the efforts of both Armies would be directed towards securing airfields which would enable us to develop the ever-growing strength of our Anglo-American air forces.' On 11th April the river Miliane was fixed as a 'boundary' between No. 242 Group R.A.F. and the Desert Air Force, while XII A.S.C. supported British and French formations on its 'front'. This was an act of common sense and convenience; not a return to an attempt to divide the air into compartments.

Tactical air operations followed their familiar pattern and the airmen who supported 5th Corps earned the thanks of 78th Division and of General Anderson. Less glamorous but of vital importance were the operations of the tactical and photographic reconnaissance aircraft which went out daily in all weathers to bring back information

---

[1] Date: 16th April 1943.

(a) Northwest African Air Forces	1,758	(1,357)
Middle East Air Command	1,298	(1,026)
Malta Air Command	185	(155)
	3,241	(2,538)

(b) The figures in the text and in this table exclude air transports.

[2] German ground crews who remained in Tunisia and were surplus to needs, were formed into *Luftwaffe* Field Companies to fight as infantry.

valuable to armies and air forces alike. And rarely did a night pass without the Wellingtons, or the Bisleys, or the French LeO 45s, or sometimes all of them, setting out to bomb targets in the battle area to deny the enemy sleep and rest or to bomb the landing grounds from which his close support aircraft operated, while Allied night-fighters covered Northern Tunisia to prevent him retaliating.

Throughout the whole of the Mediterranean area the growing might of the Allied air forces was making itself felt. From 29th March to the night of the 21st/22nd April, the eve of operation 'Vulcan', described in a later chapter, N.A.A.F. and Middle East Air Command together flew an estimated daily average of 1,102 sorties (excluding anti-shipping operations) compared with 705 in the previous four weeks, and the daily effort was still rising as more and more Allied squadrons entered the theatre. And whereas Allied aircraft losses amounted to 203, so far as is recorded, the German figure reached 270 and from what few records exist it is known that the Italians lost 46 operational aircraft and almost their entire remaining air transport fleet.

The more closely the 1st and 8th Armies approach each other, the more often must the narrative jump from front to front. On 12th April 8th Army's 10th Corps took over the Kairouan area from 9th Corps which withdrew to get ready for its part in the assault on Tunis. 1st British Armoured Division left 10th Corps, preparatory to joining 9th Corps, when its vehicles changed their sandy desert paint for the dark green of 1st Army. On 13th April the New Zealand Division pushed in light rearguards and by early afternoon its leading troops were looking at part of the 'Enfidaville Line'. The peaks of Djebel Garci and Takrouna were dominant and grim, and Brigadier Kippenberger (5th N.Z. Brigade) very quickly decided that the former must be tackled by a division. He decided to try his luck at Takrouna but shells soon warned him that the enemy was not to be rushed, and he had no supporting artillery. Next day and on the 15th, 10th Corps closed up to the Enfidaville positions. 19th Corps was still skirmishing at Djebel Sefsouf some miles on the west. General Montgomery decided that 10th Corps must break into the Enfidaville position on 20th April and advance to Bou Ficha. 8th Army estimated that about eight German battalions, and many more feeble Italian, faced 10th Corps which should be able to break through and be on the way to Cape Bon by 23rd April. General Horrocks was not so confident and foresaw a difficult operation. Yet he was not unhopeful because he assumed that the enemy's morale must be very low owing to the long retreat and many defeats.

Moreover he did not think that there was an alternative plan in the circumstances. The circumstances are described in two paragraphs of Alexander's Operation Instruction of the 16th.

> 'The Allied forces will start offensive operations to destroy or capture the enemy forces in Tunisia, and by relentless pressure will combine with Naval and Air Forces to prevent the enemy's withdrawal by air or sea. . . .
> Eighth Army will:
> (a) draw enemy forces off First Army by exerting continuous pressure on the enemy.
> (b) by an advance on the axis Enfidaville—Hammamet—Tunis prevent the enemy withdrawing into the Cap Bon Peninsula . . .'

The same day Montgomery signalled to Alexander . . . 'All my troops are in first class form and want to be in the final Dunkirk . . .' It is a fair inference from events that he very reasonably interpreted the Operation Instruction as pointing to Cape Bon, or even Tunis. It would have been more than human not to hope perhaps that the 8th Army might reach these places before the 1st.

At Enfidaville the 8th Army was facing an area of ground of a sort new to most of it. This was a mountainous tract, twenty to thirty miles deep, and having a single good south to north route. This route began in a funnel, never more than seven thousand yards wide, through which ran the coastal road to Bou Ficha and to Hammamet, where it branched, right to Cape Bon, left to Hammam Lif and Tunis. Enfidaville, militarily merely a name and a landmark, lay on the southern edge of this tract in a rough, cultivated plain, upon which frowned Takrouna, a precipitous, rocky knoll, 500 feet high, and its western neighbour Djebel Garci. Garci was a complex feature, 1,000 feet high, abounding in steep, bald, rock faces, gullies and abominations. Four miles north of it was Djebel Mdeker, bigger and equally forbidding. East of Djebel Mdeker the jagged ridges of Djebel Mengoub and Djebel Tebaga prolonged the obstacle towards Sebkra Kralifa and the sea. Northwards other barriers showed the family likeness. Horrible country sometimes helps an attacker, and sometimes does half the defender's work as here it did. There were gullies, crags, bare slopes, and false crests to swallow the infantry and send mad their gunners, to make porters and pack-mules the only useful form of transport, and to promise very agreeable shooting to the enemy's machine-gunners and mortar-men.

Messe held his positions in depth, and placed their forward edge, with outposts beyond, on the line Sebkra Kralifa—Takrouna—Djebel Garci—westward. He 'sandwiched' Italian and German units, although from east to west the array of divisions was: 90th Light, Young Fascist, Trieste, Pistoia (in process of absorbing Centauro's remnants), 164th Light, Spezia, and in reserve 15th Panzer Division. Takrouna was held at first by the Italian 1st/66th Infantry Regiment (of Trieste Division), and Garci was held by the Pistoia Division with, on its right and rear, 164th Light Division defending the hills and passes around Saouaf. On 14th April there were 83 German and approximately 177 Italian guns in *AOK 1*, 44 German guns in *D.A.K.*, which on 25th had about 60 Italian guns.[1] 15th Panzer Division had four tanks fit for battle, and twenty-one under repair. Formations held a half-'issue' of ammunition each, and fuel for thirty miles except for the Panzer Division which had enough for sixty miles.

H.Q. 10th Corps, by the 18th, was sure that the enemy was in strength. The Corps' intention was to prepare to advance to Bou Ficha. To begin with, the 50th Division was to hold and patrol the eastern sector, the New Zealand Division was to capture Takrouna and exploit northwards; 4th Indian Division was to capture Djebel Garci and another mountain (Djebel Biada) north-east of it; 7th Armoured Division was to guard the west flank. The main feature of the next phase of the plan was for 4th Indian Division to capture Djebel Mdeker and then climb and fight for twelve miles north-east until it came out above the coast road at Sebkra Kralifa. Meanwhile the New Zealanders would go on making ground. The New Zealand and 4th Indian were two-brigade divisions, and therefore each had six infantry battalions instead of nine. Moreover their transport, apart from a few commandeered animals, was mechanized as was their artillery. They were, in fact, so unsuitably equipped for a long mountain battle that the bold and ambitious plan was also impracticable.

By this time the Desert Air Force was becoming established on some of the airfields and landing grounds from which the enemy had been driven. It could deploy 8 squadrons of day-bombers, 22 squadrons of fighters, and 4 (equivalent) squadrons of reconnaissance aircraft.[2]

Both New Zealand brigades attacked, an hour before midnight on the 19th. 6th Brigade, on the right, took without difficulty its objectives which were features north-east of Takrouna. 5th Brigade's objectives included a small hill just east of Takrouna and Takrouna itself. 28th (Maori) Battalion, on the right, went across mines and through shells and the cross-fire of automatic weapons to gain a brittle foothold on the small hill. Most of 21st Battalion, on the left, in spite of intense fire penetrated deeply west of Takrouna, but their

---

[1] As the Allied net closes upon them, the Axis armies in Tunisia become less separate. Units are transferred back and forth and therefore orders of battle and states of equipment constantly vary.

[2] In these totals are included 2 American and 1 French squadrons of day-bombers, and 8 American squadrons of fighters.

foothold too was uncertain and the knoll itself was not taken. Meanwhile 23rd Battalion had been called from reserve into the battle, and had heavy casualties, especially in officers.[1] However it pushed dourly on, passing below Takrouna on the east, though one forward company had left only twenty unscathed men and the other seventeen. At length 23rd and 28th Battalions linked. At daybreak Sergeant Rogers and eleven men of 28th Battalion, reinforced by Sergeant W. J. Smith, 23rd Battalion, who had temporarily lost himself, assaulted Takrouna. Somehow this party reached the top of the knoll, and began to engage the enemy who were mostly in a little village just below it. A few reinforcements and artillery observers rushed up to Sergeant Rogers and there the New Zealanders stayed in spite of continual shelling and a counter-attack. The 20th found both brigades committed and holding fast, but as there were no reserves they could not change their holds or better them.

4th Indian Division began its attack at 9.30 p.m. on the 19th, earlier than the New Zealanders to allow for a very difficult approach. 5th Indian Infantry Brigade was to capture Djebel Garci; 7th Indian Infantry Brigade was to help if necessary, and then to capture Djebel Mdeker. The 1st/4th Essex broke the outposts and fought their way up to their objective. Then 4th/6th Rajputana Rifles went through and a furious mêlée began. 1st/9th Gurkhas were sent in to add a dash of the kukri. Towards 4 a.m. the enemy counter-attacked savagely and was met savagely. Here Havildar Major Chhelu Ram of the Rajputana Rifles won the V.C. for courage and leadership sustained from the beginning of the battle until, fighting to the last, he died of his wounds. Jemadar Dewan Singh of the 1st/9th Gurkhas, who survived twelve wounds, later described a moment '... My hands being cut about and bloody, and having lost my kukri, I had to ask one of my platoon to take my pistol out of my holster and to put it in my hand. I then took command of my platoon again ...' At daybreak another counter-attack was beaten off. By noon it was clear that 5th Brigade was firmly holding, but only a fraction of Garci. Tuker brought forward 7th Brigade and soon four of his six battalions were committed while his division's task, taken as a whole, had barely begun. Yet there seemed to be no way of continuing it except by holding on and smashing counter-attacks. This is what happened, and in it the very powerful artillery (eight field and three medium regiments) under the division's control or at call, hammered the enemy mercilessly, switching concentrations from target to target. For example

---

[1] Lieutenant-Colonel R. E. Romans, commanding 23rd Battalion, was wounded. '... Sgts were promoting themselves to Platoon Commanders, Corporals to Sgts and so on and in many cases they no sooner promoted themselves than they were wounded ...' All Battalion Commanders in 5th Brigade were hit, and one in 6th Brigade.

'... FOO [Forward Observation Officer] reported that enemy infantry had got within 300 yards when the full weight of the Divisional Artillery came down. The DF [Defensive Fire] ... fell slap amongst them. When the smoke and dust had cleared away nothing was seen of them afterwards.'

On 21st April the New Zealanders cleared Takrouna, but the balance-sheet for them and for 4th Indian Division was unsatisfactory. Both had fought grimly in a fine feat of arms, and had suffered heavy loss for a little ground, and the hope '... that Boche was getting a really bloody nose everywhere ...' This phrase from a Gunner's log sums up this 'Soldiers' Battle'. von Arnim interpreted the battle as the first stage of the Allies' offensive, and expected further attacks, and Kesselring's Intelligence Staff appreciated that the Allies were now able to attack in any sector at any time. Both were perfectly correct, as 1st Army's activities show.

32. Royal Air Force Bostons over Tunisian mountains.

33. Tunisia. Longstop Hill (Djebel el Ahmera), from north-west.

34. Tunisia. Pack mules. Tanngoucha area.

35. Tunisia. Crags above Kelbine, near Chaouach.

36. Tunisia. Heidous Hill.

37. Tunisia. British 7.2-inch howitzer.

38. Landing Ship Infantry *Cathay* on fire off Bougie, after air attack.

39. Anti-aircraft fire at night. Algiers.

CHAPTER XVI

THE WAR AT SEA

March, April, and May 1943

See Maps 23 and 24

WE have already told how the Allies tried to cut Axis communications with Tunisia during the first four months following the 'Torch' landings. In November and December 1942 they failed to do this decisively mainly because the Axis held ideally placed air bases from which they could protect their shipping and transport aircraft where it was vital to do so, that is within the triangle Sicily—Tunisia—Sardinia. During January and February 1943, however, the Allies gradually overcame this Axis advantage and by the beginning of March British and American aircraft, though still from rather distant airfields, held the upper hand over the triangle and waters and ports of the Tyrrhenian Sea as well. As the Allies gained control of the area the enemy's supply position in Tunisia grew steadily worse and during the opening months of 1943 Axis leaders high and low were looking for ways to avert disaster.

Estimates of the size of the problem varied because there was no agreed policy for Tunisia. In February and early March von Arnim and Rommel were trying to convince their High Command that their armies could neither withstand an all-out Allied assault, nor mount a decisive offensive, unless they had ample reserves, particularly of fuel and ammunition, in addition to their daily needs.

In mid-March Hitler told a conference of his Service chiefs that if the Axis was to hold Tunisia its troops must be supplied at the rate of 150,000 to 200,000 tons a month and not at *Comando Supremo's* 'inadequate amount' of 80,000 tons. His solution of the difficulty of means was to say that more ships must be available. In fact the task utterly exceeded the capacity of the shipping that so far it had been possible to provide, and air transport could not lift more than 10,000 tons monthly at the most. The 94,000 tons disembarked in Libyan and Tunisian ports in November proved to have been a flash in the pan, and deliveries direct by sea to Libya ceased in early January 1943. Against mounting Allied opposition, coupled with some exceptionally bad weather, the average for the next three months was only 64,600.[1] To better this figure, or even to prevent it falling, more supply ships and stronger air and surface escorts were needed. So far the capacity of the ports had proved sufficient. In spite of Allied bombing which upset dock labour and damaged cranes and quays, Bizerta and Tunis could take twice the tonnage that was arriving.

Therefore the barrel was scraped for supply ships. Some French merchant ships, commandeered after the Axis had occupied Vichy and Tunisian ports, seemed suitable but inspection showed that most needed large refits. So did French destroyers and smaller French warships which the Axis had recently seized. German war transports, Naval ferry barges and Siebel ferries had proved their worth, particularly on the short run from Trapani. More ferries were being built in Italy and at Toulon, but congestion in the yards and shortage of labour and of steel prevented yet more building. Kesselring's drive added a number of motor fishing-vessels, rounded-up in the Adriatic, to the supply fleet.

If it was difficult to increase the number of supply ships, it was still more difficult to protect those in service against the increasing Allied attack. The first need was more fighters to cover the convoys and the ports, and more bombers to assail Allied airfields, surface warships and submarines. Recent reinforcements for the German Air Force, however, were insufficient to offset losses and also to match the growing number of Allied aircraft directed at targets in the Sicily—Tunisia—Sardinia triangle. Nor could the right surface escorts be found to replace those sunk. Destroyers, in particular, were wanted for several duties at once and they continued to be switched from convoy escort to troop-carrying or to minelaying, and even held in reserve in case the larger warships put to sea. For anti-aircraft defence the Italians accepted a German offer of additional weapons for escorts and of German gun crews for escorts and supply ships.

While the men on the spot had been discussing supplies Hitler and Mussolini had been exchanging letters in which they agreed that Tunisia must be held but differed about the administrative means. The *Duce* wanted more German aircraft and the *Führer* more ships and escorts. But Hitler does not seem to have applied himself to tackling Mediterranean problems in earnest until March when he returned from the Russian front. He then immediately sent Dönitz to Rome with proposals. The Admiral acted vigorously and soon the

---

[1] The figures are from '*The Italian Navy in World War II*' (Annapolis, Maryland, 1957) by M. A. Bragadin. They are higher than those quoted in other official sources, probably because tanks, guns and motor transport are included by weight as opposed to numbers. It is interesting that the average monthly tonnage unloaded in Libya in the eighteen months between June 1941 and the end of 1942 works out at much the same figure as that quoted above, namely 63,000. The conditions during those months were, however, in many ways not comparable with those of 1943.

Italians accepted all he proposed, including mixed German and Italian staffs in *Comando Supremo* and in all naval echelons of command. Vice-Admiral Ruge, hitherto responsible for German convoy protection in north-west European waters, was to be attached to *Supermarina* with a German naval staff. He would be subordinate to Riccardi and would co-operate closely with the Italians in the control, administration and protection of transports running between Italy and Africa. Dönitz had already removed Weichold from the post of German Admiral in Rome on the grounds that he had become too pro-Italian.

Here it is relevant to say that German-Italian relations, though not yet at their worst, were bad. It was evident that Italians were sick of the war. Mass strikes in Turin and Milan had recently been staged demanding peace and liberty. Italian dislike for Germans was widespread, and the chief reciprocal emotion was distrust.[1] The Duce was sick, ageing, and losing control. Hitler was determined to revive him, but it was not until April that the two met near Salzburg, as told in the previous chapter. When Mussolini went back to Italy and no longer had the forceful *Führer* at his side he soon became as depressed and feeble as before.

In spite of many words and some measures, the Axis tonnage arriving in Tunisia continued to fall. Discord between the Axis partners was partly to blame, but the true cause was that by March 1943 it was too late to avert disaster in Africa. The Allies had assembled superior forces in the Mediterranean. The Germans could not withdraw enough aircraft from other fronts to challenge Allied superiority in the air; at sea a sortie by the Italian Fleet could have done little but present the British with a most welcome opportunity to rid themselves of the nuisance of an enemy fleet in being. It followed that on land the Axis armies were faced with the defeat inevitable to an overseas expedition whose communications are relentlessly being destroyed.

In the event, during March and April confusion grew in the Axis system of supply and results dwindled. The bulk of the cargo continued to be transported from Naples in ships ranging from 1,500 to 8,000 G.R.T. The rest was carried mostly in ferries and landing-craft sailing from Trapani and Marsala. As before, many of the tanks, guns and motor transport were sent by this route. Destroyers and air transports shared the carriage of reinforcements, and Allied counteraction had so far had little success. Convoys from Naples to Bizerta and Tunis now took around thirty-six hours for the passage

---

[1] The First Secretary to the Italian Embassy in Berlin recorded that many Germans were convinced that the transfer of Count Ciano on 5th February from Minister of Foreign Affairs to Ambassador at the Vatican had been for the purpose of negotiating with the Allies for a separate peace.

if no stops were made; those from Trapani about fourteen hours and the troop-carrying destroyers from Trapani seven hours or less. Timing remained haphazard for a number of reasons, among them the weather—which was astonishingly bad during the last eight days of March—and because escorts had sometimes to wait several days for fuel. As for routes, the Italians had come to believe that some relief from air attack could be obtained if convoys kept well to the west, towards Sardinia, when crossing the Tyrrhenian Sea, thereby keeping out of range of torpedo-bombers from Malta. However, to the hard-driven crews of the Italian merchantmen and their escorts the sky, by March, seemed crowded with enemy aircraft and the hazards of the voyage continuous. To the risks of air, submarine and surface attack was added the increasingly difficult task, intricate even in fine weather, of navigating among their own and British minefields.[1] Though not many ships struck mines, the narrow swept channels left little room for error, or freedom of manoeuvre when convoys were subjected to bombing. Admiral Cunningham has written '... It was always a surprise to me how the Italian seamen continued to operate their ships in the face of the dangers that beset them ... the fact that they stood up to it should be remembered to their credit.'

The chief cause of Axis distress was the greatly increased strength of the Allied air forces. In March, in the Mediterranean as a whole, Allied aircraft accounted for more than half the ships and craft sunk at sea and in port, and of the ships employed in supplying Tunisia a still higher proportion. Aircraft continued to concentrate on the Sicily—Tunisia—Sardinia triangle. During March, April and May scarcely a ship was sunk at sea by air attack outside this area although by no means all the victims were employed in supplying Tunisia. The best hunting was obtained at focal points off the western tip of Sicily, off Cape Bon, and in the approaches to Tunis and Bizerta. Yet the air effort was shifting more from the open sea to the ports until, in April, the tonnage of ships sunk in port was more than that sunk at sea—largely the result of the greater part played since the beginning of March by the U.S.A.A.F. As a corollary Malta's share of the sinkings was on the wane and the Middle East, which had long since sent most of its torpedo-bombers to Malta, was also concentrating on the ports, the U.S. IX Bomber Command's effort in

---

[1] Along the French North African coast during the winter and spring of 1942–43 the weather was unusually stormy. 'The blue Mediterranean where he lay, lulled by the coil of his crystalline streams ...' is not always a true picture of that region.

April being more than double that of the previous month.[1] Bad weather during the second half of April lessened sinkings at sea by air attack.

The Coastal and Strategic Air Forces of the newly organized Northwest African Air Forces now played the principal role in the Air/Sea warfare. The Coastal Air Force was mainly British, and the Strategic Air Force American. The Coastal Air force was responsible for sea reconnaissance, shipping sweeps, anti-submarine operations including escorts to convoys and, in addition, for the fighter defence of ports and of convoys within range of shore bases. The Strategic Air Force was primarily responsible for the bombing of Axis ports and convoys. Yet as far as possible the most appropriate aircraft for the task were made available. For example, to make up for a shortage of long-range aircraft in the Coastal Air Force, a R.A.F. torpedo-carrying squadron of Marauders was turned over completely to reconnaissance. A force of strike aircraft consisting of two squadrons of U.S. Mitchells of the Strategic Air Force was loaned daily to the Coastal Air Force to follow up sightings of ships.

A yardstick is required to measure the effect of the examples of the sinking of ships which follow. A rough and ready one is that the loss of even a ship of 3,000 G.R.T. could represent the loss of two days' requirements for the entire Axis forces in North Africa. Alternatively, it could mean the loss of several weeks' supply of one commodity, for example, aviation spirit. These losses which hit all ranks of the enemy, hit hardest his commanders who had to plan operations, offensive or defensive, without knowing whether they would have the requisite supplies.

By the end of March the enemy was living from hand to mouth, in northern and central Tunisia as well as in the south. During this month the U.S.A.A.F. had contributed largely to the enemy's predicament by accounting for two-thirds of the tonnage sunk by air attack, sinking slightly more at sea than in harbour. On 7th March, six U.S. Mitchells escorted by fourteen Lightnings caught a convoy of three ships, carrying anxiously awaited ammunition and fuel, north-east of Cape Bon, and sank the merchant ships, totalling over 10,000 tons, and damaged several of the surface escort. On the night of 12th/13th the 10,500-ton tanker *Sterope*, carrying 4,000 tons of fuel, was sunk off the north-west corner of Sicily by torpedoes from Beauforts of No. 39 Squadron and F.A.A. Albacores from Malta. On the 22nd, thirteen escorted American Marauders attacked another convoy north-east of Cape Bon. The *Monti*, 4,300 tons, was sunk, and the *Ombrina* was set on fire but struggled into Bizerta where she

---

[1] On 29th March Air Vice-Marshal T.A. Langford-Sainsbury became the A.O.C. No. 201 (Naval Co-operation) Group in the Middle East in place of Air Commodore Scarlett-Streatfeild.

blew up. On the same day twenty-four U.S. Fortresses escorted by twenty-seven Lightnings made a highly successful raid on Palermo. An ammunition ship exploded, devastating much of the dock area and helping to sink seven other ships totalling 11,500 tons. The port, which was already working feebly, became practically unusable for several weeks. Two more ships, the *Capo Mele*, 3,010 tons, and the *Albisola*, 4,097 tons, and four motor torpedo-boats were sunk in a raid on Cagliari on the 31st. This port, too, suffered much damage. The destroyer *Genere* in Palermo and the torpedo-boat *Monsone* in Naples were sunk in bombing raids on the 1st of March. During the last week of the month Fortresses of the N.A.A.F. switched to the unloading ports, and Bizerta, Ferryville and Sousse were all hard hit, although no ship of over 500 tons was sunk. From Malta Beauforts and Albacores continued their minelaying operations in harbour approaches, Spitfire fighter-bombers raided Sicilian airfields and Wellingtons and Albacores bombed a number of the smaller harbours. From Cyrenaican airfields R.A.F. and U.S. bombers added their attacks to those of the N.A.A.F. and Malta on Naples, Messina, Palermo and Catania, and also bombed the Tunisian ports of Sfax and Sousse.[1]

Meanwhile, submarines of the 8th and 10th Flotillas were ranging widely. Patrols off the north coast of Sicily were the most rewarding. Here, during March, *Trooper*, *Thunderbolt*, *Sibyl* and *Splendid* sank seven ships, including a naval tanker, totalling 22,000 tons. Another four ships fell to *Turbulent*, *Torbay* and *Unbending* off the west coast of Italy, and the remainder of the month's bag to *Taurus* and the Dutch *Dolfijn* further afield. The bag counts only ships of large or medium tonnage. Many smaller craft were sunk or damaged by torpedoes or gunfire in the course of a normal patrol. Shelling and sabotage of railway tracks, tunnels and trains continued whenever opportunity offered.

Three British submarines were lost in March without survivors. *Tigris* was probably the first to go, although how is uncertain. She disappeared during her return passage to Algiers after a patrol off Naples and may have hit a mine on the 10th of the month. Two days later, *Turbulent* was sunk by Italian anti-submarine craft sent out from Bastia (Corsica). Her fate, like that of more than one earlier sister boat, was the sadder because she was about to return to the U.K. after this last of many successful patrols, for which Commander J. W. Linton, her commanding officer, was awarded the Victoria Cross. The third British submarine lost during March was H.M.S. *Thunderbolt*, sunk on the 14th by the Italian corvette *Cicogna* to the north-west of Cape St. Vito (Sicily).

---

[1] The total sorties for March to May will be found in Table IV page 418.

Surface forces had a disappointing month. Repeated sweeps had no better reward than sundry brushes with E-boats. On the 12th, in one of these, the destroyer *Lightning* was hit by two torpedoes and later sank. She was replaced in Force Q by the Polish destroyer, *Blyskawica*, which had escaped from the Baltic in 1940 and had since seen much service in British home waters.

Early in March the fast minelayer *Abdiel* added 320 mines in two operations to her previous lays in the Sicilian channel. The submarine *Rorqual* laid fifty mines off Trapani on the 22nd and M.T.Bs laid a total of sixty-six in five lays off Bizerta, Plane Island and Zembra Island. Wellingtons, Albacores and Marauders dropped magnetic mines in La Goulette, Sfax and Sousse. Mines do not seem to have sunk any Axis merchant ship during March but two Italian destroyers, the *Malocello* and the *Ascari*, ferrying German troops, sank after striking mines north of Cape Bon on the 24th. Over 600 men were drowned. These were the first Italian destroyers to be sunk while transporting troops.

There was another important loss during March. On the 28th the 8,000-ton *Catarina Costa* blew up in Naples harbour. The cause of the explosion is unknown but she was carrying a mixed cargo of fuel and ammunition, a highly dangerous combination to which the Italians had agreed under heavy German pressure, and which afterwards they loaded only in less valuable ships.

The biggest ship sunk by aircraft during April was the 9,646-ton *Sicilia* which Fortresses destroyed in Naples on the 4th. Fortresses, two days later, sank the 8,564-ton *Roverto* and the 6,013 *San Diego* off Bizerta.[1] American bombs also accounted for three ships in Palermo, three in Trapani and two in Porto Torres, a harbour on the north coast of Sardinia in use because of damage and congestion elsewhere. The sinking of the 5,324-ton *Monginevro* between Zembra and Zembretta islands on the 16th/17th was the combined work of M.T.Bs 634 and 656 and F.A.A. Albacores of No. 826 Squadron, while a few hours earlier the *Giacomo C* of 4,638 tons, torpedoed by the submarine *Unbroken*, was finished off in Palermo by bombs from American aircraft. By comparison, the R.A.F's score was modest: on the 11th/12th, Wellingtons of No. 458 (R.A.A.F.) Squadron from Malta sank the 2,943-ton *Fabriano* north of Sicily; on the 23rd/24th Malta Beauforts of No. 39 Squadron torpedoed the 5,079-ton *Aquino* north-west of Marittimo Island and she sank after a second attack. The *Aquino* had already been bombed and left burning off Marittimo Island by Fortresses of the N.A.A.F. On the 28th the 1,599-ton *Teramo* was set ablaze off Kelibia by South African

---

[1] High altitude bombing of shipping by Fortresses proved to be extremely effective. It was found that a pattern of 28 tons of bombs was required to sink a medium-sized ship. The normal formation of eighteen Fortresses carried double this load.

Kittyhawk fighter-bombers of the Desert Air Force and became a total loss.

During April aircraft scored notable successes against the Italian Navy. Two of its three remaining heavy cruisers, *Trieste* and *Gorizia*, were still at Maddalena. On the 10th, sixty Fortresses attacked them in two waves, dropping 360 one-thousand pound bombs from 18,000 feet. *Trieste* was sunk. *Gorizia* was severely damaged and again by another attack three days later, but managed to reach Spezia under her own steam. On the night of the 13th/14th, United Kingdom R.A.F. Bomber Command laid 32 mines in the approaches to Spezia, and on the 18th/19th 162 of its heavy bombers dropped over 300 tons of bombs on the port itself. The battleship *Littorio* had a turret damaged, the destroyer *Alpino* was sunk and a number of smaller warships were sunk or damaged. Other losses of Italian warships from air attack included the torpedo-boat *Medici* sunk in a raid on Catania on the 16th and, on the last day of the month, two destroyers *Pancaldo* and *Lampo*—both previously sunk and salved—which were caught by American and British fighter-bombers of the Desert Air Force, the first off Cape Bon shortly after mid-day and the other a few hours later twenty miles to the south-east. The *Pancaldo* was carrying German troops to Tunisia as was the German-manned destroyer *Hermes* (formerly the Greek *Vasilefs Giorgios I*). The *Hermes* was severely damaged in this attack.

Of the ships of over 500 G.R.T. sunk by submarines during April, three fell to *Saracen* and *Taurus* in the waters around Corsica, two to *Safari* close to Cagliari and three off the north and west coasts of Sicily to *Unison* and *Sahib*. The *Francesco Crispi*, 7,600 tons, the *Tagliamento*, 5,448 tons, and the *Marco Foscarine*, 6,406 tons, were the biggest ships sunk, the first two by *Saracen* and the last by *Unison*. On the 16th, as mentioned previously, *Unbroken* shared with American aircraft the sinking of the *Giacomo C*. On the 28th *Unshaken* sank the Italian torpedo-boat *Climene* in the Sicilian Narrows.

Three British submarines were lost. *Splendid*, on the 21st April, was sunk off Capri by the destroyer *Hermes*, which picked up thirty survivors. *Sahib*, on the 24th off the north coast of Sicily, was forced to the surface after depth charge attacks and scuttled, though fortunately all but one of her company were picked up by the Italians. Shortly before, or on, 1st May, *Regent* was lost in the neighbourhood of Brindisi with all hands.

Surface forces had a more lively month than in March. Besides the 5,324-ton *Monginevro*, which M.T.Bs shared with the F.A.A. on the night of 16th/17th, M.T.Bs sank two merchant ships totalling 6,912 tons and a Siebel ferry on the 1st of the month south of Cani Rocks. Early on the 16th, the destroyers *Pakenham* and *Paladin* of Force K encountered two Italian torpedo-boats, *Cigno* and *Cassiopea*, fifteen miles south of Marittimo Island. *Cigno* was sunk but *Pakenham* received a hit in the engine room which stopped her. *Paladin* took her in tow but progress was slow and enemy airfields very close. From Malta Admiral Bonham-Carter ordered that *Pakenham* must be sunk. Five nights later *Laforey*, *Loyal* and *Lookout* of Force Q on a sweep from Bône to the western end of Sicily sank the German war transport *K.T.7* fifteen miles west of Marittimo Island. Both Force Q and Force K had further encounters with enemy craft during the last three nights of April and in one of these a small merchant ship, the *Fauna*, employed in supplying Pantelleria, was sunk by *Nubian* and *Paladin*. Commando parties were landed by M.T.Bs on several occasions. In mid-April the cruiser *Dido* left Force Q for the U.K. and was replaced by the *Newfoundland*.

Early in April *Abdiel* laid a further 320 mines in the Sicilian Channel. *Rorqual* laid 100 mines off Marittimo Island towards the end of the month and aircraft continued to drop magnetic mines in the entrances to ports. In most of these lays the mines were set to sink before the first of May. The only loss attributed to mines during April was one Siebel ferry.

For the Axis, transport aircraft became more important as a means of ferrying men and supplies to Africa as the difficulties of getting them there by sea grew. Towards the end of March it had been estimated that the daily average arrivals of Axis transport aircraft—Ju. 52s, Ju. 90s and Ju. 290s, and the giant Me. 323s—in Tunisia had risen to 200. Most flights assembled at Naples and used one of the airfields in western Sicily as a staging post, although some went directly to Tunisia, making a rendezvous over Trapani with a fighter escort. An Allied plan ('Flax') had been drawn up in February to dislocate the Axis transport system completely. It comprised fighter sweeps of the Sicilian Narrows combined with bombing of the terminal and staging-post airfields. The plan was postponed because of the Axis offensive at Kasserine and on other counts but at length it was put into action on 5th April.

At 8 a.m. on the 5th, a few miles north-east of Cape Bon, a fighter sweep of 26 U.S. Lightnings intercepted 50–70 Ju. 52s, a few dive-bombers, and about 25 German fighters some of which appeared to be escorting a sea convoy. At about the same time and in the same neighbourhood 18 U.S. Mitchells attacked shipping, and their escort of 32 Lightnings joined in the general air mêlée. 15 Ju. 52s and two Me. 109s were shot down for the loss of two Lightnings. Next, U.S. Fortresses attacked the terminal airfields of Sidi Ahmed and El Aouina with fragmentation bombs. Around noon other Fortresses and Mitchells went for the Sicilian staging posts, to catch the second daily flight of transports, and at Milo (Trapani) the Fortresses destroyed thirteen German aircraft (including eight Ju.

52s) and eight Italian aircraft. At least 27 German and most likely three Italian air transports were lost that day.

During the following two and a half weeks similar operations with the object of intercepting transport flights were carried out very successfully. For example: on the 10th U.S. Lightnings and Mitchells bagged four Ju. 52s and one Me. 109; the next day U.S. Lightnings shot down a total of 17 Ju. 52s, an Italian S.82 and two Me. 110s; and on the 18th American fighters of the Desert Air Force destroyed 32 Ju. 52s out of a force of about 100 (believed to be evacuating personnel from Tunisia) and two German and probably three Italian fighters.

The climax came on 22nd April. Kittyhawks of Nos 2, 4, and 5 Squadrons S.A.A.F., Spitfires of No. 1 Squadron S.A.A.F. and the Polish Flight, and Kittyhawks of U.S. 79th Fighter Group intercepted 21 huge Me. 323s, heavily escorted as were most transports, routed the escort and shot down 16 Me. 323s, 1 M.C. 202, and 1 Re. 2001. Each Me. 323 carried ten tons of petrol and they burned like torches as they fell. Göring, in fury, forbade all transport flights to Africa, but after a few days and protests from Kesselring, allowed night-flights. Nevertheless these produced only 60–70 sorties a night in contrast with a 24-hour total ranging from 100 to 250 which had been not uncommon before 'Flax' had got into its swing.

To sum up the results of this struggle: the monthly tonnage transported to Tunisia by sea, which in December, January and February had averaged around 64,000 (almost exactly that estimated as possible by the Italians), dwindled in March to 43,000 and in April to 29,000.[1] In May (included here for convenience) supplies arriving up to the date of the Axis capitulation amounted to about 3,000 tons. The figures for tonnage transported by air were March 8,000, April 5,000 and May 837. The air figures are for German supplies. The Italian figures are not known. During March 12,000 German reinforcements were transported to Tunisia by air and 8,400 Germans and 11,000 Italians by sea. In April the figures were 9,000 Germans by air and 2,800 Germans and an unknown number of Italians by sea. In May only three hundred German reinforcements were flown in to Tunisia. Destroyers made twenty-four successful trips as troop carriers in March and lost two of their number on mines while on this duty. Destroyers were available for troop-carrying only for the second half of April and made eight trips at the

---

[1] These figures are based on M. A. Bragadin's '*The Italian Navy in World War II*', and include the tonnage for both German and Italian forces. In German documents however it appears that about half the tonnage transported in March and April 1943 was for purely German needs.

Table I
Cargoes disembarked in North Africa and percentage lost on passage
(From figures given by the Italian Official Naval Historian)

Month 1943	Type	Cargo disembarked in North Africa (tons)	Percentage lost on the way
March	General Military cargo and fuel.	43,125	41·5
April	,, ,, ,, ,, ,,	29,233	41·5
May	,, ,, ,, ,, ,,	3,000 approx.	77

Table II
Number and tonnage of Italian and German merchant ships of over 500 tons G.R.T. sunk at sea or in port in the Mediterranean March, April and May 1943
(Compiled from Italian post-war and German war records)

Month	By Surface ships	By Submarine	By Aircraft	Shared	From other causes	Total
March	—	16–39,872	18– 62,453	—	2– 9,156	36–111,481
April	3– 7,487	10–35,492	15– 59,566	3–11,904	2– 1,774	33–116,223
May	1– 3,566	4–10,733	30– 89,628	—	4– 8,807	39–112,734
Total	4–11,053	30–86,097	63–211,647	3–11,904	8–19,737	108–340,438

Table III
A breakdown of the figures in Column 4 (by aircraft) of Table II

Month	Sunk by U.S.A.A.F. In port	Sunk by U.S.A.A.F. At sea	Shared by British and U.S. aircraft	Sunk by R.A.F. or F.A.A. In port	Sunk by R.A.F. or F.A.A. At sea	Total
March	9– 18,608	6–24,752	—	—	3–19,093	18– 62,453
April	10– 35,368	2–14,577	1– 5,079 (at sea)	—	2– 4,542	15– 59,566
May	24– 64,386	2–10,292	2– 9,088 (1 at sea and 1 in port)	1–5,164	1– 698	30– 89,628
Total	43–118,362	10–49,621	3–14,167	1–5,164	6–24,333	63–211,647

cost of the *Pancaldo* sunk. In these two months, trips by Siebel ferry, landing craft, barge and many other types of small craft ran into several hundred, and losses among them were heavy.

Some of these results are included in Tables I and II from which the changing pattern of Allied achievement can be seen.

During these three months some 230 vessels of less than 500 tons G.R.T., totalling 25,000 tons, were also sunk, the majority in U.S.A.A.F. attacks on Italian and Tunisian ports and a number by gunfire from submarines.

Table IV

Sorties (calculated from available records) flown by 'Torch', Malta and Middle East Air Forces in searching for and attacking enemy ships (including submarines) at sea and against enemy ports of loading and unloading during March, April and May 1943.

Month	Target		'Torch'		Malta	Middle East		Totals on target each month
			R.A.F. & F.A.A.	U.S.A.A.F.	R.A.F. & F.A.A.	R.A.F. & F.A.A.	U.S.A.A.F.	
March	Ships at sea		477	395	273	555	—	1,700
	Ports	Loading	24	150	24	108	104	410
		Unloading	49	157	—	—	—	206
April	Ships at sea		532	560	259	1,211	514	3,076[1]
	Ports	Loading	27	375	151	76	263	892
		Unloading	84	79	—	70	—	233
May	Ships at sea		640	668	272	1,626	693	3,899[1]
	Ports	Loading	316	1,552	127	205	385	2,585
		Unloading	—	126	—	89	9	224[2]
TOTALS: March—May 1943								
	Ships at sea		1,649	1,623	804	3,392	1,207	8,675
	Ports	Loading	367	2,077	302	389	752	3,887
		Unloading	133	362	—	159	9	663
	Grand Totals		2,149	4,062	1,106	3,940	1,968	13,225

[1] The figure for April includes 1,133 sorties flown in the last week of the month by fighters and fighter-bombers, mainly from the Desert Air Force which also provided most of the 1,881 fighter and fighter-bomber sorties included in the May figure and flown in the first ten days of that month.

[2] Attacks ceased mid-May with the capture of all enemy unloading ports in Africa.

The foregoing account has tried to show by some rather detailed examples that each loss directly or indirectly affected the enemy's power to continue to fight in Tunisia. This generalization is neither new, nor peculiar to the Tunisian campaign. Ever since German forces had come to the help of the Italians in the Mediterranean and Middle East in 1941 (to take a memorable date) the events of the war, land, sea, and air, had influenced each other though not coincidentally in time. In this interplay Malta's changing fortunes were particularly important. However in Tunisia, recently, the events of war in the three elements and their effects, one upon another, had been more closely linked in time. If we single out one factor, and for a moment enter the deceitful country of 'Might-Have-Been', two thoughts occur. Had the Allies been able to get a tighter strangle-hold on the Axis communications immediately after the 'Torch' landings, they might have won the gamble of the Tunisian campaign by the end of 1942, and victory in Africa as a whole might have been close. Conversely, the Axis might have staved off for a long time their defeat in May 1943 had their forces received the supplies they needed. These speculations ignore many other factors and possibilities, e.g. that dream of all commanders, a crushing and irreversible tactical victory; or an endurance of starvation and the absence of nearly all necessaries of war like that shown by Masséna and his troops outside the Lines of Torres Vedras.

A most interesting idea suggested by the tables in this chapter and in Chapters VIII and X is that the Axis, in the Mediterranean as a whole, had been losing each month for many months the means of carrying sufficient cargo to supply amply their forces in Africa.[1] The British in their hungry years had experienced time and again the want of many things that modern forces require to wage war, not that the Axis had wallowed in abundance. But as 1942 passed into 1943 the Axis forces were becoming starved. Their seamen and indeed their airmen persisted in trying to keep their forces supplied, and the forces showed a dogged endurance which matched that of the Allies in their bad times. Both sides deserve the respect and admiration of fighting men.

Meanwhile the Allies brought in their own reinforcements and supplies with almost clockwork precision to French North Africa and to the Middle East. The Allies' machinery of supply was directed by men who trusted and respected one another even in their disagreements, and this was a weighty advantage. In both March and April two fast convoys carrying men and two with material arrived at Algiers from the United Kingdom. The like number arrived at Oran

---

[1] Calculation has been founded on the generally accepted ratio between G.R.T. and cargo tons or deadweight tonnage of five to eight. Aircraft have been left out because of the very many intricate factors which affect their power to carry freight. Moreover ships and seamen enjoyed the experience of centuries; aircraft and airmen of 30 or 40 breakneck years.

from the United States. The small fast L.S.I. plying between these ocean terminals and ports nearer the front line were reduced when *Royal Scotsman* and *Royal Ulsterman* returned to the United Kingdom to refit, leaving only *Queen Emma* and *Princess Beatrix* from the four which had done such fine service since the opening days of 'Torch' ferrying British troops forward to Bône. In mid-April five new American-built British L.S.T. arriving at Oran were loaded and despatched to Philippeville and Bougie, and six American L.C.T. moved forward to Bône to help with the transfer of stores for the 2nd U.S. Corps to La Calle and Tabarka.

On 16th March, Vice-Admiral H. K. Hewitt, U.S.N., assumed command of all U.S. Naval Forces in North West African waters and set up his H.Q. at Algiers alongside Admiral Cunningham. Force H, commanded by Vice-Admiral A. U. Willis, who had succeeded Sir Harold Burrough on 4th March, now comprised the battleships *Nelson* and *Rodney*, the aircraft carrier *Formidable*, and escorting destroyers. When not covering one of the ocean convoys on its passage inside the Mediterranean, Force H usually berthed at Mers-el-Kebir or Gibraltar, but during the first ten days of March, on Admiralty instructions, Force H remained at Gibraltar because there were indications that German warships might be about to make another raid into the Atlantic from northern Norway.

The arrival of the anti-aircraft cruiser *Carlisle* early in March powerfully strengthened the defence of local convoys, and with the steady improvement in radar equipment and fighter direction made air attack on Allied ships at sea and in port increasingly costly to the enemy. In April the anti-submarine defences were augmented by an all-round strengthening of light coastal forces. Five flotillas of motor launches were in future to operate from French North African ports: two flotillas from Algiers, two from Oran and one from Bougie. Of four M.T.B. flotillas, one of them American, three were now based on Bône and one on Malta. After Sousse was opened to the Allies' use on 12th April, six of the Malta flotilla were sent to operate from that port pending the capture of Bizerta. With these changes, Captain, Coastal Forces (A.G.V. Hubback) shifted his headquarters from Malta to Algiers. Another means of harassing U-boats was introduced in April when instructions were issued that aircraft in transit were to be routed whenever practicable over the sea.

The Allies' defence measures could not, however, prevent all loss and damage from enemy action. In the Western Basin four or five German U-boats were usually operating between Alboran Island and Bougie and two or three Italians between Bougie and Bône, and there were still some German and Italian bombers and torpedo-bombers available in Sardinia, Tunisia and Sicily to strike at ships and ports. Bône continued to be the main target for the enemy's air attacks but Algiers also received attention. A new type of weapon, the circling torpedo, which appeared first in an attack on Tripoli on 19th March, was used at Algiers on 26th of the month.[1] Nine torpedoes were dropped, but with negligible results. Losses in March at sea included two ships sunk by U-boats in the Atlantic from an outward bound United Kingdom slow convoy. Within the Mediterranean the most serious loss was that of the 19,000-ton Union Castle line *Windsor Castle* sunk on March 23rd north-west of Algiers by German torpedo-bombers, which, in the same neighbourhood during the following four days, also sank the 1,524-ton *Prinz Willem III* and the *Empire Rowan* of 9,545 tons. On the 30th, *U.596* sank the 7,133-ton *Fort à la Corne* and the 9,551 (Norwegian) *Hallanger* in a coastal convoy north of Cape Tenez. Besides these sinkings eight Allied merchant ships were damaged at sea in the Western Basin by air and submarine attack during March.

In April the ships sunk by the enemy, all by U-boat, dropped to five, three of which were Frenchmen. Other than these, no ships were damaged at sea during April.

The four German U-boats lost in the Mediterranean during March and April were sunk in the Western Basin, *U.83*, *U.77* and *U.602* by air attack, and *U.343* by depth charges dropped by an A/S trawler. The *Delfino*, the only Italian submarine sunk in these two months, probably struck a mine in the Gulf of Taranto. Two German boats passed through the Straits of Gibraltar in March but none in April, leaving eighteen German U-boats in the Mediterranean at the end of this month.

Meanwhile the Levant Command was running convoys from Alexandria to keep the 8th Army supplied and to stock Malta. In June 1942, some ten months earlier, a Malta convoy, heavily attacked from the air and threatened by the main Italian Fleet, had had to return to Alexandria, while its counterpart from the west lost four out of six supply ships. Now, the enemy rarely attempted to interfere. The losses of the Allies at sea in the Eastern Mediterranean during March and April were all inflicted by *U.593* off the hump of Cyrenaica. In March this U-boat sank two medium-sized merchant ships on the 18th and the 5,157-ton *City of Guildford* on the 27th, and on 10th April the 1,858-ton *Runo*.

In harbour, during March, by a curious coincidence, three well-found ships, totalling 14,430 tons, were lost as a result of fire, one in

---

[1] This circling torpedo was of Italian design. It was dropped with a parachute attached to its tail which was released when the torpedo struck the water. Rudders were put over automatically at intervals to cause a turning circle of between 150 and 200 feet diameter. The torpedo ran on the surface and experience soon proved that it was easy to sink by small-arms or machine-gun fire.

the Red Sea, one in Alexandria and one in Malta. Losses in harbour from enemy action were confined to Tripoli. The enemy knew well how much the 8th Army depended on this port and persisted in frequent raids in the face of strong fighter and gun defences, soon augmented by a balloon barrage and smoke-producing equipment. On 19th March twelve Ju. 88s made a determined attack in pouring rain, using bombs and, for the first time, circling torpedoes. Two merchant ships, the *Ocean Voyager* of 7,174 tons and the *Varvara* of 1,354 tons were sunk by bombs. The only damage caused by the new weapon, of which thirteen were subsequently accounted for, was to the destroyer *Derwent* which had to be beached for temporary repairs. As the *Derwent* was not hit until half an hour after the torpedoes had been dropped it was evident that this method of attack was a good one in a crowded harbour.

Despite the air attacks cargo unloaded at Tripoli rose steadily. In March the daily average was 2,280 tons, the highest figure of 5,000 tons being achieved on the 27th. In April the daily average climbed to well above 4,000 tons and this did not include bulk petrol. Much of the stores and equipment unloaded at Tripoli was transhipped for onward passage in smaller vessels to Gabes, Sfax and Sousse, ports which were brought speedily into use after capture, largely as a result of the good work of Captain Wauchope's Inshore Squadron and the port parties mentioned in Chapter IX. Even before these ports were in Allied hands the Naval Mobile Beach Party was unloading stores on nearby open beaches. Since the opening of the campaign in October this small party of thirty officers and men under Commander F. H. Ashton R.N. had unloaded 6,500 tons on to beaches close to the front line.

As the Allied armies closed in on Bizerta and Tunis night patrols of destroyers and M.T.Bs increased in the Sicilian Channel. By day the area was left to the Allied air forces because there were not enough fighters to cover warships as well. As has been seen, by mid-April the Axis supply situation was already desperate and although four merchant ships reached Tunisia between the 15th and 20th of that month the tactical problems that arose immediately thereafter, when the Allies began their final offensive, became critical because of shortage of fuel. By 30th April it was not even possible to move tanks from the workshops where they had been repaired to the front, as no fuel could be spared. Even fighter aircraft, a large number of which had been transferred to Sicily from Tunisia, were used to transport petrol, but their capacity was small and the only cargo vessels larger than ferries and coastal craft which arrived in Tunis and Bizerta between 21st April and the end of the month were the 1,200-ton

German war transports. The war transports made as many as ten trips during the last half of the month and had only one loss. On the 28th General von Arnim reported that the administrative state of his Army Group could only be described as 'catastrophic'.

The largest vessel arriving and discharging its cargo in the first days of May was the *Belluno*, carrying 2,070 tons of supplies. She left Trapani at 7 p.m. on the 3rd May and arrived at Tunis at 7 a.m. next morning. But she was the last merchant ship to get through. During the next night *Nubian*, *Paladin* and *Petard* of Force K sank the *Campo Basso* and her torpedo-boat escort, *Perseo*, eight miles east of Kelibia. From Naples the *Campo Basso* had reached Trapani and then Pantelleria, from where she had hoped to dodge across to a beach near Cape Bon on which she could discharge guns, vehicles and 3,877 tons of supplies. Further afield, on the 5th, U.S. Fortresses sank the *San Antonio* off the north-west tip of Sicily. She had been bound from Naples to Bizerta with 5,600 tons of supplies. On the 7th, the day the Allied armies entered Tunis and Bizerta, the destroyer *Hermes*, severely damaged on 30th April in the air attacks which sank the *Pancaldo*, was bombed again and after being towed into Tunis roads was scuttled in La Goulette. The same day in Tunis itself R.A.F and U.S.A.A.F. bombers sank the 5,700-ton *Arlesiana*, and outside in the Gulf U.S. Kittyhawk fighter-bombers caught the *Belluno*, as she sought to escape, and sank her and her escort, the torpedo-boat *Tifone*. On the evening of the 7th the last three available German war transports, *KT5*, *9* and *21*, fully loaded with petrol and ammunition, left Trapani for the Cape Bon peninsula and all seaworthy craft down to open motor-boats were mobilized to take supplies through to the end. Of a number of U-boats diverted from other operations to act as fuel and store transports (each could carry twenty tons), only one reached the Tunisian coast and she was unable to find a suitable beach on which to discharge her cargo of ammunition. On the 9th, after steaming up and down the coast in search of discharging points, the three German transports were sunk, *KT5* and *21* by *Laforey*, *Tartar* and *Loyal* north of Cape Bon and *K9* by British and American aircraft north of Bizerta. The German Naval Commander in Tunisia had spent the evening of 8th May desperately trying to signal to the German transports, which were lying offshore, to jettison the equipment which they were carrying on deck so that they could get at the fuel cargo and throw it overboard, in the hope that it would be washed up on some attainable beach. The ships were however under constant air attack and he failed. Early the next morning Army Group reported that none of its formations could move because there was no fuel left.

This was the end to the blockade of supplies and reinforcements to Tunisia and the beginning of the blockade to ensure that nothing came out. For, on 8th May, Admiral Cunningham ordered operation 'Retribution', the destruction of all forces that might attempt to escape by sea, and made a memorable signal to his ships. 'Sink, burn and destroy. Let nothing pass'. The air forces had earlier issued a directive for their part in this operation.

The capture of many of the enemy's remaining Tunisian airfields set fighters free to cover warships in the Narrows and daylight destroyer patrols were begun, while coastal and Malta convoys were stopped temporarily so that their escorts could join in this final operation. It was arranged that the air forces were to continue to attack enemy shipping and small craft within five miles of the Tunisian shore, namely within range of enemy artillery, while surface forces were to have complete freedom of action elsewhere. By night the inshore area was to be occupied by patrols of motor gunboats and motor torpedo-boats of the United States and Royal Navies.

From 9th May onwards, some ten or twelve destroyers were constantly on patrol off the Cape Bon peninsula, and a like number of coastal craft in the inshore area by night. Air cover resulted in almost complete freedom from interference by enemy aircraft and there were few cases of mistaken identity, although it became necessary to order destroyers to paint their upperworks red to make recognition more certain. In an area which had been thickly sown with mines by both sides it was fortunate that no destroyers suffered damage. Most British mines, however, had been set to sink at the beginning of May and knowledge of enemy minefields was judged reliable enough to distinguish areas where the risk was great from those where it could be accepted. In the event, the enemy made very few attempts to escape. Some 800 Germans and Italians were captured from various small craft.

Minesweepers had been assembled at Bône as soon as the fall of Bizerta seemed imminent and by 11th May had swept a channel through to that port from the west. The advance Naval port party arrived on the 9th. Bizerta and the naval yard at Ferryville had been badly damaged and the entrance to the canal had been blocked with fourteen wrecks. A great British and American combined effort blasted a way through these obstructions and on 14th May 1,000 tons were unloaded. Already on the 10th, L.C.T. had been able to discharge their cargoes.

Meanwhile the main minesweeping task of clearing the whole Sicilian Channel was under way. The sweepers comprised the 12th, 13th and 14th Minesweeping Flotillas, two groups of minesweeping trawlers, and motor launches and motor minesweepers. By 15th May a channel two miles wide had been cleared from the Galita Channel around Cape Bon as far as Sousse and from there on to

Tripoli. This had been achieved at the price of one motor minesweeper sunk and the minesweeper *Fantome* damaged. The passage through the Mediterranean was clear and the first convoy from Gibraltar of four fast ships escorted by *Carlisle* and four destroyers reached Tripoli on the 22nd. At Tripoli four more merchant ships and additional destroyers joined and on the 26th, two years and fourteen days after operation 'Tiger', a through convoy again reached Alexandria. A regular series of through convoys in both directions now began.

Many were the calculations of what saving in shipping had been achieved by the opening of the Mediterranean. The principal gain was, of course, the tonnage saved in voyages to the Middle East and India for which the route around the Cape of Good Hope was no longer necessary. In addition there was the balance sheet for 'Torch,' the operation which had had so great a share in this happy result. This account was not so clearly advantageous. The Allied gain of French ships from French North African ports (around half a million tons) had to be set off against the greater number seized by the Axis in the Mediterranean ports of Metropolitan France (around 875,000 tons). Then there had been heavy Allied losses in 'Torch' itself (a quarter of a million tons), particularly in the first month, while at the same time the many ships drawn away from the North Atlantic traffic by the demands of 'Torch' reduced British imports by one million tons. The short term advantage to the Allies was not therefore great but the long term gain in time and hence tonnage was immense.

The Axis surrender in Tunisia made little difference to the activities of the Allied bombers except to free more of them for attacks on the ports and airfields of Sicily, Sardinia and the Italian mainland, and these attacks continued with devastating effect. By the end of May the figures for ships destroyed by air attack had far surpassed those for any previous month: twenty-six ships of over 500 G.R.T., totalling 75,000 tons, sunk in harbour and four, totalling 15,000 tons, at sea, with a further 100 or so smaller vessels, totalling 12,000 tons, most of which had been sunk during bombings of the ports. Because very few enemy ships put to sea it is not surprising that Allied submarines found few targets during May. Besides the losses of surface warships already mentioned, three Italian torpedo-boats were sunk during heavy air raids, the *Groppo* at Messina on the 25th, and the *Antares* and the *Bassini* in a devastating raid by 70 Fortresses on Leghorn on the 28th. Four German and two Italian U-boats were also lost in May, *U.447* sunk on the 7th by Hudsons of No. 233 Squadron R.A.F. west of Gibraltar, the *Mocenigo* in an air raid on Cagliari on the 13th, *U.303* by the British submarine *Sickle* off Toulon on the 21st, the *Gorgo* also on the 21st, by U.S.S. destroyer

Nields north of Oran, *U.414* near Cape Tenez on the 25th by the British corvette *Vetch*, and *U.755* on the 28th by a Hudson of No. 608 Squadron R.A.F. west of the Balearics.

There was still a sting left in the Axis attack which was not to be despised. On 1st May a large convoy from Alexandria was attacked by sixteen Heinkels north of Benghazi, shortly before it split into halves for Tripoli and Malta. The Commodore's ship, *Erinpura*, of 5,143 tons, and the tanker *British Trust*, of 8,466 tons, were sunk. *Erinpura* had on board 1,000 men of the Basuto Pioneer Corps of whom some 600 were lost. On the 8th Gibraltar experienced, once again, attack from Italian human torpedoes. This time three torpedoes manned by the customary two-man crew and armed with two warheads apiece were launched through the underwater doors which had been secretly constructed in the interned Italian merchant ship, *Olterra*, still lying alongside the jetty at Algeciras. In spite of vigilant British patrols and boisterous weather each crew succeeded in mining one target and three large merchant ships were severely damaged by the resulting explosions. The human torpedoes all returned to the *Olterra* in safety. On the 18th an attack by *U.414* on a United Kingdom slow convoy north-east of Cape Tenez sank the 5,979-ton *Empire Eve*. These were all the Allied merchant ship casualties in May, with the exception of the small 645-ton *Dorset Coast* which narrowly escaped a bomb only to be capsized by the explosion, and no Allied warships larger than coastal craft were lost.

A number of changes in British naval commands were brought about in May through Vice-Admiral Stuart Bonham-Carter falling sick. Rear-Admiral A. J. Power was appointed as Vice-Admiral Malta in his place, Rear-Admiral C. H. J. Harcourt succeeded Power in the 15th Cruiser Squadron, comprising *Newfoundland* (Flag), *Euryalus* and *Orion*, and Captain W. G. Agnew, as Commodore, succeeded Harcourt in the 12th Cruiser Squadron, comprising *Aurora* (Broad Pennant), *Penelope*, *Sirius*, *Cleopatra* and *Delhi*. At Gibraltar during May the battleships *King George V* and *Howe* arrived to relieve *Rodney* and *Nelson* and on the 7th Rear-Admiral A. W. La T. Bissett hoisted his flag in *King George V* as Rear-Admiral Force H. Towards the end of the month Vice-Admiral Willis returned for the time being to the U.K. in *Nelson*. An important change in Italian naval appointments had taken place during April when Admiral Angelo Iachino, who had been Commander-in-Chief Afloat for more than two years, was succeeded by his second-in-command, Admiral Carlo Bergamini.

The opening up towards the end of May of the ports of Tunis and Bizerta and the surer protection which could be afforded to Allied convoys now that all Tunisia was in Allied hands, meant that men and supplies could be brought to Bizerta and Tunis without transhipment into small ships at Algiers or Oran. Small ports such as Bône, Bougie and Sousse consequently lost some of their importance in the chain of communications, yet remained just as busy because they became increasingly absorbed in the training and administrative arrangements for 'Husky'. Preparations for this next step were already well advanced—it was only two months ahead. Admiral Sir Bertram Ramsay, who was to be the Senior Naval Officer in command of the British landings, had arrived with his staff and established his headquarters in Cairo as long ago as 1st March. At the end of April two Combined Operations Headquarters ships, *Bulolo* flying the flag of Rear-Admiral T. H. Troubridge and *Largs* that of Rear-Admiral R. R. McGrigor, had arrived at Aden in company with a number of Landing Ships. In home waters a third Headquarters Ship for the Sicilian landings, H.M.S. *Hilary*, was shortly to hoist the flag of Rear-Admiral Sir Philip Vian. Among the preliminaries deemed necessary to ensure the success of 'Husky' was the capture of Pantelleria, where it was hoped to base some of the fighters for support of the western landings, and on the 13th and 31st May the cruiser *Orion* bombarded the island with the object of testing the strength of its defences. The assault on the island was not, however, to begin until the second week of June and the story will therefore be told in the next volume of this history.

On 21st May, Malta, which of all the bases earmarked for use in the Sicilian landings was to be the most important, was bombed for the first time since December 1942 and another raid followed on the 31st. Unlike so many that Malta had earlier experienced, these bombings caused little, if any, damage.

During the months of March, April and May Malta's aircraft had destroyed an estimated total of 64 German aircraft in the air and on the ground—almost equal numbers of fighters, bombers and air transports. It is also possible that Malta was responsible for a considerable proportion of the 38 German aircraft lost on operations in that general area of the Mediterranean, though by whose hand is not ascertainable. Italian losses are unknown. Malta's own casualties amounted to an estimated total of fifty-three aircraft, just over half of which were fighters and fighter-bombers.

It is fitting to end the story of the North African campaign, so far as maritime events are concerned, with references to Malta. Earlier in this chapter something has been said of the interplay of fortunes on land and sea and in the air and of the dominating role played by Malta—a role long sustained with great hardship. Admiral Cunningham's message to the island, as he was about to relinquish his Mediterranean Command in April 1942, in which he stressed Malta's offensive role against enemy shipping is apt. '. . . The very extent of the success of the forces based on Malta [he wrote] has led to the ceaseless battering of the fortress, but one has only to think of the air effort the enemy is diverting to this purpose to realize that this is but another of the services that Malta is rendering to the Empire.'[1] The enemy was equally conscious of Malta's importance. Rommel himself recorded, 'Malta has the lives of many thousands of German and Italian soldiers on its conscience'.

Happily the days of Malta's battering and starvation were now over and with them the leading role so long played by Malta-based submarines in attacking enemy shipping had gradually passed to the aircraft although the score of each in terms of tonnage sunk was about equal. Surface forces, too, had used Malta as their principal base for anti-shipping operations when conditions permitted. They had had several spectacular successes, devastating to enemy morale and effective over a long term as a deterrent to enemy movement by sea. Towards the end North African bases as well as Malta had been used increasingly by air and sea forces alike. Mention must also be made of the mining operations which in the last months had added a note of nightmare to the hazards of Axis convoys. As will be seen in the next volume of this series, Malta was to contribute much to the Allies' plans in the Mediterranean. The island was to hold a key-position in the invasion of Sicily.

---

[1] Admiral of the Fleet Viscount Cunningham: *A Sailor's Odyssey*, (London 1951) p. 460.

CHAPTER XVII

'...WE ARE MASTERS OF THE NORTH AFRICAN SHORES.'
(22nd April to 15th May 1943)

See Map 37

1ST and 8th Armies, composing 18th Army Group, and the entire North West African Tactical Air Force directly supporting them, now were gathered together. Their prey was in front of them, but still full of fight, and the chase was not to end in an eagle's kill. Battles seldom end in that way. In Tunisia the final act was a series of battles, without well marked stages, and occurring over a period of nearly three weeks. Therefore a short summary will help the narrative.

The enemy held the perimeter of his bridgehead from the northern coast near Kef Abbed to the Gulf of Hammamet near Enfidaville. In between, the line ran across all sorts of country—from Djebels Azzag and Ajred, across the broken and hilly country rising to the long ridge of Djebel Ang and Heidous, across the Medjerda River east of Medjez, taking in Djebel Bou Aoukaz, across the plain of Goubellat to a spear-point below Djebel Mansour and skirting Djebel Fkirine to Enfidaville and the sea. 1st Army attempted to break the northern part of this perimeter in an almost simultaneous offensive by three of its Corps, its fourth joining in three days later. 8th Army attacked the southern part of the perimeter with one Corps. Thus in 1st Army, on 22nd April, 9th Corps tried to break through the plain of Goubellat. A few miles away on this Corps' left flank, 5th Corps attacked on both sides of the Medjerda River on 23rd April, and between 5th Corps' left flank and the northern coast 2nd U.S. Corps attacked, also on 23rd April. On the right flank of 18th Army Group, 8th Army's 10th Corps attacked northwards from Enfidaville, on 22nd April. On 25th April, 1st Army's 19th (French) Corps, between its parent army and the 8th, attacked towards Pont du Fahs and Zaghouan.

Almost all these offensives, which must be considered as one though their courses are diverse, brought on hard, often bitter, fighting. Allied victory was certain, but towards the end of April the general offensive was slowing down and it was clear that the victory was not coming in exactly the shape planned. General Alexander paused, checked the 8th Army's attack, reinforced 1st Army from 8th, and with 1st Army delivered a final stroke on 6th May. von Arnim's defence was cracking and therefore there was no dramatic climax on the battlefield. The enemy broke into groups which, in one week more, were cornered or hunted into surrender.

General Alexander's intentions for the general offensive (named 'Vulcan'), expressed in his directive of 16th April were:

'... First Army will:
(a) Capture Tunis.
(b) Co-operate with 2 U.S. Corps in the capture of Bizerta.
(c) Be prepared to co-operate with Eighth Army should the enemy withdraw to Cap Bon Peninsula.
2nd U.S. Corps will:
(a) Secure suitable positions for the attack on Bizerta, covering the left flank of First Army.
(b) Advance and capture Bizerta with the co-operation of First Army on their right flank ...'

Alexander tactfully met American wishes by keeping 2nd U.S. Corps formally under his own command, but in fact authorised Anderson to give to it all necessary orders and instructions.

Alexander's directions to Montgomery were:

'... Eighth Army will:
(a) draw enemy forces off First Army by exerting continuous pressure on the enemy
(b) by an advance on the axis Enfidaville—Hammamet—Tunis prevent the enemy withdrawing into the Cap Bon Peninsula ...'

April 22nd was fixed as the offensive's opening date.

Air Marshal Coningham's whole tactical air force was to support 18th Army Group in Vulcan. No. 242 Group R.A.F., U.S. XII Air Support Command and North West African Tactical Bomber Force were to work with 1st Army, and the Western Desert Air Force with 8th Army though this allotment was alterable. Coningham planned first to neutralize the hostile air forces by bombing 'round-the-clock', beginning on the night 18th/19th April, their seven principal airfields and two main air transport bases.[1] N.A.S.A.F. was asked to tackle the airfields outside Africa from which reinforcements usually came, e.g. Bari, and to intercept air transports on passage. N.A.C.A.F. was asked to continue the intruder operations of its Beaufighters. The main object of the second part of Coningham's

---

[1] 'Airfield' here denotes groups e.g. of landing grounds as well as single fields.

plan was directly to help the land forces. Therefore the day-bombers and low-flying fighters were continuously to attack targets in the battle area. N.A.S.A.F. was asked to engage targets outside this area. There was to be constant air reconnaissance during both stages of the plan.

So much for N.A.T.A.F., but in fact the whole Mediterranean Air Command, unified, experienced, and formidable was to make an onslaught upon the enemy in Tunisia, and outside it at those points, whatever their nature, which chiefly sustained him. Air Chief Marshal Tedder's 3,241 operational aircraft represented air power of a different order from that of Air Marshal Longmore's 370 in 1940. The German Air Force, though greatly outnumbered and in process of withdrawing from Tunisia, was game but virtually on its own. For it is the harsh truth that the contribution of the Italian Air Force was now almost valueless.

Before continuing the story from the Allied side it is worth while to glance at the enemy. Kesselring on April 20th issued an Order of the Day in which he said that the Allies were flexing their muscles for a decisive blow in the Mediterranean and might try to set foot on European soil as well. However if every German soldier justified the reliance of Führer and Fatherland upon him by fighting, in an historic hour, with bravery and unshakeable resolution, '...we shall destroy the enemy's hopes and victory will be ours.' von Arnim echoed Kesselring in a similar Order.

No Orders however altered the fact, described in previous chapters, that the muscles of the Axis had wasted severely for want of nourishment. On 23rd April, to take a single example, Army Group's opinion was that shortage of fuel paralysed all except local tactics. Yet on the same day Kesselring sent an appreciation to Dönitz, Jodl and Göring, of which the gist was that Army Group Africa, in spite of the Allies' numerical superiority could hold the Tunisian bridgehead provided that large amounts of ammunition, fuel, and new weapons were sent to it. Dönitz shared Kesselring's views, but it is unlikely that this appreciation had much practical effect in high quarters. Had not the Dictators already ruled that Tunisia was to be held until the end? Between 20th April and 4th May no merchant ships reached Tunisia although small craft sneaked to and fro. Mussolini, at the end of April, reluctantly released some destroyers for the service of supply, but these were soon withdrawn because they attracted fierce air attacks.

In view of the disaster which befell Army Group Africa, a word about evacuation is relevant. A general evacuation of Tunisia was contrary to the policy of the High Commands and though discussed, was not seriously contemplated, so that on 16th April Kesselring told Messe '... there can no longer be any question of getting away 300,000 men.' In Rome there had been some inconclusive conferences about withdrawing valuable specialists and officers, but when General Schmundt, Chief of the German Army Personnel Branch, proposed this to Jodl, the latter rejected it after consultation with Kesselring. Mussolini, who was assured by Kesselring on 4th May that the Tunisian stuation was not desperate, on the 5th refused a scheme secretly to withdraw selected commanders and staffs. Thereafter it was taken for granted that everyone would stay at his post. According to Warlimont, unpalatable information was expunged from reports of operations in Tunisia before these were shown to Hitler, and it was not until the 7th May (according to Goebbels) that the Führer judged the situation to be 'pretty hopeless'.

Since Alexander had decided to use 1st Army to capture Tunis and Bizerta, to that army we return. Re-grouping it for the offensive had exacted difficult staff-work, nowhere better performed than by the British-American staffs in moving 2nd U.S. Corps from Tebessa to near Djebel Abiod. This formation, some 90,000 strong, together with 1st British Armoured Division moving north to join 9th Corps, went north in four days, at a rate of 2,400 vehicles a day, across 1st Army's heavily-used east-west roads and railways, without blocking them. To the air forces goes the credit for that protection from aerial attack which made the move possible.

General Anderson's main formations were:

5th Corps (Lieut.-General C. W. Allfrey)
  1st British Infantry Division (Major-General W. E. Clutterbuck);
  4th Infantry Division (Major-General J.L.I. Hawkesworth);
  78th Infantry Division (Major-General V. Evelegh);
  25th Tank Brigade (Brigadier R. H. Maxwell)less 51st R.T.R.
9th Corps (Lieut.-General J. T. Crocker, then Lieut.-General B. G. Horrocks)
  1st British Armoured Division (Major-General R. Briggs);
  6th Armoured Division (Major-General C. F. Keightley);
  46th Infantry Division (Major-General H. A. Freeman-Attwood);
  51st R.T.R. (Lieut.-Colonel R. B. Holden).
2nd U.S. Corps (Lieut.-General Omar N. Bradley)[1]
  1st U.S. Armoured Division (Major General Ernest N. Harmon), less one armoured regiment;
  1st U.S. Infantry Division (Major-General Terry de la M. Allen);

---

[1] Lieut.-General Omar N. Bradley succeeded Lieut.-General George S. Patton in command of 2nd Corps on 15th April, because General Patton was required to take over the American 7th Army for the invasion of Sicily.

9th U.S. Infantry Division (Major-General Manton S. Eddy);
34th Infantry Division (Major-General Charles W. Ryder);
1st, 2nd, 3rd Bns Corps Franc d'Afrique (Colonel Magnan);
4th and 6th Tabors marocains (Captain Verlet, Major Labataille).[1]

19th French Corps (General Koeltz) Division du Maroc (General Mathenet);
Division d'Alger (General Conne);
Division d'Oran (General Boissau);
Armoured Group (General Le Coulteux);
1st King's Dragoon Guards (Lieut.-Colonel M. J. Lindsay).[2]

The administrative state of the army was undoubtedly satisfactory, except for stocks of 25-pdr artillery ammunition. 343,000 rounds were allotted, virtually the entire amount in North Africa, though 105,000 rounds were expected from the United Kingdom at the end of April. In fact ammunition expenditure in 'Vulcan' proved to be very great, by 24th April some rationing was introduced, salvage dumps were scoured, and 100,000 rounds were borrowed from 8th Army. The end of the campaign came, however, before a crisis about shells.

General Anderson had not changed his intention of annihilating or capturing the forces opposed to him. He thought that the enemy's vitals (to put it that way) lay in the area Peter's Corner (a well-known point on the Tunis road, eight miles east of Medjez el Bab)—Longstop Hill—El Bathan and Massicault In fact he was correct. South of a line from approximately Massicault to Goubellat was Hermann Göring Division, and north of this line was 334th Division, whose positions then ran north-east, including Longstop and Djebel Ang. 10th Panzer Division came into the area on Hermann Göring's left flank on 22nd April. In this area was the Sebkret el Kourzia, and west of it, the hills fringing the Goubellat plain. Anderson planned his attack on this part of his front as follows. 5th Corps was to take the line approximately Djebel Ang, Longstop Hill, thence to Peter's Corner, and then to push on to El Bathan—Massicault. At the same time, 9th Corps was to capture with its infantry the entrances to the Goubellat plain. Then its two armoured divisions were to push quickly north-east towards Massicault. Anderson judged it likely that the enemy would commit his armour east of the Medjerda, and he intended 9th Corps' armour to engage

---

[1] The Corps Franc d'Afrique had been raised in 1942 at the instance of General Giraud. The officers were mostly French reservists; the men included Frenchmen resident in Algeria and Morocco, or who had escaped from France; pensioned Foreign Legionnaires; Moroccan and Algerian Mohammedans; Spanish political refugees.

A Tabor was a unit of Moroccan Irregulars under French officers. The men were known as *goumiers* from the Arabic word *qum* = a band or troop.

[2] Besides the French troops mentioned above, some 5,600 regulars and 14,000 irregulars were performing useful duties for the Allies by guarding communications, vital points, and depots in Morocco, Algeria, and Tunisia.

and destroy it, and then to cut off any enemy who were still opposing 5th Corps' advance to El Bathan—Massicault. The way to Tunis would then be open.

Next for Bizerta—the objective of 2nd U.S. Corps. This Corps was to cover 5th Corps' left flank by taking the high ground at Chouigui: simultaneously it was to advance on Bizerta by way of Sedjenane and Mateur, and also by the River Sedjenane. Between the Americans and Chouigui was about half of Weber's 334th Division, and on Weber's right was von Manteuffel Division.

There remains 1st Army's extreme east flank. Here was 19th Corps which, when ordered by Anderson, was to advance north-east on Pont du Fahs and Djebel Fkirine. In its path lay *D.A.K.* General Anderson expected severe fighting at first but that his whole offensive would succeed within nine days.

See also Map 39

On 17th April Schmid, acting commander of Hermann Göring Division, had suggested a spoiling attack, and on the 19th von Arnim approved. A strong force was collected, mainly from Hermann Göring and 334th Divisions.[1] During the small hours of 21st this force attacked at a place about five miles east of Medjez el Bab, called 'Banana Ridge' by the British, held by 1st British Division's 3rd Brigade, and at Djebel Djaffa five miles south of Medjez, held by 4th Division's 10th Brigade. British Intelligence had got wind of the plan, but there was none the less sharp fighting, and some danger to British artillery which was assembling far forward in readiness for 'Vulcan', before the enemy was beaten off with over 300 casualties. The spoiling attack spoiled nothing, and at 3.40 a.m. on 22nd April 9th Corps opened the offensive. 1st Army's four Corps entered the offensive at intervals like the voices in a quartette, and it will be simpler to follow them one by one.

46th Division attacked on a two-brigade front with the support of 224 guns and 51st R.T.R. Its objective was some low hills about three miles west of Sebkret el Kourzia, because once these were gripped, 6th Armoured Division could aim at penetrating about six miles deeper to an area which may be defined by two features— Djebel bou Kournine and Djebel es Srassif. 128th Brigade on the right found the enemy stubborn and well dug-in, and fell short; 138th Brigade on the left gained its objectives by noon. 6th Armoured Division therefore began to advance later than had been hoped, was

---

[1] The force included two battalions of Hermann Göring's Parachute Regiment, and one of its Grenadier Regiment 1; Grenadier Regiment 754 (334th Division); Panzer Regiment 7 (10th Panzer Division); *Panzerabteilung 501* (which on 20th April had 13 Tiger tanks operational).

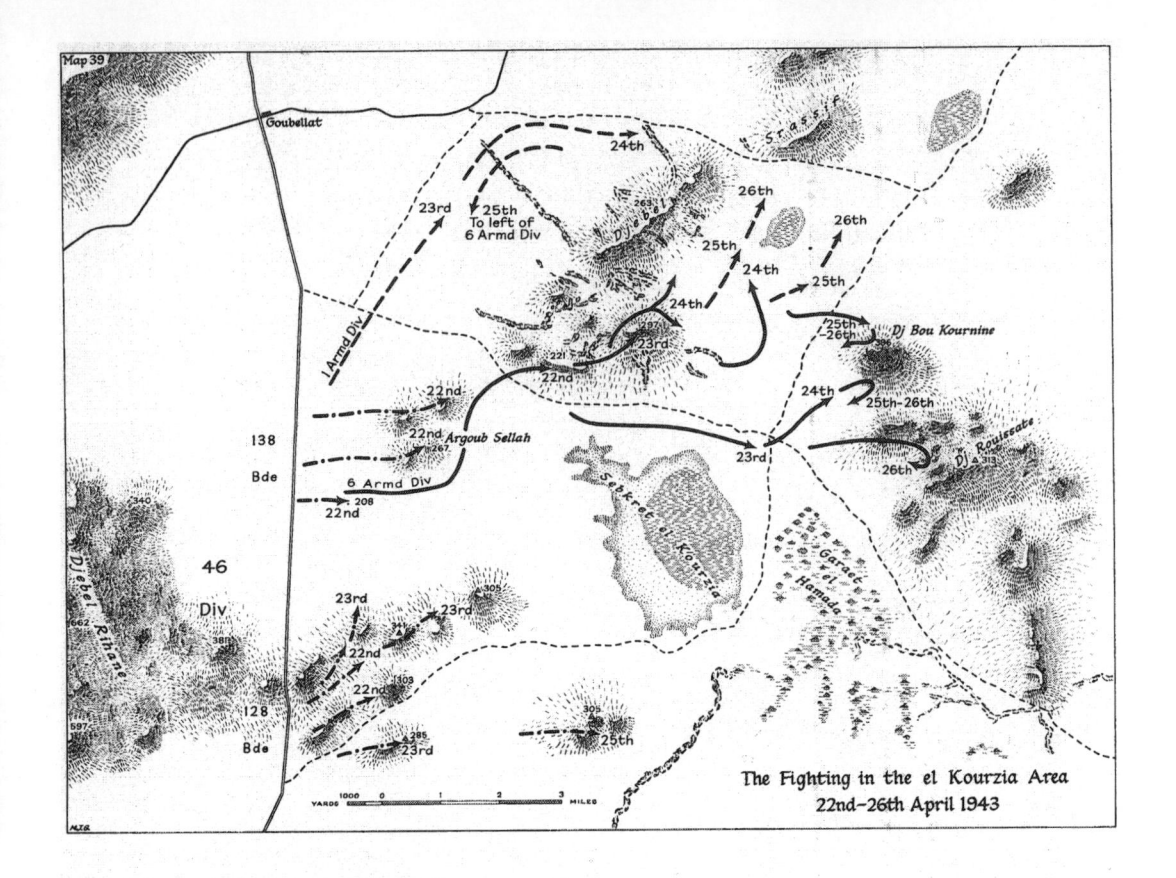

The Fighting in the el Kourzia Area
22nd–26th April 1943

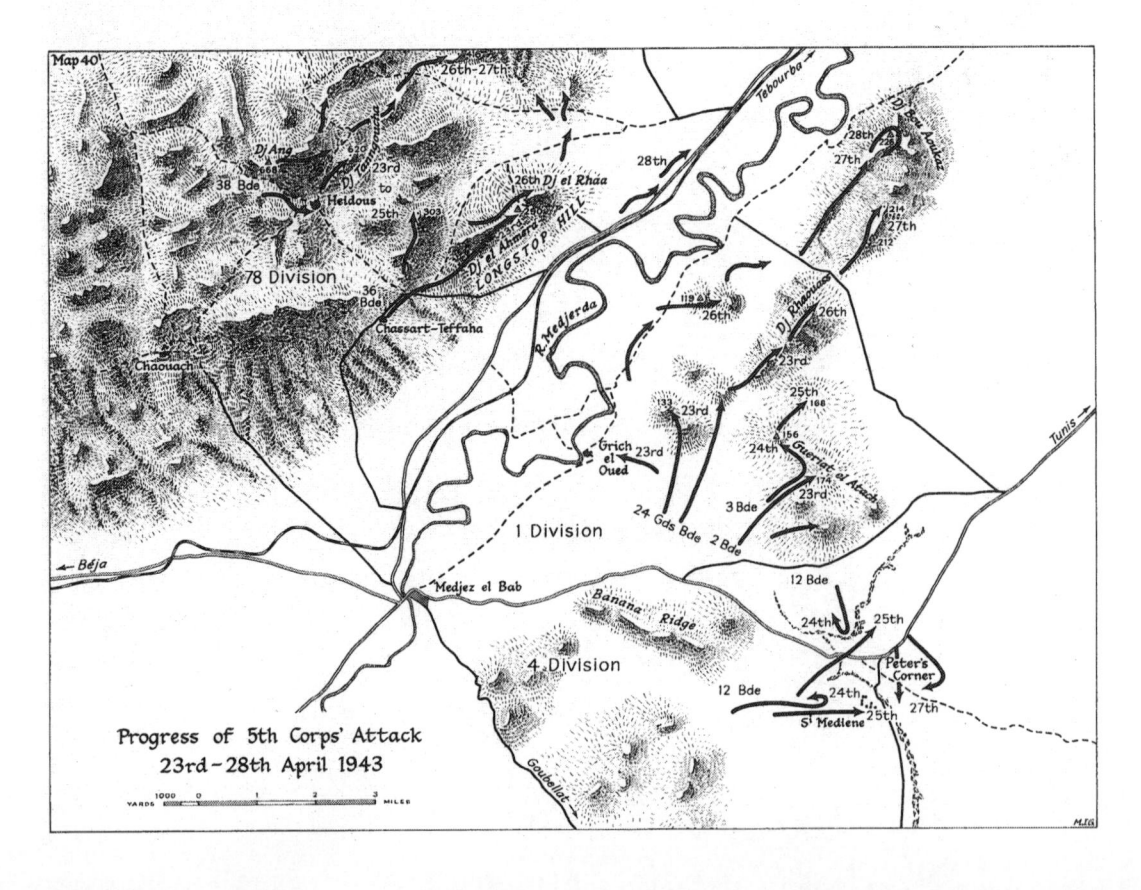

Progress of 5th Corps' Attack
23rd–28th April 1943

further delayed by difficult wadis, and got little beyond 138th Brigade's positions. The enemy however summed up the fighting as a deep penetration of Hermann Göring Division's positions which had been checked by his armour.[1]

On the 23rd April 6th Armoured Division had to face determined opposition, notably from Panzer Regiment 7 and *Panzer Abteilung 501*. Difficult ground again restrained manoeuvre and therefore progress was slow, yet ten miles in all had been gained by evening. 1st British Armoured Division had advanced, rather slowly because of the many mines scattered in standing crops, to a point west of Djebel es Srassif.

On the 24th 6th Armoured Division pressed 10th Panzer Division hard. Yet Crocker saw that the '... real but, no doubt, fleeting opportunity to thrust deep into enemy country and anticipate his reactions . . .' had passed. On the night 24th/25th he swung his 1st Armoured Division round behind the 6th and on the 25th began to pass it through that division. 6th Armoured then swung south against Djebel bou Kournine. Crocker's aim was to quicken the pace by thrusting hard with both divisions on a narrower front. But the Hermann Göring and 10th Panzer Divisions held on stubbornly, taking full advantage of the ground which offered hull-down positions

---

[1] *46th Division.* Main Formations:
   128th Infantry Brigade (Brigadier M. A. James).
      1st/4th and 2nd/4th Hampshire Regiment; 5th Hampshire Regiment.
   138th Infantry Brigade (Brigadier G. P. Harding).
      6th Bn The Lincolnshire Regiment; 2nd/4th The King's Own Yorkshire Light Infantry; 6th Bn The York and Lancashire Regiment.
   139th Infantry Brigade (Brigadier R. E. H. Stott).
      2nd/5th Leicestershire Regiment; 16th Bn The Durham Light Infantry; 5th Bn The Sherwood Foresters.
      46th Reconnaissance Regiment; 70th, 71st, 172nd Field Regiments R.A.; 58th A/Tk Regiment R.A.; 115th L.A.A. Regiment R.A.; 270th, 271st, 272nd Field Companies R.E.
6th Armoured Division. Main Formations:
   26th Armoured Brigade (Brigadier G. P. B. Roberts).
      16th/5th Lancers; 17th/21st Lancers; 2nd Lothian and Border Horse; 10th Rifle Brigade.
   1st Guards Brigade (Brigadier S. A. Foster).
      3rd Grenadier Guards; 2nd Coldstream Guards; 3rd Welsh Guards.
      1st Derbyshire Yeomanry; 12th Regiment R.H.A.; 152nd Field Regiment R.A.; 72nd A/Tk Regiment R.A.; 51st L.A.A. Regiment R.A.; 8th and 625th Field Squadrons R.E.
1st British Armoured Division. Main Formations:
   2nd Armoured Brigade (Brigadier R. C. G. Joy).
      The Queen's Bays; 9th Lancers; 10th Hussars; 9th Bn The King's Own Yorkshire Light Infantry (The Yorkshire Dragoons).
      Tank Strength on 25th April 1943; Sherman and Grant 81, Crusader II 17, Crusader III 18.
   7th Motor Brigade (Brigadier T. J. B. Bosville).
      1st Bn The King's Royal Rifle Corps; 2nd The Rifle Brigade; 7th The Rifle Brigade.
      12th Lancers; 2nd, 4th, 11th (H.A.C.) Regiments R.H.A.; 76th A/Tk Regiment R.A.; 42nd Light A.A. Regiment R.A.; 1st and 7th Field Squadrons R.E.; 1st Bn Royal Northumberland Fusiliers.

to tanks, and lurking-places pleasing to anti-tank guns, mortars and machine guns. Though the enemy was beginning to fear a breakthrough, his defence continued resolutely during the 26th.

Anderson meanwhile had been thinking of drawing 9th Corps closer in towards 5th Corps, and directing it on Tunis by an axis north of Djebel es Srassif. 5th Corps, as will be related, was making steady gains, and on the 26th Anderson, after a visit to Crocker, translated some of his thought into action. He directed 6th Armoured Division into Army Reserve for the purpose of exploiting in 5th Corps' sector, and ordered Crocker to go on trying to advance north-eastwards with 1st British Armoured and 46th Divisions. 9th Corps' attack had not fulfilled his hopes but was certainly fulfilling a large part of his purpose by inflicting upon the enemy losses which he could not afford; for example 10th Panzer Division was reduced to about 25 'fit' German tanks, and perhaps ten Italian.

See also Map 40

5th Corps, after earlier preliminaries, attacked on 23rd April on both sides of the Medjerda. 78th Division had attempted Longstop Hill and the Tanngoucha ridge nine days earlier, and now its 36th Brigade was to attack the first, and its 38th Brigade the second, of these features.[1] It may be that the ghosts of good soldiers gathered to watch—soldiers of the 1st Guards Brigade, the U.S. 18th Infantry, 69th Panzer Grenadiers and 754th Grenadiers, and others, valiant dust on the 'Christmas Mountain.'

During the night 22nd/23rd April the Royal West Kents and the Buffs won a part of the western slopes but too late for the Argylls to continue the advance under cover of dark. Therefore this battalion went in by day and in spite of heavy artillery support had many casualties. Nevertheless Major J. T. McK. Anderson took the survivors of the assault companies forward until with thirty men he captured the western summit. For this feat he was awarded the V.C. Reinforcements came up and by evening the hills except Djebel el Rhaa had been taken. An attempt to storm this during the night failed.

By this time the enemy had turned Heidous into a most unpleasant place—machine guns and mortars tucked in among the machicolated rocks were well nigh impossible to spot and to neutralize although

---

[1] *36th Infantry Brigade* (Brigadier B. Howlett). Main Units:
5th Bn The Buffs; 6th Bn The Royal West Kent Regiment; 8th Bn The Argyll and Sutherland Highlanders.
38th Infantry Brigade (Brigadier N. Russell).
6th Bn The Royal Inniskilling Fusiliers,
1st Bn The Royal Irish Fusiliers;
2nd Bn The London Irish Rifles.

112 field guns, 16 mediums, 4 heavy, and 6 3·7″ howitzers were in support. 38th Brigade's three battalions fought all day on 23rd April and into the night. A company of the Inniskillings reached the top of Tanngoucha and was dislodged by a counter-attack. The enemy confirms that the fighting was hard. On the 24th 78th Division paused to reorganize.

We must now step back to the day before (23rd) and to 1st Infantry Division on the right bank of the Medjerda. Its first objectives were a ridge of low hills between Grich el Oued and Gueriat el Atach. 2nd Infantry Brigade, supported by five field regiments, one medium regiment, and three heavy batteries, reached Gueriat el Atach easily but found the ground too hard for quick digging-in. The Germans counter-attacked very quickly with infantry and tanks under heavy mortar bombardment. 2nd Brigade lost some ground and then retook it, but at length was pressed backward along the ridge. The fighting was heavy and the casualties amounted to 57 killed, 262 wounded, and 190 missing, while 142nd Royal Armoured Corps which had come up in support ended the day with only 16 undamaged tanks out of 45, though only 8 men were killed and 11 wounded. Lieutenant W. A. S. Clarke, 1st Loyals won a posthumous V.C., dying within a few feet of a machine-gun after destroying several others single-handed.

On 24th April 4th Division entered the battle on 1st Division's right. The 12th Infantry Brigade attacked towards Peter's Corner to prepare the way for a deeper thrust by 10th Brigade. Here too the enemy fought hard, and 10th Brigade did not get its opportunity. On the afternoon of this day, in 1st Division, 3rd Infantry Brigade recaptured quite easily the whole Gueriat el Atach ridge, only to be plagued by tanks, mortars, and *nebelwerfers* hidden in near-by fields of growing corn. The ridge was securely held, though the 2nd Sherwood Foresters and 1st K.S.L.I. had 329 casualties between them. The casualties on Gueriat el Atach have been given to illustrate a point, often forgotten, about the infantry battalion of World War II. The number of very necessary 'specialists' was high; therefore a 'rifle' company—and it was the rifle companies who usually took most knocks—was in theory no more than 127 strong, and in practice very much less. Casualties therefore quite soon unbalanced a battalion as a fighting instrument, even though its fighting spirit was unimpaired.

Since the 23rd 2nd U.S. Corps, on the northern flank in difficult country, had been fighting towards Djebel Ajred and Djebel Azzag.

von Arnim, taking account of the fact that the Allies had not broken through, and assessing their losses as heavy, yet saw that *Pz AOK 5's* main defences had been penetrated at several points, and that it had not enough reserves to wipe out the intruders. He therefore ordered this Army to retire about five miles during the night 24th/25th, and *D.A.K.* to new positions pivoting on Pont du Fahs.[1] These movements were completed on the 25th. On this date *AOK 1*, which had already been ordered to send to von Vaerst (now commanding *Pz AOK 5*) the two German Reconnaissance Units, and all its armour (15 German tanks and 29 Italian armoured fighting vehicles) was told to send as well 90th Light Division's Engineer Battalion, two weak Bersaglieri battalions, and a little less than four German and Italian batteries.

von Arnim's re-dispositions explain a lull on 25th during which 78th Division occupied Tanngoucha and Heidous, though the enemy stayed—uneasily, one imagines—on Djebel el Rhaa. 1st and 4th Divisions patrolled; 2nd U.S. Corps went on advancing in spite of some administrative troubles; in 19th Corps the Division du Maroc and the Division d'Alger began to move on Pont du Fahs.

Meanwhile, as will be told later, large attacks by 8th Army at Enfidaville had been discontinued and there were differences of opinion about what it should do next.

On 26th April 1st and 4th Divisions had sharp, though small, actions at points in the enemy's new positions. 36th Brigade (78th Division) took Djebel el Rhaa—5th Buffs advancing along the upper slopes of Longstop Hill, while B Squadron and two troops of A Squadron North Irish Horse pushed their tanks through on the lower slopes. A patrol of the Argylls and another squadron of tanks caused a diversion on the other flank. This neat co-operation and the appearance of Churchill tanks on such unlikely ground were quickly successful. On the 27th 4th Division's 12th Brigade made some ground north-east of Peter's Corner but in the evening a strong counter-attack by the Hermann Göring's Parachute Regiment and tanks dislodged 6th Black Watch and almost wiped out a squadron of 12th R.T.R. The 24th Guards Brigade (1st Division) just failed to carry Djebel Bou Aoukaz on the east bank of the Medjerda. The French were now approaching the road Pont du Fahs—Enfidaville; on the far northern flank the Americans entered Sidi Nsir. 9th Corps was still engaged north-east of Sebkret el Kourzia. Its commander General Crocker was accidentally wounded during a demonstration of the capricious PIAT and Major-General R. Briggs took over.

von Arnim and von Vaerst this day agreed that the situation was extremely serious. The thrusts made by 1st and 78th Divisions in 334th Divisions' sector, and the American advance against von Manteuffel were very dangerous because there were no reserves. All troops were unmistakably exhausted and strengths were dropping.

---

[1] *D.A.K.* at this time had under command 21st Panzer Division, parts of 999th Division, and Superga Division.

von Arnim concluded that if supplies were the yardstick, he could maintain his defence only for a 'very limited period'.

Next day, the 28th, the only important event was that 24th Guards Brigade, after a morning's fighting, took Djebel Bou Aoukaz but was counter-attacked and dislodged by a battle-group led by Oberst Irckens of Panzer Regiment 8.[1] In the fighting for Djebel Bou Aoukaz two V.Cs were won. On the 27th Captain The Lord Lyell, 1st Scots Guards, as the climax of several gallant acts, destroyed an 8·8-cm gun and crew but himself was killed. On the 29th Lance-Corporal J. Kenneally, 1st Irish Guards, saw a number of German infantry preparing to counter-attack, charged like a one-man whirlwind and dispersed them and, unhurried and unhurt, rejoined his platoon.

During the eight days 22nd to 29th April, No. 242 Group R.A.F., U.S. XII A.S.C., and N.A.T.B.F. (reinforced on occasion by N.A.S.A.F.) had most actively supported 1st Army. Though the weather had been unfavourable or bad for flying on five days, only on the 24th had the sorties flown fallen to 229, which may be compared with a daily average of 650. The battle-area was small in proportion to the numbers of aircraft in the air, but the choice of targets was great—headquarters, enemy positions, troops on the move, guns, tanks, vehicles, and focal points on road and rail on the fronts of 9th, 5th and 2nd U.S. Corps. For example, on the 22nd 24 British Bostons bombed enemy positions in the area of Longstop Hill and east of it, and 90 American Bostons other positions between Medjez el Bab and Tebourba as well as guns elsewhere; a task shared by 36 American Kittyhawk fighter-bombers. An equal force of Hurricane fighter-bombers attacked the railway station at Sidi Nsir and enemy positions on Djebel Azzag. Next day, in better weather, the effort was much greater and the targets more varied, but on the 24th the bombers were grounded because their airfields were hemmed in by the cloud-covered surrounding hills. These conditions, perversely, suited the enemy because his airfields in the plain were free from such hazards, and the poor visibility enabled his pilots to play tip and run, but the weather did not prevent the Allied fighters carrying out low-flying attacks, and patrols and sweeps over the battle area. Unfortunately that same day (the 24th) also demonstrated again how accurate was the enemy's *flak* which shot down no less than ten Spitfires. In contrast, and though the weather was far from perfect, the 25th proved to be a very good day for air support, 1,629 sorties

---

[1] Irckens's Battle Group had begun to form on 27th April. Its composition indicates the difficulties of *Pz AOK 5* in finding reserves. Detachments Panzer Regiments 5, 7, 8; one coy *Panzer Abteilung 501*; 2nd Bn Grenadier Regiment 47; C.-in-C's escort (2¼ platoons); one anti-tank company; one battery (8 guns); two A.A. batteries (13 8·8-cm guns); some unspecified Italian tanks; 5 Italian guns.

being flown by the Allied tactical air forces (including W.D.A.F.) in support of the armies. A particularly successful bombing attack was made by 30 British Bostons against troops, tanks, A.F.Vs and guns holding up 6th Armoured Division which had also had the benefit of fighter-bomber support. From the 26th to the 28th the pilots had to contend with poor visibility and on the 29th the weather was bad. Nevertheless a great many sorties were flown during these four days, and despite the conditions on the 29th No. 242 Group R.A.F., at the request of 1st Army, carried out concentrated and continuous attacks in the Ksar Tyr area from early afternoon until dusk.

Throughout, the fighters kept up constant attacks, as did the fighter-bombers which were less handicapped than the day-bombers by the weather and they kept up a steady average of about five attacks daily. The daily tactical reconnaissance work by American and British aircraft, which maintained a close watch on enemy movements, was very valuable. The record of sorties given in the footnote tells its own tale.[1] By night N.A.T.B.F. made the best of the weather to keep up the pressure by attacking roads leading from Tunis to the front. The Bisleys were out on three occasions flying a total of 52 sorties, and the French LeO 45s twice flying a total of 12. The Beaufighters ranged over the whole of northern Tunisia, as well as the battle area, and only once were they grounded by the weather —three German and most probably three Italian aircraft fell to their guns.

The enemy air forces fought stubbornly, the Germans being by far the more prominent. Their fighters were encountered on many occasions, and their Ju. 88 bombers and strafing aircraft, including Hs. 129s and Me. 210s, turned the weather to advantage when they could and there was plenty of opportunity, particularly on the 24th when at least half of the 30 Allied tanks lost were accounted for by air attack. On the 25th enemy air activity noticeably increased, most probably because the German reconnaissance aircraft had observed the Allied movements from the south to the Sebkret el

---

[1] Sorties flown (excluding the tactical contribution by N.A.S.A.F.).

	No. 242 Group R.A.F.	U.S. XII A.S.C.	N.A.T.B.F. (day)	TOTALS
22nd April	334	171	126	631
23rd April	429	191	199	819
24th April	194	35	—	229
25th April	445	316	124	885
26th April	298	258	96	652
27th April	349	225	124	698
28th April	395	205	118	718
29th April	291	206	72	569
	2,735	1,607	859	5,201

Kourzia sector, and next day 108 enemy aircraft were counted in the air. But on the 29th few were seen, no doubt because of the weather.

Some idea of the severity of the fighting in the air and of the opposition from the ground during daylight in a quite small area can be formed from the aircraft losses on both sides, in these operations alone, in the eight days: Allied 50 (eleven of them to A.A. fire); German 25 (two to A.A. fire); Italian most probably two. The Allies also lost one by night; the Germans three in the air and seven on the ground outside the immediate battle area, and three at night; and the Italians most probably three at night, too.

By 29th April Alexander and Anderson knew that 5th Corps' offensive was slowing down. By coincidence Gause, von Arnim's Chief of Staff, wrote at this time that experience showed that the British maintained the momentum and drive of a major offensive for two or three days. If then they had not achieved unmistakable success they paused, on the defensive, for from four to six days and reorganized their troops and supplies for a fresh effort. Alexander and Anderson were now thinking seriously of a half-formed plan of Anderson's for a direct drive on Tunis, using 6th Armoured and 78th Divisions, and possibly 1st British Armoured Division. Alexander had these thoughts for the armour '... tk. losses must be accepted, atk guns will be found in olive groves etc., there will not be a clean gap, but using all the artillery support they can ... and with their power of manoeuvre they must get on with it ...' But before Anderson could put his ideas into definite shape the details, if not the broad intention, were much affected by the situation of 8th Army.

See also Map 38

The understandable failure of N.Z. and 4th Indian Divisions to plunge into the mountains north of Takrouna and Djebel Garci caused General Montgomery to decide on 21st April that 10th Corps should advance for about three miles astride the coast road and then swing westward. It was proposed that 4th Indian Division, the N.Z. Division, and 56th Division should undertake this task. 56th (London) Division (Major-General E. G. Miles) had just arrived, or rather its 169th Brigade, because 167th Brigade did not reach the forward area until the 28th. The division had come overland from Kirkuk in Iraq, a journey of 3,200 miles in 32 days. It was without experience in battle because it had not left England until August 1942 when it was sent to Middle East and then to Persia and Iraq Command.¹ Neither General Tuker nor General Freyberg liked the plan. Tuker pointed out that Garci was costly to hold but presumed that, as an observation point, it had been counted worth the cost. He thought that the plan suggested would split 10th Corps, disperse its resources and leave Garci isolated. But the alternative was drab: to subdue the enemy's positions in the hills one by one, until the way was clear to send the armour through. The 'fact was that there was no battle to be won in these parts . . .' Horrocks has since declared that both he and Montgomery disliked the plan but that Montgomery had told him to carry on with preparations because it was essential for the 8th Army to break through. Both of them, Horrocks continues, felt that the 1st Army's front was where the main effort should be made. Montgomery, it is true, in a signal of the 29th, told Alexander that he was '. . . not happy about present plan for finishing off this business . . .' yet three days earlier he had told Freyberg that 'the big issues are so vital that we have got to force this through here.' During this rather perplexing time he was absent in Cairo between 23rd and 26th April in order to examine plans for the Sicilian invasion and on returning to Tunisia was unwell with tonsilitis. Horrocks issued on 26th April orders that 10th Corps would break through between Djebel Chabet el Akam and the sea on 1st May. These orders involved five divisions in three series of reliefs and two attacks. The first of these attacks was to capture a line from Djebel Tebaga to the coast—4th Indian Division on the left, to take Tebaga, 56th Division on the right Terhouna—during the night 28th/29th.

Meanwhile the N.Z. Division and 201st Guards Brigade had been making small local attacks to maintain pressure and gain ground. On the 23rd and 24th a battalion of 6th N.Z. Brigade attacked two features, Djebel Terhouna and Djebel es Srafi, which would overlook the flank of 4th Indian Division's proposed line of advance on Tebaga. The New Zealanders were unable to take the whole of these features which were strongly held, and no one knew exactly who was where when on the night 26th/27th 169th Brigade (56th Division) took the sector over as part of the series of reliefs which we have

---

¹ *56th Division.* Main formations:
167th Infantry Brigade (Brigadier J. C. A. Birch)
    8th and 9th Battalions The Royal Fusiliers; 7th Battalion The Oxfordshire and Buckinghamshire Light Infantry.
169th Infantry Brigade (Brigadier L. O. Lynne)
    2nd/5th, 2nd/6th, and 2nd/7th The Queen's Royal Regiment.

    44th Reconnaissance Regiment; 64th, 65th, 113th Field Regiments R.A.; 67th Anti-Tank Regiment R.A.; 100th Light A.A. Regiment R.A.; 220th, 221st, 501st Field Companies R.E.; 6th Bn (M.G.) The Cheshire Regiment.

mentioned. On the 28th Brigadier Lynne (169th Brigade) pointed out that the enemy held parts of the features, and the dangers which resulted. Horrocks decided that 56th Division must take Djebels Terhouna and Srafi during the night 28th/29th, and 169th Brigade did this, but on 29th morning was counter-attacked, lost Srafi, and fell into some disorder. This incident, unimportant in itself, caused Montgomery to realize that 56th Division must have time to learn the ways of battle, and that his plan to carry the 8th Army to Cape Bon and Tunis was not practicable. He asked Alexander to visit him, and Alexander, on the 30th, decided that further large operations by 8th Army would be very costly in casualties and uncertain of success. He directed Montgomery to carry on local operations mainly to prevent von Arnim from transferring troops from Messe to von Vaerst. He arranged too that Montgomery was to transfer forthwith to 1st Army 7th Armoured Division, 4th Indian Division, and 201st Guards Brigade. These were to reinforce Anderson's final thrust to Tunis in a revised plan. Alexander had asked for the 8th Army's best and it was a happy coincidence that those which Montgomery chose had been among the first in the field in the Desert War.[1]

Meanwhile the Desert Air Force had been giving as much support as was possible to 8th Army, having regard to bad weather, and to the policy of the moment which directed most of its attention to the air and sea approaches to Tunisia. It was not until 23rd April that the fighter-bombers were able to intervene in the land battle, and even then their activities were quickly curtailed by the weather. The day-bombers made their first appearance the following day, 74 of the 92 sorties flown being expended in four attacks north-west of Enfidaville, mainly on gun positions, but on the 24th they were grounded again. Next day there was an improvement, the British day-bombers flying 125 sorties and the American 16, attacking enemy positions in the Enfidaville sector. Thereafter the weather closed in on the hills once more. Only 407 day-bomber sorties had been flown in support of 8th Army during 22nd—29th April. Operations then ceased until 4th May for want of suitable targets. There was virtually no armour to attack, and the hostile infantry and guns were tucked into folds and crevices of the hills and were often concealed by low cloud. The sorties flown by W.D.A.F. on

---

[1] 7th Armoured Division, in Egypt before the outbreak of war, and known first as The Mobile Division and secondly as The Armoured Division (Egypt)) joined the Western Desert Force on 17th June 1940. Its war service in the Western Desert may be said to have begun on 28th August 1939. 4th Indian Division began to land in Egypt in August 1939. 201st Guards Brigade (then known as 22nd Guards Brigade) joined the Western Desert Force on 11th April 1941. Compositions of course changed; traditions continued.

tactical air operations from 22nd April to dusk on 5th May are shown in the footnote below.[1]

The weather, too, plagued the night-bombers of No. 205 Group R.A.F. in their attempts to help 8th Army. On 23rd/24th April the Wellingtons bombed the airfields in the Cape Bon Peninsula within easy range of the Enfidaville sector, but they did not operate again until 4th/5th May. Single F.A.A. Albacores operated on four occasions against roads and M.T.

If attempts to support 8th Army had been frustrating for the Desert and Middle East air forces, events on 26th April in another direction certainly served to bring them considerable consolation. That day 36 British and 31 American day-bombers struck at Soliman south landing ground at the base of Cape Bon peninsula destroying six Me. 109s on the ground and a Ju. 88 in the air. Further afield, in Italy, 63 Liberators of U.S. IX Bomber Command heavily bombed Bari airfield destroying 107 and damaging 45 German aircraft on the ground—five Italian aircraft were also destroyed.[2] It was a day of disaster for the *Luftwaffe* in the Mediterranean area, its total losses on the ground and on operations on the 26th in all areas amounting to no less than 124 aircraft.

The opinions of General Gause, the Army Group's Chief of Staff, at the end of April are interesting, and apt at this point. He believed that the Allied High Command was at last planning operations in singleness of purpose. The Allied commanders knew the fine fighting

---

[1] Sorties flown by W.D.A.F. (excluding anti-shipping operations and shipping protection):

		British				U.S.		
	Fighter-bomber	Fighter	Day-bomber	Tac. R.	Fighter-bomber	Fighter	Day-bomber	Total
April								
22nd	12	260	—	3	—	92	—	367
23rd	—	195	68	11	—	108	24	406
24th	—	73	—	5	—	71	—	149
25th	12	380	125	5	—	206	16	744
26th	—	199	36	10	—	94	31	370
27th	—	198	—	7	—	—	—	205
28th	—	195	36	11	—	36	—	278
29th	—	228	53	14	—	24	18	337
30th	—	314	—	5	—	84	—	403
May								
1st	—	321	—	7	96	84	—	508
2nd	—	167	—	8	20	36	—	231
3rd	—	153	—	6	—	36	—	195
4th	—	322	70	10	—	112	35	549
5th	—	424	18	9	—	108	—	559
	24	3,429	406	111	116	1,091	124	5,301

[2] The German aircraft destroyed were: Hs. 129, 3; Me. 109, 40; Ju. 87, 16; Fiesler Storch, 6; F.W. 190, 41; W34 (glider), 1. Italian types are not recorded.

qualities of Axis troops and that Tunisia would be defended to the last. But the Allies wished to expel the Axis from Africa very quickly in order to gain political and military advantages, for example perhaps to open a second front before the fourth year of war ended—provided that Germany was still pinned down in Russia. Their commanders were very cautious, avoided casualties, and had several times failed to use opportunities for a decisive break-through, preferring to abide by small successes, and seemingly choosing a series of small attacks all along the fronts as the means of breaking the Axis defence. The 8th Army were the best troops, experienced and recovered from their reverses. The Americans, excellently equipped and supplied, were unstable and lacked élan.[1] The French were badly equipped and their morale was not high. Allied tactics were very methodical and were applied step by step, always from a firm base. But the absence of really bold planning behind the tactics would involve the Allies in many wearisome and costly engagements before a final victory could be assured.[2]

Although Kesselring's Intelligence staff continued until 2nd May to assert that the Allies' final stroke would be delivered from the area of Pont du Fahs, von Arnim continued to believe that it would come from the west. He therefore held to his policy of reinforcing *Pz AOK 5* at the expense of *AOK 1*, and by the beginning of May Messe had transferred all his tanks, most of his 8·8-cm guns, some heavy artillery, and the remainder of 15th Panzer Division.[3] Plans to give von Vaerst some of *D.A.K's* German units were mostly spoiled by want of petrol to move them, for the Army Group as a whole was down to half a consumption unit by 3rd May. At the end of April and in early May certain senior German officers fell ill, were sent out of Tunisia, and thus escaped capture later. They were Weber (334th

---

[1] The American official historian of the campaign has written:
'... It had required actual combat and casualties to make the average American soldier sufficiently wary and determined. Even then, the soldiers not only had to know what to do and how to do it, but also to be under the unremitting control of officers who knew their business'. George F. Howe, *Northwest Africa: Seizing the Initiative in the West* (Washington 1957) p. 671.

[2] Curiously, some German training instructions from March 1943 read very like British ones of 1941-42; e.g. all troops, and not only tanks and anti-tank units, must deal with tanks; fire should be opened on A.F.Vs at 800 metres range or less; when co-operating with tanks the infantryman fights as one and not as a tank-jackal.

[3] Not all transfers from *AOK 1* to *Pz AOK 5* are recorded but the following details indicate the trend:
  1 German infantry battalion; 1 engineer battalion.
  15th Panzer Division, including: 15 German tanks, two infantry battalions, an engineer and an anti-tank battalion, two batteries.
  2 German Reconnaissance Units.
  1 Battery German Army Artillery (8 10-cm guns; 6 heavy guns).
  2 Batteries German A.A. Artillery (13 8·8-cm guns).
  8 Troops German A.A. Artillery (29 8·8-cm guns). (to *D.A.K.*).
  3 Italian Infantry Battalions.
  14 Italian 7·5-cm self-propelled guns.
  3 Batteries Italian Artillery (149-mm and 10-cm guns—numbers unknown.)

Division), von Manteuffel (Manteuffel Division), and Bayerlein, Messe's German Chief of Staff. In the same order of names, Major-General Krause, Major-General Buelowius, and Oberst Markert replaced them. Gause was summoned to a conference in Italy on 4th May, and Schmid (Hermann Göring Division) on 9th May was ordered to fly out by Göring.

After visiting Montgomery on the 30th April, General Alexander flew to see Anderson and with him settled the new version of the plan to finish the campaign (Operation 'Strike'). The same evening Anderson conferred with Horrocks, who that morning had taken over 9th Corps from Briggs, because 9th Corps had the main task—to break through.[1] 9th Corps was to use 4th British Division and 4th Indian Division to break into the enemy's defences on a narrow front. 6th and 7th Armoured Divisions were then immediately to dash through and break into the inner defences of Tunis—the high ground some six miles west of the city—before the enemy had time to man them.[2] 5th Corps was to capture Djebel Bou Aoukaz, as a preliminary, to protect 9th Corps' left flank; and was to hold ready a division or more to back it up.[3] 2nd U.S. Corps was to capture the high ground east and west of Chouigui, the river crossings at Tebourba and Djedeida, and finally Bizerta. 19th Corps was to take Zaghouan. Alexander laid stress on some points. 9th Corps was to do its utmost to pass its armoured divisions through on the same day that its infantry attacked, to deny the enemy time to throw out a strong anti-tank screen. A break-through on a narrow front was the aim and mopping-up could come later. To get to Tunis at speed would result in cutting off all troops north of that place from their chance of escape to the Cape Bon peninsula. In any event, action to prevent the enemy withdrawing to Cape Bon was not to interfere with the chief object—the capture of Tunis.

General Horrocks, and his divisional commanders Hawkesworth, Tuker, Keightley, and Erskine, made their plans between 1st and 4th May. Shortly, the two infantry divisions—4th Indian on the left, 4th British on the right—were to capture a knoll-studded ridge between Montarnaud and Furna on the Medjez el Bab—Tunis road. It was thought that strong field-works might be concealed in the

---

[1] In 8th Army Lieut.-General Freyberg took command of 10th Corps.
[2] *9th Corps.* Main Formations:
    6th and 7th Armoured Divisions; 4th British and 4th Indian Divisions; 25th Tank Brigade (less two battalions); 201st Guards Brigade.
        1st British Armoured Division, which was under strength in tanks owing to its recent casualties, was placed in Army reserve, as were 139th Infantry Brigade (46th Division), 1st King's Dragoon Guards and 51st R.T.R.
[3] *5th Corps.* Main Formations:
    1st Division, 46th Division (less 139th Infantry Brigade); 78th Division.

springing crops and plentiful scrub, and there was keen discussion about the best method of ensuring the infantry's success against defenders who enjoyed very good fields of fire. Two methods chiefly commended themselves: a carefully controlled daylight attack behind barrages, or a more venturesome night attack taking advantage of artillery concentrations. In the end a balance was struck: the attack to begin at 3 a.m.; first objectives to be taken by 7 a.m.; then at 8.30 a.m. the final assault. Fire support included counter-battery, barrages, and concentrations, choice of the two last being left mostly to divisional commanders. 25th Tank Brigade and some Scorpions were at their disposal. The guns numbered some 442 for a 3,000 yard front.[1]

The armoured divisions were to be ready to move from 7 a.m.—7th Armoured north of the Medjez el Bab—Tunis road and 6th Armoured south of it. The first objectives were: for 7th the high ground about three miles north of La Mornaghia, for 6th the high ground the same distance south of that place. Next both divisions were to break through the perimeter defences of Tunis on either side of the road. General Horrocks had left no divisional commander in doubt about the key-words: speed and success. A special force of artillery under the Commander, Corps Royal Artillery was closely to follow the armoured divisions to give extra and immediate support. The date of 9th Corps' attack was fixed as 6th May, and 5th Corps therefore was ordered to capture Djebel Bou Aoukaz on 5th May. General Anderson wished to confuse the enemy '... from whom [he] could scarcely hope to conceal the colossal traffic movement (reminiscent of Derby Day) and the dust around Medjez...' Therefore on the 3rd 18th Army Group Camouflage Section erected seventy dummy tanks near Bou Arada and it was hoped that these, with 1st British Armoured Division, might draw the enemy's eyes in that direction or puzzle him by making it seem that Anderson had split his armour. Administratively there were no very intractable problems except traffic congestion owing to the facts that two Corps were using the same axis, and that there was but one bridge over the Medjerda at Medjez el Bab (there were no sites for others because of very difficult approaches); and a possible shortage of ammunition.

Air Marshal Coningham's plan to support the 1st Army's final attack had been settled on 2nd May. Air Commodore K. B. B. Cross, Commander of No. 242 Group R.A.F., was given operational control of the whole of N.A.T.A.F. and of the medium bombers of N.A.S.A.F. which could be spared for tactical operations, because he was the Air Officer best situated to co-ordinate and direct air

---

[1] Including the guns of 5th Corps, the total was 652. Ammunition worked out at 350 r.p.g., this quantity being determined by the transport available for dumping.

power in support of the Army. There would be preliminary bombing on the night 5th/6th May to shake the enemy, and on the 6th the day-bombers of N.A.T.B.F. (including those of W.D.A.F.) would drop a moving curtain of bombs ahead of the advancing troops. The remainder of the tactical air force would continue to attack targets in the area of battle.

By 1st May von Arnim knew (mainly from intercepted wireless messages) of the reinforcement of 1st Army by 8th, and that the blow would fall between Medjez el Bab and Pont du Fahs. Since 29th April he had known only too well the actions of 2nd U.S. Corps, and succeeding days brought no comfort in that quarter. Yet at 5th May his Intelligence Staff, and Kesselring's expected a few more days' grace. The general attitude was of dogged and combative resignation, apart from some perhaps wishfully hopeful statements by Kesselring and Gause. The administrative situation was almost at rock-bottom. Artillery ammunition stood at less than one issue, and the dumps were empty of shell for field and anti-tank guns.[1] Radio communications were breaking down.

On 29th April 5th Corps found that the enemy was still aggressive in his defence, though in eight days it had advanced about ten miles on a front of fifteen. 2nd U.S. Corps was meeting strong resistance and counter-attacks. 19th Corps' patrols were in contact. On 1st May 34th U.S. Division by what Anderson called 'a particularly fine piece of work' took hills, very valuable as observation points, north and east of Sidi Nsir including the rugged feature Tahent, held by the Barenthin Regiment. Along the Sedjenane river 9th U.S. Division and the Corps Franc d'Afrique were advancing well. These two penetrations compelled von Manteuffel to withdraw all his troops, including those west and south-west of Mateur. 1st U.S. Armoured Division, following closely on von Manteuffel's heels, pushed through Mateur on the 3rd. Immediately that the enemy evacuated the Djebel Azzag position, 9th U.S. Division was directed northwards to move round Garaet Achkel and then towards Bizerta.

On 30th April American Bostons and Mitchells, including some from N.A.S.A.F., attacked targets on 5th Corps' front while British Bostons concentrated on enemy strongpoints and positions north-west of Ksar Tyr and west of Furna, N.A.T.B.F's share amounting to 66 sorties. Thereafter activity rapidly became less and the day-bombers were grounded on 3rd and 4th May, but on the 5th with some improvement in the weather they were busy once more.

---

[1] Alexander, in his despatch dated 23rd May 1947, says that the enemy 'contrary to reports at the time' were well supplied with ammunition of all natures. von Arnim, writing after the war, says that the dumps were filled with spent cases.

American Bostons and Mitchells supported by Marauders from N.A.S.A.F. attacked enemy positions in the north while the British Bostons supported 1st Division's attack on Djebel Bou Aoukaz. It was left to the fighter-bombers to fill in the gaps in air support and in the six days they flew 191 sorties spread over the Tebourba, Ksar Tyr, Massicault and Zaghouan areas. The sorties flown by the northern tactical air forces are shown in the footnote below.[1]

The Desert Air Force day-bombers of N.A.T.B.F. in the south reserved their energies for daylight operations, but on the night of 4th/5th May No. 205 Group R.A.F. (which had been placed under Coningham's operational control on 3rd May) began its operations in support by attacking roads leading from Tunis to, and targets in, the battle area.

On the evening of 5th May 1st Division's 3rd Brigade, supported by more than six hundred guns, captured Djebel Bou Aoukaz, thus securing the left flank of 9th Corps' start-line from molestation. At 3 a.m. on 6th May the artillery began its programme in support of 4th Indian and 4th British Divisions. The weight of fire was great: in two hours 16,632 shells fell upon the enemy facing 4th British Division, and in the first twenty-four hours the whole artillery averaged 368 rounds per gun or rather more than during a like period of El Alamein. To this must be added the tactical air support, which will be described. It was the weight of support which perhaps explains why it is otiose to pick out for description this or that incident in the battle. There was some stiff opposition at first but in general the infantry divisions fought methodically and punctually from objective to objective, and had broken the back of the position by noon.

6th Armoured Division's 26th Armoured Brigade began to move out from the area of Gueriat el Atach at 7.30 a.m. and found the going slow because of a single gap through a scattered minefield and because tanks, supporting 4th British Division, had not cleared the

---

[1] Sorties flown 30th April—5th May:

	242 Group R.A.F.	XII A.S.C.	N.A.T.B.F.	Total
30th April	275	144	66	485
1st May	232	65	21	318
2nd May	243	143	12	398
3rd May	238	114	—	352
4th May	305	125	—	430
5th May	275	177	71	523
	1,568	768	170	2,506

front.[1] By 10.45 a.m. the armour was moving into an area about two miles short of Furna and soon afterwards was engaged by some anti-tank guns and scattered tanks.

Meanwhile 7th Armoured Division had also been on the move, 22nd Armoured Brigade leading.[2] Horrocks told Tuker that the Division would be slipped as soon as a knoll in the middle of 4th Indian Division's third objective had been taken. This occurred at 10.30 a.m., and 22nd Armoured Brigade then passed through to a short distance eastward, directed to high ground just north of Massicault and then to the neighbourhood of St. Cyprien. Nevertheless from about noon both armoured divisions lost impetus, although at twenty minutes before one o'clock 9th Corps H.Q. had the '... General impression the enemy not aware of direction of our attacks and are now pulling out as fast as they can ...' Both armoured divisional commanders were anxious to form firm bases before pushing their tanks far ahead, and to bring up 131st Brigade (7th Armoured Division) and 201st Guards Brigade (6th Armoured Division) took time. By 5 p.m., with two and a quarter hours to go before sunset, 7th Armoured Division had settled into position just north of Massicault, and 6th Armoured Division about two miles east of it—that is approximately eight miles beyond the infantry's positions.

On 6th May the air forces concentrated their tactical support in an area four miles deep by three and a half miles across, in which lay Massicault and St. Cyprien. At first light N.A.T.B.F's day-bombers from the north in the shape of 67 American Bostons bombed enemy positions forward of Furna, and they were followed soon afterwards by the Bostons of Nos. 18 and 114 Squadrons R.A.F. Then from 7.30 a.m. until 8 a.m. the Desert Air Force's day-bombers from the south took over, thickening and extending the artillery's fire. In the afternoon 89 day-bombers from the north and south answered calls from the armoured divisions, eighteen aircraft coming in every two minutes. This and other forms of support continued throughout the day. XII Air Support Command launched seven fighter-bomber attacks, and Hurricane fighter-bombers of No. 242 Group R.A.F. nine. The fighters escorted bombers, and made continual sweeps during one of which 12 aircraft of No. 72 Squadron R.A.F. sighted 16 Me. 109s, north of Tunis, and shot down five. Tactical and artillery reconnaissance aircraft steadily pursued their tasks throughout the hurly-burly. The total air support from dusk on 5th May until dusk on the

---

[1] *26th Armoured Brigade* (Brigadier G.P. Roberts).
  Main units: 16th/5th Lancers; 17th/21st Lancers; 2nd Lothian and Border Horse; 10th The Rifle Brigade.
[2] *22nd Armoured Brigade*(Brigadier W. R. N. Hinde).
  Main units: 1st and 5th R.T.R.; 4th County of London Yeomanry; 1st The Rifle Brigade.

40. Royal Air Force Mosquito over Malta.

41. United States 'Flying Fortresses' (over Europe).

42. United States Mitchells (top and left). South African Air Force Baltimores.

43. Tunis. A 'grave-yard' of enemy aircraft (M.C. 202s) wrecked by Allied air attack.

44. Tunis. Seaplane hangars wrecked by Allied air attack.

6th amounted to 1,958 sorties—a figure never before approached in Africa in 24 hours of direct support of troops.[1]

The failure of the armoured divisions to carry out Alexander's exhortation of 29th April '... with their power of manoeuvre they must get on with it ...'—now seems to be more an anti-climax than a misfortune because Army Group Africa's report of the 6th gives us the enemy's story. The Hermann Göring and 334th Divisions had been worn down by the fighting since 22nd April and von Arnim had reinforced the sector with the whole of what was left of 15th Panzer Division on the 5th.

> '... Between the Medjerda and the Medjez—St. Cyprien road the enemy has achieved his decisive break-through to Tunis. This sector was heroically defended by 15th Panzer Division ... but these troops could not survive an assault mounted by numerically far superior infantry and armoured formations with massive artillery support, and accompanied by air attacks of an intensity not hitherto experienced. The bulk of 15th Panzer Division must be deemed to have been destroyed[2] ... There can be no doubt that on 7th May the road to Tunis will be open to the enemy, and that the fall of the city of Bizerta is only a question of time ...'

For the moment however, 2nd U.S. Corps was meeting a defence even stronger than before, although 1st U.S. Armoured Division captured the high ground between Mateur and Ferryville.

In practical terms von Arnim and his senior commanders, German and Italian, lost control on the 6th, but they continued to try to exercise it. On the evening of the 6th von Arnim ordered a step by step retreat into the 'fortress area' of Bizerta and the mountainous area Hammam Lif—Zaghouan—Enfidaville. Accordingly *Pz AOK 5* was to pull its centre and left back to the line Tebourba—La Mohammedia—Djebel Oust; *D.A.K.* was to draw its right into the area Zaghouan—Djebel Oust, and later to take under command 10th Panzer and Hermann Göring divisions. *AOK 1* was to hold its present positions, and to be responsible for coast defence of the Cape

---

[1]

	N.A.A.F.	*Sorties*	*M.E.A.C.*	*Sorties*
5th/6th May	N.A.T.B.F.	42	No. 205 Group	46
	N.A.C.A.F. (Beaufighter)	6		
6th May	No. 242 Group	469	W.D.A.F. (R.A.F. & U.S.).	*733
	XII A.S.C.	419		
	N.A.T.B.F.	243		
		1,179		779 Grand Total 1,958

* Excluding shipping protection.

[2] 15th Panzer Division arrived in Africa in April and May 1941—it had been one of the best German formations.

Bon peninsula. von Arnim moved his own Headquarters from the peninsula south to Sainte Marie du Zit; the petrol for the move came from the lucky find of a drum on the beach. During the afternoon von Vaerst had ordered the port installations at Bizerta and Ferryville to be destroyed. von Arnim wrote after the war that he and von Vaerst together decided not to defend Tunis or Bizerta, and Messe states that he was not told of this decision.

For the moment no directions came from Germany or Italy. Then on the 7th or 8th, Hitler issued orders to resist until the last man and the last round. Hitler probably meant his words; Army Group Africa—and who will blame it?—interpreted them to mean that the troops were to fight until they had shot off their ammunition and destroyed weapons and vehicles. Then commanders might decide to cease fighting. On the evening of the 8th Keitel reaffirmed that the Dictators were resolved to continue the battle in Tunisia for as long as possible, and he authorized Kesselring to reinforce Tunisia or not to do so, and to amalgamate formations and units in Tunisia and to evacuate staffs thus thrown up. On the 7th *Comando Supremo* sent a rather similar instruction to von Arnim and Messe. von Arnim may not have received this and these High Command directives were too late to have practical effects.

To return to 1st Army. On the 7th morning 6th and 7th Armoured Divisions went forward and met only scattered resistance. At 2.30 p.m. 26th Armoured Brigade had its first sight of Tunis. In 7th Armoured Division 22nd Armoured Brigade engaged a few tanks and 8·8-cm guns east of La Mornaghia and by 2 p.m. had disposed of them. It was now clear that there would be no serious fighting around Tunis and at 3.15 p.m. Erskine ordered his division to close in on the town. A patrol of 'C' Squadron 1st Derbyshire Yeomanry and one of 'B' squadron 11th Hussars reached the centre of the town twenty-five minutes later. It was raining, and enemy soldiers were drifting about. Some threw grenades and fired random shots; others surged up to surrender. Excited civilians added to the confusion from which the patrols prudently withdrew a little. Soon 1st/7th Queens (131st Brigade) and some tanks of 1st R.T.R. arrived. They quelled any parties who showed fight, seized intact all important buildings and bridges and restored order.

> '... The sight as the Bn entered the town was an unforgetable [sic] one. Despite the pouring rain, dense crowds of wildly enthusiastic French, men and women lined the streets, throwing flowers over the vehicles, attempting to jump on them and in many case throwing their arms round the troops and kissing them. In the midst of this was the smoke and flames from burning vehs [vehicles] and buildings, and the noise of rifle and M.G. fire from the enemy still holding out in various buildings...'

At 4.30 p.m. 6th Armoured Division received Anderson's orders to turn south-east towards Soliman and Grombalia to stop the enemy taking positions to defend the Cape Bon peninsula. The armoured brigade pushed on to La Mohammedia by nightfall. In 2nd U.S. Corps 1st U.S. Armoured Division entered Ferryville in the afternoon and at 4.15 p.m. part of 894th Tank Destroyer Battalion of 9th Division entered Bizerta. Enemy guns still fired from south-west of the town, and inside it, as at Tunis, there was shooting. There were many booby traps and mines and extensive destruction which were cleaned up by 15th and 20th Engineers. 19th French Corps occupied Pont du Fahs, but opposite 8th Army the enemy stood fast.

The Axis formations continued to resist in whatever groups they found themselves. In 9th Corps 1st British Armoured Division replaced the 7th and swung east to Creteville on 8th May. 6th Armoured Division found that the enemy was holding the defile between the hills and the Gulf of Tunis at Hammam Lif, and in fact in this area was *D.A.K.*, the remains of Hermann Göring Division and most of *AOK 1*'s heavy anti-tank guns. 7th Armoured Division turned north into the 'bulge' above Tunis, fighting at times, clearing up Carthage and La Marsa and gathering in prisoners, guns, and grounded aircraft. 2nd U.S. Corps' four divisions swept the country from the Wadi Tine in the north, east and south of Bizerta, and down to Chouigui, there linking with 5th Corps. Boissau's division and Le Coulteux's armoured group had made good progress north-eastward but struck stiff opposition west of Zaghouan. Conne's division and Mathenet's were labouring up the spurs of Djebel Zaghouan. In 10th Corps (8th Army) both 56th and New Zealand Divisions were opposed when they staged local attacks.

It is now necessary to impose an order upon events in which there was no particular order, for when large enemy forces are fighting or surrendering over an area some 100 miles long and from 30 miles to a grenade-toss deep, soldiers on the winning side may be scratching their bewildered heads in safety at one place while elsewhere others, grimly purposeful, find that death and wounds remain death and wounds. On 9th May 2nd U.S. Corps cornered von Vaerst and what remained of *Pz AOK 5*, and at 10 a.m. German *parlementaires* sought terms from Major-General Harmon (1st U.S. Armoured Division). General Bradley demanded unconditional surrender, in accordance with the policy agreed at the Casablanca Conference, and by noon von Vaerst had yielded. His was the second German army to capitulate in this war—the first, that of Field-Marshal Paulus, had done so at Stalingrad on 2nd February 1943.[1] von Arnim and his

---

[1] Paulus himself had surrendered on 31st January 1943.

Headquarters joined Cramer and the Headquarters of *D.A.K.* Messe with *AOK 1* was sitting tight, and in fact his troops inflicted upon 167th Brigade (56th Division) casualties of 63 killed, 221 wounded, 104 missing when this brigade made a local attack.

6th Armoured Division, on the 9th, continued to fight at Hammam Lif. The narrow gap between cliff-like hills and the sea was well covered by anti-tank guns; the Guards Brigade, though it had taken the hills, could not quickly get down into the gorge; and shelling had apparently little effect. By noon however 2nd Lothians and Border Horse attacked slap at the enemy from the front and also from the flank, driving along the beach and in the sea. 17th/21st Lancers followed along the beach, and by 4 p.m. the defile was forced. 6th Armoured Division pushed steadily on towards Hammamet and began to gather in crowds of prisoners. 22 Shermans had been lost in this bold and rewarding action. 4th Indian Division (now under 5th Corps) was ordered to swing east to cut in between the armour and 19th Corps, which was preparing to advance round and across the Zaghouan massif against opposition. But *D.A.K.* had no fuel for manoeuvre and was beginning to crumble. '... In effect the Corps was waiting for the end and was mainly preoccupied in ensuring that its long service in Africa be brought to an honourable conclusion,' as Messe later wrote. On the 10th 1st Army continued to drive south-east, south, and east, drawing the net tighter round von Arnim and Messe.

On the 11th *Group Arnim* and *Group Messe* were formed and though the enemy was in his death-struggle he was still dangerous. Mathenet's Division du Maroc cut into 21st Panzer Division, Le Coulteux's tanks pressed west and north of Zaghouan, and on his left Boissau linked with 4th Indian Division. The spasmodic German messages recorded stiff fighting, and von Arnim was now cut off from Messe. 6th Armoured Division swept south to Bou Ficha and at about 10 a.m. 26th Armoured Brigade made wireless touch with 56th Division, and later observed fire for 10th Corps' artillery—possibly a very rare example of troops of one army moving southwards, spotting for the gunners of another army shooting northwards. 1st Division came down to Grombalia, stopping movement to or from the Cape Bon peninsula, and 4th Division began to clear the peninsula itself. 4th Indian Division was closing in on Sainte Marie du Zit. The French armour got there that evening.

After 6th May the quickly changing and often confused situation on the ground made it almost impossible that calls for air support from the troops could be acted on. The higher Army/Air headquarters therefore directed the aircraft wherever it seemed, from air or other reports, that they could best be used further to disorganize the already disorganized enemy. This policy led to attacks by day-bombers, fighter-bombers and fighters in the areas of Bizerta, Tunis, Zaghouan, and the Cape Bon peninsula. The sea also was watched but attacks were confined within a distance of five miles off-shore to avoid mishaps between Allied aircraft and naval vessels all keyed-up to let nothing pass that floated. Air attacks were thus, at first, directed to roads leading to Bizerta and Tunis, and between them, to those in the Cape Bon peninsula, and to the few remaining hostile airfields and landing grounds. This pattern soon changed to one of free-lance attacks and strafing of whatever targets could be found. On the 9th the *Luftwaffe* withdrew to Sicily and Pantelleria, and by the 12th the Italians had followed suit with their remaining 57 aircraft. The anti-aircraft gunners had to be reckoned with until the end. The island of Pantelleria attracted special attention because the enemy used it as a staging-post for aircraft and small vessels. On the 8th 122 day-bombers of the Western Desert Air Force (British Bostons and Baltimores, American Mitchells) attacked the island. On the 9th 121 day-bombers attacked again, and again, twice on the 10th. A great deal of damage was done. The air forces therefore harried and distracted the enemy to the end, as the few surviving reports testify. The number of sorties flown was high—on the busiest day, 9th May, the 'Northern' air forces flew 1,014 sorties, the Desert Air Force 643.[1]

At night all the available bomber effort was devoted to ensuring that the enemy should have no respite. From the north the Bisleys of N.A.T.B.F., grounded for two nights, came out in strength as soon as the weather cleared. For three nights beginning on 8th/9th they bombed concentrations of M.T. and troops wherever they could be found in the La Goulette—Cape Bon area. The 10th/11th was the Bisleys' finale in the Tunisian Campaign when nearly all of them

---

[1] Sorties flown 7th—11th May:

	No. 242 Group R.A.F.	XII A.S.C.	N.A.T.B.F. (Day)	Total
7th	431	174	94	699
8th	475	306	213	994
9th	444	286	284	1,014
10th	330	207	130	667
11th	241	117	116	474
	1,921	1,090	837	3,848

Western Desert Air Force (excluding shipping protection)

	British				U.S.			
	Fighter -bomber	Fighter	Day-Bomber	Tac. R.	Fighter -bomber	Fighter	Day-Bomber	Total
7th	12	268	—	5	—	123	9	417
8th	12	208	89	13	—	74	33	429
9th	76	332	87	10	104	—	34	643
10th	83	231	158	11	116	24	70	693
11th	60	132	66	13	—	44	18	333
	243	1,171	400	52	220	265	164	2,515

were out twice during the night, bringing their total sorties since the 8th/9th to 137—and after that there was no more work for them to do. Meanwhile the Beaufighters of No. 600 Squadron patrolled overhead and farther afield, a Ju. 88 being shot down on the 6th/7th and an He. III on the 11th/12th when three other German aircraft may well have fallen to the A.A. guns. From the south, since the Desert Air Force bombers were fully occupied by day, the Halifaxes, Wellingtons and F.A.A. Albacores of No. 205 Group R.A.F. threw their whole weight into direct support of 1st Army's advance. Operating from Gardabia east of Tripoli, which meant a round trip of 800 miles, they attacked focal points on roads and railways, and troops. In seven consecutive nights from the 4th/5th to the 10th/11th May they flew 215 sorties and dropped 400 tons of bombs—after which they, too, had no more work to do.[1] The night-flying Hurricanes of No. 73 Squadron were also out. This squadron, which had arrived in the Middle East at the end of 1940, had begun its operations in support of the Desert Army on New Year's Day 1941. Flying at maximum intensity, and reaching 22 sorties during one of the four nights ending on the 11th/12th, it brought its long and gallant record in Africa to a close by strafing enemy flare-paths, M.T. and any other targets that could be found in the Cape Bon area, including boats offshore, and adding four Ju. 52s to its list of aircraft destroyed.

Throughout 'Vulcan', and except on the rare occasions when they took part in tactical air operations, the activities of the strategic bombers were not visibly related to the fighting on the ground, and understandably so. It is therefore convenient to treat them separately and as a whole, bearing in mind that there was but one war.

By far the greatest part of their effort was devoted to attacks on shipping and on ports, which have been described in Chapter XVI. The remainder was expended on attacks against the enemy's principal airfields in the Central Mediterranean and on those in Tunisia where L. of C. and tactical targets were also bombed in support of the N.A.T.A.F. plan. Against airfields outside Africa N.A.S.A.F. flew 246 sorties, 70 of them against Sardinia and the rest roughly divided between Sicily and Italy. M.E.A.C. made only one such attack, the magnificently successful bombing of Bari airfield by U.S. IX Bomber Command on 26th April already described. Against airfields in Tunisia the Wellingtons of N.A.S.A.F. attacked those at Sidi Ahmed and El Aouina and the Wellingtons of No. 205 Group R.A.F. principally Soliman south landing ground, 58 sorties being flown all told. The tactical air operations by No. 205 Group R.A.F. in support of 1st Army from 4th/5th to 10th/11th which have already

---

[1] It is not easy to picture a number of tons of bombs. 400 tons would represent nearly 3,600 × 250 lb bombs.

been described are included in the table of sorties in the footnote.[1]

Including attacks on ports but excluding anti-shipping operations, the Northwest African and Middle East air forces had flown a daily average of 1,165 sorties of all kinds from 22nd April to 15th/16th May, rather more than in the first three weeks of April and half again as much as in March.

This for practical purposes is the end of operations. At this point we must take leave of 1st Army for its headquarters was soon to be disbanded, and many of its troops were to be absorbed in the Allied forces for the invasion of Sicily and Italy. 1st Army had, in the words of its commander, 'achieved a great esprit de corps and pride of being, and these things count for much in war.' The Army's achievements are the best witnesses of the qualities of its commander, General Anderson, a fine soldier.

Some of the circumstances of the surrender in Africa must be described from the records of that time because the passing years sometimes transmute surrenders more strangely than they do other military events. Just after midnight on the 12th/13th Cramer sent his last signal (except a 'hail-and-farewell' to Rommel) to Army Group Africa and *OKH*. This last signal from the most famous of the German formations in Africa is worth quoting as an example of prevailing attitudes.

> 'Ammunition shot off. Arms and equipment destroyed. In accordance with orders received *D.A.K.* has fought itself to the condition where it can fight no more. The German Afrika Korps must rise again. Heia Safari. Cramer, General Commanding.'

In fact on the 10th and 11th Freyberg had summoned von Sponeck (90th Light) to surrender, but had not been answered.

On the morning of 12th May von Arnim ordered all wireless installations of his Headquarters to be destroyed, thus cutting communications between himself and his troops and his superiors outside Africa.[2] The surrenders of the Axis commanders and troops

---

[1] Sorties flown (excluding operations against shipping and ports) 22nd April to 15th/16th May.

	Day	Night
N.A.S.A.F.		
U.S. Fortresses	197	—
R.A.F. Wellingtons	—	85
M.E.A.C.		
U.S. Liberators	64	—
R.A.F. Halifaxes	—	11
R.A.F. Wellingtons	—	218
F.A.A. Albacores	—	12
Totals	261	326

[2] At 9.5 p.m. on 12th May *OKH's* intercepting station picked up a Reuter report: 'Allied G.H.Q. North Africa; von Arnim taken prisoner.'

were to form an untidy and disjointed series. General Anderson however, on the 12th, issued orders that the enemy must give unconditional surrender; cease forthwith to destroy material of military value; provide complete maps of his minefields. No other terms were offered and it is certain that the Axis forces in Africa surrendered unconditionally, although the manner of surrendering varied. von Arnim waited until British troops were on the hills overlooking his Headquarters and then sent three staff officers, the senior of whom was Oberst H. W. Nolte, Chief of Staff of *D.A.K.*, to negotiate surrender. Nolte arrived at the positions of 1st Battalion The Royal Sussex Regiment (Lieut.-Colonel J. B. A. Glennie) of 7th Indian Infantry Brigade, and was taken to General Tuker at H.Q. 4th Indian Division. Meanwhile 1st/2nd Gurkhas were mopping up in the area and Lieut.-Colonel L. J. G. Showers spotted a white flag. With Rifleman Sarghana Limbu he went to investigate, discovered that it was H.Qs of von Arnim and of *D.A.K.*, and was met by a German officer who explained Nolte's mission. Colonel Showers was on his way to report his find when Colonel Glennie arrived to place guards over the enemy.

General Tuker, with General Allfrey (Commander, 5th Corps), then went to von Arnim's H.Q. and interviewed this distinguished prisoner of war. von Arnim tried to evade the issue of surrendering on behalf of all Axis troops still fighting in Tunisia, pleading that he was not in communication with all his subordinates and that he could only surrender the two Headquarters and staffs on the spot, i.e. of Army Group Africa and *D.A.K.* Allfrey and Tuker split no hairs with him, and von Arnim, Cramer, their Chiefs of Staff, and A.D.Cs were sent, prisoners, to General Anderson. von Arnim passed on to Alexander's Headquarters, thence to a P.O.W. camp near Algiers, and therefore disappears from this narrative.

We turn now to Messe. *AOK 1*, though out of signal touch with Army Group Africa, continued in touch with *OKW* and *Comando Supremo*. At 11.15 a.m. on the 12th Messe received from Mussolini permission to negotiate an honourable surrender.[1] At about 1 p.m. Messe sent a wireless message to the '8th Army' to the effect that he was ready to negotiate a surrender with the honours of war, bearing in mind that his troops were still holding their positions intact. N.Z. Divisional Signals picked up the message and at 8.30 p.m. sent this reply. 'Commander First Italian Army from Commander 10 Corps. Hostilities will not cease until all troops lay down their arms and surrender to the nearest Allied unit.' There is some discrepancy

---

[1] No copy of this signal is known to us. Messe, in '*La Ia Armata in Tunisia*,' gives 'As the aims of your resistance can be considered achieved, your Excellency is free to accept an honourable surrender. I again express my high admiration and praise to you personally and to the heroic remnants of the Italian First Army. Mussolini'.

in the details of what happened next, and the nearest contemporary account is that of Messe's Italian Chief of Staff, General Mancinelli, dated 30th May 1943. The discrepancy does not affect the outcome and is summarized in a footnote.[1] At 10.33 p.m. New Zealand signals received this reply: 'From Italian First Army to 10 Corps Eighth Army. Reference your message our representatives have left to meet yours at 10 p.m. your time.' General Mancinelli, Oberst Markert and Major Boscardi, after a roundabout journey, arrived at H.Q. 10th Corps at 8.30 a.m. on the 13th. General Freyberg refused discussion and handed to Mancinelli demands exactly expressing Anderson's orders. Freyberg said that Messe had until 12.30 to accept, if he did not wish hostilities to be resumed.

Mancinelli said that he had no power to accept these orders and that he must obtain Messe's decision. Freyberg courteously advised him that there was not a moment to spare, and Mancinelli left. At the same time a message was sent to *AOK 1* saying: 'Your representatives with a British officer carrying instructions have left for your headquarters. I have ordered my troops to cease fire pending your acceptance of these terms by 1230 hours today.' Mancinelli reached Messe at 12.20 p.m., and Messe then surrendered his German and Italian troops. He had been promoted Marshal of Italy on the day before. Later on the 13th, Messe, with Major-General von Liebenstein surrendered in person to General Freyberg.

At 1.15 p.m. on 13th May the German Radio Control station in Rome reported to *OKW:* 'The last German radio station in Africa [Army Station XIII with *AOK 1*] closed down at 1312 hours. Radio Control Rome is no longer in radio communication with Africa.' At 1.16 p.m. on the same day General Alexander originated this message to the Prime Minister: 'Sir, it is my duty to report that the Tunisian campaign is over. All enemy resistance has ceased. We are masters of the North African shores.'

No satisfactory contemporary calculation of the casualties sustained by the Axis forces in the last phases of the campaign in Africa

---

[1] According to Axis sources 10th Corps' signal, referred to above, was received at 3 p.m. Messe decided not to reply and informed *Comando Supremo* that the fight would go on pending orders to be contrary. At about 5 p.m. 1st Army, by wireless, asked *AOK 1* if the message from 10th Corps had been received. Messe replied that it had, and that he stood by his proposal to surrender with the honours of war. Next, 1st Army suggested that he should send officers to meet a British 'delegation' on the road between Bou Ficha and Enfidaville, and at 10 p.m. Messe replied, to 10th Corps, that his officers would reach Bou Ficha at about 11 p.m. and that until they returned to him 'an armed truce' would be observed. 1st Army's records do not confirm.

have been found in Axis records. The closest Allied record is that of the unwounded prisoners actually held on 25th May. This gives:

    German: 101,784
    Italian: 89,442
    Nationality unspecified: 47,017

or a grand total of 238,243. The American Official History gives an estimated total of 275,000, and an 18th Army Group calculation of prisoners taken from 20th March to 13th May gives German: 157,000; Italian: 86,700, or a grand total of 244,500.[1] Between 22nd April and 15th/16th May the Germans lost 42 bombers, 166 fighters, 52 air transports, and 13 Fiesler Storch in the Mediterranean area. Only 17 Italian aircraft can be recorded with certainty as destroyed. Besides these aircraft destroyed, the Allies found over 600 German and Italian aircraft abandoned in the areas of Bizerta, Tunis, and Cape Bon, which provided much new technical information.

These varying figures may disappoint lovers of statistics, but nevertheless show clearly the disaster which had befallen the Axis forces in Africa. When the dust and excitement of the closing scenes had subsided qualified observers formed these impressions from the prisoners of war. Morale of both Germans and Italians was good, though most had been eager to surrender as soon as ordered. The atmosphere in the cages was of relief that the campaign was over although the German troops were anxious that their country should judge that they, as soldiers, had done their whole duty. Physique and health of the troops seemed excellent, and German equipment was of very good quality. There was no doubt that ammunition and fuel were very scarce.

The Allied casualties in Tunisia were of this order:

	Killed	Wounded	Missing
British (all Imperial troops) 1st Army from 8th November 1942	4,094	12,566	9,082
8th Army from 9th February 1943	2,139	8,962	1,517
United States Forces from 12th November 1943	2,715	8,978	6,528
French	2,156	10,276	7,007

Between 22nd April and 15th/16th May the Royal Air Force lost 12 bombers and 47 fighters; the U.S.A.A.F. 32 bombers and 63

---

[1] Rommel's estimate was 130,000 Germans; von Arnim's was Germans 100,000, Italians 200,000.
    On 3rd May the Staff Officer responsible for compiling the rations strength of Army Group Africa stated that this could not be given in detail because the relevant documents had been destroyed.

fighters; the French one bomber—or a total of 45 bombers and 110 fighters.[1]

As was felicitous, the closing days of the campaign in Africa were set off by many messages of congratulation from personages and bodies, exalted or of lesser degree, to the Allied commanders and their forces, not forgetting those now distant from the battle in the Middle East. There were, for example, messages from His Majesty King George VI, both Houses of Parliament, the Prime Minister, the War Cabinet, the Combined Chiefs of Staff, and Premier Stalin. A parade to celebrate the victory was held in Tunis on 20th May. Detachments representative of the British, American, and French troops of 1st and 8th Armies, and of the Royal Air Force marched past, and the Royal Air Force performed a Fly Past.[2] General Eisenhower with Generals Alexander and Giraud took the salute, and at the saluting-base were many Allied officers of high rank and of all Services. It is agreeable to remark that Admiral Cunningham was greatly struck by the fine appearance of this parade and that, even at the Victory March in London in June 1945, his mind '. . . instinctively went back to Tunis in May 1943, and the magnificent bronzed and battle-hardened young men . . .' who had marched past. Admiral Cunningham was a judge of men and knew soldiers for, as a Midshipman, he had served alongside them in the Naval Brigade for seven months of the South African War, and in 1915 the guns of H.M.S. *Scorpion* under his command had given close support to soldiers at Helles.

'. . . We had come a long and troublous way . . .' wrote Admiral Cunningham in 1945. 1943 in Africa marked the end of one of the great stages on that way, and therefore a description, in very general terms, of the feelings of some of the wayfarers may find a place here. The dramatic circumstances, the ceremonial, the ormolu phrases of congratulation, the honours which accompany the end of a splendid campaign are very often taken to represent the thoughts of the fighting men. But laurels on the head are not the same as the very human thoughts inside it—we speak only of British troops; to speak of the Allies is beyond our scope. Keenness and high spirits were at a peak; there was a settled confidence in the high command, in Alexander and in Montgomery who was immensely popular; there was respect, confidence and goodwill between men and officers. There was

---

[1] Though these losses, and those of the Axis on the previous page, cover the whole Mediterranean area they were all suffered by the Allied and Axis air forces in direct or indirect support of their armies in Tunisia. For example, the attacks by Axis aircraft on Allied ports, bases and L. of C. well behind the front line in Tunisia, and those of the Allies on airfields many miles away in Sardinia, Sicily and Italy from where these aircraft operated, were all part of the struggle on the Tunisian battlefield itself. The air was one vast battlefield.

[2] The order of precedence in marching past was French—American—British.

respect and admiration, too, between 1st and 8th Armies although each was pleasantly aware that it was much better than the other. 'Spit and polish' was grumbled over and, if unwisely exacted, was resented. 'What next?' was in most minds because armies like action and are quickly bored. In the 8th Army there were hopes of a spell at home, and when the Secretary of State for War announced that this, for good reason, would not be possible but that a generous provision of wireless sets ('Hear home—not go home') would be made, there were gibes.[1] 'There were no doubts about victory but many men vaguely believed that if war ended today a boat would be alongside tomorrow, and that at the end of the voyage they would find ' . . . a nicer house than before with unlimited new furniture arriving in plain vans, and the gardens that they never cultivated full of beautiful flowers . . . ' In short, these men of the 1st and 8th Armies, and their fellows of the Royal Navy and the Royal Air Force, were not pasteboard heroes or carefree schoolboys. They were 'such men . . . as made some conscience of what they did.' It was certain that they, steadfast, enduring, and brave, would continue and end the work that they had begun.

---

[1] A letter-writer commented '. . . The well-meaning but hopeless imbecile responsible for that scheme, no doubt switches off his wife every night, and goes to bed with a wireless set . . .'

APPENDIX I

Principal Commanders and Staff Officers in the Mediterranean and Middle East

(The ranks given are in some cases 'acting' ranks.
Some brief temporary appointments are omitted.)

ROYAL NAVY IN WESTERN MEDITERRANEAN

Naval Commander Expeditionary Force: (from 1st November 1942) Admiral of the Fleet Sir Andrew Cunningham, and, from 20th February 1943, Commander-in-Chief Mediterranean
Chief of Staff: Commodore R. M. Dick
Deputy Naval Commander Expeditionary Force: (from 1st November 1942) Admiral Sir Bertram Ramsay (from February 1943 he began planning the Assault of the British element in 'Husky')
Chief of Staff: Commodore C. E. Douglas-Pennant
Flag Officer Force H: Vice-Admiral Sir Neville Syfret; Vice-Admiral Sir Harold Burrough (from 27th January 1943); Vice-Admiral A. U. Willis (from 4th March 1943)
V. A. Aircraft Carriers: Vice-Admiral A. L. St. G. Lyster (to mid-November 1942)
R. A. Force H: Rear-Admiral A. W. La T. Bissett (from 7th May 1943)
Commander Eastern Naval Task Force: Vice-Admiral Sir Harold Burrough
Commander Central Naval Task Force: Commodore T. H. Troubridge
R.A. 12th Cruiser Squadron: Rear-Admiral C. H. J. Harcourt (from 25th November 1942); Commodore W. G. Agnew (from 28th May 1943)
S.N.O. Inshore Squadron ('Torch' Area): Commodore G. N. Oliver
Commodore Algiers: Rear-Admiral J. A. V. Morse (from 25th December 1942)
Flag Officer Commanding North Atlantic: Admiral Sir Frederick Edward-Collins
Flag Officer-in-Charge Bizerta: Admiral Sir Gerald Dickens (Retd.) (from 20th May 1943)

ROYAL NAVY IN CENTRAL AND EASTERN MEDITERRANEAN

Commander-in-Chief Mediterranean: Admiral Sir Henry Harwood (to 20th February 1943)
Commander-in-Chief Levant: Admiral Sir Henry Harwood (from 20th February 1943); Vice-Admiral Sir Ralph Leatham (from 27th March 1943)
Chief of Staff: Commodore J. G. L. Dundas
Additional Chief of Staff, R.N., at Middle East H.Q. Cairo: Commodore H. G. Norman; Commodore E. B. K. Stevens (from March 1943)
R.A. 15th Cruiser Squadron: Rear-Admiral A. J. Power; Rear-Admiral C. H. J. Harcourt (from 28th May 1943)

Commodore Destroyers: Commodore P. Todd
Vice-Admiral in Charge, Malta: Vice-Admiral Sir Ralph Leatham; Vice-Admiral Sir Stuart Bonham-Carter (from 29th January 1943); Vice-Admiral A. J. Power (from 7th May 1943)
R. A. Alexandria: Rear-Admiral G. H. Creswell; Rear-Admiral A. Poland (from 1st November 1942)
Flag Officer Commanding Red Sea and Canal Area: Vice-Admiral R. H. C. Hallifax
Senior Naval Officer Persian Gulf: Commodore C. F. Hammill
Directorate of Combined Operations Middle East: Rear-Admiral L. E. H. Maund
S.N.O. Inshore Squadron (8th Army Area): Captain C. Wauchope

UNITED STATES

Commander Western Naval Task Force: Vice-Admiral H. Kent Hewitt
Commander Northern Attack Group: Rear-Admiral Monroe Kelly
Commander Central Attack Group: Captain Robert R. M. Emmet
Commander Southern Attack Group: Rear-Admiral Lyal A. Davidson

THE ARMY

(The reader is referred also to: Lieutenant-Colonel H. F. Joslen, *Orders of Battle*. Vols I and II. H.M.S.O. 1960.)

Allied Force Headquarters

Allied Commander-in-Chief, North African Theatre: General Dwight D. Eisenhower
Deputy Allied Commander-in-Chief: Lieutenant-General Mark W. Clark; General the Hon. Sir Harold Alexander (from 19th February 1943)
Principal Staff Officers
   Chief of Staff: Major-General Walter Bedell Smith
   Chief Administrative Officer: Major-General H. M. Gale

General Headquarters Middle East

Commander-in-Chief: General the Hon. Sir Harold Alexander; General Sir Maitland Wilson (from 16th February 1943)
Principal Staff Officers
   General Staff branch: Lieutenant-General R. L. McCreery; Lieutenant-General R. M. Scobie (from 22nd March 1943)
   Quarter-Master-General's branch: Major-General G. Surtees
   Adjutant-General's branch: Major-General C. D. Moorhead
   Lieutenant-General, Adminstration: Lieutenant-General Sir Wilfrid Lindsell

18th Army Group
General the Hon. Sir Harold Alexander

1st Army
Lieutenant-General K. A. N. Anderson

8th Army
General Sir Bernard Montgomery

9th Army
Lieutenant-General W. G. Holmes

APPENDIX 1

10th Army
General Sir Edward Quinan

Malta
Governor and Commander-in-Chief: Field-Marshal the Viscount Gort, V.C.
General Officer Commanding: Major-General R. M. Scobie; Major-General W. H. Oxley (from 27th March 1943)

Persia and Iraq Command
General Sir Maitland Wilson; General Sir Henry Pownall (from 23rd March 1943)

British Troops, Egypt
Lieutenant-General R. G. W. H. Stone

Tripolitania Base and Tripolitania District
Major-General Sir Brian Robertson

Formations
(As mentioned in the text of the volume)

5th Corps: Lieutenant-General C. W. Allfrey
9th Corps: Lieutenant-General J. T. Crocker; Lieutenant-General B. G. Horrocks (from 30th April 1943)
10th Corps: Lieutenant-General H. Lumsden; Lieutenant-General B. G. Horrocks (from 9th December 1942); Lieutenant-General Sir Bernard Freyberg, V.C. (from 30th April 1943)
13th Corps: Lieutenant-General B. G. Horrocks; Lieutenant-General M. C. Dempsey (from 12th December 1942)
30th Corps: Lieutenant-General Sir Oliver Leese
New Zealand Corps: Lieutenant-General Sir Bernard Freyberg, V.C.
1st Armoured Division: Major-General R. Briggs
6th Armoured Division: Major-General C. F. Keightley
7th Armoured Division: Major-General A. F. Harding; Major-General G. W. E. J. Erskine (from 24th January 1943)
8th Armoured Division: Major-General C. H. Gairdner
10th Armoured Division: Major-General A. H. Gatehouse; Major-General H. L. Birks (from 12th January 1943)
1st Division: Major-General W. E. Clutterbuck
4th Division: Major-General J. L. I. Hawkesworth
44th Division: Major-General I. T. P. Hughes
46th Division: Major-General H. A. Freeman-Attwood
50th Division: Major-General J. S. Nichols; Major-General S. C. Kirkman (from 14th April 1943)
51st Division: Major-General D. N. Wimberley
56th Division: Major-General E. C. Miles; Major-General D. A. H. Graham (from 5th May 1943)
78th Division: Major-General V. Evelegh
9th Australian Division: Lieutenant-General Sir Leslie Morshead

2nd New Zealand Division: Lieutenant-General Sir Bernard Freyberg, V.C. who was also G.O.C. 2nd New Zealand Expeditionary Force.
1st South African Division: Major-General D. H. Pienaar
4th Indian Division: Major-General F. I. S. Tuker

Certain Allied Formations

United States

2nd U.S. Corps: Lieutenant-General Lloyd R. Fredendall; Lieutenant-General George S. Patton (from 6th March 1943); Lieutenant-General Omar N. Bradley (from 16th April 1943)
1st U.S. Armoured Division: Major-General Orlando Ward; Major-General Ernest N. Harmon (from 5th April 1943)
1st U.S. Infantry Division: Major-General Terry de la M. Allen
9th U.S. Infantry Division: Major-General Manton S. Eddy
34th U.S. Infantry Division: Major-General Charles W. Ryder

French

French North African Forces: Général d'Armée H. Giraud
French North African Land Forces: Général de Corps d'Armée A. Juin
19th Corps: Général de Corps d'Armée L. M. Koeltz
Tunisian Troops: Général de Division G. Barré
Division de Constantine: Général de Division J. E. Welvert; Général de Brigade J. Schwarz (from 10th April 1943)
Division d'Alger: Général de Brigade Conne
Division du Maroc: Général de Brigade Mathenet
Division d'Oran: Général de Division Boissau
Armoured Group: Général de Brigade Le Coulteux
'L' Force: Général de Division Leclerc
1st F.F. Division: Général de Division de Larminat

ROYAL AIR FORCE AND UNITED STATES ARMY AIR FORCE

MEDITERRANEAN
(Mediterranean Air Command formed 17th February 1943)

Command Headquarters

Air Commander-in-Chief: Air Chief Marshal Sir Arthur Tedder
Deputy Air Commander-in-Chief: Air Vice-Marshal H. E. P. Wigglesworth
Chief of Staff: Brigadier-General H. A. Craig, U.S.A.A.F.
Director of Operations: Brigadier-General P. W. Timberlake, U.S.A.A.F.
Director of Maintenance and Supply: Air Vice-Marshal G. G. Dawson

MIDDLE EAST
(Became Middle East Air Command 18th February 1943)

Air Headquarters, Royal Air Force
Air Officer Commanding-in-Chief: Air Chief Marshal Sir Arthur Tedder; Air Chief Marshal Sir William Sholto Douglas (from 11th January 1943)

APPENDIX 1

Deputy Air Officer Commanding-in-Chief: Air Marshal R. M. Drummond; Air Marshal Sir John Linnell (from 6th May 1943)

Senior Air Staff Officer: Air Vice-Marshal H. E. P. Wigglesworth; Air Vice-Marshal Sir Hugh Lloyd (from 1st October 1942); Air Vice-Marshal W. A. Coryton (from 26th March 1943)

Air Officer-in-Charge of Administration: Air Vice-Marshal G. C. Pirie; Air Vice-Marshal E. B. C. Betts (from 26th March 1943)

Chief Maintenance and Supply Officer (appointment lapsed on 17th February 1943): Air Vice-Marshal G. G. Dawson

No. 201 (Naval Co-operation) Group R.A.F.: Air Vice-Marshal Sir Leonard Slatter; Air Commodore J. R. Scarlett-Streatfeild (from 3rd February 1943); Air Vice-Marshal T. A. Langford-Sainsbury (from 29th March 1943)

No. 205 Group R.A.F.: Air Commodore A. P. Ritchie; Air Commodore O. R. Gayford (from 22nd December 1942)

No. 216 Group R.A.F. (re-formed on September 1st 1942 as a 'Transport and Ferry Group'): Air Commodore Whitney W. Straight

Air Headquarters, Egypt

(became Air Headquarters, Air Defences Eastern Mediterranean, 4th March 1943)

Air Officer Commanding: Air Vice-Marshal W. A. McClaughry; Air Vice-Marshal R. E. Saul (from 5th January 1943)

No. 209 Group R.A.F. (Levant) (formed 15th December 1942): Group Captain G. M. Buxton; Group Captain E. W. Whitley (from 6th February 1943)

No. 210 Group R.A.F. (Tripolitania) (formed 8th February 1943): Group Captain J. Grandy

No. 212 Group R.A.F. (Cyrenaica) (transferred from Western Desert Air Force to Air Headquarters, Egypt, 25th November 1942 and re-formed 1st December 1942): Group Captain H. A. Fenton; Group Captain A. J. Rankin (from 1st December 1942); Air Commodore K. B. B. Cross (from 20th January 1943); Air Commodore G. M. Lawson (from 22nd February 1943); Air Commodore A. H. Wann (from 26th March 1943)

No. 219 Group R.A.F. (Egypt) (formed 6th December 1942): Group Captain K. B. B. Cross; Group Captain G. A. G. Johnson (from 19th January 1943)

Air Headquarters, Levant

Air Officer Commanding: Air Commodore L. O. Brown; Air Commodore M. L. Taylor(from 6th December 1942); Group Captain J. E. G. H. Thomas (from 1st May 1943)

No. 213 Group R.A.F. (reduced to a nucleus Group 12th November 1942 and re-formed same day for duties in Syria): Group Captain S. D. Macdonald; Group Captain R. A. R. Mangles (from 2nd October 1942); Group Captain F. M. Denny (from 14th February 1943); Group Captain T. Humble (from 28th May 1943)

Air Headquarters, Iraq
(became Air Headquarters, Iraq and Persia, 1st January 1943)

Air Officer Commanding: Air Vice-Marshal H. V. Champion de Crespigny

No. 214 Group R.A.F. (merged with No. 217 Group R.A.F. 30th November 1942 and re-formed at Castel Benito 1st May 1943 to administer R.A.F. units in Tripolitania): Group Captain R. M. Foster; Group Captain R. Pyne (from 10th September 1942); Air Commodore J. P. Coleman (from 1st May 1943)

No. 215 Group R.A.F.: Air Commodore H. B. Russell; Air Commodore G. L. Carter (from 2nd May 1943)

No. 217 Group R.A.F. (formed as 'Persian Group' 1st September 1942 and became No. 217 Group 18th September 1942. Absorbed No. 214 Group R.A.F. 30th November 1942. Reduced to number basis 1st May 1943): Group Captain S. D. Macdonald; Group Captain C. Hallawell (from 30th January 1943)

Air Headquarters, Deeforce (formed 1st October 1942)

Air Officer Commanding: Air Commodore R. M. Foster; Group Captain C. W. Hill (from 26th February 1943)

Headquarters, British Forces, Aden

Air Officer Commanding: Air Vice-Marshal F. G. D. Hards; Air Vice-Marshal F. H. Macnamara (from 12th January 1943)

No. 203 Group R.A.F. (Sudan) (reduced to a number basis 10th May 1943 and re-formed at Heliopolis as a Training Group same day): Air Commodore R. G. Parry; Group Captain G. M. Buxton (from 26th March 1943); Air Commodore M. L. Taylor (from 10th May 1943)

No. 207 Group R.A.F. (became Air Headquarters, East Africa, 16th November 1942): Air Commodore M. L. Taylor; Air Vice-Marshal H. E. P. Wigglesworth (from 1st October 1942); Air Commodore G. S. Shaw (from 7th February 1943); Air Vice-Marshal H. S. Kerby (from 5th March 1943)

UNITED STATES ARMY MIDDLE EAST AIR FORCE

(formed 28th June 1942. Became United States Ninth Air Force 12th November 1942)

Air Headquarters

Commanding General: Major-General L. H. Brereton, U.S.A.A.F.

United States IX Bomber Command (formed unofficially 12th October and officially recognized 27th November 1942): Brigadier-General P. W. Timberlake, U.S.A.A.F.; Colonel (later Brigadier-General) U. G. Ent, U.S.A.A.F. (from 19th March 1943)

United States IX Fighter Command (an advanced detachment arrived in the Middle East 23rd December 1942): Colonel John C. Kilborn, U.S.A.A.F.; Brigadier-General Auby C. Strickland, U.S.A.A.F. (from January 1943)

United States IX Air Service Command (formed 12th November 1942. Originally the United States IX Air Force Service Command): Brigadier-General E. E. Adler, U.S.A.A.F.; Colonel (later Brigadier-General) Robert Kauch, U.S.A.A.F. (from 4th January 1943); Colonel John D. Corkille, U.S.A.A.F. (from 22nd March 1943)

APPENDIX 1

WESTERN DESERT AIR FORCE

(placed under the operational control of Northwest African Tactical Air Force 23rd February 1943 but remained under Royal Air Force, Middle East, for administration)

Air Headquarters

Air Officer Commanding: Air Vice-Marshal Sir Arthur Coningham; Air Vice-Marshal Harry Broadhurst (from 1st February 1943)

No. 211 Group R.A.F.: Group Captain G. L. Carter; Group Captain R. L. R. Atcherley (from 2nd February 1943)

No. 212 Group R.A.F. (formed unofficially 15th September 1942 and transferred to Air Headquarters, Egypt, 25th November 1942): Group Captain H. A. Fenton

Desert Air Task Force

(United States Army Air Force Headquarters for the control and co-ordination of operations of U.S.A.A.F. squadrons with the Western Desert Air Force. Formed 22nd October 1942. Became Desert Air Task Force, United States Ninth Air Force, 15th February 1943 and Advanced Headquarters, United States Ninth Air Force, 13th March 1943)

Commanding General: Under direct command of Major-General L. H. Brereton, U.S.A.A.F., Commanding General U.S.A.M.E.A.F. until 1st March 1943; Brigadier-General Auby C. Strickland, U.S.A.A.F. (from 1st March 1943); Colonel C. Darcy, U.S.A.A.F. (from 13th March 1943)

MALTA

(Became Malta Air Command 18th February 1943 but remained under Royal Air Force, Middle East, for administration)

Air Officer Commanding: Air Vice-Marshal Sir Keith Park

NORTH WEST AFRICA

Allied Air Force (formed 5th January and became Northwest African Air Forces 18th February 1943)

Commander-in-Chief: Major-General Carl Spaatz, U.S.A.A.F.

Allied Air Support Command (formed 22nd January 1943 and became Northwest African Tactical Air Force 18th February 1943): Brigadier-General L. S. Kuter, U.S.A.A.F.; Air Marshal Sir Arthur Coningham (from 17th February 1943)

EASTERN AIR COMMAND

(absorbed by Northwest African Air Forces 18th February 1943)

Air Headquarters

Air Officer Commanding: Air Marshal Sir William Welsh

Senior Air Staff Officer: Air Commodore G. M. Lawson; Air Commodore F. W. Long (from 8th November, 1942)

Air Officer-in-Charge of Administration: Air Commodore A. MacGregor.

No. 242 Group R.A.F. (raised from nucleus to Group status 6th December 1942 and became part of Northwest African Tactical Air Force 18th February 1943): Air Commodore G. M. Lawson; Air Commodore K. B. B. Cross (from 22nd February 1943)

APPENDIX 1

WESTERN AIR COMMAND
(absorbed by Northwest African Air Forces 18th February 1943)
Air Headquarters
(also Headquarters, United States Twelfth Air Force)

Commanding General: Major-General James H. Doolittle, U.S.A.A.F.
Chief of Staff: Colonel Hoyt S. Vandenberg, U.S.A.A.F.
United States XII Bomber Command (absorbed by Northwest African Strategic Air Force 18th February 1943): Colonel Claude E. Duncan, U.S.A.A.F.
United States XII Fighter Command (absorbed by Northwest African Coastal Air Force 18th February 1943): Colonel (later Brigadier-General) Thomas W. Blackburn, U.S.A.A.F.
United States XII Air Support Command (became part of Northwest African Tactical Air Force 18th February 1943): Brigadier-General J. K. Cannon, U.S.A.A.F.; Brigadier-General H. A. Craig, U.S.A.A.F. (from 10th January 1943); Colonel Paul L. Williams, U.S.A.A.F. (from 21st January 1943)

NORTHWEST AFRICAN AIR FORCES
(formed 18th February 1943)
Air Headquarters

Commanding General: Major-General Carl Spaatz, U.S.A.A.F.
Deputy: Air Vice-Marshal J. M. Robb
Chief of Staff: Colonel E. P. Curtis, U.S.A.A.F.
Air Officer-in-Charge of Administration: Air Commodore A. MacGregor
Northwest African Strategic Air Force (formed 18th February 1943): Major-General James H. Doolittle, U.S.A.A.F.
Northwest African Coastal Air Force (formed 18th February 1943): Group Captain G. G. Barrett; Air Vice-Marshal Sir Hugh Lloyd (from 14th March 1943)
Northwest African Tactical Air Force (formed 18th February 1943): Air Marshal Sir Arthur Coningham
Northwest African Tactical Bomber Force (formed 20th March 1943 under Northwest African Tactical Air Force): Air Commodore L. F. Sinclair
Northwest African Troop Carrier Command (formed 18th March 1943): Colonel (later Brigadier-General) R. A. Dunn, U.S.A.A.F.
Northwest African Photographic Reconnaissance Wing (formed 18th February 1943) : Lieutenant-Colonel Elliot Roosevelt, U.S.A.A.F.
Northwest African Air Service Command (formed 18th February 1943): Brigadier-General (later Major-General) Delmar H. Dunton, U.S.A.A.F.

GIBRALTAR

(Under command of Coastal Command, Royal Air Force, but the Air Officer Commanding was placed under the control of the Commander-in-Chief, Allied Expeditionary force, for Operation 'Torch')
Air Officer Commanding: Air Commodore S. P. Simpson
   Note: Air Vice-Marshal J. M. Robb was attached to Air Headquarters from 21st October to 30th November 1942 to control air preparations and operations in support of Operation 'Torch'.

APPENDIX 2

Appointments held by some German and Italian Commanders and Staff Officers during the period of this volume

(Some Acting or Temporary Appointments are omitted)

GERMAN

Arnim, Colonel-General Jürgen von: commander Pz AOK 5, later of Army Group Africa in succession to Rommel, from March 1943

Bayerlein, Major-General Fritz: Chief of Staff D.A.K., later of German-Italian Panzerarmee, later German Chief of Staff AOK 1

Borowietz, Major-General Willibald: commander 15th Panzer Division, from November 1942 in succession to von Vaerst

Broich, Major-General Freiherr Fritz von: commander Division von Broich, later of 10th Panzer Division

Buelowius, Major-General Karl: Chief Engineer of German-Italian Panzerarmee, later of Army Group Africa; temporarily commanded D.A.K. Assault Group and von Manteuffel Division

Burckhardt, Lieutenant-General: commander 19th Flak Division

Cramer, General Hans: commander D.A.K. from March 1943

Dönitz, Grand Admiral Karl: Commander-in-Chief German Navy, succeeded Raeder in January 1943

Fehn, General Gustav: commander D.A.K. November 1942–January 1943

Fischer, Lieutenant-General Karl: commander 10th Panzer Division

Frantz, Major-General Gotthard: commander 19th Flak Division from January 1943

Gause, Lieutenant-General Alfred: Chief of Staff to Rommel 1941–42, later Chief of Staff Army Group Africa

Göring, Marshal of the Reich Hermann: C.-in-C. German Air Force

Hagen, Colonel Walter: Fliegerführer 3

Harlinghausen, Major-General Martin: Fliegerführer Tunisia. Commanded Fliegerkorps II in succession to Loerzer from March 1943

Heigl, Colonel Heinrich: Q.M.G. Panzerarmee 5

Jodl, Lieutenant-General Alfred: Chief of Operations Staff OKW

Keitel, Field-Marshal Wilhelm: Chief of OKW

APPENDIX 2

Kesselring, Field-Marshal Albert: Commander-in-Chief South, and commander Luftflotte 2

Kosch, Colonel Benno: Fliegerführer 2

Krause, Major-General Fritz: Artillery commander German-Italian Panzerarmee, later 334th Division

Liebenstein, Major-General Freiherr Kurt von: commander 164th Light Division; acting commander D.A.K. January—February 1943

Loerzer, General Bruno: commander Fliegerkorps II until March 1943

Manteuffel, Major-General Hasso von: commander Division von Manteuffel (formerly Division von Broich)

Markert, Colonel Anton: German Chief of Staff AOK 1 in succession to Bayerlein

Nehring, General Walther: commander XC Corps

Neuffer, Major-General Georg: commander 20th Flak Division

Otto, Lieutenant-Colonel Walter: Q.M.G. German-Italian Panzerarmee 1941–March 1943

Raeder, Grand Admiral Erich: Commander-in-Chief German Navy until January 1943

Rintelen, General Enno von: Military Attaché and German General at H.Q. Italian Armed Forces, Rome

Rommel, Field-Marshal Erwin: commander German-Italian Panzerarmee, then of Army Group Africa until March 1943

Ruge, Vice-Admiral Friedrich: Chief of German Staff at Italian Admiralty from March 1943

Schmid, Major-General Josef: acting commander Hermann Göring Division

Seidemann, Major-General Hans: Fliegerführer Africa, then commander Fliegerkorps Tunis

Sponeck, Lieutenant-General Graf Theodor von: commander 90th Light Division

Stumme, General Georg: acting commander German-Italian Panzerarmee, September–October 1942

Vaerst, General Gustav von: commander Pz AOK 5 in succession to von Arnim

Waldau, Lieutenant-General Otto Hoffman von: commander Fliegerkorps X

Warlimont, Lieutenant-General Walter: Deputy Chief of Operations Staff OKW

Weber, Major-General Friedrich: commander 334th Division

APPENDIX 2

Weichold, Vice-Admiral Eberhard: German Naval Commander Italy until March 1943

Westphal, Major-General Siegfried: Chief of Operations Branch, H.Q of C-in-C South

Ziegler, Lieutenant-General Heinz: Chief of Staff Pz AOK 5, and acting commander D.A.K. February–March 1943

ITALIAN

Ambrosio, General Vittorio: Chief of Staff Italian Armed Forces from February 1943 in succession to Cavallero

Arena, General Francesco: commander Ariete Division

Bacchiani, Colonel Augusto: commander Settore Aeronautico Centrale, later Nord

Barbasetti di Prun, General Curio: Head of Delegation from Comando Supremo (Delease)

Bastico, Marshal Ettore: Commander-in-Chief Armed Forces in North Africa until February 1943

Bergamini, Admiral Carlo: Commander-in-Chief Afloat, in succession to Iachino

Bernasconi, General Mario: commander 5th Squadra in succession to Marchese

Biani, Colonel Vincenzo: commander Settore Aeronautico Sud from March 1943 in succession to Drago

Bonomi, Brigadier-General Ruggero: commander Settore Aeronautico Ovest

Boschi, Brigadier-General Mario: acting commander of reinstituted Comando Aeronautica Tunisia formerly commanded by Gaeta

Calvi di Bergolo, General Count Carlo: commander Centauro Division

Cavallero, Marshal Ugo: Chief of Staff Italian Armed Forces until February 1943

Drago, Colonel Carlo: commander Settore Aeronautico Est, later Sud

Falugi, General Guglielmo: commander Pistoia Division

Frattini, General Enrico: commander Folgore Division

Gaeta, Brigadier-General Giuseppe: commander of all Italian Air Force units in Tunisia November 1942–February 1943

Iachino, Admiral Angelo: Commander-in-Chief Afloat until April 1943

Imperiali de Francavilla, Brigadier-General: commander 'L' Special Brigade

La Ferla, General Francesco: commander Trieste Division

Lorenzelli, General Dante: commander Superga Division

Mancinelli, Brigadier-General Giuseppe: Italian Chief of Staff AOK 1

Marchese, General Vittorio: commander 5th Squadra until October 1942

Mattioli, Brigadier-General Enrico: Liaison Officer to Comando Supremo

Messe, General Giovanni: commander AOK 1. Promoted Marshal 12th May 1943

Navarrini, General Enea: commander 21st Corps

Riccardi, Admiral Arturo: Chief of Staff Italian Navy

Rossi, General Silvio: Chief of Operations Branch Comando Supremo

de Stefanis, General Giuseppe: commander 20th Corps

APPENDIX 3

Certain messages between Hitler, Rommel, and Comando Supremo, of 2nd, 3rd and 4th November, 1942 during the Battle of El Alamein. Referred to on pages 72 and 85. German time was two hours behind 8th Army's time.

(a) *Rommel to OKW 7.50 p.m. on 2nd November.*
'After ten days of extremely hard fighting against overwhelming British superiority on the ground and in the air the strength of the Army is exhausted in spite of today's successful defence. It will, therefore, no longer be in a position to prevent new attempt to break through with strong enemy armoured formations which is expected to take place tonight or tomorrow. An orderly withdrawal of the six Italian and two German non-motorized divisions and brigades is impossible for lack of MT. A large part of these formations will probably fall into the hands of the enemy who is fully motorized. Even the mobile troops are so closely involved in the battle that only elements will be able to disengage from the enemy. The stocks of ammunition which are still available are at the front but no more than nominal stocks are at our disposal in rear. The shortage of fuel will not allow of a withdrawal to any great distance. There is only one road available and the Army, as it passes along it, will almost certainly be attacked day and night by the enemy air force.

In these circumstances we must therefore expect the gradual destruction of the Army in spite of the heroic resistance and exceptionally high morale of the troops'.

(Signed) Rommel
No. 132/42

(b) *Hitler to Rommel. 3rd November. This telegram is headed '3rd November 23.30 hrs' which must be an error for 11.30 hrs, vide the start of message (d) below. Moreover, it was received at Panzerarmee at about 1.30 p.m. on the 3rd.*

'The German people join with me in following, with full confidence in your leadership and in the bravery of the German and Italian troops under your Command, the heroic defence in Egypt. In your present situation nothing else can be thought of but to hold on, not to yield a step, and to throw every weapon and every fighting man who can still be freed into the battle. Strong air reinforcements will be sent to OB Süd in the next few days, and the Duce and Comando Supremo will do their utmost to provide you with the means to carry on the struggle. Despite his superiority the enemy must also have exhausted his strength. It would not be the first time in history that the stronger will has triumphed over the enemy's stronger battalions. You can show your troops no other road than to victory or death.'

Adolf Hitler

(c) *Comando Supremo to Italian Liaison Staff at HQ Panzerarmee. 11 a.m. 3rd November.*

'Please inform Field Marshal Rommel that the Duce considers it essential, whatever the cost, to hold the present front. In the opinion of Comando Supremo nowhere else in Egypt is suitable except to offer resistance for a short time while formations are being reorganized. As a measure of extreme caution Delease was ordered a few days ago to occupy the Sollum-Halfaya positions with small units and whatever artillery is available.[1] Naturally no forces allocated to the Panzerarmee will be employed for this purpose. Everything possible will be done to get supplies across by sea and air.'

(d) *Rommel to Hitler. 3rd November. Untimed.*

'With reference to the signal of 3 November 1130 hrs, I report that during the night 2/3 November the Italian Divisions and the Ramcke Brigade in the southern sector were withdrawn behind a general line El Taqa—Bab el Qattara—south of Deir el Murra in order to shorten the front. They have orders to defend themselves to the last. The German divisions are engaged in the northern sector in extremely heavy fighting with greatly superior enemy forces. They are defending the area Deir el Murra—Sidi Abd el Rahman. All the available German Forces have already been thrown in. Up to now the German losses in Infantry, Panzerjäger, and Engineers amount to about 50%, in Artillery about 40%. 24 tanks are at present available to D.A.K. Of 20th Corps, the Littorio and Trieste divisions have been practically wiped out. The Ariete which has, up to now, been in the southern sector, was brought up during the night 2/3 November to positions directly adjoining D.A.K.

Every last effort will continue to be made to hold the battlefield.'

Rommel
No. 133/42

(e) *Rommel to Hitler. 11.15 a.m. 4th November.*

'In the last day or two the enemy has broken through the main line in the northern sector on a front 10 km. wide and up to 15 km. deep with 400–500 tanks and strong infantry forces and has almost wiped out the troops holding the front line. We are continuing to do our utmost to retain possession of the battlefield. But our losses are so high that there is no longer a connected front.

We cannot expect any new German forces. Added to this the Italian troops have no more fighting value because of the enemy's great superiority

---

[1] Delease was an Italian organization set up in August 1942 as a link between Comando Supremo and the Panzerarmee. Its duties were almost wholly administrative but it had some responsibility for the defence of the L. of C. See Vol. III, Chapter XV.

on the ground and in the air. Some of the Italian infantry has already abandoned secure positions without orders.

I am fully aware of the necessity for holding this position to the last and not yielding a step.

But I believe that the British tactics of destroying one formation after another by the maximum concentration of fire and continual air attacks are turning against us and wasting our strength increasingly.

At the present time, therefore, I see mobile warfare, in which the enemy has to fight for every foot of ground, as the only possible way of damaging our opponent further and of continuing to prevent the loss of the African theatre.

I ask for your consent to carry out this plan.

If this is granted I intend to carry out a fighting withdrawal bit by bit to a new position running south from Fuka. On this line, which is approximately 70 km. long, the southern sector—to a width of about 30 km.—is practically impassable for tank formations.'

Rommel
135/42

(f) *Hitler to Rommel. 4th November. 8.50 p.m.*

'In reply to your No. 135/42 of 4 November. I have caused the Duce to be informed of my views. In the circumstances . . . I consent to your decision. The Duce has given orders accordingly through Comando Supremo.'

Adolf Hitler

(g) *Comando Supremo to Rommel. 4th November. 8.45 p.m.*
'. . . The Duce, after informing himself of OKW's point of view has recognized that it is appropriate for you to be given freedom of action to withdraw the army bit by bit to Fuka positions as you suggested. You must, however, make certain that the non-motorized units are withdrawn too . . .'

APPENDIX 4

Some types of landing ships and craft in use in 1942

(a) *Ships*

Type	Short Title	In Service. Remarks
Landing ship infantry (large)	L.S.I.(L)	'*Karanja*' and '*Glen*' class liners converted to carry L.C.A. and L.C.P. (see next table).
Landing ship infantry (medium)	L.S.I.(M)	'*Queen Emma*'. Dutch (Harwich to Hook service).
Landing ship infantry (small)	L.S.I.(S)	'*Prince Charles*'. Belgian (Dover to Ostend service).
Landing ship (gantry)	L.S.G.	'*Dale*' class oilers fitted to carry L.C.M. (see next table), and with gantries to hoist them out.
Landing ship tank	L.S.T.	Maracaibo oilers. Shallow-draught oilers designed to cross sandbars in Lake Maracaibo, Venezuela. Load: 20 heavy tanks or 30 trucks. Door and ramp in bows. 60-foot bridge to span water gap.
Headquarters ships	L.S.H.	H.M.S. *Bulolo* and *Largs*. Specially fitted for the purpose, e.g. with elaborate signals equipment. A few ships were fitted as Brigade H.Q. ships.

APPENDIX 4

(Appendix 4—contd.)

(b) *Craft*

Type and Short Title	Length & Beam (to nearest foot)	Displacement (tons)	Speed (knots) max. and cruising	Load
Landing craft assault L.C.A.	41 / 10	$13\frac{1}{2}$	$8\frac{1}{2}$ / —	35 equipped men. (Not more than 24 when lowering.)
Landing craft personnel (large) L.C.P.(L)	37 / 11	9	$10\frac{1}{2}$ / $9\frac{1}{4}$	25 equipped men.
Landing craft personnel (medium) L.C.P.(M)	38 / 10	$7\frac{1}{4}$	$7\frac{1}{2}$ / 6	20 equipped men.
Landing craft support (medium) L.C.S.(M)	As for L.C.A.			$2 \times 0.5''$ machine-guns. One 4-in. Smoke Mortar. One projector and ten rockets. Smoke generators.
Landing craft mechanized (1) L.C.M.(1)	45 / 14	37	$7\frac{1}{2}$ / $6\frac{1}{2}$	16 tons.
Landing craft mechanized (3) L.C.M.(3)	50 / 14	52	8 / 7	30 tons.
Landing craft tank (3) L.C.T.(3)	192 / 31	300	$10\frac{1}{2}$ / 9	260 tons.
Landing craft tank (4) L.C.T.(4)	187 / 39	350	10 / $8\frac{1}{2}$	300 tons.

NOTES: The above figures might vary slightly with different constructors and types of engine. L.C.A., L.C.M. and L.C.T. had ramps. L.C.A. were armoured against small-arms fire.

All craft were shallow draught, e.g. L.C.A. (loaded)   *Forward*   *Aft*
                                    1 ft 10 ins   2 ft 3 ins
                L.C.T.4   ,,   3 ft   4 ft 2 ins.

APPENDIX 5

Main strength of The Royal Navy in Mediterranean waters between early November 1942 and mid-May 1943

(Because of essential maintenance not all the ships in this list would be available continuously for immediate service, but no ship out of action at the times shown for more than a few days has been included)

SHIPS BASED ON PORTS IN THE WESTERN BASIN

	Early November 1942	Mid-February 1943	Early May 1943
Capital Ships:	Duke of York Rodney Renown	Nelson Rodney	King George V Nelson
Aircraft Carriers:	Formidable Victorious Furious Argus	Formidable	Formidable
Cruisers, 6-inch:	Sheffield Bermuda Jamaica Aurora	Aurora Penelope	Aurora Newfoundland Penelope
5·25-inch:	Argonaut Charybdis Scylla Sirius	Dido Sirius	Sirius
A.A. Cruisers:	Delhi	None	Carlisle
Destroyers:	47	31	33
Submarines:	12	15	15
Fast Minelayers:	Welshman	Abdiel	—

480

APPENDIX 5

SHIPS BASED ON PORTS IN CENTRAL AND EASTERN BASINS

		Early November 1942	Mid-February 1943	Early May 1943
Cruisers, 6-inch:		Arethusa Orion	Orion	Orion
5·25-inch:		Cleopatra Dido Euryalus	Cleopatra Euryalus	Cleopatra Euryalus
Destroyers:		16	21	22
Submarines:		18	13	18
Fast Minelayers:		Manxman	None	Abdiel

APPENDIX 5

Italian Fleet and German Submarines in the Mediterranean

(Ships seriously damaged and under repair are not included)

Early November 1942	Mid-February 1943	Early May 1943
Battleships: Littorio Vittorio Veneto Roma Duilio Cesare Doria	Littorio Vittorio Veneto Duilio ⎫ Cesare ⎬ † Doria ⎭	 Duilio ⎫ Cesare ⎬ † Doria ⎭

Cruisers, 8-inch:
    Trieste
    Gorizia
	Trieste
	Gorizia
		None

6-inch:
    Eugenio di Savoia
    Duca D'Aosta
    Montecuccoli
    Garibaldi
    Duca degli Abruzzi
    Cadorna
	Cadorna	Eugenio di Savoia
		Garibaldi
		Duca degli Abruzzi
		Cadorna

5·25-inch: Attilio Regolo	None	None
Fleet Destroyers: 22	16	11

Submarines:
    Italian* 38
    German   19
	21
	22
		26
		18

† Maintained in material readiness for sea but without fuel and with reduced crews.

* These figures are for submarines operating in the Mediterranean; in addition there were a number operating in the Atlantic.

APPENDIX 6

Outline distribution of British Land Forces in the Middle East and Mediterranean Theatre at mid-November 1942

NOTE: The Order of Battle of large modern land forces is a big document: a typical example, of Middle East Forces in 1943, consists of 130 pages and some 5,000 entries. A complete list of forces in the theatre would therefore be unmanageable in a volume such as this. On the other hand a selective list would be misleading because of the frequent movement and temporary regroupings of units. This Appendix attempts no more than an outline. Discrepancies may be noticed between this and the more detailed composition of some formations, which appears in the text or in footnotes. The explanation lies in the movements and regroupings to which we have referred. Much valuable information is to be found in 'Orders of Battle. Second World War 1939–1945' by Lieut.-Colonel H. F. Joslen. Two volumes. H.M.S.O. 1960.

8TH ARMY
10th Corps:
  1st Armoured Division
  7th Armoured Division
  New Zealand Division

13th Corps:
  44th Division
  9th Australian Division
  4th Indian Division

30th Corps:
  10th Armoured Division
  50th Division
  51st Highland Division
  24th Armoured Brigade
  21st Indian Infantry Brigade
  Tank Re-Organization Group

9TH ARMY
  201st Guards Motor Brigade
  25th Infantry Brigade
  10th, 20th, 26th Indian Infantry Brigades
  Four unbrigaded battalions

Egypt: 1st South African Division; 74th Armoured Brigade; 4th New Zealand Armoured Brigade; 132nd Infantry Brigade.
  Unbrigaded: four regiments R.A.C.; one regiment I.A.C.; fourteen battalions.
Sudan: Sudan Defence Force; four unbrigaded battalions.

Palestine: 1st Army Tank Brigade; one regiment R.A.C.; two unbrigaded battalions.
Aden: Three battalions.
Malta: Four infantry brigades.

1ST ARMY[1]
    Advanced H.Q. 1st Army
    One Regimental Group 6th Armoured Division
    78th Division (less one brigade)
    1st Parachute Brigade
    22nd and 52nd A.A. Brigades.

---

[1] An Order of Battle of 5th Corps on 6th December 1942 is given as Appendix 7.

APPENDIX 6

Outline distribution of British Land Forces in the Middle East and Mediterranean Theatre at the end of April 1943

8TH ARMY
  10th Corps:
    1st Armoured Division[a]
    7th Armoured Division[a]
    New Zealand Division
    51st Highland Division
    56th Division
    4th Indian Division[a]
  [a] Temporarily under command of 1st Army.

  H.Q. 30th Corps
  50th Division
  Four unbrigaded battalions.

9TH ARMY
  10th Armoured Division
  8th Indian Division
  10th Armoured Brigade
  10th, 20th, 25th Indian Infantry Brigades.

Egypt: 6th South African Armoured Division; 4th New Zealand Armoured Brigade; 168th and 231st Infantry Brigades.
  Unbrigaded: three regiments R.A.C.
Sudan: Sudan Defence Force; two unbrigaded battalions.
Palestine: 1st Army Tank Brigade; six unbrigaded battalions.
  13th Corps: 5th Division.
Aden: Three battalions.
Malta: Three infantry brigades.

1ST ARMY
  9th Corps: 5th Corps:
    1st Armoured Division[a]   1st Division
    6th Armoured Division   4th Division
    7th Armoured Division[a]   78th Division
    46th Division
    4th Indian Division[a]
  [a] Temporarily under command from 8th Army.

APPENDIX 7

On 6th December 1942, the date on which 5th Corps (Lt.-General C. W. Allfrey) became committed as a Corps to action in Tunisia, the Order of Battle was in outline:

Corps Troops: 9th/13th, 14th/16th Medium Batteries R.A.; 456th, 457th Light Batteries R.A.; 265th/45th L.A.A. Battery R.A.; 5th Corps Signals; 564th, 751st Fd Coys R.E.; 103rd Corps Bridge Coy R.A.S.C.

6th Armoured Division (Major-General C. F. Keightley)
Divisional Troops: 1st Derbyshire Yeomanry; 12th Regiment R.H.A.; 152nd Fd Regt R.A.; 72nd A/Tk Regt R.A.; 51st L.A.A. Regt R.A.; 5th Fd Squadron R.E.
26th Armoured Brigade (Brigadier C. A. L. Dunphie) 16th/5th The Queen's Royal Lancers; 17th/21st Lancers; 2nd Lothians and Border Horse; 10th Bn The Rifle Brigade.
38th Infantry Brigade (Brigadier N. Russell) 6th Bn Royal Inniskilling Fusiliers; 1st Bn The Royal Irish Fusiliers; 2nd Bn London Irish Rifles.

78th Division (Major-General V. Evelegh)
Divisional Troops: 56th Bn Reconnaissance Regt; 132nd, 138th Fd Regts R.A.; 64th A/Tk Regt R.A.; 49th L.A.A. Regt R.A.; 237th, 256th Fd Coys R.E.; 281st Fd Park Coy R.E.
1st Guards Brigade (Brigadier R. A. V. Copland-Griffiths) 3rd Bn Grenadier Guards; 2nd Bn Coldstream Guards; 2nd Bn The Hampshire Regiment.
11th Infantry Brigade (Brigadier E. E. E. Cass) 2nd Bn The Lancashire Fusiliers; 1st Bn The East Surrey Regiment; 5th Bn The Northamptonshire Regiment.
36th Infantry Brigade (Brigadier A. L. Kent-Lemon) 5th Bn The Buffs; 6th Bn The Queen's Own Royal West Kent Regiment; 8th Bn The Argyll and Sutherland Highlanders.

1st Parachute Brigade (Brigadier E. W. C. Flavell) 1st, 2nd, 3rd Parachute Battalions.

6th Commando

American Troops
Combat Command 'B' (Brigadier-General Lunsford F. Oliver) 13th Armoured Regiment: 1st and 2nd Bns, and 1st Bn 1st Armoured Regiment.
1st and 2nd Bns, 6th Armoured Infantry Regiment.
27th Field Artillery Bn.
One Coy 701st Tank Destroyer Bn.
One Coy 16th Armoured Engineers.

APPENDIX 7

Other American Units
   5th Field Artillery Bn.
   175th Field Artillery Bn.
   106th Coast Artillery (AA) Bn.
   Two Coys 701st Tank Destroyer Battalion.
   Coy 3rd Bn 39th Infantry Regiment.
   67th Armoured Regiment (25 tanks).
     Not all units in Combat Command 'B' or elsewhere were complete.

APPENDIX 8

Orders of Battle
Royal Air Force and
United States Army Air Forces

(a) Royal Air Force, Middle East Command
    and
    United States Army Middle East Air Force.
(b) Eastern Air Command (N.W.A.) (initially No. 333 Group, R.A.F.)
    November 1942—February 1943.
(c) Western Air Command (United States Twelfth Air Force)
    November—December 1942.
(d) Northwest African Air Forces, Malta Air Command and Middle East Air Command Mid-April 1943.

NOTES

1. The Orders of Battle include only operational chains of command and control, and operational formations and units, except for air transport and troop carrier aircraft, which are included because they were particularly closely connected with the fighting. The less closely connected non-operational flying units, which have been omitted, performed duties such as: meteorological flights, operational conversion, operational training, air communications in rear areas, calibration of radar and radio stations, and many another. In fact, until the middle of 1942, the number of aircraft engaged on non-operational duties was much greater than the number operationally employed. When American operational units arrived in the Middle East in mid-1942, and the Allied air forces for 'Torch' in French North Africa, the number of Allied operational aircraft in the Mediterranean theatre quickly increased. But non-operational commitments increased almost as quickly, so that by mid-April 1943 there were over 3,000 non-operational aircraft as against the 3,400–3,500 which were operational.

2. The Orders of Battle do not include the many administrative and ground units of all kinds which supported the flying squadrons. Examples are: maintenance and repair and salvage units; supply and transport columns; radar and wireless observer units; signals units; R.A.F. armoured car companies and the R.A.F. Regiment. The nature of the theatre explains the need for, and the number of, these units. In the Middle East there was no aircraft industry and no engineering industry that deserved the name, and therefore the R.A.F. had to be self-sufficient in repair and other technical requirements. Distances were vast, and the civil telephone and telegraph system was small, and so the R.A.F. had to maintain a

large signal-system. In French North Africa the need for administrative and ground units was as great, though not of the same size and kind, as in the Middle East.

Besides the units mentioned in this note, there were many others which were essential, and which employed large numbers of men.

ABBREVIATIONS

A.C.—Army Co-operation; A.O.P.—Air Observation Post; A.S.—Anti-submarine; A.T.—Air Transport; B.R.—Bomber Reconnaissance; B.T.—Bomber Transport; C.—Coastal Duties; Com.—Communications; Det.—Detached or Detachment; F.—Fighter; F.B.—Fighter-bomber; G.R. General Reconnaissance; H.B.—Heavy Bomber; L.B.—Light Bomber; M.B.—Medium Bomber; N.F.—Night-Fighter; P.F.—Pathfinder, including flare-dropping; P.R.—Photographic Reconnaissance; R.C.M.—Radar and Radio Counter-measures; S.E.—Single-engine; S.O.E.—Special Duty Operations; Strat. R.—Strategical Reconnaisance; Sur. R.—Survey Reconnaissance; Tac. R.—Tactical Reconnaissance; T.B.—Torpedo-bomber; T.C.—Troop Carrier; T.D.—Tank Destroyer; T.E.—Twin-engine.

N.A.A.S.C. — Northwest African Air Service Command.
N.A.C.A.F. — Northwest African Coastal Air Force.
N.A.P.R.W. — Northwest African Photographic Reconnaissance Wing.
N.A.S.A.F. — Northwest African Strategic Air Force.
N.A.T.A.F. — Northwest African Tactical Air Force.
N.A.T.B.F. — Northwest African Tactical Bomber Force.
N.A.T.C. — Northwest African Training Command.
N.A.T.C.C. — Northwest African Troop Carrier Command.
W.D.A.F. — Western Desert Air Force.

27th OCTOBER, 1942

R.A.F. MIDDLE EAST COMMAND

NOTE: OPERATIONAL COMMAND AND CONTROL ONLY
TOTAL AIRCRAFT ESTABLISHMENT: 1628

H.Q., R.A.F., M.E.

	Sqdn.	Role	Aircraft Est.	Type
	No. 2 P.R.U.	P.R.	24	Spitfire VB/Hurricane I
	No. 60 (S.A.A.F.)	Sur. R.	(Det. from W.D.A.F.)	Maryland
See FN	No. 162	R.M.C./M.B.	8	Wellington IC

No. 201 GROUP, R.A.F.

	Sqdn.	Role	Aircraft Est.	Type
	No. 1 G.R.U.	G.R.	6	Wellington D.W.I.
	No. 15 (S.A.A.F.)	L.B.	24	Blenheim V/Bisley
	No. 47	S.E.F.	16	Beaufort I/Wellesley
	No. 94			Spitfire VB/C
	No. 203	G.R.	(Det. from Egypt)	Blenheim IV/Bisley
				Baltimore I/II/III/Maryland
	No. 230	G.R.	6	Sunderland I/II/III/D.O. 22
	Nos. 252, 272	T.E.F.(C)	Total 32	Beaufighter IC/VIF
	No. 459 (R.A.A.F.)	G.R.	16	Hudson III
	No. 701 (F.A.A.)	G.R.	12	Walrus
See FN	No. 815 (F.A.A.), 826 (F.A.A.)	T.B.,P.F.	Total 24	Swordfish
				Albacore

No. 235 Wing, R.A.F.

	Sqdn.	Role	Aircraft Est.	Type
	No. 13 (Hellenic)	G.R.	16	Blenheim IV/Bisley
	No. 47	G.R.	(Det. see above)	Wellesley
	No. 459 (R.A.A.F.)	G.R.	(Det. see above)	Hudson III
	No. 701 (F.A.A.)	G.R.	(Det. see above)	Walrus

No. 247 Wing, R.A.F.

	Sqdn.	Role	Aircraft Est.	Type
	No. 38	M.B.,T.B.	(Det. see below)	Wellington IC/VIII
	No. 39	T.B.	(Det. see below)	Beaufort I/II
	No. 203	G.R.	(Det. see below)	Blenheim IV/Bisley
				Baltimore I/II/III/Maryland
	No. 221	T.B.	(Det. see below)	Wellington IC/VIII

No. 248 Wing, R.A.F.

	Sqdn.	Role	Aircraft Est.	Type
	Nos. 38, 458 (R.A.A.F.)	M.B.,T.B.	Total 32	Wellington IC/VIII
	No. 39	T.B.	16	Beaufort I/II
	No. 221	T.B.	16	Wellington IC/VIII

No. 203 GROUP (SUDAN), R.A.F.
L.B./Tac. R./P.R. (Det. from Egypt)
(Operated from Kufra to support 'Lightfoot'.)

	Sqdn.	Role	Aircraft Est.	Type
See FN	No. 15 (S.A.A.F.)			Blenheim V/Bisley

No. 205 GROUP, R.A.F.

	Sqdn.	Role	Aircraft Est.	Type
	Special Liberator Flight	S.O.E.	10	Liberator II

No. 231 Wing, R.A.F.

	Sqdn.	Role	Aircraft Est.	Type
See FN	Nos. 37, 70	M.B.	Total 32	Wellington IC

No. 236 Wing, R.A.F.

	Sqdn.	Role	Aircraft Est.	Type
See FN	Nos. 108, 148	M.B.	Total 32	Wellington IC

No. 238 Wing, R.A.F.

	Sqdn.	Role	Aircraft Est.	Type
See FN	No. 40	M.B.	16	Wellington IC
See FN	No. 104	M.B.	16	Wellington II

No. 242 Wing, R.A.F.

	Sqdn.	Role	Aircraft Est.	Type
	No. 160	H.B.	16	Liberator II

No. 245 Wing, R.A.F.

	Sqdn.	Role	Aircraft Est.	Type
*See FN	No. 14 (R.A.A.F.)	L.B./M.B.	16	Boston III/Marauder
	No. 462	H.B.	16	Halifax II

Footnote—Available to reinforce W.D.A.F. in support of 'Lightfoot' but not under its control.
(* Transferred to No. 201 Group 29th October 1942 for G.R. duties.)

No. 207 GROUP, R.A.F.
(Became A.H.Q., East Africa 16th November 1942)

	Sqdn.	Role	Aircraft Est.	Type
	No. 16 (S.A.A.F.) Flight	L.B.	16	Beaufort I/Maryland
	No. 34 (S.A.A.F.) Flight	G.R.	6	Anson
	No. 35 (S.A.A.F.) Flight	G.R.	6	Blenheim IV
†	No. 209	G.R.	6	Catalina I
	No. 321 (Dutch)	G.R.	(Det. from No. 222 Group, Ceylon)	Catalina IVB
	No. 803 (F.A.A.)	A.S.	12	Fulmar II
	No. 805 (F.A.A.)	S.E.F.	6	Martlet III
	No. 1433 Flight	Sur. R.		Lysander
	No. 41 (S.A.A.F.)	S.E.F./L.B.	32	Hurricane IIB/Hartbeest

(† Operationally controlled by No. 222 Group, Ceylon.)

No. 246 Wing, R.A.F.

No. 216 GROUP, R.A.F.
(Advance Unit—'Air Transport Force'—with W.D.A.F.)

	Sqdn.	Role	Aircraft Est.	Type
See FN	No. 117	A.T.	16	Hudson VI
See FN	No. 173	Com.	16	Boston III/Lodestar
See FN	No. 267	A.T.	16	Bombay/Hudson III/VI/Lodestar
		A.T.		Hudson III/VI/Lodestar/Dakota

No. 283 Wing (ERITREA), R.A.F.

	Sqdn.	Role	Aircraft Est.	Type
	No. 163	A.T.	16	Hudson VI

H.Q., BRITISH FORCES, ADEN

	Sqdn.	Role	Aircraft Est.	Type
	No. 8	G.R.	16	Blenheim I/IV/Bisley
	No. 459 (R.A.A.F.)	G.R.	(Det. from Egypt)	Hudson III
	Defence Flight	S.E.F.	8	Hurricane IIB

A.H.Q., EGYPT

	Sqdn.	Role	Aircraft Est.	Type
	No. 234 Wing, R.A.F.	S.E.F.	12	Fulmar II/Hurricane IIC
	No. 250 Wing, R.A.F.			
	No. 89	T.E.F. (N.F.)	16	Beaufighter IF/VIF
	No. 94	S.E.F.	16	Hurricane IIC/Spitfire VB/C
	No. 252 Wing, R.A.F.			
	No. 46	T.E.F. (N.F.)	16	Beaufighter IF/VIF
	No. 417 (R.C.A.F.)	S.E.F.	16	Hurricane IIC/Spitfire VB/C

A.H.Q., MALTA

	Sqdn.	Role	Aircraft Est.	Type
	No. 69	G.R./P.R.	12	Wellington V/VIII/Baltimore I/II/Spitfire P.R. IV
	No. 89	T.E.F. (N.F.)	(Det. from Egypt)	Beaufighter IF/VIF
	Nos. 126, 185, 1435 Flight	S.E.F.	Total 68	Spitfire VB/C
	No. 227	S.E.F.	20	Beaufighter IC/F/VIF
	No. 249	S.E.F.	16	Hurricane IIC/Spitfire VB
	No. 828 (F.A.A.) ('Y' Flight)	T.B.	3	Albacore
	No. 830 (F.A.A.) ('X' Flight)	T.B.	3	Swordfish

(a)

(a) contd.

W.D.A.F.

Sqdn.	Role	Aircraft Est.	Type
Nos. 12 (S.A.A.F.), 24 (S.A.A.F.)	No. 3 (S.A.A.F.) Wing		
	L.B.	Total 48	Boston III
No. 21 (S.A.A.F.)	L.B.	24	Baltimore I/II/III
	No. 232 Wing, R.A.F.		
Nos. 55, 223	L.B.	Total 48	Baltimore I/II/III
Attached			
82nd, 83rd, 434th (all U.S.A.A.F.)	M.B.	Total 39	Mitchell II
	No. 285 Wing, R.I.F.		
No. 2 P.R.U.	P.R.	(Det. from Egypt)	
No. 40 (S.A.A.F.)	Tac. R.	18	Hurricane I/IIA,B Maryland
No. 60 (S.A.A.F.)	Sur. R.	12	Hurricane IIA/B
No. 208 (S.A.A.F.)	Tac. R.	18	
No. 1437 Flight	Strat. R.	8	Baltimore I/II/III

No. 211 GROUP, R.A.F.
*No. 6, 7 (S.A.A.F.) (one Flight) — T.D. — Total 32 — Hurricane IID
(* Nos. 6 and 7 (S.A.A.F.) Squadrons were transferred to No. 212 Group when the Axis retreat began.)
Attached
†64th (U.S.A.A.F.) — S.E-F./F.B. — 25 — Kittyhawk II/III
†65th (U.S.A.A.F.) — S.E-F./F.B. — 25 — Kittyhawk II
(† Operated under the control of No. 211 Group as the equivalent of an R.A.F. Wing.)

No. 233 Wing, R.A.F.
Nos. 2 (S.A.A.F.), 4 (S.A.A.F.) — S.E-F./F.B. — Total 32 — Kittyhawk I/II/III
No. 5 (S.A.A.F.) — S.E-F./F.B. — 16 — Tomahawk
No. 260 — S.E-F./F.B. — 16 — Kittyhawk I/II

No. 239 Wing, R.A.F.
Nos. 3 (S.A.A.F.), 112, 250, 450 (R.A.A.F.) — S.E-F./F.B. — Total 64 — Kittyhawk I/II/III
Attached
66th (U.S.A.A.F.) — S.E-F./F.B. — 25 — Kittyhawk II

No. 244 Wing, R.A.F.
No. 73 — S.E-F. (N.F.) — 16 — Hurricane IIC
No. 92 — S.E-F. — 16 — Spitfire VB C
Nos. 145, 601 — S.E-F. — Total 32 — Spitfire VB

No. 212 GROUP, R.A.F.
No. 80 — No. 7 (S.A.A.F.) Wing — S.E-F. — 16 — Hurricane IIC
No. 127, 335 (Hellenic) — S.E-F. — Total 32 — Hurricane IIB
No. 274 — S.E-F. — 16 — Hurricane IIE

No. 243 Wing, R.A.F.
Nos. 1 (S.A.A.F.), 33, 213, 238 — S.E-F. — Total 64 — Hurricane IIC

A.H.Q., LEVANT

Sqdn.	Role	Aircraft Est.	Type
No. 2 P.R.U.	P.R.	(Det. from Egypt) 8	Hurricane I
No. 1438 Flight	Strat. R.		Blenheim IV
	No. 213 GROUP, R.A.F.		
	No. 241 Wing, R.A.F.		
No. 451 (R.A.A.F.)	Tac. R.	18	Hurricane I
	No. 259 Wing, R.A.F.		
No. 451 (R.A.A.F.)	Tac. R.	(Det. see above)	Hurricane I

A.H.Q., IRAQ
(Also responsible for the R.A.F. in Persia)

Sqdn.	Role	Aircraft Est.	Type
No. 240	G.R.	(Det. from No. 222 Group, Ceylon)	Catalina II
No. 413 (R.C.A.F.)	G.R.		Catalina I/IB/IVB
	No. 214 GROUP, R.A.F.		
	No. 237 Wing, R.A.F.		
No. 52	L.B.	24	Blenheim IV
No. 237 (Rhodesian)	Tac. R.	18	Hurricane I
	No. 215 GROUP, R.A.F.		
No. 244	G.R.	12	Blenheim IV/Bisley/Vincent
'X' Flight	S.E-F.	4	Gladiator

A.H.Q., *Defence*
(Nucleus formation in Persia)
No. 1434 Flight — Sur. R. — 4 — Blenheim IV

close liaison and co-operation → **U.S.A.M.E.A.F.**

(Became United States Ninth Air Force 12th November 1942)

*U.S. IX BOMBER COMMAND.
*U.S. 1st (Provisional) Heavy Bombardment Group
Halverson Squadron — H.B. — 8 — Liberator II
9th — H.B. — 8 — Fortress IIA

U.S. 98th Heavy Bombardment Group
343rd, 344th, 345th, 415th — H.B. — Total 32 (+3 Liberator II for Group H.Q.)

* Under the strategic direction of R.A.F. Middle East.
(† Became the U.S. 376th Heavy Bombardment Group 1st November 1942.)

U.S. DESERT AIR TASK FORCE

U.S. 12th Medium Bombardment Group
(Squadrons under operational control of W.D.A.F., with the exception of the 81st Squadron which had 13 Mitchell IIs plus 5 for Group H.Q.)

U.S. 57th Fighter Group
(Squadrons under operational control of W.D.A.F.—5 Kittyhawks II/IIIs with Group H.Q.)

APPENDIX 8

(b)

EASTERN AIR COMMAND (N.W.A.)

(Initially No 333 Group, Royal Air Force)
NOVEMBER 1942—FEBRUARY 1943

A.H.Q., E.A.C.

(Advanced A.H.Q. set up at ALGIERS 13th November 1942.)
(Absorbed by N.A.A.F. 18th February 1943)

No. 242 GROUP, R.A.F.

(Raised from nucleus to full Group status 6th December 1942 with H.Q. at AIN SEYMOUR)

No. 322 Wing, R.A.F.

(Mobile Wing. H.Q. set up at MAISON BLANCHE 8th November 1942)

Sqdn.	Role	Arrival in North West Africa		Aircraft Type
		As planned	Actual	
Nos. 81, 154, 242	S.E.-F.	8/11/42	8/11/42	Spitfire VB
No. 225	A.C.	12/11/42	13/11/42 (Aircraft 14/11/42)	Hurricane IIE

No. 323 Wing, R.A.F.

(Non-mobile Wing. H.Q. set up at MAISON BLANCHE 8th November 1942)

No. 43	S.E.-F.	8/11/42	8/11/42	Hurricane IIC
No. 253	S.E.-F.	8/11/42	10/11/42	Hurricane IIC
No. 4 P.R.U.	P.R.	12/11/42	13/11/42	Spitfire P.R.IV

(Began operations at Gibraltar 6/11/42).

No. 324 Wing R.A.F.

(Mobile Wing. H.Q. set up at MAISON BLANCHE 13th November 1942)

No. 111	S.E.-F.	22/11/42	11/11/42	Spitfire VB
No. 93	S.E.-F.	22/11/42	13/11/42	Spitfire VB
No. 152	S.E.-F.	22/11/42	14/11/42	Spitfire VB
No. 255	T.E.-F. (N.F.)	6/12/42	15/11/42	Beaufighter VIF
No. 72	S.E.-F.	22/11/42	16/11/42	Spitfire VB

No. 325 Wing, R.A.F.

(Mobile Wing. H.Q. set up at ALGIERS 22nd November 1942)

No. 600	T.E.-F. (N.F.)	6/12/42	18/11/42	Beaufighter VIF
No. 241	A.C.	22/11/42	22/11/42 (Aircraft 29/11/42)	Hurricane IIE
No. 32	S.E.-F.	6/12/42	7/12/2 (Aircraft 10/12/42)	Hurricane IIC
No. 87	S.E.-F.	6/12/42	7/12/42 (Aircraft 17/12/42)	Hurricane IIC
Nos. 232, 243	S.E.-F.	6/12/42	7/12/42 (Aircraft 3/1/43)	Spitfire VB

APPENDIX 8

No. 326 Wing, R.A.F.
(Semi-mobile Wing. H.Q. set up at BLIDA 13th November 1942)

No. 18	L.B.	12/11/42	11/11/42	Bisley
No. 114	L.B.	22/11/42	15/11/42	Bisley
Nos. 13, 614	B.R.	22/11/42	17/11/42	Bisley

No. 328 Wing, R.A.F.
(Non-mobile Wing. G.R. Operations Room set up at TAFARAOUI 10th November and H.Q. at BLIDA 17th November 1942)

No. 700 (F.A.A.)	A.S.	Not planned	8/11/42	Walrus
No. 813 (F.A.A.)	A.S./T.B.	12/11/42	10/11/42	Swordfish
(Transferred from Gibraltar)				
No. 500	G.R.	6/12/42	11/11/42	Hudson V
(Began operations at Gibraltar 5/11/42)				
No. 608	G.R.	12/11/42	13/11/42	Hudson V
(Began operations at Gibraltar 8/11/42)			(Aircraft 16/12/42)	

Additional Units

Sqdn.	Role	Arrival in North West Africa As planned	Actual	Aircraft Type
No. 651	A.O.P.	By convoy. Aircraft to be erected on arrival.	12/11/42	Auster I
No. 153	T.E.-F. (N.F.)	Not planned	19/11/42	Beaufighter VIF
No. 89	T.E.-F. (N.F.)	Not planned	26/11/42	Beaufighter VIF
Nos. 142, 150	M.B.	To be called forward	18–19/12/42	Wellington III
	TOTALS	28 Squadrons	31 Squadrons	

COASTAL COMMAND, ROYAL AIR FORCE

*H.Q., R.A.F., GIBRALTAR
(Less squadrons transferred later to North West Africa)

8th NOVEMBER 1942

Sqdn.	Role	Aircraft Type
No. 10 (R.A.A.F.)	G.R.	Sunderland II/III
No. 202	G.R.	Catalina I
No. 210	G.R.	Catalina I/IB
No. 233	G.R.	Hudson III
No. 235 (Det. from U.K.)	T.E.-F.	Beaufighter VIF
No. 540 (Det. from U.K.)	P.R.	Mosquito P.R.I/IV
No. 544 (Det. from U.K.)	P.R.	Spitfire P.R. IV

* The A.O.C. was placed under the control, and all the air facilities at Gibraltar at the disposal, of the Commander-in-Chief, Allied Expeditionary Force, for Operation 'Torch'.

APPENDIX 8

(c)

WESTERN AIR COMMAND
(United States Twelfth Air Force)
(Absorbed by N.A.A.F. 18th February 1943)
NOVEMBER—DECEMBER, 1942

Area	Role	Arrival of squadrons in North West Africa		Aircraft Type
		As planned	Actual	

Squadrons available for Phase I (8th—14th November)

Area	Role	As planned	Actual	Aircraft Type
*ALGERIA	S.E.-F.	6	6	Spitfire VB
	T.E.-F./F.B.	–	1–3	Lightning II
	B.R.	1	–	—
	L.B.	–	1	Boston I
	M.B.	1	–	—
	A.T.	–	4	Dakota I
*MOROCCO	S.E.-F.	6	3	Kittyhawk II
	S.E.-F./F.B.	–	3 (Aircraft on 27/12/42)	Airacobra I
	Tac. R.	1	–	—
	L.B.	1	–	—
	A.T.	–	3–4	Dakota I

Squadrons available for Phase II (15th November—25th December) (Includes squadrons planned for and which arrived in Phase I)

Area	Role	Arrival of squadrons in North West Africa		Aircraft Type
		As planned	Actual	
	S.E.-F.	12	9	Kittyhawk II
	S.E.-F./F.B.	–	6 (Aircraft on 27/12/42 or later)	Airacobra I
	T.E.-F.	6	–	—
ALGERIA	T.E.-F./F.B.	–	3	Lightning II
&	Tac. R.	2	2	Airacobra I
MOROCCO	P.R.	1	1	Lightning F.4
	B.R.	2	2	Boston I
	L.B.	5	5	Boston I/III
	M.B.	12	11–12	3–4 Mitchell II / 8 Marauder I
	H.B.	8	9†	Fortress IIA
	A.T.	8	8	Dakota I
	G.R.	–	2	Catalina III

Reserves (Assessed only in terms of aircraft and aircrews)

Area	Role	As planned	Actual	Aircraft Type
	S.E.-F.	3	–	—
ALGERIA	T.E.-F.	3	5	Lightning II
&	P.R.	1	1	Lightning F.4
MOROCCO	M.B.	4	4	Marauder I
	A.T.	4	4	Dakota I
TOTALS (including Reserves)		71	72–73	

* Though the total number of American squadrons shown as having arrived in North West Africa in Phase I is known to be correct, the locations shown are based on the assumption that those given in the 'Torch' plan were adhered to.

† Early in December one group of Liberators (not planned for 'Torch' but lent by the

APPENDIX 8

United States Eighth Air Force) was sent from North West Africa to the Western Desert in exchange for one squadron of Fortresses. These Liberator squadrons have been omitted from the above tables, but the additional Fortress squadron has been included.

Note. The roles of the squadrons have been given in Royal Air Force terminology. For example, 'Observation Bomber' is shown as 'Bomber Reconnaissance (B.R.)' and 'Fighter Observation' as 'Tactical Reconnaissance (Tac. R.)'; and the role of two flying boat squadrons has been shown as 'General Reconnaissance (G.R.)'.

MID-APRIL, 1943

NORTHWEST AFRICAN AIR FORCES

NOTE:- OPERATIONAL COMMAND AND CONTROL ONLY
TOTAL AIRCRAFT ESTABLISHMENTS
Northwest African Air Forces — 2,086
Malta Air Command — 218
Middle East Air Command — 1,012
GRAND TOTAL —— 3,516

N.A.T.A.F.

N.A.T.B.F.

Sqdn.	Role	Aircraft Est.	Type
Huitième Groupement (F.F.A.F.)	M.B.	16	LeO 45

U.S. 12th Medium Bombardment Group

	Role	Aircraft Est.	Type
81st, 82nd	M.B.	Total 26	Mitchell II

(* Detachment on loan from W.D.A.F.)

U.S. 47th Light Bombardment Group

	Role	Aircraft Est.	Type
84th, 85th, 86th, 97th	L.B.	Total 52	Boston I, III

No. 326 Wing, R.A.F.

	Role	Aircraft Est.	Type
Nos. 13, 18, 614	L.B.	Total 48	Bisley
No. 114	L.B.	16	Boston III

W.D.A.F.

	Role	Aircraft Est.	Type
No. 821 (F.A.A.)	P.F.		Albacore

(Det. from Malta)

No. 3 (S.A.A.F.) Wing, R.A.F.

	Role	Aircraft Est.	Type
No. 12 (S.A.A.F.), 24 (S.A.A.F.)	L.B.	Total 32	Boston III
No. 21 (S.A.A.F.)	L.B.	16	Baltimore III, IIIA

U.S. 12th Medium Bombardment Group

| 83rd, 434th | M.B. | 26 | Mitchell II |

No. 232 Wing, R.A.F.

| Nos. 55, 223 | L.B. | Total 32 | Baltimore IIIA |

No. 249 Wing, R.A.F.

| Nos. 117, 216 | A.T. | (Det. from Egypt) | Hudson VI |

No. 211 GROUP, R.A.F.
No. 7 (S.A.A.F.) Wing, R.A.F.

| Nos. 2, 4, 5 (all S.A.A.F.) | S.E.F.B. | Total 63 | Kittyhawk I |

U.S. 57th Fighter Group

| 64th, 65th, 66th, 314th | S.E.F. | Total 80 | Kittyhawk II/III |

U.S. 79th Fighter Group

| 85th, 86th, 87th, 316th | S.E.F. | Total 80 | Kittyhawk II/III |

No. 239 Wing, R.A.F.

| No. 3 (R.A.A.F.), 260 | S.E.F.B. | Total 42 | Kittyhawk II/III |
| No. 112, 250, 450 (R.A.A.F.) | S.E.F. | 63 | Kittyhawk II/III |

No. 244 Wing, R.A.F.

Nos. 1 (S.A.A.F.), 417 (R.C.A.F.), 601	S.E.F.	Total 38	Spitfire VB/C
No. 6	T/D.	16	Hurricane IID
Nos. 92, 145*	S.E.F.	42	Spitfire VB/C/IX

(*Includes Polish Flight.)

No. 285 Wing, R.A.F.

| No. 40 (S.A.A.F.) | Tac. R. | 18 | Hurricane IIA/B Spitfire VB |
| *No. 60 (S.A.A.F.) | Sur. R. | 7 | Baltimore II, III, Mosquito II, Maryland |

| †No. 73 | S.E.F. (N.F.) | 21 | Hurricane IIC |
| No. 680 | P.R. | (Det. from Egypt) | Spitfire VB, VI |

| No. 1437 Flight | Strat. R. | 8 | Baltimore II |

(*Operationally controlled by H.Q., R.A.F. M.E.)
(†Operationally controlled by No. 211 Group.)

N.A.C.A.F.

Sqdn.	Role	Aircraft Est.	Type
No. 813 (F.A.A.)	T.B.	12	Swordfish
No. 826 (F.A.A.)	T.B.	12	Albacore

U.S. 1st (Provisional) A.S. Wing

| 1st, 2nd | A.S. | Total 16 | Liberator III |

U.S. 2nd AIR DEFENCE WING
U.S. 81st Fighter Group

| 91st, 92nd, 93rd | S.E.F. | Total 75 | Airacobra I |

U.S. 350th Fighter Group

| 345th, 346th, 347th | S.E.F. | Total 75 | Airacobra I |

No. 323 Wing, R.A.F.

| No. 32, 87, 253 | S.E.F. | Total 48 | Hurricane IIC |
| No. 43 | S.E.F. | 16 | Spitfire VB/C |

No. 325 Wing, R.A.F.

| No. 153, 255, 600 | T.E.F. (N.F.) | Total 48 | Beaufighter VIF |

No. 328 Wing, R.A.F.

| No. 14 | T.B. | 16 | Marauder I |
| Nos. 500, 608 | G.R. | 32 | Hudson V |

N.A.P.R.W.

| No. 682 (R.A.F.) | P.R. | 12 | Spitfire VC, IX |

U.S. 3rd P.R. Group

| 5th, 12th | P.R. | Total 26 | Lightning F4/5 |
| 15th | P.R. | | Fortress I |

U.S. XII AIR SUPPORT COMMAND
U.S. 31st Fighter Group

| 307th, 308th, 309th | S.E.F. | Total 75 | Spitfire VB, IX |

U.S. 33rd Fighter Group

| 58th, 59th, 60th | S.E.F. | Total 75 | Kittyhawk IV |

U.S. 52nd Fighter Group

| 2nd, 4th, 5th | S.E.F. | Total 75 | Spitfire VB, IX |

U.S. 68th Observation Group

| 154th | Tac. R. | 18 | Airacobra I, Lightning F4, F5, Mustang II |

No. 242 GROUP, R.A.F.
No. 322 Wing, R.A.F.

No. 81	S.E.F.	16	Spitfire IX
No. 152	S.E.F.	16	Spitfire VC
Nos. 154, 232	S.E.F.	Total 32	Spitfire VB C
No. 242	S.E.F.	16	Spitfire VB

No. 324 Wing, R.A.F.

No. 72	S.E.F.	16	Spitfire IX
No. 93	S.E.F.	16	Spitfire VC
No. 111	S.E.F.	16	Spitfire VC
No. 225	Tac. R.	16	Spitfire VB/C/Mustang II
No. 241	S.E.F.B.	16	Hurricane IIE
No. 243	S.E.F.	16	Spitfire VB

N.A.S.A.F.

Sqdn.	Role	Aircraft Est.	Type
Nos. 142 (R.A.F.), 150	M.B.	Total 32	Wellington III

U.S. 5th HEAVY BOMBARDMENT WING
U.S. 97th Heavy Bombardment Group

| 340th, 341st, 342nd, 414th | H.B. | Total 32 | Fortress II |

U.S. 99th Heavy Bombardment Group

| 346th, 347th, 348th, 416th | H.B. | Total 32 | Fortress II |

U.S. 301st Heavy Bombardment Group

| 32nd, 352nd, 353rd, 419th | H.B. | Total 32 | Fortress II |

U.S. 1st Fighter Group

| 27th, 71st, 94th | T.E.F. | Total 75 | Lightning II |

U.S. 47th MEDIUM BOMBARDMENT WING
U.S. 17th Medium Bombardment Group

| 34th, 37th, 95th, 432nd | M.B. | Total 52 | Marauder IA |

U.S. 310th Medium Bombardment Group

| 379th, 380th, 381st, 428th | M.B. | Total 52 | Mitchell II |

U.S. 319th Medium Bombardment Group

| 441st, 442nd, 443rd, 444th | M.B. | Total 52 | Marauder IA |

U.S. 321st Medium Bombardment Group

| 445th, 446th, 447th, 448th | M.B. | Total 52 | Mitchell II |

U.S. 82nd Fighter Group

| 95th, 96th, 97th | T.E.F. | Total 75 | Lightning II |

U.S. 325th Fighter Group

| 317th, 318th, 319th | S.E.F. | Total 75 | Kittyhawk II/III |

N.A.T.C.C.
U.S. 51st TROOP CARRIER WING
U.S. 60th Troop Carrier Group

| 10th, 11th, 12th, 28th | T.C.A.T. | Total 52 | Dakota I |

U.S. 62nd Troop Carrier Group

| 4th, 7th, 8th, 51st | T.C.A.T. | Total 52 | Dakota I, III |

U.S. 64th Troop Carrier Group

| 16th, 17th, 18th, 35th | T.C.A.T. | Total 52 | Dakota I, III |

(*U.S. 60th Troop Carrier Group detached to N.A.A.S.C.)
(†8th Squadron of U.S. 62nd Troop Carrier Group detached to N.A.T.C.)

(d) contd.

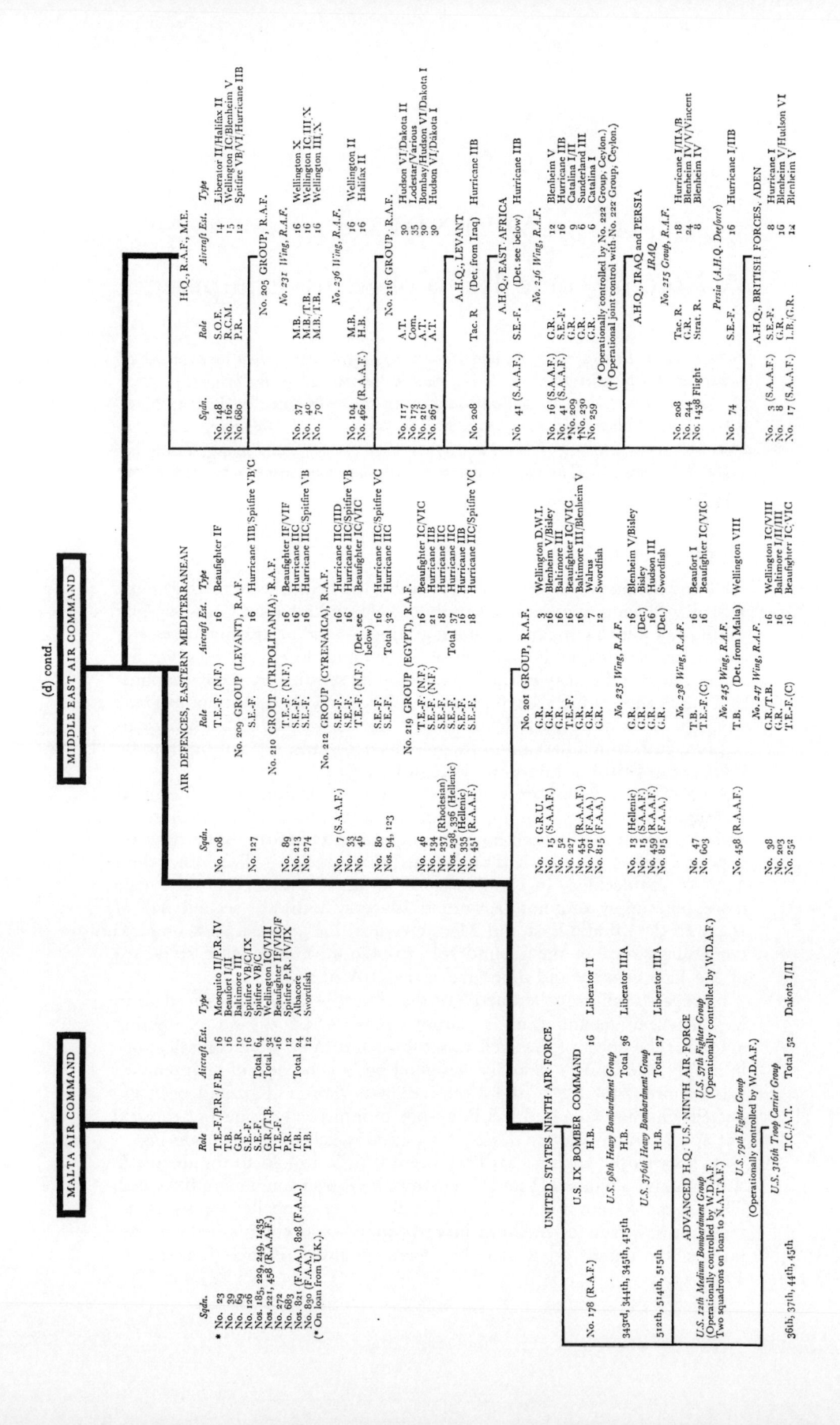

MALTA AIR COMMAND

Sqdn.	Role	Aircraft Est.	Type
No. 23	T.E.-F./P.R./F.B.	16	Mosquito II/P.R. IV
No. 39	T.B.	16	Beaufort I/II
No. 69	G.R.	10	Baltimore III
No. 126	S.E.-F.	16	Spitfire VB/C/IX
Nos. 185, 229, 249, 1435	S.E.-F.	Total 64	Spitfire VB/C/IX
Nos. 221, 458 (R.A.A.F.)	T.E.-F.	Total 32	Wellington IC/VIII
No. 272	T.E.-F.	16	Beaufighter IF/VIC/F
No. 683	P.R.	12	Spitfire P.R. IV/IX
Nos. 821 (F.A.A.), 828 (F.A.A.)	T.B.	Total 24	Albacore
No. 830 (F.A.A.)*	T.B.	12	Swordfish

(* On loan from U.K.).

MIDDLE EAST AIR COMMAND

AIR DEFENCES, EASTERN MEDITERRANEAN

Sqdn.	Role	Aircraft Est.	Type
No. 108	T.E.-F. (N.F.)	16	Beaufighter IF

No. 209 GROUP (LEVANT), R.A.F.

Sqdn.	Role	Aircraft Est.	Type
No. 127	S.E.-F.	16	Hurricane IIB, Spitfire VB/C

No. 210 GROUP (TRIPOLITANIA), R.A.F.

Sqdn.	Role	Aircraft Est.	Type
No. 89	T.E.-F. (N.F.)	16	Beaufighter IF/VIF
No. 213	S.E.-F.	16	Hurricane IIC
No. 274	S.E.-F.	16	Hurricane IIC, Spitfire VB

No. 212 GROUP (CYRENAICA), R.A.F.

Sqdn.	Role	Aircraft Est.	Type
No. 7 (S.A.A.F.)	S.E.-F.	16	Hurricane IIC/IID
No. 33	T.E.-F. (N.F.)	(see below)	Hurricane IIC/Spitfire VB
No. 46	S.E.-F.	16	Beaufighter IC/VIC
No. 80	S.E.-F.	16	Hurricane IIC/Spitfire VC
Nos. 94, 123	S.E.-F.	Total 32	Hurricane IIC

No. 219 GROUP (EGYPT), R.A.F.

Sqdn.	Role	Aircraft Est.	Type
No. 46 (Rhodesian)	T.E.-F. (N.F.)	16	Beaufighter IIB
No. 134	S.E.-F.	21	Hurricane IIB
Nos. 237, 336 (Hellenic)	S.E.-F.	18	Hurricane IIC
Nos. 238, 336 (Hellenic)	S.E.-F.	Total 37	Hurricane IIC
No. 335 (Hellenic)	S.E.-F.	16	Hurricane IIC
No. 451 (R.A.A.F.)	S.E.-F.	18	Hurricane IIC/Spitfire VC

No. 201 GROUP, R.A.F.

Sqdn.	Role	Aircraft Est.	Type
No. 1 G.R.U.	G.R.	3	Wellington D.W.I.
No. 15 (S.A.A.F.)	G.R.	16	Blenheim V/Bisley
No. 52	G.R.	16	Baltimore III
No. 227	T.E.-F.	16	Beaufighter IC/VIC
No. 454 (R.A.A.F.)	G.R.	16	Baltimore III/Blenheim V
No. 701 (F.A.A.)	G.R.	7	Walrus
No. 815 (F.A.A.)	G.R.	12	Swordfish

No. 235 Wing, R.A.F.

Sqdn.	Role	Aircraft Est.	Type
No. 13 (Hellenic)	G.R.	16	Blenheim V/Bisley
No. 15 (S.A.A.F.)	G.R.	(Det.)	Bisley
No. 459 (R.A.A.F.)	G.R.	16	Hudson III
No. 815 (F.A.A.)	G.R.	(Det.)	Swordfish

No. 238 Wing, R.A.F.

Sqdn.	Role	Aircraft Est.	Type
No. 47	T.B.	16	Beaufort I
No. 603	T.E.-F.(C)	16	Beaufighter IC/VIC

No. 245 Wing, R.A.F.

Sqdn.	Role	Aircraft Est.	Type
No. 458 (R.A.A.F.)	T.B. (Det. from Malta)	16	Wellington VIII

No. 247 Wing, R.A.F.

Sqdn.	Role	Aircraft Est.	Type
No. 38	G.R./T.B.	16	Wellington IC/VIII
No. 203	G.R.	16	Baltimore I/II/III
No. 252	T.E.-F.(C)	16	Beaufighter IC/VIC

H.Q., R.A.F., M.E.

Sqdn.	Role	Aircraft Est.	Type
No. 148	S.O.F.	14	Liberator II/Halifax II
No. 162	R.C.M.	15	Wellington IC/Blenheim V
No. 680	P.R.	12	Spitfire VB/VI, Hurricane IIB

No. 205 GROUP, R.A.F.

Sqdn.	Role	Aircraft Est.	Type
No. 37	M.B.	16	Wellington X
No. 40	M.B.T.B.	16	Wellington IC III X
No. 70	M.B.T.B.	16	Wellington III X

No. 236 Wing, R.A.F.

Sqdn.	Role	Aircraft Est.	Type
No. 104	M.B.	16	Wellington II
No. 462 (R.A.A.F.)	H.B.	16	Halifax II

No. 216 GROUP, R.A.F.

Sqdn.	Role	Aircraft Est.	Type
No. 117	A.T.	30	Hudson VI/Dakota II
No. 173	Com.	35	Lodestar/Various
No. 216	A.T.	30	Bombay/Hudson VI/Dakota I
No. 267	A.T.	39	Hudson VI/Dakota I

A.H.Q., LEVANT

Sqdn.	Role	Aircraft Est.	Type
No. 208	Tac. R (Det. from Iraq)		Hurricane IIB

A.H.Q., EAST AFRICA (Det. see below)

Sqdn.	Role	Aircraft Est.	Type
No. 41 (S.A.A.F.)	S.E.-F.		Hurricane IIB

No. 246 Wing, R.A.F.

Sqdn.	Role	Aircraft Est.	Type
No. 16 (S.A.A.F.)	G.R.	12	Blenheim V
No. 41 (S.A.A.F.)	S.E.-F.	16	Hurricane IIB
*No. 209	G.R.	6	Catalina I/II
†No. 239	G.R.	9	Sunderland III
No. 259	G.R.	6	Catalina I

(* Operationally controlled by No. 222 Group, Ceylon.)
(† Operational joint control with No. 222 Group, Ceylon.)

A.H.Q., IRAQ and PERSIA

IRAQ

No. 215 Group, R.A.F.

Sqdn.	Role	Aircraft Est.	Type
No. 208	Tac. R.	18	Hurricane I/IIA/B
No. 244	G.R.	24	Blenheim IV/V/Vincent
No. 1438 Flight	Strat. R.	8	Blenheim IV

Persia (A.H.Q. Defore)

Sqdn.	Role	Aircraft Est.	Type
No. 74	S.E.-F.	16	Hurricane I/IIB

A.H.Q., BRITISH FORCES, ADEN

Sqdn.	Role	Aircraft Est.	Type
No. 3 (S.A.A.F.)	S.E.-F.	8	Hurricane I
No. 8 (S.A.A.F.)	G.R.	16	Blenheim V/Hudson VI
No. 17 (S.A.A.F.)	L.B./G.R.	12	Blenheim V

UNITED STATES NINTH AIR FORCE

U.S. IX BOMBER COMMAND

	Role	Aircraft Est.	Type
No. 178 (R.A.F.)	H.B.	16	Liberator II

U.S. 98th Heavy Bombardment Group

	Role	Aircraft Est.	Type
343rd, 344th, 345th, 415th	H.B.	Total 36	Liberator IIIA

U.S. 376th Heavy Bombardment Group

	Role	Aircraft Est.	Type
512th, 514th, 515th	H.B.	Total 27	Liberator IIIA

ADVANCED H.Q. U.S. NINTH AIR FORCE

U.S. 12th Medium Bombardment Group (Operationally controlled by W.D.A.F.)
U.S. 57th Fighter Group (Operationally controlled by W.D.A.F.)
Two squadrons on loan to N.A.T.A.F.

U.S. 79th Fighter Group (Operationally controlled by W.D.A.F.)

U.S. 316th Troop Carrier Group

	Role	Aircraft Est.	Type
36th, 37th, 44th, 45th	T.C./A.T.	Total 52	Dakota I/II

APPENDIX 9

A Note on some Items of Army Equipment

[*Some notes on British, German, and Italian artillery weapons from the outbreak of the war until September 1942 are to be found in Volume III of this history, p. 427–33. Notes on tanks, armour, and anti-tank guns are to be found in Volume II, p. 341–45, and Volume III, p. 434–444. The purpose of the following note is to summarize some points of interest concerning these weapons, and mines, during the period of Volume IV. The note is not technical, but supplements references in the narrative.*]

ARTILLERY (See Table A)

During the period covered by this volume the British were predominant in artillery owing to an ample supply of field and medium guns—25-pdr gun/how, 4·5-inch gun, and 5·5-inch gun/how—and to steadily increasing skill in artillery methods and tactics. A demand developed however for longer range and a heavier shell than could be satisfied by these weapons. In Tunisia the 7·2-inch howitzer provided a heavy shell, but not as great range (its maximum was 16,900 yards) as was wanted. The American 155-mm gun, with a maximum range of 25,700 yards, did not begin to be available to British artillery until August 1943.

A belief too had been growing in the value of air burst H.E. for lethal and moral effect, and with it a demand for a suitable shell other than the anti-aircraft shell. The shell however required a time fuze, but a decision of policy, before the war, had abandoned this fuze for artillery other than A.A. It was decided, in October 1940, to make this type of fuze once more, but supply did not become satisfactory until the second half of 1943. In the Middle East and Mediterranean the 3·7-inch A.A. gun was increasingly used in the ground role to take advantage, as a stop-gap, of the high velocity and time fuze of the H.A.A. shell.

As regards self-propelled artillery the 'Priest'—the American 105-mm M7 howitzer mounted on a Grant chassis—had earned conflicting opinions: the effect of the shell was valued but there were complications in supply; the Grant's mobility was good but a good deal of maintenance was required; the life of the piece itself was shorter than had been expected. Opinion favoured a S.P. 25-pdr of improved design but this did not appear in our theatre during the period which we are considering.

As regards the enemy's artillery there is little to add to the details in Table A and Volume III and it remained heterogeneous and unbalanced. The Germans were not satisfied with their few self-propelled guns—15-cm medium howitzers or medium infantry guns—and complained particularly of the chassis on which they were mounted, French Lorraine or Pzkw II.

APPENDIX 9

ANTI-TANK GUNS (See Table B)

The 17-pdr Mark I and Mark II began to arrive in the Middle East in December 1942, and in Tunisia in January 1943. Most of these guns were mounted on 25-pdr carriages. They had few chances of firing shots in anger during the closing stages of the campaign in Africa, but showed that it was possible to dispose of any Axis tanks at 1,500 yards' range. As regards the 6-pdr, the Mark IV (long) gun did not begin to reach Africa until April 1943, but the earlier Mark IIs were very satisfactory, and had penetrated the side-armour of the German Tiger tank at up to 900 yards' range. Early in 1943 it was decided in principle that the 6-pdr should no longer be carried (portée) on the large and vulnerable 3-ton wheeled vehicle, but should be towed by a 15-cwt armoured truck. The change was delayed by want of these vehicles.

In October 1942 the German staff recognized that they must have in Africa an anti-tank gun (*Panzerabwehrkanone*) more powerful than the 5-cm Pak 38 in order to deal with the Grant tank. The new gun was the excellent 7·5-cm Pak 40, but it is unlikely that more than about 80 altogether were in action. There was also the 7·62-cm Pak 36, an improved version of the 7·62-cm Pak (R). Here too must be mentioned the newest version of the famous dual-purpose '88'. This was the 8·8-cm Flak 41, specially designed for anti-tank fighting with low silhouette, an improved shield, and impressive hitting-power. There were at least 25, all told, of these in use by March 1943.

TANKS (See Tables C and D)

British attempts to up-gun Crusader Mark II and Valentine Mark II by replacing the 2-pdr by a 6-pdr gun were not very rewarding. Crusader III, in spite of its good gun, was the same rather unreliable, thin-skinned tank as Mark II. Valentine Mark IX, though it acquired a 6-pdr, lost its 7·92-mm machine gun—a disadvantage. In the Sherman Marks II and III however there appeared a tank which deservedly won a great reputation. It was American-built and had features of design and layout, e.g. the turret, which were the fruits of British experience. Mark II was powered by a radial petrol-engine; Mark III by twin Diesel engines. Mark III proved to be faster and to have much greater endurance than Mark II. Other desirable features of the Sherman were its strong tracks, thick, well-sloped armour, and good protection for the gun-mounting and turret ring. Its main armament, the 75-mm M3 gun was a great improvement on the 75-mm M2 gun of the Grant. Its muzzle-velocity was higher and the latest shell (APCBC M.61) was more effective, e.g. against German face-hardened armour. The HE M.48 shell proved very useful. The gun was mounted high in a turret with all-round traverse, whereas the Grant's 75-mm gun had been mounted low in a sponson on the hull. It is noticeable that almost all the good points of the Sherman, praised by its users, were ruefully recognized by the enemy.

The Churchill tanks Marks I and III were the other most important newcomers. The main armament of Mark I was the 2-pdr, and a 3-inch howitzer mounted as a hull gun; of Mark III the 6-pdr. The Churchill was reliable mechanically, and had outstanding performance across country or in climbing. Suspension and tracks were sturdy, and the armour gave good protection against the 5-cm Pak but not against heavier guns. Weak points were the mantlet, turret-ring and side-door, and inadequate protection for ammunition.

On the enemy's side points of interest relate only to German tanks. The short 5-cm gun (5-cm Kwk L/42—Kwk is the abbreviation of *Kampfwagenkanone*) was a thing of the past. But now an increasing number of Pzkw III were mounting the short 7·5-cm Kwk L/24 gun, formerly the standard main armament of Pzkw IV. The reasons why the 7·5-cm short gun was gaining favour at the expense of the long 5-cm gun (5-cm Kwk 39 L/60) seem to have been mainly two. The nature of the fighting tipped the balance towards H.E. rather than armour-piercing shell, while the introduction of hollow-charge ammunition for the 7·5-cm gun in the summer of 1942 improved its all-round usefulness. All Pzkw III now carried spaced armour, although when the tank mounted a 7·5-cm gun, spaced armour on the mantlet was omitted. Pzkw IV did not yet carry spaced armour.

The dramatic German newcomer however was Pzkw VI or Henschel Tiger I, known usually as the 'Tiger'. This was the biggest tank yet seen— 56 tons against the 23·25 tons of Pzkw IV Model F2. Its thickest armour was 102 mm, of machineable quality. Its main armament was the 8·8-cm Kwk 36 L/56. This was a formidable tank. On the other hand its characteristics restricted its value. It needed much maintenance; it was a large target; a very large and heavy object to recover or transport; too heavy for most bridges, and too wide (12 feet, 3 inches with 'wide' tracks) for narrow places. The first Tiger to be captured by the British fell to 72nd Anti-Tank Regiment, R.A. (6-pdrs) on 31st January, and an immediate and accurate technical examination led to a sound appreciation of the tank's powers and limitations. There were about 20 of these tanks in action—all in Tunisia.

MORTARS (See Table E)

If the British artillery was predominant the enemy had plenty of mortars, and used them particularly well. The types here considered are the German 8-cm mortar and the Italian 81-mm, and German newcomers, the 15-cm *Nebelwerfer 41* and 21-cm *Nebelwerfer 42*.[1] Concerning the first two named the German mortar outranged the British 3-inch by about 1,000 yards, the Italian mortar (using the 7·25 lb bomb) by nearly 3,000. Both enjoyed a higher rate of fire. The fragmentation of the bombs (7·7 lb German; 7·25 lb or 15 lb Italian) was very good.

The history of the *nebelwerfer* in Africa is complicated. In October 1942 OKH planned to send two *Werfer* regiments, each of 9 troops. Part of a *Werfer* Battery began to arrive on 6th November, and appears to have been absorbed by *Werfer* Regiment 71 which began to arrive in January 1943. This unit ultimately consisted of two battery headquarters and seven *nebelwerfer* troops. A troop of 6 projectors possessed 36 barrels if armed

---

[1] Literally, 'nebel' means 'smoke' and 'werfer' means 'projector'.

APPENDIX 9

with the six-barrelled 15-cm projector, and 30 if armed with the five-barrelled 21-cm projector. The 15-cm model was first used in action at the Kasserine Pass in February, while the 21-cm appeared at Mareth though without much ammunition. On 14th April there were in Africa thirty 15-cm and ten 21-cm projectors. These weapons were fairly light and therefore very mobile in comparison with guns, and fired very heavy bombs to extreme ranges of 6,000–8,000 yards depending on type. Accuracy was very fair and defects compensated by the wide-spread fragmentation of the bombs.

The British 3-inch mortar was a useful weapon limited by its short range. To increase this meant strengthening the base-plate and barrel and using a more powerful charge—in fact a re-design which did not bear fruit during the period which this volume covers.[1] The 4·2-inch mortar was intended as both a weapon for chemical warfare and to give close support with H.E. to infantry. It was, at first, in the hands of C.W. Companies R.E., of which there was one in 8th Army and four in 1st Army. The weapon made a shaky start and was not popular. It was criticized as cumbrous and inaccurate, possibly an example of giving a dog a bad name because later this mortar became quite well-regarded.

MINES

It is likely that in scarcely any other scene of war did the mine, anti-tank and anti-personnel, play a greater part than in the Middle East and Mediterranean. In 1942–43 when the mine became generally available in the very large numbers which are necessary if it is to be profitably used, it was on the whole the Axis troops who laid mines, and the British who cleared them. This was the natural result of the fact that at the eastern end of the theatre from October 1942 the 8th Army was advancing, while at the western end 1st Army too was most usually the attacker. On the Axis side the mine became a principal defensive and delaying weapon, and the Germans, even more than the Italians, used it in masterly and ingenious fashion.

Of the several types of enemy mine the anti-tank Tellermine (model T.Mi.35) and the anti-personnel S mine (model S.Mi.35) were the most common. The Tellermine was a powerful breaker of tanks' tracks and could severely damage their suspensions and sometimes their hulls; it usually wrecked wheeled vehicles, and whether the occupants escaped death or injury depended upon whether some sort of protection (e.g. sand-bags) had been fitted, and upon luck. The S mine worked on the principle of a 'Jack in the Box'—a charge in the base of the mine threw a small canister into the air; this burst, often at about waist-height, scattering 'shrapnel' pellets and fragments all round. The mine was difficult to spot. Many improvements were made to mines, e.g. non-magnetic casings to defeat detectors, and anti-lifting devices.

---

[1] A 3-inch mortar, in theory at any rate, could put down 200 lb of projectiles in one minute of 'rapid' fire.

The anti-tank mine could be laid in various ways. There was, for example, the regular 'field' of various patterns, which was usually marked; there were mines deep-laid in roadside verges and similar places; there were scattered mines or unmarked patches and even fields. Airfields were nearly always mined. Anti-lifting devices and anti-personnel mines made the life of the mine-clearer at best one of sharp wariness and strain, and at worst, short. Anti-personnel mines increased steadily in numbers between October 1942 and the end of the campaign. The booby-trap was a near relative of the anti-personnel mine. Almost anything could be booby-trapped—a bait was laid for inquisitiveness, or acquisitiveness, and an explosive charge then deadened these emotions.

In the British forces mine-clearing (which includes disposal) was widely and well taught but the unenvied duty fell naturally, and because of their tradition as overcomers of obstacles, to the engineers, and they did it magnificently. Whatever method or aid might be used, the mine-clearer was a man in extreme danger. The simplest, and sometimes the best method, was prodding with a bayonet. There were electrical mine-detectors of various patterns, usually efficient but very vulnerable to unavoidable rough handling and rather heavy. There were several types of vehicle devised to destroy mines or to check that these had been dealt with or were absent. The most successful was the Scorpion which has been described in Chapter I. This vehicle was steadily improved, as time went on. Scorpion Mark II was still a Matilda tank but the auxiliary engine which drove the flail was housed in a turret instead of in a thinly armoured box. The cooling and air-filtering systems, formerly a common cause of breakdowns, had been improved also. Mark III was a diesel-engined Grant with a lighter frame for the flail, and was a better traveller from one place of operations to another than Marks I and II. The Crab was another advance: the tank kept its gun, the flail was driven by the tank's main engines, could be kept at a constant height from the ground, and had a device for wire-cutting.[1]

There were other special vehicles: the Valentine tank pushing a Fowler spiked roller; and Middle East and Mediterranean inventions such as the 3-ton sandbagged lorry pushing one roller and pulling another (a pilot-vehicle), or towing devices called 'Slug' and 'Centipede'. The last two were designed to flatten crops and long grass in which—in Tunisia—mines were hidden, and to detonate S mines. The Slug and Centipede came too late for use in operations in Africa. A useful but not greatly used vehicle was the Snail—a 30-cwt lorry, protected with sandbags, from which dripped Diesel oil to mark a track which could be seen in the dark. This too was a pilot-vehicle.

It is true however to say that in spite of all the ingenuity and courage which was devoted to defeating it, the mine remained a most dangerous enemy.

---

[1] The lineage of the main handlers of Scorpions was: at El Alamein, detachments of 1st Army Tank Brigade; then 41st R.T.R.; then 'T' Scorpion Regiment R.A.C.; then No. 1 Scorpion Regiment R.A.C.

APPENDIX 9

TABLE A

Some particulars of the Principal Field Branch Artillery Weapons used in the Middle East and North Africa

The table includes information given in Volume III about British weapons or weapons used by the British. Weapons used by the United States or French forces are not included. Of enemy weapons, newcomers only, during the period of this volume, are mentioned —for others the reader is referred to Volume III pages 431–433.

British

(1) Weapon	(2) Weight in action (tons)	(3) Calibre (inches)	(4) Weight of HE projectile (lb.)	(5) Maximum range (yards)	(6) Remarks
18-pdr gun	1·55	3·3	18	9,800	
3·7-inch how	0·75	3·7	20	6,800	
4·5-in. how	1·5	4·5	35	6,600	
18/25-pdr	1·6	3·45	25	11,800	
25-pdr gun/how	1·75	3·45	25	13,400	Also fired an AP shot.
60-pdr gun	5·5	5	60	15,100	
4·5-in. gun	5·7	4·5	55	20,500	
6-in. how	4·5	6	100	11,400	
5·5-in. gun/how	5·7	5·5	100	16,200	
U.S. 105-mm SP how	22·5	4·1	33	10,500	The 'Priest'. Mounted on Grant chassis.
7·2-in. how	10·5	7·2	202	16,900	

German

(1) Weapon	(2) Weight in action (tons)	(3) Calibre (inches)	(4) Weight of HE projectile (lb.)	(5) Maximum range (yards)	(6) Remarks
17-cm (K.18) gun	17·2	6·8	138	32,375	Mounted on howitzer carriage.

APPENDIX 9

ANTI-AIRCRAFT ARTILLERY

The British anti-aircraft guns shown below were all provided with S.A.P., A.P., and H.E. types of ammunition. The German anti-aircraft gun was provided also with suitable natures of ammunition for field and anti-tank roles.

BRITISH

(1) Weapon	(2) Weight in action (tons)	(3) Calibre (inches)	(4) Weight of projectile (lb.)	(5) Muzzle velocity (feet per second)	(6) Ceiling (feet)	(7) Practical rate of fire (rds per minute)	(8) Remarks
Bofors (40-mm)	2·0 to 2·5	1·58	2	2,800	23,600	120	
3-in.	8	3	16½	2,000	25,200	20 to 25	
3·7-in. (Marks I to III)	7·5 to 8	3·7	28	2,600	41,000	8 to 10*	*Increased to 20 by use of automatic and fuze-setting gear.

GERMAN

8·8-cm Flak 41 L/74	11·1	3·5	20¾	3,280	49,200	15	

TABLE B
Tank and Anti-Tank Guns

Expected penetration in millimetres of homogeneous armour plate

An angle of impact of 30° to the normal has been taken simply as a basis for comparison. In battle the angle of impact may be anything from 0° to 90°. As a rough guide it may be taken that at short ranges the penetration of a shot striking normally to the surface would be about one and a quarter times that of the figure given for 30°. But while the figures give an idea of the relative expected performances of the various projectiles, they cannot be taken as a definite forecast of how any one particular shot or shell will behave.

BRITISH

(1) Weapon	(2) How moved or mounted	(3) Weight of shot or shell (lb.)	(4) Muzzle velocity (feet per second)	(5) 250 yds.	(6) 500 yds.	(7) 750 yds.	(8) 1000 yds.	(9) 1500 yds.	(10) 2000 yds.
2-pdr	Towed or portée; and tank gun of Crusader and Valentine	2 AP shot 2 AP high velocity shot	2600 2800	58 64	52 57	46 51	40 45	— —	— —
6-pdr Marks I and II	Towed or portée; tank gun of Crusader, Valentine, Churchill	6·25 AP shot	2675	—	79	72	65	52	—
17-pdr	Towed	17 APC shot	2900	—	—	120	113	96	82
75-mm M2	Sponson of Grant	14 AP shot M72	1930	—	61	—	53	46	38
		15 APCBC shell M61	2030	—	66	—	61	56	51
75-mm M3	Turret of Sherman	15 APCBC shell M61	2030	—	66	—	61	56	51

TABLE B (continued)

GERMAN

(1) Weapon	(2) How moved or mounted	(3) Weight of shot or shell (lb.)	(4) Muzzle velocity (feet per second)	(5) 250 yds.	(6) 500 yds.	(7) 750 yds.	(8) 1000 yds.	(9) 1500 yds.	(10) 2000 yds.	
5-cm Pak 38	Towed	4·5 APCBC	2700	67	61	56	50	—	—	German weapons were provided also with a H.E. shell a little lighter than the AP projectile. The figures under German guns give the length in calibres.
5-cm Kwk 39 L/60	In Pzkw III Special	1·94 Pzgr 40	3930	109	77	46	—	—	—	
7·5-cm Kwk L/24	In Pzkw III N	14·9 APCBC 9·75 hollow charge	1350 1476	— about 75-mm irrespective of range	46	42	41	—	—	
7·5-cm Pak 40 L/46	Towed	15 APCBC shell	2460	—	92	—	84	75	66	
7·5-cm Kwk 40 L/43	In Pzkw IV Special	16·7 APCBC shell	2430	—	92	—	84	75	66	
7·62-cm Pak 36(R)	Towed; SP version on Pzkw 38 (Czech chassis)	21 APCBC shell	2600	—	112	—	103	92	83	
8·8-cm Flak 36 L/56	Towed									
8·8-cm Kwk 36	In Pzkw VI. Tiger									
8·8-cm Flak 41 L/74	Towed	21 APCBC shell	3214	—	177	—	162	146	132	

ITALIAN

(1) Weapon	(2) How moved or mounted	(3) Weight of shot or shell (lb.)	(4) Muzzle velocity (feet per second)	(5) 250 yds.	(6) 500 yds.	(7) 750 yds.	(8) 1000 yds.	(9) 1500 yds.	(10) 2000 yds.
47/32 Model 37	Towed; and in M 14/41 and 42 tank	3·25 AP shell	2060	—	(400 yds.) 48	38	32	—	—

APPENDIX 9

TABLE C

Thickness in Millimetres of some of the plates on certain British and German Tanks

The number of degrees shows the inclination of the plate to the vertical. Where no inclination is given the plate is vertical.

British

Type	Hull		Superstructure		Turret		Remarks
	Front nose plate	Sides	Front Glacis plate	Driver's front plate	Front	Sides	
Crusader III	33 at 29°	28	20 at 60°	40	51	24 at 45°	
Sherman II and III	50 rounded	38	50 at 53°	50 at 43°	76 rounded	50	†102-mm rounded } on Mk I
Churchill III	88 at 20°	76	38 at 70°	88	88†	76*	*88-mm

German

Pzkw III Model N	50 at 52°	30	25 at 84°	50+20 at 9°	57 at 15°	30 at 25°	
Pzkw IV Model F2	50 at 12°	30	25 at 73°	50 at 10°	50 at 11°	30 at 26°	
Pzkw VI Tiger E	102 at 24°	82	61 at 80°	102 at 10°	100 at 10°	82	Gun mantlet was 97.

TABLE D
Some particulars of certain British, German and Italian Tanks

British

Type	Weight tons	Crew	Main Armament	Type of Ammunition	Secondary Armament[1]	Thickest Armour	Engine B.H.P.	Cross country speed m.p.h.[2]	Remarks
Valentine Mark II Mark IX	16	3	One 2-pdr One 6-pdr	AP shot AP shot	One 7·92-mm m.g. *	65-mm	131	8	*In later designs a 7·92-mm m.g. was added.
Crusader Mark II Mark III	19 19·75	4 3	One 2-pdr One 6-pdr (short)	AP shot AP shot H.E.	One 7·92-mm m.g. One 7·92-mm m.g.	49-mm 51-mm	340 340	12 12	
Churchill Mark III	38·5	5	One 6-pdr (short)	AP shot H.E.	Two 7·92-mm m.g	88-mm	350	6	
Grant Mark I	28·5	6	One 75-mm in sponson One 37-mm in turret	75-mm AP shot and H.E. 37-mm APCBC shot	One, two, or three ·30-inch m.g.s.	57-mm	340	10	Mark I mounted one 2-pdr and one 7·92-mm m.g co-axially in turret, and one 3-inch how in hull.
Sherman Mark II Mark III	30 31	5	One 75-mm (long)	APCBC shell H.E.	Two ·30-inch m.g.	76-mm	400 375		

[1] A.A. m.g.s. are omitted
[2] Speed across country is greatly affected by the nature of the 'going'. These figures are a guide to speeds in the desert.

APPENDIX 9

TABLE D (continued)

GERMAN

Type	Weight tons	Crew	Main Armament	Type of Ammunition	Secondary Armament[1]	Thickest Armour	Engine B.H.P.	Cross-country speed m.p.h.[2]	Remarks
Pzkw III Model J	22	5	One 5-cm (long)	APCBC Pzgr 40 H.E.	Two 7·92-mm m.g.	50-mm	300	12	
Model N	22	5	One 7·5-cm (short)	Hollow charge H.E.	Two 7·92-mm m.g.	57-mm	300	12	
Pzkw IV Model F2	23·25	5	One 7·5-cm (long)	APCBC	Two 7·92-mm m.g.	50-mm	300	10	
Pzkw VI Tiger E	56	5	One 8·8-cm L/56		Two 7·92-mm m.g.	102-mm	700	12	

ITALIAN

M 14/41 and 42	14·7	4	One 47-mm	AP H.E.	Three 8-mm m.g.	40-mm	125	8	

[1] A.A. m.gs. are omitted.
[2] Speed across country is greatly affected by the nature of the 'going'. The figures are a guide to speeds in the desert.

TABLE E

Some particulars of certain British, German, and Italian Mortars

Weapon	Total Weight (lb.)	Weight of H.E. bomb (lb.)	Maximum Range (yds.)
British			
3-in. Mark 5	89	10	1600
4·2-in.	980	20	4100
German			
8-cm s.GW 34	124	7·7	2625
15-cm Nebelwerfer 41 6 barrels	1298	75	7546
21-cm Nebelwerfer 42 5 barrels	1331	248	8585
Italian			
81-mm Model 35	129	7·25	4429
		15	1640

APPENDIX 10

Some particulars of Allied and Enemy Aircraft in use in the Middle East and Mediterranean Theatre during the period of this volume

The figures in these tables are no more than a general guide to the characteristics and capabilities of each type of aircraft. The performance is affected by the climate, the skill of the pilot, the accuracy of navigation, and the uncertainties of flying in the presence of the enemy. For these reasons a safety margin has to be imposed, so that the operational range—not to be confused with the radius of action—is always much less than the still air range. Broadly speaking, after allowing for the running of the engines on the ground and for the climb to the height quoted, the still air range is the distance that can be flown in still air until the tanks are empty.

NOTES:
(i) The most economical cruising speed is the speed at which the greatest range is achieved.
(ii) The height given in column IV is the optimum height for the maximum speed.
(iii) In some instances the American and British names of an aircraft of American design and manufacture vary. For example, the American Warhawk fighter is known to the British as the Kittyhawk. To avoid confusion only the British names of such aircraft are used in these tables.
(iv) Particulars of Allied and enemy aircraft in use during the period of this volume but not included in the following tables may be found in the relevant appendices in previous volumes.

FIGHTER AIRCRAFT

BRITISH

Aircraft	Fuel and Still Air Range at Most Economical Cruising Speed		Most Economical Cruising Speed in Miles per hour	Maximum Speed in Miles per hour	Armament	Remarks
	Galls.	*Miles*				
Beaufighter Mk. I C and F Twin-engine monoplane Crew 2	550	1,515	226 at 15,000 ft.	324 at 11,750 ft.	6 × ·303 4 × 20 mm	
Beaufighter Mk. VI C and F Twin-engine monoplane Crew 2	550 610(a)	1,480 1,640	243 at 15,000 ft.	333 at 15,000 ft.	6 × ·303 4 × 20 mm	(a) With extra tanks.
Hurricane Mk. II C Single-engine monoplane Crew 1	97 183(a)	470 960	212 at 20,000 ft.	339 at 22,000 ft.	4 × 20 mm	(a) With two extra tanks. Could carry 2 × 250 lb bombs in lieu of tanks. The performance of the Sea Hurricane IIC was virtually the same as that of this aircraft.
Hurricane Mk. II E Single-engine monoplane Crew 1	97	495	176 at 2,000 ft.	314 at 13,500 ft.	2 × ·303 2 × 40 mm	Developed for low-flying attacks. Could also carry bombs or rocket projectiles in lieu of 40-mm guns.
Kittyhawk Mk. II Single-engine monoplane Crew 1	131 174(a)	795 1,075	240 at 20,000 ft.	345 at 14,700 ft.	4 or 6 × ·50	American design and manufacture. Fitted with Packard Merlin engine. (a) With extra tank. Could carry one 500 lb bomb in lieu of tank.

APPENDIX 10

FIGHTER AIRCRAFT

BRITISH

Aircraft	Fuel and Still Air Range at Most Economical Cruising Speed		Most Economical Cruising Speed in Miles per hour	Maximum Speed in Miles per hour	Armament	Remarks
	Galls.	Miles				
Kittyhawk Mk. III Single-engine monoplane Crew 1	123 166(a)	750 1,017	210 at 15,000 ft.	345 at 5,000 ft.	4 or 6 ×·50	American design and manufacture. (a) With extra tank. Could carry one 500 lb bomb in lieu of tank.
Mosquito P.R. Mk. I Twin-engine monoplane Crew 2	539 687(a)	1,690 2,180	255 at 15,000 ft.	382 at 14,000 ft.	Nil	(a) With extra tanks.
Mosquito Mk. II F Twin-engine monoplane Crew 2	400 551(a)	1,205 1,705	255 at 15,000 ft.	370 at 14,000 ft.	4 ×·303 4 × 20 mm	(a) With extra tanks.
Mosquito P.R. Mk. IV Twin-engine monoplane Crew 2	536 657(a)	1,640 2,025	260 at 15,000 ft.	381 at 14,000 ft.	Nil	(a) With extra tanks.
Mustang Mk. II Single-engine monoplane Crew 1	140 390(a)	1,000 2,450	225 at 15,000 ft.	402 at 12,000 ft.	4 ×·50	(a) With extra tanks. Could carry 2 × 500 lb bombs in lieu of tanks. American design and manufacture. Fitted with Packard Merlin Engine.
Seafire Mk. I B Single-engine monoplane Crew 1	85 130(a)	492 770	215 at 20,000 ft.	365 at 16,000 ft.	4 ×·303 2 × 20 mm	(a) With extra tank.

APPENDIX 10

FIGHTER AIRCRAFT
BRITISH

Aircraft	Fuel and Still Air Range at Most Economical Cruising Speed		Most Economical Cruising Speed in Miles per hour	Maximum Speed in Miles per hour	Armament	Remarks
	Galls.	*Miles*				
Seafire Mk. II C Single-engine monoplane Crew 1	85 130(a)	460 730	219 at 20,000 ft.	364 at 13,000 ft.	4 × ·303 2 × 20 mm	(a) With extra tank. Could carry 1 × 500 lb bomb in lieu of tank.
Spitfire P.R. Mk. IV Single-engine monoplane Crew 1	217	1,460	228 at 22,000 ft.	365 at 22,000 ft.	Nil	
Spitfire Mk. V C Single-engine monoplane Crew 1	84 174(a)	469 1,135	226 at 20,000 ft.	369 at 19,500 ft.	4 × ·303 2 × 20 mm or 8 × ·303 or 4 × 20 mm	(a) With extra 90 gallon tank, jettisoned when empty.
Spitfire Mk. VI Single-engine monoplane Crew 1	84 174(a)	510 1,170	239 at 20,000 ft.	364 at 22,000 ft.	4 × ·303 2 × 20 mm	(a) With extra tank, jettisoned when empty.
Spitfire Mk. IX Single-engine monoplane Crew 1	85 255(a)	434 1,355	220 at 20,000 ft.	408 at 25,000 ft.	4 × ·303 2 × 20 mm	(a) With extra 170 gallon tank, jettisoned when empty. Could carry one 500 lb and 2 × 250 lb bombs in lieu of tank.

APPENDIX 10

BOMBER AIRCRAFT
BRITISH

Aircraft	Still Air Range with Associated Bombload		Most Economical Cruising Speed in Miles per hour	Maximum Speed in Miles per hour	Armament	Remarks
	Miles	*Bombload*				
Baltimore Mk. III/IIIA Twin-engine monoplane Crew 4	950	2,000 lb.	190 at 15,000 ft.	302 at 11,000 ft.	10 × ·30 4 × ·303	American design and manufacture.
Beaufort Mk. II Twin-engine monoplane Crew 4	1,285	1 Torpedo or 1,650 lb	160 at 5,000 ft.	260 at 14,500 ft.	4 × ·303	
Bisley (Blenheim Mk. V) Twin-engine monoplane Crew 3	1,230	1,000 lb	170 at 15,000 ft.	244 at 6,000 ft.	5 × ·303	
Boston Mk. III Twin-engine monoplane Crew 4	1,020	2,000 lb	200 at 15,000 ft.	304 at 13,000 ft.	8 × ·303	American design and manufacture.
Catalina Flying Boat Mk. IV B Twin-engine monoplane Crew 9	1,395 2,950	2,000 lb Nil	123 at 5,000 ft.	177 at 5,000 ft.	2 × ·303 2 × ·50	American design and manufacture. Performance of Mk. I, IB and II was very similar to that of Mk. IVB.
Dakota Mk. I and II Twin-engine monoplane Crew 3	1,520 (a) 1,910 (b) 3,220 (c)		160 at 10,000 ft.	220 at 10,000 ft.	None	Transport aircraft. American design and manufacture. (a) With 31 troops (b) With 26 troops (c) With 8 troops

BOMBER AIRCRAFT
BRITISH

Aircraft	Still Air Range with Associated Bombload		Most Economical Cruising Speed in Miles per Hour	Maximum Speed in Miles per Hour	Armament	Remarks
	Miles	*Bombload*				
Halifax Mk. II Four-engine monoplane Crew 6	2,100 650	1,500 lb 13,000 lb	205 at 20,000 ft.	253 at 19,000 ft.	9 × ·303	
Hudson Mk. VI Twin-engine monoplane Crew 4	1,140 2,240	1,400 lb Nil	150 at 5,000 ft.	253 at 5,600 ft.	7 × ·303	American design and manufacture. Performance of Mk. V was similar to that of Mk. VI.
Marauder Mk. I Twin-engine monoplane Crew 6	387 1,870	5,000 lb Nil	190 at 15,000 ft.	293 at 14,000 ft.	2 × ·30 3 × ·50	American design and manufacture.
Sunderland Flying Boat Mk. II Four-engine monoplane Crew 10	2,070 2,310	1,900 lb Nil	144 at 5,000 ft.	194 at 3,000 ft.	7 × ·303	
Sunderland Flying Boat Mk. III Four-engine monoplane Crew 10	2,500 3,120	1,900 lb Nil	143 at 5,000 ft.	212 at 1,500 ft.	7 × ·303	
Wellington Mk. III Twin-engine monoplane Crew 6	1,200 2,040	4,500 lb 1,500 lb	180 at 15,000 ft.	261 at 12,500 ft.	6 × ·303	
Wellington Mk. X Twin-engine monoplane Crew 6	1,325 1,885	4,500 lb 1,500 lb	180 at 15,000 ft.	255 at 14,500 ft.	6 × ·303	

FIGHTER AIRCRAFT
UNITED STATES

Aircraft	Fuel and Still Air Range at Most Economical Cruising Speed		Most Economical Cruising Speed in Miles per hour	Maximum Speed in Miles per hour	Armament	Remarks
	Galls.	*Miles*				
Airacobra Mk. I Single-engine monoplane Crew 1	100 246(a)	630 1,520	215 at 15,000 ft.	363 at 6,500 ft.	Probably 1 × 37-mm and 4 × ·30, 2 × ·50 or 6 × ·50	(a) With extra tanks. Could carry one 500 lb bomb in lieu of tanks.
Kittyhawk Mk. II Single-engine monoplane Crew 1	131 174(a)	795 1,075	240 at 20,000 ft.	345 at 14,700 ft.	4 or 6 × ·50	Fitted with Packard Merlin engine. (a) With extra tank. Could carry one 500 lb bomb in lieu of tank.
Kittyhawk Mk. III Single-engine monoplane Crew 1	123 166(a)	750 1,017	210 at 15,000 ft.	345 at 5,000 ft.	4 or 6 × ·50	(a) With extra tank. Could carry one 500 lb bomb in lieu of tank.
Kittyhawk Mk. IV Single-engine monoplane Crew 1	123 166(a)	845 1,138	195 at 15,000 ft.	355 at 12,000 ft.	4 × ·50	(a) With extra tank.
Lightning Mk. II Twin-engine monoplane Crew 1	242 492(a)	620 1,240	220 at 15,000 ft.	408 at 28,000 ft.	4 × ·50 1 × 20 mm	(a) With extra tanks.
Mustang Mk. II Single-engine monoplane Crew 1	140 390(a)	1,000 2,450	225 at 15,000 ft.	402 at 12,000 ft.	4 × ·50	(a) With extra tanks. Could carry 2 × 500lb bombs in lieu of tanks.

BOMBER AIRCRAFT
UNITED STATES

Aircraft	Still Air Range with Associated Bombload		Most Economical Cruising Speed in Miles per hour	Maximum Speed in Miles per hour	Armament	Remarks
	Miles	*Bombload*				
Baltimore Mk. IIIA Twin-engine monoplane Crew 4	950	2,000 lb	190 at 15,000 ft.	302 at 11,000 ft.	10×·30 4×·303	
Boston Mk. III Twin-engine monoplane Crew 4	1,020	2,000 lb	200 at 15,000 ft.	304 at 13,000 ft.	8×·303	
Catalina Flying Boat Mk. III Twin-engine monoplane Crew 9	1,100 2,280	4,000 lb Nil	126 at 5,000 ft.	179 at 5,000 ft.	2×·303 2×·50	
Dakota Mk. I and II Twin-engine monoplane Crew 3	1,520(a) 1,910(b) 3,220(c)		160 at 10,000 ft.	220 at 10,000 ft.	None	Transport aircraft. (a) With 31 troops (b) With 26 troops (c) With 8 troops
Fortress Mk. I Four-engine monoplane Crew 7 to 9	1,867 2,863	7,400 lb Nil	230 at 30,000 ft.	325 at 28,000 to 30,000 ft.	1×·30 5×·50	
Fortress Mk. II Four-engine monoplane Crew 8	840 2,320	12,800 lb 2,000 lb	195 at 20,000ft.	290 at 25,000 ft.	9×·50	Performance of Mk. IIA was slightly superior.

BOMBER AIRCRAFT
UNITED STATES

Aircraft	Still Air Range with Associated Bombload		Most Economical Cruising Speed in Miles per hour	Maximum Speed in Miles per hour	Armament	Remarks
	Miles	*Bombload*				
Liberator Mk. III/IIIA Four-engine monoplane Crew 8	1,290 3,280	12,800 lb Nil	200 at 20,000 ft.	275 at 20,000 ft.	4 × ·303 8 × ·50	
Marauder Mk. IA Twin-engine monoplane Crew 6	387 1,870	5,000 lb Nil	190 at 15,000 ft.	293 at 14,000 ft.	2 × ·30 3 × ·50	
Mitchell Mk. II Twin-engine monoplane Crew 5	1,150	3,000 lb	210 at 15,000 ft.	295 at 15,000 ft.	1 × ·30 4 × ·50	

FIGHTER AIRCRAFT

GERMAN

Aircraft	Fuel and Still Air Range at Most Economical Cruising Speed		Most Economical Cruising Speed in Miles per hour	Maximum Speed in Miles per hour	Armament	Remarks
	Galls.	*Miles*				
Av. 196 Single-engine monoplane Crew 2	132	600	120 at 6,000 ft.	195 at sea level	3 × 7·9 mm 2 × 20 mm	Used mainly for reconnaissance. Could carry 220 lb of bombs.
F.W. 190 Single-engine monoplane Crew 1	115 180(a)	530 820	220 at 18,000 ft.	395 at 17,000 ft.	2 × 7·9 mm 4 × 20 mm	(a) With extra tanks.
Me. 109G Single-engine monoplane Crew 1	88 155(a)	590 1,020	210 at 18,000 ft.	395 at 22,000 ft.	2 × 7·9 mm 3 × 20 mm	(a) With extra tanks.
Me. 210 Twin-engine monoplane Crew 2	550	1,700	227 at 16,500 ft.	365 at 20,000 ft.	2 × 7·9 mm 2 × 20 mm	
Me. 410 Twin-engine monoplane Crew 2	528	994	257 at 18,000 ft.	390 at 22,000 ft.	2 × 7·9 mm 2 × 13 mm 2 × 20 mm	Could carry 1,100 lb of bombs.

BOMBER AIRCRAFT

GERMAN

Aircraft	Still Air Range with Associated Bombload		Most Economical Cruising Speed in Miles per hour	Maximum Speed in Miles per hour	Armament	Remarks
	Miles	*Bombload*				
B.V. 222 Flying Boat Six-engine monoplane Crew 11	1,612	Nil	155 at sea level	198 at sea level	4 × 7·9 mm 2 × 13 mm 1 × 20 mm	Transport aircraft. Could carry at least 10 tons of freight.
Do. 24 Flying Boat Three-engine monoplane Crew 6	1,118	2,200 lb	161 at 6,560 ft.	195 at 5,900 ft.	4 × 7·9 mm	Used mainly for reconnaissance.
Do. 217E Twin-engine monoplane Crew 4	1,090 1,005	4,400 lb. 6,600 lb.	230 at 17,000 ft.	314 at 16,400 ft.	4 × 7·9 mm 4 × 20 mm	
Hs. 129 Twin-engine monoplane Crew 1	348	770 lb	150 at 6,600 ft.	275 at 9,000 ft.	2 × 20 mm 1 × 37 mm	Army co-operation aircraft.
Ju. 52 Three-engine monoplane Crew 3 to 4	530–790	Nil	132 at sea level	165 at sea level	5 × 7·9 mm	Transport aircraft. Freight 4,000–5,060 lb.
Ju. 87D Single-engine monoplane Crew 2	720	2,200 lb	180 at 15,000 ft.	255 at 13,500 ft.	4 × 7·9 mm	

BOMBER AIRCRAFT

GERMAN

Aircraft	Still Air Range with Associated Bombload		Most Economical Cruising Speed in Miles per hour	Maximum Speed in Miles per hour	Armament	Remarks
	Miles	*Bombload*				
Ju. 88 Twin-engine monoplane Crew 4	1,310	2,200 lb	194 at 16,400 ft.	295 at 14,000 ft.	7 × 7·9 mm 1 × 20 mm	
Ju. 90 Four-engine monoplane Crew 5	810	Nil	155 at 5,000 ft.	218 at 3,600 ft.	4 × 7·9 mm	Transport aircraft. Freight 9,000 lb.
Ju. 290 Four-engine monoplane Crew 4 to 6	2,000	Nil	162 at 6,500 ft.	243 at 18,000 ft.	2 × 7·9 mm 3 × 20 mm	Transport aircraft. Freight close on 10 tons.
Me. 323 Six-engine monoplane Crew 5	500	Nil	130 at sea level	170 at sea level	5 × 13 mm	Transport aircraft. Could carry up to 20 tons of freight.

FIGHTER AIRCRAFT

ITALIAN

Aircraft	Fuel and Still Air Range at Most Economical Cruising Speed		Most Economical Cruising Speed in in Miles per Hour	Maximum Speed in Miles per Hour	Armament	Remarks
	Galls.	*Miles*				
M.C. 202 Single-engine monoplane Crew 1	96	445	190 at 18,000 ft.	345 at 18,000 ft.	2 × 12·7 mm	
M.C. 205 Single-engine monoplane Crew 1	96	580	190 at 18,000 ft.	385 at 22,000 ft.	2 × 7·7 mm 2 × 12·7 mm	
Re. 2001 Single-engine monoplane Crew 1	146	900	190 at 18,000 ft.	345 at 18,000 ft.	2 × 7·7 mm 2 × 12·7 mm	

BOMBER AIRCRAFT
ITALIAN

Aircraft	Still Air Range with Associated Bombload		Most Economical Cruising Speed in Miles per Hour	Maximum Speed in Miles per Hour	Armament	Remarks
	Miles	*Bombload*				
B.R. 20 Twin-engine monoplane Crew 4	1,350	2,200 lb	175 at 13,000 ft.	255 at 13,500 ft.	2 × 7·7 mm 1 × 12·7 mm	
Ca. 313 Twin-engine monoplane Crew 3 to 4	960	880 lb	160 at 13,000 ft.	270 at 13,000 ft.	4 × 7·7 mm	
Cant Z. 1007 b Three-engine monoplane Crew 4 to 5	1,650	1,100 lb	160 at 15,000 ft.	280 at 15,000 ft.	2 × 7·7 mm 2 × 12·7 mm	
R.S. 14 Twin-engine monoplane Crew 3	1,450	880 lb	150 at 13,000 ft.	237 at 13,000 ft.	2 × 7·7 mm 1 × 12·7 mm	
S.79 Three-engine monoplane Crew 4 to 5	1,190	2,750 lb	155 at 13,000 ft.	255 at 13,000 ft.	2 × 7·7 mm 3 × 12·7 mm	Used, when modified, as a torpedo-bomber.
S.84 Three-engine monoplane Crew 4 to 5	1,360 1,230	1,760 lb 4,400 lb	170 at 15,000 ft.	280 at 15,000 ft.	4 × 12·7 mm	

APPENDIX 11

Telegram from General Eisenhower to his Chief of Staff in London dated 5th December 1942

'Deliver following to General Ismay at once as personal message for Prime Minister:

It seems clear that certain messages despatched from here regarding operations and situation have never been received by Chiefs of Staff. Therefore, I am giving you this personal account to bring you reasonably up to date on situation, as it now exists.

In accordance with my intention, announced to you before leaving London, I initially directed that every manner of risk be taken in the attempt to be ahead of the Axis in the Tunisian area. Consequently, as soon as troops began getting ashore at this port [Algiers] we started pushing them to eastward by sea and land, although at that time we were not sure of future attitude of local French. This policy has been consistently pursued, and every atom of strength that could be used by Anderson has been gathered up over the area and pushed forward to him. We have even sent forward 25 of our Shermans from the Casablanca force, although these had to go by slow train and without transport, spare parts and other ordinarily necessary auxiliaries. In the rush forward, using every conceivable kind of transportation including air, naval, railway and all types of nondescript vehicles on the roads, we have outrun present possibilities of minimum supply, of immediate reinforcement and, what is even more important, of reasonable air support for ground forces. We did not succeed in getting into the critical points ahead of the Axis, largely because of the senselessness of French officials in Tunisia who chose to follow Vichy instead of Darlan. During the period of the 9th to 15th November, if French forces in that area had resisted even feebly our gamble would have won.

Anderson's two latest detailed situation reports have been transmitted to you practically verbatim so that you should be well acquainted with the tactical situation on the front. You know that the counter-attacks of 1st to 3rd December set us back considerably and caused us material losses. This morning's G-2 report places the total Axis strength in Tunisia at more than 31,000 troops, of which the bulk is north of Sousse.

The Allied force was initially loaded and despatched with a principal purpose of getting ashore and seizing three main ports. To accomplish this mission, it came woefully short in motor transport and other auxiliaries normally making up the "train" of an army. Although we have worked the railroad to the maximum, we finally came to a situation where all sidings were blocked and distribution impossible because of lack of transport and service troops. All the native labour deserts the second a bomb falls in the neighbourhood. Troops finally were without reserves of supplies and ammunition, although these were forward in ample quantities at various points along the lines of communication. Our fighter aircraft were trying to support the front lines from airdromes 120 miles distant, while the enemy had to fly only 15 miles. We reached the point where practically by air alone the enemy could break up every attempted advance.

A breathing space in attempt [sic] reinforcement, untangling of supply and betterment of air support was manifestly called for. That period started yesterday morning. The wisdom of the move was made more manifest by the receipt this morning of Anderson's report of his defensive fighting on 3rd December. Our temporary reverses were due to the conditions I have outlined.

During this breathing space, our one hope of achieving a better relative position, aside from the measures already outlined, is to hammer heavily with our bombers on the supply lines of the enemy. I have already ordered down from the United Kingdom an additional U.S. group of Liberators, which I intend to use for the next few days as temporary reinforcements. We also asked General Andrews to consult Middle East Commanders-in-Chief to determine whether they could loan us some of their American heavy bombers for a few days. To that request we received no reply. Daily reports show that Malta is straining every nerve to help us, and I have nothing but praise for the work Park has done.* In addition you have undoubtedly received reports of what the Navy has done by night in interrupting supply lines. However, the enemy can do this work largely by day under strong fighter cover because of the shortness of the trip, and we cannot tell whether or not he is reinforcing materially.

I want to assure you that every individual along the line, both in the battle itself and along the line of communication, has performed heartbreaking work without relief and has devoted himself unreservedly to success in the big gamble we took. It is my personal belief that if we could have had, during the period 18th November to 1st December, a half-dozen motor transport companies over and above the forces we actually did have, this battle could have been over. But we could not have both the combat strength and the motor transport we so desperately needed.

Position of main front line troops has been already indicated in prior messages. That part of the 6th Armoured Division so far landed concentrating area south of Béja by 7th December. On 2nd December, French detachments were on general line Bou Arada—Maktar—Sbiba—Sbeitla—Feriana—Gafsa. At last three mentioned places they are supported by United States forces, strength about one battalion and additional weapons. Two battalions of guards brigade will reach Souk El Arba on 7th.†

In the political field it is easily apparent that our communications

---

* [Air Vice-Marshal K. R. Park was A.O.C. Malta].
† [The third battalion of 1st Guards Brigade was 2nd Hampshire Regiment which had been sent ahead to reinforce 11th Infantry Brigade.]

APPENDIX 11

system has not served us well in attempting to keep you fully informed. This has been aggravated by the fact that difficulties in censorship here have permitted stories to go out that have no foundation in fact. Among these stories is one that the American military authorities are dealing with Darlan on matters that have nothing to do with the local military situation, and are supporting him in his claims to a permanent authority rather than as merely the temporary head of the local government. Nothing could be further from the truth. Admiral Cunningham, Mr. Mack and Brigadier Whiteley and other British officers are kept closely and intimately informed of every move made, both in our local dealings with Darlan and in the weary process we have been going through straightening out the Dakar tangle. At every meeting [with] Darlan I tell him, that so far as this headquarters is concerned, he is the head of a local *de facto* organization through which we are enabled to secure the co-operation, both military and civil, that we need in the prosecution of this campaign. He knows that I am not empowered to go farther than this. I assure you again that we are not entering a cabal designed to make Darlan the head of anything except the local organization. Here he is absolutely necessary, for he, and he alone, is the source of every bit of practical help we have received. If you will picture the situation existing along our lines of communication, which extend 500 miles from here through mountainous country to Tunisia, you can understand that the local French could, without fear of detection, so damage us that we would have to retreat hastily back on to ports from which we could supply ourselves by sea. Giraud quickly gave up in trying to help us and it was only through Darlan's help that we are fighting the Boche in Tunisia instead of somewhere in the vicinity of Bône or even west of that. It appears to us that both Boisson and Darlan have committeed themselves irrevocably to an Allied victory; and my conversations with them this morning, in which Cunningham participated, dealt with their desire to get French naval forces at Dakar quickly into the fight against the enemy. They are also convinced that Godfroy will soon be brought around through the medium of the French emissaries that Cunningham has sent from here to Cairo. Boisson cannot go back to Dakar except with something concrete to show the governors of the nine provinces which he controls. He strikes us as an honest man, and there is no question that he hates the Boche. He wants immediately to start a tour of his whole region, creating by personal contact a real war spirit that will allow him to assist actively as well as passively.

I earnestly hope that we may get some kind of an expression to-day from the Combined Chiefs of Staff that will allow us to sign a tentative memorandum of co-operative effort. Incidentally, we explained to the C.C./S. in messages following up the original text of the tentative memorandum, that the French were perfectly willing to substitute "United States and Allied Forces" wherever the item "United States" appeared, provided the vexatious question of prisoners could be settled. Even this last they offered to leave completely out of the memorandum and put the latter [sic] off for further negotiation. I was somewhat fearful that the British Government could not accept this last proposal, for the reason that

I understand several hundred British prisoners are now held in French West Africa.

The military outlook depends upon several factors, of which the most important is our ability to build up fighter cover over our ground troops. This, in turn, depends upon getting supplies, establishing forward fields and keeping up a rapid flow of fighter craft until the battle is won. It also depends upon weather, until we can get steel mats on all our mud-fields. The next thing we must accomplish is to get forward every available atom of ground reinforcement and replacements for troops now in the line, who need a short rest. Finally, we must get our lines of communication working so well that all ground and air troops can be assured of adequate reserves when more intensive fighting begins again. The third great factor is the prevention of rapid reinforcement by the enemy. Our bombing-fields are so far removed from targets that the scale of our air bombing is not what we should like, but we are doing our best. Finally, during all this process, we must provide adequate protection for our land and sea lines of communication, particularly our ports. All these jobs strain our resources and keep everyone going at maximum pace, but we shall yet get it done. But all this shows you how dependent upon French passive and active co-operation we are and, to date, we have had no evidence of reluctance on Darlan's part to help us.

Permit me to express to you my warmest regard and best wishes for your continued health.'

APPENDIX 12

Operational Code Names

BRITISH

'Brimstone'	Plan for the capture of Sardinia
'Crusader'	British offensive, Western Desert November 1941
'Flax'	Allied air operation to disorganize the enemy's system of air transport to Africa. April 1943
'Gymnast'	Plan for British landing in French North Africa
'Super Gymnast'	Plan for Anglo-American landing in French North Africa (These 'Gymnasts' later became 'Torch')
'Husky'	Plan for the capture of Sicily
'Lightfoot'	Opening phase of the Battle of El Alamein, October 1942
'Pedestal'	Convoy to Malta from the west, August 1942
'Portcullis'	Convoy to Malta from the east, December 1942
'Round up'	Plan for Allied landing in north-western France in 1943
'Sledgehammer'	Plan for Allied landing in Cherbourg peninsula in 1943
'Stoneage'	Convoy to Malta from the east, November 1942
'Strike'	Final phase of 1st Army's assault on Tunis and Bizerta, May 1943
'Supercharge'	(a) Last phase of the Battle of El Alamein October—November 1942 (b) British attack at 'Tebaga Gap', March 1943
'Torch'	Allied landings in French North Africa, November 1942
'Vulcan'	18th Army Group offensive to destroy Axis forces in Tunisia, April—May 1943

ENEMY

Ausladung	('Unloading') Pz AOK 5 operation (von Manteuffel), northern Tunisia, February to mid-March 1943

'Eilbote' ('Express Messenger') Pz AOK 5 operation, northern Tunisia, January 1943

'Frühlingswind' ('Spring Breeze') Pz AOK 5 operation, central Tunisia, February 1943

'Morgenluft' ('Morning Air') D.A.K. Assault Group operation, central and southern Tunisia, February 1943

'Ochsenkopf' ('Bull's Head')
    (a) Pz AOK 5 operation (Weber), northern Tunisia, February—early March 1943
    (b) Term used in Pz AOK 5 to describe *'Ausladung'* and (a) above when considered together as a single offensive.

INDEX

Ships of all nationalities are in their alphabetical places *in italics*. Groups, Wings, Squadrons and other units of the R.A.F. are under Royal Air Force. Squadrons of the F.A.A. are under Fleet Air Arm. Squadrons of the R.A.A.F. and S.A.A.F. are under Royal Australian Air Force and South African Air Force. Corps, Divisions, Brigades and Battalions of the British forces are under those headings. Cavalry and armoured units are listed under Regiments. Other units and branches of the Army are under their titles: e.g. Royal Artillery. Formations and units of the United States Army Air Forces and of the French Air Force are found under those headings. Corps, divisions, regimental combat teams, regiments and all units of the United States Army and of the French Army are listed under those headings. Formations and units of the German and Italian Armies are under German Army and Italian Army; of the German Air Force under *Luftwaffe*, and of the Italian Air Force under that heading.

Abdiel, H.M.S.: minelaying by, 245, 249, 413, 415
Admiralty: 130, 256-7, 420
Agedabia: air attacks on, 100
Agnew, Captain, W. G.: 426
Agostino Bertani: 243
Aine-el-Turk: capture of, 150
Aircraft: particulars of, 511-24
  Hurricane IID: use of, 63
  Me. 109G: advantage of, 393
  F.w. 190: description of, 171n; advantage of, 283, 393
  Mustang II: superiority of, 393
  Spitfire IX: superiority of, 393
Air Headquarters, Air Defences, Eastern Mediterranean: 355
Air Headquarters, Egypt (late Air Headquarters, Air Defences, Eastern Mediterranean): 221, 258, 355
Air Officer Commanding-in-Chief, Coastal Command: 129
Air Officer Commanding, Gibraltar: *see* Simpson
Air Officer Commanding-in-Chief, Middle East: *see* Tedder *and* Douglas *and, for joint action*, Commanders-in-Chief
Air Officer Commanding, Western Desert Air Force: *see* Coningham *and* Broadhurst
Air Support: in pursuit to El Agheila, 88, 99, 221-2; in operation 'Torch', 128-9, 168-9, 307-8; in advance into Tunisia, 182-3, 185, 190, 400; in operation 'Husky', 265; co-ordination of, 310-11; in Battle of Mareth, 354-5; in operation 'Vulcan', 439-41, 443; in operation 'Strike', 448-51, 454-6
Ajax, H.M.S.: 245
Alam el Halfa: Battle of, 2, 7, 24, 79
Albisola: 412
Alcamo: 247
Alexander, General the Hon. Sir Harold: *see also* Commanders-in-Chief; and Persia and Iraq Command, 1; and Montgomery, 1-3, 443, 446; and operation 'Lightfoot', 2, 4-5, 47, 66; and CDL, 8n; on air support, 78; and operation 'Torch', 113; visits Tripoli, 255-6; mentioned, 257, 389, 458; and operation 'Husky', 265, 316; succeeded by Wilson, 266; and fighting in Tunisia,

Alexander, General—*cont.*
  289n, 316, 376, 397-8, 402; commands 18th Army Group, 289n, 303-4; and American troops, 294, 376; and Eisenhower, 303-4; and Anderson, 304-5, 383, 398; and Battle of Mareth, 320, 329, 336, 339-40; and Battle of Wadi Akarit, 357-8, 373; and fighting at Fondouk, 381-2; on securing airfields, 400; and operation 'Vulcan', 430, 432, 441-3; and operation 'Strike' 446, 448n, 451; on end of Tunisian campaign, 459; at victory parade, 461
Algerino: 100
Algiers: landing at, 143-4, 159-60; occupation of, 145, 160; air attacks on, 252-3
Allen, Major-General Terry de la M.: 296, 376n, 432
Allfrey, Lieut.-General C.W.: commands 5th, Corps, 165n; and operation 'Torch' 183-4, 186-8; and fighting in Tunisia, 383; and operation 'Vulcan', 432; and von Arnim, 458
Allied Air Support Command: 271, 311
Almack, U.S. combat loader: 155-6
Alpino: 414
Ambrosio, General Vittorio: replaces Cavallero, 268; and Axis command, 269; and supplies, 276, 361; and fighting in Tunisia, 288, 305, 322, 326, 329-30, 359-60, 392; and Army Group Africa, 305
Amsterdam: 201
Anderson, Private E.: 370
Anderson, Major J. T. McK.: 436
Anderson, Lieut.-General K. A. N.: and operation 'Torch', 113, 126, 129, 152-3; commands 1st Army, 153; Eisenhower's directives to, 165, 270-1, 304-5; and fighting in Tunisia, 169, 174-7, 179, 181-3, 186-8, 204-5, 276, 281-2, 285, 288n, 289, 292, 294, 300, 304, 315-6, 383-4, 389, 397; and control of French troops, 176, 270-1; mentioned, 296n, 359; and Alexander, 304-5, 383, 398, 430, |446; tasks of, 305; and air support, 307-8, 400; and operation 'Vulcan', 432-3, 436, 441, 443; and operation 'Strike', 446-7, 453; qualities of, 457; and Axis surrender, 458-9
Andrews, Lieutenant-General Frank M: 83n

531

Ankara: 245-6
D'Annunzio: 100, 244
Antares: 425
Anti-tank mines: 29-30, 38-40
XXI Aprile: 249
Apuania: 20
Aquino: 413
Aquitania, s.s.: 259
Ardeola, s.s.: 196
Arethusa, H.M.S.: 197-9
Argonaut, H.M.S.: 139, 205-6
Argus, H.M.S.: and operation 'Torch', 138-140, 144, 154; air attack on, 157
Arlesiana: 423
Armies:
  1st: and operation 'Torch', 125, 128, 153, 165-7; mentioned, 126, 169, 179, 239, 264, 270, 299, 304, 308, 319, 358-9, 364n, 383, 386, 389, 395, 398, 402; command of, 153, 271, 303; and fighting in Tunisia, 165, 173, 186, 189, 199, 281-2, 284-5, 289, 292-4, 296, 298, 323, 327, 389-90, 395-8, 405, 429; strength and state of, 165, 167, 383, 432-3; reinforcements and supplies for, 273, 275, 284, 385-8, 430, 443, 448; reorganization of, 315; at Fondouk, 379; joins 8th Army, 397, 401, 429; and operation 'Vulcan', 430, 432, 434, 442; air support for, 439-40, 447, 456; and operation 'Strike', 452, 454; achievements of, 457, 462; and Axis surrender, 459n; at victory parade, 461
  7th U.S.: 432n
  8th: strength and state of, 2-3, 10, 13, 30, 52, 57, 76, 316, 334, 445; and operation 'Lightfoot', 2-3, 5, 12, 14-9, 30, 32, 35-8, 51-2, 60; reorganization of, 7, 16, 220; air support for, 13, 76, 78, 88, 98-100, 221-2, 231, 318-9, 321, 354, 368-9, 374, 443-4; supplies and reinforcements for, 15-7, 30, 101-6, 200, 213, 215-6, 220, 233, 252, 256-8, 316-7, 320n, 368, 421-2, 448; and Dog-fight, 57; and operation 'Supercharge', 65n, 72; in Battle of El Alamein, 76, 78-9, 133; losses of, 78, 375; and pursuit to El Agheila, 88, 96, 107, 215, 221-2; mentioned, 110, 165, 186, 197, 212, 230, 232, 255, 264, 304-5, 350, 359n, 361, 363, 386, 389, 399-400, 446n, 458-9; enters Benghazi, 199; in advance to Tripoli, 213, 215, 226-7, 238-9, 264n; Prime Minister visits, 267; and fighting in Tunisia, 276, 284, 301, 315, 322-3, 384, 398, 402; command of, 303; and Battle of Mareth, 320-2, 329, 331, 334, 341-4, 348, 352-3; at Medenine, 326; and Battle of Wadi Akarit, 357-8, 365, 369, 373, 375, 377, 383; joins 1st Army, 397, 401, 429; and operation 'Vulcan', 430, 438, 441, 443, 453; at victory parade, 461; tribute to, 462
Army Group, 18th: formed, 282, 386; mentioned, 289n, 305, 364n, 380, 383n, 388, 398n, 429; command of, 289n; and Army/Air co-operation, 312n, 358, 430; and

Army Group—*cont.*
  action at Maknassy, 376; and action at Fondouk, 382; and fighting in Tunisia, 389; and operation 'Vulcan', 430, 447; and prisoners, 460
Armistice, French: 134
Arnim, Colonel-General Jürgen von: his command, 184, 269; and fighting in Tunisia, 186-7, 268, 274, 276n, 278, 287-9, 291, 293-5, 300-1, 305-6, 322, 326-9, 378, 394-5, 397, 405, 430, 434; and supplies, 246, 250, 359-61, 407, 423; mentioned, 269, 290, 441, 443; and Battle of Mareth, 330-1, 348; and Battle of Wadi Akarit, 360, 372-3; and operation 'Vulcan', 437-9, 445; and operation 'Strike', 448, 451-4; surrenders, 457-8; on prisoners, 460n
Arnold, Lieut.-General Henry H.: 110n
Artillery Weapons: notes on, 498, 503-4
Ascari: 413
Ashton, Commander F. H.: 422
Assault Forces: *see also* Naval Task Forces: in operation 'Torch', 138
  Central (Oran): 126, 134
  Eastern (Algiers): and operation 'Torch', 126, 134, 140, 165-6, 196
  Western (Moroccan): 126, 134
Attendolo: 211
Attilio Regolo: 202
Auchinleck, General Sir Claude: 4
Augusta: U.S.S.: 139
Augustus: 131
Auphan, Admiral: 161, 163
Aurora, H.M.S.: and operation 'Torch', 139, 147, 149-50; at Bône, 205, 245; mentioned, 426
Avenger, H.M.S.: and operation 'Torch', 138-140, 144, 154; sinks, 156
Aviere: 207
Avon Vale, H.M.S.: 253
Awatea, L.S.I.: 153-4

Baalbeck: 249
Bachaquero, s.s.: 149
Bacchiani, Colonel Augusto: 273, 393n
Bantam, s.s.: 198
Barbasetti di Prun, General Curio: 55, 219n
Barham, H.M.S.: 157
Barré, General G.: and operation 'Torch', 162-3, 170-1, 174, 190; and fighting in Tunisia, 276, 279
Barrett, Group Captain, G. G.: 271
Bari: air attacks on, 444, 456
Bassini: 425
Bastico, Marshal Ettore: and Cavallero, 93; and Rommel, 94, 219, 229; and Comando Supremo, 230; returns to Italy, 268
Bateman, Brigadier D. R. E. R.: 365
Battalions:
  1st, The Argyll and Sutherland Highlanders: 21n
  7th, The Argyll and Sutherland Highlanders: and Battle of El Alamein, 74-5; in fighting in Tunisia, 326n, 366n, 370, 372

INDEX

Battalions—*cont.*
  8th, The Argyll and Sutherland Highlanders: 327n, 396n, 436
  9th, The Argyll and Sutherland Highlanders: 153n
  2/23rd Australian: 58
  2/24th Australian: 49, 61
  2/32nd Australian: 61-2
  2/48th Australian: 49, 61
  2/3rd Australian Pioneer: 61
  2nd, The Bedfordshire and Hertfordshire Regiment: 388n
  1st, The Black Watch: 326n, 366n
  5th, The Black Watch: 223, 366n
  6th, The Black Watch: 388n, 398, 438
  7th, The Black Watch: 366n, 370, 372
  1st, The Buffs: 92
  5th, The Buffs: lands at Bougie, 153n; in fighting in Tunisia, 276n, 396n; in operation 'Vulcan', 436, 438
  2nd, The Cheshire Regiment: 325n, 366n
  6th, The Cheshire Regiment: 442n
  2nd, Coldstream Guards: 187-8, 380n, 435n
  3rd, Coldstream Guards: 326n, 335
  2nd, The Duke of Cornwall's Light Infantry: 388n
  1st, The Duke of Wellington's Regiment: 388n
  6th, The Durham Light Infantry: 338, 340
  8th, The Durham Light Infantry: 66n, 338
  9th, The Durham Light Infantry: 66n, 338, 340
  16th, The Durham Light Infantry: 327n, 396n, 435n
  1st, The East Surrey Regiment: and operation 'Torch', 142n, 144-5; and fighting in Tunisia, 176, 180-1, 396n, 399
  1/6th, The East Surrey Regiment: 388n
  5th, The East Yorkshire Regiment: and Battle of Mareth, 335, 340; in fighting in Tunisia, 366n, 370, 372
  1st/4th Essex Regiment: 365, 404
  1st, The Gordon Highlanders: 56, 223, 236
  5/7th The Gordon Highlanders: 74-5, 223
  6th, The Gordon Highlanders: 388n
  6th, The Green Howards: 366n, 371-2
  7th, The Green Howards: 338, 366, 370
  3rd, Grenadier Guards: 380n, 435n
  5th, Grenadier Guards: 388n
  6th, Grenadier Guards: 326n, 335
  1/2nd Gurkha Rifles: 369-70, 458
  1/9th Gurkha Rifles: 370, 404
  1st/4th, The Hampshire Regiment: 327n, 380n, 435n
  2nd, The Hampshire Regiment: 180-1, 296, 396n
  2nd/4th, The Hampshire Regiment: 327n, 380n, 435n
  5th, The Hampshire Regiment: in fighting in Tunisia, 327n, 328; at Fondouk, 380n, 381; in operation 'Vulcan', 435n
  1st, Irish Guards: 388n, 439
  2nd/4th, The King's Own Yorkshire Light Infantry: 435n

Battalions—*cont.*
  9th, The King's Own Yorkshire Light Infantry (The Yorkshire Dragoons): 435n
  1st, The King's Royal Rifle Corps: 223n, 351n, 435n
  2nd, The King's Royal Rifle Corps: 54, 71, 232n
  1st, The King's Shropshire Light Infantry: 388n, 437
  2nd, The Lancashire Fusiliers: and operation 'Torch', 142n, 145, in fighting in Tunisia, 396n, 399
  2/5th, The Leicestershire Regiment: 298-9, 327n, 435n
  6th, The Lincolnshire Regiment: 327n, 435n
  2nd, The London Irish Rifles, 399, 436n
  1st, The Loyal Regiment: 388n, 437
  28th (Maori): in operation 'Supercharge', 66; in fighting in Tunisia, 326n, 403-4; in Battle of Mareth, 350, 352
  1/7th Middlesex Regiment: 366n
  21st New Zealand: in pursuit to El Agheila, 94; in fighting in Tunisia, 326n, 403; in Battle of Mareth, 349, 350n
  23rd New Zealand: 326n, 350, 404
  24th New Zealand: 350
  25th New Zealand: 350n
  26th New Zealand: 350n, 367n
  7th, The Northamptonshire Regiment: and operation 'Torch', 142n, 144-5, 153; in fighting in Tunisia, 177, 180, 187-8, 396n, 399
  2nd, The North Staffordshire Regiment: 388n
  7th, The Oxfordshire and Buckinghamshire Light Infantry: 442n
  1st Parachute: 170
  2nd Parachute: 177, 327n
  3rd Parachute: 154, 276n
  3/1st Punjab Regiment: 351n
  4/16th Punjab Regiment: 365n
  5th, The Queen's Own Cameron Highlanders: 66n, 366n, 370
  1st, The Queen's Own Royal West Kent Regiment: 388n
  1/5th, The Queen's Royal Regiment: 24, 326n
  1/6th, The Queen's Royal Regiment: 24, 326n
  2nd/5th, The Queen's Royal Regiment: 442n
  2/6th, The Queen's Royal Regiment: 442n
  1/7th, The Queen's Royal Regiment: in action at Munassib, 24; casualties in, 43n; in fighting in Tunisia, 326n; enters Tunis, 452
  2/7th, The Queen's Royal Regiment: 442n
  6th Rajputana Rifles: 365n
  4th/6th Rajputana Rifles: 365n, 372, 404
  1st, The Rifle Brigade: 43, 450n
  2nd, The Rifle Brigade: in Battle of El Alamein, 39n, 54-6; in fighting in Tunisia, 351n, 435n
  7th, The Rifle Brigade: 351n, 435n

Battalions—*cont.*
   10th, The Rifle Brigade: in fighting in Tunisia, 297n, 299, 380n; in operation 'Vulcan', 435n, 450n
   1st, The Royal Fusiliers, 351n
   2nd, The Royal Fusiliers: 388n
   8th, The Royal Fusiliers: 442n
   9th, The Royal Fusiliers: 442n
   6th, The Royal Inniskilling Fusiliers: 277, 396n, 436n
   1st, The Royal Irish Fusiliers: 396n, 399, 436n
   1st, The Royal Northumberland Fusiliers: 21n, 352, 435n
   1st, The Royal Sussex Regiment: 365n, 370, 458
   4th, The Royal Sussex Regiment: 56-7
   5th, The Royal Sussex Regiment: 70
   6th, The Royal West Kent Regiment: and operation 'Torch', 145, 153n, in fighting in Tunisia, 396n, 436
   2nd, The Seaforth Highlanders: and Battle of El Alamein, 70; in fighting in Tunisia, 366n, 370, 372
   5th, The Seaforth Highlanders: and Battle of El Alamein, 66n; in fighting in Tunisia, 366n, 370, 372
   1st, Scots Guards: 388n, 439
   2nd, Scots Guards: 325-6
   2nd, The Sherwood Foresters: 388n, 437
   2nd/5th The Sherwood Foresters: 327n
   5th, The Sherwood Foresters: 435n
   3rd, Welsh Guards: 380n, 381-2, 435n
   6th, The York and Lancashire Regiment: 435n
Bayerlein, Colonel (later Major-General) Fritz: commands D.A.K., 85n; with *AOK* 1, 270; and Battle of Mareth, 339, 345, 351, 354; and Battle of Wadi Akarit, 369, 371-4; and withdrawal in Tunisia, 378; on air attacks, 378; leaves Tunisia, 446
Beak, Brigadier, D. M. W.: 337, 339
Beamish, Air Commodore G. R.: 15, 272
Bedell Smith, Brigadier-General Walter: 112
Belluno: 423
Benghazi: air attacks on, 20, 91, 100; raid on, 20-1; capture of, 103, 199; as a supply base, 103-4, 232
Bennehoff, Captain O. R.: 137
Benson, Colonel Clarence C.: 376, 378, 397
Bergamini, Admiral Carlo: 426
Bermuda, H.M.S.: 139, 145-6
Bernasconi, General Mario: 273
Bersagliere: 246
Birch, Brigadier J. C. A.: 442n
Bir Dufan: air attacks on, 234
Bissett, Rear-Admiral A. W. La T.: 426
Biter, H.M.S.: 139-40, 149
Bizerta: and operation 'Torch', 152; air attacks on, 169, 179, 183, 185, 188, 242, 278, 412; mining of, 208; capture of, 453
Blackburn, Commander J. F.: 21n
Blyskawica: 413
Boissau, General: 400, 433, 453-4
Boisson, M.: 115, 163
Bolzano: 244
Bombardiere: 246

Bomber Command (United Kingdom): 414
Bône: air attacks on, 174-5, 179, 252-3
Bonham-Carter, Vice-Admiral Sir Stuart: 257, 415, 426
Bonomi, Brigadier-General Ruggero: 273
Boscardi, Major: 459
Boschi, Brigadier Mario: 272-3, 393n
Bosville, Brigadier T. J. B.: 40, 435n
Bourne, Lieut.-General A. G. B.: 121n
Bradley, Lieut.-General Omar N.: 432, 453
Breconshire, H.M.S.: 245, 258
Brereton, Major-General Lewis H.: commands U.S.A.M.E.A.F., 10; and Cs.-in-C's Committee, 11n; commands U.S. Ninth Air Force, 83n; and Tedder, 265
Brigades & Brigade Groups:
   Armoured:
      1st Army Tank: 8n
      21st Army Tank: 388n
      25th Army Tank: 432, 446n, 447
      1st: 16, 65, 68
      2nd: and operation 'Lightfoot', 8, 40-1, 44; strength and state of, 9, 65n, 71, 84n, 351n; and Dog-fight, 54, 56; and operation 'Supercharge', 65n, 67-8, 70-1; and pursuit to El Agheila, 84, 89; and Battle of Mareth, 347, 351-2; and Battle of Wadi Akarit, 367; and operation 'Vulcan', 435n
      3rd: 449
      4th Light: and operation 'Lightfoot', 8, 42; strength and state of, 9, 83n; and Dog-fight, 57; and operation 'Supercharge', 65n, 68; and pursuit to El Agheila, 81, 83, 84n, 86-7, 94, 96-7, 221n, 223; and advance to Tripoli, 225-6, 232n, 234, 236; and fighting in Tunisia, 325
      8th: and operation 'Lightfoot', 8, 40-1, 45-7; strength and state of, 9, 65n, 71, 84n, 324, 367n; air attacks on, 47; and operation 'Supercharge', 65n, 67, 70-1, 75; and pursuit to El Agheila, 81, 84, 86, 90-1, 221n, 224; and advance to Tripoli, 226, 232n, 234; and Battle of Mareth, 320, 337n, 343-5, 347, 350-2; and fighting in Tunisia, 325; and Battle of Wadi Akarit, 367, 373, 375; mentioned, 377
      9th: strength and state of, 9, 65n, 66-7, 83n; and operation 'Lightfoot', 31, 37-8, 45-7; and Dog-fight, 52, 57; and operation 'Supercharge', 65, 67; and pursuit to El Agheila, 81, 83, 84n, 90
      22nd: and operation 'Lightfoot', 8, 42-3, 45-6; strength and state of, 9, 65n, 84n; and operation 'Supercharge', 65n; and pursuit to El Agheila, 87, 90, 95; and advance to Tripoli, 227n, 231, 236; and fighting in Tunisia, 325, 450, 452; mentioned, 366n
      23rd: strength and state of, 9, 367n; and operation 'Lightfoot', 37; and

INDEX

Brigades and Brigade Groups—*cont.*
  Armoured—*cont.*
    operation 'Supercharge', 74; and advance to Tripoli, 231, 236; mentioned, 366n
    24th: and operation 'Lightfoot', 8, 14, 40-1, 45-7; 65n; strength of, 9; and Dog-fight, 54-5; and operation 'Supercharge', 65n
    26th: in fighting in Tunisia, 296, 298-9, 380n, 381-2; in operation 'Vulcan', 435n; in operation 'Strike', 449, 450n, 452, 454
  Infantry:
    20th Australian: 7, 58
    24th Australian: 7, 58
    26th Australian: and operation 'Lightfoot', 7; and Dog-fight, 48-9, 58, 60-1
    2nd (British): 388n, 437
    3rd (British): 388n, 434, 437
    9th (British): 7
    10th (British): 388n, 434, 437
    11th (British): and operation 'Torch', 126, 140-2, 144-5, 153; in fighting in Tunisia, 169, 176, 180-1, 184, 396, 399; casualties in, 177n
    12th (British): 388n, 398, 437-8
    36th (British): and operation 'Torch', 126, 140-1, 153; in fighting in Tunisia, 165, 169-70, 173, 176-7, 276, 284, 396; casualties in, 177n, in operation 'Vulcan', 436, 438
    38th (British): 396, 399, 436-7
    69th (British): and Battle of El Alamein, 8; and Battle of Mareth, 335, 338, 340-1; and Battle of Wadi Akarit, 366, 370
    128th (British): in fighting in Tunisia, 327, 379-81; in operation 'Vulcan', 434, 435n
    131st (British): and operation 'Lightfoot', 8, 42-3, 45-6; attacks Deir el Munassib, 23; and Dog-fight, 57; and advance to El Agheila, 221n; and fighting in Tunisia, 325, 326n, 450, 452
    132nd (British): 8, 24
    133rd (British): and operation 'Lightfoot', 8, 14, 40-1, 45-6; and Dog-fight, 54, 56; and operation 'Supercharge', 66, 70; and pursuit to El Agheila, 90-1
    138th (British): 327n, 389, 434-5
    139th (British): 327, 435n, 446n
    151st (British): and Battle of El Alamein, 8, 57, 66, 69n; and Battle of Mareth, 337-41
    152nd (British): and operation 'Lightfoot', 7; and operation 'Supercharge', 57, 66, 70, 74-5; and advance to El Agheila, 221n; and Battle of Wadi Akarit, 366, 371-2
    153rd (British): and Battle of El Alamein, 7, 38; in advance to Tripoli, 221n, 223; and Battle of Wadi Akarit, 366

Brigades and Brigade Groups—*cont.*
  Infantry—*cont.*
    154th (British): and Battle of El Alamein, 7, 69n, 74; in advance to Tripoli, 221n; mentioned, 324; and fighting in Tunisia, 326n; and Battle of Wadi Akarit, 366, 370, 372
    167th (British): 441, 454
    169th (British): 441-3
    1st Fighting French: 8, 42-3
    2nd Fighting French: 8
    1st Greek: 8, 221n
    1st Guards: in fighting in Tunisia, 187, 282, 296; at Fondouk, 380n, 381-2; in operation 'Vulcan', 435n, 436
    24th Guards: 388n, 438-9
    201st Guards: in fighting in Tunisia, 320, 324-5, 326n; and Battle of Mareth, 335; and Battle of Wadi Akarit, 365; and operation 'Vulcan', 442; transferred to 1st Army, 443
    5th Indian: and operation 'Lightfoot', 7; and operation 'Supercharge', 69n, 74-5; and pursuit to El Agheila, 84, 94; and Battle of Mareth, 341; and Battle of Wadi Akarit, 365, 370, 372
    7th Indian: and operation 'Lightfoot' 7; and Battle of Mareth, 341; and Battle of Wadi Akarit, 365, 369; in fighting in Tunisia, 404; mentioned, 458
    11th Indian: 364
    161st Indian: 7
    4th New Zealand: 8
    5th New Zealand: and Battle of El Alamein, 7, 46, 69n; and pursuit to El Agheila, 84n, 86, 221n; in advance to Tripoli, 225-6; and fighting in Tunisia, 326n, 403-4; and Battle of Mareth, 337n, 344, 347, 349-50; and Battle of Wadi Akarit, 367n; mentioned, 401
    6th New Zealand: and Battle of El Alamein, 7; and pursuit to El Agheila, 83-4; in advance to Tripoli, 221n, 225-6; and Battle of Mareth, 337n, 343, 347, 350; and Battle of Wadi Akarit, 367n; in fighting in Tunisia, 403-4, 442
    1st South African: 8
    2nd South African: 8
    3rd South African: 8
  Motor:
    7th: and operation 'Lightfoot', 8, 40-1; and Dog-fight, 54, 56; and operation 'Supercharge', 67, 70; in Battle of Mareth, 351n, 352; and Battle of Wadi Akarit, 367n; in operation 'Vulcan', 435n
  Parachute:
    1st (British): in fighting in Tunisia 183, 282, 327n, 389

Briggs, Major-General R.: commands 1st Armoured Division, 8; and Dog-fight, 54; and Battle of Mareth, 347, 352; and operation 'Vulcan', 432; commands 9th Corps, 438; mentioned, 446
Brilliant, H.M.S.: 149
British Trust, tanker: 426
'Brimstone': 263-4
Brioni: 68n, 202
British Government: *see* War Cabinet, *and* Defence Committee
British Joint Staff Mission: 261
Broadhurst, Air Commodore (later Air Vice-Marshal) H.: at A.H.Q., Western Desert, 221n; mentioned, 271; and fighting in Tunisia, 346-7, 354
Broich, Colonel (later Major-General) Freiherr Fritz von: 173, 187, 306
Broke, H.M.S.: 143-4
Brooke, General Sir Alan, Chief of the Imperial General Staff: and operation 'Lightfoot', 47, 60; as Chief of Staff, 110n; and operation 'Torch', 125; and reopening of Tripoli harbour, 256-7; at Casablanca, 262-3; and 'Husky', 263-4; visits Middle East and Turkey, 266-7; Alexander reports to, 304
Brooklyn, U.S.S.: 139
Browne, Captain L. H.: 223n
Buck, Captain H. C.: 21n
Buelowius, Major-General Karl: commands D.A.K. Assault Group, 288n, 295; and fighting in Tunisia, 297, 300; replaces von Manteuffel, 446
Bulolo, H.M.S.: in operation 'Torch', 139, 141-2, 144, 146; and operation 'Husky', 427
Burrough, Vice-Admiral Sir Harold: commands Eastern Naval Task Force, 129, 134, 139; and operation 'Torch', 141-3, 146; commands Force H, 254; succeeded by Willis, 420

Cadogan, Sir Alexander: 267
Cagliari: air attacks on, 248, 425
Cameronia, s.s.: 211
Campbell, Lieut.-Colonel Lorne: 372
Campo Basso: 423
Capo Mele: 412
Capo Orso: 247
Carlisle, H.M.S.: 420, 425
Casey, Rt. Hon. R. G.: 60, 256
Cass, Brigadier E. E. E.: and operation 'Torch', 141, 143, 177, 181; commands 11th Infantry Brigade, 396n
Cassiopea: 414
Castel Benito: air attacks on, 235, 237
Castelverde: 207
Castelvetrano: air attacks on, 392n
Casualties: in raids on Tobruk and Benghazi, 23; in operation 'Lightfoot', 52; in operation 'Torch', 155; in Tunisia, 326, 460; in Battle of Wadi Akarit, 375; in operation 'Vulcan', 436-7
Catania: air attacks on, 412, 414
Caterina Costa: 413

Cathay, L.S.I.: 153-4
Cavallero, Marshal Ugo: and operation 'Lightfoot', 26; and withdrawal to El Agheila, 93-4, 219; and Allied landings, 135; and 15th Panzer Division, 230; replaced by Ambrosio, 268; and Messe, 269; mentioned, 329
Centauro: 203
Chakmak, Marshal: 267
Chaouach: capture of, 396
Chapman, Captain, A. C.: 199
Charybdis, H.M.S.: 138-9
Chatel, M.: 161
Chenango, U.S.S.: 139
Chhelu Ram, Havildar-Major: 404
Chief of the Imperial General Staff: *see* Brooke
Chief of Staff, 8th Army: *see* de Guingand
Chiefs of Staff: named, 110n; and operation 'Round-up', 111-12; and operation 'Torch', 114, 124-5, 165; and advance into Tunisia, 182, 276; and Malta, 193-4, 196, 200, 204; and Mediterranean Commands, 207; and Casablanca Conference, 261-2, 264; and operation 'Husky', 264
Chrystal, Captain P. D.: 223
Churchill, Rt. Hon. Winston S.: *see* Prime Minister
Ciano, Count: 229, 268, 409n
Cicogna: 412
Cigno: 414-5
City of Guildford, s.s.: 421
Clark, Major-General Mark W.: and operation 'Torch', 112, 133, 161; signs agreement with Darlan, 163; and French Fleet, 163; mentioned, 201
Clarke, Lieutenant W. A. S.: 437
Cleopatra, H.M.S.: and 'Stoneage' convoy, 197-8; at Malta, 205; bombards Zuara, 244; mentioned, 426
Cleveland, U.S.S.: 139
Climene: 414
Clutterbuck, Major-General W. E.: 388, 432
Clyde, H.M.S.: 196
Coastal Command:
  (in Gibraltar): and operation 'Torch', 128-9, 131-2, 137-8; 144, 150, and anti-submarine patrols, 252
  (in Gambia): and operation 'Torch', 129, 131
  (in U.K.): and operation 'Torch', 129, 131, 138
Col di Lana: 247
Colvin, Brigadier R. B. R.: 388n
Comando Aeronautica Tunisia: *see* Boschi
  Settore Aeronautico Centrale: *see* Bacchiani
  Settore Aeronautico Est: *see* Drago
  Settore Aeronautico Nord: *see* Bacchiani
  Settore Aeronautico Ovest: *see* Bonomi
  Settore Aeronautico Sud: *see* Drago
Comando Supremo: *see* Italian High Command
Combined Chiefs of Staff: and operation 'Round-up', 110; directive to Eisenhower, 114, 165; Eisenhower reports to, 182, 186, 188; and 'Husky', 263-4; on end of Tunisian campaign, 461

Combined Operations: 119-23
Combined Operations Organization: 120-21
Commander-in-Chief, Middle East: *see* Alexander, and, *for joint action*, Commanders-in-Chief
Commanders-in-Chief: and operation 'Torch', 2; and control of U.S.A.M.E.A.F., 11; and raids on Benghazi and Tobruk, 20; and Malta, 200; and Mediterranean Commands, 207; and reopening of Tripoli harbour, 257
Commanding General, U.S.A.M.E.A.F.: *see* Brereton
Commandos:
  1st: and operation 'Torch', 126, 140-1, 143-4; in advance into Tunisia, 177, 183, 327n
  6th: and operation 'Torch', 126, 141, 143, 145, 154; in advance into Tunisia, 183, 276n
Conferences: at Washington, 110, 112, 264n; at Casablanca, 207, 216, 261-6, 276, 282, 303, 316, 322, 453; (with Turks) at Adana, 266-7
Coningham, Air Vice-Marshal (later Air Marshal) Sir Arthur: and Tedder, 3; and operation 'Lightfoot', 6, 13, 32-3; and control of American squadrons, 11, 78; and operation 'Supercharge', 78; and pursuit to El Agheila, 82, 99, 221-2; and advance to Tripoli, 222, 231; commands N.A.T.A.F., 271, 303, 310-11; and advance into Tunisia, 298n, 310; and air support, 311-12; and Battle of Mareth, 321; and operation 'Vulcan', 430; and operation 'Strike', 447, 449
Conne, General,: 433, 453
Convoys: *see also* 'Stoneage' *and* 'Portcullis': (British): to Malta, 2, 77, 97, 116, 193-4, 196-200, 213, 257-8, 421, 424, 426; and operation 'Lightfoot', 15; and operation 'Supercharge', 77; to North Africa, 103, 175, 233, 257, 385-8, 419-22, 426; and operation 'Torch', 127-31, 134, 165-7; losses, 211, 253, 421-2; to Middle East, 252-4, 425
  (enemy): to Africa, 193, 201-11, 240-1, 243-52, 259, 407-18, 422-3, 431; losses, 200-3, 205-11, 250, 417, 423
Cooke-Collis, Brigadier E. C.: 335, 366n
Copland-Griffiths, Brigadier F. A. V.: 187-8
Corps:
  5th: mentioned, 165; in operation 'Torch', 167; in advance into Tunisia, 183-4, 186, 188, 276, 279, 282, 284, 295, 315, 383-4, 389-90, 395-9; mentioned, 302, 447n, 454; and air support, 308, 400, 439; and Battle of Wadi Akarit, 359; and operation 'Vulcan', 429, 432, 434, 436; and operation 'Strike', 446-8, 453
  9th: and fighting in Tunisia, 358-9, 377, 384, 389, 397-8, 401, 429; at Fondouk, 379, 381-3; and operation 'Vulcan', 432-4, 436, 438, 446, 450, 453

Corps—*cont.*
  10th: and operation 'Lightfoot', 5, 7-8, 13, 18, 31, 34-6, 39-42, 47; formation of, 7; strength and state of, 9, 84; casualties in, 52; and Dog-fight, 52, 54, 57; and operation 'Supercharge, 65, 67-9, 71-2; and pursuit to El Agheila, 81-4, 86, 89, 91, 96, 98n, 220-1; supplies for, 105; and advance to Tripoli, 227, 231, 232n, 233; and Battle of Mareth, 320, 338, 342, 347, 353; and Battle of Wadi Akarit, 357, 363-5, 367, 371-5; mentioned, 377, 399, 458-9; and advance into Tunisia, 378, 397, 401, 403, 429, 441-2, 453-4; command of, 446n
  13th: and operation 'Lightfoot', 5, 8, 18, 34, 36, 42-7; strength and state of, 9; casualties in, 52; and Dog-fight, 48, 52, 57; and operation 'Supercharge', 65, 68, 72; and pursuit to El Agheila, 81, 92-3, 220
  30th: and operation 'Lightfoot', 5, 7, 18, 31, 34-45, 47; strength and state of, 9, 324; mentioned, 51, 82n, 337, casualties in, 52, 227n; and Dog-fight, 48, 52, 54, 57; and operation 'Supercharge', 64, 68-9, 72, 74; and pursuit to El Agheila, 81, 86, 107; and advance to Tripoli, 220-1, 224-7, 231-2, 234; and Battle of Mareth, 320, 331, 334-5, 338-9; and fighting in Tunisia, 324-6, 341, 343-4, 353; and Battle of Wadi Akarit, 357, 363, 365, 367-8, 371-3, 375, 377
Corsica: Italians occupy, 162
Cowdray, H.M.S.: 146
Coventry, H.M.S.: 22
Craig, Brigadier-General Howard: 113
Cramer, General Hans: commands D.A.K., 288n, 323n, 324; and fighting in Tunisia, 372-3, 454, 457; surrenders, 458
Crete: reinforcement of, 24; air attacks on, 100, 228
Crocker, Lieutenant-General J. T.: commands 9th Corps, 358, 432; at Fondouk, 380-2; and operation 'Vulcan', 435-6; wounded, 438
Crook, Lieut.-Colonel A. A.: 188
Cross, Air Commodore K. B. B.: 271, 447
Cruiser Squadrons:
  12th: 426
  15th: 426
'Crusader': mentioned, 100n, 102, 110, 182n
Crüwell, Lieut.-General Ludwig: 172n
Cunningham, Admiral of the Fleet Sir Andrew: *see also* Commanders-in-Chief: on Combined Chiefs of Staff's Committee, 110n; commands Western Mediterranean, 113; and operation 'Torch', 113, 152, 156, 161; mentioned, 164n, 420; and Darlan, 191; and Malta, 200, 427-8; and 'sink at sight' zone, 202; and Force Q, 205; on minelaying, 245; becomes C.-in-C. Mediterranean, 254; and operation 'Husky', 265-6; on Italian seamen, 410; and operation 'Retribution', 424; at victory parade, 461

Cunningham, Admiral Sir J. H. D.: 257
Currie, Brigadier J. C.: 37, 46, 66
Custance, Brigadier E. C. N.: 40, 45-6

D.A.K. (Deutsches Afrika Korps): air attacks on, 49, 65-6, 377; strength and state of, 57, 64, 67, 290, 403, 454, 457; and operation 'Supercharge', 64-5, 67, 69, 72-3, 81; and withdrawal to El Agheila, 81-2, 84-7, 89, 91, 95-8; command of, 172n, 288n, 372; in retreat to Tripoli, 230n, 235; mentioned, 323n, 359n, 371, 394, 454, 458; in fighting in Tunisia, 324 377-8, 382, 438, 451, 453-4; and Battle of Mareth, 330; and Battle of Wadi Akarit, 360, 374
D.A.K. Assault Group: command of, 288n; in defence of Tunisia, 289, 291, 293, 295, 297-300, 305
Darlan, Admiral Jean François: in Algiers, 134, 159; orders 'cease fire', 145, 151, 161-2; under arrest, 160; and Pétain, 162; signs agreement with Clark, 163; and Toulon Fleet, 163-4; mentioned, 169; and Barré, 170; collaborates with Allies, 190-1; assassinated, 190, 266; his contribution to Allied cause, 191
Darwen, Wing Commander J.: 100, 347
Dasher, H.M.S.: 139-40, 149
Da Verazzano: 201
Dawson, Air Vice-Marshal G. G.: 312
Decimomannu: air attacks on, 392n
de Gaulle, General: and 'Fighting France', 2n, 158, 266; mentioned, 158-9; difficulties with, 190; meets Giraud, 266
de Guingand, Brigadier F. W.: and Montgomery, 5; and operation 'Lightfoot', 35-6, 45, 46n; and Dog-fight, 59; and Battle of Mareth, 344n
Deindl, Major-General: 23
Deir el Munassib: action at, 23-4, 26
de Laborde, Admiral: 163-4
'Delease': 219
Delfino: 421
Delhi, H.M.S.: 147, 426
Denbighshire, s.s.: 198
Dennis, Brigadier M. E.: 36
Derrien, Admiral: 162, 190
Derwent, H.M.S.: 422
De Stefanis, General: 94
Devonshire, H.M.S.: 259
Dewan Singh, Jemadar: 404
Dickinson, Captain N. V.: 153
Dido, H.M.S.: and 'Stoneage' convoy, 197-8; at Malta, 205; in Force Q, 206, 245; leaves Force Q, 415
Dill, Field-Marshal Sir John: 110n, 261
Divisions:
  Armoured:
    1st (British): and operation 'Lightfoot,' 7-8, 31, 39-41, 44, 47; strength and state of, 9, 65n, 351n, 367n, 446n; and Dog-fight, 48, 53, 57; and operation 'Supercharge', 65n, 67-8, 70-2, 75; and pursuit to El Agheila, 81, 84, 86-7, 89-91; supplies for,

Divisions—*cont.*
  Armoured—*cont.*
105n; and advance to Tripoli, 227n; and Battle of Mareth, 320, 341, 344-7, 350-2; and Battle of Wadi Akarit, 357, 364-7, 369; under 9th Corps, 359n; mentioned, 377; in fighting in Tunisia, 378, 397, 401; and operation 'Vulcan', 432-3, 435-6, 441; and operation 'Strike', 447, 453
    6th: and operation 'Torch', 166, 183-4, 187; mentioned, 273, 380n, 396n, 449; in advance into Tunisia, 276, 279, 284-5, 296, 298, 315, 397; re-equipment of, 302; under 9th Corps, 359n; at Kairouan, 377, 380; at Fondouk, 381; and operation 'Vulcan', 432-6, 440-1; and operation 'Strike', 446-7, 450, 452-4
    7th: and operation 'Lightfoot', 8, 34, 42-4, 46; strength and state of, 9, 65n, 367n; and Dog-fight, 48, 51-2, 57; and operation 'Supercharge', 65n, 68, 70, 79; and pursuit to El Agheila, 81, 84, 86-7, 90-1, 94-8, 107, 221, 223-4; supplies for, 105n; and advance to Tripoli, 227, 231-2, 235-6; at Medenine, 316; and Battle of Mareth, 320, 341, 346; mentioned, 324, 335; and fighting in Tunisia, 325, 377-8, 403, 446-7, 450, 452-3; transferred to 1st Army, 443
    8th: and operation 'Lightfoot', 7-8; and pursuit to El Agheila, 81
    10th: and operation 'Lightfoot', 7-8, 14, 18-9, 31, 39n, 40-1, 44-7; strength and state of, 9, 14; and Dog-fight, 52, 54, 57; and operation 'Supercharge', 65n; and pursuit to El Agheila, 81, 84, 86, 90-1; mentioned, 221n, 369
  Infantry:
    9th Australian: and operation 'Lightfoot', 7, 31, 37-8, 43-4, 47; strength of, 9; mentioned, 50-1; casualties in, 52; and Dog-fight, 48, 52-3, 56, 58-60; and operation 'Supercharge', 74-5; returns to Australia, 220, 259
    1st (British): and fighting in Tunisia, 315, 364n, 388, 396; and operation 'Vulcan', 432, 434, 437-8
    4th (British): and fighting in Tunisia, 388, 396-9, 432, 434; in operation 'Vulcan', 437-8; in operation 'Strike', 446, 449, 454
    5th (British): 264
    44th British): and operation 'Lightfoot', 8, 42, 46; mentioned, 23; and Dog-fight, 48, 57; and pursuit to El Agheila, 92; disbanded, 220
    46th (British): and fighting in Tunisia, 284, 315, 327, 389, 397; mentioned, 299, 396n, 446n; and 9th Corps, 359n; 384; at Fondouk, 379

INDEX

Divisions—*cont.*
  Infantry—*cont.*
    50th (British): and operation 'Lightfoot', 8; and Dog-fight, 48, 57; and operation 'Supercharge', 66; and advance to Tripoli, 220; 227n, 231; and Battle of Mareth, 320, 334–5, 337–42; and Battle of Wadi Akarit, 364–7, 372–3; and fighting in Tunisia, 403
    51st (Highland): and operation 'Lightfoot', 7, 18, 31, 38, 44–5; casualties in, 52, 375; and Dog-fight, 48, 52–4, 56–8; and operation 'Supercharge', 66, 70, 72, 74; mentioned 83; and pursuit to El Agheila, 107, 221; and advance to Tripoli, 223–4, 227n, 231–2, 234–6; at Medenine, 316; and Battle of Mareth, 320, 335, 338, 353; and fighting in Tunisia, 325, and Battle of Wadi Akarit, 364, 366–7, 370, 372–3, 375, 377
    56th (British): and operation 'Husky', 264; and fighting in Tunisia, 441–3, 453–4
    78th (British): and operation 'Torch', 140–1, 166, 168–9; in fighting in Tunisia, 175–6, 179, 183, 187, 284, 296, 315, 327n, 396–7, 399; and operation 'Husky', 264; and air support, 308, 400; and operation 'Vulcan,' 432, 436–8, 441; and operation 'Strike', 446n.
    4th Indian: and operation 'Lightfoot', 7, 31, 36n, 42; and Dog-fight, 57; and advance to Tripoli, 220, 227n; and Battle of Mareth, 320, 335, 338–9, 341, 345–6, 353; mentioned, 344, 458; and Battle of Wadi Akarit, 364–6, 369, 371–3; and fighting in Tunisia, 403–5, 441–2, 446, 449–50, 454; transferred to 1st Army, 443
    New Zealand: and operation 'Lightfoot', 7, 13, 18, 31, 37–8, 41, 43–7; strength and state of, 9, 52; casualties in, 52; and Dog-fight, 52, 54, 57–9; and operation 'Supercharge' 65–8; 72; mentioned, 75; and pursuit to El Agheila, 81–3, 84n, 85, 87–8, 90–1, 94, 96, 107, 221–4; supplies for, 105n; and advance to Tripoli, 226–7, 231–2, 234, 235n, 236; and fighting in Tunisia, 325, 378, 401, 403, 441–2, 453; and Battle of Mareth, 337, 339, 344–5, 347, 352–3; and Battle of Wadi Akarit, 357, 364–5, 367, 369, 373, 377; under 30th Corps, 357n
    1st South African; and operation 'Light foot', 8, 31, 38–9; casualties in, 52; and Dog-fight, 54, 57; to return to Union, 220
Dog-fight: 48–57
Dolfijn: 412

Dönitz, Grand Admiral Karl: replaces Raeder 254; visits Rome, 329, 408–9; and defence of Tunisia, 431
Doolittle, Brigadier-General (later Major-General) James H.: 113, 147, 271
Dorset Coast, m.v.: 426
Douglas, Air Chief Marshal Sir Sholto: *see also* Commanders-in-Chief; becomes A.O.C.-in-C. Middle East, 227; and Mediterranean Air Command, 265, 271n
Drago, Colonel Carlo: 273
Drake, Colonel Thomas D.: 290
Duke of York, H.M.S.: 139, 211
Dundas, Commodore J. G. L.: 255–6
Dunphie, Brigadier C. A. L.: 296–9

Easonsmith, Major J. R.: 23
Eastern Air Command: formed, 128; in operation 'Torch', 154, 166, 168, 307; strength and state of, 168, 174, 177, 189, 204–5; losses of, 154–5, 177, 179, 185–6, 189, 280; and advance into Tunisia, 169–70, 174, 177, 179–80, 182–3, 185–6, 188–90, 204, 248, 277, 280, 283–4, 293; mentioned, 242; and N.A.A.F., 248; attacks transport aircraft, 249; and convoy protection, 252; and air support, 307–9, 311; supply and maintenance in, 309–10
Edda: 243
Eddy, Major-General Manton S.: 376n, 433
Edwards-Collins, Vice-Admiral Sir F.: 132
'Eilbote': 277–8, 280, 283–4
Eisenhower, Lieut.-General Dwight D.: becomes C.-in-C., Allied Expeditionary Force, 112; and operation 'Torch', 112–114, 123–5, 129–30, 133, 161, 164, 166; directive to; 114, 165; and Allied air forces, 128; and control of French troops, 176; and advance into Tunisia, 182, 184, 186, 188, 275–6, 281–2, 289, 292; and Darlan, 191; and Tedder, 206; and Macmillan, 261; and assault on France, 262; and operation 'Husky', 264–5; and command in Tunisia, 270–1; and Anderson, 270–1; mentioned, 308, 322, 358; and fighting at Fondouk, 382; at victory parade, 461
El Agheila: capture of, 224
El Alamein: Battle of, 31–79
El Aouina: air attacks on, 169, 185, 203, 280, 284
El Daba: air attacks on, 32, 44, 63, 73
El Guettar: capture of, 336
El Hamma: air attacks on, 349, 354
Elmas: air attacks on, 248, 284
Elmhirst, Air Commodore T. W.: 16
Emma: 243
Empire Eve, s.s.: 426
Empire Patrol, m.v.: 196
Empire Rowan, m.v.: 421
Epervier: 148. 150
Erinpura, H.M.S.: 426
Erskine, Major-General G. W. E. J.: 446, 452
Estéva, Admiral: 162, 190
Etiopia: 91, 209
Ettrick, m.v.: 155–6

Eugenio: 211
Euryalus, H.M.S.: and 'Stoneage' convoy, 197-9; at Malta, 205; bombards Zuara, 244; mentioned, 426
Evelegh, Major-General V.: and operation 'Torch', 141; and fighting in Tunisia, 175-7, 180-2; and operation 'Vulcan', 432
Evill, Air Marshal D. C. S.: 110n

Fabriano: 413
Fantome, minesweeper: 425
Fauna: 415
Favor: 245
Fedala: capture of, 151
Fehn, General Gustav: 288n
Feriana: evacuation of, 294
Ferryville: air attacks on, 242, 278, 412; capture of, 453
Field Maintenance Centres: 104-5, 386
'Fighting France': 2n, 158, 266
Fighting French Flying Column: 316n, 320
Firth, Lieut.-Colonel C. E. A.: 365n
Fischer, Major-General Wolfgang: 172, 180-1, 184
Fisher, Brigadier A. F.: 40
Flag Officer Commanding, Gibraltar: 133
'Flax': 249, 358, 415-6
Fleet Air Arm: and operation 'Lightfoot', 13; and pursuit to El Agheila, 86, 100; in operation 'Torch', 137, 141, 144-5, 149-50, 154; losses of, 149, 154n; and advance into Tunisia, 180, 444; attacks enemy shipping, 201, 203, 206-7, 242, 414, 417-8
Squadrons:
    No. 800: 140
    801: 140
    802: 140
    804: 140
    807: 140
    809: 140
    815: 198
    817: 140
    820: 140
    821: 74n, 205, 336
    822: 140
    826: 74n, 413
    828: 204n
    830: 204n
    832: 140
    833: 140
    880: 140
    882: 140
    883: 140
    884: 140
    885: 140
    888: 140
    891: 140
    893: 140
Fliegerführer Afrika: 227, 272n
Fliegerführer Tunisia: 272
Fliegerführer 2: *see* Kosch
Fliegerführer 3: *see* Hagen
Folgore, destroyer: 205
Fondouk: action at, 379-83
Force A: 20-2
Force B: 20-2

Force C: 20-2
Force G: 127
Force H: and operation 'Torch', 127, 134, 137-140, 157; and Italian Fleet, 157; returns to Gibraltar, 211; human torpedo attack on, 212; and convoy protection, 254; strength and state of, 420; command of, 426
Force K: and operation 'Torch', 149; at Malta, 205; operations of, 206-7, 244, 247, 249, 414-5, 423
Force O: 138-9
Force Q: operations of, 205, 207, 240, 247, 249, 415; air attacks on, 245, mentioned, 413
Force X: 21, 23
Formidable, H.M.S.: 139-140, 144, 420
Fort à la Corne, s.s.: 421
Fort Sidi Ferruch: occupation of, 145
Foscolo: 209
Foster, Brigadier S. A.: 380n, 435n
Franco, General: 115
Fredendall, Major-General Lloyd R.: and operation 'Torch', 126, 147; and fighting in Tunisia, 281, 288n, 289, 294, 296, 298; and Battle of Mareth, 336; succeeded by Patton, 376n
Free French Air Force:
    Huitième Groupement: 328
Freeman-Attwood, Major-General H. A.: 432
French Armistice: 159
French Army: strength of, 116; British relations with, 176; fights well, 190
    Corps:
        19th: mentioned, 133, 273, 282; command of 170n; constituted, 279n; strength and state of, 281; and fighting in Tunisia, 284, 296, 315, 380, 383-4, 398-9, 401; and operation 'Vulcan', 429, 433, 438; and operation 'Strike', 446, 448, 453-4
    Corps Franc D'Afrique: 433, 448
        1st Bn.: 433
        2nd Bn.: 433
        3rd Bn.: 433
    Divisions:
        Constantine: 170n, 399
        d'Alger: mentioned, 170n; and operation 'Vulcan', 433, 438, 453
        du Maroc: 433, 438, 453-4
        d'Oran: 400, 433, 453
        Tunisian: 171, 174
    Armoured Group: 433, 453
    'L' Force: 316, 337, 367n
    Tabors marocains:
        4th: 433
        6th: 433
French Fleet: strength of, 116; and operation 'Torch', 127, 133, 137-8, 147, 151, 160; its resentment against British, 152, 159; scuttles at Toulon, 163-4; at Alexandria, 164n; and Darlan, 190-1; and Force H, 211
French North Africa: significance of, 109-10; 'cease fire' in, 151, 157, 162; agreement on responsibilities in, 163; and Darlan, 191; command in, 303; end of operations in, 457

Freyberg, Lieut.-General Sir Bernard: commands New Zealand Division 7; and operation 'Lightfoot', 35, 44, 46; and Dog-fight, 57; and operation 'Supercharge', 65, 68; and pursuit to El Agheila, 83-7, 96, 223-4; and advance to Tripoli, 225-6; and Battle of Mareth, 337, 343-5, 347, 352-4; and Battle of Wadi Akarit, 357, 372-3; and operation 'Vulcan', 442; commands 10th Corps, 446n; and surrender in Tunisia, 457, 459
Frith, Brigadier E. H. C.: 24
Fuka: air attacks on, 63
Fullriede, Lieut.-Colonel: 379, 381-2
Furious, H.M.S.: 139-40, 149, 196

Gabes: Axis occupy, 173; air attacks on, 179, 185, 242, 248, 277-8, 280, 283, 319, 349, 354
Gaeta, Brigadier-General G.: 272-3
Gafsa: Axis raid, 173; Allies leave, 292; Allies capture, 336
Gairdner, Major-General C. H.: 8, 81
Gale, Major-General H. M.: 114
Gamtoos, salvage vessel: 255-6
Gascoigne, Brigadier J. A.: 326n, 335
Gatehouse, Major-General A. H.: commands 10th Armoured Division, 8, 14; and operation 'Lightfoot', 45-6; and pursuit to El Agheila, 84
Gause, Lieutenant-General Alfred: mentioned, 329, 448; and reinforcements, 363; and fighting in Tunisia, 372, 441, 444; leaves Tunisia, 446
Gayford, Air Commodore O. R.: 227
Genere: 412
Genoa: air attacks on, 131
Gentry, Brigadier W.: 343
Gerd: 247
German Air Force: *see* Luftwaffe
German Army: *see also* D.A.K.: 3, 92
  Armies:
    Panzerarmee Afrika (*later* Deutsch-Italienische Panzerarmee *and* AOK 1): mentioned, 7, 24, 58n, 270, 389; strength and state of, 10, 25-6, 30, 51, 229, 362-3, 403; supplies and reinforcements for, 27, 30, 50, 68n, 172, 189, 242, 274, 359n; and Italian commanders, 29; and operation 'Lightfoot', 31, 50-1; renamed, 50n, 269; and operation 'Supercharge', 69-70, 72-4, 77; losses of, 78-9; in Battle of El Alamein, 79; in retreat to El Agheila, 82, 85, 93-8, 101, 215; and Tunisian harbours, 135; in retreat to Tripoli, 227, 229-30, 235, 238; command of, 269, 322; in fighting in Tunisia, 275, 276n, 287, 305, 326, 378-9, 394-5, 438, 451, 453-4; and Battle of Mareth, 330-1, 346, 348-9, 351; and Battle of Wadi Akarit, 359-63, 369, 371-2, 374-5; reinforces Pz AOK 5, 445; and Axis surrender, 458-9

German Army—*cont.*
  Armies—*cont.*
    Pz AOK 5: created, 184; in defence of Tunisia, 187, 229n; command of, 269-70; strength and state of, 274-5, 280-1, 297, 439n; tasks of, 278; and fighting in Tunisia, 287-9, 295, 305, 322, 326, 394, 437-8, 451, 453; supplies for, 295, 359n, 445
  Corps:
    90th: 171-2
  Groups:
    Army Group Africa: command of, 269; formed, 305; mentioned, 322, 359-60, 395, 457-8; and supplies to Tunisia, 323, 423, 431, 445; and fighting in Tunisia, 330, 371, 374, 378-9, 382, 394, 451-2; and Battle of Mareth, 349; air support for, 355
    Saharan: 363, 374, 378
  Divisions:
    22nd Air Landing: 26
    Hermann Göring: strength and state of, 275; in fighting in Tunisia, 276n, 306, 394n, 434-5, 451, 453; mentioned, 399, 446
    von Manteuffel (formerly von Broich): 306, 394n
    334th Infantry: mentioned, 187, 394n, 399, 445-6; in fighting in Tunisia, 278, 279n, 306, 328, 397, 433-4, 438, 451
    90th Light: and operation 'Lightfoot', 29, 42; and Dog-fight, 51, 55-6, 59, 62; strength and state of, 64, 86, 95n, 363; and operation 'Supercharge', 69, 72-3; and withdrawal to El Agheila, 82, 84-7, 89, 91-2, 97-8; and retreat to Tripoli, 230n, 235-6; and Battle of Mareth, 320, 333, 335, 353; and fighting in Tunisia, 323, 378, 394n, 395, 402; and Battle of Wadi Akarit, 359, 361-5; air attacks on, 377; mentioned, 438
    164th Light: mentioned, 49n; and Battle of El Alamein, 50, 55, 69, 72; strength and state of, 87n, 95n, 363; in retreat to Tripoli, 230n, 235n; and Battle of Mareth, 320, 333, 336, 343-6, 349, 353n; in fighting in Tunisia, 323, 324n, 378, 394n, 403; and Battle of Wadi Akarit, 359, 363, 373
    10th Panzer: and operation 'Torch', 172-3, 180, 184, 187, 188n; in fighting in Tunisia, 276n, 279, 287-8, 290-5, 297, 299-300, 305-6, 323-4, 378, 433; strength and state of, 290, 325, 436; mentioned, 302n, 394n, 434n; and Battle of Mareth, 330-1, 333n, 343-4; and operation 'Vulcan', 435-6
    15th Panzer: strength and state of, 9, 50-1, 64, 87n, 95n, 325, 333n, 363, 378, 403, 451; and operation 'Lightfoot', 28, 40, 44, 47, 49-50; air

542   INDEX

German Army—*cont.*
  Divisions—*cont.*
    attacks on, 47, 62; and Dog-fight, 50, 55, 57, 59; and operation 'Supercharge', 69, 71; in retreat to El Agheila, 87; in retreat to Tripoli, 225, 230n; reinforced, 230; and fighting in Tunisia, 287–8, 324–5, 378, 394n, 395, 403, 451; and Battle of Mareth, 320, 331, 333n, 335, 339–40, 342, 344–5, 348, 351–3; and Battle of Wadi Akarit, 359, 363, 371–2, 374; transferred to Pz AOK 5, 445, 451
  21st Panzer: strength and state of, 9, 59, 64, 87n, 90, 95n, 287, 290, 325, 333n; and operation 'Lightfoot', 28, 40; and Dog-fight, 48, 51, 55, 57, 59, 62; and operation 'Supercharge', 64, 71; in retreat to El Agheila, 84, 86–7, 89–91; in retreat to Tripoli, 230; in fighting in Tunisia, 276n, 282–3, 288–95, 297, 300, 305, 323–5, 378, 454; mentioned, 302n, 394n, 438n; and Battle of Mareth, 330–1, 333n, 343–6, 351–3; and Battle of Wadi Akarit, 359
  999th Africa: for Tunisia, 275; mentioned, 379n, 395, 399, 438n
  von Manteuffel: 394n, 434, 446
  Regiments and Units:
    190th Anti-Tank Unit: 363
    155th Artillery Regiment: 290n
    334th Artillery Regiment: 279n
    Barenthin Glider Regiment: 172, 276n, 327n
    52nd Flak Regiment: 279n
    1st Grenadier Regiment: 434n
    47th Grenadier Regiment: 187, 328, 333, 439n
    754th Grenadier Regiment: at Longstop Hill, 187n, 188n; and operation 'Vulcan', 434n, 436
    47th Infantry Regiment: 26n, 55
    961st Infantry Regiment: 379
    962nd Infantry Regiment: 399
    756th Mountain Regiment: 279n, 399
    Panzer Grenadier Africa: 230, 295–6, 335
    5th Panzer Regiment: 290n, 351, 439n
    7th Panzer Regiment: and operation 'Torch', 172, 180n, 187n; and fighting in Tunisia, 290n, 327n; and operation 'Vulcan', 434n, 435, 439n
    8th Panzer Regiment: 295, 297, 439
    Panzer Grenadier Regiment Africa: 297
    69th Panzer Grenadier Regiment: and operation 'Torch', 187n; and fighting in Tunisia, 279n, 290n; and operation 'Vulcan', 436
    86th Panzer Grenadier Regiment: 290n, 327n
    104th Panzer Grenadier Regiment: 64, 171, 290n

German Army—*cont.*
  Regiments and Units—*cont.*
    115th Panzer Grenadier Regiment: 54
    125th Panzer Grenadier Regiment: and Battle of El Alamein, 49, 59, 61–2, 69; in Battle of Mareth, 351
    133rd Panzer Grenadier Regiment: 54
    200th Panzer Grenadier Regiment: in fighting in Tunisia, 324, 339, 363, 369, 372
    361st Panzer Grenadier Regiment: and Battle of El Alamein, 62; in fighting in Tunisia, 324, 363, 371, 373; air attacks on, 377
    433rd Panzer Grenadier Regiment: 352
    5th Parachute Regiment: 171–2, 434n, 438
    3rd Reconnaissance Unit: in retreat to El Agheila, 84; in retreat to Tripoli, 230n; in fighting in Tunisia, 324n; in Battle of Mareth, 351
    33rd Reconnaissance Unit: and operation 'Supercharge', 69; in retreat to Tripoli, 230n; and fighting in Tunisia, 295–6; in Battle of Mareth, 351
    580th Reconnaissance Unit: 69, 230n
  Battalions:
    Brandenburg: 399
    10th Motor Cycle: 180n
    190th Panzer: 172, 176n
    501st Panzer: 172, 176n
    33rd Panzer jäger: 54, 71
    90th Panzer jäger: 180n
    605th Panzer jäger: 71
    1st Parachute: 174
    11th Parachute Engineer: 171, 173, 276n
    190th Signals: 176n
German Naval Staff: 25
German Navy: 274
German U-boat Command: 155
Giacomo C: 413–4
Giraud, General Henri: as Algerian liberator, 159; his command, 161, 270; and operation 'Torch', 170; and control of French troops, 176, 270; succeeds Darlan, 190, 266; mentioned, 201, 270, 271n; and Corps Franc d'Afrique, 433n; at victory parade, 461
Giulia: 222
Giulio Giordani: 100, 203
Glennie, Lieut.-Colonel J. B. A.: 458
Godfroy, Admiral R. E.: 164, 256
Goebbels, Dr.: 432
Gore, Lieut.-Colonel A. C.: 297n
Gorgo: 425
Göring, Marshal of the Reich, Hermann: and Rommel, 219; and transport flights, 416; and defence of Tunisia, 431; and Schmid, 446
Gorizia: 414
Gort, Field-Marshal the Viscount, Governor and Commander-in-Chief, Malta: on supplies for Malta, 193, 199; on offensive operations from Malta, 200; on sick leave, 257n

Gott, Lieut.-General W. H. E.: 113
Graham, Lieutenant-Colonel Miles: 317n
Gratwick, Private P. E.: 49
Groppo: 425
'Gymnast': 110

Hagen, Colonel Walter: 272-3, 393n
Hallanger: 421
Hanson, Lieutenant-Colonel F. M. H.: 367n
Harcourt, Rear-Admiral C. H. J.: 138, 153, 426
Harding, Major-General A. F.: 8, 235n
Harding, Brigadier G. P.: 327n, 435n
Harlinghausen, Colonel: 171
Harmon, Major-General Ernest N.: commands 1st U.S. Armoured Division, 367n, 377, 432; and Axis surrender, 453
Hartland, H.M.S.: 148-9, 155
Harvey, Brigadier C. B.: 223, 343
Harwood, Admiral Sir Henry: *see also* Commanders-in-Chief; his command, 113, 256-7; mentioned, 213, 255; as C.-in-C. Levant, 266; and Prime Minister, 256-7
Haselden, Lieut.-Colonel J. E.: 21n, 22
Hawkesworth, Major-General J. L. R.: 388, 432, 446
Hecla, H.M.S.: 155
Heraklion: air attacks on, 222
Hermes: 414, 423
Hewitt, Vice-Admiral H. Kent: and operation 'Torch', 127, 134, 139; his command, 420
Hildebrandt, Major-General Hans-Georg: 351
Hillary, H.M.S.: 427
Hinde, Brigadier W. R. N.: 450n
Hitler, Adolf: and Russian campaign, 24, 219; and Mediterranean theatre, 24, 219, 239, 268, 323; mentioned, 26; and Rommel, 50, 55, 72-3, 81, 85, 93, 187n, 219, 229, 250, 268; and operation 'Supercharge', 72-3, 81; and withdrawal to El Agheila, 85, 93-5; and defence of Tunisia, 134-6, 170, 183-4, 219, 229, 274, 323, 329-30, 393-5, 431-2, 452; on reinforcements, 245, 247, 250, 407-8; and Raeder, 254; and Axis command, 268-9; and Akarit position, 260; and Mussolini, 409
Hogshaw, Brigadier J. H.: 388n
Holden, Lieut.-Colonel R. B.: 432
Home Fleet: 127
Homs: capture of, 235
Honestas: 207
Hopkins, Harry L.: 112
Hornet, U.S.S.: 113n
Horrocks, Lieut.-General B. G.: commands 13th Corps, 8; and action at Deir el Munassib, 24; and operation 'Lightfoot' 43, 52; and pursuit to El Agheila, 92; and advance to Tripoli, 220; and Battle of Mareth, 344-5, 347, 352-4; and Battle of Wadi Akarit, 357, 371-3; and advance in Tunisia, 401, 442-3, 432, 446-7, 450; commands 9th Corps, 432, 446
Houldsworth, Brigadier: 74
Howe, H.M.S. 426
Howlett, Brigadier, B.: 327, 396n

Hubback, Captain A. G. V.: 420
Hughes, Major-General I. T. P.: 8
Hull, Brigadier R. A.: 388n
Human torpedo attacks:
  (British): 244, 254-5
  (Italian): 211-12, 426
'Husky': plan for, 263-5, 316, 398, 427

Iachino, Admiral Angelo: 426
Ibis, H.M.S.: 157
Imperiali di Francavilla, Brigadier-General: 172, 179, 187
Ile de France, s.s.: 259
Inönü, Mr.: 267
Inshore Squadron: 103, 233, 422
Isaac Sweers: 155-6
Irwin, Brigadier-General Le Roy: 300
Italian Air Force: strength and state of, 3, 116, 157, 195, 213, 222n, 252, 324, 334, 368, 400, 431; losses of, 19-20, 23, 78, 154, 179, 189, 195, 208n, 222, 228, 234, 238, 277, 355, 358n, 392n, 416, 444, 460; in Battle of El Alamein, 78; short of fuel, 135; and operation 'Torch', 135, 154, 157; in Tunisia, 152, 179, 186, 277, 394; leaves Tunisia, 455
Squadra:
  5th: 32, 273, 393n
Italian Army: strength and state of, 3; supplies and reinforcements for, 50n; losses of, 78-9
Corps:
  10th: 69, 72-3, 85
  20th: and operation 'Lightfoot', 50; operation 'Supercharge', 69, 72-3, 81; in retreat to El Agheila, 85, 81, 97; mentioned, 94; in retreat to Tripoli, 230; and Battle of Wadi Akarit, 362, 364, 372
  21st: and Battle of El Alamein, 69, 72-3; in retreat to El Agheila, 84-5, 91; in retreat to Tripoli, 219, 230; and Battle of Wadi Akarit, 363-4
  30th: 394
Divisions:
  Ariete: strength and state of, 10, 64; and operation 'Lightfoot', 28, 40; and Dog-fight, 48, 52, 55n; and operation 'Supercharge', 69, 71, 73; in retreat to El Agheila, 84-5, 224
  Centauro: and retreat to El Agheila, 93; and retreat to Tripoli, 230n; in fighting in Tunisia, 291, 402
  Folgore Parachute: 24, 92
  Littorio: strength and state of, 10, 50-1, 57, 64, 78; and operation 'Lightfoot', 28, 40, 44, 49-50; and Dog-fight, 57, 59; air attacks on, 62; and operation 'Supercharge,' 71
  Pavia: 23
  Pistoia; and retreat to Tripoli, 219, 230; and Battle of Mareth, 320, 333, 353n; and Battle of Wadi Akarit, 363, 369, 371, 374-5; strength and state of, 363; in

Italian Army—*cont.*
  Divisions—*cont.*
    fighting in Tunisia, 378, 394n, 395, 402-3
    La Spezia: and retreat to El Agheila, 93; and retreat to Tripoli, 219, 230n; and Battle of Mareth, 320, 333, 353n; strength and state of, 325n, 363, 375; and Battle of Wadi Akarit, 363, 369, 371-2, 374-5; mentioned, 394n; in fighting in Tunisia, 403
    Trento: 50, 78, 85
    Superga: and operation 'Torch', 172, 187; in fighting in Tunisia, 278-9, 394; mentioned, 438n
    Trieste: strength and state of, 10, 64, 78, 325n, 363; and operation 'Lightfoot', 29, 51; and Dog-fight, 59; and operation 'Supercharge', 64, 70; and retreat to Tripoli, 219, 230n; and Battle of Mareth, 320, 333, 353n; and Battle of Wadi Akarit, 363, 371-2, 374; in fighting in Tunisia, 394n, 395, 402
    Young Fascist: and retreat to El Agheila, 93; and retreat to Tripoli, 230n; and Battle of Mareth, 320, 333, 335, 339, 353n; and Battle of Wadi Akarit, 362, 374; strength and state of, 363; in fighting in Tunisia, 394n, 395, 402
  Regiments and Other Units:
    5th Bersaglieri: 297, 395
    10th Bersaglieri: 172, 327n
    36th Regiment: 369
    125th Regiment: 369
    66th Infantry Regiment: 403
    Nizza Reconnaissance Battalion: 230n
Italian Fleet: strength and state of, 116, 197, 213, 409, 482; and operation 'Torch', 127, 135, 137, 157, 202; short of fuel, 135, 211, 249; and landings on Corsica, 162; and 'Stoneage' convoy, 197; air attacks on, 211; losses of, 211; mentioned, 421
  Cruiser Divisions:
    3rd: 211
    8th: 211
Italian High Command: and Rommel, 24n, 50, 89, 93, 219n, 229, 274, 288, 295, 305, 323; and Panzerarmee Afrika, 50n; and reinforcements, 89, 407; and retreat to El Agheila, 93-4; and defence of Tunisia, 134-5, 172, 184, 274-5, 287-8, 293, 295, 301, 322-3, 394, 452, 458; and retreat to Tripoli, 229-30, 235; and Kesselring, 268, 270; and von Arnim, 269-70, 287, 293, 359, 361; and Battle of Mareth, 330-1, 362; and Battle of Wadi Akarit, 360-2, 375; and Dönitz, 409
Ivor-Moore, Brigadier T.: 388n

Jalo: action at, 21, 23; air attacks on, 100
Jamaica, H.M.S.: 139, 147, 150
James, Brigadier J. G.: 388n

James, Brigadier M. A.: 327, 380n, 435n
Javelin, H.M.S.: 206, 244
Jean Bart: 116, 151
Jervis, H.M.S.: 206
Jodl, Lieut.-General Alfred: 359, 361-2, 431-2
Joy, Brigadier R. C. G.: 435n
Juan di Estigarraja: 249
Juin, General A.: mentioned, 134; represents Darlan, 145; and operation 'Torch', 160-1; his command, 170n; and fighting in Tunisia, 279

Kairouan: air attacks on, 277, 292
Karanja, L. S. I.: 153-4
Katena: air attacks on, 336
Keightley, Major-General C. F.: at Fondouk, 380, 382; and operation 'Vulcan', 432; and operation 'Strike', 446
Keitel, Field-Marshal: 135, 250, 452
Kelvin, H.M.S.: 206, 244
Kenchington, Brigadier A. G.: 40
Kenneally, Lance-Corporal J.: 439
Kent-Lemon, Brigadier A. L.: 141, 153
Kesselring, Field-Marshal Albert: and Mediterranean defences, 24-5; his command, 24n, 268; and Rommel, 55, 201, 219, 268, 301n, 323; and Schürmeyer, 170; and fighting in Tunisia, 171, 180, 187, 274-5, 276n, 278, 283, 287-8, 295, 300-1, 305, 322-3, 326, 329-30, 393, 399, 431-2, 452; and von Arnim, 184, 187, 246, 305, 322, 326, 359, 361, 394-5; mentioned, 247, 405, 445; and Axis command, 268-70; and Army Group Africa, 305; and Battle of Mareth, 348; and Battle of Wadi Akarit, 360-1; and operation 'Flax', 416; and operation 'Strike', 448
Keyes, Admiral of the Fleet Sir Roger: 121n
Kibby, Sergeant W. H.: 61
King, Admiral Ernest J.: 110n, 112
King George V, H.M.S.: 426
King George VI: 461
Kippenberger, Brigadier H. K.: 94, 326n, 401
Kirkman, Brigadier S. C.: 5
Kisch, Brigadier F. H.: 5, 375
Koeltz, General L. M.: and operation 'Torch', 170, 190; and fighting in Tunisia, 279n, 280, 296; and operation 'Vulcan', 433
Koenig, Brigadier-General M-P.: 42
Kosch, Colonel Benno: 272, 393n
Krause, Major-General Fritz: 446
KT 5: 423
KT 7: 415
KT 9: 423
KT 21: 423
Kuter, Brigadier-General L. S.: 271

Labataille, Major: 433
La Fauconnerie: air attacks on, 369, 373
Laforey, H.M.S.: 245, 415, 423
La Goulette: air attacks on, 278
Lalbahadur Thapa, Subedar: 370
La Maddalena: air attacks on, 392n, 414

INDEX

La Marsa: air attacks on, 392
Lammerton, H.M.S.: 154
Lampedusa: air attacks on, 208, 248
Lampo: 414
Landing Craft: in Combined Operations, 119–123; particulars of, 478–9; losses in, 151
Lang, Colonel Rudolf: 187n, 188n, 328
Langford-Sainsbury, Air Vice-Marshal T. A.: 411n
Largs, H.M.S.: 139, 147, 427
La Senia: air attacks on, 149; capture of, 149–50
La Surprise: 148
Laval, Pierre: 163
Lawson, Air Commodore G. M.: and operation 'Torch', 141, 174, 183; and air support, 174, 183, 308–9; and No. 242 Group, 183, 271–2
Leahy, Admiral William D.: 110n, 261
Leatham, Vice-Admiral Sir Ralph: 257
Leclerc, General: 316, 337
Le Coulteux, General: 433, 453–4
Lederer, Colonel: 171–2
Lee, Brigadier A. W.: 40, 56
Leedstown, U.S.S.: 146
Leese, Lieut.-General Sir Oliver: commands 30th Corps, 7; and operation 'Lightfoot', 35, 44; and operation 'Supercharge', 68; and pursuit to El Agheila, 107, 220, 223; and Battle of Mareth, 340–1; and Battle of Wadi Akarit, 364, 371, 373
Leghorn: air attacks on, 425
Le Patourel, Major H. W.: 181
Le Tre Marie: 249
Levant Command: 421
Libya: end of campaign in, 289
Liebenstein, Major-General Freiherr Kurt von: commands D.A.K., 288n; and fighting in Tunisia, 345, 348, 351–2, 353n; and Battle of Wadi Akarit, 363; surrenders, 459
'Lightfoot': timing of, 2, 60; plan for, 4–8, 17–19, 31, 34–5; supplies for, 8–10, 15–17, 30; air support for, 10–12, 14–15, 19–20, 32–4, 42, 44, 47–9; training for, 12, 14; operations related to, 20–4; the operation, 36–49; naval support for, 41–2; reviewed, 51–2, 64, 76–7; losses in, 51–2, 65n; mentioned, 62, 82n, 106; and operation 'Supercharge', 64
Lightning, H.M.S.: 245, 413
Lindsay, Lieut.-Colonel M. J.: 433
Lindsell, Lieut.-General Sir Wilfrid: 101, 238
Linton, Commander J. W.: 412
Littorio: 157n, 414
Lloyd, Air Vice-Marshal Sir Hugh P.: 271
Longmore, Air Chief Marshal Sir Arthur: 431
Long Range Desert Group: operations by, 20–3, 223, 316; mentioned, 333n
Longstop Hill: action at, 187–8
Lookout, H.M.S.: 245, 415
Lorenzelli, General Dante: 172
Louisburg, H.M.C.S.: 253
Lovett, Brigadier O. D. T.: 365n
Loyal, H.M.S.: 245, 415, 423
Luck, Major von: 337

Luftwaffe: strength and state of, 3, 32, 88, 208, 368, 400, 408, 431; reinforcement of, 26, 88–9, 171; attacks Malta, 32, 427; mentioned, 92n, 170; and operation 'Torch', 146, 154; losses of, 146, 154, 208, 228, 234, 237–8, 249, 355, 358n, 392n, 401, 415–6, 427, 460; and withdrawal to Tripoli, 234, 237; and shipping protection, 247, 253; and reinforcement of Tunisia, 274, 415–6; command of, 393n; attacks Tripoli, 422; attacks shipping, 426

(in Greece, Crete and Aegean): attacks shipping, 22; strength and state of, 32, 258; and 'Stoneage' convoy, 197

(in North Africa): strength and state of, 3, 32, 88, 222n; losses of, 19–20, 33, 51, 68, 74, 78, 88, 91, 99, 222; attacks shipping, 22; and operation 'Lightfoot', 32; and Dog-fight, 55; and operation 'Supercharge', 68, 73–4; in Battle of El Alamein, 78; reinforcements for, 88–9

(in Sicily and Sardinia): strength and state of, 116, 157, 195, 213, 252, 258; and operation 'Torch', 157, 160; attacks Malta, 194–6; losses of, 195, 203, 253, 392n; and 'Stoneage' convoy, 197

(in Tunisia): strength and state of, 153, 171, 213, 272, 324, 334; arrival of, 162, 170; and fighting in Tunisia, 171, 174, 179, 182–3, 186, 189, 277, 281, 283, 291–3, 298n, 318, 378, 392n, 393–4; losses of, 179, 186, 189, 277–8, 280, 283–4, 292, 294, 302, 319, 323, 326, 369, 374, 441, 444, 456; and Battle of Mareth, 336, 349; and operation 'Vulcan', 440; withdrawal of, 455

Luftflotte 2: 272
Fliegerkorps II: 24n, 171
Fliegerkorps X: 24n
Fliegerkorps Tunis: 272, 330, 342
19th Flak Division: mentioned, 30n; strength and state of, 71n, 95n, 363; in withdrawal to Tripoli, 230
Ramcke Parachute Brigade: at Deir el Munassib, 24; and Rommel, 28; mentioned, 30n; and operation 'Supercharge', 69, 72; in retreat to El Agheila, 85, 92; strength and state of, 95n; in retreat to Tripoli, 230n, 235n
Flak Regiment 102: 10
Flak Regiment 135: 10
Lüder, Major: 279
Luisiano: 59, 63
Lumsden, Lieut.-General H.: commands 10th Corps, 8; and operation 'Lightfoot', 34–5, 44–6; and Dog-fight, 54; and operation 'Supercharge', 70; mentioned, 77n; and pursuit to El Agheila, 81, 84, 87, 96–8, 107; and advance to Tripoli, 220
Lupo: 206
Luqa: air attacks on, 195–6
Lyell, Captain The Lord: 439
Lynne, Brigadier L. O.: 442n, 443
Lyster, Rear-Admiral A. L. St. G.: 138, 211

Macfie, Captain A. N.: 21n
Macmillan, Rt. Hon. Harold: 261
Magnan, Colonel: 433
Maison Blanche: air attacks on, 174
Maknassy: capture of, 376
Malcolm, H.M.S.: 143
Malcolm, Wing Commander H. G.: 185
Maleme: air attacks on, 63, 71
Malocello: 413
Malta: *for* Governor and C.-in-C. *see* Gort, *for* Vice-Admiral *see* Leatham, Bonham-Carter *and* Power, *for* A.O.C. *see* Park; reinforcements and supplies for, 2, 193–4, 196–9, 204–5, 257–8, 421; air attacks on, 32, 194–6, 204, 427; importance of, 193; as striking base, 194, 200, 203–4, 254–5, 420, 427–8; air forces at, 195, 198; defence and defences of, 195, 198; 204, 427; and Roosevelt, 212–13; under Cunningham, 266, 427–8; command in, 303, 306; and operation 'Husky', 427
Mancinelli, Brigadier-General Giuseppe: 329, 459.
Mannerini, General Alberto: 345
Manteuffel, Colonel (later Major-General) Hasso von: and fighting in Tunisia, 306, 326, 448; leaves Tunisia, 446
Manxman, H.M.S.: 194, 196, 208
Marchese, General Vittorio: 273
Mareth: defence of, 274; Battle of, 276, 329–54; air attacks on, 318, 336; description of, 332
Markert, Colonel Anton: 446, 459
Marnix, L.S.I.: 153
Maron, m.v.: 157
Mars: 91
Marsala: air attacks on, 228
Marshall, General George C.: 110n, 112, 262–4
Martin, H.M.S.: 156
Mason-MacFarlane, Lieut.-General F. N.: 133
Massachusetts, U.S.S.: 139, 151
Mast, Major-General Charles: and operation 'Torch', 133, 145, 159–60: mentioned, 201
Mathenet, General: 276, 279, 453–4
Mattioli, Brigadier-General Enrico: 360, 375
Maund, Captain L. E. H.: 121n
Maxwell, Brigadier R. H.: 432
Maxwell, Major-General Russell L.: 83n
McCreery, Major-General R.: 289n, 304
McGrigor, Rear-Admiral R. R.: 427
McQuillin, Brigadier-General Raymond E.: 290
Medenine: air attacks on, 237, 280, 284, 318; action at, 324–6
Medici: 414
Mediterranean Air Command: organization of, 265, 271, 303, 306, 355; mentioned, 310, 383; losses of, 355; strength and state of, 400; and operation 'Vulcan', 431
Mediterranean Fleet: and operation 'Lightfoot', 6, 41–2; and enemy convoys, 25, 79, 205, 246, 412–7, 423; and operation 'Supercharge', 66; and Battle of El Alamein, 79; and operation 'Torch', 126–30, 154–5; in attack on French Fleet,

Mediterranean Fleet—*cont.*
147; casualties of, 155; and 'Stoneage' convoy, 197, 205; and Italian Fleet, 213; carries supplies for 8th Army, 232, 238, 254; and reopening of Tripoli harbour, 255–7; tribute to, 462; strength of, 480–1
Medjez el Bab: Germans occupy, 174
Merchant Navy: 127, 254
Messe, General Giovanni: and Hitler, 268; his command, 269; and fighting in Tunisia, 288, 305–6, 322–6, 378–9, 394–5, 402, 432, 452, 454; mentioned, 329, 377, 382, 443, 446; and Battle of Mareth, 331, 335, 339, 345, 348–9, 354; and Battle of Wadi Akarit, 361–2, 369–70, 372–3, 375; and reinforcement of Pz AOK 5, 445; surrenders 458–9
Messina: air attacks on, 248, 412, 425
Mezan, Captain Paul: 332
Mezzouna: air attacks on, 342, 369
Micklethwait, Captain St. J. A.: 21n, 22
Middle East: reinforcement of, 1; command in, 1, 303; review of situation in, 1–2, 212–3, 239–40, 267, 419, 461
Middle East Base: 101–6
Middle East Command and Malta, 204
Middle East Defence Committee 256, 303
Middleton, Flight-Sergeant R. H. 131
Milan: air attacks on, 131
Miles, Major-General E. G. 441
Miller, Major-General C. H. 304, 386n
Minesweeping Flotillas:
12th: 424
13th: 424
14th: 424
Misoa, s.s.: 149
Mocenigo: 425
Monginevro: 413–4
Monscne: 412
Montecuccoli: 211
Montgomery, General Sir Bernard: and Alexander, 1–3, 443, 446; and operation 'Lightfoot', 2, 5–7, 17–18, 31, 35, 40, 42–7, 60, 76; forms 10th Corps, 7; and 8th Army, 13, 35n; and raids on Benghazi and Tobruk, 20; and Dog-fight, 49, 51–3, 57–8; and operation 'Supercharge', 59, 64–6, 68–70, 72, 74, 77; on air support, 63; and Coningham, 78; and Battle of El Alamein, 76–9; and pursuit to El Agheila, 81–3, 87, 95–8, 101, 220–1, 224; and New Zealand Division, 82n; and operation 'Torch', 113; and advance to Tripoli, 215, 226, 231–6; thanks Navy, 254; on reopening of Tripoli harbour, 256–7; and fighting in Tunisia, 316, 324, 325n, 397, 402; and supplies, maintenance, 317, 320n, 387n; and Battle of Mareth, 320–2, 331, 333, 337, 339–41, 343–7, 352n, 353–4; and Battle of Wadi Akarit, 357–8, 363–5, 371, 373, 375n; and operation 'Vulcan', 430, 442–3, popularity of, 461
Monti: 411
Moore, Brigadier E. E. J.: 388n
Moore, Lieut.-Colonel Anderson T. W.: 296, 298
Mormacmoon, s.s.: 198

INDEX

Morshead, Lieut.-General Sir Leslie: commands 9th Australian Division, 7, 219n; and operation 'Lightfoot', 35; and Dogfight, 49, 60
Mountbatten, Commodore Lord Louis: 120–21
Murphy, Robert D.: reports from, 115; and French co-operation, 133–4, 159–61; and French Fleet, 163; at Casablanca, 261
Murray, Brigadier J. E. S.: 66n
Murray, Brigadier G.: 366n
Mussolini, Benito: and lack of ships, 24; mentioned 26; and Panzerarmee, 29, 72, 229; and operation 'Supercharge', 72–3; and retreat to El Agheila, 93–4, 219; and defence of Tunisia, 135, 184, 219, 274, 329, 393–5, 408, 431–2, 452; and retreat to Tripoli, 229; and African theatre, 268, and Axis command, 268–9; and Ambrosio, 360; state of, 409; and Axis surrender, 458

Naples: air attacks on, 211, 222, 228, 392n, 412–3
Narkunda, s.s.: 157
Nation, Lieutenant B. H. C.: 145
Naval Task Forces: *see also* Assault Convoys; 134n, 137–9
  Algiers (Eastern): command of, 134; and operation 'Torch', 137–40, 142, 156; air support for, 307
  Moroccan (Western): 134, 138–9, 150–1
  Oran (Central): 134, 137–40, 147
Nehring, General Walther: 172–4, 179–80, 184
Nelson, H.M.S.: 211, 420, 426
Newfoundland, H.M.S.: 415, 426
New York, U.S.S.: 139
New Zealand Artillery:
  5th, Field Regiment: 326n
New Zealand Engineers:
  6th Field Company: 231n
  8th Field Company: 367n
New Zealand Expeditionary Force, 2nd: 343
Ngarimu, Second-Lieutenant: 352
Nichols, Major-General J. S.: commands 50th Division, 8; and Battle of Mareth, 334, 339–41; and Battle of Wadi Akarit, 372
Nicholson, Brigadier C. G. G.: 298–9, 300
Nields, U.S.S.: 426
Nieuw Zeeland: 156, 259
Noguès, M.: 161–2
Nolte, Oberst H. W.: 458
Northwest African Air Forces: formed 248, 271, 272n, 310; organization of, 306–7; operations and losses of, 393, 401, 412–4, 439–41, 451n, 457; strength of, 400n
  Northwest African Service Command: 272n, 307
  Northwest African Coastal Air Force: functions of, 252, 271, 355, 411; command of, 271; organization of, 272n, 307, 311; operations of, 301, 430, 451n
  Northwest African Photographic Reconnaissance Wing: command of, 271; organization of, 272n

Northwest African Strategic Air Force: operations of, 248, 301–2, 311, 318–9, 321, 329, 355, 391n, 392, 411; organization of, 271, 272n, 307, 411; command of, 271, 447; and Battle of Mareth, 334, 336, 342; strength and state of, 391; mentioned, 440n; and operation 'Vulcan', 430–1, 439, 448–9, 456–7; and operation 'Strike', 448–9, 456–7
Northwest African Tactical Air Force: formed, 271, 272n; operations and losses of, 298, 300–1, 318, 321, 336, 348; and Desert Air Force, 306; organization of, 307, 310; and air support, 311, 313, 318, 321, 355, 429, 431, 456; strength and state of, 368; control of, 447
Northwest African Tactical Bomber Force: formed 272n, 311n; operations and losses of, 294, 336, 342, 377; mentioned, 312; strength and state of, 368; and operation 'Vulcan', 430, 439–40; and operation 'Strike', 448–50, 451n, 455
Northwest African Training Command: 272n
Northwest African Troop Carrier Command: 272n
Noto: 242
Nubian, H.M.S.: operations, 206, 244, 415, 423

Ocean Voyager, s.s.: 422
Oliver, Commodore G. N.: 175
Oliver, Brigadier-General Lunsford E.: 184
Olterra: 212, 426
OKH: Rommel reports to, 26, 55, 94n; and reinforcements for Panzerarmee, 27, 55; mentioned, 31; and Tunisia, 186; and Kesselring, 268, 270; and von Arnim, 270; and air effort, 355; and Cramer, 457
OKW: and Rommel, 26, 55, 79, 89, 94, 229, 250, 322; and Panzerarmee Afrika, 50n; and operation 'Torch', 135; mentioned, 170, 330, 458–9; and Kesselring, 268, 275, 323; and Axis command, 269
Olga: 244
Ombrina: 411
Oran: landings at, 146–50; occupation of, 150, 162
Orion, H.M.S.: 197–8, 426–7
Ostia: 63, 202

P.35, H.M.S.: 201
P.44, H.M.S.: 246
P.46, H.M.S.: 202
P.48, H.M.S.: 212
P.212, H.M.S.: 243
P.219, H.M.S.: 133, 201
P.222, H.M.S.: 212
P.311, H.M.S.: 244
Pakenham, H.M.S.: 244, 414–5
Paladin, H.M.S.: 244, 414–5, 423
Palermo: mining of, 208; air attacks on, 248, 358n, 392n, 412–3
Pancaldo: 414, 418, 423
Panther: H.M.S.: 137

Pantelleria: air attacks on, 248. 455; bombardment of, 427
Panuco: 27
Paolo: 248
Parham, Brigadier: 299
Park, Air Vice-Marshal Sir Keith, Air Officer Commanding, Malta: 205, 265, 271n
Parthian, H.M.S.: 196
Patton, Major-General George S.: 126, 376–7, 432n
Paulus, Field-Marshal: 453
'Pedestal': 116, 193, 211n
Penelope, H.M.S.: 245,426
Percy, Brigadier J. E. C.: 66n
Perseo: 423
Persia and Iraq Command: 1, 267, 442
Pétain, Marshal: 158–64
Petard, H.M.S.: 423
Peters, Captain F. T.: 148–9
Philadelphia, U.S.S.: 139
Pienaar, Major-General D. H.: 8, 35
Pistoia: 242
Platino: 253
Pont du Fahs: air attacks on, 280; capture of, 453
Portal, Air Chief Marshal Sir Charles, Chief of the Air Staff: as Chief of Staff, 110n; and operation 'Torch', 124, 132; at Casablanca 262
'Portcullis': 199
Portofino: 91
Porto Torres: air attacks on, 413
Pound, Admiral of the Fleet Sir Dudley, First Sea Lord and Chief of Naval Staff: as Chief of Staff, 110n; and operation 'Torch', 124; and reopening of Tripoli harbour, 256; and Harwood, 256–7
Power, Rear-Admiral A. J.: 198–9, 205, 426
Pownall, General Sir Henry: 267
Pozarica, m.v.: 253
Pozzuoli: 247
Primauguet: 151
Prime Minister and Minister of Defence (Rt. Hon. Winston S. Churchill): and Persia and Iraq Command, 1, 267; and operation 'Torch', 2, 110–12, 114, 125; and 10th Corps, 7; and operation 'Lightfoot', 37, 60; on enemy minefields, 76; Alexander reports to, 78; on Battle of El Alamein, 79; mentioned, 131, 162n, 237; and Godfroy, 164; on air support, 182; visits Tripoli, 255–6; and Harwood, 256–7; at Casablanca, 261, 263–4, 266; and operation 'Husky', 263–4; and de Gaulle, 266; visits Middle East and Turkey, 266–7; Alexander reports to, 304, 459; and Montgomery, 375n; on end of Tunisian campaign, 461
Princess Beatrix, L.S.I.: 175n, 252, 420
Prinz Willem III, m.v.: 421
Prisoners: in operation 'Lightfoot', 51; in operation 'Supercharge', 75; in Battle of El Alamein, 79; in retreat to El Agheila, 92–3, 226; in Tunisia, 280n, 294n, 302n, 460; in Battle of Wadi Akarit, 375
Proserpina: 50n, 201

Qotafiya: air attacks on, 44
Queen Elizabeth, H.M.S.: 259
Queen Emma, L.S.I.: 175n, 420
Queen of Bermuda, s.s.: 259
Quentin, H.M.S.: 205–6
Quiberon, H.M.S.: 205

Raeder, Grand Admiral Erich: 254
Ramcke, Major-General: 92
Ramsay, Admiral Sir Bertram: 113, 427
Ranger, U.S.S.: 139
Regent, H.M.S.: 414
Regiments:
    4th, County of London Yeomanry: 366, 371, 450n
    1st Derby Yeomanry: 379, 380n, 397, 435n, 452
    Household Cavalry: 92
    3rd Hussars: 66–7, 83n
    10th Hussars: 351n, 435n
    11th Hussars: in pursuit to El Agheila, 95, 97–8; in pursuit to Tripoli, 236; enter Tunis, 452
    1st King's Dragoon Guards: in advance to Tripoli, 223; in Battle of Mareth, 337n; and operation 'Vulcan', 433; in Army reserve, 446n
    16th/5th Lancers: mentioned, 284n, 296; in fighting in Tunisia, 380n, 382; in operation 'Vulcan', 435n, 450n
    9th Lancers: 39n, 351n, 435n
    12th Lancers: and Battle of Ll Alamein, 41; in pursuit to El Agheila, 89, 97; in fighting in Tunisia, 351n, 378, 397; in operation 'Vulcan', 435n
    17th/21st Lancers: and operation 'Torch', 180: in fighting in Tunisia, 299; at Fondouk, 380–2; in operation 'Vulcan', 435n, 450n, 454
    2nd Lothian and Border Horse: in fighting in Tunisia, 297n, 299; at Fondouk, 380n; and operation 'Vulcan', 435n, 450n, 454
    New Zealand Divisional Cavalry: 367
    North Irish Horse: 438
    Nottinghamshire Yeomanry: and Battle of El Alamein, 41, 71; and Battle of Mareth, 337n, 350
    The Queen's Bays: and Battle of El Alamein, 39n, 41; strength and state of, 351n; in operation 'Vulcan', 435n
    1st Reconnaissance Regiment: 388n
    4th Reconnaissance Regiment: 388n
    44th Reconnaissance Regiment: 42–3, 92, 442n
    46th Reconnaissance Regiment: 435n
    56th Reconnaissance Regiment: 142n, 145
    1st The Royal Dragoons: and Battle of El Alamein, 41, 66, 71, 75; in pursuit to El Agheila, 97–8; in advance to Tripoli, 223n, 232n, 234
    The Royal Scots Greys: 42–3, 223–5, 232n
    The Royal Wiltshire Yeomanry: 45n, 67, 83n
    Staffordshire Yeomanry: and Battle of El Alamein, 41; in pursuit to Tripoli, 224;

INDEX 549

Regiments—*cont.*
  Staffordshire Yeomanry—*cont.*
    in Battle of Mareth, 337n, 350; in Battle of Wadi Akarit, 373
  Warwickshire Yeomanry: 67, 83n
  Royal Tank Regiment:
    1st Battalion: 450n, 452
    3rd Battalion: 337n, 350–1, 373
    5th Battalion: 43, 341, 450n
    8th Battalion: 66, 74–5
    12th Battalion: 388n, 438
    40th Battalion: and Battle of El Alamein, 48, 58, 61–2; in pursuit to Tripoli, 236n; and Battle of Wadi Akarit, 366, 372
    42nd Battalion: 14
    43rd Battalion: 388n
    44th Battalion: 14
    46th Battalion: 58
    50th Battalion: and Battle of El Alamein, 44, 66, 70; in pursuit to Tripoli, 236; and Battle of Mareth, 335n, 338–40; strength and state of, 339n; and Battle of Wadi Akarit, 366, 370
    51st Battalion: in action at Fondouk, 379, 380n, 381; and operation 'Vulcan', 432, 434; in Army reserve, 446n
  South African Armoured Car Regiment, 4/6th: 71, 75, 77
  142nd Royal Armoured Corps: 437
  145th Royal Armoured Corps: 388n
Renown, H.M.S.: 139
'Retribution': 424
Richards, Brigadier G. W.: 37
Richardson, Lieutenant J. H. D.: 378, 397
Richelieu: 116
Riddell-Webster, Lieut.-General Sir Thomas: 101
Reina de Pacifico: 149
Rime-Bruneau, General: 332
Rintelen, General Enno von: 219, 395
Ritchie, Air Commodore A. P.: 227
Robb, Air Vice-Marshal J. M.: 132
Roberts, Brigadier G. P. B.: commands 22nd Armoured Brigade, 42; commands 7th Armoured Division, 235n; commands 26th Armoured Brigade, 380n, 435n, 450n
Roberts, H.M.S.: 154
Robertson, Brigadier (later Major-General) Sir Brian: at H.Q. 8th Army, 5; and Montgomery, 232n; achievement of, 238; commands 'Tripbase', 317
Robinett, Brigadier-General Paul McD.: 279, 292, 298
Robin Locksley, s.s.: 198
Rodney, H.M.S.: and operation 'Torch', 139, 149–50; in Force H, 420; relieved, 426
Roddick, Brigadier M. G.: 42
Rorqual, H.M.S.: 196, 245, 413
Roma: 157n
Rommel, Field-Marshal Erwin: mentioned, 1, 29n, 37, 92, 172, 187, 193, 202, 208, 221, 278, 287, 360, 457; and Battle of Alam el Halfa, 2, 17; supplies and reinforcements for, 10, 25–6, 50, 55, 63, 89, 173, 187n, 201,

Rommel—*cont.*
  219, 229, 242, 250, 291, 407; and operation 'Lightfoot', 17, 26–8, 76; and Comando Supremo, 24n, 50, 89, 219n, 229; his health, 26, 77, 269, 301n; reports to OKH and OKW, 26, 55, 89, 229; plans deeper defences, 26–8; resumes command of Panzerarmee, 50. 77; and Dog-fight, 50–1, 53, 55–6, 59, 62; and operation 'Supercharge', 68–70, 72–3, 77; and Battle of El Alamein, 78, 81; and withdrawal to El Agheila, 84–5, 87–9, 93–7, 101, 133, 189, 215, 217, 219–20, 222, 224; and Hitler, 219, 268–9; and withdrawal to Tripoli, 225–6, 229–30, 234–8; and Kesselring, 268; leaves Africa, 269, 329; and fighting in Tunisia, 274, 287–9, 291, 293–5, 297–8, 300–2, 305–6, 322–7, 330; and Akarit position, 362; on prisoners, 460n
Roverto: 413
Roosevelt, President: and operation 'Torch', 110, 112, 114, 125, 133, 160; and Darlan, 190; at Casablanca, 261, 263–4, 266; and operation 'Husky', 263–4 and de Gaulle, 266
Roosevelt, Colonel E.: 271
Rorqual, H.M.S.: 208, 243, 249; minelaying by, 415
Rossi, General Silvio: 360
'Round-up': 110–12, 123, 263
Royal Air Force: Orders of Battle, 488–97
  Groups:
    No. 201 (Naval Co-operation): and operation 'Lightfoot', 13, 19; mentioned, 20, 194 204n, 205; and pursuit to El Agheila, 83, 221; strength and state of, 197; and 'Stoneage' convoy, 197–8; attacks enemy shipping, 201; command of, 247n, 411n; and convoy protection, 258; and Malta, 258; in Aegean, 258
    205: and operation 'Lightfoot', 13, 32–3, 45; and Dog-fight, 63; and pursuit to El Agheila, 82–3, 221–2; strength and state of, 205, 334, 391; command of, 227; and advance to Tripoli, 234; and Malta, 258; and advance into Tunisia, 318, 391–2, 444, 449, 456; at Gardabia, 319; and Battle of Mareth, 321, 342, 346, 348–9, 354; and Battle of Wadi Akarit, 374
    208: 43
    209: 221
    210: 258n, 319
    211: 11, 99, 319
    212: 11, 221, 258
    213: 68
    216: 13, 99, 227
    219: 221, 258
    242: formed 183, 308; control of, 271, 272n, 311; operations and losses of, 302–3, 310, 313, 321,

Royal Air Force—*cont.*
  Groups—*cont.*
        328, 355; maintenance of, 312; and Desert Air Force, 400; and operation 'Vulcan' 430, 439–40; mentioned, 447; and operation 'Strike', 449n, 450, 451n, 455n
    333: 128
  Wings:
    No. 232: 11, 319
      233: 11, 221
      239: mentioned, 11, 231, 234; operations of, 221, 227
      243: 11, 221, 258n
      244: mentioned, 11, 231n, 319; operations of, 221
      248: 205
      285: strength of, 13; operations of, 221, 331; mentioned, 231n
      322: 144
      323: 144
      326: 311n
  Squadrons:
    No. 4: 168
      6: 74n, 346
      18: 185, 311n, 450
      23: 205
      33: 68, 74
      37: 74n, 336
      39: operations of, 68n, 242, 247, 411, 413; at Malta, 204n
      40: 74n, 204n, 336
      43: 144
      46: 205
      47: 201
      55: operations of, 32, 61, 74n, 349
      69: 27, 204n
      70: 74n
      72: 174, 450
      73: operations of, 33, 74n, 221, 321, 456
      80: 74
      81: 144, 154, 169
      89: 204n
      92: 74n
      93: 174
      104: 74n, 204n, 336
      108: 74n
      111: 154, 169, 301
      112: 74n
      114: 311n, 450
      126: 204n
      127: 74
      142: 242, 278
      145: 74
      148: 74n
      149: 131
      150: 242, 278
      152: 301
      154: 144, 154, 169
      160: 71
      162: 74n
      178: 319
      185: 204n
      203: 198
      208: 74n, 93

Royal Air Force—*cont.*
  Squadrons—*cont.*
      213: 74n, 100
      221: 242
      223: 32
      225: operations of, 168–9, 301, 328n; mentioned, 174
      227: 204n
      229: 204
      233: 425
      235: 204n
      238: 68. 74, 100
      241: 328n
      242: 144, 169
      243: 283
      248: 204n
      249: 204n
      250: 74n, 237
      252: 198, 201
      243: 174
      260: 74n, 237
      272: 201, 203, 204n
      274: 74n
      335 (Hellenic): 74n
      600: 456
      601: 74n
      608: 426
      651: 168
      654 Air Observation Post: 359n
      680: 319
      985 Balloon: 245
  Flights:
    No. 1435: 204n
      1437: 74n
      Polish: 416
  Other Units:
    No. 2 Armoured Car Company: 99
    No. 1 Forward Salvage Unit: 216
    No. 2 Photographic Reconnaissance Unit: 74n
    R.A.F. Regiment: 17, 144, 389
    Servicing Commandos: 144, 153n, 309
Royal Air Force Bomber Command: 129, 131, 414
Royal Air Force in Gibraltar: *see* Coastal Command
Royal Air Force in Middle East, *later* Middle East Air Command: *see also* Western Desert Air Force; and aircraft maintenance, 17, 216–7; attacks enemy shipping, 25, 203–4, 241–2, 246–7; strength and state of, 30, 128n, 400n; and convoy protection, 197, 232; and advance to Tripoli, 228, 237–8; losses of, 228, 237, 401; attacks enemy ports, 243, 247–8, 254, 277, 284; attacks transport aircraft, 249; total sorties by, 391n, 401, 541n, 456–7
(in North Africa): and operation 'Lightfoot', 14–17, 19–20, 33, 36, 42, 44–5, 47; losses of, 19–20, 22, 33, 44, 51, 55, 68, 74, 78, 83, 91, 100–1, 222; attacks Benghazi, 21, 23; attacks Tobruk, 22; attacks Deir el Munassib, 24; strength and state of, 30; supports 8th Army, 30, 44, 48, 98–100, 222, 237; and Dogfight, 48–50, 55–7, 61–4; and operation 'Supercharge'. 65–8, 71, 73–4; in

INDEX

Royal Air Force in Middle East—*cont.*
  (in North Africa)—*cont.*
    Battle of El Alamein, 78, 82; and pursuit to El Agheila, 82–3, 86–92, 98–100, 222; and advance into Tunisia, 186, 189
  (in Malta) *and* Malta Air Command: and operation 'Lightfoot', 19, 33; attacks enemy shipping, 100, 194, 203, 206–7, 240–2, 247, 410–11, 418; and operation 'Torch', 131, 138, 169–70; and advance into Tunisia, 180, 185–6, 188–9, 248, 277, 284; strength and state of, 195, 204, 400n; defends Malta, 195; losses of, 195–6, 199, 207–8, 250, 427; and 'Stoneage' convoy, 198–9; attacks enemy air bases, 203, 207–8, 412; minelaying by, 243, 412; attacks Sicily and Italy, 243, 412; attacks enemy aircraft, 249, 427; attacks Tripoli, 254

Royal Army Service Corps:
  No. 10 Pack Transport Company: 396n
  No. 11 Pack Transport Company: 396n

Royal Artillery: *see also* Royal Horse Artillery
  Brigades:
    12th Anti-Aircraft: 237
  Regiments:
    14th Anti-Tank: 388n
    57th Anti-Tank: 337n
    58th Anti-Tank: 299, 327n, 435n
    67th Anti-Tank: 442n
    72nd Anti-Tank: 296, 380n, 435n
    73rd Anti-Tank: 326n
    76th Anti-Tank: 351n, 352, 435n
    81st Anti-Tank: 388n
    93rd Anti-Tank: 296, 297n, 299n
    102nd (Northumberland Hussars) Anti-Tank: 335n, 366n
    149th Anti-Tank: 365n
    102nd Army Field: 327n
    2nd Field: 379, 388n
    19th Field: 388n
    22nd Field: 388n
    23rd Field: 299
    30th Field: 388n
    64th Field: 442n
    65th Field: 442n
    67th Field: 388n
    70th Field: 282n, 327n, 435n
    71st Field: 299, 435n
    77th Field: 388n
    11th Field: 337n
    113th Field: 442n
    132nd Field: 142n, 145
    138th Field: 153n
    152nd Field: 380n, 435n
    171st Field: 327n
    172nd Field: 327n, 435n
    54th Heavy: 389, 396
    56th Heavy: 273, 389, 396
    42nd Light Anti-Aircraft: 351n, 435n
    51st Light Anti-Aircraft, 380n, 435n
    53rd Light Anti-Aircraft: 337
    90th Light Anti-Aircraft: 388n
    91st Light Anti-Aircraft: 388n
    100th Light Anti-Aircraft: 442n
    115th Light Anti-Aircraft: 435n

Royal Artillery—*cont.*
  Regiments—*cont.*
    5th Medium: 327n
    58th Medium: 379
    64th Medium: 337n
  Batteries:
    155th: 328
    229th Anti-Tank: 299
    239th Anti-Tank: 55
    276th Anti-Tank: 366n
    288th Anti-Tank (Northumberland Hussars): 366n
    90th/100th Field: 299
    322nd Field: 176–7
    450th Field: 299
    41st Light A.A.: 323n
    84th Light A.A.: 142n
    456th Light: 327n
    457th Light: 327n
    15th/17th Medium: 327n
    64th Medium: 323n

Royal Australian Air Force:
  Squadrons:
    No. 3: 74n, 349
    450: and Battle of El Alamein, 32, 74n; and 'Stoneage' convoy, 198; and Battle of Mareth, 342
    458: 413
    459: 198
    462: 71, 336

Royal Engineers:
  86th Chemical Warfare Company: 299
  7th Field Company: 388n
  23rd Field Company: 388n
  42nd Field Company: 366n
  59th Field Company: 388n
  220th Field Company: 442n
  221st Field Company: 442n
  225th Field Company: 388n
  233rd Field Company: 366n
  237th Field Company: 142n
  238th Field Company: 388n
  248th Field Company: 388n
  256th Field Company: 153n
  270th Field Company: 435n
  271st Field Company: 435n
  272nd Field Company: 435n
  274th Field Company: 366n
  275th Field Company: 366n
  276th Field Company: 366n
  501st Field Company: 442n
  505th Field Company: 366n
  571st Field Company: 39n
  572nd Field Company: 39n
  573rd Field Company: 39n
  586th Field Company: 379
  751st Field Company: 379
  1st Field Squadron: 351n, 435n
  2nd Field Squadron: 231n
  3rd Field Squadron: 39n
  4th Field Squadron: 42
  7th Field Squadron: 39n, 351n, 435n
  8th Field Squadron: 380n, 435n
  9th Field Squadron: 39n, 339
  21st Field Squadron: and Battle of El Alamein, 42; and pursuit to El Agheila, 86n; in advance to Tripoli, 223n. 231n

Royal Engineers—*cont.*
  625th Field Squadron: 380n, 435n
  1st Field Park Squadron: 351n
  141st Field Park Squadron: 39n
Royal Horse Artillery:
  Regiments:
    2nd: 351n, 435n
    3rd: 223n
    4th: 351n, 435n
    11th (Honourable Artillery Company): 351n, 435n
    12th: 435n
Sappers and Miners, 4th Field Company Bengal: 341, 365n
Sappers and Miners, 12th Field Company Madras, 341, 365n, 370n
Royal Marines: 20, 22
  Battalions:
    11th: 21n
    12th: 380n
Royal Scotsman, L.S.I.: 175n, 420
Royal Ulsterman, L.S.I.: 175n, 420
Ruge, Vice-Admiral Friedrich: 409
Ruhr: 242
Runo, s.s.: 421
Russell, Brigadier D.: 75
Russell, Brigadier N.: 396n, 436n
Russell, Lieutenant T. C. D. A.: 21n
Ryder, Major-General Charles W.: and operation 'Torch', 126, 140–1, 145; and fighting in Tunisia, 296, 376n, 380; and operation 'Vulcan', 433

Saetta: 249
Safari, H.M.S.: 207, 248, 414
Safi: capture of, 151
Sahib, H.M.S.: 207, 414
St. *Day*, Tug: 146
Ste. Marie du Zit: air attacks on, 392; capture of, 454
Salemi: 248
Samphire, H.M.S.: 253
Sanders, Air Vice-Marshal A. P. M.: 113
San Diego: 413
Sangamon, U.S.S.: 139
San Antonio: 423
Sant Antioco: 207
Santa Rita: 248
Santee, U.S.S.: 139
Saracen, H.M.S.: 414
Saracoglu, Mr.: 267
Saturno: 241
Savannah, U.S.S.: 139
Scarlett-Streatfeild, Air Commodore J. R.: 247n
Schmid, Major-General Josef: 399, 434, 446
Schmundt, General: 432
Schürmeyer, Captain: 170
Schwarz, General J.: 400
Scillin: 202
Scorpion, H.M.S.: 461
Scylla, H.M.S.: 138–9
Seagrim, Lieut.-Colonel D. A.: 338
Seidemann, Major-General Hans: commands Fliegerkorps Tunis, 272, 330; and 'Eilbote', 281; commands Luftwaffe in Africa, 393n

Sfax: Axis occupy, 173; air attacks on, 179, 185, 189, 242–3, 277–8, 283, 369, 391, 412
Sfax el Maou: air attacks on, 342
Sheffield, H.M.S.: 138–9, 146, 153
Shipping: summaries of attacks on enemy 417–8
Showers, Lieut.-Colonel L. J. G.: 458
Sibyl, H.M.S.: 412
Sicily: air attacks on, 203; invasion of, 259 262
Sickle, H.M.S.: 425
Sicilia: 413
Sidi Ahmed: air attacks on, 185, 278, 284, 392n, 415
Sidi Haneish: air attacks on, 49, 63
Sikh, H.M.S.: 20–2
Simpson, Air Commodore S. P.: 133
Sirio: 222
Sirius, H.M.S.: and operation 'Torch', 139, at Bône, 205, 245; mentioned, 426
Sladen, Captain G. M. S.: 244
Slatter, Air Vice-Marshal Sir Leonard: 247n
'Sledgehammer': 111–12
Soliman: air attacks on, 444, 456
Souk el Arba: air attacks on, 179
Sousse: plan for British landing at, 170n; Axis occupy, 173; air attacks on, 179, 185, 189, 228, 234, 242, 248, 277–8, 280, 412; mining of, 208
South African Air Force:
  Wings:
    No. 3: 11, 221, 231n
    7: 11, 319
  Squadrons:
    No. 1: 68, 74n, 416
    2: and Battle of El Alamein, 32, 74n; attacks Gambut, 99; and Battle of Mareth, 342; in operation 'Flax', 416
    4: and Battle of El Alamein, 32, 74n; attacks Gambut, 99; in operation 'Flax', 416
    5: and Battle of El Alamein, 74n, 99; and fighting in Tunisia, 342; in operation 'Flax', 416
    7: 74n
    12: 14, 74n, 349
    15: 74n, 198, 201
    21: 61, 74n, 349
    24: and smoke-laying, 14; and Battle of El Alamein, 61, 74n; and Battle of Mareth, 349
    40: 74n, 334n
    60: 74n
Smith-Dorrien, Lieut.-Colonel G. H. G.: 92
Spaatz, Major-General Carl: and allied air co-ordination, 207, 310–11; commands N.A.A.F., 265n, 271n, 310; and fighting in Tunisia, 298n, 310–11
Special Air Service Brigade, 1st Battalion: 21n
Special Service Regiment, 1st: 20–22
Spey, H.M.S.: 137, 146
Spezia: air attacks on, 414
Splendid, H.M.S.: operations of, 207, 243, 249, 412; loss of, 414
Spolete: 242

INDEX

Sponeck, Lieut.-General Graf Theodor von: and fighting in Tunisia, 324, 326, 369; and Axis surrender, 457
Stack, Colonel Robert I.: 292
Stalin, Premier: 264, 461
Stark, Colonel Alexander N.: 296, 298
Sterope: 411
Stirling, Lieut.-Colonel A. D.: 21n, 23
Stirling, Brigadier J. E.: 326m, 366n
Stolz, Colonel: 173, 279n
'Stoneage': air cover for, 77, 97, 198; the operation, 196–9; mentioned, 205
Stott, Brigadier R. E. H.: 327, 435n
Strathallan, s.s.: 211
'Strike': 446–56
Stromboli: 244
Stumme, General Georg: commands Panzerarmee Afrika, 26; and operation 'Lightfoot', 26–9, 36, 50; supplies and reinforcements for, 27; death of, 50
Submarines:
    (British): and operation 'Torch', 138, 202; carry supplies to Malta, 196; and enemy convoys, 201–3; losses of, 212
    (French): strength of, 116
    (German): strength of, 116, 211, 253, 482; operations of, 130–1, 157, 253; losses of, 157, 211, 253
    (Italian): strength of, 116, 156, 482; operations of, 156–7, 253; losses of, 157, 211, 253
Submarine Flotillas:
    British:
        1st: and French Fleet, 138; mentioned 194; operations of, 201–2, 258
        8th (Gibraltar): and operation 'Torch', 138, 201–2; patrols by, 243, 412
        10th (Malta): and operation 'Torch', 138, 201; patrols by, 243, 412
    Italian:
        Tenth Light: 211–12
Sudan Defence Force: 21
'Supercharge': plan for, 53, 59, 64–5; the operation, 65–79; mentioned, 62, 96, 106
'Supercharge' (Tebaga Gap): 346–7, 369
'Super Gymnast': 110
'Superlibia': 219, 269
Supermarina: 409
Surtees, Brigadier G.: 102
Suwanee, U.S.S.: 139
Syfret, Vice-Admiral Sir Neville: commands Force H, 127; and operation 'Torch', 127, 138–9; at Gibraltar, 211; his illness, 254
Syracuse: air attacks on, 228

Tadorna, s.s.: 196
Tafaraoui: air attacks on, 149; capture of, 149–50
Taku, H.M.S.: 22
Tanks:
    American: distribution of, 9; losses of, 52
        M3 (Grant): distribution of, 9; losses of, 52n
        Sherman: description of, 8; distribution of, 9, 273; losses of, 52n

Tanks—*conts*.
    American—*cont*.
        Sherman Crab (mine-clearing): 38n
        Stuart- distribution of, 9; losses of, 52n
    British: distribution of, 9; losses of, 52
        Churchill: description of, 273; for 1st Army, 273
        Crusader: distribution of, 9; losses of, 52n; replaced by Sherman, 273
        Crusader Mark III: description of, 8; distribution of, 9; losses of, 52
        Matilda: and CDL, 8n
        Scorpion (mine-clearing): description of, 14; in operation 'Lightfoot', 38, 43
        Valentine: distribution of, 9; losses of, 52n; replaced by Sherman, 273
    German: distribution of, 9, 30, 95n, 290, 325, 334, 367; losses of, 328n; serviceable in Africa, 363n; Pzkw VI Henschel Tiger I, description of, 172n, 500
    Italian: distribution of, 10
    Notes on tanks, armour and anti-tank guns: 499–502, 505–10
Tarano: 244
Tartar, H.M.S.: 423
Tasajera, s.s.: 149
Tauorga: air attacks on, 234
Taurus, H.M.S.: 412, 414
Tebaga: air attacks on, 342
Tebourba: air attacks on, 280
Tedder, Air Chief Marshal Sir Arthur: *see also* Commanders-in-Chief; and Coningham, 3; and operation 'Lightfoot', 3; forces of, 3; and control of U.S.A.M.E.A.F., 11; and raids on Behghazi and Tobruk, 20; and Beaufort IIs, 201n; and Malta, 205; visits Eisenhower, 206–7; on air command in Mediterranean, 207, 265; becomes A.O.C.-in-C. Mediterranean Air Command, 227, 265, 271n; and Hurricane tank-destroyers, 377; and air power, 431
Teramo: 413
Tergestea: 50n
Teviot Bank, H.M.S.: 259
Texas, U.S.S.: 139
Thelepte: evacuation of, 294
Thoma, Lieut.-General Ritter von: commands Panzerarmee, 50; and Dog-fight, 56; and operation 'Supercharge', 64, 69, 73; taken prisoner, 85
Thomas Stone, U.S. transport: 137, 146
Thorsheimer: 247
Thunderbolt, H.M.S.: 244, 254–5, 412
Tiessenhausen, Captain: 157
Tifone: 423
'Tiger': 425
Tobruk: air attacks on, 20, 22, 33, 91, 100, 318; raid on, 20–3, 26; capture of, 97, as a supply base, 103–4, 232
Torbay, H.M.S.: 249, 412
'Torch': preparation of, 1, 110–12, 114, 123–5; timing of, 2, 77, 123; and operation 'Light' foot', 60; and operation 'Supercharge', 77; mentioned, 93, 107, 119, 121, 123, 171, 186, 189–90, 200n, 202, 204, 209, 239, 261, 307, 407, 419, 425; Allied command for,

112–14; plan for, 114, 125–33, 151, 313; French attitude to, 115, 125, 127, 133–5, 141, 158–61; adverse conditions in, 117–9, 124, 127; training for, 130; landings in, 135, 138–51, 153–6, 162, 166; Axis unaware of, 135–6, 170; limitations of, 152; casualties in, 155; and enemy U-boats, 155–8; reviewed, 164, 310
Tornade: 149
Toukabeur: capture of, 396
Tramontane: 149
Trapani: air attacks on, 248, 358n, 392n, 413, 415
Traveller, H.M.S.: 212, 244
Trevor, Lieut.-Colonel T. H.: 145
Trieste: 244, 414
Tigris, H.M.S.: 412
'Tripbase': 317
Tripoli: air attacks on, 100, 222, 228, 234, 237, 254, 277–8, 284, 318, 422; description of, 228; capture of, 236–7, 248, 264n; Naval operations at, 254–5; harbour reopened, 255–7
Tripolino: 63, 202
Triton: 212
Trooper, H.M.S.: 244, 412
Troubridge, Commodore T. H.: and operation 'Torch', 134, 139, 147–8; mentioned, 427
Truscott, General Lucian K.: 270
Tuker, Major-General F. I. S.: commands 4th Indian Division, 7; and Battle of Wadi Akarit, 364, 369–73; and fighting in Tunisia, 404, 442, 446, 450; and surrender, 458
Tunis: air attacks on, 179, 183, 185, 188, 228, 248, 277, 280, 284; mining of, 208; capture of, 452
Tunisia: political situation in, 162–3; reinforcements for, 240, 246–7; 274, 358, 407–19, 431; Axis surrender in, 453, 457
Turbulent, H.M.S.: 243, 249, 412
Turin: air attacks on, 131
Turner, Lieut.-Colonel V. B.: 54, 56
Turkey: aid for, 267
Tuscaloosa, U.S.S.: 139
Typhon: 148, 150
Tynwald, H.M.S.: 154

U.77: 421
U.83: 421
U.118: 253
U.130: 155
U.155: 155
U.173: 155, 158
U.303: 425
U.331: 157
U.343: 421
U.375: 208
U.380: 156
U.407: 156
U.414: 426
U.415: 155
U.431: 156, 158
U.447: 425
U.515: 155
U.562: 211

U.593: 421
U.596: 421
U.602: 421
U.617: 258
U.755: 426
Ulpio Traiano: 244
Umbra, H.M.S.: 207
Una, H.M.S.: 249
Unbending, H.M.S.: 249, 412
Unbroken, H.M.S.: 243, 413–4
Unison, H.M.S.: 414
Unrivalled, H.M.S.: 249
Unruffled: H.M.S. 249
Unseen, H.M.S.: 248
United States Air Force: Orders of Battle, 488–97
  Commands:
    IX Bomber: formed, 11, 83n; strength and state of, 391; operations of, 391, 410–11, 444, 456
    316th Troop Carrier Command: 216, 227
  Groups:
    XII Air Support: control of, 271, 272n, 311; and fighting in Tunisia, 294, 300, 302–3, 307, 310–11, 321, 328, 377; and Battle of Mareth, 336; functions of 355, 400; and operation 'Vulcan', 430, 439, 440n; and operation 'Strike', 449n, 450, 451n, 455
    14th Fighter: 174
    57th Fighter: 11, 221, 231n
    79th Fighter: 416
    93rd Heavy Bombardment: 319n
    12th Medium Bombardment: in Desert Air Force, 11; and advance to Tripoli, 221, 231n; moves to Tripoli area, 319
  Squadrons:
    64th: 74n, 99
    65th: 74n, 99
    66th: 74n
    82nd: 74n
    83rd: 74n, 349
    308th: 150
    309th: 150
    434th: 74n, 349
United States Army: strength 'in Torch' 167
  Combat Command 'A': 290–4
  Combat Command 'B': and operation 'Torch', 181, 184, 186n; and fighting in Tunisia, 279n, 284, 289, 292–4, 297–9
  Combat Command 'C': 290, 292–4
  Corps:
    2nd: and fighting in Tunisia, 270–1, 275, 285, 289, 315, 320, 384, 397–8; air support for, 328, 377, 439; command of, 329, 376n; and Battle of Mareth, 329, 336, 343; and Battle of Wadi Akarit, 357–8, 360, 373–4; strength and state of, 376, 432; at Fondouk, 379; supplies for, 420; and operation 'Vulcan', 430, 432, 434, 437–8; and operation 'Strike', 446, 448, 451, 453

INDEX

United States Army—*cont.*
　Divisions:
　　Armoured:
　　　1st U.S.: and operation 'Torch', 126, 166; and fighting in Tunisia, 279, 282, 285, 289, 292, 294, 296, 298, 315, 376; losses of 292n, 302; and Battle of Mareth, 336n; mentioned, 364n, 376n, 453; command of, 377; and operation 'Vulcan', 432; and operation 'Strike', 448-9, 451, 453
　　Infantry:
　　　1st U.S.: and operation 'Torch', 150, 166; and fighting in Tunisia, 315, 376; mentioned 364n, 376n; and operation 'Vulcan', 432
　　　9th: and fighting in Tunisia, 296, 299, 315, 376, 384; and Battle of Mareth, 336n; and operation 'Vulcan', 433; and operation 'Strike', 448, 453
　　　34th: and operation 'Torch', 140-1, 166, 169: command of, 271, 376n; and fighting in Tunisia, 284, 290, 296, 315; losses of, 302; and Battle of Mareth, 336; at Fondouk, 379-82, 389; strength and state of, 380n; and operation 'Vulcan', 433; and operation 'Strike', 448
　Groups :
　　1st Tank Destroyer: 376n
　Regimental Combat Teams:
　　16th: 126, 146, 150
　　18th: and operation 'Torch', 126, 146, 150, 186n; and fighting in Tunisia, 296
　　26th: and operation 'Torch', 126, 146, 150; and fighting in Tunisia, 296, 298
　　39th: and operation 'Torch', 126, 137, 140-1, 145
　　168th: and operation 'Torch', 126, 140-3, 145; and fighting in Tunisia, 290-1, 302
　Regiments:
　　1st Armoured: and operation 'Torch', 176, 180; and fighting in Tunisia, 290-1, 292n, 397; losses of, 302; mentioned, 376n
　　13th Armoured: and operation 'Torch', 176, 181; and fighting in Tunisia, 279n, 296; mentioned, 376
　　19th Combat Engineers: 296-7
　　509th Parachute: 170
　Battalions:
　　13th Field Artillery: 376n
　　27th Field Artillery: 181n, 279n, 300
　　33rd Field Artillery: 296
　　34th Field Artillery: 300n
　　36th Field Artillery: 186n, 296
　　60th Field Artillery: 300n
　　65th Field Artillery: 376n
　　68th Field Artillery: 376n

United States Army—*cont.*
　Battalions—*cont.*
　　84th Field Artillery: 300n
　　91st Field Artillery: 290n
　　125th Field Artillery: 380n
　　175th Field Artillery: 296, 380n
　　185th Field Artillery: 380n
　　2nd/509th Parachute: 179
　　1st Ranger: 126, 146-7, 296
　　81st Reconnaissance: 376n
　　751st Tank Destroyer: 380n
　　601st Tank Destroyer: 279n
　　701st Tank Destroyer: 290n
　　751st Tank Destroyer: 380n
　　805th Tank Destroyer: 296
　　813th Tank Destroyer: 380n
　　894th Tank Destroyer: 453
　　899th Tank Destroyer: 376n
　Companies:
　　47th Cannon: 300n
　　60th Cannon: 300n
　Infantry:
　　18th: 187, 436
　　1st/26th: 296
　　39th: 376n
　　3rd/39th Infantry: 296
　　133rd: 380n, 381
　　135th: 380n, 381
　　168th: 380n
　　1st/168th Infantry: 296
　　1/6th Armoured: 181
　　2/6th Armoured: 181, 279n
　　6th Armoured: 376n
　　3/6th Armoured: 297
United States Army Middle East Air Force: *then see* United States Ninth Air Force; control of, 10-11; and operation 'Lightfoot', 11, 19-20, 33, 44; strength and state of, 12n, 128n; losses of, 20, 33, 44, 78, 91, 101, 154n, 155; and Dog-fight, 48, 55-6; and operation 'Supercharge', 68-9, 74; in Battle of El Alamein, 78; and pursuit to El Agheila, 82, 88, 91, 100; becomes U.S. Ninth Air Force, 83n; and operation 'Torch', 128-9, 150-1
United States Chiefs of Staff: as Joint C.O.S., 110n; and operation 'Round-up', 111; and operation 'Torch', 124-5; and Casablanca conference, 261
United States Eighth Air Force: 129, 319n
United States Navy: and operation 'Torch', 126-7
United States Ninth Air Force: mentioned, 11n; formed, 83n; operations and losses of, 202-4, 211, 222, 228, 233-4, 237, 243, 246-8, 277-8, 284, 319, 320
　Desert Air Task Force: 320
United States Twelfth Air Force: and advance into Tunisia, 179, 183, 204, 277, 280, 283-4, 291-2, 294; losses of, 179, 283, 292, 294; strength and state of, 204-5; attacks enemy shipping, 241-2; attacks enemy ports, 247-8, 277; and N.A.A.F., 248; and convoy protection, 252; and air support, 311
Unruffled, H.M.S.: 207, 244
Unshaken, H.M.S.: 414

INDEX

Unwin, Lieut.-Colonel E. H. M.: 21n
Utilitas: 249
Utmost, H.M.S.: 212

Vaerst, General Gustav von: commands Pz AOK 5, 270; and operation 'Vulcan', 438, 443; mentioned, 445; and operation 'Strike', 452–3; surrenders, 453
Valsavoia: 248
Vansittart, H.M.S.: 149
Varvara, s.s.: 422
Velox, H.M.S.: 137
Vercelli: 242
Verlet, Captain: 433
Verona: 242
Vetch, H.M.S.: 426
Vian, Rear-Admiral Sir Philip: 427
Viceroy of India, s.s.: 156
Vichy France: Germans move into, 162–3
Vichy Government: 110, 160–2, 170–1
Victorious, H.M.S.: 138–40, 144–5, 211
Villacidro: air attacks on, 248
Viminale: 244
Vittorio Veneto: 157n
'Vulcan': 430–4, 436–43

Wadi Akarit: description of, 362, Battle of, 369–75
Ward, Major-General Orlando: commands U.S. 1st Armoured Division, 289; and fighting in Tunisia, 292, 298, 376n, 377
Warlimont, General: and operation 'Torch', 170; on supplies, 250, 274; and defence of Tunisia, 274, 432
Walney, H.M.S.: 148–9, 155
War Office: 16, 317
Warwick Castle, m.v.: 155
Water, Lieut.-Colonel John K.: 290
Wauchope, Captain C.: 255, 422
Wavell, General Sir Archibald: 304
Weber, Major-General Friedrich: and fighting in Tunisia, 279, 306, 326–8; mentioned, 278, 390, 434; leaves Tunisia, 445
Weichold, Vice-Admiral Eberhard: 409
Welsh, Air Marshal Sir William: and operation 'Torch', 113, 129, 144; and advance into Tunisia, 183; on need to replace Bisleys, 185; and air support, 308
Welshman, H.M.S.: carries supplies for Malta, 194, 196, 200, 258; and minelaying, 245, 258; loss of, 249, 258; moves troops, 258
Welvert, General J. E.: 296, 399

Western Air Command: and operation 'Torch', 128, 147; strength and state of, 168; and advance into Tunisia, 185–6, 188–90; losses of, 186, 189
Western Desert Air Force: strength and state of, 3, 11, 13, 76, 78, 334, 368, 403; and operation 'Lightfoot', 3, 6, 11, 13–17, 19, 30, 32–3, 44; reorganization of, 11, 221, 319; supplies and reinforcements for, 16–17, 101–6, 216–7, 309; and Dog-fight, 62–3; and operation 'Supercharge', 73–4; in Battle of El Alamein, 76, 78, 82; and pursuit to El Agheila, 82, 88, 95–6, 98–100, 107, 215, 221; and 'Stoneage' convoy, 99, 197–8; and V.H.F. radio-telephone, 199n; in advance to Tripoli, 213, 215, 225–7, 231, 233–5, 237; losses of, 234, 349, 374, 377–8; attacks Zuara, 244–5; mentioned, 258n, 320, 326, 391; N.A.T.A.F. controls, 271, 272n, 306; and fighting in Tunisia, 284, 317, 321, 359, 377–9, 400; and Battle of Mareth, 336, 342, 346, 348–9; functions of, 355, 400; and Battle of Wadi Akarit, 369, 373–4; attacks shipping, 414; in operation 'Flax', 415–6; and operation 'Vulcan', 430, 440, 443–4; and operation 'Strike', 448–50, 451n, 456; attacks Pantelleria, 455
Westphal, Major-General Siegfried: 329, 360
Weyburn, H.M.C.S.: 254
Weygand, General Maxime: 115, 159
Wheatland, H.M.S.: 154
Whistler, Brigadier L. G.: 24, 326n
Whitehead, Brigadier D. A.: 48
Wichita, U.S.S.: 139
Willis, Vice-Admiral A. U.: 420, 426
Wilson, General Sir Maitland: *see also* Commanders-in-Chief; 266–7
Wimberley, Major-General D. N.: 7, 234–5, 364
Windeyer, Brigadier W. J. V.: 58
Windsor Castle, s.s.: 421
Wishart, H.M.S.: 137, 146

Zara: 68n, 202
Zarat: air attacks on, 342
Zetland, H.M.S.: 143
Ziegler, Lieut.-General Heinz: arrives at Tunis, 184; and D.A.K., 288n; and fighting in Tunisia, 290–1, 293–4, 323
Zitouna: air attacks on, 369
Zuara: bombardment of, 244; air attacks on, 244–5, 318
Zulu, H.M.S.: 20–2

HISTORY OF THE SECOND WORLD WAR
UNITED KINGDOM MILITARY SERIES

Reprinted by the Naval & Military Press in twenty two volumes with the permission of the Controller of HMSO and Queen's Printer for Scotland.

THE DEFENCE OF THE UNITED KINGDOM

Basil Collier

Official history of Britain's home front in the Second World War, from the Phoney War, through the Battle of Britain and the Blitz to victory in Europe.
ISBN: 1845740556
Price £22.00

THE CAMPAIGN IN NORWAY

T. H. Derry

The catastrophic 1940 campaign which caused the downfall of Neville Chamberlain and brought Winston Churchill to power.
ISBN: 1845740572
Price: £22.00

THE WAR IN FRANCE AND FLANDERS 1939-1940

Major L. F. Ellis

The role of the BEF in the fall of France and the retreat to Dunkirk.
ISBN: 1845740564
Price £22.00

VICTORY IN THE WEST
Volume I: The Battle of Normandy

Major L. F. Ellis

The build-up, execution and consequences of D-Day in 1944.
ISBN: 1845740580
Price: £22.00

Volume II: The Defeat of Germany

Major L. F. Ellis

The final stages of the liberation of western Europe in 1944-45.
ISBN: 1845740599
Price £22.00

www.naval-military-press.com

THE MEDITERRANEAN AND MIDDLE EAST

Volume I: The Early Successes against Italy (to May 1941)

Major-General I. S. O. Playfair

Britain defeats Italy on land and sea in Africa and the Mediterranean in 1940.
ISBN: 1845740653
Price: £22.00

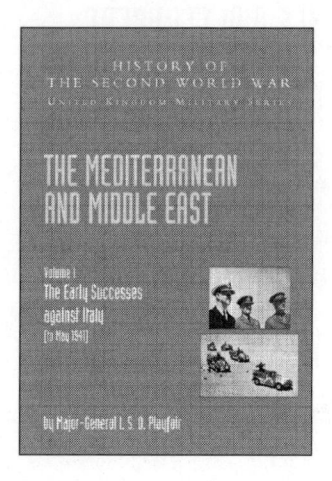

Volume II: The Germans Come to the Help of their Ally (1941)

Major-General I. S. O. Playfair

Rommel rides to Italy's rescue, Malta is bombarded, Yugoslavia, Greece and Crete are lost, and Iraq and Syria are secured for the Allies.
ISBN: 1845740661
Price: £22.00

Volume III: (September 1941 to September 1942) British Fortunes reach their Lowest Ebb

Major-General I. S. O. Playfair

Britain's darkest hour in North Africa and the Mediterranean, 1941-42.
ISBN: 184574067X
Price: £22.00

Volume IV: The Destruction of the Axis Forces in Africa

Major-General I. S. O. Playfair

The battle of El Alamein and 'Operation Torch' bring the Allies victory in North Africa, 1942-43.
ISBN: 1845740688
Price: £22.00

Volume V: The Campaign in Sicily 1943 and the Campaign in Italy — 3rd Sepember 1943 to 31st March 1944

Major-General I. S. O. Playfair

The Allies invade Sicily and Italy, but encounter determined German defence in 1943-44.
ISBN: 1845740696
Price: £22.00

Volume VI: Victory in the Mediterranean Part I: 1st April to 4th June 1944

Brigadier C. J. C. Molony

The Allies breach the Gustav, Hitler and Caesar Lines and occupy Rome.
ISBN: 184574070X
Price: £22.00

Volume VI: Victory in the Mediterranean Part II: June to October 1944

General Sir William Jackson

The 1944 Italian summer campaign breaches the Gothic Line but then bogs down again.
ISBN: 1845740718
Price: £22.00

Volume VI: Victory in the Mediterranean Part III: November 1944 to May 1945

General Sir William Jackson

The messy end of the war in Italy, Greece, and Yugoslavia.
ISBN: 1845740726
Price: £22.00

THE WAR AGAINST JAPAN

Volume I: The Loss of Singapore

Major-General S. Woodburn Kirby

The fall of Hong Kong, Malaya and Singapore in 1941–42.
ISBN: 1845740602
Price: £22.00

Volume II: India's Most Dangerous Hour

Major-General S. Woodburn Kirby

The loss of Burma and Japan's threat to India in 1941–42.
ISBN: 1845740610
Price: £22.00

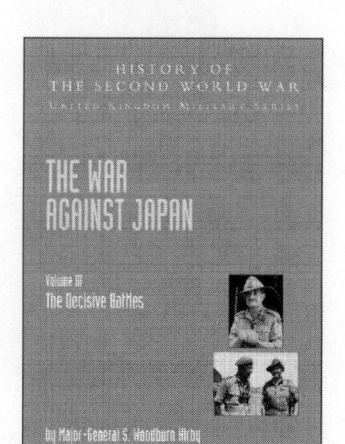

Volume III: The Decisive Battles

Major-General S. Woodburn Kirby

Turning the tide in the war against Japan at the battles of Kohima, Imphal and the Chindit campaigns.
ISBN: 1845740629
Price: £22.00

Volume IV: The Reconquest of Burma

Major-General S. Woodburn Kirby

The reconquest of Burma by Bill Slim's 'forgotten' 14th Army.
ISBN: 1845740637
Price: £22.00

Volume V: The Surrender of Japan

Major-General S. Woodburn Kirby

Victory in South-East Asia in 1945 - from Rangoon to Nagasaki.
ISBN: 1845740645
Price: £22.00

www.naval-military-press.com

THE WAR AT SEA - 1939–1945

Captain Roskill has long been recognised as the leading authority on The Royal Navy's part in the Second World War. His official History is unlikely ever to be superceded. His narrative is highly readable and the analysis is clear. Roskill describes sea battles, convoy actions and the contribution made by technology in the shape of Asdic & Radar.

Volume I: The Defensive

Captain S. W. Roskill, D.S.C., R.N.

2004 N&MP reprint (original pub 1954).
SB. xxii + 664pp with 43 maps and numerous contemporary photos.
ISBN: 1843428032
Price: £32.00

Volume II: The Period of Balance

Captain S. W. Roskill, D.S.C., R.N.

2004 N&MP reprint (original pub 1956).
SB. xvi + 523pp with 42 maps and numerous contemporary photos.
ISBN: 1843428040
Price: £32.00

Volume III: Part I The Offensive
1st June 1943-31 May 1944

Captain S. W. Roskill, D.S.C., R.N.

2004 N&MP reprint (original pub 1960).
SB. xv + 413pp with 21 maps and numerous contemporary photos.
ISBN: 1843428059
Price: £32.00

Volume III: Part 2 The Offensive
1st June 1944-14th August 1945

Captain S. W. Roskill, D.S.C., R.N.

2004 N&MP reprint (original pub 1961).
SB. xvi + 502pp with 46 maps and numerous contemporary photos.
ISBN: 1843428067
Price: £32.00

www.naval-military-press.com

990923

Printed in Great Britain by
Amazon.co.uk, Ltd.,
Marston Gate.